Praise for
Buffett

D1322007

"In this engaging biography, Roger Lowenstein tells not only how Mr. Buffett made it but how he has managed to avoid spending it—the most fascinating part of the story . . . a delightful portrait of a homespun capitalist."

—*The New York Times*

"Lively, smoothly written, and elaborately researched . . . the best book by far on this legendary character."

—*BusinessWeek* (Top 10 Business Books of 1995)

"A delightful portrait."   —*The New York Times Book Review*

"A significant contribution to the craft of biography as well as an illuminating and comforting story for investors everywhere."   —*Chicago Tribune*

"Thoroughly researched and perceptive . . . a highly readable account."

—*Financial Times*

"Lowenstein has accomplished something remarkable."

—*Los Angeles Times*

"*Buffett* throws a lot of light on the character of a man who is now almost as famous for his homespun aphorisms as he is for the prowess which has made him the second wealthiest individual in the United States."

—*The Independent* (London)

"Lowenstein's excellent . . . biography . . . burnishes the Buffett myth while deconstructing it with heavy doses of reality." —*Barron's*

"Many people know of Warren Buffett's riches and investment savvy. But here you'll get to know the boy who searched the local golf course for 'used but marketable golf balls' and started a lemonade stand on a heavily trafficked street in front of a friend's house instead of his own quieter street. And you can explore the psyche of a father of three who, while married to one woman, lived with another, among other personal details about the man behind the investments." —*U.S. News & World Report*

"*Buffett* is a landmark portrait of a uniquely American life—a portrait that offers an enthralling, precisely documented, full-fleshed characterization of an American icon. It is a work that should be required reading in every business curriculum, for it relates directly to the current and future interests of individual and corporate investors throughout America."

—*Business Book Review*

"Anyone who reads this will walk away from the experience with a much richer sense of who Warren Buffett is and what makes him a great investor, perhaps enhancing their own investment returns as well . . . one heck of a good book." —*The Motley Fool*

"As much a history of investing in the latter half of the 20th century as it is a penetrating look at Buffett . . . splendid." —*Salon.com*

"[An] excellent biography . . . [that provides] personal glimpses of a very private man." —*Publishers Weekly*

"Lowenstein does a remarkable job of telling the financial story of Buffett's rise to securities fame . . . [in this] highly interesting, fascinating . . . near hagiographic biography."
—*Library Journal*

"The first definitive, inside account of the life and career of this American original."
—Ingram

"The prose [Roger Lowenstein] displays here is an admirable mixture of the clear-eyed and the poetic. The book is both empathetic and intelligent, without ever slopping over into fawning."
—*The Washington Monthly*

"This work of art from Roger Lowenstein . . . chronicles the intimately private as well as the investing life of one of the greatest investors ever."
—MarketThoughts.com

BUFFETT

BUFFETT

THE BIOGRAPHY

ROGER LOWENSTEIN

Duckworth Overlook

Published in 2008 by
Duckworth Overlook
90-93 Cowcross Street
London, EC1M 6BF
Tel: 020 7490 7300
Fax: 020 7490 0080
info@duckworth-publishers.co.uk
www.ducknet.co.uk

Grateful acknowledgment is made to the following for permission to print both
previously published and unpublished material:
WARREN E. BUFFETT: Excerpts from letters, reports to the Buffett
Partnership and Berkshire Hathaway, and annual reports.
Reprinted by permission of Warren E. Buffett.
FORBES: Excerpt from "Look at All Those Beautiful, Scantily Clad Girls Out There"
(November 1, 1974). Copyright © 1974 by Forbes Inc.
Reprinted by permission of Forbes magazine.
OMAHA WORLD-HERALD: Excerpts from "Susie Sings for More Than Her Supper"
by Al Pagel (April 17, 1977) and "Klewitt Legacy as Unusual as His Life" by Warren
Buffett (January 20, 1980). Reprinted by permission of the Omaha World-Herald.
THE WALL STREET TRANSCRIPT: Excerpt from "Pension Fund and Money Managers"
(December 23, 1974), excerpt from editors' interview tih Eric T. Miller (April 23,
1973), and excerpt from "Some Thoughts for Financial Analysis" (June 17, 1974).
Copyright © 1973, 1974 by The Wall Street Transcript Corporation. Reprinted
by permission of The Wall Street Transcript.

A catalogue record for this book is available
from the British Library

ISBN 978 0 7156 3830 9

Printed in Great Britain by
Creative Print & Design, Blaina, Wales

Author's Note/Acknowledgments

I came to the study of Warren Buffett as a longtime investor in Berkshire Hathaway, the company that Buffett controls, and also as a veteran of a dozen years of financial reporting at the *Wall Street Journal*. Ideally, this book has the benefit of an investor's familiarity and a reporter's objectivity. Whether such noble hopes have been fulfilled may best be judged by the reader.

I began the project in the fall of 1991, when Buffett was engaged in the rescue of Salomon Brothers. Buffett advised me then that he would not collaborate in any way, but that neither would he attempt to interfere with the project. Specifically, he promised not to either discourage or encourage potential sources. He lived up to both pledges. However, Buffett's voluminous writings, which he has allowed me to quote, were an invaluable source.

This book is primarily the result of interviews with people who did agree to cooperate—Buffett's family members, his friends, his associates in business, and others—and I am grateful to every one of them. With a very few exceptions for those requesting anonymity, sources are identified in the text or in the source notes. In some cases in which the source seems obvious, I did not include a note. For instance, the source for most of the unattributed conversations or incidents involving Buffett and a second party was an interview with that other party.

A few sources deserve special mention. There were others, but Roxanne Brandt, Ken Chace, Bob Goldfarb, Stan Lipsey, Barbara Morrow, and Charlie Munger responded to my repeated pleas for help with a spirit of inquiry worthy of the best reporter. Buffett's two sisters, Doris and Roberta, and his three children, Susie, Howie, and Peter, were at once loyal siblings and offspring and invaluable and generous guides to the Buffett family.

In a computerized age, Bruce Levy at the *Wall Street Journal* and Jeanne Hauser and Stephen Allard at the *Omaha World-Herald* proved that good librarians are as irreplaceable as ever. Also, my editors at the *Wall Street Journal* were unusually generous in granting me an extended leave.

I owe special thanks to my sharp-eyed but gentle readers—Neil Barsky, Robert Goodman, Andrea Lowenstein, Louis Lowenstein, and Jeffrey Tannenbaum. Melanie Jackson, my agent, had the audacity to believe in this book from the beginning, and I am grateful for it. Ann Godoff, my editor, provided unflinching but—alas—unerring criticism, without which this would have been a far lesser work. For my young children, Matthew, Zachary, and Allison, this project has occupied half a lifetime. (I have missed you, too.) Finally, I must allude to the many gifts I have gotten from my two parents, among which was the exposure to my father's love of finance and unwavering ethics.

—ROGER LOWENSTEIN
January 1995

Contents

Berkshire Hathaway vs. the Dow Industrials

Monthly closing prices

Source: Datastream International, Baseline

INTRODUCTION

In the annals of investing, Warren Buffett stands alone. Starting from scratch, simply by picking stocks and companies for investment, Buffett amassed one of the epochal fortunes of the twentieth century. Over a period of four decades—more than enough to iron out the effects of fortuitous rolls of the dice—Buffett outperformed the stock market, by a stunning margin and without taking undue risks or suffering a single losing year. This is a feat that market savants, Main Street brokers, and academic scholars had long proclaimed to be impossible. By virtue of this steady, superior compounding, Buffett acquired a magical-seeming net worth of $15 billion, and counting.

Buffett did this in markets bullish and bearish and through economies fat and lean, from the Eisenhower years to Bill Clinton, from the 1950s to the 1990s, from saddle shoes and Vietnam to junk bonds and the information age. Over the broad sweep of postwar America, as the major stock averages advanced by 11 percent or so a year, Buffett racked up a compounded annual gain of 29.2 percent.[1]

The uniqueness of this achievement is more significant in that it was the fruit of old-fashioned, long-term investing. Wall Street's modern financiers got rich by exploiting their control of the public's money: their essential trick was to take in—and sell out—the public at opportune moments. Buffett shunned this game, as well as the more venal

excesses for which Wall Street is deservedly famous. In effect, he rediscovered the art of pure capitalism—a cold-blooded sport, but a fair one.

The public shareholders who invested with Buffett also got rich, and
in exactly the same proportion to their capital that Buffett did. The
numbers themselves are almost inconceivable. If one had invested
$10,000 when Buffett began his career, working out of his study in
Omaha in 1956, and had stuck with him throughout, one would have
had an investment at the end of 1995 worth $125 million.[2]

And yet, the numbers alone do not account for the aura that Buffett
cast on Wall Street. Once a year, disciples and money men would flock
to Omaha like pilgrims on a hajj, to hear Buffett deconstruct the in-
tricacies of investing, business, and finance. His annual meetings became a piece of Americana, like an Elvis concert or a religious revival.
Financial groupies arrived in Omaha clutching Buffett's writings like a
Bible and reciting his aphorisms like excerpts from the Sermon on the
Mount.

His grasp of simple verities gave rise to a drama that would recur
throughout his life. Long before those pilgrimages to Omaha, long
before Buffett had a record, he would stand in a corner at college parties, baby-faced and bright-eyed, holding forth on the universe as a
dozen or two of his older, drunken fraternity brothers crowded around.
A few years later, when these friends had metamorphosed into young
associates starting out on Wall Street, the ritual was the same. Buffett,
the youngest of the group, would plop himself in a big, broad club
chair and expound on finance while the others sat at his feet.

On Wall Street, his homespun manner made him a cult figure.
Where finance was so forbiddingly complex, Buffett could explain it
like a general-store clerk discussing the weather. He never forgot that
underneath each stock and bond, no matter how arcane, there lay a
tangible, ordinary business. Beneath the jargon of Wall Street, he
seemed to unearth a street from small-town America.

It is a curious irony that as more Americans acquired an interest in
investing, Wall Street became more complex, more abstruse, more arcane, and more forbidding than ever. When Buffett was born, in the
midst of the Depression, the few Americans who did have capital felt
personally equipped to manage it. This they did by salting it away in
blue chips and triple-A bonds. The Depression cast a long shadow, but
the postwar prosperity eclipsed it. Today, tens of millions have at least a

small grubstake, but very few feel comfortable with handling it, and fewer still have the old habit of prudence. At best, they anxiously scan the financial pages, as though each day's twitch in the data on housing or inflation might bring the long-awaited "answer." At worst, they switch in and out of mutual funds with an impatience that would have shocked their grandparents.

In such a complex age, what was stunning about Buffett was his applicability. Most of what Buffett did was imitable by the average person (this is why the multitudes flocked to Omaha). Buffett's genius was largely a genius of character—of patience, discipline, and rationality. These were common enough virtues, but they were rare in the heat of financial passions, and indispensable to anyone who would test his mettle in the stock market. In this sense, Buffett's character and career unfolded as a sort of public tutorial on investing and on American business. Buffett was aware of his role from the very beginning, and he nurtured a curious habit of chronicling his escapades even as he lived them.

As an investor, Buffett eschewed the use of leverage, futures, dynamic hedging, modern portfolio analysis, and all of the esoteric strategies developed by academics. Unlike the modern portfolio manager, whose mind-set is that of a trader, Buffett risked his capital on the long-term growth of a few select businesses. In this, he resembled the magnates of a previous age, such as J. P. Morgan, Sr.

But the secretive Morgan was a Wall Street archetype; Buffett, a plainspoken Midwesterner, was its antithesis. He was famous for quipping that it was the bankers "who should have been wearing the ski masks,"[3] or that, as he said to a friend who had been offered a job in finance, "you won't encounter much traffic taking the high road in Wall Street."[4] He once wrote that he would no more take an investment banker's opinion on whether to do a deal than he would ask a barber whether he needed a haircut.[5] This commonsensical crackerbarrel wit made him an archetype of something larger, and far more basic, to the country's past. It answered to a deeply American need for authentic heroes.

This has always been America's secular myth: the uncorrupted commoner from the Midwest or West who stands up to the venal Easterners, be they politicians, bankers, big businessmen, or other. It is a ransom to the country's origins, a remembrance that the first authentic and pure Americans were destroyed. Let Europe have its princes; the American ideal has always been a self-made man from the midcountry—a Lincoln, a Twain, a Will Rogers. In an age without heroes, this, too, is what Buffett's disciples were seeking in Omaha.

As Jack Newfield wrote of Robert Kennedy, Buffett was not a hero, only a hope; not a myth, only a man.[6] Despite his broad wit, he was strangely stunted. When he went to Paris, his only reaction was that he had no interest in sight-seeing and that the food was better in Omaha. His talent sprang from his unrivaled independence of mind and ability to focus on his work and shut out the world, yet those same qualities exacted a toll. Once, when Buffett was visiting the publisher Katharine Graham on Martha's Vineyard, a friend remarked on the beauty of the sunset. Buffett replied that he hadn't *focused* on it, as though it were necessary for him to exert a deliberate act of concentration to "focus" on a sunset.[7] Even at his California beachfront vacation home, Buffett would work every day for weeks and not go near the water.

Like other prodigies, he paid a price. Having been raised in a home with more than its share of demons, he lived within an emotional fortress. The few people who shared his office had no knowledge of the inner man, even after decades. Even his children could scarcely recall a time when he broke through his surface calm and showed some feeling.

Though part of him is a showman or preacher, he is essentially a private person. Peter Lynch, the mutual-fund wizard, visited Buffett in the 1980s and was struck by the tranquillity in his inner sanctum. His archives, neatly alphabetized in metal filing cabinets, looked as files had in another era. He had no armies of traders, no rows of electronic screens, as Lynch did. Buffett had no price charts, no computer—only a newspaper clipping from 1929 and an antique ticker under a glass dome. The two of them paced the floor, recounting their storied histories, what they had bought, what they had sold. Where Lynch had kicked out his losers every few weeks, Buffett had owned mostly the same few stocks for years and years. Lynch felt a pang, as though he had traveled back in time.[8]

Buffett's one concession to modernity is a private jet. Otherwise, he derives little pleasure from spending his fabulous wealth. He has no art collection or snazzy car, and he has never lost his taste for hamburgers. He lives in a commonplace house on a tree-lined block, on the same street where he works. His consuming passion—and pleasure—is his work, or, as he calls it, his canvas. It is there that he revealed the secrets of his trade, and left a self-portrait.

BUFFETT

OMAHA

Almost from the day that Dr. Pollard awakened him to the world, six pounds strong and five weeks early, Warren Buffett had a thirst for numbers. As a boy, he and his friend Bob Russell would pass an afternoon on the Russells' front porch, which overlooked a busy intersection, recording the license-plate numbers of passing cars. When the sky darkened, they would go inside and spread open the *Omaha World-Herald*, counting how often each letter appeared and filling entire scrapbooks with progressions of numbers, as though they held the key to some Euclidean riddle. Often, Russell would reach for the almanac and read out a list of cities. One by one, Warren would spit back the populations. "I'd say a city, he'd hit it on the nose," Russell would recall, half a century later. "I might say, 'Davenport, Iowa; Topeka, Kansas; Akron, Ohio.' If I gave him ten cities, he'd hit every one." Baseball scores, horse-racing odds—every numeral was fodder for that precocious memory. Combed, scrubbed, and stuffed into a pew of Dundee Presbyterian Church, Warren would pass the time on Sundays calculating the life spans of ecclesiastical composers. He would stand in the living room with a paddle and ball, counting, counting by the hour. He would play Monopoly for what seemed forever—counting his imagined riches.

Blue-eyed, with a fair complexion and pink cheeks, Warren was intrigued not merely with numbers, but with *money*. His first possession was a nickel-coated money changer, given to him by his Aunt Alice at Christmas and thereafter proudly strapped to his belt. When he was five, he set up a gum stand on his family's sidewalk and sold Chiclets to passersby. After that, he sold lemonade—not on the Buffetts' quiet street, but in front of the Russells' house, where the traffic was heavier.

At nine, Warren and "Russ" would count the bottle caps from the soda machine at the gas station across from the Russells' house. This was not idle counting, but a primitive market survey. How many Orange Crush caps? How many Cokes and root beers? The boys would cart the caps in a wagon and store them in Warren's basement, *piles* of them. The idea was, which brand had the highest sales? Which was the best *business*?

At an age when few children knew what a business was, Warren would get rolls of ticker tape from his stockbroker father, set them on the floor, and decipher the ticker symbols from his father's Standard & Poor's. He would search the local golf course for used but marketable golf balls. He would go to Ak-Sar-Ben* racetrack and scour the saw-dusted floors, turning over torn and discarded stubs and often finding a winning ticket that had been erroneously thrown away. In the sweltering Nebraska summers, Warren and Russ would carry golf clubs for the rich gentlemen at the Omaha Country Club and earn $3 for the day. And at dusk, as they rocked on the Russells' front-porch glider in the stillness of the Midwestern twilight, the parade of Nashes and Studebakers and the clanging of the trolley car would put a thought in Warren's mind. All of that traffic with no place to go but right by the Russells' house, he would say—if only there were a way to make some money off it. Russell's mom, Evelyn, recalled Warren after fifty years. "All that *traffic*," he would say to her. "What a shame you aren't making money from the people going by." As if the Russells could set up a toll booth on North 52nd Street. "What a *shame*, Mrs. Russell."

What, then, was the source?

Warren was the second of three children, and the only son. His mother was a petite, feisty woman from a small town in Nebraska. She had a lively temperament and, as was said of women relegated to a supporting role, "a good head for numbers." Warren's father, a serious

*Nebraska spelled backward.

but kind man, was surely the dominant influence in his life. Opening to Warren's eyes the world of stocks and bonds, he must have planted a seed, but insofar as such things are knowable, Howard Buffett's acumen for numbers was not on a par with his son's. Nor was his passion for making money. What was it, then, that prompted Warren to turn from that mannered, comfortable household—to crawl along the floor of the racetrack as though it were a bed of pearl oysters? What was it that would enable him, years later, to stun his colleagues in business—time and again—by computing columns of figures in his head, and by recalling encyclopedic volumes of data as easily as he had the population of Akron? Warren's younger sister, Roberta, said flatly, "I think it was in his genes."

The Buffetts were said to be gentle and sweet-natured, traits that endured. They were skilled at business and loath to spend a dollar. The earliest known Buffett (pronounced *Buff*ett) in America, John Buffett, was a serge weaver of French Huguenot origin. He married Hannah Titus, in Huntington, on the north shore of Long Island, in 1696.[1] The Buffetts remained on Long Island, as farmers, until after the Civil War. But they had a streak of ambition, which clashed with the family's frugal ways. In 1867, Sidney Homan Buffett was employed at clearing land for Zebulon Buffett, his grandfather. On hearing of his fifty-cent-per-diem wage, Sidney became so disgusted that he put down his ax and headed west. He took a job driving a stage out of Omaha, and in 1869 opened the S. H. Buffett grocery. With Omaha still in its frontier beginnings, the Buffetts were ensconced in the city's commercial life, a mile and a half from the wooded site of the future office of America's richest man.

Omaha was a cluster of frame and log buildings, set against the rugged bluffs rising from the Missouri River. Though the plains stood at its door, the town itself was hilly. The area had been wilderness until 1854, when a treaty with the Maha Indians (later the Omahas) opened the Nebraska Territory to settlement. The seminal moment in its growth was in 1859, when an Illinois railroad lawyer named Abraham Lincoln visited the area and took a parcel of land as collateral for a defaulted loan. A few years later, President Lincoln designated the city as the eastern terminal of the Union Pacific Railroad.[2]

Sidney Buffett opened his store, with impeccable timing, three months after the railroads joined the continent. Omaha was already "the great jumping-off place" for engines belching across the plains.[3] It soon was teeming with settlers, drifters, speculators, Civil War veterans, railroad men, ex-convicts, and prostitutes, many of whom happened upon the Buffett grocery, where Sidney sold quail, wild ducks, and prairie chickens over the counter. Zebulon was highly dubious of his prospects. Writing to his twenty-one-year-old grandson, Zebulon stressed that prudence in business was the Buffetts' watchword.

> You can't expect to make much, but I hope business will get better in the spring. But if you can't make it, do leave off in time to pay your debts and save your credit, for *that is better than money*.[4]

But the young city prospered, and Sidney prospered with it. By the 1870s, Omaha had cast-iron architecture and an opera house. By the turn of the century, it had skyscrapers, cable cars, and a swelling population of 140,000. Sidney built a bigger store and brought two sons into the business. The younger of these, Ernest—the future grandfather of Warren—had the family knack for business. He quarreled with his brother over a girl, and married her, whereupon the brothers stopped speaking. In 1915, Ernest left the downtown store and established a new one—Buffett & Son—in the city's western reaches.

Once again, the Buffett timing was shrewd. Omaha's population was migrating west from the river. Sensing opportunity in the suburbs, Ernest cultivated a delivery trade and sold on credit. Soon, rich families' cooks were phoning orders to Buffett & Son. The business grew, and Ernest hewed to the Buffetts' tightfisted ways. He paid the stock clerks the lordly sum of $2 for an eleven-hour shift, accompanied by a lecture on the evils of the minimum wage and similar "socialistic" mandates. Tall and imposing, Ernest did not merely run the store—he tyrannized it.

Ernest's son Howard—Warren's father—had no interest in becoming a third-generation grocer. Howard was independent-minded, like Ernest, but warmer and without the bluster. He worked briefly on an oil pipeline in Wyoming, but his true interests were in the life of the mind. At the University of Nebraska in Lincoln, Howard was editor of the *Daily Nebraskan*, and aspired to a career in journalism. Though not particularly handsome, he had dark hair and an arresting gaze. As fraternity president, he had his pick of society belles. But in his senior year, Howard met a hardscrabble country girl who was anything but society.

Leila Stahl had grown up in West Point, Nebraska, a bleak, rural town of 2,200 people. Her father, John Ammon Stahl, owned a weekly paper, the *Cuming County Democrat*. Most of the people in town were Germanic, and the English-speaking Stahls were outsiders. Leila's mother felt particularly isolated and spent much of the time bedridden and depressed. Leila and her brother and two sisters had to fend for themselves, and Leila had to help her father at the *County Democrat*. From the fifth grade on, she would sit on a high stool and set type by hand, and later by Linotype. Sometimes when a train stopped in West Point she would rush on board and interview passengers to fill the news columns. On Thursdays, this slight schoolgirl stood beside the fly of the giant press, firmly gripping the sheets of newsprint and taking care to pull each one at just the right moment. In time, Leila developed pounding headaches, synchronized with the press run of the *County Democrat*.

After Leila graduated from high school, at sixteen, she had to work three more years to afford tuition at Lincoln. She appeared in Howard Buffett's office, looking for a job at the *Daily Nebraskan*, having survived her childhood with a tart tongue and a wry sense of humor. She was pretty, just over five feet, with soft features and wavy light brown hair. As she would put it, she "majored in marrying"[5]—not an unreasonable course of study for a woman facing the prospect of returning to West Point.

Howard hired her, and immediately asked her for a date. The attraction was immediate on both sides. When his graduation neared, Howard asked for her hand. John Stahl, an educated man, had hoped that his daughter would finish college, but gave his blessing. The wedding was in West Point, the day after Christmas, 1925, in ten-below-zero weather. According to a memoir that Leila wrote for her grandchildren, Howard later told her, "When I married you it was the best bargain I ever made." There was no thought of a honeymoon. Directly the wedding ended, they boarded a bus for Omaha.

Howard had been offered a newspaper job, the stuff of his dreams, but a friend of his father's had a $25-a-week spot for him in an insurance company. Howard's capitulation was a commentary on the times. As Leila noted, "He deferred to his father, who had paid for college."[6]

The couple moved into a two-bedroom white clapboard bungalow with a coal furnace, on Barker Avenue. For Leila, it was a hard beginning. Raised by an invalid mother, she was unprepared as a homemaker. As Howard used the car, Leila walked to the streetcar when she took temporary secretarial or printing jobs—sometimes, in those first years, making more in a week than he did. Then she would walk back to a load of housework. In 1927, Leila had an eye operation, after which her headaches began to recur. The next year, when Doris, her first child, was born, Leila ran a fever of 105, alarming everyone. Two years later the couple had a son, Warren Edward. It was a humid summer's day—August 30, 1930—a cloudburst breaking the eighty-nine-degree heat.

From the start, Warren was cautious beyond his years. When he learned to walk, it was with his knees bent, as if ensuring that he wouldn't have far to fall. When his mother took Doris and Warren to church-circle meetings, Doris would explore and get lost, but Warren would sit dutifully by her. "Never much trouble as a little child," Leila would write.

In a picture taken when Warren was two, he appears as a chunky, blondish boy in white laced boots and white socks, one hand grasping a cube-shaped block, with a slight smile and a deep gaze. His hair, reddish blond at first, turned to auburn, but his temperament didn't change. He didn't wander where he was unfamiliar, nor did he cause trouble or get into fights. Roberta, younger than Warren by three years, would protect him from neighborhood bullies. Once, Howard brought home some boxing gloves and invited a boy over to box with Warren. "They were never used afterwards," Leila noted. So gentle was Warren's nature that he inspired in his sisters, as he would in others, a protective instinct. He didn't seem *equipped* to fight.

Warren's first years were difficult ones for the family. Howard was working as a securities salesman with Union Street Bank. The curmudgeonly Ernest thought it a dubious profession. He summed it up in a letter to Warren's Uncle Clarence:

I know all there is to know about stocks, and in a few words that means that any man who has been able to save a few dollars up to the time he is fifty years old is a darn fool to play the stock market, and I don't mean maybe.[7]

Howard scribbled in the margin, "A real booster for my business!" But within a year, Ernest looked prophetic. On August 13, 1931—two weeks shy of Warren's first birthday—his father returned from work with the news that his bank had closed. It was the defining, faith-shattering scene of the Great Depression. His job was gone, his savings were lost.[8] Ernest gave his son a little time to pay the grocery bills—a bitter pill, for Howard had inherited the Buffett disdain for borrowing. "Save your credit, for that is better than money." His prospects were so bleak that he considered moving the family back to West Point.

But in short order, Howard announced that Buffett, Sklenicka & Co. had opened its doors in the Union State Bank building on Farnam Street—the same street where Warren would later live and work. Howard and a partner, George Sklenicka, peddled "Investment Securities, Municipal, Corporation and Public Utilities, Stocks and Bonds." Howard now drew on his courage and will, for the market crash had tarnished the public's trust. Omaha, at first, had thought itself immune to the Depression, but by 1932, wheat prices had plunged and farmers were eating in soup kitchens. Staunchly Republican Omaha voted Roosevelt in a landslide; the next year, eleven thousand registered for relief. Born in those meanest of times, Buffett Sklenicka appears at first to have been a business only in name—a place where Howard could hang his hat and work on commission. His first sales were long in coming, and the commissions were small. Ernest, who was president of the Omaha Rotary, informed his fellow Rotarians that as his well-intentioned son didn't know much about stocks, they would be advised *not* to give him their business.[9] Leila managed to put dinner on the table, but she often skipped herself to give Howard a full portion. The family was so strapped that Leila stopped going to her church circle for want, of twenty-nine cents to buy a pound of coffee.

And the Buffetts were wracked by those extremes of nature that in the Midwest seemed as if fused with the Depression itself. "The Great Depression began," Leila wrote, with "a terrible, 112-degree heat." Dust storms blew in from Oklahoma, and Omahans vainly sealed their homes against the locusts. On the day of Warren's fourth birthday party, a "high searing wind" blew the paper plates and napkins off the table and buried the porch in red dust. Warren and Doris would bear the suffocating heat outside, waiting for the ice man to hop from his horse-drawn cart and hand them ice slivers to suck on. Worse than the heat was the bitter winter cold. Bundled up, Warren and his sister would walk eight long blocks to the Columbian School, in weather so frigid that salesmen kept their motors running as they paid their calls, for fear that they wouldn't be able to restart their engines.

By the time that Warren began school, his father's fortunes were rapidly improving. When Warren was six, the Buffetts moved to a more spacious Tudor brick home with a sloping, shingled roof, on suburban North 53rd Street. The bad times in the Buffett home were not discussed; they were banished.

But they seem to have deeply affected Warren. He emerged from those first hard years with an absolute drive to become very, very rich. He thought about it before he was five years old. And from that time on, he scarcely stopped thinking of it.

When Warren was six, the Buffetts took a rare vacation to Lake Okoboji, in northern Iowa, where they rented a cabin. Warren managed to buy a six-pack of Cokes for twenty-five cents; then he waddled around the lake selling the sodas at five cents each, for a nickel profit. Back in Omaha, he bought soda pop from his grandfather's grocery and sold it door-to-door on summer nights while other children played in the street.

From then on, such endeavors were unceasing. And Warren's moneymaking had a *purpose*. He wasn't thinking about getting pocket money for then, but about advancing toward his great aspiration.

When Warren was seven, he was hospitalized with a mysterious fever. Doctors removed his appendix, but he remained so ill that the doctors feared he would die. Even when his father fetched his favorite noodle soup, Warren refused to eat. But left alone, he took a pencil and filled a page with numbers. These, he told his nurse, represented his future capital. "I don't have much money now," Warren said cheerfully, "but someday I will and I'll have my picture in the paper."[10] Purportedly in his death throes, Warren sought succor not in soup but in dreams of money.

Howard Buffett was determined that Warren would never repeat his own experience of hardship. Also, he resolved that as a parent, he would never follow the example of Ernest and demean *his* son. He unfailingly expressed confidence in Warren and supported him in whatever he did. And though Warren had his mother's high spirits, his universe revolved around his father.

Six feet tall, Howard towered over the family, physically and in other respects. He worked hard at supporting the family, owning not only his brokerage but also the South Omaha Feed Co., a small business by Omaha's stockyards. But he was not excited by money; his passions were religion and politics. He was a self-consciously moral man and had the courage of his beliefs, which were conservative in the extreme. ("To the right of God," a local banker said.)

Convinced that Roosevelt was destroying the dollar, Howard gave gold coins to his children and bought pretty things for the house—a crystal chandelier, sterling silver flatware, and oriental throw rugs—all with a view that tangibles were better than dollars. He even stocked up on canned foods and purchased a farm, intended to be the family's refuge from the hellfire of inflation.

Howard also stressed a principle that was more enduring than any of his political opinions, namely, the habit of independent thought. With his children at his side, Howard would recite a favorite maxim from Emerson:

> The great man is he who in the midst of the crowd keeps with perfect sweetness the independence of solitude.

Howard drilled the children in religious values, but also in secular ones. He taught an adult Sunday school class, but he also served on the public school board. Scarcely a week went by without his reminding Warren and his sisters of their duty—not just to God, but to community. He was fond of telling them, "You are not required to carry the whole burden—nor are you permitted to put down your share."

As was not, perhaps, so uncommon for a man of that era, he not only mouthed such aphorisms but did his best to live by them. He did not ever drink or smoke. When a favored customer's securities turned out poorly, Howard felt bad enough to repurchase them for his own account.

"You are a good citizen," he would respond when told of some social malady. "What are you going to do about it?"

He sat, always, in a red leather chair in the living room, with a Victrola at his ear blaring out Stephen Foster and cherished hymns and marches. A creature of habit, the dimpled stockbroker would take the family to Sunday dinner at the bustling terra-cotta Union Station, and then to Evans Ice Cream on Center Street. Though he dressed soberly in dark suits, he smiled easily. Herbert Davis, at one time Howard's associate, said, "He was exactly what you'd want in a father."

His children lived in fear of disappointing him. Doris refused to even sit with friends who were drinking beer, lest her father see them and associate her with such sinfulness. "He had all these high principles," Roberta recalled. "You felt you *had* to be a good person."

Warren idealized him the most of all. He was close to his dad, and loose and easy with him. In church, once, Warren told his rather off-key father, "Pops, either you can sing or I can sing, but we both can't sing at the same time." Howard affectionately called him "Fireball."

When Warren was ten, Howard took him to New York—as he did, in turn, each of his children—on the overnight train. Leila watched Warren go off with his "best friend" in hand and his big stamp album under his arm. Their itinerary included a baseball game, a stamp display, and "some place with Lionel toy trains."[11] On Wall Street, Warren went to the stock exchange.

Warren was already as fascinated by stocks as other boys were by model aircraft. He frequently visited Howard's now prosperous brokerage, which had moved to the marble-columned Omaha National Bank Building, at 17th and Farnam. Up in his father's office, Warren would gaze at the stock and bond certificates, stowed behind gold-painted bars and endowed, in Warren's eyes, with a mysterious allure.[12] Often, he would race down the steps to the Harris Upham brokerage, which was in the same building and was frequented by financial men in Omaha as a source of stock quotations. Jesse Livermore, the infamous East Coast speculator, would stop by when he was in town, scribble an order on a piece of paper, and silently depart. And the Harris Upham brokers indulged the young, big-eared Warren by allowing him to chalk the prices of stocks on the blackboard.[13]

At home, Warren began to chart the prices of stocks on his own. Observing their ups and downs, he was bewitched by the idea of deciphering their patterns. At eleven, he took the plunge and bought three shares of Cities Service preferred, as well as three shares for his sister Doris, at $38 a share. "I knew then he knew what he was doing," Doris would recall. "The boy lived and breathed numbers." But Cities Service plunged to 27. They sweated it out, and the stock recovered to 40, whereupon Warren sold, netting, after commission, his first $5 of profit in the market. Directly he sold, Cities Service climbed to 200. It was his first lesson in patience.

Warren did better at the track. Intrigued by the mathematics of odds-making, he and Russell developed a tipping system for horse players. After a few days, they noticed that the system worked, so they penciled out their picks under the banner *Stable-Boy Selections* and took a pile of copies to Ak-Sar-Ben racetrack. Quoting Russell: "We found out we could sell it. We were waving them around, calling 'Get your *Stable-Boy Selections*.' But we didn't have a license and they shut us down."[14]

Warren's exploits were always based on numbers, which he trusted above all else. In contrast, he did not subscribe to his family's religion. Even at a young age, he was too mathematical, and too logical, to make the leap of faith. He adopted his father's ethical underpinnings, but not his belief in an unseen divinity. In a person who is honest in his thoughts, and especially in a boy, such untempered logic can only lead to one terrifying fear—the fear of dying. And Warren was stricken with it.[15]

Every week, no matter if the snows were four feet high, Leila and Howard insisted that Warren go to Sunday school. But it didn't sustain him. When he sat in church, calculating the life spans of the ecclesiastics, there was a purpose to it. He wanted to know whether faith would result in living a longer life.[16] Not faith in an afterlife, as a believer would have had, but a concern for living longer in *this* one.

He and Bob Russell would be sitting on the Russells' front-porch glider, in the stillness of an afternoon, and as if brought on by a sudden prairie twister, Warren would say, "Russ, there is one thing I am scared of. I am afraid to die." He brought it up maybe every year or so—often enough so that it stuck in Russell's mind. It seemed disconnected from everything else that Russell knew of Warren, who was usually so buoyant. Sometimes Russell would put birdseed on the floor of the milk box and trap a bird inside and invariably, Warren would beg him not to harm it. Russell would pull a string, tied to the door of the milk box, and let it go. But he couldn't release Warren from the fear of his *own* mortality.

"If you do what God gave you the talent to do, you can be successful and help others and die with a smile," Russell would say.

"Bob, I'm just scared," Warren would reply.

Russell, a Roman Catholic, did not understand. He would wonder where it came from, why a guy who had so much going for him was so afraid. But there was an aspect of Warren's life at home that Russell did not know about.

To outside appearances, the Buffett household was the ideal: loving, prosperous, inspired by high morals, and centered on the family. And such particulars were genuine. Leila would refer to the day she met Howard as "the luckiest day of my life."

She treated her husband like a king—a benevolent king, but a king nonetheless. A practical woman, Leila had ideas of her own about stocks, but she didn't mention them to Howard. Even when Leila had pounding headaches, she was careful not to bother Howard or disturb his reading. Her aim was to be a perfect wife. Warren's friends knew her as a tiny, cheerful woman with a pretty smile—sweet and sociable and all *atwitter*, like the good witch of the North.

But when the strain of trying to be perfect was too much for Leila, she would turn on Warren and his sisters with the wrath of God. Without warning, that good-humored woman would become furious beyond words, and rage at her children with an unrelenting meanness, some-times not letting up for hours. She scolded and degraded her children. Nothing they had done measured up. She compared, criticized, and dredged up every imaginable failing.

In Leila's fury, she seemed as if driven by some horrible injustice. Nothing that Warren or his sisters had done would escape her notice; no transgression, however slight, was too small for one of her vicious rebukes. Even when they had committed no crime, her imagination supplied one.

As far as Warren and his sisters knew, Leila's moods were wholly unpredictable, and therefore all the more terrifying. And when one came over her there was no escape. She was a strong woman, strong as the girl who had run the Linotype at age eleven. If they tried to break free she would snap at them, *"I'm not finished."*[17] And then, suddenly, the tempest would be over. Then the sweet little woman would return.

Once, in more recent years, one of Warren's sons, who was home from college, called Leila to say hello. She suddenly lit into him with all her fury. She called him a terrible person for not calling more often, and detailed his supposedly innumerable failings of character, and went on for two entire hours. When Warren's son put down the phone, he was in tears. Warren said softly, "Now you know how I felt every day of my life."

Sometime after Leila left West Point, her family suffered repeated tragedies. One of her sisters committed suicide; another sister and Leila's mother were institutionalized. Whatever the streak of madness or emotional imbalance that the Stahl women suffered, Leila at least survived.

But Warren and his sisters had to deal with the shrapnel from her fury on their own. There was certainly no discussion of it in the Buffett home. One morning, when Warren was young, Howard came down-stairs and warned him, "Mom is on the warpath again."[18] But more often, after Howard had left the house, Warren and the girls would listen for the telltale tone of her voice and warn one another. Their parents didn't argue; the conflict was between Leila and her kids. And it was a conflict that Warren and his sisters had no chance of winning.

Warren coped with this hopeless battle by *not* fighting back. "He didn't get mad. He kept it to himself," his sister Roberta said. Jerry Moore, who lived across the street, observed that Warren didn't fight with anyone. He shied away from the usual neighborhood scrapes—from any sort of conflict.

He didn't mention his mother's "moods" to his friends, and there was nothing in his upbeat manner that would have betrayed them. But some of the boys noticed that Warren spent more time with them at their homes than he did at his own. Mrs. Russell used to say, "I put him out with the cat and brought him in with the milk." Byron Swanson, a classmate, would come home—in that halcyon time when Americans left their homes unlocked—and find Warren, innocently and rather charmingly, sitting in his kitchen, drinking a Pepsi and eating potato chips. Walter Loomis said his mother had to chase Warren out when Loomis's father came home so the family could have dinner. (In retro-spect, he added dryly, "Too bad we kicked him out.")

Later, Warren's son Peter would wonder if his father's success was driven in part by the urge to get out of the house. The question is unan-swerable, but he had the urge from *somewhere*. Warren would sit on the fire escape at Rosehill elementary school and flatly tell his chums that he would be rich before he was thirty-five.[19] He never came across as being a braggart, or swell-headed. (In Russell's homely phrase, "his cap always fit.") He just had this *conviction* about himself.

He would bury himself in a favorite book, *One Thousand Ways to Make $1,000*, an exhortation to future Rockefellers with stories such as "Building a Business on Homemade Fudge" and "Mrs. MacDougall Turned $38 into a Million." How vividly did Warren imagine himself as the man in the illustration—dwarfed by a mountain of coins that brought more ecstasy than any mountain of candy! Surely, he was the reader of the editor's dreams—so well did he seize on the book's advice to "begin, begin" whatever schemes one might, but, by all means, not to wait.

On 53rd Street, Warren was known as a bookworm, and was certified in the neighborhood lore as having a "photographic memory." He was tall for his age, and liked to play sports, but was rather ungainly. He talked up his financial exploits, however, with a contagious passion. And when Warren talked, his friends perked up their ears. He didn't *persuade* the other boys to join him so much as he attracted them—a fireball, as his father said, drawing moths. Warren recruited Stuart Erickson, Russell, and Byron Swanson to go to Ak-Sar-Ben to scavenge for tickets. He enlisted half the neighborhood to gather golf balls. Soon he had bushel baskets of golf balls in his bedroom, organized by brand and price. Bill Pritchard, a neighbor, recalled, "He'd hand out a dozen golf balls. We'd sell 'em, and he'd take his cut." Warren and Erickson even set up a golf-ball stand at Elmwood Park, until, as Erickson recalled, business was so good that "somebody snitched on us and the pro threw us out."

A *Saturday Evening Post* profile of the Omaha of those years saw a barren city—in the telling quip, west of civilization, which stopped in Des Moines, and east of the scenery, which began with the Rocky Mountains.[20] It was distinguished only for its "conformity"; extreme only in its weather. Its contribution to culture was the Swanson dinner. Overlaid on this myth of Omaha as a cultural wasteland was a more romantic view of Omaha as an unspoiled refuge from the sinful East— as "simple" and vaguely pastoral. While this had an element of truth, it was greatly exaggerated. It would partly account for a later tendency to describe Buffett as oracular, rather than as talented and savvy, as a New Yorker would have been described—as the "Oracle of Omaha" or, repeatedly, the "Wizard of Omaha." (The Wizard of Oz did hail from Omaha.)

But Omaha was not a barren place to Warren. The Buffetts and their neighbors were educated and urban and part of the cultural mainstream. Fred Astaire learned to dance at the Chambers Academy on Farnam Street; Henry Fonda, a local boy, appeared on Omaha stages. Warren's Omaha was a small city—220,000 people—but by no means a small town. Carl Sandburg, who shoveled coal there, called it "Omaha, the roughneck, [which] feeds armies, eats and swears from a dirty face."[21]

The summer that Warren was eleven, Howard, who wanted his children to experience the supposed purity of farm life, took out an ad for a rural home. For a few weeks, Warren and Doris were boarded by a farmer named Elmer Benne. Warren savored Mrs. Benne's pies, but he didn't care for cows or stalks of corn. A silo was just as remote to him as the modern Art Deco skyscrapers of Omaha were to a farm boy. Warren was a *city* kid.

On 53rd Street, he knew the people in every house. And there was a sameness to the homes, with their twin gables, brown brick, and center doorways. He recognized the truck from Roberts Dairy, and the music of the trolley and the not-too-distant freight trains, and the aroma of coffee from the roasting plant downtown, and even, when a wind blew from the south on warm summer evenings, the thick, intolerable smell of the meatpacking plants. Whether on foot, on his three-speed, or by streetcar, he could fan out over the city, to the golf courses, to his father's office, to his grandfather's store. Whatever Warren's problems with his mother or his torment in church, his city was his great, sustaining constant.

But the violent shock that upset all America in December 1941 also threatened Warren's life in Omaha. The Sunday of Pearl Harbor, the Buffetts were paying a visit to Grandpa Stahl, in West Point. On the drive home, they listened to martial music. For the next few months, as America got used to war, Warren's life went on as before.

But in 1942, the Republicans in Nebraska's second congressional district were unable to find a candidate who would run against the party of a popular wartime president. In desperation, the GOP turned to an outspoken New Deal hater: Howard Buffett.

Howard, an isolationist, was given little chance of winning. On the stump, his venom was directed not at Hitler or Mussolini but at Franklin Roosevelt.

I am fully aware of the odds against a Republican candidate today. He fights against the most powerful Tammany political machine the world has ever known. This ruthless gang, under cover of war, is making plans to fasten the chains of political servitude around America's neck.[22]

Inveighing against inflation and big government, Howard was forty years ahead of his time. But in Omaha, he was personally popular. He had little money—his expenses would amount to only $2,361—but he campaigned tenaciously.

On election day, Howard typed out a concession speech and retired at nine o'clock. The next day, he discovered he had won. He would call it "one of the happiest surprises" of his life.

Warren realized his fate with a jolt: for the first time in his twelve-plus years, he was leaving Omaha. In a family photograph taken just after the election, Warren looked decidedly uneasy, his handsome face set in a vague stare, his tightly pursed lips managing only the slightest suggestion of a smile.

As space in wartime Washington was scarce, Howard rented a home in the charming but remote Virginia town of Fredericksburg. The house stood on a hill, overlooking the Rappahannock River. It was a rambling white Colonial place with a front porch and roses. To Roberta, it looked "like something out of the movies." Warren hated it.

Cinematic though it may have been, Fredericksburg was isolated, Southern, and unfamiliar. Any change would have been unwelcome to Warren, and this one turned his world upside down. Not only had he been yanked away from friends and neighborhood, but he was separated during the week from his father, who was residing at the Dodge Hotel, in Washington, fifty miles north. The freshman congressman told his family that he would serve only one term, but that didn't comfort his son. Away from Omaha and from all that he knew, Warren was "miserably homesick."[23]

Though he was desperate to leave, it was not in his nature to confront his folks. He merely told them that he was suffering from a mysterious "allergy" and that he couldn't sleep at night. Of course, his Zen-like stoicism was perfectly calculated to unnerve them. He would recall, "I told my parents I couldn't breathe. I told them not to worry about it, to get a good night's sleep themselves, and I'd just stand up all night."[24] Naturally, they were worried sick about him.* Meanwhile,

---

*Asked years later whether Warren was in fact standing up, Doris said, "Goodness, no. He was sleeping."

Warren wrote to Grandpa Ernest and told him that he was unhappy. In short order, Ernest wrote back and suggested that Warren move in with him and his Aunt Alice and finish the eighth grade in Omaha. After a few weeks in Fredericksburg, his parents agreed.

Warren went back on the train, sharing an overnight compartment with Hugh Butler, a Nebraska senator. At daybreak, Senator Butler, noticing that the youngster had passed the night soundly, commented, "I thought you couldn't sleep." Warren replied airily, "Oh, I got rid of that in Pennsylvania."[25]

In Omaha, Warren's spirits revived. Aunt Alice, a free-spirited home economics teacher, was a kind guardian, and she took an interest in Warren. Like other teachers, she was attracted to his brightness and curiosity.

Grandpa Ernest, an instinctive teacher, also took a shine to him. Ernest was working on a book, and each night he dictated a few pages to Warren.[26] The recherché title was "How to Run a Grocery Store, and a Few Things I Have Learned About Fishing." The thrust of it is evident from a letter in which Ernest confidently declared that supermarkets were a passing fad:

> Kroger, Montgomery & Ward, and Safeway, I think have seen their high points. The chain stores are going to have a hard time from now on.[27]

Fortunately, "How to Run a Grocery Store" was never published.

But Warren went to work at Buffett & Son, where he observed his grandfather's maxims firsthand. Ernest took it upon himself to deduct two pennies a day from Warren's meager salary—a gesture which, along with his lectures on the work ethic, was intended to impress upon Warren the intolerable costs of government programs such as Social Security. For a twelve-year-old boy, the work itself was hard: lifting crates, hauling soda pop. Warren didn't care for it. He didn't like the *smell* of groceries. When fruit spoiled, he had to clean the bins.[28]

But he liked the store. Buffett & Son was a cozy nook of a grocery, with squeaky wooden floors, rotating fans, and rows of wooden shelves that reached to the ceiling. When someone wanted a can from the upper shelf, Warren or another clerk would move a sliding ladder to the proper spot and ascend to the summit.

It was the first successful business that Warren had seen. His Uncle Fred, who stood behind the counter, had a cheerful word for every shopper. With its pungent, fresh-baked breads, ripe cheeses, and un-wrapped cookies and nuts, Buffett & Son had *something*—an adher-ence, perhaps, to Grandpa's penny-pinching virtues—that pulled people back.[29]

Charlie Munger, Warren's future business partner, worked there on Saturdays (though he did not meet Warren until years later). Munger saw in the store the inculcation of a culture, something out of a Nor-man Rockwell painting. Nobody *ever* loafed. "You were just goddam busy from the first hour of morning to night." When Bill Buffett, War-ren's cousin, would trudge in a few minutes late, he would be greeted by his portly, white-haired grandfather, pocket watch in hand, bellow-ing from a second-floor balcony, "Billy, what *time* is it?"

While living at Ernest's, Warren often went to the home of Carl Falk, his father's then business partner, for lunch. He would curl up with an investment book from Falk's study—much more his cup of tea than groceries—while Mrs. Falk made lunch. One time, while Warren was slurping Mary Falk's chicken noodle soup, he declared that he would be a millionaire by age thirty—and enigmatically added, "and if not, I'm going to jump off the tallest building in Omaha."

Mary Falk was horrified, and told him not to repeat it. Warren looked at her and laughed. Nonetheless, she couldn't resist his charm, and always made him welcome in the Falk home. Mary Falk seems to have been the first to ask: "Warren, why this drive to make so much money?"

"It's not that I *want* money," Warren replied. "It's the fun of making money and watching it grow."

The final months of eighth grade, Warren enjoyed a reprieve. He was reunited with his chums, and he had the run of the city, from the Buffett store in the western suburbs to the cobblestone streets down-town, bustling with open-air markets and red-brick and cast-iron ware-houses, where Sidney, the first Buffett in Omaha, had set up his store, three-quarters of a century earlier. Already the fourth generation of Buffetts in Omaha, Warren was immensely at home there. He had the city's informal style, its plain prairie syntax, and also its opaque, une-motional cover. He was hardly "simple," but in his essential features—his dawning self-reliance, his ambitious but prudent capitalist zeal, and his composed, calm exterior—he was unmistakably Midwestern. Alas, by the fall of 1943, Warren had run out of excuses for not joining the family in Washington. His reprieve had run out.

Chapter 2

RUNAWAY

The Buffetts had moved to a four-bedroom house in Spring Valley, an outlying section of Washington, on Northwest 49th Street. The home was white-painted brick, with an open porch in front and a driveway that sloped to the rear. It was a typically modest young congressman's home—the Richard Nixons would be their neighbors—a short walk from Massachusetts Avenue. Behind the house was nothing but woods.

Warren's new life revolved around his job as a carrier for the *Washington Post*. Now thirteen, he kept a record of his earnings and filed a tax return—and defiantly refused to let his dad pay the taxes.[1]

But aside from his paper route, Warren was profoundly unhappy. At Alice Deal Junior High, he caused a bit of trouble for his teachers, and his grades were mediocre.[2] Young for his class, having skipped a grade, he was bespectacled and out of the social stream. His appearance was so slovenly that the principal warned Leila that he had better shape up.[3]

In June, at the end of that first, unhappy year, Warren ran away—the first real rebellion of his life. He and Roger Bell, the son of a Missouri congressman, and one other chum put out their thumbs for Hershey, Pennsylvania. Warren knew of a golf course there and thought they could stay a few days and caddie. But for once, economics were not his motivation. He was mad at his folks, mad at being in Washington—mad all around.[4]

The boys arrived at nightfall, without so much as a toothbrush, and checked into a room at the Community Inn. In the morning, no sooner were they out the door than the police stopped them. Bell was short, while Warren and the other boy were close to six feet. From a distance, the police thought Bell much younger—perhaps a kidnap victim—and took the trio in for questioning. One may imagine Warren, just shy of fourteen, glibly persuading the authorities of their innocence without saying much about what they *were* doing. The police let them go, but their balloon was pricked. They thumbed their way home that day.

It seems unlikely that Warren was of a mind to continue his rather halfhearted revolt. His spurts of acting out at school had been pretty tame; according to his sister Roberta, "rebellious" was "a pretty strong word" for him.

But Howard and Leila were shocked. Though they were gentle with Warren when he returned to Washington, Howard resolved to nip his mutiny in the bud. He told Warren that he would have to improve his marks or give up his paper route.

This worked on Warren's grades like a tonic. Far from relinquishing the paper route, he expanded it. He promptly procured a route with the *Times-Herald*, the *Post*'s morning competitor, covering the same territory as he had with the *Post*. As Buffett would recall, if a subscriber canceled one paper and wanted the other, "there was my shining face the next day."[5] Soon Warren had *five* delivery routes, and close to five hundred papers to deliver each morning. Leila would arise early to make his breakfast; Warren was out the door by five-twenty to catch the bus down Massachusetts Avenue. On the rare occasion when he was ill, Leila did the route, but she didn't go near the money. "Collections were everything to him," she wrote. "You didn't dare touch the drawer where he kept his money. Every penny had to be there."

Warren's crown jewel was the Westchester Apartments, a cluster of red-brick, eight-story high-rises on Cathedral Avenue. He quickly developed an assembly-line approach that was worthy of the young Henry Ford. He would drop off half of the papers for each building on the eighth-floor elevator landing and half on the fourth floor. Then he would run through the building on foot, floor by floor, sliding the papers in front of each apartment. On collection day, he left an envelope at the front desk, sparing him from having to go door-to-door. When the Buffetts returned to Omaha for the summer, Warren entrusted the route to a friend, Walter Diehl, and lectured him on how to handle it. Diehl remembered, "There was this pile of papers sitting in front of you—a *mountain*. But it only took an hour and a quarter or so. It was a beautiful route. All the buildings were connected underground. You never had to go outside."

Figuring that he could increase his profits by adding to his product line, Warren peddled magazines at the apartments, too. The trick was to offer subscriptions at just the right time. Some of his customers, Buffett would recall, "left their magazines out on the stairwell. You could tell by tearing off the address label when the expirations were. So I would keep track of when everybody's subscriptions expired."[6]

Though the apartments were considered classy—Warren saw Jacqueline Bouvier in the elevator—he had a problem with deadbeats. In wartime Washington, people were frequently moving in and out, sometimes neglecting to pay him. So Warren made a deal with the elevator girls. They got free papers; Warren got tipped off when anyone was planning to move![7]

In short, Warren had turned his paper routes into a business. He was earning $175 a month—what many a young man was earning as a full-time wage—and saving every dime.[8] In 1945, when he was still only fourteen, he took $1,200 of his profits and invested it in forty acres of Nebraska farmland.

World War II, of course, was the omnipresent backdrop to Warren's Washington years. There were bond drives at school and blackout curtains at home. Nevertheless, the war had little direct impact on him. The single exception was in August 1945, when the Buffetts were spending the summer in Omaha. Warren heard the news about Hiroshima and had a lively discussion about the atom bomb with Jerry Moore, his Omaha neighbor. Warren, Moore recalled, was quite concerned. He viewed relativity as he did religion—with unshaking, terrifying *logic*. "We were talking—I remember it vividly—on my front lawn. He was afraid of the implications of the chain reaction . . . of the possible devastation of the world."

Back in Washington, at Woodrow Wilson High, Warren was fitting in a bit better. His paper routes had given him an escape from homesickness, and he began to develop a set of friends. As in Omaha, he got a crew to hunt for golf balls. He also was a pretty good golfer and joined the school team.

Robert Dwyer, the golf coach, was another teacher-figure that Warren cultivated. Dwyer thought him funny—eager without being pushy. He took Warren to the track and taught him how to read the *Daily Racing Form*. In the summer after Warren's junior year, Dwyer and Warren happened to be playing golf on the day of the All-Star game. It started to rain, so they went to Dwyer's car and turned on the game. Charlie Keller, the New York Yankee slugger, was up. Dwyer said, "If you give me twenty-to-one odds, I'll bet you he hits a home run." Warren said, "I'll take a dollar's worth." Keller, of course, hit one. Dwyer was kind enough to lose the $20 on another bet.

But as both of them knew, Warren was making more money than his coach.[9] Marooned in a strange city, he was trying to jump-start his career at a time when he was barely capable of shaving. He was reading every business book he could get his hands on, poring over actuarial tables, running his paper route. Donald Danly, a Wilson student who became a good friend, thought Warren "was charting his way toward a [financial] target."

Danly, the son of a Justice Department attorney, was a serious and brilliant student. At first glance, he and Warren had little in common. Danly had a good-looking girlfriend, whereas Warren didn't date. And Danly was chiefly interested in science. But Danly, who had lost his mother, began to spend a lot of time at the Buffetts' after the war, when Danly's father went to Japan to prosecute war criminals. The two played music together, Warren strumming on the ukulele while Danly played the piano. Then they discovered that Danly's love of science and Warren's obsession with business had a shared language—numbers. They would calculate the odds of poker hands, or the chances, in a room with a dozen people, that two would have the same birthday. Or Danly would rattle off a series of two-digit numbers, waiting for Warren to spit out the sum.

In their senior year, Danly bought a used pinball machine for $25, and Warren and he played it by the hour. The machine often broke, and as Danly tinkered with it, Warren took note of his friend's mechanical skill. Warren had an idea: why not put the machine in the barber shop on Wisconsin Avenue and rent it out?[10]

Warren approached the barber, who agreed to a fifty-fifty split. At the end of the first day, they found $14 in the machine. Within a month or so, Warren and Danly had machines in *three* barbershops. Prospering, they expanded to seven. Warren—living a real-life fantasy—thought of a name, the Wilson Coin Operated Machine Company. "Eventually we were making $50 a week," he recalled. "I hadn't dreamed life could be so good."[11]

Wilson Coin Op had a natural division of labor. Warren put up most of the capital for the machines, secondhand arcade games that cost from $25 to $75 apiece. Danly repaired them. Warren kept the books and typed a monthly financial statement. Barbers were instructed to call Danly if a machine broke—one was always breaking—and the two of them would show up pronto in Danly's 1938 Buick, which had had the backseat removed.

Fearing that the pinball business was controlled by the mob, Warren stuck to small, out-of-the-way locations. Also, he and Danly hinted that they were merely legmen for a going concern that was not to be taken lightly. Buffett recalled:

> The barbershop operators were always pushing us to put in new machines, and we'd always tell them we'd take it up with the boss. We pretended like we were these hired hands that were carrying machines around and counting money.[12]

Once a week they made the rounds, sometimes with Danly's girlfriend, Norma Jean Thurston. Warren would return to the car with a funny description of the barber, or of what he'd said to him, and the three of them would howl. Warren could see the twist—the irony of these kids acting out the role of being big-time businessmen.

Norma Jean thought Warren was especially funny. She was pretty and slender, with arched eyebrows and striking blond hair. Her nickname was "Peroxide." Danly was "Duck," but Warren was simply "Buffett." Their elders had fought a war, but Buffett, Duck, and Peroxide were still in a state of innocence. Though they were natural hams, they didn't smoke or use swear words, and Warren didn't drink anything but Pepsi-Cola. All the girls that Norma Jean knew were virgins; in her crowd there was hardly *any* sex. But Warren was a shade more innocent still. He didn't go to the Friday-night dances; "he didn't have the moves other guys had," Norma Jean said. "He didn't try."

He walked with his shoulders hunched forward and bent toward the ground, *tramp, tramp,* like a billy goat. At times, he carried a clunky-looking change purse strapped to his belt.[13] To his Wilson classmates, Warren's footwear marked him as a hayseed, and they remembered it after decades. "We used to get a kick out of Warren and his sneakers," remembered Casper Heindl. "He used to wear 'em year-round. I don't care if the snow was a foot deep, he had sneakers on." And Robert Moore said, "I remember him very well. The one thing we used to joke about—he didn't wear anything other than tennis shoes. Even in the dead of winter."

Warren seemed to take a perverse delight in those sneakers. "Most of us were trying to be like everyone else," Norma Jean noted. "The girls all buttoned their sweaters in the back. I think he *liked* being different." Though he was high-spirited and perpetually kidding, there was something of the odd man out about him. When his quirks were pointed out, he would stick to his guns, or kid himself, with self-depreciation. Norma Jean said, "He was what he was and he never tried to be anything else."

At the dinner table at home, Warren was getting a nightly seminar on sticking to one's guns. Howard, who despite his pledge to serve one term was reelected in 1944 and again in 1946, was in the fabled do-nothing Congress, so named for fighting Truman at every turn. In the evenings, he would expose the family to a drumbeat of dire alarums. Once, when the family was discussing what to get one of Howard's aides for Christmas, little Roberta piped up, "How about a savings bond—or does he know that they're no good?"

Another time, after having voted against a popular labor measure, Howard took Warren to a baseball game in Omaha. When the congressman was introduced to the crowd, he was roundly booed.[14] But he showed Warren no sign that he minded.

Unshakably ethical, Howard refused offers of junkets and even turned down a part of his pay. During his first term, when the congressional salary was raised from $10,000 to $12,500, Howard left the extra money in the Capitol disbursement office, insisting that he had been elected at the lower salary.

Leila said her husband considered only one issue in voting on a measure: "Will this add to, or subtract from, human liberty?" But his view of liberty was decidedly cramped. His single interest was in rolling back the enlarged government that Roosevelt, and World War II, had made permanent.

During the war, he coauthored a letter demanding that the United States "elaborate" on its policy of seeking an unconditional German surrender and posing the curious question "What are we fighting for?"[15] Did uprooting Nazism not constitute "an addition to human liberty?"

After the war, he voted against aiding bombed-out Britain, against school lunches, against European grain exports, and against the Bretton Woods monetary scheme.[16] At his worst, his Americanism lapsed into xenophobia and Red-baiting. As the Buffetts drove past the still-lit British embassy in the evenings, Howard would growl, "They even stay up late to think of ways to get our money."[17] He opposed the Marshall Plan to rebuild Western Europe as "Operation Rathole," and as possibly having Stalin's secret backing.[18]

On several issues, Howard was remarkably prescient. One of his few proposals was a measure to protect the owners of U.S. savings bonds against inflation. Yet the broad sense of his tenure is that of a moralist disfigured by parochial, and extremist, claims.

Warren mouthed his father's politics,[19] and probably believed them superficially, but he didn't commit himself to them. He absorbed his father's patriotism, but not his bitter isolationism. A few years later, Warren wryly alluded to his father's dogmatism in a letter to a college friend. "I had better knock this off," Warren wrote, "and go out and help my dad conduct a crusade against something or other."[20]

He did inherit his father's scruples and concern for society. (Indeed, Warren would later revile the corporate theft of other people's money in much the same terms that Howard critiqued the government's.) But for Warren, who had witnessed the Depression and the war as a child, government was society's defender, not its enemy. Given his utter devotion to his father, his political awareness, though still undeveloped, suggested a stirring of independence.

Warren had already decided that he would not follow his father into government. When Norma Jean asked whether he might make a life in Washington, Warren replied without hesitation, "No. I'm going to live in Omaha."

By his senior year, he was planning on a career not just in business, but specifically in investing. Sitting in the breakfast nook at home, at an age when other boys didn't get past the sports pages, he was already studying the stock tables. And word of his supposed expertise had followed him to school, where his teachers tried to pick his brain about the market.[21]

In a wily effort to capitalize on his renown, Warren shorted—that is, bet against—shares of American Telephone & Telegraph Company, because he knew that his teachers owned it. "They thought I knew about stocks and I thought if I shorted AT&T, I would terrorize them about their retirement."[22]

Why this mild repute as an oracle? Warren hadn't had any coups in the market. Yet people sensed that he knew. He had something innate: not merely a precocious store of knowledge, but an ability for casting it in logical terms. Faith didn't move him, but facts he could assemble in a smooth and sensible train. Quoting Danly: "He just seemed to have tremendous insight. He would say things in a way that didn't leave any doubt that he knew what he was talking about."

Warren graduated in June 1947, finishing sixteenth in a class of 374. (Danly was tied for first.) The Wilson yearbook captured him with bright, eager eyes, neatly parted hair, and a sheepish grin. The caption: "Likes math . . . a future stockbroker."

Howard suggested the nearby Wharton School of Finance and Commerce at the University of Pennsylvania. Warren replied that college would be a waste. He had delivered almost 600,000 papers and in the process earned over $5,000.[23] Money was coming in from newspapers, from Wilson Coin Op, and from a Nebraska tenant farmer. What's more, he had read at least one hundred books on business. What, in short, did he have to learn?

Howard gently pointed out that Warren was still two months shy of his seventeenth birthday. Finally, Warren capitulated. In August, Wilson Coin Op was sold for $1,200 to a returned war veteran. Warren pocketed his share and headed for Wharton.

This time, though, Howard had been wrong. Despite Wharton's fine reputation, its curriculum was lacking in beef. Warren disgustedly reported that he knew more than the professors. His dissatisfaction—a forerunner of his general disaffection for business schools—was rooted in their mushy, overbroad approach. His professors had fancy theories but were ignorant of the practical details of making a profit that Warren craved.

When Warren visited Omaha, Mary Falk warned him not to neglect his studies. He replied insouciantly, "Mary, all I need to do is open the book the night before and drink a big bottle of Pepsi-Cola and I'll make 100."

In fact, he was spending a lot of his time at a brokerage office in Philadelphia, following various stocks.[24] But he didn't have a system for investing—or if he did, it was haphazard. He would study the charts, he would listen to tips. But he didn't have a framework. He was searching.

In his freshman year, Warren roomed with Charles Peterson, an Omaha boy (and later, among Warren's first investors). He also made fast friends with Harry Beja, a Mexican who was as displaced on a northeastern campus as Warren was. Beja was *the* most serious student on campus, but Warren would kid him about living with the "Indians" in Mexico. The two of them matched A+'s in Industry 1, but Beja couldn't help but notice how much harder he had worked in the course than Warren had. Nonetheless, though he resented Warren's easy success, Beja had to admit that he *liked* Warren. Beja saw him as the type of American he had idealized: the honest and unassuming Midwesterner with a common touch.

Warren found another kindred soul in Beja's roommate, a Brooklyn boy named Jerry Orans. They met in the weight room, and the broad-shouldered Orans instantly decided that Warren was a "genius." Like Warren, Orans felt a bit out of the swing; he was dreadfully homesick and spent much of the first year in tears.[25] But he had a rapier wit and a warm smile, and was very bright himself. Warren and Orans became close friends.

Unwittingly, Warren was sowing the seeds for a future pool of investors.* But at the time, he felt he was going nowhere. After a year at Penn, he wanted out, but his father insisted that he try another year. In Washington for the summer, Warren found a comical outlet for his rich-man strivings—once again with Don Danly. His pinball partner had plunked down $350 for an old Rolls-Royce. Warren went with Danly to a Baltimore junkyard to pick it up and followed him back to

---

*Orans would be a Buffett investor and a lifelong admirer. He later suggested that Beja also invest, but Beja was determined to prove that he could do as well on his own. Thereafter, he said, Orans would call him a couple of times a year to tell him what Warren was worth. "It would just go up and up."

Washington. Just inside the District line, they were stopped by the police. Danly recounted:

> I had no plates, the taillights didn't work. The cop was fixing to write up a ticket. Warren said, "Look, officer, we just have to get it home to my garage so we can fix it up to meet all of the safety requirements." He was talking and talking and he just kept talking until the cop said okay.

Danly kept the Rolls in the Buffetts' garage. They spent the summer fixing it up—though, of course, Danly was the one who was under the chassis. Warren would sit on a stool, entertaining his friend with business stories and reading from a book they thought was a scream—*How to Lose Friends and Alienate People.*

The Rolls was a 1928 Ladies' Shopping Car. It had a single seat in front and a wide berth in back, and a hand crank for show. Danly and Norma Jean painted it dark blue. They rented it out a few times, but the real point was to be seen in it. Warren proposed that they drive downtown, posing as a rich couple with their chauffeur—but *he* would play the rich "aristocrat," Danly the chauffeur. Danly put on Howard Buffett's black overcoat and took the wheel, and Warren, wearing a muskrat coat and top hat, sidled in next to Norma Jean. As they approached the *Times-Herald* building, Danly, following a script, cut off the ignition and coasted to a stop. Then he got out and started tinkering under the hood, as if he were trying to figure out what was wrong. When people started to stare, Warren—the aristocrat—tapped on the windshield glass with a cane and pointed, as if indicating where the trouble might be. Danly fiddled a bit more and—behold—it was "fixed."*

But without a script, Warren was hardly so suave. He dated Norma Jean's cousin, Barbara Worley, over the summer, and took her to hear Billie Holiday. But though Warren was a lively companion, he ruined any hope of romance by subjecting Worley to an unending series of riddles and "brainteasers"—presumably, an activity that relieved Warren's awkwardness. When he finally screwed up his courage and invited her for a weekend at Penn, Worley turned him down.

---

*Danly went on to have an accomplished career as a chemical engineer with Monsanto. In retirement, he bought a Jaguar.

In his sophomore year, Warren lived at the Alpha Sigma Phi house, a Victorian mansion on Spruce Street with high ceilings and a stately spiral stair. He was ambivalent toward his fraternity brothers—not aloof, but not quite part of their rituals, either. After lunch, he would plop himself in a curved bridge chair by a bay window and join in a game of hearts or bridge. In a conversational setting, such as at meal-times, Warren was very alive—loose and confident with his opinions. In those years, fraternity members were served by waiters and dressed in jackets and ties for dinner. Anthony Vecchione, recalling Warren's table chatter, said, "When he was on he was fun—a lot of laughs."

> He was a very funny kid, very clever. It wasn't boffo slapstick, it was dry. He had a semicynical view of the way things worked. I remember he said if he ever got rich, he'd install steam-heated toilet seats in the bath-room. He said that had to be the ultimate.

But Warren was aching for some sort of intellectual—or financial—stimulus. Penn was a rah-rah school; campus life in 1948 revolved around pep rallies and the top-ten football team. Ironically, Warren was portrayed on the cover of *Penn Pics*, a student magazine, as the model fan, decked in a derby hat and raccoon coat, one hand waving a banner, the other offering a brandy flask to his apparent date, with a cigar extending from a jaunty grin, all against a photographic montage depicting the Penn marching band and a leather-helmeted ball carrier.

The cover was a joke; Warren's friend Jerry Orans was one of the editors. In truth, Warren was everything that the cover boy was not. He was a nondrinker, was uncomfortable with women, and was not a big socializer. On a campus with so many older students—returned GIs—he even looked out of place. With his hair unslicked, the skinny eigh-teen-year-old student looked like a visiting kid brother.

His youthfulness was especially apparent in the context of sex. Be-sides being inexperienced with women, he was noticeably ill-at-ease with the fellows' locker-room humor. "I remember distinctly," said Vecchione, the son of a Long Island subcontractor, "when people started talking about sex, he'd look at the floor. His face would get flushed."

On weekends, when Alpha Sigma threw beer parties, the monastic frat house was flooded with women. Warren usually did not have a date, but—of importance for a future investor—he was comfortable without being part of the crowd. While most of the guys had their arms around a date, Warren would sit on the couch and entertain the party with a little dissertation on the gold standard. He was so captivating that the fellows made a party routine of having Warren stand in a corner and peppering him with questions about economics and politics. "He'd start holding forth, and before a minute or two had gone by he'd have an audience, maybe ten to twenty people," remembered William Wayne Jones, a fellow nondrinker and a future Methodist missionary. "He would do it so humbly you were just in thrall. He'd say, 'I really don't know much about this, but it looks to me . . .' "

Warren's fraternity mates were in awe of his intellect.[26] He would read a chapter, they recalled, and recite it by rote. In class, when a graduate lecturer would parrot an answer from the text, Warren, who had it memorized, would burst out, "You forgot the comma."[27] Moreover, the way he glibly critiqued the faculty left his fellows spellbound. One of the frat brothers, Richard Kendall, said, "Warren came to the conclusion that there wasn't anything Wharton could teach him. And he was right."

When the brothers returned to Wharton in the fall of 1949, they were stunned to find that Warren wasn't there. Vecchione said, "He just evaporated at the end of the second year. Nobody ever heard from him again."[28] In short, he had run away once more. His father had been defeated in 1948 and had returned with the family to Omaha, leaving Warren alone in the East. In Wharton, there had been nothing to keep him—no paper route, no pinball. He transferred to the familiar University of Nebraska at Lincoln, where his parents had met. "I didn't feel I was learning that much," Warren explained. "Nebraska called, Wharton repelled."[29]

Among his Alpha Sigma brothers, the memory that stuck was of Warren's playing bridge, in an alcove by the great bay window. Otherwise, he almost seemed not to have been there.

From the time he returned to Nebraska, Buffett was a student only in name. In fact, he was launching his career. During the summer, he took a job at J.C. Penney, where he was offered (but declined) a position for after college. Feeling more comfortable on his home turf, he also began to date more. Writing to "Dear Monster" (Jerry Orans), a jocular Buffett was feeling his oats:

> The latest girl I have been dating casually mentioned to me that she played tennis so thinking I would impress the little gal with a show of cave-man masculinity I offered to give her the opportunity to see me work out from across the net. She trounced me.[30]

He planned a Herculean load—five courses in the fall of 1949 and six in the spring of 1950, mostly in business and economics. But his focus was off-campus. Buffett had taken a newspaper job, he explained to Orans, that involved "50 little boys calling me 'Mr. Buffett.' " He was supervising paperboys in six rural counties for the *Lincoln Journal*, traveling southeastern Nebraska in a 1941 Ford. The job paid seventy-five cents an hour. Mark Seacrest, the head of circulation, was dubious that a student could handle the load. But Buffett was "all charged up." He would come in each week to get his assignments and be off in a flash. To Buffett, it was a man-sized job. In his words:

> If you have a down route in Seward or Pawnee City or Weeping Water, Nebraska, you're looking for a kid to deliver fifteen papers a day or something of the sort and you got to find him late in the afternoon or early in evening while you're attending college—it's an education.[31]

In Lincoln, Buffett lived with Truman Wood, then affianced to Warren's sister Doris, in the upstairs of a Victorian house on Pepper Avenue. Buffett would come back from his newspaper work in the late afternoon, read the *Wall Street Journal*, and go out with Wood to a greasy spoon for a dinner such as mashed potatoes, beef, and gravy. Wood, intrigued that Buffett had read the Bible three or four times and remained agnostic, could not resist trying to convert him. They had the usual debates about faith and the afterlife, but Buffett was immovable. For every argument that Wood raised, Buffett had a deadly logical response.

Apart from their bull sessions, Buffett was rushing to finish college in three years, working a virtually full-time job, keeping up his bridge game, and racking up A's. Also, as he wrote to Orans in the fall, he had submitted a dozen entries in the hopes of winning a $100 Burma-Shave jingle contest,* and had lined up a date with "a German gal that looks all right."

In the winter, Buffett revived his golf-ball business—this time as a serious enterprise, with Orans as his agent in Philadelphia. In January 1950, Buffett implored his friend to get down to business.

> I don't imagine the boys back there are playing much golf yet and I can guarantee March 1st delivery on the type of balls you want so don't hesitate on getting orders.[32]

Buffett promised to make good the losses on any "duds" and assured Orans that the quality of his golf balls was okay. Nonetheless, he added, "don't get them near any real heat." As an afterthought, Buffett mentioned that he had gotten through finals "pretty good" and listed his courses for the spring. In April, having sent Orans a shipment, he sent his chum a lighthearted—but pointed—reminder that "Buffett's Golf Enterprises" was not a charitable venture.

> By this time I imagine you are bathing in luxury with the enormous profits you undoubtedly reaped from the sale of those gleaming beauties I mailed your father's partner in crime. However, don't forget that Philadelphia's prosperity is not shared by Lincoln until you dispatch a check for the token sum of $65.94.[33]

In the summer, Buffett continued his breakneck pace, moving in with his parents and taking three courses in Omaha so he could get the credits to graduate. By July, he had sold 220 dozen golf balls and had reaped $1,200 from them.[34] From all his ventures combined, he had saved $9,800.

That trifling grubstake would be the source of every dollar that Buffett would earn.[35] He had tracked every penny—the Cities Service stock, the paper route, the golf-ball sales, the pinball—in squiggly, uneven handwriting. So prophetic was his ledger of later exploits that it called to the mind of one journalist the papers that "Horatio Alger might have donated to the Baker Library at the Harvard Business School."[36]

---

*Buffett's best: "If missin' on kissin'—Hey Listen, try thissen—Burma-Shave."

Buffett had in fact applied to Harvard Business School. He confidently wrote to Orans, who had opted for Columbia Law School: "Egad! Big Jerry, reconsider and join me at Harvard."[37] In the summer, Buffett took a train to Chicago to meet an alumnus. Scrawny and unpolished, and merely nineteen, he struck his interviewer as not quite Harvard. The session was over in ten minutes.[38] Writing "Big Jerry" on July 19, Buffett needed five paragraphs to work up to the news. He informed his friend that he was taking a tax course and learning "all the shrewd angles that clip the dollars from the return." There followed talk of his "famous cannonball serve," get-well wishes for Orans's convalescing father, and an update on golf-ball sales.

> Now for the blow. Those stuffed-shirts at Harvard didn't see there [*sic*] way clear to admit me to their graduate school. They decided 19 was too young to get admitted and advised me to wait a year or two. Therefore I am now faced with the grim realities of life since I start paying room and board here in four weeks. My dad wants me to go on to some graduate school but I'm not too sold on the idea.

Two weeks later, there was no holding back. "Dear Big Jerry," he wrote.

> To tell you the truth, I was kind of snowed when I heard from Harvard. Presently, I am waiting for an application blank from Columbia. They have a pretty good finance department there; at least they have a couple of hot shots in Graham and Dodd that teach common stock valuation.[39]

Buffett was being a bit too nonchalant. Benjamin Graham, in fact, was the dean of the securities profession; he and his colleague David Dodd had written the seminal textbook in the field, *Security Analysis*. And Buffett had read Graham's new book, *The Intelligent Investor*, while at Lincoln, and had found it highly captivating. Wood, Buffett's housemate, said, "It was almost like he had found a god."[40] His jocular reference to Columbia's "hot shots" may be taken as posturing at a moment when he feared being rejected again. But in August, Buffett got some good news. He was going to New York, to study with the master.

Chapter 3

GRAHAM

Mr. Market is very obliging indeed.
Every day he tells you what
he thinks your interest is worth.

BENJAMIN GRAHAM,
THE INTELLIGENT INVESTOR

Buffett had been fascinated by stocks since he had first chalked them up on the blackboard. He had traded stocks, studied the market, consulted oracles, and looked for the great epiphany—some mystical correlation in the charts, some system that would make him rich. Yet he was no further, really, than when he had combed the floor of the racetrack, looking for discarded ticket stubs. Some stocks would place, but many more would not.

Ben Graham opened the door, and in a way that spoke to Buffett personally. He gave Buffett the tools to explore the market's manifold possibilities, and also an approach that fit his student's temper. Armed with Graham's techniques, Buffett could dismiss the oracles and make use of his native talents. And steeled by the example of Graham's character, Buffett would be able to work with his trademark self-reliance—with the "sweetness" of Emersonian independence of which Buffett had heard from his father.

Yet Graham was far more than Buffett's tutor. It was Graham who provided the first reliable map to that wondrous and often forbidding city, the stock market. He laid out a methodological basis for picking stocks, previously a pseudoscience similar to gambling. Investing without Graham would be like communism without Marx—the discipline would scarcely exist.

And groundbreaking as they were, Graham's writings did not explain in full the hold he had on his disciples. Unlike other Wall Street practitioners, Graham was open with his thoughts and freely shared his ideas. Wall Street interested him merely as an abstraction—the money meant nothing to him. In a field that was filled with narrow minds, Graham was also classical scholar, a student of Latin and Greek, a translator of Spanish poetry, and the author of a Broadway play—which closed in four nights. Oddly, for one who revolutionized investing, he spent much of his time working on quirky avocations and inventions, such as a new kind of slide rule and "more practical" pieces of furniture. (That was abstract, too; it is unlikely that Graham ever held a hammer.)[1] He was short, with penetrating, light blue eyes and thick lips—"a funny little guy, sort of ugly," as an associate said—but possessed of a spark.[2]

He came into the world as Benjamin Grossbaum, in London, in 1894.[3] When he was a year old, his father moved the family to New York to open a branch of a china-importing business. However, he died when Ben was nine. His mother put her savings in the market, and was wiped out in the panic of 1907. Ben took odd jobs, excelled at Boys High in Brooklyn, and entered Columbia. When he graduated, in 1914, he was offered posts in three departments—English, mathematics, and philosophy. But he took the advice of a college dean and went to Wall Street.[4]

Graham started at the lowest rung, earning $12 a week chalking prices on a blackboard.[5] While there were no securities analysts in those days, merely "statisticians," he quickly made his mark as an investor and also began to write. By the late 1920s, he was lecturing on finance after work.

His Wall Street lectures reflected his passion for geometry. Namely, he was anxious to systematize investing—to devise a set of Euclidean principles that would work for the stock market.

Graham's approach—an oddity in the speculative climate of the late 1920s—was to look for companies that were so cheap as to be free of risk. In 1926, for example, he discovered that Northern Pipe Line, an oil transporter, owned, in addition to its pipeline assets, a portfolio of railroad bonds worth $95 for each of its shares. Yet the stock was trading for only $65. Graham bought two thousand shares, and suggested that the company sell its bonds as a means of recouping its buried portfolio value. The management, which was controlled by the Rockefellers, refused. But Graham mounted a proxy fight and was elected to the board. Northern Pipe capitulated, liquidated its bonds, and paid a $70-a-share dividend.

By 1929, the "Benjamin Graham Joint Account," Graham's partnership, had $2.5 million of capital, and Graham was riding high.[6] By then, of course, Wall Street was full of rich men. Speculators were driving prices to the moon. That very year, the unfortunate Professor Irving Fisher of Yale proclaimed: "Stock prices have reached what looks like a permanently high plateau."[7]

Graham, though, was careful. When the Crash came, the Joint Account lost a tolerable 20 percent. In 1930, Graham—like so many—was convinced that the worst was over. He borrowed on margin and plunged into stocks. And then the bottom fell out. "The singular feature of the great crash," as John Kenneth Galbraith observed, "was that the worst continued to worsen."[8]

The smart money—the fellow who had waited out the panic—was wiped out with the rest. By 1932, the Joint Account had fallen 70 percent. Graham was close to ruin. His family left its park-view duplex in the Beresford for the relative austerity of a small rear apartment in the nearby El Dorado, where space was going empty. His wife, a dance teacher, went back to work. Graham was ready to quit, but a relative of Jerome Newman, Graham's partner, put up $75,000 of capital that enabled the firm to survive.[9] When Security Analysis appeared, in 1934, its forty-year-old coauthor had gone five straight years without being paid.[10]

Graham, in the introduction, frankly acknowledged that investing in common stocks seemed "discredited."[11] At the market's recent lows, a third of American industry was selling at less than its liquidation value.[12] The experts who only a few years back had seen in Wall Street a place of unending milk and honey now advised, as one said, that "common stocks as such are not investments at all."[13] Gerald M. Loeb, a commentator whose popular book The Battle for Investment Survival appeared at about the same time as Security Analysis, held that investing for profit was impossible. If the Dow Jones Industrial Average could register 381.17 in 1929 and 41.22 in 1932, who was to say what "real" value was? "I do not think anyone really knows," he averred, "when a particular security is 'cheap' or 'dear.' " Instead, Loeb counseled, "It is necessary to speculate . . . to foresee [the] tides."[14]

Loeb stressed that the thing to watch was not the earnings of an enterprise but the public psychology:

> The importance of full consideration of popular sentiment, expectations and opinion—and their effect on the price of the security—cannot be overstressed.[15]

Yet how was one to gauge the public sentiment? The chief method was to follow the prices of stocks themselves, to "watch the tape." If a stock declined it should be sold, and quickly; if it advanced, it should be purchased. It was not enough to buy something cheap—one must only buy "just as it starts to get dearer."[16]

If Loeb failed to grasp the paradox of millions of investors each reacting to one another and yet all trying to stay a step ahead of the crowd, it was not lost on Graham and Dodd:

> For stock speculation is largely a matter of A trying to decide what B, C and D are likely to think—with B, C and D trying to do the same.[17]

Security Analysis offered an escape from such a trap. Graham and Dodd urged that investors pay attention not to the tape, but to the businesses beneath the stock certificates. By focusing on the earnings, assets, future prospects, and so forth, one could arrive at a notion of a company's "intrinsic value" that was *independent of its market price*.

The market, they argued, was not a "weighing machine" that determined value precisely. Rather, it was a "voting machine," in which countless people registered choices that were the product partly of reason and partly of emotion.[18] At times, these choices would be out of line with rational valuations. The trick was to invest when prices were far below intrinsic value, and to trust in the market's tendency to correct.

Given that the Depression had far from run its course, it was a remarkable time to assert one's faith in markets. Many companies' shares were being quoted for *less than the value of their cash in the bank*.[19] But Graham, a classicist, could recognize Wall Street's gloom as part of an all-too-human cycle:

> That enormous profits should have turned into still more colossal losses, that new theories should have been developed and later discredited, that

unlimited optimism should have been succeeded by the deepest despair are all in strict accord with age-old tradition.[20]

Graham dissected common stocks, corporate bonds, and speculative senior securities (what Michael Milken would call junk bonds) as the biologist did the frog. At first blush, then, *Security Analysis* was a textbook for a profession still in the making.* But written during the madness of 1929 and its aftermath, the book was also a call to arms against the sins of speculation. In that sense, it was a total break. Loeb's speculator regarded stocks as pieces of paper, worth however much or little the next fellow might pay. His aim was to anticipate that next fellow, and the fellow after that. The Graham-and-Dodd investor saw a stock as *a share of a business*, whose value, over time, would correspond to that of the entire enterprise.

> It is an almost unbelievable fact that Wall Street never asks, "How much is the *business* selling for?"[21]

That was the question Graham and Dodd proposed as a guide to valuing stocks. It was not an exact science, but (and this was key) one did not need exactitude—only the skill to identify the occasional company that was priced well below its value.

> To use a homely simile, it is quite possible to decide by inspection that a woman is old enough to vote without knowing her age, or that a man is heavier than he should be without knowing his weight.[22]

Left unresolved was the nagging question of what to do when a cheap stock, after its purchase, became even cheaper. For if prices were sometimes wrong, the authors admitted, it could take an "inconveniently long time" for them to adjust.[23]

The answer appeared the year before Buffett arrived at Columbia. *The Intelligent Investor* boiled Graham's philosophy down to three words—"margin of safety."[24] An investor, he said, ought to insist on a gap—a big gap—between the price he was willing to pay and his estimate of what a stock was worth. This was identical to leaving room for

---

*The New York Society of Security Analysts was established three years later, in 1937. Graham was a cofounder.

error in driving an automobile. If the margin was great enough, the investor ought to be safe. But what if he was not? Suppose, that is, that the stock kept dropping. Assuming that nothing about the *business* had changed, Graham said, the investor should pay no heed to the ticker, no matter how grim its tidings.

Indeed, an investor who became unduly discouraged by a market drop and who allowed himself to be stampeded into selling at a poor price was "perversely transforming his basic advantage into a basic disadvantage."[25] *Basic advantage?* Most investors did not know they had one. Graham explained in a parable:

> Imagine that in some private business you own a small share that cost you $1,000. One of your partners, named Mr. Market, is very obliging indeed. Every day he tells you what he thinks your interest is worth and furthermore offers either to buy you out or to sell you an additional interest on that basis. Sometimes his idea of value appears plausible. . . . Often, on the other hand, Mr. Market lets his enthusiasm or his fears run away with him, and the value he proposes seems to you a little short of silly.[26]

The true investor was in that very spot. He could take advantage of the daily market quote or choose to ignore it—Mr. Market would always return with a new one.

To Buffett, these ideas were the Rosetta stone. He had already run the gamut of speculative technique; he had done stock tips, Magee charts—one system after another in the name of keeping up with the trend. But here was an approach to investing that absolved him from having to imitate "B, C and D"—that required only the sweet independence that he had learned from his father. Buffett experienced it as a revelation, "like Paul on the road to Damascus."[27] Quite simply, he had found his idol.

At Columbia, Buffett found that Graham was personally captivating. He looked a good deal like Edward G. Robinson, and his lectures had an air of drama. In one class, Graham depicted the vastly different balance sheets of Company A and Company B. It turned out that each was Boeing—at an up and down moment in the aircraft manufacturer's history.[28]

Graham had twenty students in 1950. Most were a good deal older than Buffett, and some were already working on Wall Street. But, almost comically, the lecture devolved into a two-way seminar.[29] Graham, who used the Socratic style, would pose a question, and even before he had the words out of his mouth the twenty-year-old from Omaha would shoot his hand skyward.

Graham would rarely say yes or no to Buffett's answer. He wouldn't wrap the universe in a ball. It was more like: "That's interesting. What line of thought brought you to *that* conclusion?"[30] And Buffett would run with it. As recalled by Jack Alexander, a Buffett classmate:

> Warren was probably the youngest person in the class—definitely the precocious pupil. He had all the answers, he was raising his hand, he was leading the discussions. He had tremendous enthusiasm. He always had more to say than anyone else.

Graham's accent was on cheap stocks—"cigar butts," or stocks that one could pick up almost for free, like spent cigars, and that might have a couple of valuable "puffs" left in them. One of his assignments that year was to research the performance of shares trading for less than $5.[31]

Buffett also learned the details of reading a financial statement, and how to spot a fraud. In essence, Graham taught him how to get from a company's published material to a fair value for its securities.

But he didn't do it in merely a theoretical way. Graham lectured about *live* stocks. He was quite indifferent to the fact that students were profiting from his ideas. By 1950, the fifty-six-year-old Graham was prosperous, but his attitude had been no different in the 1930s.

"These smart Wall Street guys," one of his students recalled, "they'd all go out and make a lot of money off Ben and he didn't seem to mind."[32] Graham was the sort of absentminded theoretician who would sleep with a notepad by his pillow—and then come to work in shoes of different colors. Marshall Weinberg, Buffett's contemporary and later his broker and friend, took Graham's course twice. He recalled:

> He was giving you ideas. Youngstown Sheet & Tube I bought at 34⅝ and sold between 75 and 80. I bought GM on his recommendation, also Easy Washing Machine. He'd say, "This is a stock that looks cheap to me"—now, *this morning*. Real Silk Hosiery was another stock. The class paid for my degree.

Buffett was fanatical about following in Graham's footsteps. He invested in stocks held by Graham-Newman Corp., Graham's investment company, such as Marshall Wells and Timely Clothes.[33] He also looked up his professor in *Who's Who* and discovered that Graham was chairman of the Government Employees Insurance Company. GEICO, as the company was known, was based in Washington. Buffett felt that anything that Graham was chairman of he wanted to know about, so he decided to pay a visit.[34] Conveniently enough, Warren's father had been reelected to Congress in 1950, and was back in Washington by the spring of 1951, during Warren's second term at Columbia.

Buffett took the train on a Saturday. Downtown Washington was desolate, but he went straight to GEICO's offices, on 15th and K streets. Finding the door locked, he banged until a janitor appeared.

"Is there anybody here I can talk to besides you?" Buffett queried.[35]

The janitor said there was a man working on the sixth floor, and agreed to take him there. Lorimer Davidson was taken aback to see a youngish student hovering at his desk—and stunned when he started peppering Davidson with questions. But the two of them talked for four hours.

> After we talked for fifteen minutes I knew I was talking to an extraordinary man. He asked searching and highly intelligent questions. What was GEICO? What was its method of doing business, its outlook, its growth potential? He asked the type of questions that a good security analyst would ask. I was financial vice president. He was trying to find out what I knew.

Davidson knew plenty—about GEICO and about Graham. GEICO had been founded in Texas in 1936 by Leo Goodwin, who had the ingenious idea of selling automobile insurance via direct mail, thus cutting out the usual network of agents. Also, GEICO sold policies only to government employees, a group with fewer than average claims. Its one-two punch of low distribution costs and superior policyholders made it a winner. In 1947, the majority owner wanted to cash out, and he hired Davidson—then an investment broker—to sell it. At first, no one took the bait. Then, in 1948, he shopped it to Graham, who saw that it was a gold mine. Graham-Newman immediately put up

$720,000—one-quarter of its assets—for a half-ownership in GEICO. Shortly thereafter, Graham-Newman divested its GEICO stock to its shareholders, and GEICO stock began to trade publicly. Davidson, meanwhile, had done such a good sales job that he had convinced himself and gone to work for GEICO.

Buffett returned to New York enamored with GEICO. With a little research, he discovered that its profit margins were five times that of the average insurer, and that its premiums and profits were soaring.[36] Then he went to see insurance experts—the B, C, and D of the day. Every one told him that GEICO's stock was overpriced. Buffett's reading of the facts was just the opposite, but he found them daunting.[37] They were experts; he was in B-school.

Every stockpicker worth his salt eventually comes to such a crossroads. It is extremely difficult to commit one's capital in the face of ridicule—and this is why Graham was invaluable. He liked to say, *"You are neither right nor wrong because the crowd disagrees with you."*[38] Picking a stock depended not on the whim of the crowd, but on the facts. And Buffett took this to heart, partly because he saw Graham in idealized terms—as a "hero," like his father.[39]

Graham had a similar effect on others. Though generally reserved, he had an almost parental fondness for his students.[40] To Jack Alexander, Graham was "almost like a father figure." In a way, it was a curious description—more likely to have been uttered by a student than by one of Graham's offspring.

With his own family, Graham was remote, a condition exacerbated by his roving eye. He left his first wife for a young model, and by the time Buffett met him, Graham was on wife number three, his former secretary, Estelle. In an incident telling of Graham's disregard for convention, the professor was lying in bed with Estelle one morning when a just-married young woman came calling. Graham suggested that she hop in with them.

Graham's children found him distant, especially after he lost a nine-year-old son.[41] They knew him as a figure of ideas, strolling around Central Park with a hat and walking stick, reciting poetry. His son Benjamin, Jr., once asked him a simple question from high school Latin, and Graham responded by reciting an oration of Cicero's from memory, as if giving a lecture. He lacked the patience for small talk, and would often disappear to read in the middle of his own dinner parties.

But to be Graham's student in the 1950s was to inhabit a special place. Wall Street was lined with cigar butts; one needed only the tools, and the cast of mind, to spot them. For the would-be money manager, the Columbia of Graham and Dodd produced a kinetic and communal surge, akin to the jolt that a young writer of the twenties might have experienced at a table at the Café des Amateurs in Paris, within earshot of Hemingway.

Buffett quickly fell in with a nucleus of Graham stalwarts. He went home with Fred Stanback, a retiring classmate from North Carolina, who reported to his mother that Buffett "just eats hamburgers and drinks Pepsi-Colas" and hence would be no trouble. Then Buffett and Stanback went to Jersey City for the annual meeting of Marshall Wells, and there met Walter Schloss, a devotee who was working for Graham-Newman. The three went to lunch and talked stocks to the point of exhaustion.

On another excursion, to the downtown Wall Street Club, Buffett met Tom Knapp, an unassuming Long Islander who had switched from chemistry to stocks after taking a night class with David Dodd. Buffett also became close to William Ruane, an earnest Harvard Business School graduate who was auditing Graham's class. Right off the bat, these students were united by their burning devotion to Graham. As Buffett would observe later, people either took to Graham right away or not at all.[42] For people of a certain temperament, no amount of persuasion worked. Buffett's new pals were hooked *immediately*. They found the Graham strategy—in a nutshell, trying to buy $1 worth of securities for fifty cents—powerful and absurdly simple, whereas most of Wall Street seemed like shooting craps. They had the beginnings of tribe, and they gravitated to Buffett, who was witty, likable, and—they knew—a step ahead of themselves. Knapp's first impression was that "Buffett knew almost every balance sheet on the New York Stock Exchange."

Oddly, when Buffett graduated, in 1951, both Graham and his father advised him *not* to go into stocks. Each had the post-Depression mentality of fearing a second visitation. Graham pointed out that the Dow had traded below 200 at some point in every year, save for the present one. Why not postpone going to Wall Street until after the next crash, his heroes counseled, and meanwhile get a safe job with someone like Procter & Gamble?[43]

It was awful advice—violating Graham's tenet of not trying to forecast markets. The Dow, in fact, never went under 200 again. "I had about ten thousand bucks," Buffett noted later. "If I'd taken their advice I'd probably still have about ten thousand bucks."[44]

Anyway, there was no way that Buffett was going to wait. Having racked up the only A+ that Graham had awarded in twenty-two years at Columbia,[45] Buffett made what seemed an irresistible offer: to work for Graham-Newman for free.

But Graham turned him down. These were the days when Jews were locked out of Wall Street's gentile firms, and Graham preferred to hold his spots for Jews.[46]* (Morgan Stanley would not hire its first Jew until 1963.)[47] It is not clear whether Buffett discovered Graham's reason then or a bit later, but when he did, it was a shocker. "It was sensitivity training for him," one of his friends would comment.[48]

It did not occur to Buffett to look anyplace else on Wall Street—that is, to work for someone he didn't know. Once again, he headed home. The Omaha National Bank offered him work, but Buffett turned it down, preferring the familiar confines of Buffett-Falk & Co., his father's brokerage. A friend of Howard's asked: "Will you be known as Buffett & Son?"

"No," Warren cracked. "Buffett & *Father*."[49]

In Omaha, Buffett began to court Susan Thompson, the daughter of a prominent Omaha minister and psychology professor. Her folks were friends of the Buffetts, and her father had managed one of Howard's campaigns. Also, Susie had roomed with Warren's sister Roberta at Northwestern University.

Susie had an enormous sparkling smile, round cheeks, and dark hair that fell to a curve at the neck—somewhat resembling Betty Boop's. Bubbly and outgoing, on first impression she struck many as light-headed and even vacuous.

The truth was to the contrary. As a girl, Susie had been sickly. She had suffered from earaches, had frequently had her ears lanced, and had spent long stretches at home with rheumatic fever. William and Dorothy Thompson had tried to make up for it by showering their daughter with attention, tenderness, and physical demonstrativeness.

---

*In later public comments, Buffett shielded Graham. He liked to joke that after he had volunteered, "Ben made his customary calculation of value to price and said no."

She grew up, she would say, with an awareness of being uncondi-
tionally loved.⁵⁰ And having overcome illness, she was conscious of a
sensation of freedom. She felt not merely healthy, but *released* from
pain. She would say, "To be free of pain is a great state of being. I
learned that at a very young age."⁵¹

By the time she reached adulthood, Susie seemed to have been put
together from all the emotional material that Warren did not have. She
took an unusual interest in reaching out to other people—a *deep* interest. Instinctively empathetic, she had a soothing way of drawing people
out, especially at a level of feelings. Faith Stewart-Gordon, a sorority
sister and later proprietress of New York's Russian Tea Room, said:

> Susie had this otherworldly side. We took the same philosophy course.
> After, she sent me this book on Zen Buddhism. She was always trying to
> get past the mundane and get to the big issues. She'd look into my eyes
> and say, "How *are* you?" When Susie said that, she meant: "How are
> you doing in life? How is your soul?"

In particular, Susie had a fascination with death. But it was the mirror image of Warren's obsession. Somewhere in her illnesses, Susie
had lost the fear of dying, and now she was eager to be with people on
their deathbeds and to ease their fears of passing on. Whereas Warren
thought about dying logically and wanted to keep the whole terrifying
subject as far away as possible, Susie related to death in spiritual terms
and was eager to wrap her hands around it.

Once he started seeing Susie, in the summer of 1951, Warren immediately fell in love with her. But Susie was anything but in love with
him. She was bored by his brainteasers and would slip out the back
door when Warren came calling. He told her that he would be rich,
which did not mean a thing to her. Besides, as Susie recalled, she was
"madly in love with somebody else." So Warren settled for courting
Susie's father. According to Susie, Warren

> went over to my parents' home every night and played the ukulele. My
> father [had] played the mandolin since he was 20, so he was really ex-
> cited about having someone to play with. So Warren did that every
> night, while I went out with this other person.⁵²

The "other person" was Milton Brown, a Union Pacific mail han-
dler's son who had dated her in high school and also at Northwestern.

Susie's parents objected to her dating a Jew and wouldn't invite Brown into the house.[53] The cash-strapped Brown wasn't welcome at Susie's sorority, either. To Susie, who was trying to break out of her sheltered, Waspish upbringing, this magnified Brown's appeal. But eventually, she gave in to her father, broke off with Brown, and hastily left Northwestern.[54]

Warren, meanwhile, was canny enough to see what was going on. He told "Doc" Thompson that he was the perfect compromise: "Jewish enough to suit Susie, and Christian enough to suit you."[55] By Jewish enough for Susie, Warren surely meant that Susie would find plenty in him to empathize with, too. Susie's sister, Dorothy, recalled:

> My dad liked him right away. He'd come over after the family had dinner. She'd be doing the dishes and he'd be sitting on a stool and playing a ukulele or a little guitar and singing. Warren had a very nice voice.

The black-haired minister, who was used to getting his way, kept telling Susie that she ought to go out with Warren. And Susie looked up to her father and respected his judgment.

Eventually, she and Warren began to date. She liked his sense of humor, and their Pat-and-Dick courtship blossomed into romance. "They were so infatuated with each other," said Warren's Aunt Katie. "Kissing, sitting on each other's laps. It was awful."

Warren, as he had predicted, was indeed "Jewish enough" for Susie. He had his buried childhood traumas, such as his tormenting mother and his forced removal to Washington, just waiting for Susie to go to work on. And Susie had a depth of understanding that was unlike anyone's in his experience. In retrospect, Warren said he had been lonely until he met her.[56]

Hidden behind an illusion veil and a gown of Chantilly lace, Susie married Warren at Dundee Presbyterian on the third Saturday in April 1952. Driving to California for a honeymoon, they stopped at the Wigwam Café, outside of Omaha, for their first meal. According to one account—perhaps apocryphal—of the trip, on the first Sunday, Warren noticed a lone Cadillac parked outside a company headquarters. He stopped the car, ducked inside, and picked the brain of the company president while his nineteen-year-old bride waited in the car, reflecting on the verities of being married to Warren Buffett.

. . .

The Buffetts started out in a $65-a-month three-room apartment.[57] Given Warren's promises of riches, Susie may have been a bit taken aback. The place was so run-down that mice crawled into their shoes at night. Warren was so tight about money that when the couple had a daughter—also named Susie—they made a bed for her in a dresser drawer.

At Buffett-Falk, Buffett was not the sort of stock salesman one meets very often. The first stock he sold was a tough sale, little-known security—GEICO. Buf Buffett, now over his own self-doubt, put $10,000— most of his savings—into it and pushed it on dubious customers all over Omaha. (His Aunt Alice got him started by buying one hundred shares.) He would cash out for a 50 percent profit the following year.[58]

What was most unusual about the young salesman was his appetite for research. Searching for ideas, he read the heavy purple-bound Moody's manuals page for page with the zest of a small boy reading comics. And he found small gems—unwanted and very cheap cigar butts such as Kansas City Life, Genesee Valley Gas, and Western Insurance Securities, all trading at three times earnings or less. It seemed too good to be true; if the stocks were so cheap, Buffett figured, *somebody* ought to be buying them. But slowly, it dawned on him. The somebody was him. Nobody was going to *tell* you that Western Insurance was a steal; you had to get there on your own.[59]

But Buffett was in the wrong job. All that research was wasted on a salesman, who stood to make the same small commission regardless if the idea was any good or not.

And customers thought he was green. Many times, a fellow would listen to Buffett's pitch, then check it out with his own, more seasoned broker and buy it from him. Daniel Monen, a friend of Buffett's in Omaha, said, "It drove Warren wild."

Buffett did learn a trick for getting in the door. He told Bob Dwyer, his old golf coach, "Just let 'em feel that you can save 'em something on taxes and nobody will keep you out."*

---

*He wasn't bluffing. After he left Wharton, Buffett had lunch with Rep. Jasper Bell, the father of his friend in Washington. The congressman said Buffett "knew more about tax law than any lawyer in the country."

But he didn't like *persuading* people to invest, particularly as he real-ized that his own interest—getting a commission—was not the same as theirs. It had an adversarial—almost a confrontational—aspect that made him highly uncomfortable.[60] Don Danly said, "I know that he abhorred it."

On the side, Buffett bought a Texaco station—sort of a twenty-some-thing version of Wilson Coin Op—and invested in real estate. But nei-ther worked out.[61] Meanwhile, he dreamed up studies to do for Ben Graham and suggested a couple of stocks to him—anything to keep his chances of working for Graham alive.[62]

Buffett's biggest step at Buffett-Falk was not an investment at all; it was taking a Dale Carnegie course on public speaking. Buffett was ter-rified of it, but he desperately wanted to master his fear.

The interesting question is, why? Why would a twenty-one-year-old stockbroker have *wanted* to learn that skill? If Buffett's only ambition was to be an investor, he would not have envisioned that he would *need* to speak in public. Much less would he have foreseen the day that he would deliver a narrative off-the-cuff so compelling, so concise, and so precisely to the point that his audience would swear it was scripted. But to what did Buffett aspire—aside from being a stockpicker—that prompted him to try?

After the Carnegie course, Buffett polished his skills by teaching a night class—"Investment Principles"—at the University of Omaha. The students were in their thirties and forties, and many of them were doctors. When the skinny, open-collared twenty-one-year-old teacher walked in, the doctors snickered.[63]

Buffett immediately began to talk about Graham. "After he talked for five minutes you were sold," said Leland Olson, an obstetrician. "And he wasn't selling. He was laid back."

Buffett, who taught several terms, based the lectures on *The Intelli-gent Investor*. But now and then he would spice the class with a homey story or word of wisdom, phrasing it simply and pacing it to perfection.

I will tell you the secret of getting rich on Wall Street. [Pause.] Close the doors. You try to be greedy when others are fearful and you try to be very fearful when others are greedy.*

---

*This excerpt is from an off-the-cuff talk to Capital Cities/ABC, in 1987. His classroom lectures were not taped.

When Buffett lectured, he would stand behind the desk and awkwardly bend his right arm, so that his elbow was at his hip and his hand was at his cheek, as if he were holding the phone. Then he'd take his left arm and hold the right elbow, as if to make sure it didn't fall off. And he would stare above his pupils' heads, as if he were afraid to make eye contact.

Yet he spoke with such an obvious fervor that the students were spellbound. Elizabeth Zahn, a Spanish teacher who enrolled with her husband, an IBM salesman, in 1953, was so struck by Buffett's manner that she made detailed descriptions of his every gesture. In particular, Zahn was puzzled by a seeming contradiction. Buffett was very "low-gear," but at the same time, he was intensely committed to what he was saying. His informal manner was set off by a *focused* quality that was other than casual. "Even in low gear, I was mesmerized by him," Zahn recalled.

When he got deep into a thought, he would pace the room, shyly keeping his head down, and just as Zahn was afraid he'd bump into the wall he'd reverse course and do it again the other way. And nothing could distract him. Buffett would go from one point to the next, railroad-track straight, as if he had a blueprint of the lecture pasted to his brain.

Unlike Graham, Buffett would not give stock tips. The students would try to get one, indirectly. They would ask about a company with seeming casualness, but Buffett would just laugh them off. Zahn even read aloud a plaintive ballad:

> Biz-whiz counselor
> This is our cry
> Why oh why won't you tell us what YOU buy?

Buffett laughed—but no dice. The young salesman actually advised the class *not* to take tips from brokers. He said they weren't to be trusted.[64] The entire subject of sharing information touched a nerve, as though he considered it fraught with the potential for abuse on either side. He regarded the majority of tips as a waste, which is why brokers passed them along. But good ideas—*his* ideas—he treated as intensely private. He regarded them as his creation—as a tiny bit sacred.

Howard Buffett, who had retired from the House in 1952, thought his son was an honest broker, and admired him for it.[65] According to Herbert Davis, a colleague, "Howard was proud of Warren long before he had a record to be proud of. He talked about him all the time, and with great affection." And Warren was extremely loyal to his father.

In 1954, a Nebraska U.S. Senate seat opened up due to the death of Senator Hugh Butler, and Howard—who very much wanted to succeed him—was a front-runner for the nomination. But moderates in the Republican Party quietly tried to stop him. The matter came down to the party's state central committee, which met with an air of intrigue at the Cornhusker Hotel, a GOP watering hole in Lincoln.

According to Warren's sister Doris, Warren secretly went to the Cornhusker to support their dad and overheard the painful news that Howard had been beaten by Roman Hruska, a moderate.* Doris said, "He went down there to help our father. He overheard them in the coffee shop. He came back and said, 'Daddy's throat was slit from ear to ear.' "[66]

As far as others recalled, Warren didn't mention it. His father had been crushed, and Warren had been crushed with him. But like his father, Warren kept it buried. And then, just as Howard's dream was squashed, Warren's was realized. Ben Graham called and said the religious barrier had been dropped[67]—and offered Buffett a job. Without bothering to ask his salary (it turned out to be $12,000 a year), Buffett was on the next plane.[68]

The Wall Street that greeted Buffett had been in a time warp. The old men who ran it lived in fear of another Depression. The younger men had never arrived. Of the most recent graduates of the Harvard Business School, merely 2.9 percent had gone to Wall Street. The new generation considered it unglamorous. Outside its gargoyled stone fortresses, black limousines waited for men with weary memories. Inside, it was masculine, aging, and unchanged by technology. At Merrill

---

*Howard had vilified Eisenhower in the 1952 primaries and backed Ike's right-wing opponent, Robert Taft. The then Nebaraska governor, Robert Crosby, later recalled: "The party was badly split between Eisenhower and Taft. Buffett was in the conservative wing. I was in the moderate wing. When Hugh Butler died, there was a big fight in the central committee—my recollection is, at some room of the old Cornhusker Hotel. I was on the telephone to my close political friends. I got them geared up to do what they could for Roman Hruska. I felt—why not be brutally frank?—Roman was a close friend."

Lynch, Pierce, Fenner & Beane, customers' orders were borne on tiny slips of paper, which were dropped onto conveyor belts to "ride jauntily on to [their] appointment with destiny."[69]

The country, it is true, was prospering, and the Dow Industrials had topped 380. But caution was the watchword. The last time that stocks had been so high had been 1929. It was hardly necessary to remind people such as Graham what had happened *then*. He was so wary of what he termed the "new speculation" that he kept handy a set of Moody's manuals from 1914—as if anything more recent were suspect.[70]

Graham-Newman was located in the Chanin Building, on 42nd Street. It had a stock ticker sitting beneath a glass bubble, making a perpetual clicking. Buffett, one of a half-dozen employees, shared a small room with Walter Schloss, and later with Tom Knapp. He wore a gray cloth jacket, like the others, and spent his time as they did, perusing the Standard & Poor's *Stock Guide* for companies. According to Knapp, Buffett

> felt very confident right from the start. I think his father offered to give him, or lend him, some money. He said no. He wanted to make a record *starting from zero*. And he wanted to make a very clean type of income. A couple of times I remember saying, "Gee, Warren, this thing isn't reported" [to the government]. And he said, "I'm putting it in."

Graham-Newman, a mutual fund, bought stocks according to a few select techniques. Graham's favorite was to hunt for stocks that traded at one-third less than their net working capital—in other words, stocks that were *insanely* cheap.* When Buffett or another associate found such a stock, he would take it to Graham. (The associates did their best to avoid Jerry Newman, Graham's partner, who was as nasty as Graham was sweet.) And Graham would decide on the spot whether to buy it. It wasn't a matter of *persuading* Graham. A stock either met his criteria or it didn't. He did it by the numbers.

Buffett's trouble was that he could find more stocks than he could sell. He went through the S&P guide—for him, a grown-up version of

---

*Net working capital is the total of current assets such as cash, inventory, and receivables (but not including plant and equipment) after deducting *all* liabilities.

One Thousand Ways to Make $1,000—like a buzz saw. He seemed to be bursting to replicate Graham's entire oeuvre.

One time, a broker in Philadelphia offered him an obscure insurance stock known as Home Protective, at 15 a share. There was no published material on it, and hence no way of valuing it. But Buffett went to the state insurance office, in Harrisburg, and dug up some numbers. What he saw convinced him that Home Protective was a steal. However, Jerry Newman rejected it. So Buffett and Knapp bought it for their own accounts. A bit later, Home Protective went winging up to 70.[71]

Buffett also found a block of Union Street Railway of New Bedford, Massachusetts, which was trading at 45 and had $120 a share in cash alone.[72] Buffett couldn't believe his luck—but Graham wasn't convinced. Once again, Buffett bought it for himself.[73]

Still, Buffett managed a coup in his first year on the job. In 1954, Rockwood & Co., a Brooklyn chocolate concern, offered to redeem some of its stock in exchange for cocoa beans, of which it had a large inventory. Buffett deduced that trading the stock for beans and simultaneously selling beans on the commodities market—where the price had soared—would produce a huge profit. As he later described it:

> For several weeks I busily bought shares, sold beans, and made periodic stops at Schroeder Trust to exchange stock certificates for warehouse receipts. The profits were good and my only expense was subway tokens.[74]

Such a trade, taking advantage of price discrepancies in separate markets, is known as arbitrage. Arbitrage was a staple in the Graham-Newman playbook—but Buffett was a couple of subway stops ahead in terms of spotting the application.

In fact, Buffett was quicker at everything. Graham would amaze the staff with his ability to scan a page with columns of figures and pick out an error. But Buffett was faster at it. Howard Newman, Jerry Newman's son, who also worked there, said, "Warren was brilliant and self-effacing. He was Graham exponential."

Warren and Susie had rented a garden apartment in White Plains, a suburb. As in Omaha, Warren was watching his pennies. Not long after they arrived, they had a son—christened Howard Graham. Though Warren was making a good living now, he borrowed a crib for him.[75]

Within their circle of young Wall Street couples, Warren and Susie, for different reasons, were both causing a stir. Roxanne Brandt, whose husband, Henry, was a stockbroker, said:

> They were different from the other young people we knew. They were simpler, or at least they seemed that way. Susie was very interested in why I had not had any children. She drew me out.

Compared to the stiff, Brooks Brothers culture of the fifties, Warren and Susie were noticeably less formal. At a dinner at the Buffetts', after young Howie had begun to crawl, Roxanne Brandt had a sense of "kids and toys all over the place." The Buffett children weren't "put away" like children at Manhattan dinner parties; they were part of the evening.

What interested Henry Brandt, who had graduated at the top of his Harvard Business School class, was that Buffett knew more about stocks than anyone. And he explained them so simply and unassumingly. When the Brandts entertained the Buffetts and other Wall Street couples, the group would settle into a curious ritual. After dinner, the men would go into the den and Buffett would nestle into a comfortable black-and-white-tweed club chair with sturdy armrests. And the other men, who were older than Buffett, would sit on the floor and listen to Buffett talk—demurely explaining the universe, just as he had at fraternity parties. Roxanne Brandt called them "Jesus and the apostles."

Graham thought that Buffett was the cream of *his* disciples[76] and recognized a similarity between them. One day, as they were going to lunch at a delicatessen near the office, Graham said, "Money won't make any difference to you and me, Warren. We'll be the same. Our wives will just live better."[77]

Graham was a thoughtful boss, and got Buffett a movie camera and a projector when his son was born—a generous gift for an employee of only a few months.[78] On Graham's own birthday, he would give out presents to the employees, figuring that he was the lucky one to have been born.[79]

But Buffett doesn't seem to have worked as closely with Graham as he had hoped.[80] In Buffett's words, Graham "had this kind of shell around him. Everybody liked him. Everybody admired him [and] enjoyed being around him . . . but nobody got close."[81] The same could have been said of Buffett.

In any case, Buffett was frustrated at Graham-Newman. The fund had only $5 million in capital, which didn't leave room for many investments. The partners also ran a private fund, Newman & Graham, but between the two operations, the office was managing only $12 million—a very small sum even then.[82] And Graham was so nervous about the stock market that he asked the partners of Newman & Graham to *withdraw* some of their capital.

In short, Buffett's opportunities were limited. At one point, he told Bob Dwyer, his high school golf coach, that he was learning a lot, but also that Graham was "sitting on $4 million, trying to decide when to get back in the market." It was hardly how Buffett wanted to start his career.

Ironically, shares of Graham-Newman were in such demand that they traded at a $200 premium to the portfolio value, roughly $1,200. (Many people bought a single share just to see the portfolio.) Had he wanted to, Graham could have turned his operation into a big business. But Graham's first goal was never to make money—it was to avoid losing any.

Because of his conservatism, he refused to analyze companies subjectively, preferring to stick to his mathematical guidelines. According to Irving Kahn, an assistant to Graham, when anyone tried to talk to Graham about a company's products, "Ben would look out the window and get bored."

Kahn said Buffett and Graham "argued on this"—a phrase that rings of overstatement, given the temperament of each. But their differences were real. Buffett was interested in what made one business better than another and wanted to pursue it. But Graham, who mistrusted corporate managements, discouraged Buffett from visiting companies.[83] And his formulaic approach cost him.

Walter Schloss tried to get him to buy Haloid, a humdrum photographic business that owned the rights to a technology known as xerography. The stock was at $21, of which Haloid's ongoing business accounted for about $17. Thus, Schloss figured that for $4 you could take a flier on the Xerox machine. But Graham wasn't interested in *any* speculation. He said, "Walter, it's not cheap enough."[84]

When the market roared ahead, Graham grew more nervous still. In 1955, the Dow hit 420—10 percent above the high of 1929. There was no reason, a quarter century having passed, why it should not have risen.

But the old-timers kept looking back to 1929. Congress was so unnerved by the prospect of a bust that it scheduled hearings. John Kenneth Galbraith went before the Senate Banking Committee in March with proofs of his forthcoming study of 1929, *The Great Crash*—which shocked the market into a sharp one-day swoon. Was the next crash on its way?

No one knew, but the real purpose of the hearings was not the stated one; it was the desire, recurring in politicians, to get to the bottom of Wall Street. From the time of J. P. Morgan, Sr., each generation had summoned the priests of finance to Washington. When Graham appeared, J. William Fulbright, the committee chairman, was all too cognizant that he had the era's preeminent stockpicker on the stand. Eager to unearth his secrets, Fulbright inquired about every aspect of the trade. At times, he sounded like a man about to call his broker.

THE CHAIRMAN: Mr. Graham, in connection with your own company
                . . . How do you determine whether a special situation
                is undervalued or not?[85]

Graham patiently took the senator to school. At one point, when Graham voiced skepticism of stock options, Fulbright tried to flatter him.

THE CHAIRMAN: I agree with your views quite often.

MR. GRAHAM: Senator, I have no intention of shaping my views with
                the expectation of your agreement.

Finally, Fulbright got to the heart.

MR. CHAIRMAN: One other question and I will desist. When you find a
                special situation and you decide, just for illustration,
                that you can buy for 10 and it is worth 30, and you take
                a position, and then you cannot realize it until a lot of
                other people decide it is worth 30, how is that process
                brought about—by advertising, or what happens?

Rephrasing: What caused a cheap stock to find its value?

MR. GRAHAM: That is one of the mysteries of our business, and it is a mystery to me as well as to everybody else. [But] we know from experience that eventually the market catches up with value.

However elliptical, his answer was the basis for Buffett's career. Stocks would rise to value; therefore, an investor who trusted his judgment could be patient.

But Graham himself no longer cared. In 1956, a year after the hearings, he retired to Beverly Hills, to teach at the University of California at Los Angeles and pursue a life of financial writing, skiing, and the classics, accompanied by his wife, and also by a French mistress. He gave much of his money to charity and offered that anyone who died with more than $1 million to his name was a fool.[86]

Graham-Newman's record had been very good, if not spectacular. Over its twenty-one-year life (1936–1956) it had earned an average of nearly 17 percent a year, compared to just under 14 percent for the Standard & Poor's index. The figure, though, does not include what was easily its best investment, its GEICO shares, which were distributed to Graham-Newman's stockholders. Investors who kept their GEICO through 1956 did twice as well as the S&P 500.[87]

But Buffett, quietly investing on his own, had done better. Since leaving college in 1950, Buffett had boosted his personal capital from $9,800 to $140,000.[88] And now that he had a kitty, he was eager to go "home"—to Omaha—yet again. Standing on the train platform surrounded by a sea of New York commuters didn't seem like a life to him.[89]

In the spring of 1956, he and Susie rented a house on Underwood Avenue, two blocks from the Buffett grocery. This time, Buffett had no thought of working for anyone else. On May 1—virtually as he arrived in Omaha—he organized a pool for family and friends. Seven limited partners—sister Doris and her husband, Aunt Alice, Doc Thompson, his ex-roommate Chuck Peterson and his mother, and Dan Monen, his lawyer—put up $105,000. Buffett, the general partner, put in $100. It was a minuscule sum, but Buffett was running money not for his father or for Ben Graham, but for a partnership of his own: Buffett Associates, Ltd.

Around that time, Homer Dodge, a physicist and Graham-Newman investor, asked Graham the question that had occurred to not a few of his investors: "Who will carry your mantle?" Graham suggested Warren Buffett. When Dodge was driving west for a summer vacation, he stopped in Omaha, a canoe strapped to his car. He had a brief chat with Buffett and left for the great outdoors—having agreed to put in $120,000.[90]

Buffett now had three tiny partnerships, which he ran from his bedroom. And he had begun to envision that his family pool might become something more. In August, he returned to New York for the final stockholders' meeting of Graham-Newman Corp. He mentioned to Ed Anderson, another Graham disciple, that he was thinking of setting up a partnership along Graham's model—maybe with a $50,000 minimum. Yet who was to say if he could carry Graham's torch? As the stockholders formally voted Graham-Newman out of existence, an investor named Lou Green offered an ironic eulogy. Green, the head of a Manhattan brokerage, averred that Graham had made "one big mistake"—that of failing to develop talent. Laying it on the line, Green elaborated: "Graham-Newman can't continue because the only guy they have to run it is this kid named Warren Buffett. And who'd want to ride with him?"[91]

Chapter 4

BEGINNINGS

*A series of market decisions
does add up, believe it or not,
to a kind of personality portrait.*

ADAM SMITH, THE MONEY GAME

With the partnerships up and running, Buffett was troubled by a seemingly bizarre concern. As he wrote to "Big Boy" (Jerry Orans), he was
afraid that his estate would eventually be so big that the money might
spoil his children. He couldn't figure out "the logical thing to do with
the dough."

> This is no problem now but viewing things optimistically it may become
> one and my thinking produces no results. I am sure I don't want to leave
> a barrel of money to my kids, unless I do it at an elderly age when I have
> time to see what the tree has produced. However, how much to leave
> them, what to do with the balance, etc. bothers me considerably.[1]

Buffett was twenty-six. He had modest savings and no steady income.
Another young man fretting over his unearned millions might be worthy of a snicker, yet in Buffett there was no hint of bravado. He knew, as
much as anyone can, that he *would* be rich—not just successful, but
rich enough to have trouble figuring out what to do with it all. He had
anxiety over spending his "dough"—before, indeed, he had any—but
not over making it.

At a time when his accomplishments were modest, Buffett's awe-
some self-confidence was the thing that propelled him. In 1957, he was

managing a mere $300,000 for just a few relatives and friends. If he was ever to be more than a quiet stockpicker in Omaha, Buffett would need *capital*, and lots of it. And if Buffett was to raise capital, what was there—besides that yawning self-assuredness—that would induce investors to trust him?

Buffett had no track record as an independent operator. He had nothing, on paper, to indicate that he was worthy of people's trust. And he did not want mere discretion over people's money, he wanted *absolute control* over it. He wanted no one to answer to for his decisions on stocks—no wary customers as at Buffett-Falk, no skeptical bosses as at Graham-Newman.

By now, Buffett was familiar with virtually every stock and bond in existence. Line for line, he had soaked up the financial pages and the Moody's books; day after day, he had built up a mental portrait of Wall Street. He could measure each stone against the skyline, and there was no one else whose analysis he trusted better than his own.

Writing to Orans, he could critique the leading mutual funds, dispense advice on Treasury securities, and rip the conventional wisdom as regards investing for capital or income in a couple of breathless paragraphs. And all of that knowledge he focused on a single, unrelenting purpose. When Orans wrote for advice on mutual funds, Buffett breezily replied:

> The objectives you mention in your letter mean nothing. That is all a lot of bull put out by the sponsors. Everyone has the same objective—to end up with more dough than they start with a minimum of risk.[2]

If Buffett's inner confidence and clear-minded design didn't gain people's trust, what would? Save for those defining aspects of his character, why would he even try?

In the summer of 1957, Buffett got a call from Edwin Davis, a prominent Omaha urologist. They had never met, but one of Davis's patients, a New York investment adviser named Arthur Wiesenberger, had known Buffett in New York.[3] Wiesenberger had heard that Buffett was trying to raise money and had suggested that Davis call him. Though skeptical about investing with a greenhorn, Davis agreed to have a look. On the appointed Sunday, he gathered his family to take the young man's measure. On first impression, Buffett was startling.

The doorbell rang and in comes this guy—egad—he looked like he was eighteen. He had very short hair, almost a butch. His collar was open, his coat was too big for him. Everybody noticed it. He talked so very fast.[4]

This was an important moment for Buffett. Dr. Davis could give him capital and, what was more, cachet. If he could sign up the Davises, he would not be investing merely for his parents and Aunt Alice; he would have his foot in the door as a professional.

But Buffett did not have the air of someone trying to please. Indeed, some of his pitch was calculated to set the Davises on notice. He warned them that he would disclose nothing about where their money was invested. He would give them a yearly summary of results, nothing more.

Also, Buffett would be "open for business" only one day a year. On December 31, the Davises could add or withdraw capital. Otherwise, the money would be Buffett's to play with (which he would do, he assured them, according to Graham's principles) and his alone. He presented this evenly, without any edge, but the message was clear. As badly as Buffett wanted the Davises' capital, he didn't want it on any terms but his.

Then he offered the terms. The Davises, as limited partners, would get all of the profits that Buffett could earn up to 4 percent. They would share any remaining profits—75 percent to the Davises and 25 percent to Buffett.[5] Thus, Buffett was not asking the Davises to gamble alone; Buffett's money would be on the same horse. If his results were mediocre or worse, Buffett would get zilch—no salary, no fee, *nada*. According to Lee Seemann, the doctor's son-in-law, "The whole thing was laid right out. We liked that. You knew where you stood with him."

After Buffett left, the Davises kicked it around. In objective terms, they had nothing to go by. But the doctor's wife, Dorothy, declared, "I like everything about this young man." Edwin Davis put up $100,000.

By year-end, Buffett was running five small partnerships, totaling in the range of $500,000. For the year, Buffett's first, his portfolios gained 10 percent, easily topping the Dow Industrials, which suffered an 8 percent drop.*

---

*All figures for the Dow are as Buffett reported them to his partners—that is, adjusted to include dividends.

With Susie expecting a third child and Warren seemingly on his way, the Buffetts bought a sprawling five-bedroom house on Farnam Street. Warren helped his daughter bid a tender farewell to the old house. Previously, four-year-old "little Susie" had developed a terrifying fantasy of a bespectacled interloper, whom she referred to as "the glasses man." Each night, before she went to sleep, Susie had insisted that her father check the balcony off her room just in case the glasses man was there. Now, as they made ready to drive away, Warren asked his daughter to step inside for a final look. Bending down, he said, "The glasses man is staying here. Tell him goodbye."

The Buffetts' new home was a 1920s gray stucco with brown trim— the picture of upper-middle-class suburbia. It fronted on a busy street but was obscured by plantings. Writing to Jerry Orans, Buffett thought it barely worth mentioning. "Not much new out here. As I may have mentioned I picked up a house. . . ." The aspect that drew his attention was the expense. "Buffett's Folly," he reported, "has lots of room, both in the house and yard," but he hadn't gone "overboard on price"—a reassurance that Orans hardly needed.[6] The house had cost $31,500.[7]

Buffett worked off the master bedroom in a sitting area, which his wife decorated with greenback wallpaper. Peter, their third child, was born that year, but mentally Warren was wrapped up in stocks and bonds. He was working virtually all the time, and loving every minute. He said he was thinking of making money before his feet hit the ground.[8]

Soon after the Buffetts moved, Tom Knapp, Buffett's Graham-New-man colleague, flew to Omaha and he and Buffett drove to Beloit, Wisconsin, to hear Graham give a speech. On the way, Knapp happened to mention that the U.S. Post Office was taking its four-cent Blue Eagle stamp out of circulation. Buffett came alive—here was a chance to earn some greenbacks! He and Knapp stopped at every post office on the drive home, "investing" in soon-to-be-scarce Blue Eagles. Eventually, they bought $12,000 worth of stamps—all of them, alas, destined for Knapp's mailroom.

Buffett did better with his stocks. His partnerships soared 41 percent in 1958—inching out the Dow, which rose 39 percent. By the end of Buffett's third year, the original partnership money had *doubled*.

He also was gathering new investors. He signed up friends such as Fred Stanback from Columbia, Don Danly, and Jerry Orans. He went to neighbors and to former students. He signed up Leland Olson, the obstetrician who had taken Buffett's class, and when Olson wanted to sign up his mother, Buffett drove his baby-blue Volkswagen Beetle through a blinding snowstorm, arriving in fine shape, as if he'd stepped out of a VW commercial. But Buffett refused to grovel or to bend his rules to get new investors.

As he was picking up steam, Jack Ringwalt, the owner of an Omaha insurance company and a friend of Buffett's Aunt Alice, called Buffett, whom he had never met, and offered $10,000 for the kid to "fool around" with.

Buffett replied that he had been counting on a big fish such as Ringwalt for $50,000. Ringwalt thought it a most ungrateful reply, but repeated his offer of $10,000.

Buffett turned him down.[9]

Around town, Buffett's fast start, coupled with his unusual gumption, was raising eyebrows. There was a luncheon at the Blackstone, a big hotel in Omaha, at which, as one of Buffett's investors recalled, "everybody was talking about Warren Buffett. Bob Storz was there. He was one of the biggest wheels in Omaha. He said that young man will be broke—it's just a new idea and you'll lose your money in less than a year."

But the impression of people who met Buffett was otherwise. It was not so much his results as his serene self-confidence. One time he went to a meeting of neighbors, who were hotly debating what to do about a city proposal that would reroute traffic onto Farnam Street. Buffett stood up and calmly suggested that everybody ought to forget about it. And that was it; people realized he was right and went home.* Buffett evoked a similar reaction from his investors. They felt that he could see simple truths that they themselves had missed.

Buffett insisted on not disclosing his stocks because he was afraid that someone would copy him—thus making it more expensive if he wanted to buy more. He wouldn't talk to *anyone*—he maintained that he was afraid to talk in bed because his wife might hear.[10]

But behind the cordon of secrecy, he was living a Graham-and-Dodder's fantasy, picking up small cheap stock after small cheap stock. His talent lay not in his range—which was narrowly focused on invest-

---

*George Payne, who had organized the meeting, immediately called Buffett and signed up for a partnership.

ing—but in his intensity. His entire soul was focused on that one splendid outlet, as it had been when he was a boy delivering papers. Company after company he analyzed and committed to memory. And when one became cheap, he pounced.

National American Fire Insurance was as obscure a company as one could find. An Omaha-based insurer, National American was controlled by Howard F. Ahmanson, the banking magnate, and his brother Hayden. The stock had been distributed to Nebraska farmers and such in the late 1920s, and then largely forgotten. The Ahmansons now were offering to buy it back for $50 a share. Their offer was cheap, but as no public market existed for the stock, shareholders were gradually selling out.

After doing some digging in state insurance files, Buffett realized that it was *extremely* cheap, but he couldn't find any stock to buy. He and his lawyer chum, Dan Monen, went to the annual meeting, but Hayden Ahmanson curtly refused to let them see the stockholders list. Then, as if asking a friend to spend an afternoon hunting for golf balls, Buffett suggested that Monen drive around the state looking for stock. Sucked in by the Buffett contagion, Monen took off in a red-and-white Chevrolet for the far corners of Nebraska, waving $100 a share at anyone he saw in rural courthouses, banks, and the like. "It sounds corny," Monen said later, reflecting on his willingness to go. "Warren Buffett is as near to Mr. Perfect as anyone I know." Mr. Perfect and his partner captured 10 percent of the stock and made more than $100,000—Buffett's first big strike.[11]

Sanborn Map, another, illustrated Buffett's debt to Ben Graham. Sanborn's once-lucrative map business had declined; however, the company had an investment portfolio, built up over its flush years, worth some $65 a share. *And its stock, reflecting its sagging map business, was trading at only 45.* This was a carbon copy of Northern Pipe Line—prized by Graham for its railroad bonds. Echoing his mentor, Buffett bought Sanborn stock throughout 1958 and 1959. He was trusting in Graham's testimony: *sooner or later a stock would rise to value.*

But it didn't. The company's directors owned merely four hundred shares (105,000 were outstanding) and were content to let the share price languish. In fact, while sitting on that huge portfolio they had cut dividends five times in eight years, though, as Buffett noted, it had not as yet occurred to the board to reduce the fees to themselves.[12]

Following Graham page for page, Buffett became a director and lobbied the management to unearth the sub rosa value in its investment portfolio. The management resisted.

In the meantime, Buffett did not mention Sanborn to *his* investors, though he did disclose that he had put 35 percent of their assets into a single stock. But he and other dissident shareholders continued to put the heat on. In 1960, Sanborn capitulated, and agreed to use its portfolio to buy out stockholders. Buffett made roughly a 50 percent profit. With the cat out of the bag, he wrote to partners that Sanborn "does point up the necessity for secrecy regarding our portfolio operations as well as the futility of measuring our results over a short span of time. . . ."[13]

Not everyone was convinced. In the midst of the Sanborn episode, John Train, a New York financial writer, met Buffett with an idea of signing up. When Train learned that Buffett would not reveal his holdings, he decided not to invest.[14]

Buffett also approached Donald Keough, a neighbor whose kids often played with Buffett's. "Don, you've got a wonderful group of children," Buffett said. "Have you given any thought to how you're going to get the kids through college?"

Keough, an up-and-coming assistant manager for a coffee wholesaler, liked Buffett, but he thought it strange that his neighbor stayed in the house all day, working in his sneakers and a T-shirt. Keough, too, turned him down.[15]

People who signed up intuitively grasped that Buffett's Garbo-like loneliness was part of the appeal. When Buffett insisted on secrecy, it was not merely to prevent leaks, but also to prevent intrusions, and to maintain that sweet independence. He wanted no amateur tipsters or second-guessers. For a stock to merit investment, Buffett had to persuade himself of it, and if he did, what was the use of other opinions? Temperamentally, he mistrusted advice-givers and financial soothsayers. If the basis for a stock was popular opinion and opinion changed, then what? He was confident that his own analysis would be less fickle.

Buffett wanted only one thing from outside: capital.

In 1960, now just shy of thirty, Buffett approached one of the more devoted of his partners, a folksy cardiologist named William Angle. "Doc Angle" had built a model train set for Buffett in his attic, and was willing to do just about anything for him. "Warren asked if I'd be interested in getting ten doctors together to put up $10,000 each," Angle recalled. "So I rounded up a group from Clarkson Hospital at a restaurant on 49th and Dodge."

Buffett had yet to appear in public as a money manager. But at the restaurant—the Hilltop House—he trotted out the speaking skills he had learned at Dale Carnegie and refined in night school. Silhouetted against a darkening summer sky, he poured out liquid couplets from Benjamin Graham and Shakespeare, interspersed with gentle self-mockery. He was done in less than an hour.

At the Clarkson coffee shop the next day, the talk was of nothing else. An obstetrician said, "We're not giving money to that young man—he could leave the country." Arthur Green, who had taken Buffett's class, declared that *he* wasn't investing because Buffett had ridiculed AT&T, which Green owned, as "an old ladies' stock." "I was stupid," Green said later. But eleven doctors decided to take a chance on him. In Omaha, at least, Buffett had made a big step forward.

The next year, Buffett bet $1 million—his biggest plunge ever—on a company that, had they known of it, would have made the doctors gasp. Dempster Mill Manufacturing was an eighty-year-old windmill and farm-implement maker in Beatrice, Nebraska, ninety miles south of Omaha. The windmill business being not exactly another Xerox, Dempster had suffered from static sales and dismal profitability. Buffett had nibbled at the stock—a cheap, typical-Graham play—a few years earlier. In 1961, he snapped up the controlling interest, giving him 70 percent—and staking a fifth of his partnerships' assets on it. Buffett appointed himself the chairman, a prophetic move (and unusual for a money manager) that signaled an ambition to be something more than just an investor.

Characteristically, Buffett roped Dan Monen onto the board, too. Every month, Buffett and the loyal Monen would drive to Beatrice, a dusty town in the plains, like a Quixote with his Sancho Panza. But Buffett couldn't get a handle on Dempster. It needed an overhaul, but working with the gritty details was not his forte. It was like cleaning the fruit bins at the Buffett store; he preferred the numerical abstractions to the business itself.[16] Each month, Buffett would entreat the managers to cut their overhead and trim the inventory, and they would give it lip service and wait for him to go back to Omaha.[17] Promptly, Buffett put the company up for sale.[18]

But he did not question the Graham-like premise that had led to its *purchase.* In fact, Graham's influence permeated the partnerships. Aside from Dempster, the money was sprinkled among forty stocks— cigar butts, arbitrages, workouts (such as liquidations)—all from the Graham-Newman playbook.[19] Buffett unashamedly aped his mentor in his letters to partners;[20] he even mimicked Graham's shortcomings. Like his teacher, Buffett ruled out any and all high-technology compa- nies as speculative. Graham had rejected Xerox; Buffett snubbed Con- trol Data at $1 a share, even though he was related (via the marriage of an uncle) to William Norris, the computer giant's founder, and was well aware of the opportunity.*

The Buffetts would visit the Grahams (staying at a *very* inexpensive strip motel) a couple of times over the summer, when the Buffett fam- ily took a vacation in California. Buffett would closet himself with Gra- ham for hours. He also struck up a friendship with Graham's wife Estelle.

Graham by then was spending much of his time in the quiet com- pany of his olive-skinned French lover, Marie Louise Amingues, a.k.a. Malou.† Estelle Graham was crushed by it. A poor girl from Brooklyn, Estelle was self-educated and enamored of the high life in Los Angeles, where she and Graham shared a box at the Hollywood Bowl and threw lavish parties. According to Rhoda Sarnat, a cousin of Graham's who lived across the street, "It wasn't all tea and crumpets living with Ben. Just because you're a genius doesn't make you the most caring person in the world."

Buffett treated Estelle kindly, and he enjoyed being there even when Graham wasn't around. Ironically, Graham's wife became Buffett's most ardent disciple. Though Graham steered others to his prize pupil, Estelle actually invested with him. She exclaimed to Sarnat: "This guy is really coming up; he's totally trustworthy, and you ought to put your oar in."

Buffett himself was far more taciturn. In any single year, he knew, Mr. Market could take a nasty turn. He warned his partners: "There are bound to be years when we are surpassed by the Dow."[21] To shoulder the expectation of having to beat it *every* year was too much. But his

---

*Buffett would not call this a "mistake." He would argue that since he did not have the technical computer expertise to value Control Data, investing in it would have been a gamble.
†Malou had previously been the companion of one of Graham's sons, who committed suicide.

brief record, even including the still-unresolved Dempster, had been phenomenal. It should be understood that in most years, most money managers do not even match the Dow Jones Industrial Average. Over the first five years, the Buffett partnerships had left it in the dust.

	PARTNERSHIPS	DOW
1957:	+10.4%	−8.4%
1958:	+40.9	+38.5
1959:	+25.9	+19.9
1960:	+22.8	−6.3
1961:	+45.9	+22.2

And the cumulative gain, after five years:

PARTNERSHIPS	DOW
+251.0%	+74.3%[22]

The last pair of figures merit a second glance. The Dow was up three-quarters, Buffett's portfolios *two and a half times*.

Word of Buffett's success spread quickly in his hometown. Acquaintances would amble over to him at Ross's Steak House and ask, with studied casualness, if he had any tips. Buffett, with perfect geniality, would advise them to take a pencil, shut their eyes, and point it at the stock tables. He would pull into the Omaha Country Club, in khaki pants and Hush Puppies, and older men in golf shoes and sportswear would descend on him like bees.[23] But they wouldn't get any honey.

Virtually every *other* stock man in the country chatted up ideas with nary a second thought. Over lunch, at golf courses, on the telephone—tens of thousands of times every day—investment people inhaled and exhaled the name of a favored stock. And most of their tips were forgotten days, if not moments, later, to be supplanted by a new hot stock. But Buffett was different. He was *possessive* about stocks, like an artist with an unfinished canvas. He liked to tell stories of his coups in the market—but only when they were wrapped up. And only of stocks that were on *his* agenda to talk about.

People liked to listen to him, because he made business sound transparent and did it with a sense of humor. In 1960, he invested in Data Documents, a tiny Omaha tab card manufacturer founded by Wayne

Eves, a friend, and John Cleary, a former aide to Buffett's father. Buffett was so quick with answers that Eves and Cleary made him chairman. Then Buffett put Bill Ruane and Fred Stanback, pals from Ben Graham's class, and Robert Malott, a friend from Chicago, on the board, too. They would fly into Omaha the night before board meetings—basically, as one said, they wanted an excuse "to eat steak at Ross's and talk to Buffett for three or four hours."[24] He was fun company.

Buffett had an astonishing circle of cronies, who overlapped with his investors. And he did not change gears from one to the other; he was fetching, understated, informal, and a bit of the teacher in either camp. He did not draw the usual line between "work" and other activities. When he got on the links, he was focused as a cat. Robert Billig, a golf partner, said Buffett "could take putting instructions better than anyone." When Billig told him how to aim, Buffett shut out everything else and turned his ethereal concentration on the golf ball. "It was amazing how often he'd make those," Billig marveled.

Buffett's passion outside of work was bridge. He had a regular game, the members of which were a sampling of Main Street, U.S.A.—ad executive, Buick dealer, judge, life insurance agent, mortgage man, railroad attorney, and American Automobile Association chapter president. Buffett would show up with a six-pack of Pepsi-Cola and entertain the guys with a stream of jokes and stories. He didn't talk about the money he was making. The point was, he didn't have to. He played so intensely he could have *been* working, only with trumps instead of with stocks and bonds.

Buffett hated to lose. He resisted playing for high stakes, meaning a penny a point, unless he thought his team had an edge. But he competed just as hard at quarter-penny stakes.[25]

What distinguished Buffett was the way he zoned in. He would stare at the cards and calculate the odds like a machine. "He was not emotional," noted James Koley, a lawyer and occasional partner. "It was just mathematics to him."

Before the first card was played, Buffett would plan the entire hand, stripping away the hateful aspect of chance. Kay Koetter, the life insurance man, recalled, "Warren used to sit there and think and think and think until he had figured out where every card in the deck was. I brought my father once—it drove him crazy."

Buffett was so consistently analytical—*unusually* so. On form, his emotional pendulum did not swing as far as other people's. There was no pushing him to an expression of, say, anger, despondency, recklessness, or other feeling outside of his customary Pepsi-drenched high spirits. He was always logical and even-tempered, always in the same, circumscribed arc.

Buffett was enormously dependent on Susie. She paid the bills, took care of the kids, ran their lives. Whatever was outside his range, Susie handled. In particular, Susie shielded Warren from his mother. Even as an adult, he would shake or go mute at the sight of that aging and shriveling tormentor. He did his best to avoid her, and at family gatherings, he would withdraw after dinner on the pretext that he needed to "nap."

One time, as Leila was leaving, she and her son passed in the hallway. When she attempted a kiss goodbye, Warren backed away, leaving his mom in tears. But save for such a rare chance encounter, Susie would cover for him. Susie would talk to Leila so that Warren wouldn't have to.[26]

Warren's need for Susie was palpable. Once, when they were visiting his sister Doris in Washington, Susie awoke at six in the morning with an extremely painful case of diverticulitis. En route to the hospital, even though Susie was the critically sick one, she was trying to comfort Warren, who had a mortal fear of hospitals and visibly was the more distraught.[27]

Even on a normal day, Warren's face would light—a touching betrayal of his feeling—when Susie entered the room. She would run her fingers through his hair, fix his tie, sit on his lap, hug him. She *sustained* him. Referring, presumably, to her soothing explorations of his childhood, Warren once declared, "Susie removed the thorns, one by one."[28] And Susie would speak of Warren like a fragile child whom she was sworn to protect. She would hint to her children that there were parts of him they didn't know about—that only Susie knew about.[29]

They were perfectly complementary—Warren, self-absorbed, Susie, reaching out to the world. She tended to an unending stream of confidants and solace-seekers—a friend going through a divorce, a neighbor with a sick relative. It seemed that anyone in Omaha who had a problem landed on Susie's "couch." On more than one occasion, she became so involved in talking to a waiter or waitress that she left the restaurant with his or her phone number.

Susie was determined to see that the Buffetts did not lead narrow lives.[30] In a trivial example, they joined a "gourmet cooking club"—a group of couples who dined on Swedish meatballs one month and French crêpes the next. Each time, though, Warren would pleasantly ask the hostess to make him a hamburger.[31] He preferred to stick to the familiar: the same city, the same foods, the same single-minded pursuit. He stuck to the arc.

At a party, the Buffetts were a study in contrasts. Susie would work the room. She'd lean into someone with her big round eyes and say, "Is everything *okay*?"[32] Warren would plop himself in a corner, "looking so young, with this cowlick sticking up, kind of cute," said Susie's friend Eunice Denenberg. But people would drift over to him. Without any apparent effort, he would start to tell a story, choosing the words precisely and pacing it to perfection, "and you would look around and suddenly people were at his feet." School was always in with him.

Buffett was a talker more than a conversationalist. Richard Holland, an Omaha advertising executive, observed that even in social settings, Buffett had a purposeful quality. Holland met Buffett in the late fifties, when Holland was serving on a creditors' committee of a bankrupt client. Buffett, who had been recommended to manage the workout, showed up in tennis shoes and an old shirt. "I thought maybe *he* was ready for bankruptcy," Holland said. They got to be good pals, and Holland also invested with Buffett. He noticed that Buffett was not a chitchatter. "He wanted to talk about *something*." But he was awkward at small talk, which he punctuated with a nervous chuckle.

Jane Orans, Jerry's wife, thought Buffett's mind "worked differently." He would pick a subject for an evening and ask everyone what he or she thought of it, as if he were leading a seminar. One year, about 1961, when Warren and Susie were visiting the Oranses in New York, Buffett spent much of the evening arguing that overpopulation was the world's most serious problem. It was a typically Buffett-like position: logical and mathematically derived. Also, it touched on his morbid fear for human survival. But Buffett wasn't confrontational about it; his touch was much lighter. Quoting Jane Orans:

> He injected it all with humor. He was very convincing, very logical, but it wasn't lecturing. He made you feel you had reached the same conclusion with him, though obviously he had given it more thought. When

he left you felt he had shaped the evening, but you didn't feel that you hadn't enjoyed it.

Buffett was also raising serious money in New York. The Buffetts would visit in the spring, both to see friends and for Warren to do business. He would ring up Orans from his hotel, usually the Plaza, and say, "Big Boy, could you bring over a six-pack of Pepsi? You can't believe what room service charges!" Meanwhile, Buffett was collecting six-figure checks.

In part, he was feeding off the Graham network. He met Marshall Weinberg, a broker and fellow Graham alumnus, at a lecture at the New School. He and Weinberg became friends, and Weinberg and his brothers invested $100,000. Henry Brandt, another broker friend, invested and steered his clients to Buffett. Laurence Tisch, tipped off by Howard Newman (formerly of Graham-Newman), was good for another $100,000.

Then there was David Strassler, a New Yorker whose family was in the business of fixing distressed companies. Strassler flew into Omaha to look into buying Dempster, the windmill company. Buffett picked him up at the airport. Quoting Strassler:

> I had the typical attitude of a New York guy meeting a hayseed. I had gone to Harvard and studied at MIT. I had just finished working out some deals. I was feeling pretty good. After we had been driving a little bit he started asking me questions about a company in which my family had a majority interest. It was Billings & Spencer, of Hartford. It made forgings and metal shears. Only [about 2%] of it was public. I'm still not sure how he knew about it. Then he started asking me questions about the balance sheet. He knew the balance sheet better than I did. That stopped me totally cold.

Strassler, the "typical" New York guy, invested on the spot.

The Buffett partnerships, begun with a $105,100 grubstake, entered 1962 with $7.2 million in capital—more than Graham-Newman at its peak. Of the total, $1 million belonged to Buffett personally. He was still small, but not unproven. And though unknown to the general public, he was no longer obscure. The original nucleus of seven investors had mushroomed to ninety, grouped in clusters from California to Vermont.[33]

Swelling with new accounts, Buffett decided that he had outgrown his sitting room. He merged the partnerships into one: Buffett Partnership, Ltd. He quadrupled the minimum investment, to $100,000. And he moved his office to Kiewit Plaza, a fourteen-story pale-green-and-white tower on Farnam Street.

Kiewit Plaza was perched at the crest of a hill on the outskirts of Omaha's business district, in a hybrid neighborhood with strip shopping, apartments, and an old steel foundry. Buffett's building was drably functional down to the industrial-carpeted halls—happily drab, as Buffett could assure his partners that he wasn't overspending. Indeed, from Buffett's point of view it was a palace. He had a secretary and an assistant to shake him loose from administrative details—thus, more time for Moody's. He had space to rent to his father, who was ailing. And the office was on the same street as his home—as though he had merely tacked on a couple of miles to the hallway linking his bedroom to his study.

Buffett spent the day reading annual reports and business publications and talking on the telephone. With more and more reports to read and stocks to analyze, he was ever in good humor. But it was rather solitary. He often lunched alone, sending out for a cheeseburger and french fries. His tiny staff knew nothing more of his stock picks than his wife did.

Buffett did have an adviser away from the office—miles away, where it suited him. His letters to his partners were peppered with references to a "West Coast philosopher" friend, a nom de guerre that only hints at this fellow's influence. Charlie Munger, six years Buffett's senior, had also grown up in Omaha, the son of a lawyer and grandson of a judge. He was a close family friend of Edwin and Dorothy Davis and had worked ("slaved") at the Buffett store on Saturdays.

After three years in college and a wartime stint studying meteorology, Munger got into Harvard Law School without a bachelor's degree. His classmates found him brilliant and opinionated to a fault. Called on by a professor when he was unprepared, Munger shot back, "I haven't read the case, but if you give me the facts, I'll give you the law."[34]

After Harvard, Munger practiced in Los Angeles, but in 1959 he returned to Omaha to close out his father's practice. Edwin Davis's son, one of Buffett's investors, was struck by his likeness to Munger and invited the two of them to lunch at the exclusive Omaha Club. They hit it off immediately.[35]

"Warren, what's your racket?" Munger inquired.

"Well, we have a partnership."

"Maybe I could do that out in Los Angeles."

Buffett peered at him and said, "Yeah, I think you could."

The next night they were reunited at Dick Holland's, a mutual friend's, and talked a blue streak. Munger was clutching the same drink the entire evening. He was so intent on babbling that as he lifted his glass and tilted his head to swallow he would raise the other hand in a stop sign so no one would cut him off.[36]

Physically, Munger was unimpressive. He had an elfin face, pasty skin, and glasses an inch thick. Though something of a snob and highly judgmental, he had a deep sense of ethics. His smarts were matched by a Churchillian self-assurance and *joie de vivre*. Asked once if he could play the piano, Munger replied, "I don't know, I never tried." Buffett saw in him a kindred intellect and blistering independence.

A friendship evolved over the summers, when the Buffetts went to California. When Buffett was home, he was constantly sprawled on the floor cradling the phone and talking to Munger. A familiar refrain at the Buffetts' dinner hour, according to little Susie, was "Oh-oh, Dad's talking to Charlie." She recalled, "They talked for hours. They anticipated each other. It was like they hardly had to say anything. It was, 'Yeah—Uh-huh—I know what you mean—Right.' "

Buffett said he and Munger thought so much alike it was "spooky."[37] But unlike so many of Buffett's friends—surely this was part of the attraction—Munger was not in awe of him. And Buffett was so enamored of Munger that he urged him to adopt his own line of work. He kept telling him that practicing law was a waste of his talent—and Munger did not disagree.

> Like Warren, I had a considerable passion to get rich. Not because I wanted Ferraris—I wanted the independence. I desperately wanted it. I thought it was undignified to have to send invoices to other people. I don't know where I got that notion from, but I had it. I had lived way under my income for years, saving money.

He started a law firm, Munger, Tolles & Hills, but barely practiced there. By 1962, as Buffett was moving into Kiewit Plaza, Munger was running his own investment partnership.

That spring, Buffett went to Munger with a problem: what to do about Dempster? Munger was no Ben Graham disciple. In his view, troubled companies, which tended to be the kind that sold at Graham-like discounts, were not easily put right.

But Munger knew a fellow, name of Harry Bottle, who might be the man for Dempster. Buffett interviewed Bottle in Los Angeles, and Bottle was on the job in Beatrice six days later. He cut costs, closed plants, and slashed the inventory. Writing to his partners of Bottle,* Buffett announced:

> Harry is unquestionably the man of the year. . . . He has accomplished one thing after another that has been labeled as impossible. . . .[38]

Bottle was doing—and doing well—the dirty work that Buffett couldn't do. He was squeezing cash from Dempster's underperforming factories, which cash Buffett was funneling into stocks and bonds. From Harry Bottle's clay, Buffett was sculpting a wholly different enterprise—one with a diversified (and steadily rising) portfolio of securities. This was the sort of alchemy that was very much within Buffett's range. He told his partners:

> To some extent, we have converted the assets from the manufacturing business which has been a poor business, to a business which we think is a good business—securities.[39]

The redeployment carried a cost. One hundred people were laid off, and Buffett met with heavy criticism in Beatrice.[40] Bill Otis, a bridge partner, asked him in a kidding vein, "How can you sleep at night after firing all those people?"

To Buffett, who had a thin skin where his reputation was concerned, it was no joke.

"If we'd kept them the company would have gone bankrupt," he said. "I've kept close tabs and most of them are better off."

---

*Buffett did not hesitate to talk about a company once he had a controlling share of it.

Though this has the ring of rationalization, Buffett hated being called a liquidator and vowed that he would "never" lay people off again.[41]

But he had no problem with the results. After a year, Dempster was trimmer but more profitable, and it had $2 million worth of securities to boot. In 1963, Buffett sold it—netting the partnership a $2.3 million profit and nearly tripling its investment.[42] Three things had made it work: the initial bargain price, Buffett's patience in holding on, and his and Bottle's turnaround. To Buffett—as ardently in Ben Graham's camp as ever—the first point outweighed the rest.

> This is the cornerstone of our investment philosophy: Never count on making a good sale. Have the purchase price be so attractive that even a mediocre sale gives good results.[43]

Chapter 5

PARTNERS

*I cannot promise results
to partners.*

WARREN BUFFETT,
LETTER TO PARTNERS, JANUARY 1963

Sol Parsow, who owned a men's shop in Kiewit Plaza, knew Warren Buffett as other than a fashion plate. Typically, Buffett would come in and order five suits—all, despite Parsow's pleading, in a dull gray—and leave on a dime.

One morning, though, Buffett came into the store seeking a bit of fashion advice—sort of. He wanted Parsow's opinion of Byer-Rolnick, a hat manufacturer.

Parsow explained that President Kennedy's bareheaded look was all the rage. "Warren," he said, "I wouldn't touch it with a ten-foot pole. Nobody is wearing hats anymore."

A bit later, Buffett returned. "Sol, what's going on with the suit industry?" Buffett asked.

"Warren, it stinks. Men aren't buying suits."

This time, he couldn't talk him out of it. Buffett Partnership bought a small stake in a New Bedford, Massachusetts, maker of suit liners—Berkshire Hathaway, Inc.—at precisely $7.60 a share.[1] In 1962, Berkshire was one more cheap stock of the sort that appealed to Ben Graham disciples. The venerable Yankee manufacturer had long been struggling against lower-cost Southern and Far Eastern competitors. But on its books, at least, Berkshire was a bargain. It had $16.50 a share of working capital—two times its share price. As a Graham-and-Dodder, Buffett liked the stock and gradually added to his position.

Despite this investment, it was clear that Buffett was becoming more than just a carbon copy of his teacher. He was bolder than Graham: more willing to load up on a stock or to ride a winner. And, of course, his results had been better.

What was not so apparent was that Buffett was also beginning to *think* differently—that is, to think in qualitative terms, as well as in the merely numerical terms that had appealed to Graham. When Buffett looked at a stock, he was beginning to see not just a frozen snapshot of assets, but a live, ongoing business with a unique set of dynamics and potential. And in 1963, the year after he invested in Berkshire, Buffett began to study a stock that was unlike any he had bought before. It had no factories and virtually no hard assets at all. Indeed, its most valuable commodity was its name.

American Express was a company divinely suited to the time. America had entered the space age, and its citizens were in a futuristic frame of mind. Few products symbolized the attainment of the modern life as aptly as those of American Express. Air travel having become affordable, the middle class was embarking on the Grand Tour, and the traveler's check had become its passport. ("Checks That Never Bounce," *Reader's Digest* gushed.)[2] Half a billion dollars of the company's scrip was in circulation, accepted as readily as money itself. Of equal import, by 1963 one million people carried the American Express card, introduced, merely five years earlier, in the innocent era in which citizens thought it necessary to travel about with hard coin. *Time* heralded the advent of the "cashless society."[3] A revolution was at hand, and American Express was its beacon.

And then the bottom fell out. The trouble began, as it often will, in a remote and seemingly minor colony of the corporate empire—in this case, a warehouse in Bayonne, New Jersey, that was owned by an American Express subsidiary.

The warehouse, in the normal course of its less than glamorous trade, accepted tank loads, supposedly of vegetable oil, from an outfit known by the unwieldy moniker Allied Crude Vegetable Oil Refining. In return for the supposed salad oil, the warehouse issued receipts to Allied, which used the receipts as collateral to obtain loans. Subsequently, Allied filed for bankruptcy. Creditors seized Allied's collateral—or rather, tried to. At this point—November 1963—American Express discovered that it had a problem: "Subsequent investigation disclosed that the tanks contained very little vegetable oil."[4] What they contained, in part, was seawater, and seawater of very high quality, though not worth its weight in salad oil. In short, the warehouse had suffered a massive fraud, by some estimates totaling $150 million.

Who would make good the losses? The responsible party was, in the first instance, Allied. But Allied was broke. The American Express subsidiary also filed for bankruptcy. Whether American Express itself had any liability was uncertain. But Howard Clark, the chief executive, grasped that for a company with its name on traveler's checks, the public trust was all. Clark, to his credit, issued a manifesto the very thought of which would have caused lesser CEOs to shudder.

> American Express Company feels *morally bound* to do everything it can, consistent with its overall responsibilities, to see that such excess liabilities are satisfied.

In other words, the parent company would stand behind the claims whether legally bound to or not. The potential loss was "enormous." Indeed, he said, it was "more than we had."[5]

The company's stock fell from 60 before the news to 56½ on November 22. When markets reopened after the Kennedy assassination, American Express tumbled to 49½.

It developed that Allied had been run by one Anthony De Angelis, a.k.a. "the Salad Oil King." De Angelis was a familiar type in American finance, possessed of the combination of brilliance and moral flexibility that produces a first-rate white-collar crook. In a previous incarnation, he had controlled a New Jersey meatpacker that had run afoul of the government and gone belly-up.[6] When he resurfaced with Allied, a supplier of vegetable oils for export, his record as a former bankrupt prevented him from getting credit. Thus his canny scheme to park "salad oil" in the American Express warehouse. Once he had receipts with that most hallowed of corporate names, De Angelis was bankable. He borrowed money, bet the house on vegetable oil futures, and lost.

In the scandal's wake, the portly De Angelis was escorted from his two-story red-brick home in the Bronx to face indictment in federal court in Newark.* And American Express, which had not missed a

---

*He was convicted and sentenced to ten years. In 1992, De Angelis resurfaced—charged with using a fraudulent letter of credit to obtain $1.1 million worth of meat. He was convicted again.

dividend payment in ninety-four years, suddenly was said to be at risk of insolvency.

As these events were unfolding, Buffett paid a visit to Ross's Steak House in Omaha, in the same inquiring spirit as when he had earlier dropped in on the clothier Sol Parsow. On this evening, Buffett was interested not in the customers' steaks, nor in their suits or hats. He positioned himself behind the cashier, chatted with the owner, and watched. What Buffett observed was that, scandal or no, Ross's patrons were continuing to use the American Express card to pay for their dinners.[7] From this, he deduced that the same would be true in steakhouses in St. Louis, Chicago, and Birmingham.

Then he went to banks and travel agencies in Omaha and found that they were doing their usual business in traveler's checks. Similarly, he went to supermarkets and drugstores that sold American Express money orders. Finally, he talked to American Express's competitors. His sleuthing led to two conclusions, both at odds with the prevailing wisdom:

1. American Express was not going down the tubes.

2. Its name was one of the great franchises in the world.[8]

American Express did not have a margin of safety in the Ben Graham sense of the word, and it is unthinkable that Graham would have invested in it. The Graham canon was quite clear: a stock ought to be purchased on the basis of "simple and definite arithmetical reasoning from statistical data."[9] In other words, on the basis of working capital, plant and equipment, and other tangible assets—stuff that one could measure.

But Buffett saw a type of asset that eluded Graham: the franchise value of American Express's name. For franchise, think: a market lock. The Cardinals own the franchise for baseball in St. Louis; no other team need apply. American Express was nearly that good. Nationally, it had 80 percent of the traveler's check market, and a dominant share in charge cards. In Buffett's opinion, nothing had shaken it, and nothing could.[10] The loyalty of its customers could not be deduced from Graham's "simple statistical data"; it did not appear on the company's balance sheet as would a tangible asset, such as the factories of a Berkshire Hathaway. Yet there was *value* in this franchise—in Buffett's view, immense value. American Express had earned record profits in each of the past ten years. Salad oil or not, its customers were not going away. And the stock market was pricing the company as if they already had.

By early 1964, the shares had plunged to 35. Wall Street's chorus, all reading the same lyrics, was chanting, "Sell." Buffett decided to buy. He put close to one-quarter of his assets on that single stock—one with a liability of unknown and potentially huge proportions. If Buffett was wrong, his accumulated profits and reputation stood to go up in flames.

Clark, the American Express president, offered $60 million to the warehouse's creditors in an effort to settle their claims. But he was sued by his own shareholders, who asserted that Clark was "wasting" their assets on a specious moral obligation.

Buffett did not agree. He dropped in on Clark and introduced himself as a friendly shareholder. "Buffett was buying our stock," Clark recalled, "and anybody who bought it then was a pal indeed."

When Buffett told Clark that he supported him, an American Express lawyer asked if he would testify. Buffett went to court and said shareholders shouldn't be suing—they ought to be congratulating Clark for trying to put the matter behind them.[11] "As far as I was concerned," Buffett would explain, "that $60 million was a dividend they'd mailed to the stockholders, and it got lost in the mail. I mean, if they'd declared a $60 million dividend, everybody wouldn't have thought the world was going to hell."[12]

Though the suits dragged on, the stock began to rise. Buffett, however, did not follow the Graham route of taking profits. He liked Clark, and he liked the company's products. Gradually, Buffett added to his position.

Berkshire Hathaway, meanwhile, was indeed going to hell. With the market for textiles mostly poor, Berkshire was losing money and gradually closing mills. But Buffett continued buying its stock, too, and the partnership won a controlling interest. As in the case of Dempster Mill, Buffett went on the board, hoping to set it straight. He also was charmed by its rugged New England plant. Despite its difficulties, he reported to his partners, "Berkshire is a delight to own."[13]

Half of his portfolio now was rooted in two very different stocks, which glared at each other like opposing bookends. In Buffett's terminology, Berkshire's appeal was "quantitative"—based on price. American Express was based on a subjective view of "qualitative" factors such as the strength of its products and management. Though he regarded the softer methodology as the less conclusive, Buffett was uncertain where the balance lay. The "main qualification is a bargain price," he wrote; but he also would pay "considerable attention" to qualitative factors.[14]

Buffett didn't disclose the American Express holding to his partners. But concurrent with his experimentation away from Graham, he began to communicate more expansively to his partners in his letters. He used the letters not just to report results, but to talk about his approach and to educate his readers in a general sense about investing. School was *in*.

Increasingly, the voice that emerged was not Ben Graham's—not phrases from *The Intelligent Investor*—but Buffett's own. It was, by turns, articulate, droll, self-deprecating, and rather more literate than one would expect from an investment manager in his thirties. For a young man, he was astonishingly comfortable with himself. Here is Buffett at thirty-two, on "The Joys of Compounding":

> I have it from unreliable sources that the cost of the voyage Isabella originally underwrote for Columbus was approximately $30,000. This has been considered at least a moderately successful utilization of venture capital. Without attempting to evaluate the psychic income derived from finding a new hemisphere, it must be pointed out that . . . the whole deal was not exactly another IBM. Figured very roughly, the $30,000 invested at 4% compounded annually would have amounted to something like $2,000,000,000,000 [two trillion]. . . .[15]

His serious point was that even trifling sums should be invested with the *utmost* care. To Buffett, blowing $30,000 represented the loss not of $30,000 but of the potential for $2 trillion.

In another letter, he chided partners for being overly influenced in their financial planning by the desire to avoid taxes. Indeed, many of life's errors were the result of people forgetting what they were *really* trying to do.

> What is one really trying to do in the investment world? Not pay the least taxes, although that may be a factor to be considered in achieving the end. Means and end should not be confused, however, and the end is to come away with the largest after-tax rate of compound.

It must be, he added, that people's *emotional* distaste for paying taxes blinded them to acting rationally—a misstep that Buffett was careful to avoid. "Ultimately," he reasoned, there were only three ways to avoid a tax: (1) to give the asset away, (2) to lose back the gain, and (3) to die with the asset—"and that's a little too ultimate for me—even the zealots would have to view this 'cure' with mixed emotions."[16]

Buffett returned to such thematic grace notes again and again. Indeed, reading the letters front to back, they are full of early sightings of later Buffett melodies. But reading them singly, one is more aware of the tone, and specifically of Buffett's intense focus on his own development. Written at night, when the rest of the house was asleep, the letters have about them a quality of self-discovery—a pimply, self-conscious honesty. The writer of these letters has the same engaging informality that Buffett did in person.

Of course, Buffett knew many of his readers on a personal basis, as family or friends. But the collective relationship that he had with them as his partners—even though, in a sense, an abstract one—had a special significance to him.

In person, he kept a distance, but as a general partner, Buffett was revealing about what was, in effect, his most intimate concern. If his work in the partnership amounted to a sort of self-portrait, the background motif of the letters was Buffett's own character. He used these semiannual missives to prepare his partners, and to align their expectations and thinking with his own. He *talked* to them.

> I am not in the business of predicting general stock market or business fluctuations. If you think I can do this, or think it is essential to an investment program, you should not be in the partnership.[17]

It was enormously important to Buffett that his partners see him as trustworthy. He and Susie put more than 90 percent of their personal money in with the partners', as did Bill Scott, Buffett's assistant. "So we are all eating our own cooking," Buffett assured them.[18]

He took pains to explain his approach *in advance*, and in concrete terms—precisely because he knew that a misunderstanding could sunder the union. One time, a partner barged into the reception area at Kiewit Plaza intent on finding out where the money was invested. Buffett, who was meeting with a banker named Bill Brown—later chairman of the Bank of Boston—told his secretary he was busy. She returned in a moment and said the man *insisted* on seeing him. Buffett disappeared for a minute and then told his secretary, "Price that guy out" [of the partnership]. Turning to Brown, Buffett added, "They know my rules. I'll report to them once a year."[19]

Buffett made no attempt to predict his results, but he was obsessed with the notion that his partners should judge him fairly—meaning unemotionally and according to a neutral, arithmetic scale. (That is how Buffett judged himself.)

> I believe in establishing yardsticks prior to the act; retrospectively, almost anything can be made to look good in relation to something or other.[20]

His own goal, stated at the outset, was to beat the Dow by an average of 10 points a year. On this topic, he took his readers deeper. The Dow, he noted, was an unmanaged group of thirty stocks. Yet most of the pros couldn't match it. Why was it, he wondered, that "the high priests of Wall Street," with their brains, training, and high pay, couldn't top a portfolio managed by no brains at all? He found a culprit in the tendency of managers to confuse a *conservative* (i.e., reasonably priced) portfolio with one that was merely *conventional*.[21] It was a subtle distinction, and bears reflection. The common approach of owning a bag full of popular stocks—AT&T, General Electric, IBM, and so forth—*regardless of price*, qualified as the latter, but surely not as the former. Buffett blamed the committee process and group-think that was prevalent on Wall Street:

> My perhaps jaundiced view is that it is close to impossible for outstanding investment management to come from a group of any size. . . .[22]

Such decision-via-consensus—then and now the rule on Wall Street—tended to produce a sameness from one fund to the next. It nourished the seductive syllogism "whereby average is 'safe'" and unorthodox is risky. In truth, Buffett countered, sound reasoning might lead to conventional acts, but often it would lead to unorthodoxy.

> In some corner of the world they are probably still holding regular meetings of the Flat Earth Society. We derive no comfort because important people, vocal people, or great numbers of people agree with us. Nor do we derive comfort if they don't.[23]

Buffett's portfolio was decidedly unconventional. With his big bets on American Express, Berkshire Hathaway, and two or three others, the lion's share of the pool was in just five stocks.[24] Ideally, Buffett would have preferred to spread his assets, *provided* that he could have found, say, fifty stocks that were equally "superior." But in the real world, he found that he had to work extremely hard to find just a few.[25]

He ridiculed the fund managers who took the opposite tack—which is to say, most of those working on Wall Street. Diversification had become an article of faith; fund managers were commonly stuffing their portfolios with *hundreds* of different stocks. Paraphrasing Billy Rose, Buffett doubted that they could intelligently select so many securities any more than a sheik could get to "know" a harem of one hundred girls.

> Anyone owning such numbers of securities . . . is following what I call the Noah School of Investing—two of everything. Such investors should be piloting arks.[26]

A portfolio with scores of securities would be relatively unaffected if any one stock fell, but similarly unaffected should an issue rise. Indeed, as the number of stocks grew, the portfolio would come to mimic the market averages. That would be a safe and perhaps a reasonable goal for the novice, but in Buffett's view, it undermined the very purpose of the professional investor, who presumably was being paid to *beat* the average. Owning so many stocks was an admission that one could *not* pick the winners.

None of this is to suggest that Buffett was a gambler. He was just as determined as Ben Graham had been to avoid taking a loss. But where Graham had insisted on substantial (if not extreme) diversification,[27] Buffett thought he could safeguard his eggs without spreading them around.* Beneath his surface modesty he was, in effect, making a very brassy claim. And he continued to live up to it. The partnership portfolio jumped an astonishing 39 percent in 1963 and 28 percent in 1964. By then, Buffett was managing $22 million. His personal net worth was close to $4 million—at that time, quite a fortune.[28]

---

*Mark Twain, though a poor investor, had a similar strategy: "Put all your eggs in the one basket and—*watch that basket.*"

This spiraling accumulation had no noticeable effect on Buffett's lifestyle. He remained partial to Parsow's gray suits, Ross's steaks, and University of Nebraska football games. During the week, aside from an occasional business trip, his X coordinate merely traversed an alley between his home and office; the Y coordinate barely moved at all. Nor was there anything in Buffett's manner that suggested money. He did add some rooms and a racquetball court to his house, the variously sloping roofs of which now seemed to ramble disjointedly over the lot. But for a multimillionaire, it was remarkably ordinary, and of course remained close to a busy suburban thoroughfare. Outside, a blinking yellow traffic light stood watch like a sentry.

Buffett scarcely thought about spending his wealth on material comforts. That wasn't why he wanted it. The money was a *proof*: a scorecard for his favorite game.

He did ask Susie to upgrade his VW, explaining that it looked bad when he picked up visitors at the airport. But he didn't have the slightest interest in it.

"What kind of car?" Susie asked.

"*Any* car. I don't care what kind."[29] (She got him a wide-finned Cadillac.)

Scott Hord, a vice president of Data Documents, the Omaha computer-card company, got to the heart of the matter when Buffett and he flew to Houston on a business trip.

"Warren, what's it feel like to be a millionaire?" Hord asked innocently. "I've never known a millionaire."

"I can have anything I want that money will buy. But I always could."

Whatever was the object of Scotty Hord's fantasies—toys, trucks, cars, paintings, jewelry, silks—Buffett could have had. But they didn't mean a thing to him. Buffett's fantasy was to be in Kiewit Plaza, piling up more money day after day.

Paradoxically, Susie projected an air of disinterest in *having* money but was a virtuoso shopper. She dropped $15,000 on a home refurnishing, which "just about killed Warren," according to Bob Billig, one of his golfing pals. Buffett griped to Billig, "Do you know how much that is if you compound it over twenty years?"

Beneath his becoming lack of acquisitiveness, Buffett had a certain obsession. In his mind, every dime had the potential of Queen Isabella's lost fortune. When a nickel today could become so much more tomorrow, spending it drove him nuts. He didn't even buy life insurance, figuring that he could compound the premiums faster than an insurance company.* Buffett said of himself that he was "working [his] way up to cheap."[30] (He was not stingy, though, about picking up the check.)

When it came to money, Buffett seemed to have twin personalities—it was nothing to him and it was everything. He had an overly reverent view of money's proper role, as if spending were a sort of sinfulness. Even when he dieted, he inserted money into the equation. He would write a $10,000 check to his daughter, payable on such-and-such a date *unless his weight had dropped.* Little Susie would try to ply him with ice cream or drag him to McDonald's—but it was useless. Her daddy didn't want the ice cream as much as he wanted to keep the money.

Buffett acknowledged his contrasting sentiments, quite comically, one summer when the family was touring San Simeon, the William Randolph Hearst mansion in California. The guide was giving a blow-by-blow account of how much Hearst had paid for every item—the drapes, carpets, antiques, and so on. Bored to tears, Buffett protested, "Don't tell us how he spent it. Tell us how he *made* it!"[31]

Buffett's money seems to have affected him politically—but not in the manner one would expect. As he became independently wealthy—roughly during the early and middle sixties—he finally asserted his political autonomy from his father. Warren based his evolving politics not on his personal economic interests, as most millionaires—and most people—do, but on his fears for society writ large. In the turbulent 1960s, several issues awakened him. The Cuban missile crisis mortified him, just as Hiroshima had. According to his friend Dick Holland:

> Warren was afraid. He was interested in studying the attitudes that led to extreme nationalism, and how wars could be prevented. He was always trying to calculate the odds of the world's blowing up.

Buffett read Bertrand Russell, the pacifist philosopher and mathematician, extensively during this period, and adopted much of Rus-

---

*There was one exception. According to Kay Koetter, an insurance agent, some of Buffett's partners were so concerned about losing their investment if Buffett dropped dead that Buffett bought a policy and named them as the beneficiary.

sell's internationalist outlook.[32] An agnostic like Russell, and deeply aware of his mortality, Buffett thought it was up to society, collectively, to protect the planet from dangers such as nuclear war. Unlike his isolationist and antigovernment father, Warren recognized a *need* for government.

This was also true on the burning issue of civil rights. Omaha had a substantial black population, and strict segregation in housing and many jobs. Howard Buffett did not have a public record on civil rights, but as an avid member of the John Birch Society,[33] he presumably did not lose sleep over it.

Warren was emphatically on the other side. He quit the Omaha Rotary Club specifically because he objected to its racist and elitist policies.[34] Discrimination collided with his belief in merit and his faith in neutral yardsticks, which lay at the heart of his investing. In the same vein, he thought it was wrong that rich kids got a big head start over everyone else.

Buffett was also being exposed to the idealism of his wife. Susie was an organizer and an active member of the Panel of Americans, a group of Omaha women of various religions and races who would speak to churches, schools, and clubs about their experiences with ethnic prejudice. The panel included a refugee from Nazi camps, a Mississippi-born black, and so on. Susie would give the Wasp perspective. In the Omaha of the early and mid-sixties, the Panel of Americans was rather daring.[35] Women of Susie's caste were expected to go to Junior League meetings. The Buffetts, though, were one of the few families in the lily-white Happy Hollow area—for a while, probably the *only* family—that regularly and routinely entertained blacks at home.

Repelled by the Republicans' indifference to civil rights, Warren decided to break from his father's party and become a Democrat. This was a major step for him. His father, his best friend, was fighting a protracted battle with cancer, and the GOP had been a huge part of his life.

In the winter of 1964, Howard was suffering greatly and stoically. Warren would go to the hospital every night. One evening, he had "a difficult conversation with him about changing parties."[36] As he explained to Charlie Munger, he wasn't sure that his father was wrong on a lot of issues, but he didn't want to be "consumed by ideology" as Howard had been. (Perhaps to spare his father anguish, Warren didn't change parties or publicly acknowledge the switch until Howard's death.)

In the spring, his father took a turn for the worse. After learning of his condition, Buffett showed up for a table tennis game at Dick Holland's looking clearly out of sorts. But he kept the awful news to himself. Not many days later, Buffett arrived home looking glummer than his daughter had ever seen him. "He was very withdrawn and sad," she recalled. "I think I asked him why he wasn't going to the hospital. He said, 'Grandpa died today.' Then he went upstairs."

Five hundred mourners attended Howard's funeral. Colleagues from both parties saluted his integrity and warmth. Warren sat through it silently. Then, he left town, without telling friends of his whereabouts.[37] When Buffett returned to Kiewit Plaza, he hung a large-size likeness of his father on the wall facing his desk. But his best friend was gone.

As his father had been with him, Warren was a moral exemplar to his own children. But Warren was the same unsentimental analyst with his kids as he was with his partners. He was a concerned parent, and a supportive one—but not demonstrative. He took Susie to the office on Saturdays, as his father had taken him; he threw a football with Howie and helped Pete with his math. But he rarely if ever talked to them about subjects—such as his own parents—that might have exposed his feelings.

He and little Susie shared a certain tenderness. But Warren's sons felt emotionally neglected by him. Howie, the second child, was a bit of a troublemaker, and was repeatedly frustrated by his dad's lack of outward feeling.[38] "I used to misinterpret his tone to mean that he didn't care about me," he said. "It's the exact same quality that makes him so good as an investor. There was no emotion in it."

Most people—high-powered executives perhaps especially—tend to compartmentalize their lives. They may be tigers at the office and kittens at home. But Buffett was all of a remarkably consistent piece. To young Peter, his father ran on an inner clock whose springs and gears never ceased to turn. Day to day, Buffett was in his own solar system.[39] "I remember I gave him a birthday card once," Peter said. "He just sort of opened it and closed it—he read it that fast. I guess I was waiting for some response." Warren was expressive in his letters, but mute with his son.

A bit later, when Peter was in a drugstore with his mother, he saw a book called *The Father's Handbook*. He said rather flippantly, "You should get that for Dad." So she did. When Warren got the book, he called Peter up to his study and said, "Hey, what's going on? What do you mean?" Peter meant there was nothing that he could tell his dad that his father wanted to know—or such was Peter's impression then. Buffett, obviously, *was* concerned. But he couldn't show it. He made efforts to reach out, but they struck Peter as halfhearted.

The Buffett house was like a storm center with Warren at its eye. As little Susie said, her father was always reading. The house was a hub of comings and goings: friends, relatives, lonely-hearts talking to Susie. Susie herself went around the house singing. The kids would climb from the attic onto the Dutch gambrel roof, or go trooping into the family room. And Warren was just *up there*, buried in his work. He would dart out of his study just long enough to grab a Pepsi with syrupy cherry flavoring or to entreat his wife to calm the kids. "Susan-O—tell them to quiet down."

His abstractedness was a running joke. One time he came downstairs and asked what had happened to the greenback wallpaper in the study. Susie had changed it a couple of *years* before.

Susie tolerated him perhaps because Warren, in his absentminded way, was unfailingly good-natured. As she said to her sister, "You can't get mad at someone who is so *funny*." Moreover, she, and even the children, understood that Warren was on a sort of spiritual mission that diverted him from the more routine aspects of family living. They referred to his office, only half-jokingly, as the "temple." His work was a "canvas"—a work of art. Susie, referring to Buffett's maestrolike self-absorption, once remarked to Marshall Weinberg, their Manhattan stockbroker chum, "Let's face it—I'm married to Artur Rubinstein."[40]

Weinberg, a music lover, knew full well. Buffett could hum the chords, and the concertinos, and even the entire symphonies of Wall Street in his sleep. Once in a while, Weinberg would play a few bars for his friend, hoping—just once—to show him something new. One time, for instance, he told Buffett about a certain cement stock that was cheap relative to its book value. Buffett shot back, "Yeah, but the book isn't worth anything. Look at the record of selling cement plants in the last seven years."[41]

As Weinberg also knew, the explanation, or part of it, lay in Buffett's relentless focusing on his craft. In 1965, after Weinberg had returned from a trip to Egypt, Warren and Susie visited him at his Manhattan apartment. Few Americans had been to Egypt, and Weinberg, who was so often impressed with Buffett, was eager to show his genius friend his slides of the pyramids.

Buffett said easily, "I have a better idea. Why don't you show the slides to Susie and I'll go into your bedroom and read an annual report." The pyramids were out of his zone, like the wallpaper.

The report that Buffett had with him may well have been Walt Disney Productions'. At around the time of his visit to Weinberg, he went to see the company's latest film, *Mary Poppins*, in Times Square. Needless to say, Buffett was not so interested in Julie Andrews, the show's star, but in Disney's stock.

Settling into a seat, with his tweeds, briefcase, and popcorn, he noticed that the other patrons were staring at him. He suddenly realized that he was the only adult unaccompanied by a child, and must have looked rather odd.[42]

But when the theater went dark, the other moviegoers forgot him. Buffett saw that they were riveted to the picture, and he asked himself, in effect, what it would be worth to own a tiny bit of each of those people's ticket revenues—for today and tomorrow and as many tomorrows as they kept coming back to Disney.

In the summer, when the Buffetts were in California, they went with the Mungers to Disneyland. While the kids did the park, Buffett and Munger dissected it financially, ride for ride, a kind of Fellini fantasy version of a corporate balance sheet.[43]

Subsequently, Buffett visited Walt Disney himself on the Disney lot. The animator, meeting him in shirtsleeves, was as enthusiastic as ever. Buffett was struck by his childlike enchantment with his work—so similar to Buffett's own.[44]

Disney's stock, meanwhile, was trading at only about ten times earnings. Buffett tried to analyze it not as a stock, but as a whole company, perhaps as a business down the street in Omaha that was willing to sell him a part ownership.[45] In Buffett's view, its most valuable feature was its library of old cartoons and films, such as *Snow White* and *Bambi*. A Ben Graham would not have been interested in such an imprecise asset. However, Buffett estimated that, on a proportional basis, the library alone was worth the price of a share.[46] Plus, he would own a slice of Disneyland, and he would have the unpretentious Mr. Disney as his partner. With such thoughts in mind, Buffett bought 5 percent of Disney for $4 million.[47] Disney himself would be dead within the year.

Buffett, it should be understood, was not abandoning the Graham credo of hunting for securities that were well below "intrinsic value." But his definition of value was changing, or rather, broadening. To Buffett, the value of Disney's film library, even though imprecise and mostly off the books, was no less real than a tangible asset such as a factory.

He was no doubt encouraged by his similar bet on American Express, which had begun to see its way clear of the salad-oil scandal. By 1965, the stock had hit 73½, double its recent low. And Buffett Partnership beat the Dow that year by a phenomenal 33 percentage points.

Buffett warned his partners not to expect a repeat.[48] In the following year he would top the Dow by 36 percentage points. But then, his doleful forecasts had long been sounding like a broken record. Fearful that success would sow the seeds of disappointment, he had repeatedly prophesied his own fall.

[January 1962:] If my performance is poor, I expect partners to withdraw. . . . [January 1963:] It is a certainty that we will have years when . . . we deserve the tomatoes. . . . [January 1964:] I believe our margin over the Dow cannot be maintained. . . . [January 1965:] We do not consider it possible on an extended basis to maintain the 16.6 percentage point advantage over the Dow. . . . [January 1966:] Those who believe 1965 results can be achieved with any frequency are probably attending weekly meetings of the Halley's Comet Observers Club. We are going to have loss years and are going to have years inferior to the Dow—no doubt about it. . . . [July 1966:] Such results should be regarded as decidedly abnormal.

That is what he said. But his wings refused to melt. Over the partnership's second five years, Buffett's record was off the charts:

	PARTNERSHIP	DOW
1962:	+13.9%	−7.6%
1963:	+38.7	+20.6
1964:	+27.8	+18.7
1965:	+47.2	+14.2
1966:	+20.4	−15.6

And the cumulative record, over ten years:

PARTNERSHIP	DOW
+1,156%	+122.9%[49]

After deducting for Buffett's share of the profits, his limited partners' investment had risen by 704.2%—six times the gain in the Dow. For an original investor, such as the Edwin Davis family, each $100,000 had grown to $804,000. (The Davises, like others, had continued to put in more money along the way.)

Buffett Partnership's total assets, as of the start of 1966, had swelled to $44 million. Buffett, in other words, was running a fair-sized enterprise (though still far smaller than the big mutual funds). And at age thirty-five, he was a very rich man. He wrote to his partners in January 1966, "Susie and I have an investment of $6,849,936, which should keep me from slipping away to the movies in the afternoon."[50]

He also got a first taste of the limelight. In May, readers of the *Omaha World-Herald* awoke to Buffett's toothy, chipmunkish grin at the top of the second section. Buffett was pictured with an ear to the phone, unstylishly short hair, and a look of unmistakable eagerness. According to the hometown *World-Herald:*

> One of the most successful investment businesses in the United States is operated in Omaha by a young man who bought his first stock at age 11.[51]

A more probing interviewer, reporting on the changes at Berkshire Hathaway for a textile-industry trade paper, zeroed in on Buffett's seeming contradictions:

> While his approach is informal, he never gives the impression of being offhand. If his manner is casual, he is obviously a man with his facts well in hand. . . . Buffett doesn't dodge questions . . . but sometimes he's a trifle oblique.[52]

The general financial press and the broader business public had not heard a word of him. But to investors such as the Davises, Buffett's stature was rising to mythological proportions. This one man—this kid— was making them *rich*. Lee Seemann, Edwin Davis's son-in-law, who was a salesman for International Harvester, who liked to hunt ducks and go to football games, who had big Lyndon Johnson ears and had no business dreaming of money, was getting *rich*. He felt he was living in a fairy tale.[53] The investors began to think of themselves as a privileged tribe—as blessed.

Buffett invited groups of them to the house once a year. The partners looked forward to these dinners with the oracle. Susie had the place spiffed up, and she would sidle up to each guest in turn and draw him or her out. And Buffett would recount his coups of the past year and spin little stories, stressing how he had gotten himself into a jam or a comical situation, such as how, when he had been trying to save Dempster, he had had to walk a very fine line because the yokels in Beatrice were convinced that he was out to destroy the company, or, going back to Wilson Coin Op, he had had to put on an act for the barbers to keep the pinball mafia from running him out of town. The hero of these cracker-barrel tales seemed to be a sort of middlingly talented but plucky Huck Finn, a modest sort who triumphed almost despite himself. And his guests hung on his words. Leland Olson, an investor, remembered the stories for years. "They would fascinate you. And he didn't talk down to you," Olson said.

The investors, in fact, were starting to *worship* Buffett. Roxanne Brandt, wife of the broker Henry, wrote in her daughter's baby book under "Three greatest minds of the era": Schweitzer, Einstein, and Warren Buffett. He was the unassuming genius who drank nothing but Pepsi-Cola and could beat the pants off Wall Street year after year.

Buffett encouraged it as only a confident and successful man may do, with modesty. The self-deprecating quips, like the humble prognostications of his own decline, merely confirmed his investors' awe of him. The worship surely delighted him, but it also made him edgy. With each successful vault, the bar of expectations climbed. The brighter his star, the darker was the shadow of a looming burnout. Buffett had been saying all along that it could not go on forever. On Wall Street, nothing does.

Chapter 6

GO-GO

I am out of step
with present conditions.

WARREN BUFFETT,
LETTER TO PARTNERS, OCTOBER 1967

Graham's generation had retired, taking its grim Depression memories
with it. Wall Street had reawakened to a younger breed, many of whom
had not been alive in 1929, and who were bored with their elders' endless recitations. More important, they had no memory of the heady
years before the Crash. For them, speculation bore no curse; the bull
market of the sixties was as fresh as first love. Even the stocks that they
traded were new—electronics issues, big conglomerates, small growth
stocks. These all required a faith, but faith there was aplenty. Stocks
were going *up*.

This had hardly bothered Buffett when his fund was small. But as his
capital swelled, he grew increasingly antsy. The combination of more
cash to invest and fewer bargains had him trapped. He complained of
being pressed for ideas and, bit by bit, of a strain. Indeed, his letters of
the later sixties read like an inverted chronicle of the age. Wall Street
waxed ever more euphoric, Buffett, more doubting.

Early in 1966, he took the fateful step of closing the partnership to
new accounts.*

---

*Buffett was also constrained by federal securities law, which restricts such partnerships to ninety-
nine partners. According to Dan Monen, his lawyer, he had far more than ninety-nine people
investing with him, but no more than ninety-nine "limited partners"—an end run accomplished
by lumping groups of investors into single entities. "It was within the letter of the law," Monen
said. "I don't know about the spirit."

The only way to make this effective is to apply it across-the-board and I have notified Susie that if we have any more children, it is up to her to find some other partnership for them.[1]

As Buffett was shutting off the spigot, Wall Street was being deluged. The war in Vietnam was pumping up the stock market to record heights. Young people, it is true, were marching in the streets, but their parents, seeing the war's expansionary effects, were queuing at brokers. Mutual funds opened by the dozen, and the Dow Jones Industrial Average broke 1,000 for the first time ever. It repeated this death-defying act on three more occasions; alas, it closed beneath the magic number each time. Then, in the spring of 1966, the market went into a steep swoon. (New money is jittery money.) Increasingly, investors were focusing on the shorter term.

Some of Buffett's partners called to "warn" him that the market might go lower still. Such calls, Buffett shot back, raised two questions:

(1) if they knew in February that the Dow was going to 865 in May, why didn't they let me in on it then; and, (2) if they didn't know what was going to happen during the ensuing three months back in February, how do they know in May?

Inevitably, the advice of such partners was to sell until the future was "clear." For some reason, market commentators suffer a peculiar blind spot. They routinely assume that once the "uncertainty" of the immediate moment is lifted they will have a plain view of the future unto Judgment Day. The fact that they did not foresee the present uncertainty does not deter them from thinking that no new clouds will trouble the future.

Let me again suggest [that] the future has never been clear to me (give us a call when the next few months are obvious to you—or, for that matter, the next few hours).[2]

Buffett avoided trying to forecast the stock market, and most assuredly avoided buying or selling stocks based on people's opinions of it. Rather, he tried to analyze the long-term business prospects of individual companies. This owed to his bias for logical reasoning. One could "predict" the market trend, as one could predict which way a bird would fly when it left the tree. But that was guesswork—not analysis. If he ever sold stocks "just because some astrologer thinks the quotations may go lower," he warned, they would all be in trouble.[3]

The Dow did go lower, into the 700s, but the broader market was frothy. In two cases, just as Buffett had begun to buy what he considered to be hot prospects, competitors snatched the stocks away. (Like most pros, Buffett built a position in a stock gradually, to avoid driving up the price while he was buying.) One of them rose to a price way out of his range; the other was taken over.[4] Nothing made him madder.

In such a climate, Buffett's obsession with secrecy rose to the level of paranoia. His brokers were given to understand that under *no* circumstance were they to speak of Buffett's stock picks, even to people in their offices. According to Kay Koetter, an Omaha bridge crony, Buffett even got the idea that his Kiewit Plaza office was being bugged via "telescopic amplification" from the nearby Blackstone Hotel. Buffett hired a security firm to check it out, Koetter added, but found nothing.

The real problem was not that people were stealing his stocks, but that he couldn't find enough that met his standards. In part, Graham's disciples had become too numerous. Aided by the computer, they were plucking the bargains off the trees.

At the start of 1967, Buffett felt compelled to advise his partners that some of the newer mutual funds had better recent returns than his own. Moreover, he warned that his stream of new ideas was down to a "trickle." Though he was working night and day to keep them coming, his tone was ominous. If his idea flow "should dry up completely, you will be informed honestly and promptly so that we may all take alternative action."[5]

It is noteworthy that Buffett was sending off these dire alarums in direct proportion to the giddiness on Wall Street. To money men, these were the Go-Go years. There was a frenzy for electronics stocks, each new issue of which was held to be the next Xerox. Had Wall Street suddenly developed an expertise in electronics? To ask the question was to misunderstand the age. Wall Street *believed* in electronics. Even a toad such as American Music Guild could become a prince by calling itself Space-Tone Electronics Inc.

The buzz for high-tech was followed by a merger wave, propelled by huge conglomerates such as International Telephone & Telegraph, Litton Industries, and Ling-Temco-Vought. The public of that confident time did not mistrust bureaucracy; it conferred on big organizations (as on technology) a mystique of competence.

Then, there was a burst of "letter stock"—unregistered shares, often of highly dubious companies, that were marked to absurd valuations. Though each of these fashions had its ebb and flow, as one bubble burst a new fad took its place, so that as the sixties ran their course Wall Street gathered an ever more intoxicating speculative momentum.

The archetype of the Go-Go era was the "performance fund," an acid-rock version of the conventional mutual fund. This new species attempted to outperform the market not over the long term, but over each successive quarter, month, week, and virtually every hour. Performance funds were run by sideburned gunslingers who were bent on making money *fast*. They switched from stock to stock, moving to the one that was hot, like an actor running from house to house to sustain the applause. The aim, in short, was to catch the momentary swing. Gerald Tsai, manager of the Manhattan Fund, was the first prodigy of the breed; it was said that a whisper of Tsai's involvement in a stock was sufficient to set off a small stampede. For the gunslinger wanted nothing of Howard Buffett's sweet independence. He was a contemporary man, young in age and devoid of memory.

> What manner of young man was he? He came from a prospering mid-dle-income background and often from a good business school; he was under thirty, often well under; he wore boldly striped shirts and broad, flowing ties; he radiated a confidence, a knowingness, that verged on insolence, and he liberally tossed around the newest clichés, "performance," "concept," "innovative," and "synergy"; he talked fast and dealt hard.[6]

Go-Go reached an epitome with Fred Carr, who drew a blaze of publicity as head of the Enterprise Fund. In 1967, he registered a gain of 116 percent, far outstripping any single year of Buffett's.[7] Carr invested in tiny, so-called emerging growth companies and heaps of unregistered letter stock. He was lionized in the press as "cool and decisive." The very model of the new breed, Carr installed a phone in his bathroom in Beverly Hills and sped to work in a Jaguar. His office was decorated with op art. His strategy was simple: "We fall in love with nothing. Every morning everything is for sale—every stock in the portfolio, and my suit and my tie."[8]

On paper, Go-Go's practitioners were getting rich. If the popular stocks were going up, why not simply buy them? The question nagged at Buffett continuously, and he kept a diary of his reactions, as much for his own benefit as for his partners'. "Fashion" investing, he wrote,

> does not completely satisfy my intellect (or perhaps my prejudices), and most definitely does not fit my temperament. I will not invest my own money based upon such an approach—hence, I will most certainly not do so with your money.[9]

According to his son Peter, Buffett identified with *The Glenn Miller Story*, the Hollywood epic in which the band leader searches to find his "sound." For Buffett, the right sound was a matter not just of making money, but of superior reasoning. Being right on a stock had something of the purity of a perfect move in chess; it had an intellectual resonance. Glenn Miller or Bobby Fischer, Buffett simply refused to go outside his ken.

> We will not go into businesses where technology which is away [*sic*] over my head is crucial to the investment decision. I know about as much about semiconductors or integrated circuits as I do of the mating habits of the chrzaszez.[10]

It seemed that the dizzier Go-Go's success, the greater was Buffett's urge to apply the brakes. Indeed, he kept a newspaper clipping of the 1929 crash in plain view on his wall, just as a reminder. He had no op art, nor anything else that might have been in vogue in Beverly Hills— just the big maroon Moody's books lined up on the radiator, and a few pictures. His office might have been that of a moderately successful dentist. The reception area had a hanging Franklinesque aphorism, "A fool and his money are soon invited everywhere," and an 1880 photograph of Wall Street. There was no sign of activity in the Fred Carr sense. Buffett did not even have a stock ticker. (Tickers give minute-by-minute readings of stock prices. Virtually every professional investor has one, or a computerized equivalent, and checks it throughout the day.)

Buffett's portfolio seemed almost as dated as his newspaper clippings. In 1966 and 1967, the partnership bought a pair of retailers, Hochschild, Kohn & Co., a Baltimore department store, and Associated Cotton Shops, a dress shop chain, for a total of about $15 million. In each case, Buffett bought not liquid shares of stock but the entire business. Among fund managers, this was unheard-of. Buffett had often bought stocks with the *intent* of holding them for the long term, but he was locked into Hochschild and Associated. He could not pick up the phone and sell them like Fred Carr's necktie. Moreover, to say that inner-city retailing was out of vogue would be a serious understatement. But both companies were cheap, and Buffett thought he could make a profit as an operator.

When he inquired about Associated, he amazed Benjamin Rosner, the sixty-three-year-old owner, with his grasp of retailing. But he understood the business only through the keyhole of finance. When Rosner offered to show him a store, Buffett declined, explaining that he wouldn't know what he was looking at. He merely wanted Rosner to read him the previous five years' balance sheets over the telephone. The next day, Buffett called back with an offer.[11] When Rosner accepted, Buffett took Charlie Munger to New York to ink the deal.

Associated was potentially a lemon. Its stores were in deteriorating, inner-city neighborhoods, and Rosner, its architect, was planning to retire. Sensing that he would need a Sancho Panza once again, Buffett demurely asked Rosner if he could stay on for six months to help him get going. Privately, Buffett shrewdly told Munger, "That's one problem we don't have. This guy won't be able to quit."

The son of Austro-Hungarian immigrants, Rosner had started with a single dress shop, in Chicago, in 1931. He was an archetypal bootstrapper, having taken a $3,200 grubstake to a business with $44 million in annual sales. Like other self-improvers, he was a slave to his work and a dictator to the staff. His penny-pinching work ethic may have reminded Buffett of his grandfather, the erstwhile monarch of Buffett & Son grocery. Rosner (Buffett loved to relate) had once counted the sheets on a roll of toilet paper to avoid being cheated—definitely Buffett's kind of guy. He flattered Rosner profusely, and though he asked him for monthly financial reports, he stayed out of Rosner's hair (and out of his stores), which suited both of them. As Buffett had predicted, Rosner soon found that he was in not, in fact, in any great hurry to retire, and began to squeeze the proverbial lemonade from lemons.*

Hochschild, the Baltimore retailer, was not so easily salvaged. Not only was the main store out-of-date (one wing had access only via a

---

*Rosner stayed for twenty years. Toward the end of his tenure, he told Buffett: "I'll tell you why it worked. You forgot you bought this business. And I forgot I sold it."

staircase), it required frequent additions of capital just to maintain its market share. And downtown Baltimore was badly decaying. Cheap price or no, it did not take Buffett long to realize that he had goofed.

Another long-term "bargain," textile maker Berkshire Hathaway, also was having problems. The suit business was depressed, just as the clothier Sol Parsow had warned. In midsummer 1967, Buffett soberly informed his partners that he did not see anything to suggest that it would improve.[12]

Wall Street, meanwhile, was feeling oh so happy. It was not only profitable but—for the first time since the twenties—fun. Trading volume was soaring. Consider; when Buffett started out, in the 1950s, volume on the New York Stock Exchange had been two million shares a day; by 1967, it was *ten* million. The buoyant spirit was mockingly captured by Abbie Hoffman, who visited the exchange that summer and threw dollar bills from the gallery while floor clerks scurried for the loot. On the West Coast, customers at Kleiner Bell stood in front of the ticker tape cheering "Go, go, go." The Dow roared back to the low 900s.

As if on cue, Congress held—what else?—hearings. In August, Paul Samuelson, the Massachusetts Institute of Technology economist, appeared before the very Senate Banking Committee that Ben Graham had faced a decade earlier. This time the subject was the rampant growth of mutual funds. Samuelson testified that fifty thousand mutual fund salesmen—one for every seventy investors—were combing the country. Most were plainly incompetent, but were sustained by the industry's abusively high fees. It was common for funds to charge their investors an up-front sales load of 8.5 percent. This did not cover annual management fees; it was merely to pay for marketing and to keep the salesman in shoe leather. (Buffett, in contrast, took a share of the profits, but nothing up-front and no management fee.) According to Samuelson:

> Only 91½ cents of my every dollar will ever work for me now to produce income and capital gains, and 9.3 percent of this amount has gone forever in the form of selling charges.[13]

A by-product of the mutual fund boom was the rise of a class of mandarin investors. For the first time, the pros—mutual funds, pensions, and the like—had more influence in markets than the individual duffer. In Buffett's view, the professional was more speculative, not less; the old saw that the pro kept his cool while the amateur fell victim to emotionalism was inside out. In the words of one canny observer:

> It might have been supposed that competition between expert professionals, possessing judgment and knowledge beyond that of the average private investor, would correct the vagaries of the ignorant individual left to himself. It happens, however, that the energies and skill of the professional investor and speculator are mainly occupied otherwise. For most of these persons are, in fact, largely concerned, not with making superior long-term forecasts of the probable yield of an investment over its whole life, but with foreseeing changes in the conventional basis of valuation a short time ahead of the general public. They are concerned, not with what an investment is really worth to a man who buys it "for keeps", but with what the market will value it at, under the influence of mass psychology, three months or a year hence.[14]

That, in fact, had been written by John Maynard Keynes, in 1936. Though Keynes, of course, is best remembered as a macroeconomist, Buffett read him for his considerable insights into markets. Indeed, Keynes's career in some ways prefigured Buffett's. Early on, he lost large sums speculating in currencies, corn, cotton, and rubber. Then, renouncing his sins, he became an apostle of long-term, selective investing.[15] He pursued the market with calm, devoting to it an hour in bed in the morning, yet compiling a stellar record for his own account and for that of King College. His speeches at the annual meetings of the National Mutual Life Assurance Society, of which he was chairman, were celebrated in the London of the 1930s for their impact on market prices.

For Buffett, Keynes's relevance during the Go-Go era was his keen understanding of how crowds could influence market prices. The stock market *is* a crowd, consisting of whoever is following prices at any given moment. This amorphous assemblage revalues prices every day, even every hour. Yet the outlook for a given business—say, a Walt Disney—changes far more slowly. The public's ardor for *Mary Poppins* is unlikely to change from a Tuesday to a Wednesday, or even over a month or two. Most of the fluctuations in Disney's shares, therefore, derive from changes not in the business but in the way that the business is *perceived*. And the pros were preoccupied merely with outwitting the crowd, that is, with staying a step ahead of its fleeting shifts in opinion. Again, Keynes:

> We have reached the third degree where we devote our intelligences to anticipating what average opinion expects the average opinion to be.[16]

One sees in Buffett a strongly similar suspicion of public opinion. Buffett viewed a crowd as a potential source of a sort of intellectual contagion. It was the author of acts and feelings which, rather than being a summing-up of the parts, no one individual among the crowd would have subscribed to alone.[17]

Buffett illustrated this with an allegory about an oil prospector, who arrived at heaven's gate only to hear the distressing news that the "compound" reserved for oilmen was full. Given permission by Saint Peter to say a few words, the prospector shouted, "Oil discovered in hell!"—whereupon every oilman in heaven departed for the nether reaches. Impressed, Saint Peter told him there was now plenty of room. Quoting Buffett:

> The prospector paused. "No," he said, "I think I'll go along with the rest of the boys. There might be some truth to that rumor after all."[18]

Buffett had heard the story from Ben Graham, though he did not set it to paper until much later. In the Go-Go era, the story was not at all far-fetched. The performance funds hopped on "story" stocks—that is, stocks with a simple concept ("Oil discovered in hell!") that might catch on in a hurry. A notorious example was National Student Marketing, which was sold to the public at 6 and vaulted to 82 within a year.

National Student Marketing was the brainchild of Cortes Wesley Randall, a thirty-something Gatsby who lumped under one umbrella a group of businesses purportedly serving college kids: books, records, youth airfare cards, and so on. He thus combined the public mania for conglomerates with a novel "story"—youth. In addition, Randell was a hell of a salesman. He flattered security analysts, took them on tours of his Virginia castle, and called them from his Learjet. Each year, Randell predicted trebled earnings. And each year, he met his target—

though not, it would develop, without some help from the company's accountants. But Wall Street believed, and pushed the stock to 140. One was reminded of Galbraith's comment, with regard to the twenties, that "perhaps it was worth being poor for a long time to be rich for just a little while."[19] No less than Bankers Trust, Morgan Guaranty, and the Harvard endowment fund bought Randell's stock.[20]

One wonders how such silk-stocking paragons could be so gullible. The answer is, they were afraid to be left behind. The choice was to buy the popular stocks, which, after all, were rising, or to risk momentarily lagging the pack. And those who lagged, even for a quarter or two, could not raise new capital. For a money manager in the Go-Go days there were no second acts.

The watershed moment was a 1967 critique from McGeorge Bundy, president of the Ford Foundation, and the very embodiment of pinstriped conservatism. Bundy sternly took his fellow endowment-fund managers to task—not for being too bold, but for being insufficiently so:

> We have the preliminary impression that over the long run caution has cost our colleges and universities much more than imprudence or excessive risk-taking.[21]

This knocked the Street on its ear. If the Ford Foundation was encouraging people to take more risk, what fiduciary need be timid? Moreover, Bundy, the former national security adviser and Vietnam War architect, backed his words with deeds. He far overspent the foundation's income, reckoning that he could make up the capital shortfall with trenchant plays in the market. He remarked to *Fortune*, with a self-assurance worthy of Camelot, "I may be wrong, but I'm not in doubt."[22]

In October 1967, months after the Bundy encyclical, Buffett, like a rival pope, issued a manifesto of his own. He was not so self-assured as Bundy; in fact, Buffett had nothing *but* doubts. The partnership had $65 million, but where would he put it? The bargains were gone, and the game had changed.

Wall Street was putting more and more chips on ever briefer spins of the wheel. It was true, Buffett told his partners, that this self-fulfilling merry-go-round had been quite profitable. It was also true that the fashionable stocks might continue to go up. Nonetheless, Buffett was "sure" that he, personally, would not do well with them. Nor did he wish to try. He could offer no proof that prices were silly, only conviction.

When the game is no longer being played your way, it is only human to say the new approach is all wrong, bound to lead to trouble, etc. I have been scornful of such behavior by others in the past. I have also seen the penalties incurred by those who evaluate conditions as they were—not as they are. Essentially I am out of step with present conditions. On one point, however, I am clear. I will not abandon a previous approach whose logic I understand even though it may mean forgoing large, and apparently easy, profits to embrace an approach which I don't fully understand, have not practiced successfully and which, possibly, could lead to substantial permanent loss of capital.[23]

Partners who had dismissed such stuff as crying wolf were taken up short. For the shocking kicker was this: Buffett was dropping his goal of beating the Dow by 10 percentage points a year. From now on, he would strive for the far more modest goal of earning 9 percent a year or of beating the Dow by 5 percentage points—whichever was less. Partners with better opportunities might "logically" decide to leave, "and you can be sure I will be wholly in sympathy with such a decision."

There was also a hint of midlife crisis. Buffett personally was worth more than $10 million; he wanted "a less compulsive approach" than when he was "younger and leaner." At the ripe age of thirty-seven he was thinking—astonishingly—of pursuing noneconomic activities or, alternatively, businesses in which the monetary payoff would not be the sole consideration.

What is notable in such musings is that, even when looking in the mirror, Buffett retains his rational, almost mechanistic objectivity. Unusually self-aware, he knew that if his stated goal remained constant he would feel compelled to run as hard as ever. Therefore, as if to change the settings on a laboratory rat, he was lowering his target.

Elementary self-analysis tells me that I will not be capable of less than all-out effort to achieve a publicly proclaimed goal to people who have entrusted their capital to me.

But it is doubtful that Buffett seriously tried to moderate his "all-out effort." No one in his family noticed a "less compulsive approach," nor did they believe that he was really capable of it. As young Susie recalled, it was virtually impossible to poke through the fog of his concentration. A while after his letter—on the day Susie got her driver's license—she went out for a spin and managed to hit another car, putting a small dent in her father's Lincoln. Naturally, the prospect of breaking such news to her father put Susie in a delicate state. "By the time I got upstairs, I was crying," she recalled. "Dad was reading the newspaper. I said, 'Dad, I *wrecked* your car.' He didn't look up. I kept crying, and after five seconds or so he said, 'Was anyone hurt?' I said, 'No.' I waited there. He didn't say anything. He didn't look up."

This was the new, less compulsive Buffett. A few minutes later, he realized that a fatherly word might be in order, and poked his head into Susie's room and said, "Suz, remember, the other guy is a jerk." And that was all he said. After dinner that night, Susie wanted the car and he gave it to her without a word.

Buffett's investing record, certainly, did not skip a beat. Shortly after his letter, he reported that in 1967 the partnership had advanced 36 percent—17 percentage points more than the Dow. Much of it was derived from American Express, which ballooned to 180 a share, and which at its peak represented 40 percent of the portfolio.[24] On that one $13 million investment, Buffett made a $20 million profit.[25] (He never did disclose the source of the bonanza to his partners.) He also made a 55 percent profit on Walt Disney.[26]

Perhaps because his results were so uncanny, his partners lost sight of the fact that it was a genuinely difficult time for him. (Some wrote to ask if he had "really" meant it about being out of step—which, Buffett assured them, he absolutely had.)[27] Just because he was willing to forgo "large, easy profits" does not mean that doing so was easy. In effect, he had pivoted his career on a single premise—that his instincts were correct and that those of "Mr. Market" were wrong. Watching the continued success of Go-Go must have been a torture for him.

Early in 1968, Buffett turned to the one person who, at very least, he felt would understand. Why not, he proposed, gather a group of former Ben Graham students at the foot of the master? Buffett invited a dozen of his old chums, including Bill Ruane, Marshall Weinberg, and Tom Knapp (and a few, such as Charlie Munger, who had not been Graham students), to meet near San Diego. He loyally asked the group not to bring "anything more current than a 1934 edition of *Security Analysis.*"[28] As is clear from the protective tone of his letter, Buffett was uneasy lest anyone try to steal the spotlight from his hero.

> I talked with Ben Graham today, and he likes the idea of the "select" group coming out on Friday, January 26, when we will engage in a little cross fertilization. Knowing of the propensity of some of you for speech making (and I feel a few fingers pointing toward me), I hasten to explain that he is the bee and we are the flowers! As I look at the addressees of this memo, I feel there is some danger of a degeneration of the meeting into a Turkish rug auction unless we discipline ourselves to see what we can learn from Ben, rather than take the opportunity to post him on how many of our great ideas he has missed.[29]

Perhaps he was worried about the outspoken Charlie Munger, who thought much of Graham's teaching rather daft, and kept prodding Buffett to rethink it.[30] In Munger's view, it was better to pay a *fair* price for a good business than a cut rate for a stinker. The cheap business, too often, was so full of problems as to turn out to be no "bargain."

Buffett, of course, knew this. In a revealing passage, not long before, he had admitted that while he thought of himself primarily as a Graham-style bargain hunter, "the really sensational ideas I have had over the years have been heavily weighted toward the qualitative side."[31] Certainly he had in mind American Express and Disney. For all that, he still considered Graham-type stocks to be his bread and butter: "the more sure money." His teacher still had a hold on him.[32]

En route to California, a few of the gang met in Las Vegas. The thought of Buffett loose on the strip is one to stir the pulse, but evidently Graham's disciples judged that playing the slots would be poor preparation for the upcoming reunion. As recalled by Walter Schloss, Buffett's former cellmate at Graham-Newman: "We went to Caesars Palace—low rates, cheap food."

The meeting with Graham was at the elegant Hotel del Coronado (the setting for the Marilyn Monroe classic *Some Like It Hot*), across the bay from San Diego. Graham arrived in a Socratic mood. "You're a bunch of smart fellows," he began. "I've got a test for you. Here are ten questions, true or false. I warn you, they are tremendously difficult." Nobody got more than half, except for Roy Tolles, Munger's law partner—who suspected a trick and wrote a T for every one. Graham's point was that an easy-looking game could well be rigged—a subtle warning regarding the Go-Go era.[33]

"We loved having Ben there," said Ed Anderson, Tom Knapp's partner. But the meeting was anticlimactic. Graham was feeling ill and left early. And he had lost interest in playing the "bee." The assembly was really the nucleus of a *Buffett* group.

His friends were bright, ambitious, and narrow. Henry Brandt was a born worrier and workaholic who walked around the Beach Point Club with his reading materials in a duffel bag. The imperious David "Sandy" Gottesman, who ran First Manhattan, an investment advisory firm, was singularly obsessed with the financial worth of himself and others. (In characteristic form at a dinner at the Harvard Business School, Gottesman turned to a woman he had just met and inquired, "Are you *rich*?")

Marshall Weinberg, an outgoing, plumpish bachelor, was an aesthete—interested in his pyramids and his Rubinstein. There were two eclectics—Ed Anderson, a chemist turned money manager who was into behavioral psychology, and Charlie Munger. But the common thread was a passion for Wall Street. They were intellectually curious about investing but could scarcely go head-to-head with Graham on Spanish literature or the ancient Greeks.

In San Diego, the disciples spent two days sharing their similarly dour view of the market. "We were all commiserating" over the lack of opportunities, Anderson said. Buffett pumped Jack Alexander, his Columbia classmate, for ideas, but was tightlipped about his own.[34] It is doubtful that he left San Diego with his view of the stock market improved.

Indeed, Buffett was starting to feel that managing a portfolio was a bit of a rat race. One puffed on a cigar butt and then tossed it out; the ephemeral quality was unsatisfying.[35] But he was getting a kick from his investments in long-term, controlled companies such as Berkshire and Associated, and from working with their managers, such as the Horatio Alger–like Ben Rosner. Admittedly, such companies were unlikely to match the heady profits of American Express. Nonetheless:

When I am dealing with people I like, in businesses I find stimulating (what business isn't?), and achieving worthwhile overall returns on capital employed (say, 10–12%), it seems foolish to rush from situation to situation to earn a few more percentage points.[36]

It is fair to ask why partners had hooked up with him if it was not to make "a few more percentage points." Strictly from the standpoint of investment returns, Fred Carr seemed to make more sense. "*We fall in love with nothing.*" Buffett, though, assuredly was falling for a few of his investments. Something other than math—an urge for continuity— seemed to lie behind it. He had stayed partial to Omaha, to Ben Graham, to his friends. All his life, he had hungered for continuity. His great fear had been the supreme discontinuity of dying. Selling was also a discontinuity. As with other philosophical puzzles that he tossed in the air, he was not sure where to draw the line—when, that is, to hang on to a favored business and when to take a profit. On Wall Street, no one else even dreamed of such a question.

In 1968, a year when the country was seized by political unrest, stock trading reached a frenzy. Volume on the Big Board averaged thirteen million shares a day—30 percent more than the record pace of 1967. On June 13, 1968, volume erupted to *twenty-one* million shares. The *kachung-kachung-kachung* of the ticker seemed to grow louder with each clash of antiwar marchers and rifle-bearing guardsmen, as though the rising political temperature were spawning a sympathetic fever on Wall Street. In that convulsive summer of riots and assassination wakes, the stock exchange was so swamped by paper that it was forced to shut down, for the first time in its history and for repeated days. One could hear in the brief silence an SOS. But the market rallied on, like a drunk intent on finishing the last bottle, oblivious to the light of dawn.

The broker Richard Jenrette dubbed it "the great garbage market."[37] There was a frenzy for new issues such as Four Seasons Nursing Center of America, Kentucky Fried Chicken, and Applied Logic. Buffett noted that spectacular sums were being made "in the chain-letter type stock-promotion vogue. The game is being played by the gullible, the self-hypnotized, and the cynical."[38] Most assuredly, he had in mind the case of Frederick Mates, a self-proclaimed Robin Hood who ran the Mates Investment Fund from an office that he dubbed a "kibbutz" and with a young staff that he deemed his "flower children." Mates put much of the fund into a tiny letter stock known as Omega Equities. Letter stock having no quoted market, its value was uncertain. Mates, in calculating his fund's assets, assigned a value to Omega of $16 a share. This was an interesting number, since Mates had acquired the stock for $3.25. Thus, with no change in Omega's outlook or prospects, the Mates Fund was showing a book profit of more than 400 percent.[39]

Though only in his late thirties, Buffett felt himself, comparatively, in the "geriatric ward."[40] His competitors, whom he had once scorned for supposed lethargy, were now evincing "acute hypertension." He noted that the manager of one fund had asserted that it wasn't enough to study stock prices week by week or day by day: "Securities must be studied in a minute-by-minute program." Buffett observed, "This sort of stuff makes me feel guilty when I go out for a Pepsi."[41]

It was easy to imagine such letters as coming from a rube, perhaps, one who had been dumped unawares on Wall Street and was writing to an uncle back home about the shocking goings-on in the city. The fact is that Buffett was in no way detached from Wall Street. He was on the line to stockbrokers and to traders virtually every day, and on many days numerous times. Art Rowsell, the chief trader at Cantor Fitzgerald, mused that he must have spoken "one hundred million words" to Buffett over the years.

And Buffett's circle of contacts was unusually wide. In fact, the dope that he had in Omaha probably was as good as, if not better than, most people's in New York. What he did gain from Omaha was a certain sense of proportion. Driving past a McDonald's one day, he told his son Howie, "It takes twenty years to build a reputation and five minutes to ruin it. If you think about that you'll do things differently."

People were surprised that a stock market wizard could get by in Nebraska, especially during such a fast-paced period. Buffett, speaking about this in 1968 to *Dun's Review*, remarked: "Omaha is as good a spot as any. Here you can see the forest. In New York, it's hard to see beyond the trees."

But what about the famed access of New Yorkers to "inside information?"

Buffett replied, "With enough inside information and a million dollars you can go broke in a year."[42]

This was a very Midwestern and revealing remark. The subtext was that virtue could be as rewarding as sin—a notion directly counter to the received wisdom on Wall Street.

It is illustrative to look at Buffett's investment in the same year, 1968, in Home Insurance. He was buying the stock over a period of weeks, using Tom Knapp's Manhattan-based company, Tweedy, Browne & Knapp, as a broker. One day, after Tweedy Browne had bought $50,000 worth of stock for him, Howard Browne, the trading partner, got a call from Omaha. He put down the phone and said, "That's odd. Warren said, 'Stop buying.' "

Home Insurance announced the next day that it was being taken over by City Investing at a big premium. Presumably, Buffett had gotten a tip. But he did not take the $50,000 worth of stock—meaning that he passed up a tidy profit.[43] Understand that taking it would have been legal—though, had anyone been watching, somewhat suspicious-looking.

Whether Buffett felt his virtue or his self-interest to be at stake—presumably, it was some of each—is almost irrelevant. He recognized that the self-interested course and the virtuous one were apt to coincide often enough so that one might as well play it safe. Needless to say, this perspective was occasionally lacking among some of his Wall Street peers.

Buffett traveled to New York quite a bit, with Susie in the spring and also at other times. He stayed at the Plaza, and saw a wide array of business people and friends, among them investment adviser Sandy Gottesman, Bill Ruane, *Fortune* writer Carol Loomis, and up-and-coming hotelier Larry Tisch—all in all, a well-heeled and well-connected crowd.

Yet Buffett in Gotham had a faint air of Mr. Deeds, not least because his speech was studded with gee-whiz, Ozzie-and-Harriet talk ("dope," "jerk," "okey-dokey").[44] Though Susie preferred the Café des Artistes, Buffett dined with chums at joints such as the Stage Delicatessen, where he would order his out-of-town-signature roast beef w/mayo on white bread. One time, the intrepid Marshall Weinberg suggested that they try something a bit less bland—a Japanese steakhouse.

"Why don't we go to Reuben's?" Buffett countered.

Weinberg pointed out that they had lunched at Reuben's, an East Side deli, the previous day.

"Right," Buffett said. "You know what you're getting."

"By that logic, we'd go there *every* day," Weinberg said.

"Precisely. Why not eat there every day?"

Another time, Buffett did lunch at the elegant Harmonie Club, with Sam Stayman, the champion bridge player and a Buffett investor, and

Stayman's wife. Josephine Stayman was smitten by Buffett's Midwestern informality. She recalled:

> Afterward I was going uptown, where we lived. Warren was going uptown, too, I think to another meeting. He said he felt very confined in New York—did I mind if we ran from 61st Street to 79th Street? This was before anybody was jogging in New York. We ran up Madison and at a very fast pace. He was in his business clothes. He wanted his freedom.

One thinks of the Washington schoolboy with the charmingly unstylish tennis shoes. People were not accustomed to seeing Omaha cowboys run up Madison Avenue. Nor were Americans, in general, used to multimillionaires who flew coach class and looked as if they had slept in their suits. What they expected of Wall Street was J. P. Morgan; what they saw in Buffett was Will Rogers.

Bob Malott, a Data Documents codirector, ran into Buffett one evening on Fifth Avenue, where Buffett was pacing up and down like a lost dog. Buffett explained that he was measuring the land underneath Best & Co., a department store. The Kansas-bred Malott concluded that Buffett was "unpretentious in a way I wouldn't think possible had he been raised in Greenwich, Connecticut."

Toward the end of 1968, the bull market showed signs of age. The conglomerate bubble burst. Gerald Tsai's Manhattan Fund plunged to a ranking of 299th out of 305 funds, prompting Tsai to quit. In December, the Securities and Exchange Commission suspended trading in Omega Equities. For Fred Mates, a.k.a. the flower child, this was really a bummer. The Mates Fund, which owned 300,000 shares of Omega, and which had been the top-ranked fund in the country, faced a sudden run on its assets. In a desperate mood, Mates persuaded the SEC to halt redemptions (equivalent to a bank's shutting the teller's window). Mates, as it happened, was due to speak on the investment outlook before a blue-chip audience at the New York Hilton. The irony of his delivering his expert opinion while his fund was going up in smoke seems to have been lost on Mates himself. "There are no more reasons for being afraid of what might happen in 1969 than there were in 1968," Mates said confidently. Subsequently, the "window" reopened and his fund traded down by 93 percent.[45]

And Mates was but a symptom. When his fund toppled, it was clear that his would not be the last. Walter Stern, of Burnham & Co., voiced a prescient fear that in a bear market the gunslingers might turn to selling as indiscriminately as they had bought.[46] Still, the market was buoyed by the Paris peace talks. In December 1968, the Dow climbed to 990, and Wall Street cast a hopeful eye toward a pair of elusive goals: an end to the war in Vietnam and a 1,000 Dow.

Buffett Partnership clocked a gain in 1968 of $40 million, or 59 percent. Its assets swelled to $104 million. Bereft of ideas, managing more money than ever, and with the market at a peak, Buffett had had his best year. He beat the Dow not by the 5 percentage points called for in his lower target, but by 50 points. He said the result "should be treated as a freak—like picking up thirteen spades in a bridge game."[47] It was his last hand.

The bull market was in a spasmodic death rattle. Wall Street was recommending the popular stocks *regardless of price*. Merrill Lynch liked International Business Machines at thirty-nine times earnings. Bache & Co. was pushing Xerox at fifty times. Blair & Co. was touting Avon Products at *fifty-six* times.[48] At that level of earnings, it would take a buyer of all of Avon half a century to get his money out. Could it possibly be "worth" that much? A fund manager, echoing the prevailing thinking, allowed that a stock was worth *whatever people think it's worth at the particular time*. Every college endowment, he noted, felt it had "to own IBM and Polaroid and Xerox and everything else. So . . . I think they will do well."[49] Buffett reminded partners of a seemingly lost distinction: "Price is what you pay, value is what you get."[50]

It no longer mattered. Finally, and irreversibly, he had despaired of finding stocks. In May 1969, *Business Week* proclaimed that Fred Carr "may just be the best portfolio manager in the U.S."[51] That same month, the man from Omaha made up his mind. Weary of jeremiads and wary of jeopardizing past profits, Buffett did a remarkable thing. He quit. He stunned his partners with the news that he was liquidating Buffett Partnership. And now, at the height of a bull market, he was getting out.

I am not attuned to this market environment, and I don't want to spoil a decent record by trying to play a game I don't understand just so I can go out a hero.[52]

The courage that lay behind his decision may be measured by its uniqueness. On Wall Street, people did not fold up and return the money—not at the top, not after their best year. It simply wasn't done. Buffett had plenty of options. He could simply have sold his stocks, put his assets in cash, and waited for opportunities. But every partner was looking to him to perform, and he felt an inescapable pressure to lead the league each year.[53] Since the watershed letter of 1967 he had tried to work less compulsively, but as long as he was "on stage," it wasn't possible.

> If I am going to participate publicly, I can't help being competitive. I know I don't want to be totally occupied with out-pacing an investment rabbit all my life. The only way to slow down is to stop.[54]

His friend Dick Holland had the impression that Buffett was contemplating his "whole life," and specifically what he could do with his money—of which he now had the astounding sum of $25 million.[55] To his partners, Buffett hinted at a change of pace:

> Some of you are going to ask, "What do you plan to do?" I don't have an answer to that question. I do know that when I am 60, I should be attempting to achieve different personal goals than those which had priority at age 20.[56]

Buffett, who had raised funds for the quixotic presidential campaign of Eugene McCarthy the year before, told the *Omaha World-Herald* that he hoped to spend the bulk of his time working "in any intelligent and effective way possible" on human problems.[57] In another interview, he said he wanted to pursue interests aside from merely making money.[58]

Buffett began one such effort immediately. Waspish Omaha did not permit Jews in the Omaha Club, a downtown eating haunt for businessmen. Buffett had quite a few Jewish friends, including one Nick Newman, who ran an Omaha grocery chain, and who was incensed at being excluded. Buffett brought it up with the board of the club, and was told, "They [the Jews] have their own club." (Omaha also had several country clubs, each of them segregated.) In Buffett's view, it was blatantly wrong:

Now there are Jewish families that have been in Omaha a hundred years, they have contributed to the community all the time, they have helped build Omaha as much as anybody, and yet they can't join a club that John Jones, the new middle-rank Union Pacific man, joins as soon as he's transferred here. That is hardly *fair*.[59]

Of course, Buffett was not about to lead a protest march outside the Omaha Club. Characteristically, he opted for a passive and indirect tactic, yet one that cleverly shifted the burden. Namely, he applied for membership to the all-Jewish Highland Country Club.

The Highland had been founded in 1923, by Jewish golfers who had been subjected to taunts of "kike" and "sheenie" on Omaha's public courses. Even in the sixties, anti-Semitic incidents were not unknown, and Omaha's Jews were neither entirely ready to assimilate nor entirely welcome in gentile society. Highland's purists vehemently opposed letting Buffett join. Their feeling was, "This is our club and they'll take it over."[60] Buffett's friends and the club liberals, which included Omaha's rabbis, favored integration. The battle was heated, but on October 1, 1969, Buffett was admitted. Then he returned to the Omaha Club and informed them that "the Jewish club" wasn't totally Jewish anymore. Now the Omaha Club had no excuse, and quickly admitted some Jews.

Buffett would later make light of his motives—with him, a telltale sign of strong feeling—by joking that he had joined Highland because "the food was better."[61] In fact, he rarely went there. Aside from his civil rights concern, one suspects that he had a feeling for Jews in particular—perhaps a subtle homage to Ben Graham, or an identification with underdogs. Rabbi Myer Kripke, whose family were frequent guests at the Buffetts', thought Buffett a "philo-Semite." (Buffett used to joke with Kripke that he had "a nice Jewish boy" picked out for his daughter.)

In the minds of Omahans, the Highland episode loomed large. It severed Buffett from his John Bircher father. Rabbi Kripke, who had taken issue with Howard Buffett over the latter's support for prayer in public schools, said Warren's gesture "was such a sharp reaction to this [his father]. I think he did it as a political statement."

Buffett also got involved in a path-breaking abortion case. Along with Susie, who was active in Planned Parenthood, Warren strongly favored legalizing abortions (then illegal in most states). In 1969, the California Supreme Court had agreed to hear an appeal from Leon Belous, a doctor convicted for referring a woman to an abortionist. Charlie Munger had read about Belous in the newspaper and called Buffett, and the two immediately decided to underwrite the appeal.

Munger turned *Belous* into a personal crusade. He organized two friend-of-the-court briefs: one signed by 178 medical school deans and professors, the other by seventeen prominent lawyers and written by Munger himself. In September 1969, Belous won a landmark victory— the first time an abortion law had been declared unconstitutional.[62]*

From Buffett's angle, the Highland episode and *Belous* had similar virtues. He characteristically sided with what he saw as community interests over sectarian ones. In his rational, stockpicker's view, society's stake in having open institutions and in minimizing the number of unwanted babies outweighed the narrower claims of segregationists and antiabortionists.

Aside from politics, Buffett spent most of 1969 liquidating the portfolio. His Uncle Fred, coincidentally, announced the closing of Buffett & Son, the family grocery begun precisely one hundred years earlier. Appropriately enough, in the fall, Warren and Susie threw a party with echoes of *fin de siècle*. They invited 180 guests and flew in sandwiches and racks of sausages from the Stage Deli. The Buffetts' door was illuminated by a string of flashing lights, flanked by a pair of three-foot Pepsi bottles. Politicians and businessmen came, blacks and whites, "the moneyed and the still struggling."[63] Women wore cocktail dresses, bell-bottoms, culottes, and miniskirts. Partygoers painted the bodies of two scantily clad girls in the solarium, and W. C. Fields and Mae West were featured on the racquetball court, with popcorn served from a machine. A guest said he hadn't known that Omaha had "all these people."

Meanwhile, Buffett's decision to quit had begun to look shrewd. The Dow had hovered close to 1,000 until May. In June, it dipped below 900. One by one, the high-fliers crashed. Litton Industries— hallmark of the conglomerate era—fell 70 percent from its peak; Ling Temco-Vought, another, plunged from 169 to 25. Wall Street broker-

*Two years later, *Belous* was cited in the appellants' brief in *Roe v. Wade* as having established "the fundamental right of the woman to choose whether to bear children."

ages closed their doors. The stock exchange slogan "Own your share in American business" was dropped without explanation.[64] Performance funds were routed.

Fred Carr, anointed by *Business Week* in May, quit in December, leaving the Enterprise Fund stuffed with illiquid letter stock. It would fall 26 percent in 1969 and by more than 50 percent before the carnage stopped.[65] Cortes Randell's National Student Marketing was modestly revalued, from 140 to 3½, taking the Harvard endowment along for the ride.* The Dow Industrials closed out 1969 at an even 800. And the slaughter went on. By May 1970, a portfolio of every share on the stock exchange was down by *half* from the start of 1969.[66] Four Seasons Nursing Center—darling of the '68 garbage market—fell from 91 to 32. Electronic Data Systems plunged 50 points on a spring day—reducing the fortune of its Napoleonic founder, H. Ross Perot, by a cool $445 million. The Ford Foundation portfolio was shattered, forcing McGeorge Bundy to swallow a severe helping of humble pie.†

Buffett eked out a 7 percent gain in 1969, the partnership's final at-bat. It was an off year, but it topped the Dow by 18 percentage points. The long-prophesied down year had never come. He had made a profit and beaten the benchmark in every season.

Had an investor put $10,000 in the Dow in 1957, his total profit over thirteen years would have amounted to $15,260. The same grubstake, if invested in the partnership, would have produced a profit—after deducting Buffett's share—of $150,270.[67] Alternatively, Buffett's portfolio grew at a compound annual rate of 29.5 percent, compared to 7.4 percent for the Dow. One might look for metaphors to other realms—in music, Mozart; in baseball, the 1927 Yankees. In the world of investing, there had never been anything like it.

Investment companies tried to buy his partners list, but Buffett turned them down.[68] However, there remained the matter of where his former investors would put their dough. Buffett gave them just one name: Bill Ruane, the straight-arrow from Graham's class, who was set-

---

*Randell would plead guilty to stock fraud. He was sentenced to eighteen months.
†Quoting from Bundy's letter in the 1971 Ford Foundation *Report:* "These sober six years have taught us a number of lessons. . . . in the mid-1960s we too easily allowed ourselves to make larger commitments than hindsight would recommend. It was easy in 1965 and 1966 to believe in the high long-term rates of total return on stocks, the low rates of total return on bonds, and the modest rates of inflation that had been the general pattern for fifteen years. The last six years, to put it very gently, have been different."

ting up the Sequoia Fund, a new mutual. Many of Buffett's partners invested in it.

Buffett said he would put much of his own money in municipal bonds, and he wrote a long last letter offering to help his partners do the same (but making it clear that he would *not* be offering continuing investment counsel). The letter was, at turns, informal, discursive, and highly detailed. At one point—recall that it was five years before any glimmer of New York City's financial trouble—Buffett interrupted his train of thought with a cautionary aside:

> You will notice I am not buying issues of large cities. I don't have the faintest idea how to analyze a New York City, Chicago, Philadelphia, etc. (a friend mentioned the other day when Newark was trying to sell bonds at a very fancy rate that the Mafia was getting very upset because Newark was giving them a bad name). Your analysis of New York City— and I admit it is hard to imagine them not paying their bills for any extended period of time—would be as good as mine. My approach to bonds is pretty much like my approach to stocks. If I can't understand something, I tend to forget it.[69]

The partnership liquidated all but two of its investments: Berkshire Hathaway and Diversified Retailing, the latter a holding company for the Ben Rosner dress chain.* Thus, each partner could take his proportional interests in Berkshire and Diversified in stock or opt to cash out. Buffett would take the stock:

> I think both securities should be very decent long-term holdings and I am happy to have a substantial portion of my net worth invested in them.[70]

He urged his partners to think of Berkshire, which was by far the bigger of the two, as he did—as a business, rather than as a "stock." But his plans were a trifle obscure. On the one hand, he didn't think much of textiles; on the other, he liked the guy in charge. He allowed that it ought to grow at 10 percent or so a year, but avoided making a firm prediction. Moreover, though he expected to play a role in setting pol-

---

*Buffett luckily managed to sell the Baltimore-based Hochschild to Supermarkets General and get out without a loss.

icy at Berkshire, his partners should understand that he was under no obligation "should my interests develop elsewhere."[71]

Sam Stayman, the bridge champ, figured that Buffett had played out his hand. He sold his Berkshire back to Buffett at $43 a share. But many partners hung on. They could not know what Berkshire Hathaway would become, nor how deeply Buffett was engaged in remaking it. But Buffett had made it plain that he was keeping *his* Berkshire. As the loyal Doc Angle saw it, "That's all anybody had to hear if they had any brains."

Chapter 7

BERKSHIRE HATHAWAY

It was the fate of New Bedford, Massachusetts, to be cursed by fleeting prosperity not once but twice. Founded by Pilgrims, it withstood a sacking by the British in the Revolutionary War and then became the center of the world's whaling trade. Its damp, salt-drenched cobblestones led ever to the wharf, which gave New Bedford a livelihood yet left the town at risk should whaling fall upon the shoals. A local seaman—Herman Melville—said, "The town itself is perhaps the dearest place to live in, in all New England." Yet whence had its riches sprung? "Go and gaze upon the iron emblematical harpoons round yonder lofty mansion, and your question will be answered. . . . One and all, they were harpooned and dragged up hither from the bottom of the sea."[1]

The whalers suffered losses in the Civil War, and they were doomed by the drilling of the first oil wells, in Pennsylvania. Yet if New Bedford shuddered it did not collapse—thanks to a prescient diversion of its capital. As early as 1847, a cotton mill, which promoters said would reduce the city's dependence on the sea, was financed by New Bedford whalers. A subsequent mill was named for the whaler *Acushnet*, symbolizing the redirection of capital. Ultimately, some $100 million was invested in textiles,[2] so that even as the harpoons were being laid to rest, ships were piling the docks with bales of Southern cotton. By the early twentieth century, New Bedford's seventy mills were spinning more fine cotton than any other city in the country.[3]

The salient lesson was that capital was mobile. Ships might rot, but the profits need not be cast overboard with the captain's lamp. This, however, was a point that would haunt the city's largest mill for nearly one hundred years.

Hathaway Manufacturing Company was founded in 1888 by Horatio Hathaway, whose family had operated China clippers since the early 1800s. It was capitalized with $400,000, largely from whalers, which was symbolically evident in its location on Cove Street—smack against the sea. The *New Bedford Evening Standard* boasted that the ambitious new venture would "employ about 450 hands and run 30,000 spindles." An original investor in Warren Buffett's cotton mill was Hetty Green, the notorious miser known by the sobriquet "Witch of Wall Street."[4]*

Hathaway's fortunes, and the industry's, rose with those of cotton. Profits boomed during World War I, thanks to the military's demand for uniforms and airplane cloth. In New Bedford, thirty thousand people—half of the labor force—worked in the mills.[5]

And then, quite suddenly, that industry also declined—or rather, it fled south to cheap labor. In the twenties, New Bedford's workers, mostly immigrants, were forced to take repeated pay cuts. In 1928, when the mill owners demanded a further 10 percent cut, the workers struck, and remained on strike for an agonizing five months. Many mills did not reopen, and those that did were soon leveled by the Depression. By 1940, the textile workforce had shrunk to a pitiful nine thousand.[6]

What is notable is the way the mill owners coolly appraised their dying industry. By the late twenties, though still earning substantial profits, they were operating their plants with antique machinery. Meanwhile, dividends were kept high—on the order of 10 percent.[7] The owners siphoned their capital to mills down South, to the stock market, to their yachts. Wherever the money went, the owners had learned the lesson of the whalers well. Once the industry was given up for dead, they did not reinvest in the mills. All with the exception of one: Hathaway Manufacturing.

*Green, a shipping heiress, was said to have wrapped herself in papers to keep warm in the winter. She died in 1916, reputedly the world's richest woman, with a $100 million fortune.

Hathaway was run by Seabury Stanton, a proud, proper New England whose grandfather had captained a whaler and whose father had been Hathaway's president. Young Seabury, born in New Bedford, graduated from Harvard in 1915, fought in France, where he was promoted to second lieutenant, and returned after the war to apprentice at Hathaway as its rightful heir. He would stay there for half a century, until his encounter with Warren Buffett.

Stanton was six-foot-two and ramrod-straight. He was formal and cool, with a stare that shot daggers. His defining moment was in 1934, at the height of the Depression. Mill after mill was folding up or moving south. But Stanton, a sailor like his forebears, looked into his soul and resolved to weather the storm. He conceived a plan to modernize, and over the next decade and a half he plowed $10 million of the company's funds back into the mill. True to his Yankee credo, Seabury and his brother, Otis, went into hock to buy Hathaway stock on the noble belief that if the shareholders' money was to be at risk, their own money ought to be on the line as well.[8] With Seabury at the helm, the red-brick mill on Cove Street gamely withstood the economic tides.

There followed some flush years, some not so flush. Hathaway branched into synthetic fibers and pioneered in the manufacture of rayon. The demand for parachute fabric in World War II gave it a lift. After the war, Hathaway exploited rayon and became the country's, and perhaps the world's, biggest producer of men's suit linings.[9]* The trouble was, the product was easily imitable. It was dogged by Southern and, increasingly, Far Eastern competition. Then, in 1954, a hurricane flooded the plant, leaving it badly damaged. Stanton got lucrative offers to relocate to the South, but the old skipper would not surrender. Unwilling to leave New England, he decided to merge Hathaway with a northern manufacturer as venerable as itself: Berkshire Fine Spinning Associates, Inc.

Berkshire's bloodlines could be traced to Samuel Slater, who had built the country's first cotton mill in 1790. Oliver Chace, a carpenter who had worked for Slater, had gone on to establish his own mill, in Rhode Island, in 1806. Under Chace's descendants, the business had thrived.[10] A century and a half later, the Chace family still controlled Berkshire, now a sprawling collection of some dozen plants making staple fabrics for sheets, shirts, handkerchiefs, and slips.

*The company had no relation to Hathaway shirts.

Like Hathaway, Berkshire had been profitable in World War II and its immediate aftermath and had endured tougher times since. But Malcolm Chace, the president, had taken a wholly different tack from Stanton. Whereas Hathaway had modernized and branched into fashion, suit linings, and curtains, Berkshire, which was based in Providence, was still running cottons on ancient machinery. Chace—another white-haired, lean New Englander, who had been in the business since 1931—felt the industry had little future in New England and was running out the string. His nephew, Nicholas Brady—later Secretary of the Treasury—appraised Berkshire for his senior thesis at the Harvard Business School in 1954 and concluded on such a glum note that he promptly sold his stock.

The two companies merged in 1955, creating Berkshire Hathaway, Inc. The new company was a colossus. It had fourteen plants, twelve thousand workers, and yearly sales of $112 million. There was some thinking that Hathaway's more modern management combined with Berkshire's cash reserves would produce a stronger whole. Headquarters were moved to New Bedford, and Stanton was given the reins as president. Chace became the chairman.

Stanton took one look at Berkshire, which was operating thousands of looms attached to pulleys on the roof, and resolved to modernize. He put in new spindles, rebuilt looms, increased their speed, and consolidated the best of its plants.

There was a certain nobility to Seabury Stanton. In his own mind, he was an extension of Samuel Slater, one of the "imaginative men [who] found a way to link the tumbling river, the turning wheel, the crude loom, and the thread, to clothe a country."[11] He was forever guided by his experience in the Depression, which he recalled as "a time when men stood alone, upon their own resources and courage."[12] Under his stewardship, Berkshire Hathaway became the largest—and, ultimately, the only—surviving textile manufacturer of any size in New England.

But from an economic standpoint, he might as well have been harpooning whales. According to one of his lieutenants, "Seabury hadn't the slightest concept of return on investment. He was concerned with only one thing—keeping the plant going."[13] He kept pouring money in, all the while low textile prices prevented him from recouping his investment.

Within his management, Stanton was increasingly isolated. He insisted on a regimen of argyle socks and white shirts for managers and gloves and stockings for the secretaries, and woe to the executive who dared appear in public in a sport jacket. Lord of his manor, he communicated almost exclusively via written reports, and he worked in a forbidding remove, known behind his back as the "ivory tower." According to Malcolm Chace:

> Seabury had an office in the penthouse on the second floor. No one could get in without going past the executive secretary. She also had a secretary. When you got called to his office you had to climb this long stairway. There was a door at the end, a long conference table, and at the other end was Seabury's desk.[14]

At noon, he would descend from the leather-appointed ivory tower to a waiting black Cadillac, which would scoot him home for lunch past the working-class wood-frame homes in the South End. Though the mill was visible from his stairway, Stanton had little contact with the rank and file. He saw the men on the night shift once a year, at Christmas, when he somberly descended from the ivory tower to shake their hands—hands that the workers had mischievously coated with grease in anticipation of their boss's visit.

Seabury was also at odds with Otis, his brother. Otis vehemently took issue with Seabury's strategy of reinvesting in textiles, and was similarly unhappy with Seabury's insistence on holding down wages at the expense of taking a strike.[15] This division between the brothers began to permeate the company.

Otis split his time between New Bedford and the company's sales office, in New York's garment district. He was outgoing and warm, and was largely responsible for the success of Hathaway's fabled rayon suit lining. It was Otis who marketed Hathaway's synthetic fabrics, including its linings, to "converters," who dyed and finished them and sold them to suit manufacturers. During the war, when other suppliers had allocated scarce fabrics on the basis of payola, Otis had remained honest. After the war, when supplies became plentiful, his customers, who liked him anyway, paid him back with their business.

However, Seabury, whose expertise was in manufacturing, invaded Otis's turf by setting up a new division to finish fabrics in-house and sell directly to manufacturers—thus cutting out the converters. This looked sensible in New Bedford but overlooked a vital fact of the trade. The weaving business was gentile. The converters were Jewish—as were the garment makers. "You had to live with them to do business with them," noted Stanley Rubin, a Berkshire vice president for sales in New York. "That was the worst mistake that Seabury made. It was the beginning of the end."

Increasingly, Berkshire was a house divided. When Seabury spoke about the industry's glorious potential, the people in New York, who marketed the company's unfinished fabrics—called "grey goods"—snickered. They could see the business sinking before their eyes. One time, a Berkshire salesman was with a customer on Fifth Avenue, trying to sell handkerchief cloth. The customer pointed out his window to the women going into Lord & Taylor and said, "You see all those women carrying pocketbooks? There is a box of Kleenex in every one. And that's the end of the handkerchief business."[16]

By the end of 1961, Berkshire was down to seven plants. In the previous three years alone, it had plowed $11 million back into the business.[17] And while its mills were enhanced, its business was not. Its "regular plain weave" fabrics were commodities—indistinguishable from those of any other manufacturer. When competitors flooded the market, Berkshire was helpless. Thus, in 1962, the year that its modernization was complete, it suffered a crushing $2.2 million loss.

By then, the blood feud between Seabury and Otis was boiling over Seabury's plan to pass the reins to his son. Jack Stanton was tall, thin, and stony-faced, like his father, but his misty blue eyes bespoke a sadness. Jack had followed Seabury to Harvard and into a world war, and had thrown a couple of no-hitters in the marines. The Philadelphia Athletics invited him to camp, but Seabury forbade it. The dutiful son gave up baseball and went to work on the looms, "shoulder to shoulder, all greased up." By 1962, dour Jack was treasurer. Seabury, then seventy, was planning to work a few more years and make him president. Otis and Malcolm Chace each thought Jack was unqualified and secretly began to look for someone else.

On Wall Street, Berkshire's stock was out of favor. Richard N. Tillison, a security analyst with Value Line, had recommended the shares at the beginning of 1955, at a price of 14¾. From then on, Tillison had suffered through years of oversupplied markets and shuttered mills. By early 1963, the stock was at 8⅛—down 45 percent from his original call.

But hope in the breast of a textile analyst never dies. In March 1963, Tillison reported that the outlook for Berkshire "now appears more promising than it has for a considerable time." In June, he crawled without his shell and predicted a modest quarterly profit. Alas, in September, he was forced to postpone his hopes once more:

> Berkshire is not now expected to break into the earnings column, as was earlier thought possible, because the rapid movement of many cotton textile producers into blended fabrics has caused temporary price weakness. . . .[18]

No profit "now" on account of "temporary" weakness. And so it had been for eight long years.

According to economic theory, when a company is so mismanaged, sooner or later an investor will decide that he can do more with its assets and take it over. It happened that Buffett had run across Berkshire at the same time as Tillison, when he was working for Graham-Newman, in the 1950s.[19] Howard Newman had gone to look at Berkshire and had come close to making an offer for it. Buffett was merely an observer of the company's troubles until late in 1962, when the stock fell below $8 a share. Since Berkshire had $16.50 per share of working capital, it seemed to be a bargain, and Buffett bought some stock, via his partnership. However, he had no thought of a takeover. He approached it as he did any other stock, assuming that he would hold for a couple of years or so.

But with Buffett's interest piqued, Daniel Cowin, a New York broker friend, found several large blocks of stock for him.[20] By 1963, Buffett Partnership was the company's biggest shareholder.[21] For a while, Buffett was able to keep his identity as a shareholder secret, and Cowin, playing the role of Buffett's stalking horse, took a seat on Berkshire's board.[22]

Then, word leaked out that Cowin's client was Buffett. Stanley Rubin, the Berkshire sales executive, who knew Buffett, called to see if he was planning to buy more.

Buffett said coyly, "I may or I may not." Still, nobody seemed to realize that Buffett might be up to something.

A short time later, Buffett visited the mill. When he found that Jack

Stanton had copies of Berkshire's financials going back to the 1920s, he got very excited and quickly made copies of them. Then he asked to see some of the plants. Jack recalled, "I was very busy, so we sent Ken Chace with him."

This was the mistake of Jack's life. Otis was already considering Ken Chace (no relation to Malcolm) as a candidate to succeed Seabury—though, of course, neither Seabury nor Jack, who coveted the throne for himself, had any idea of it. Chace, an unpretentious late-fortyish chemical engineer who drove a Chevrolet, was also a local boy. He had attended something called the New Bedford Textile School, joined Hathaway in 1947 to work on synthetic fibers, and worked his way up to the lofty position of vice president of manufacturing.

For two days, the square-jawed Chace took Buffett through the mills. They must have looked to Buffett like something out of Samuel Slater's sketchbook—the thick wads of cotton-candy raw stock disappearing into giant hoppers, their fibers being combed into glossy, transparent webs, their ropelike strands being twisted into yarn on hundreds of spinning frames, aligned like soldiers. Whatever Buffett grasped of it, there was something compelling in their unsung industry, something close to the soul of New England. According to Chace:

> Warren asked questions like crazy. About the marketing, the machinery, about what I thought should be done, where I thought the company was going, the technical end of it, what kind of products were we selling, who we were selling to. He wanted to know everything.

Chace spoke candidly about the company's problems, and Buffett decided he had found his man. Buffett didn't say much, but when the tour was over, he dropped an intriguing clue.

"I'll be in touch with you, Ken."

Meanwhile, Stanton finally sensed that he was under siege. In 1964, Berkshire made repeated offers to buy back shares—thereby raising the proportion of stock under Stanton's control. Buffett was on the brink of selling out to him, but he thought that Stanton was chiseling him on the price.

"They were three-eighths of a point apart" or Buffett would have sold, according to Charlie Munger. "It was an absolute accident that Berkshire became his vehicle."

As a corporate vehicle, Berkshire had nothing to recommend it. But now, Buffett, who felt that Stanton hadn't been square with him,[23] was unwilling to step aside. He and Stanton were bitterly at odds over an understanding that Buffett felt had come undone—though Buffett, as usual, let someone else do his fighting.

Dan Cowin and Stanton had a heated argument over it in the ivory tower. Stanton loudly proclaimed that no one would tell *him* what to do. Knowing that Cowin was representing Buffett, Edmund Rigby, an executive vice president, rushed in and warned Stanton, "You shouldn't talk that way to a major shareholder."

Events now rushed to a climax. Ken Chace, the plainspoken executive who had shown Buffett the plant, was so worried about Berkshire's future that he had been talking to a competitor in South Carolina. Stanley Rubin called Chace early in 1965 and pleaded with him to stay put. When Chace asked why, Rubin mysteriously told him to take his word for it.

A month or so later, Rubin called again. "You remember that Warren Buffett fellow? He's going to control Berkshire Hathaway. He's been holding stock under Street [brokerage-house] names." Rubin said Buffett had something to discuss with Chace and wanted Chace to meet him at the Plaza Hotel in New York.

It was one of the first fine days of spring. Buffett and Chace walked to the little park in front, and Buffett bought a couple of ice cream bars on sticks.

Wasting no time, Buffett said, "I'd like to have you become president of Berkshire Hathaway. How do you feel about that?"

Chace was forty-eight. The man who was proposing to catapult his career was thirty-four.

By the time Chace could blurt out his consent, Buffett added that he had enough stock to pull it off at the next directors' meeting, and that Chace should keep quiet in the meantime. As regards Berkshire's future, he said, "Figure out what you'll need. It'll be your baby." Buffett was finished with him in ten minutes. Chace left in a state of shock.

What he didn't know was that Buffett had gone to the chairman, Malcolm Chace, and offered to buy him out. Chace refused, citing his long history with the company, but some of Chace's family agreed to sell.

Buffett had one hill left to climb. Would Otis Stanton sell his shares—and undermine his brother? Stanley Rubin set up a lunch with Buffett and Otis at the Wamsutta Club in New Bedford. After Buffett made his pitch, Otis agreed to sell—provided that Buffett make an equivalent offer to buy out Seabury. That was the break. Though Jack was primed for a proxy fight, Seabury didn't have the stomach for it. With the Stantons' shares, Buffett Partnership owned 49 percent of the stock, at an average cost of about $15 a share.[24]

Jack Stanton, who had been too busy to show Buffett the plant, now realized—too late—that he ought to meet with him. Jack and his then wife, Kitty, hurried to New York and had breakfast with Warren and Susie at the Plaza. But Jack was awed, and in over his head. According to Ralph Rigby, a fabric salesman, Kitty pled harder than Jack did. Buffett joked later, "If I had hired anybody, I would have hired Kitty."

Perhaps eager to change the subject, Buffett told Jack about his own career, recounting his rise as an investor. Jack asked, "How do you do it?" Buffett said he read "a couple of thousand" financial statements a year.

Shortly before the May board meeting, Buffett was secretly named a director.[25] On the morning of his big takeover, Buffett flew into New Bedford, crew-cut, his suit tightly buttoned and noticeably creased, with an attaché and an oversized valise and something of the appearance of a down-at-the-heels but earnest traveling salesman.

Buffett made for the office on Cove Street, and Seabury emerged from the ivory tower for a final time. Calling the meeting to order, Seabury read through the agenda, showing nothing. And then Seabury Stanton resigned. It merely remained to pass the poison cup to Jack. Without a word, the two stormed out of the elegant wood-paneled boardroom. Ken Chace was voted president, Buffett chairman of the executive committee. Otis, in a final stab at his brother, voted with the majority and remained on the board. Though Malcolm Chace retained the title of board chairman, Buffett was now in charge of Berkshire. The stock closed that day—May 10, 1965—at $18 a share.

Buffett's tidy script was nearly wrecked when a messenger burst in with a copy of the afternoon *Standard-Times*, revealing the shake-up on the front page. Seabury had leaked the story, blaming his departure on a rift with "certain outside interests."[26] Buffett, fearing he would be seen as a liquidator—the hated epithet from Dempster Mill—was visibly enraged. But he papered it over in public, praising the departing

Stantons and soft-pedaling his plans. Quoted in the next day's edition, Buffett promised "to sell the same goods from the same plants to the same customers."

Over the previous decade, Berkshire had closed all but two of its mills and accumulated a net loss of $10.1 million.[27] Its assets had shrunk by half, and merely 2,300 workers—one of every five from the 1955 merger—remained. But its fortunes now seemed on the mend. Demand for synthetics was strong, and the company was—finally—in the black. One yearns to hear what Tillison would have made of Buffett's arrival, but, alas, the dutiful analyst was benched at the same juncture as Seabury Stanton. Value Line's May report on Berkshire was signed by a new analyst, who observed that the plans of "the new controlling interest" were not known.

After the board meeting, Buffett and Ken Chace strolled past the historic mill and sat down to talk. Chace now made ready to hear the new owner's plans for the mill. But Buffett said anything to do with warps and looms would be up to Chace. Buffett would watch the money.

Then, in his blunt fashion, he outlined what each of them should expect. The first point was deflating: Buffett would not approve of stock options for Chace or for anyone else.

Buffett opposed options for the reason that most CEOs were enamored of them. Options conferred potential—sometimes vast—rewards, but spared the recipients any risk, thus giving executives a free ride on the shareholders' capital.

More subtly, Buffett wanted managers whose personal interests were in line with those of the stockholders. A manager who owned options, as distinct from shares, had nothing to lose, and would be more inclined to gamble with the shareholders' capital.

However, Buffett offered to cosign a loan so that Chace could borrow $18,000 and buy a thousand shares. For Chace, who was making less than $30,000, and who normally didn't like to borrow a shoelace, that was a huge amount. But Buffett was a supersalesman, especially when he was selling himself. Like some of those early partnership investors, Chace had a feeling that good things would happen with Buffett in charge. Chace took the plunge.

Then Buffett explained to Chace the basic theory of return on investment. He didn't particularly care how much yarn Chace produced, or even how much he sold. Nor was Buffett interested in the total profit as an isolated number. What counted was the profit *as a percentage of the capital invested*. That was the yardstick by which Buffett would grade Chace's performance.

To Chace, who had been reared, like most managers, to think of growth as an absolute good, this idea was new. But he grasped that it was pivotal to Buffett's capitalist credo, and Buffett put it in terms that Chace could understand.

"I'd rather have a $10 million business making 15 percent than a $100 million business making 5 percent," Buffett said. *"I have other places I can put the money."* He flew back to Omaha that night.

Buffett was serious about having "other places" to put the money. He leaned on Chace to keep the inventory and overhead as low as possible. As Chace said, "One thing Buffett wanted was to come up with cash quickly."

Buffett also followed through with his promise of autonomy. He told Chace not to bother with quarterly projections and other time-wasters. He merely wanted Chace to send him a monthly financial report and to warn him of any unpleasant surprises.

Indeed, Buffett sculpted the relationship to get the most out of it with a minimum of personal contact. He was easy to reach, but this had the perverse effect of restraining Chace from calling except when he really needed to. And when Chace did call, Buffett didn't linger on the phone.

"I'd give the results, and the estimate for the year, and he'd remember them forever," Chace noted.

Once, Buffett said Chace had switched a figure from an earlier call—which Chace disputed. After he checked his notes, Chace saw that Buffett was right. From then on, he carefully checked his data *before* he called.

Chace's freedom had one boundary. Only Buffett could allocate capital. And as most of the previous capital that Seabury had poured into textiles had gone for naught, Buffett was extremely reluctant to put in more.

Still, Chace tried. He would propose an investment, backed by careful research and good-looking projections. And Buffett would reply, "Ken, you won't beat the historical average."

J. Verne McKenzie, Berkshire's treasurer, who had gotten to know

Buffett as the outside auditor for Buffett Partnership, said, "Try to remember, Ken. Warren uses the same rule for measuring a $5,000 in-
vestment as he does for $5 million."

During the first two years of the Buffett/Chace regime, textile markets boomed. Profits were earned; however, they were not reinvested in
textiles. Chace trimmed inventories and fixed assets, just as Buffett had
demanded. In a symbolic step, he abandoned the ivory tower. And the
company's cash position grew.[28] Buffett paid out a meager ten-cent
dividend in 1967—but quickly thought better of it.* From then on, Buffett hung on to the money—just as he said he would.

To Berkshire's shareholders, most of whom lived in New England,
there was no outward sign that the big decisions were being made in
Omaha. The headquarters remained in New Bedford, and the annual
reports were signed by Ken Chace and Malcolm Chace. But a close
reader of those reports might have wondered at the hand behind the
tiller.

> The Company has been searching for suitable acquisitions within, and
> conceivably without, the textile field.[29]

Shortly after those words were written, Buffett struck. For some time,
he had been studying an Omaha insurance firm, National Indemnity
Co. The majority owner was Jack Ringwalt, who had once laughed off
Buffett's request for a $50,000 investment in the partnership. Since
then, Ringwalt had heard about Buffett's record, and Buffett had
learned a lot about Ringwalt.

A college dropout with a rogue wit, Ringwalt had started by providing insurance for taxicabs in the Depression. This led him to conclude
that the way to make money was to write policies for risks that other
insurers did not want to touch.

> This was particularly true in my case since my competitors had more
> friends, more education, more determination, and more personality
> than I.[30]†

---

*Buffett later said, "I must have been in the bathroom" when the dividend was declared. He
never paid another.
†Ringwalt's memoir, *Tales of National Indemnity Company and Its Founder*, is a hilarious romp
past the characters, not always savory, in the back alleys of the insurance business.

His bread and butter was unusual-risk auto insurance, but Ringwalt was willing to insure any risk—bootleggers, lion tamers, you name it—that nobody else wanted, since the premiums on such were typically higher. He was known for underwriting radio station treasure hunts in cities around the country. Typically, a station would broadcast a series of clues, hinting at the location of a $100,000 bank draft. Ringwalt was liable if the draft was discovered—quite unlikely, given that it was Ringwalt who hid them, usually in a lipstick container underground. His clues were obscure, along the lines of "A dandelion is not a rose; you are within a block when you pass by Joe's."[31] He had to pay up only once, in San Francisco.

Ringwalt stated his philosophy in simple terms: "There is no such thing as a bad risk. There are only bad rates."[32] This was an insight worth its weight in gold. Buffett, who had learned this truth at the racetrack, felt that Ringwalt was another of his guys. Each liked to take risks, but only when the odds favored them. Ringwalt also was possibly the cheapest of the long line of tightwads in Buffett's acquaintance. He even left his coat in the office when he went downtown for lunch so as to avoid a coat check.

In 1967, Buffett asked if Ringwalt could stop by Kiewit Plaza to discuss a matter that Buffett said would take only fifteen minutes. By then, Buffett had learned from Charles Heider, an Omaha broker, how much it would take to persuade Ringwalt to part with National Indemnity.

"How does it happen that you never sold your company?" Buffett asked.

"Because only crooks and bankrupt people have wanted it."

"What other reason?"

"I would not want the other stockholders to take less per share than I would receive myself."

"What else?" Buffett prodded him.

"I would not want my employees to worry about losing their jobs."

"What *else?*" Buffett insisted.

"I would want it to remain in Omaha."

"What else?"

"Isn't that enough?"

"What is your stock worth?" Buffett asked, getting to the point.

"The market value is $33 per share, but the stock is worth $50 per share."

"I will take it," Buffett said.[33]

The total price was $8.6 million. The apparent riddle was why a New Bedford fabric mill would want to acquire an Omaha insurance company. But Buffett did not think of Berkshire as *necessarily* a textile company, but as a corporation whose capital ought to be deployed in the greenest possible pastures.

Whereas textiles, which required reinvestment in plant and equipment, were cash-consuming, insurance was cash-*generating*. Premiums were collected up-front; claims were paid out only later. In the interim, an insurance company could invest the funds, known in the trade as the "float."

Traditionally, insurers had managed their float conservatively, keeping far more capital than needed. But Buffett, who had thought long and hard about insurance since his early fling with GEICO, thought that float from insurance could be as dynamic as rocket fuel. Float was merely money, and an insurance firm was, in effect, a conduit for investable cash.

Buffett's view would soon be a commonplace, but at the time, insurance was a backwater.* Many insurance companies didn't even bother to publish their earnings, and few investors were interested in seeing them. Charles Heider, who brokered the deal, said, "Buffett understood float before anyone in the country."

Once Buffett had gobbled up National Indemnity, Berkshire had a stream of funds for him to play with. In successive years, Berkshire acquired Sun Newspapers of Omaha Inc., a group of weekly papers in Omaha, and the far bigger Illinois National Bank & Trust, in Rockford, Illinois. The Rockford bank was run by Eugene Abegg, who had taken charge in 1931, when it was virtually worthless and when other banks in town were failing. He was another of the nose-to-the-grindstone, Depression-schooled, Grandpa Buffett–type figures that Buffett seemed to produce from central casting whenever he bought a business. From his 1930s beginnings, Abegg had proceeded to build a $100 million base of deposits and an earnings-to-assets ratio (the key measure in banking) that was close to the highest among large commercial banks.[34]

---

*Within a year or two of the National Indemnity deal, Buffett was imitated by financial operators such as Saul Steinberg, Carl Lindner, Harold Green, Maurice Greenberg, and Larry Tisch, all of whom pursued insurance-company takeovers.

Most older entrepreneurs such as Abegg are eager to retire when they sell out, and the new owners (while praising their storied careers) usually are anxious to show them the door. Buffett was different. Running a bank, a claims office, or a retail chain was out of his arc, and he had no desire to try. Indeed, he felt, if he didn't like the way the business was run, why buy it?

He looked for a type: the self-starter with a proven record. What is interesting is that they stuck with him. Abegg, who was seventy-one when he sold to Buffett, continued to manage under Buffett's ownership—as did Jack Ringwalt at National Indemnity and Ben Rosner at Diversified. (Abegg would run the bank until he was eighty.)

None of these multimillionaires needed to work, but Buffett understood that most people, regardless of what they say, are looking for appreciation as much as they are for money. He made it clear that he was depending on them, and he underlined this by showing admiration for their work and by trusting them to run their own operations.

One time, a discontented fabric buyer at Sears, Roebuck called Buffett and tried to pull an end run around Ken Chace. The buyer reminded Buffett that they had a common friend from college, and asked him to change the salesman on his account. Buffett despised the old-boy routine (it appealed to sentiment, not reason) and bluntly told the man from Sears that such matters were up to Chace.[35] Naturally, such shows of loyalty only increased Chace's dedication to Buffett.

But as Buffett plowed Berkshire's capital into insurance, banking, and publishing, he continued to siphon it out of textiles. In 1968—three years after promising to sell the same goods from the same plants—he closed the smaller of Berkshire Hathaway's mills, in Rhode Island, which was irreversibly tied to cotton fabrics and was doomed by the dwindling market for such niceties as petticoats and dress stiffeners. The onetime king of cotton was down to a single mill—the factory in New Bedford. A year later, even the Cove Street plant stopped spinning cotton, the business launched by Horatio Hathaway, leaving only rayon linings and synthetic curtains.

And Buffett was keeping his thumb on every capital outlay down to the office pencil sharpener. The minutes of Berkshire's "finance committee"—convened, one summer, over the telephone between New Bedford and Buffett's vacation haunt in California—suggest that no expense was too trifling to escape his scrutiny:

Voted: To approve the purchase of a secondhand Reiner Warper and Creel at an approximate cost of $11,110.

Voted: To approve the purchase of 50 secondhand 64 inch XD looms at an approximate cost of $71,160, installed.

Voted: To approve the repair of office building roofs at an approximate cost of $9,340, and the repair of the shipping room floor at an approximate cost of $9,940.[36]

Corresponding with Chace on the risk of deadbeats, Buffett specifically reminded him not to trust in anything but cash:

> Also, let's look at all of our customers especially hard so that no one gets into us too heavily. If anyone is slow in paying, let's make sure we don't ship them more goods until they pay whatever amount is past due, *and the check has cleared*.[37]

Buffett made no exceptions, even for a very "special" customer. Susie came to Berkshire's New York office in the early seventies to buy some draperies. Ralph Rigby, the salesman, said, "We gave her the highest price we could. It was a good thing. Buffett called and asked what we had charged."

In 1970, with the dissolution of Buffett Partnership, Buffett personally became the owner of 29 percent of Berkshire's stock. He installed himself as chairman and, for the first time, composed the letter to shareholders in Berkshire's annual report.

Writing to the investors, Buffett used the same yardstick as he had in private with Ken Chace: the return on equity capital—that is, the percentage profit on each dollar invested. Buffett was extremely consistent abut such things. He did not have one yardstick in Kiewit Plaza, another in New Bedford, and another for the public.

Moreover, in measuring investments, Buffett was absolutely unwilling to relax his standards. Many a portfolio manager has been known to explain, "This doesn't look so hot, so we're only investing a little." Buffett refused to make such compromises, and he could be brutally honest about shooting down a prospect. Scotty Hord, his Omaha Data

Documents cohort, discovered this in the period that Buffett was reinventing Berkshire. Hord had gotten a cash windfall, and he was hoping to buy a business of his own. Buffett offered to check out any prospects before he went ahead. Hord recounted:

> I brought him four or five companies. I went to his house each time. One of them made a new product—a kind of dispenser of thin sheets of paper for hospitals, restaurants. They wanted me to put up $60,000. Buffett said, "What do you think the odds of this thing making it are?" I said, "Pretty good. One out of two." He said, "Do you think that's good? Why don't you go up in an airplane with a parachute that opens one out of every two times and jump?" I brought him another one—Jubilee Manufacturing Co. It made novelty automobile horns. I said, "Do you think enough of it to invest with me?" He said, "No." I said, "Do you think enough of *me* to invest in it with me?" He said: "No." He said it that quick. It was so refreshing to hear, without all kinds of excuses.

Buffett increasingly believed that textiles amounted to the same sort of wishful parachute drop. No matter how much they invested, manufacturers couldn't raise prices, because the product was a commodity and usually in oversupply. Thus they never recouped their investment.

In 1970, Berkshire's profits from textiles were a laughable $45,000. Meanwhile, it earned $2.1 million from insurance and $2.6 million from banking, both of which, at the start of the year, were working with roughly the same amount of capital as textiles.

In his annual report, Buffett saluted Ken Chace's attitude and effort, but noted that textiles were "swimming against a strong tide." Pointedly, he noted that Berkshire's return was 10 percent, merely average for corporate America, and that "it is considerably in excess of what would have been achieved had resources continued to be devoted exclusively to the textile business."[38]

Of course, the question of whether Buffett, an outsider, would close the mill had hung over him from the start. Malcolm Chace claimed that he knew from day one that Buffett "didn't have any intention of putting more money into the brick and mortar of textiles." Jack Stanton, watching bitterly from the sidelines, concluded that Buffett was merely a liquidator.

But from time to time Buffett did reinvest modest amounts. He did not want to be known for closing New Bedford's last mill. In a final letter to his partners he had written:

I like the textile operating people—they have worked hard to improve the business under difficult conditions—and, despite the poor return, we expect to continue the textile operation as long as it produces near current levels.[39]

He felt a debt to Ken Chace, who had provided him the cash to diversify, and in whom Buffett saw the qualities he most admired: frankness and self-reliance. Once, when Chace put himself down, Buffett threw him a look. He said, "Ken, you worked your way up from nothing."

He was stingy about paying Chace, who made less than competitors at other textile mills.[40] In 1970, after Chace had been at the helm for five years, his salary was $42,000 a year. Also, Buffett tightened up considerably—as did other textile companies—on the pension plan. "Warren had a strong negative feeling about management benefiting at the expense of shareholders," Chace noted.

Yet Chace deeply appreciated his autonomy under Buffett and was extremely devoted to him. This says a lot about Buffett's effect on people. Though he wouldn't loosen his wallet, he was uncanny as a motivator.

Chace wondered whether Buffett would shut him down, but he sensed that his overseer did not want the tumultuous upheaval of a mill closing. Buffett, he knew, did not like change. "Warren tends to hang on," Chace noted. "He keeps his old friends."

According to Buffett's capitalist credo, he probably *should* have closed the mill. But viscerally, he felt an affection for this relic of a factory, whose past seemed oddly more alive than its future.[41] He was willing to tolerate a mediocre return, as long as the mill didn't become a drain on cash and require him to put in more capital. Spiritually, though no longer financially, the Hathaway mill embodied the New England work ethic that Buffett revered. So Buffett made a Faustian pact between his conscience, his comfort, and his wallet. Textiles would be bled to the bone, but the looms on Cove Street would continue to hum.

Chapter 8

RETURN OF
THE NATIVE

Now is the time to get rich.

WARREN BUFFETT, 1974

Coming off the golf green with his chum Bob Billig in the summer of
1970, Buffett noticed a commotion by the club patio and asked what
was going on. "That's your fortieth birthday celebration, watching us,"
Billig said dryly. As Buffett stood uncertainly, the crowd approached,
bursting into the familiar refrain. Though he kept his composure, Buffett was deeply touched. Now at midlife, he was mildly celebrated. In
Omaha, he was a somebody: chairman of the weekly *Sun*, a director of
the Omaha National Bank. As a visitor observed on a walk through
downtown Omaha, Buffett could "rattle off the financial characteris-
tics of every building and business he passes."[1]

Yet with his partnership liquidated, Buffett no longer had a full-time
job. Keeping a vigil over Ken Chace and the Hathaway mill took only
so much time. His three children were teenagers. A profile in the *Lincoln Journal & Star* portrayed him as a man in limbo, monitoring his
investments from a four-room suite and living a "pretty easy life." To a
younger money manager who had sought his counsel, Buffett curtly
replied, "I am no longer in the investment management business and,
therefore, have had to decline all requests, including yours"—sounding as if Wall Street were not to hear from him again.[2]

After his fortieth birthday, Buffett reconvened the Graham group, in
Williamsburg, Virginia, this time without Graham. Oddly, Buffett was

the only one not active in stocks. The market was unattractively high, and he was asking quite natural questions—such as, with $25 million, what was the point of accumulating more? Writing in *Fortune*, his friend Carol Loomis said Buffett had "a strong feeling that his time and wealth should now be directed toward other goals than simply the making of more money."[3] Bill Ruane urged him to run for President.

In fact, Buffett was thinking seriously of public service. He did not want to run; he was far too private—and, he admitted, thin-skinned—for that carnival test.[4] But he was dabbling backstage. He supported Democratic presidential hopefuls, such as Harold Hughes and Allard Lowenstein. He was getting chummy with politicians, such as Senators Frank Church and Richard Clark and Governor Jay Rockefeller. Geoffrey Cowan, a *Village Voice* writer, had dinner at the Buffetts' along with John Culver, a candidate for U.S. senator. Strangely, the talk at this multimillionaire's dinner table was all about liberal politics.

Howard Buffett had championed America as a finished product, as a sort of perfect, closed society unneedful of change. Warren, who had the American sympathy for the underdog, identified with the up-and-coming Ben Rosners and Ken Chaces. Like his father, he hated free riders (e.g., his disdain for stock options), but he saw more of them within the country clubs and boardrooms than without. Once, at a formal dinner, when a guest complained about the cost of welfare programs for the poor, Buffett replied tartly, "I'm a lot more concerned about welfare for the rich."[5]

This was reflected in Buffett's lifestyle. He lived more or less on the $50,000 salary that he received from Berkshire. His children went to public schools, and Warren encouraged them to do something that they enjoyed, irrespective of what they would earn. In fact, Peter realized the extent of his father's fortune only when he read of it in the newspaper. Young Susie said:

> We didn't live any differently from anyone else. I could charge clothes and never get in trouble—that was the only difference. I didn't have a car. I had to get a job at sixteen—at the Carriage Shop, as a salesperson.

Buffett generally tried to make light of his money. When his wealth attracted publicity, alarming his family, Buffett joked, "We'll just put a sign on the door that says it's Bill Scott's [his assistant's] night to keep the money." Or, he would crack, "And to Peter, who wants to be mentioned in my will: 'Hi, Pete!' " Of course, this was not really a joke. Warren had strong feelings about his money and warned his kids that they should not expect a penny of it. He seemed to fear that even a droplet of his money would spoil them.

This may have been obsessive, but as a consequence, the Buffett household had an unmoneyed, informal spirit and an egalitarian air. At a Halloween apple-bobbing party, the Buffetts invited in every passing trick-or-treater—a gesture one would not have expected from a J. P. Morgan or a Henry Kravis.[6] People dropped in unannounced to use Buffett's racquetball court, and in such numbers that he took to calling it the "YMCA."

Under the influence of the hip elder Susie, the house became a refuge from Woodstock-era generational conflict. Layne Yahnke, a friend of little Susie's, said it was a "safe house." People could just walk in and raid the fridge. "If the snow fell and the city stopped—that's where you went," Yahnke recalled. "Sitting in the family room was so damned nice."

Susie had done the house in her trademark sunshiny oranges and yellows. There were paintings by artists that she had taken under her wing, and Aquarius-age posters such as the ubiquitous *War Is Unhealthy for Children and Other Living Things*. The man of the family might come down to make some popcorn, but—"retired" from money management or not—he was generally upstairs, working. Again, Layne Yahnke:

> Saturday nights the family room would be full of kids. Mrs. Buffett would be there; we'd be playing our music for her; she'd be playing music for us. Long about twelve-thirty in the morning you'd hear "Susan-O—you coming up?" There were never any rules. When he went to bed, we turned down the music.

In 1971, "big Susie" talked Warren into buying a $150,000 vacation home in Laguna Beach, south of Los Angeles. It was near the ocean but not fronting it, as the more expensive homes were, and was casually furnished with rattan chairs. The first summer, thirteen teenagers stayed there. Buffett would get a daily package of papers from his office and go off by himself, but he was pretty tolerant of his kids' friends.

One evening he took a a big crew of them to dinner. After the meal, the waiter came back with his credit card and said, "You're at your limit." Buffett arched his eyebrows at his wife and handed the waiter a second card, without so much as a word to suggest that he was, indeed, good for the bill.[7]

While Warren was pondering a political role for himself, Susie was spending a lot of time in north Omaha, the black quarter (and the birthplace of Malcolm X). Besides being president of a local volunteer agency, she would make the rounds of schools and always seemed to have an errand or a mission on the north side. (Tom Rogers, a nephew, satirized her thusly: "Oh, are you black? Are you poor?—How much do you need?")

Encouraged by Susie, Warren put his toe in the water. Their private trust, the Buffett Foundation, began to provide more than fifty scholarships a year to black college students.[8] In the early seventies, Rodney Wead, a friend of Susie's who was promoting black-run business ventures, asked Warren to get involved. In particular, Wead, who had visions of "black capitalism," thought Buffett would be just the guy to help him get his Community Bank of Nebraska off the ground.

Buffett agreed. He and Nick Newman (his country-club co-conspirator) joined the bank's advisory board and devoted a fair amount of time to it. Buffett also made a nominal investment—1.4 percent of the bank's capital.[9] However, unlike Susie, Warren was far from an innocent. He repeatedly warned the bank's directors that a disproportionate number of minority banks had failed because of bad loans. As the bank was getting under way, Buffett sent the board a nervous note, enclosing a copy of a newspaper story about a similar bank in Denver that had failed.

> You will notice that the President of the bank said, "When we started business, it was our plan to aid minority investors and the so-called little guy. This we did, but some of them didn't treat us very well in paying their debts, and that was our downfall." The President is making a mistake in blaming the borrower. Every bank gets offered lots of bad loans, and it is the banker's fault if he accepts them.[10]

When the Community Bank began to flounder, Buffett distanced himself. Wead suggested that Buffett take some black students under his wing and teach them finance, but Buffett did not respond. "Warren is an enigma," Wead concluded. "He's gracious. He's honest. He's hardworking. But he's never understood his role as a wealthy man in our beleaguered community." When bad loans mounted—just as Buffett had feared—he pointedly refused to invest more capital.[11]

Wead complained that Buffett "didn't understand the cycle of poverty." The truth was to the contrary. Buffett understood the cycle well enough to keep his wallet zipped. Without the hope of a return, he was no more willing to invest in the Community Bank than he was in textiles.

Despite his ideals, Buffett was suspicious of the liberal impulse to simply spend money. George McGovern, then running for the Democratic presidential nomination, stayed at Buffett's house and seemed to win Buffett's favor—until, soon after, he announced that a President McGovern would favor giving each person in the United States a $1,000-a-year stipend. Buffett dropped him like a hot potato and voted for Richard Nixon.[12]

Partly, Buffett was just tight, but he genuinely did not think people or organizations (or his kids) benefited from easy cash. He measured social projects through the same lens as business ventures: he wanted a return. Good works required that one proceed on the basis of trial and error, even on faith. Buffett was incapable of such a leap. Indeed, the very discipline that made him a good investor crippled what could have been a powerful inclination to work for societal changes. He needed a *yardstick*. "In investment you can measure results," he admitted to a reporter. "With some of this other stuff, you don't know in the end whether you've won or lost."[13]

Like many another mogul, Buffett thought he would be able to play both the citizen and the capitalist in publishing. Jay Rockefeller had introduced him in the late sixties to Charles Peters, a former Peace Corps administrator who was starting a magazine, the *Washington Monthly*. The *Monthly* espoused just the hardheaded liberalism Buffett admired. He invested $32,000 and brought in Joe Rosenfield, a liberal friend from Des Moines, as a partner. Full of high-minded ideals, Buffett told Rosenfield, "It'll be interesting and if it breaks even it'll be worth it."

Peters immediately blew his capital. Buffett and Rockefeller took it upon themselves to go to New York and hire a consultant to see if the magazine was worth saving. Concluding that it was, Buffett agreed to put in $50,000 more. Then he began to doubt whether it would, as he had said, be "worth it." He called Peters and told him he wanted out—which would have been a death blow. The fast-talking Peters assured him that the *Monthly* would be a big breadwinner, which neither of them believed. They went back and forth on the telephone, Buffett referring to his accursed numbers, Peters desperately trying to reel him in. Finally, Buffett agreed.

The amount of money was trivial, but as Ken Chace had learned, that didn't matter. "Warren wanted annual reports—all that shit," Peters noted. The *Monthly* was precisely the editorial voice that Buffett had hoped for—influential and at times ground-breaking. But as a business the *Monthly* was a joke. Though it was understaffed and run on a shoestring (Peters earned $24,000), Buffett was most annoyed because Peters didn't produce an *annual report*. Even in a venture that couldn't possibly make a buck, he needed that yardstick.

Buffett complained to Rosenfield, "They *talk* about open government but they don't send statements." Peters said that Buffett was "torn—between his pro bono side, and his side that didn't want it on his tombstone that he had invested capital in the *Washington Monthly*."

Buffett did care about the journalism. In 1971, he called the *Monthly* with what he said was a pretty hot tip. Two young editors rejected it, reckoning that if it came from a millionaire it wouldn't be much good.[14]

Then Buffett took the story to the *Sun*, the group of Omaha-area weekly papers that he had purchased for Berkshire. Stanford Lipsey, the publisher, and Buffett were pretty chummy. Lipsey would go over to Buffett's and, liquefied with Pepsi-Colas, the two would talk for hours about how to improve the paper and how to use it as a social force in Omaha. They had tried their hand at kingmaker, vigorously pushing a candidate for mayor (who lost). One time, Buffett called Lipsey to tell him that an editorial on President Nixon's wage-and-price controls was terrific. "Warren, you gave it to me," Lipsey reminded him.

Buffett's tip concerned Boys Town, a revered Omaha institution. It had been founded in 1917 by Edward J. Flanagan, an Irish priest, as a home for wayward youths, and celebrated in an Oscar-winning 1938 movie starring Spencer Tracy. Buffett had a source who told him that

Boys Town was sitting on a ton of money and was straying pretty far from Father Flanagan's dream.[15]

The story was tailor-made for the *Sun*, a feisty paper but a weak second fiddle to the *Omaha World-Herald*. And Buffett gave Lipsey a crucial lead: Boys Town had been required, for the first time, to file an independent tax return.[16] The return showed that Boys Town had accumulated an astonishing $162 million investment portfolio—twice the endowment of the University of Notre Dame. Meanwhile, it was serving fewer boys and operating a heart-tugging direct-mail campaign under the guise of poverty.

This was the sort of story that fired Buffett's conscience. He invested a godlike faith in capital, because any amount of it, even Queen Isabella's pittance, bore the seeds of future trillions. To squander or misdirect it was a sin.

The Boys Town project was reported in secret, and Buffett, Lipsey, and the editor proofread the eight-page exposé in the editor's living room. Buffett topped the story with a line from scripture (Luke 16) that could have been his refrain for anyone in public life, or in business, who had misused capital: *"Give an account of thy stewardship."*

The story, published in March 1972, won a Pulitzer Prize.

Buffett liked newspapers. He was nostalgic about his boyhood exploits as a *Washington Post* carrier; he liked the inky feel of newspapers. But he was dissatisfied with the Omaha *Sun*. Like other quasi-social ventures, such as the Community Bank and the *Washington Monthly*, the *Sun* didn't quite cut it for him. Though he was proud of the Pulitzer, he wanted a profit.

And the *Sun* was a poor business. When it raised its rates, its circulation dropped, rather sharply. "Warren didn't anticipate that," Lipsey noted. The experience seems to have jolted him. Buffett suddenly wanted to learn all there was to know about newspapers. He began to study the economics of newspapers, and of other media properties, in great detail. As once, after discovering GEICO, he had immersed himself in insurance, now he wouldn't sleep until he *knew* the newspaper business from the bottom up. And the more he learned, the more he knew that the *Sun*, as a secondary paper, was hopeless. Not long after the Boys Town story, Buffett wrote to a colleague:

I mentioned that in 1910 there were 1207 cities in the country with daily papers, of which 689 had two or more competing papers. In 1971, there

were 1511 cities with daily papers, of which 37 had two or more competing papers. Since I wrote that letter, the Washington *Daily News*,
backed by the enormously powerful Scripps-Howard chain, has folded,
as has the Boston *Herald-Traveler* and the Newark *Evening News*. . . .
The owners learned by bitter experience that having a paper which is
second in consumer acceptance and community importance produced
rivers of red ink which the best of management and the deepest of pocketbooks cannot reverse.

Referring to the Omaha *Sun*, Buffett emphasized that socially redeeming stories would in no way guarantee a profit.

Suggestions are constantly made to me—frequently by academicians
who are somewhat unhappy with the editorial views of the local monopoly daily—that a wonderful future would await us if we would convert to
a daily paper. This advice is well intended and sincere. The inescapable
fact that it has never been done . . . doesn't register on these theoreti-
cians.[17]

But it had registered on Buffett that it would be "wonderful" indeed
to own a *dominant* newspaper. Such a paper, he would tell his pals,
would be like the only bridge in a small town.[18] Anyone who had to get
across would have to pay the toll. An advertiser in a one-paper city was
in the same boat. A department store in Omaha *had* to advertise in the
Omaha World-Herald, the monopoly daily—which meant that the
paper had relative freedom to raise its rates. It had the protected franchise that lesser businesses, such as the Hathaway mill, could only
dream of.

Buffett would have liked to buy the *World-Herald*, but it was not for
sale.[19] So he began to nose around in publishing circles, trying to find a
paper. He checked out possibilities in California and Maryland. He
made a bid for the *Cincinnati Enquirer*, but got turned down.

He also got Bill Ruane to set up a dinner with Tom Murphy, a Harvard classmate of Ruane's. Murphy was chairman of Capital Cities
Communications and a rising star in the broadcasting business. The
two of them hit it off. Murphy took Buffett to the Republican Convention in Miami and decided he wanted to get Buffett on his board. Taking a tip from Ruane, Murphy went to Omaha, where he could see
Buffett without distractions.

They had "a hell of a game of racquetball," after which Buffett bought Murphy a steak dinner. Sensing Murphy's purpose, Buffett never let him pop the question.

"You know, Murph," he said, "I couldn't become a director of your company without a major position, and your stock's much too high. But any way I can help, you feel free to call me."

High stock prices had been a problem for Buffett all around. Since folding the partnership, he had not been able to find bargains. Going into 1972, Berkshire's insurance company had a portfolio worth $101 million, of which only $17 million was invested in stocks. Buffett had put the rest in bonds.

But little by little, he began to creep back into the game. Once again, the catalyst for his metamorphosis was Wall Street. Fund managers, who had been stunned by the collapse of Go-Go, had retreated into a shell. Their funds were now clustered in a group of big, well-known growth stocks, such as Xerox, Kodak, Polaroid, Avon, and Texas Instruments, which were dubbed the nifty fifty. In the prevailing view, these companies, unlike the small high-fliers of the Go-Go era, would grow forever. They were thus said to be "safe"—indeed, *safe at any price*.

By 1972, the nifty fifty were trading at an astronomical eighty times earnings. Wall Street had drawn a moral from Go-Go, but not the right one. The funds had converged on "safer" stocks, but risk is never wedded to one stock or another; it is present wherever investors mindlessly imitate one another.

Buffett, meanwhile, began to find bargains outside the nifty fifty, and to buy them for Berkshire's insurance company. One day it was California Water Service, the next 1st Citizens Bank & Trust of Smithfield, then General Motors. And there were more: Scripps-Howard Investment, Cleveland Cliffs Iron, Vornado, the Omaha National.

In 1973, the nifty fifty began to crack. Fund managers recoiled in horror. The "safe" stocks were falling. Where was one to turn? The Dow, which had broken above 1,000, backpedaled to 950. The broad market staggered. Wall Street, now thoroughly cured of the mania of Go-Go, retreated into a malaise. Brokerage reports dried up; analysts were sent packing. Companies that had gone public in 1969 saw their stocks fall by half.

This spiritual anemia produced a corresponding but contrary reaction in Buffett. His transformation was uncannily familiar and yet inverted, like a filmstrip of the previous decade being run in reverse. In the Go-Go years, his ideas and desire had slowly drained, but now, with the market sinking, he was running like a colt.

Looking over Berkshire's brokerage activity in 1973, one has an impression of Buffett sweeping down the aisles of a giant store—here grabbing National Presto Industries, there Detroit International Bridge, in the other lane Sperry & Hutchinson.[20] On it went—U.S. Truck Lines, Munsingwear, Handy & Harman. As the market fell, he raced down the aisles all the faster—J. Walter Thompson, Coldwell Banker, Dean Witter, King's Department Stores, Morse Shoe, Ford Motor, Pic N Save, Mitchum Jones & Templeton, Grand Union, Studebaker-Worthington.

Ralph Rigby, the textile salesman, visited Omaha and found Buffett in a state of ecstasy. "He said a lot of guys studied baseball stats or the *Racing Form*," Rigby said, "He just had a hobby that made him money. That was relaxation to him."

One time, Judge John Grant, Buffett's bridge partner, mentioned that he had been having fun trying an interesting case. Buffett's eyes twinkled. "You know," he said, "some days I get up and I want to *tap*-dance."

In the evenings, Buffett would go to Cris Drugstore, on 50th Street, for the late edition of the *World-Herald*, which carried the closing stock prices. Then he would go home and read a stack of annual reports. For anyone else it would have been work. For Buffett it was a night on the town.

He did not merely do this nine-to-five. If he was awake, the wheels were turning. He would offer to help Peter with his homework, but Peter knew it wasn't what his father really wanted to do.[21] One day, when Buffett arrived home, he found his adolescent son wincing in pain on the stair landing. Peter had thrown his back out while changing a lightbulb. Buffett, in his customary haste to get to his study, blew past him up the stairs. Later, he realized how unfeeling he had been, and apologized.

In a sense, Buffett was the boy of the house. His total delight in his work to the exclusion of all else, like his unrefined and immature eating habits, his fear of change, his dependence on Susie, even his perpetual energy and good humor, had a juvenile quality not uncommon to prodigies. A woman friend said that when she was with him, she felt as if they were "kids shooting marbles."[22]

His immersion in stocks was terribly difficult for his wife, in manifold ways. According to what Susie told her confidantes, she yearned for more of the usual sort of sharing that one would have with a spouse. When—as occurred periodically—Howie, their middle child, had some problems, Susie had to turn to her own father, the psychologist, for guidance. Her spellbound hubby was in a dream chamber. It was not that Warren was uncaring about the family. He was never mean— they knew he wouldn't *knowingly* hurt a flea. As Peter said, he had blinders on.

The entire family did a fair amount of rationalizing about those blinders.[23] They treated his work like some great, soulful endeavor that no one could disturb. And in a sense, that was appropriate. Something was happening in that dream chamber. And in the early to middle seventies, it was happening as never before.

Buffett would pick up the phone and return the most ordinary "How are you?" with a riveting exclamation, as if he couldn't contain his pleasure. According to Clifford Hayes, of Chiles Heider & Co., one of the brokerages where Buffett did business, Buffett would call "two, three, four, five times a day."

> He just wanted the information; he didn't want opinions. He'd ask about a company he was interested in. I'd say, "What do you want, five thousand shares? Ten thousand shares?" He'd say, "Buy it!"

He would run his finger down the price-earnings column of the stock table, and practically every P-E was in single digits. It was one of those rare times on Wall Street: America was being given away, and nobody wanted it. Buffett's reaction was instinctive: *Be greedy when others are fearful.*

Now he had more ideas than cash—a complete reversal from the sixties. In 1973, Bob Malott, who ran FMC Corp., asked Buffett to be a fly on the wall while some candidates to manage FMC's pension fund made presentations. They were rather esoteric, and Buffett did not think much of them. "For two days," Buffett recalled, "we sat there and listened to it. And at the end he asked me what I thought and I told him it was all a waste of time."[24]

Then Malott asked if Buffett would take a crack at managing some of FMC's pension money himself. Buffett said, "Okay, but understand that FMC will get the dregs of my ideas. I'm going to service Berkshire first, Warren and Susie Buffett second, and FMC third."[25] The point was, he had enough ideas to go around.

For Malott, it was a coup. No one—not FMC's pensioners, nor its shareholders, nor the public—knew that Buffett was running money for him. It was as if Joe DiMaggio had ripped off his Yankee suit and was playing American Legion ball incognito in his spare time. (Over the five years that he managed it, Buffett's FMC portfolio rose 51 percent, compared with just under 3 percent for the Dow.)[26]

Buffett's first concern, as he said, was Berkshire. Early in 1973, he wanted to raise money for it, and hired Salomon Brothers to raise $20 million in senior notes. Denis Bovin, an investment banker fresh from Harvard, met Buffett in Laguna Beach. They mapped out the deal while sipping Pepsis, in view of the Pacific. Bovin, who was unfamiliar with Buffett's Wall Street reputation, next saw Buffett at Salomon's headquarters, in New York. As they strolled through the great open trading room, Buffett was spotted and shouts erupted from traders—a foreshadowing of Buffett's later dramatics at the firm. Robert Spiegel, the head stock trader, ran over and blurted out, "Warren, I got a big block of—" and tried to peddle a stock to him.

Buffett's decision to sell notes was based on a Buffett rule of thumb: get the money when it is cheap. (If you wait to borrow until you *need* a loan, it is likely to be when others are also borrowing, when—perforce—rates will be higher.)

Lenders were not exactly eager. Salomon had to persuade them that the money was for Buffett—not for textiles. The offering document reassuringly noted that Berkshire had reduced the capital in textiles from $24 million to $11 million. Even so, lenders insisted on a term enabling them to demand repayment if Buffett sold his stock. But he got the money at 8 percent. Some months later, Salomon's Donald Mutschler sent Buffett a congratulatory note:

> Just as an aside, the money markets have certainly verified the famed Buffet [*sic*] financial acumen. I am not sure whether it would be possible at all to do your financing today and if it were . . . the rate would be north of 9%. . . . Your timing was perfect.[27]

Mutschler did not know the half of it. Buffett had started to nibble on the Washington Post Co. In February, Berkshire bought 18,600 shares at 27.* In May, the stock fell to 23. Berkshire, armed with the cheap money from Salomon, bought 40,000 shares more. As the price fell further, Buffett continued buying. In September, he bought a huge block of 87,000 shares, at 20¾. By October 1973, Berkshire, though unknown to the public, was the largest outside investor in the *Washington Post*, the newspaper that Buffett had once delivered, and the dominant media property that he craved.

The Post, run by Katharine Graham, also owned four television stations, *Newsweek* magazine, and newsprint mills. Such assets often traded in private sales, and were not hard to value. Buffett figured that they were worth $400 million. But the stock market was valuing the entire company at $100 *million*.

The people selling—professional fund managers—would not have disputed those numbers. Why, then, were they selling? Quite simply, they were afraid that the shares would drop further. They were afraid that *other people* might sell.

As Buffett analyzed the Post, sweetly and in his lonesome, he saw it as that all too rare opportunity. Mr. Market had turned gloomy—actually, seriously depressed. In such times, stock prices bore no relation to underlying values. One simply couldn't find such a bargain in the real world. Buffett would explain:

> It's a lot different going out to Kalamazoo and telling whoever owns the television station out there that because the Dow is down 20 points that day he ought to sell the station to you a lot cheaper. You get into the real world when you deal with a business. But in stocks everyone is thinking about *relative* price. When we bought 8 percent or 9 percent of the Washington Post in one month not one person who was selling to us was thinking that he was selling us $400 million [worth] for $80 million. They were selling to us because communication stocks were going down, or other people were selling, or whatever reason. They had nonsensical reasons.[28]

We know their reasons. As Buffett was investing in the Post, the *Wall Street Transcript* assembled a group of Wall Street media analysts to assess the industry. They agreed that, based on the "fundamentals," newspaper stocks were selling at point-blank range. But to a man, they

*For comparison with current prices, by 1995 Post shares had split four-for-one.

were fearful of pulling the trigger. Kendrick Noble, of Auerbach, Pollak & Richardson, allowed that "the *Washington Post* is certainly a dominant newspaper with good potential growth." But Noble had the fatal Wall Street habit of looking over his shoulder:

> I think the market is disregarding fundamentals. And with the horizons of our economic scenario, we think this market coolness may continue. . . . It's a tough time for a fundamental analyst.[29]

It was, in fact, a marvelous time for a fundamental analyst. Media stocks were dirt-cheap, a fact that could be demonstrated by simple math. The media analysts did not have a complicated job. They were on earth for one purpose—to evaluate shares of media companies. The stocks being at their nadir, this was their moment. And they let it pass.

In August, Affiliated Publications, owner of the *Boston Globe*, went public. In the prevailing group-think, the fact that it owned only that property made it risky. Never mind that the *Globe* had two-thirds of its market. The fear was, if something happened—if Bostonians no longer wanted to read about the Red Sox—you'd be in trouble. You'd be second-guessed.

First Boston, the underwriter, had to price it on the cheap. Knowing of Buffett's interest in newspapers, the investment bank put out a feeler to Omaha. Buffett was noncommittal.

Privately, he was doing cartwheels. Controlled by two old Boston families, Affiliated had published the *Globe* since 1872. Its circulation, revenue, and profits were rising, and these trends were accelerating. As Buffett knew, the rival *Herald Traveler* had folded the previous year. Boston was becoming—Lord be praised!—a one-paper town, or, as Buffett would have envisioned it, a monopoly toll bridge spanning the Charles. To Buffett, Affiliated's simplicity was not a weakness but a virtue, because its crown jewel was undiluted.

When the offering came to market, Berkshire was the biggest buyer. Buffett explained his rationale in a letter to William Taylor, Affiliated's president.

> Harold Andersen [publisher of the *Omaha World-Herald*] is a good friend of mine, and can tell you of my enthusiasm for excellent newspapers. I am equally enthusiastic about bargain securities. A combination

of the two in a single product is irresistible to me. When the stock market values the *Boston Globe* at under $30 million, it strikes me as ludicrous.[30]

The trick in such markets was to have the cash to exploit the moment—as Buffett put it, "to have your check clear."[31] Owing to Buffett's timely sale of notes, Berkshire had the money. It was buying stocks, especially media stocks, at every turn: Booth Newspapers, Multimedia, Harte-Hanks Newspapers, and on it went.

Around this time, Buffett asked his Omaha buddy Dick Holland an innocent-sounding question about the merits of owning an ad agency. Suspecting nothing, Holland rattled on about how great it was to be his own boss. He soon discovered Buffett's true interest: Berkshire was buying major chunks of two big agencies, Interpublic Group and Ogilvy & Mather International.*

Buffett saw advertising as a free ticket on the media business. Why free? Unlike, for instance, a certain mill in New Bedford, an ad agency did not require capital—merely a desk and a couple of pencils. To Buffett, the lack of assets was a plus, because the profits flowed directly to the owners.

The Wall Street wisdom was directly opposite. Since an agency's "assets" went down the elevators at night, the agencies were seen as evanescent. An agency was like Gertrude Stein's Oakland—there was no there there, just some English majors fiddling with slogans. Theoretically, anyone could do it. Bill Ruane, who was buying the same ad stocks as Buffett, got a bit huffy over this point with the *Wall Street Transcript*:

TRANSCRIPT: Well that [advertising] is kind of wide open. Anybody can become an ad agency. Tomorrow.

RUANE: We are not talking about a couple of long-haired artists in a loft in Greenwich Village. We are talking about a

---

*Buffett was still as secretive as possible. However, all investors are required to disclose 5 percent holdings.

> worldwide business [Interpublic] with clients like Coca-Cola, General Motors and Exxon, [with] gross revenues of approximately $150 million.[32]

In fact, the big agencies had been quite stable. What's more, because Wall Street was so gloomy, Buffett and Ruane were buying them in the subbasement range of three to four times earnings.

By 1974, Berkshire owned 17 percent of Interpublic. Alarmed that Buffett might be thinking takeover, Carl Spielvogel, an executive vice president, called to ask what his plans were.

Buffett chuckled. "My *plans?*"

Now, Spielvogel was really worried. Buffett invited him to stop in Omaha the next time he flew to the West Coast. "By coincidence, I'm going to California next week," Spielvogel lied. In Omaha, he remembered, "it must have been about minus ten degrees. I was slipping and sliding. I wasn't wearing galoshes because I was supposedly on my way to California."

Buffett assured Spielvogel that he had bought Interpublic as an investment. He spun out his philosophy: toll bridges, Ben Graham . . . the entire catechism. To Spielvogel, it all sounded too simple. Being wise to Madison Avenue, he was not prepared for a prairie philosopher. He didn't believe Buffett.[33]

This was not surprising. Despite Buffett's activity in the market, he was still rather invisible. His letters in Berkshire's annual reports were factual and terse, with none of the flourish of his partnership letters. And Berkshire Hathaway was more invisible still.

Its annual meetings were held in New Bedford, in Seabury Stanton's old ivory tower. After the formal business, Buffett would throw the meeting open to questions. It was a once-a-year shot to ask Buffett about investing. But hardly anyone showed up. Conrad Taff, who had taken Graham's class with Buffett, and Taff's brother Edwin, a security analyst, would attend, so Buffett would spend hours taking questions from the Taffs.[34]

There was so little interest in Berkshire that newspapers didn't quote its share price. Anyone in the public could have bought the stock and gotten a free rid on Buffett's coattails (without paying an override, as in the partnership). But interest in it was nil. After hitting a high of 87 in mid-1973, Berkshire slumped with the general market. In 1974, it re-treated, sickeningly, to 40. According to Edwin Taff:

> There was a general disinterest, even among investment pros who knew Warren. One guy said he'd rather buy it at 80. He wanted to see it move. Warren's announcement that he was retired threw people off.

Buffett, though, seemed to have some future for Berkshire in mind. *He* was steadily buying more of it. He even told his friends in the securities business to lay off, so that when some of the thinly traded stock became available he could get first dibs.[35] Charles Heider, Buffett's broker in Omaha, said, "Warren didn't like *anyone* buying Berkshire." Buffett was so set on firming up his control that he asked Verne McKenzie, the treasurer, not to invest in his own company. (Buffett finally told McKenzie he could go ahead in 1978—twelve years after McKenzie had been hired.)

Meanwhile, the stocks Buffett had bought for Berkshire were sinking. By the end of 1973, the market value of Berkshire's portfolio, which had cost a total of $52 million, had sunk to only $40 million. Buffett wrote to the Rockford Bank's Gene Abegg:

> However poorly you may think the [bank] Plan did during 1973, be assured that my record was even worse. It's a good thing for my partners that I terminated the Partnership when I did.[36]

His paper losses worsened significantly in 1974. And his net worth, as measured by Berkshire's price, fell by half. Yet it seemed to dampen his spirits not at all. Stan Perlmeter, a money manager who also worked in Kiewit Plaza, said, "You couldn't tell from talking to him that Warren was aware of it."

Buffett's rare ability to separate his emotions from the Dow Jones Industrial Average was a big part of his success. In the sixties, when he had been making tons of money, he had been full of fearful prophecies. But now, with his portfolio underwater, he was salivating. Writing to Berkshire's shareholders, his optimism was evident:

> We consider several of our major holdings to have great potential for significantly increased values in future years, and therefore feel quite comfortable with our stock portfolio.[37]

One such holding, Affiliated, reported a 40 percent earnings increase for 1973. Nonetheless, the stock fell like a stone. Having gone public at 10 a share, it sank within months to 9, 8, 7½—less than five times earnings. This was the acid test of an investor. When a stock drops by 25 percent, it is only human to wonder if one has made a mistake. Buffett, though, truly believed that he knew better than the crowd. On January 8, 1974, he bought more Affiliated—and more still on January 11 and January 16. He was back in the market on February 13, 14, 15, 19, 20, 21, and 22. He went on all year, like a thirsty man holding a bucket out in the rain. He bought Affiliated on 107 days, down to a low of 5½ a share.

The market collapse of 1973–74 has been oddly ignored in the annals of investing. Yet it was truly epochal, and on a par with the 1930s. Stocks fell from the sky and sat like overripe fruits. Fund managers who had been eager to buy the nifty fifty at *eighty* times earnings were unwilling to buy Affiliated at five times. What these managers feared was the possibility not of being wrong, but of being out of step. They were worried about being second-guessed—not over the long term, but quarter by quarter. An interview with Eric T. Miller, a manager at Oppenheimer, in the *Wall Street Transcript*, stands as a sort of period piece. Miller lived in the pristine suburb of Bronxville, New York. He enjoyed racquet sports. He did not enjoy bear markets.

> I wish we could say that we have strong preferences for areas that are unique right now, but we don't, partly because we don't think it's time to try to be a hero . . . to be terribly venturesome, unless you could put me on [an] island and we were taking a three-year view.[38]

It was, it needs repeating, the *ideal* time to be a hero. Yet where managers had once been willing to gamble on the most dubious of stocks, they now refused the soundest. Where optimism had been second nature, it was now unknown. Fear was all they had left.

The headlines in 1974 described the ever-worsening funk. *Business Week*: "Whistling Past the Graveyard"; *Forbes*: "Why Buy Stocks?" *Business Week*: "The Sickening Slide"; *Barron's*: "Running Scared"; *Forbes*: "The Gloom Is Deepening"; *Forbes*: "Uncharted Waters"; *For-*

tune: "A Case for Gloom About Stocks"; *Forbes:* "Is the Economic Situation out of Control?"

The economy was in a recession, and the usual solution of priming the pump was unavailable. Inflation in 1974 was 11 percent. This was a novel predicament, unknown even in the thirties: inflation *and* recession. The cure for each seemed ruled out by the presence of the other. Economists coined an ugly word: "stagflation." Interest rates soared to twentieth-century highs. Government was at a loss—and increasingly distracted by the question of what the President knew about Watergate and when he had known it. Nixon ventured the opinion that he was not a crook. Wall Street held its breath. In political circles, the talk was of impeachment; in financial circles, of depression.

Internationally, American capitalism was in retreat. The Third World was organizing cartels, spurred by the success of OPEC. Economists held that the millennium of growth was over; it only remained to divide a fixed pie into smaller shares. The evidence was plain at the corner gas station.

Wall Street wore the country's dismal mood for a mask. The nifty fifty stocks plunged by 80 percent. Peak to trough, Polaroid went from 149 to 14⅛, Xerox from 171 to 49, Avon from 140 to 18⅝. Morgan Guaranty, the largest pension-fund manager on the Street and a rigid adherent of the nifty fifty, lost an estimated two-thirds of its clients' money. Bankers Trust stopped buying equities for its trust accounts altogether. Paradoxically, it was time to be buying every stock in sight.

The Dow ended July at 757. By September, it had plunged to 607. As measured by the Dow, 40 percent of American industry had evaporated into thin air. But the Dow did not begin to measure the damage. Since 1968, the average stock had fallen an astonishing 70 percent.[39] On a single summer day, 447 stocks touched new lows. The old-timers' refrain that things had been much worse in the Depression no longer played. The bear market was in its sixth year—twice as long as the bear of 1929–32.

Buffett was as fearful of inflation as anyone. His response was to hunt for stocks, such as newspapers, that would be able to raise rates in step. Similarly, he avoided companies with big capital costs. (In an inflationary world, capital-intensive firms need more dollars to replenish equipment and inventory.)

What Buffett did *not* do was buy or sell stocks on the basis of macroeconomic predictions. In an extreme case, Yarnall, Biddle & Co. of Philadelphia urged clients to sell shares of Coca-Cola, Pepsico, Dr Pepper, and Seven-Up because of the energy crisis:

> Already supermarkets are noticing a trend for shoppers to make fewer trips while buying more per trip. Shoppers may be increasingly unwilling to load up on the relatively bulky soft drinks. . . .[40]

Invited to speak at the Harvard Business School—which had stunned him with a rejection years earlier—Buffett remarked that investors were behaving in an irrational and "manic depressive" fashion. Perhaps he had in mind Howard Stein, who had appeared the previous week at the New York Society of Security Analysts. Stein was the chairman of Dreyfus, an investment firm known for a long-running television commercial in which a lion prowled the byways of Wall Street. But now, the lion sounded more like Chicken Little. Stein admitted that stocks were cheap, but he was obsessed with "the enormity of the problems confronting us." He envisioned a fearful new world of scarcity, in which the standard measures of value would no longer apply:

> Price-earnings ratios, historic gains in earnings, projections of earnings per share and the many other analytical devices that you and I work with seem to have little relevance of late. . . . For so much that will affect security prices, I feel, will be influences emanating from outside any particular industry—causing the better analyst to lift his eyes and stretch his imagination *beyond the immediate realm of his specialty.*[41]

In Stein's apocalyptic vision of a world spinning off its axis, earnings per share no longer mattered. Buffett chose to ignore this view and stay within "the realm of his specialty." He could not size up how the country's problems would influence the shares of the Washington Post. His genius was in not trying. Civilization is too variegated, its dynamics far too rich, for one to foresee its tides, let alone the waves and wavelets that affect securities prices. Wars would be won and lost; prosperity would be hailed as everlasting and bemoaned as ne'er recurring, as would politics, hemlines, and the weather enjoy their seasons. Analyzing them was Wall Street's great game—and its great distraction. In its floating salon, everything was interesting and nothing was certain—the President, the economy, the effect of OPEC on sales of Pepsi-Cola.

None of these would substitute for critically evaluating an individual stock. When you purchased a share of Washington Post stock, ultimately you would not be rewarded on the basis of whether war broke out in the Middle East. You were buying nothing more, nothing less, than a share of the business—a claim on the future profits of its publishing and television assets. Yet if you knew what the Post, or any one business, was worth, it rang with the clarity of a single note. That was the sound Buffett strained for. Nothing else mattered, least of all the thousand cacophonous voices debating the future. Stein was searching for a glimpse of "more stable and anticipatable times," but Buffett was unwilling to wait. As he had once told his partners, the future was never clear. What was very clear to him was that certain securities were available for less—far less—than the value of their assets. Everything else—his son's strained back, the cries of Chicken Little—he cleared away.

There remained Stein's labored question as to whether the old standards of value had been outlived. One recalls Graham's response to Senator Fulbright, who had asked him two decades back: Why would stock prices, even if cheap, necessarily go up?

That is one of the mysteries of our business.

In September, Graham emerged from retirement to speak to security analysts, urging them to awaken to what he termed a "renaissance of value." Investing, he reminded them, did not require a genius.

> What it needs is, first, reasonably good intelligence; second, sound principles of operation; third, and most important, firmness of character.[42]

There were others, such as Bill Ruane and John Neff, who said publicly that it was time to take the plunge. But in the main, the Street indulged in a Hamlet-like exercise in navel-gazing. "To Be or Not to Be—in Stocks," wondered the Wall Street brokerage Hayden Stone. The facts were clear; P-Es were at postwar lows, stocks were cheap. Yet Hayden Stone agonized:

> So many problems remain that this time things may not work out. . . . our whole social structure is so different. . . . no one can predict. . . . can we comprehend and cope?[43]

It made one's head hurt. Hayden Stone advised postponing major stock purchases "until there is more certainty." Would someone kindly ring a bell, advising Hayden Stone in advance of the market's turn? What was missing was not intelligence but, as Graham suggested, moral fiber: the "firmness of character" to act on one's beliefs. At that point— early in October 1974—Buffett, for the first time in his life, made a public prediction about the stock market. The occasion was an interview with *Forbes*. The Dow Jones Industrial Average was at 580.

"How do you feel?" *Forbes* asked.

"Like an oversexed guy in a whorehouse. This is the time to start investing," Buffett said.

His doubts about the future had vanished. His stock was at a low, but his sap had never been higher. Berkshire was stuffed with securities, and Buffett was buying them day by day.

> I call investing the greatest business in the world because you never have to swing. You stand at the plate, the pitcher throws you General Motors at 47! U.S. Steel at 39! and nobody calls a strike on you. There's no penalty except opportunity lost. All day you wait for the pitch you like; then when the fielders are asleep, you step up and hit it.[44]

He had quit in 1969, but now, with the market at a low, his spikes were laced and his bat was cocked. There was no "To Be or Not to Be," no equivocation. As he said to *Forbes*, "Now is the time to invest and get rich." Buffett was back.

Chapter 9.

ALTER EGO

Howard Buffett, Warren's older son, thought his father was the second-most-intelligent man he knew. The smartest, in his estimation, was his father's West Coast philosopher friend Charlie Munger. To the writer Morey Bernstein, Munger was "the real mystery man," the quirky thinker who stood a heartbeat away. Munger was Buffett's sounding board; Munger—and only Munger—he let into the tent. The two of them had a peculiar symbiosis and, as in a good marriage, an aura of inevitability. Dr. Edwin Davis, who had helped to arrange their meeting, had been impressed by their similar mannerisms and wit. Buffett's daughter thought them "clones," walking with the same foot forward and even bearing a slight resemblance.

Yet where Buffett was cheerful, his Los Angeleno compadre was dour. He lacked Buffett's easy grace and suffered fools not at all. Frequently, he did not bother to say goodbye, preferring to bolt from his chair at the conclusion of his business.

Munger was so deeply skeptical of his fellow man that Buffett dubbed him "the abominable no-man." This, in fact, provided a clue to Munger's unique talent as Buffett's consigliere. His approach to life—of particular use to an investor—was to ask what could go wrong. He liked to quote the algebraist Carl Jacobi: "Invert, always invert." Thus, at a high school commencement, Munger gave a sermon not on the qualities that would lead to happiness, but on those that would guarantee a miserable life. *Always invert.*

Buffett had used Munger as his lawyer in a couple of acquisitions, and Munger owned a tiny slice of Diversified Retailing, which Buffett controlled. Otherwise, their careers were separate. Since the sixties, Munger had been managing Wheeler, Munger & Co., an investment partnership, located in a convenient but decrepit pipe-strewn office on the mezzanine deck of the Pacific Stock Exchange. This setup suited Munger, as it showcased his contempt for pretentious corporate suites. Just to grace the point, Munger put his secretary in the private room in back; he and his partner worked in the open anteroom.

Scarcely an hour would pass but that Munger would roar at the secretary, "Get me Warren!" Ira Marshall, Munger's partner, had the sense that Munger was cultivating Buffett, and that he wanted to become his partner. Yet, oddly, their professional linkage was accidental. Each, independently, had been buying stock in a Los Angeles company known as Blue Chip Stamps.[1] Buffett bought it for himself, personally, and also for Berkshire Hathaway. By the early seventies, Buffett was the biggest owner of Blue Chip, and Munger was the second-biggest.

Blue Chip belonged to a fading slice of Americana. It collected a fee from supermarkets that distributed its trading stamps and redeemed these stamps for "free" toasters, lawn chairs, and the like. Buffett, of course, had no interest in toasters. He was interested in the money.

The secret of its appeal was that Blue Chip gathered in cash up-front, but disgorged its funds only over time, as shoppers brought in stamp books. Often the stamps were stuffed into drawers and forgotten. In the interim, Blue Chip had free use of the float. To Buffett, Blue Chip was simply an insurance company that wasn't regulated.

Its "premiums"—that is, the stamps sold to retailers—amounted to $120 million a year. This gave Buffett a hefty bankroll, in addition to the one he had at Berkshire. He and Munger went on Blue Chip's board, took over the investment committee, and began to put the float to work.

For Buffett, this was a dangerous game. An investor operating two pools of capital is working for competing, and potentially conflicting, masters. Oddly, given Buffett's concern for his reputation, this did not occur to him. He and his friend were having too good a time buying cheap stocks together. When Buffett was in California, which was not infrequently, they would laugh about the pickings, making it sound so *easy*.[2]

One example was Source Capital, a closed-end mutual fund, also in Los Angeles. Source had been started by Fred Carr, the Go-Go manager, in 1968. In the early seventies, after Carr quit, its stock crashed. Indeed, it fell, as many stocks did, by *too* much. Though Source had $18 a share in asset value, the price slumped to 9. Blue Chip scooped up 20 percent of the fund. Thus, Buffett and Munger finally came around to Go-Go, but only when everyone else had left the party.

Munger, representing Blue Chip, went on Source's board and took a sledgehammer to anything he didn't like. One time, looking over the bond portfolio, he noticed that Source owned some less-than-safe names. He bluntly told the portfolio manager, "This is a perfectly respectable Baa list. For Source Capital I don't want anything but A1."[3] Buffett could not have asked for a better proxy—especially since he was ill suited to playing the tough cop and tried to avoid unpleasantness.

In 1971, Buffett and Munger got what was potentially the opportunity of a lifetime—a "good business" of the sort that Munger preferred, as distinct from the cheap Ben Graham type. Robert Flaherty, an investment adviser to Blue Chip, learned that See's Candy Shops, a premier chocolate chain in California, was for sale. William Ramsey, a Blue Chip executive, was hot to buy it. He went over to Flaherty's office, and they put in a call to Buffett, who was at his home in Omaha.

"Gee, Bob," Buffett said. "The *candy* business. I don't think we want to be in the candy business." Then the phone went dead.

Ramsey, who had heard this on the speaker phone, began to pace the floor frantically while they tried to get Buffett back. It seemed like an eternity. The secretary mistakenly dialed Buffett's office, where no one answered.

After three or four minutes, they got hold of him. Before they could say a word, Buffett said, "I was taking a look at the numbers. Yeah, I'd be willing to buy See's at a price."

What the "numbers" told Buffett was that California chocoholics were willing to pay a premium price for the See's well-regarded brand. But the price for the company was $30 million. Buffett and Munger were dissuaded by the paltry level of the See's book value, and would go no higher than $25 million.[4] There the talks ended. In this case, Buffett had made a common mistake.

Investors often assume that book value approximates, or at least is suggestive of, what a company is "worth." In fact, the two express quite different concepts. Book value is equal to the capital that has gone *into* a business, plus whatever profits have been retained. An investor is concerned with how much can be taken *out* in the future; that is what determines a company's "worth" (or its "intrinsic value," as Buffett would say).

Suppose, for a moment, that a new company invested in candy-making equipment, stores, and inventory identical to those of See's. Its book value would be the same, but the name on its candy box would be unknown. And this upstart, having far less earning power, would be worth far less. Since book value is blind to intangibles such as brand name, for a company such as See's it is meaningless as an indicator of value.

But Buffett and Munger got lucky. See's rang back and took the $25 million—Buffett's biggest investment by far. With seeming suddenness, his empire now included candy, textiles, retail, insurance, banking, publishing, and trading stamps.

Buffett's trick was to compartmentalize these holdings as though each were an only child. Wearing his See's hat, he did a cram course on sugar futures. His letter to Chuck Huggins, president of See's, shows Buffett delving into surprising detail.

My reluctant inclination . . . is to take prices up on Sunday, December 29. My present thinking is 20¢ to 30¢ per pound. . . . If sugar futures keep falling as they have the last few days, I would be inclined to hold off on purchases until we get some reaction in the market for refined sugar.[5]

Buffett also pestered Huggins about enhancing the See's brand name. Ironically, Buffett's inadequacy as an epicure enlightened him as to what the company was really "selling."

Maybe grapes from a little eight-acre vineyard in France are really the best in the whole world, but I have always had a suspicion that about 99% of it is in the telling and about 1% is in the drinking.[6]

Then Buffett would tunnel his attention onto trading stamps. Discount supermarkets had been taking business from stamp-dispensing stores, which were increasingly seen as a bad deal for shoppers. Buffett bombarded Blue Chip with ideas on how to counter this perception, but he conceded, in a revealing bit of self-analysis, that marketing was out of his range:

> The problem I have is that I think like an accountant or an actuary. My reaction is to explain all the facts and do all the mathematics for the consumer, to show her just how much better off she is by getting our stamps. I think I could convince a group of mathematicians, actuaries, security analysts or accountants . . . but [not] the housewife.[7]

Buffett also put $45 million of the "float" from Blue Chip into bank stocks, mimicking his capital reallocation at Berkshire.[8]

But now his dangerous game was well along. He was investing on behalf of three companies, Berkshire, Blue Chip, and Diversified, that had separate groups of shareholders, and he was obliged to each to get the best deals. Into which pocket would he put the Washington Post and which the See's Candy? Understand that Buffett was scrupulously fair about it. Even so, the conflict of interest was inherent and inescapable. The arrangement was complex beyond call, and for Buffett quite out of character. And where matters are complex, the securities cops rightfully pay attention.

In the midst of this merry game, a broker offered Buffett a block of Wesco Financial, a Pasadena, California, company that owned a savings and loan. Buffett knew Wesco in his sleep. He had read its annual report—as he did those of hundreds of savings and loans—every year since the mid-sixties.[9] Wesco was trading in the low teens, less than half its book value.* Buffett checked with Munger, who agreed that it was cheap, and Blue Chip snapped up 8 percent of the shares.[10] At the time—the summer of 1972—Wesco was a minor, $2 million investment. But in January 1973, Wesco announced a plan to merge with another California savings and loan, Financial Corp. of Santa Barbara.

Buffett and Munger instantly reached the same conclusion: Wesco was giving away the store. Under the merger terms, holders of Wesco would exchange their *undervalued* stock for shares in Santa Barbara—which seemed highly *overvalued*. Quoting Buffett:

---

*Book value *is* a useful gauge for most banks. Since a bank's assets consist of loans and other financial assets, intangibles such as brand names are usually insignificant.

I read these terms, and I didn't believe them. And I told [Munger] the
terms as announced and he couldn't believe it as I couldn't believe it.
But it was there in black and white on the Dow Jones tape.[11]

Munger wanted to buy *more* stock in Wesco, in the hope of defeating the merger, which would be subject to a vote of shareholders. Buffett, who was stoic about taking an occasional loss, did not. He said,
"To hell with it; we made a mistake."[12] But Munger persevered. For the
next six weeks, Blue Chip bought every Wesco share in sight, accumulating 20 percent of the stock.

However, they still could not stop the merger. And now Blue Chip
was in deep. As Munger said, they were like the rat in the trap who
decides it no longer wants the cheese.

In February, Munger paid a call on Louis R. Vincenti, Wesco's president. Using an odd choice of words, Munger said that Blue Chip had
been buying stock "in the hope of creating a climate" in which Vincenti and the other Wesco directors would not feel any "moral obligation" to carry out the merger.

Vincenti stuck to the script. He observed that Blue Chip was free to
vote no, and to solicit other shareholders to do the same. To Munger,
such a populist course reeked of vulgarity. He had come as a man of
honor, confident that between two such men no problem was irresolva-
ble. He declared that he liked Wesco's management, and that Vincenti, in particular, was Buffett's and Munger's sort of fellow. In fact,
Munger declared several times that if Vincenti *personally* asked him,
man to man, so to speak, Blue Chip would stop buying shares.[13]

Vincenti thought it most odd. He did not understand Munger's appeal to morality in the midst of a routine business transaction. Yet it
went to the core of what distinguished Munger, which was an adher-
ence to old-school ethics. He never tired of quoting Benjamin Franklin, whose aphorisms he judged more useful than most of what was
taught in business school.

In and out of business, Munger subscribed to the gentleman's
code. He was headstrong about getting his way, but indifferent to as-
sessing blame or credit for the results. When a doctor botched a cata-
ract operation, ruining his eyesight, he uncomplainingly observed that
it happened in a tiny percentage of such cases and took to studying
ophthalmology.[14]

In private life, Munger was enormously active. Following the *Belous* abortion case, he was a driving force for instituting abortion clinics in Los Angeles.[15] As a volunteer chairman of Good Samaritan Hospital, he totally revamped the hospital's mission and menu of specialties. Yet he bullied the doctors, as he did his fellow trustees at the local Planned Parenthood. Where Buffett had a common touch, the Republican Munger reeked of *noblesse oblige*. He would lope into a boardroom, thinking out loud and telling stories that he found uproarious, a half-blind philosopher-king with a hugely magnifying and terrifying lens.[16]

"Charlie is very funny, and also very pompous," said a member of Buffett's circle. "He believes in the aristocratic point of view, that there is a select group of accomplished, talented people in the world, and that he is one of them."

Munger was wont to joke about establishing a Munger "dynasty." When he divorced his wife, "the first duchess," he read obituaries in the hope of finding a widow with the desired attributes for his intended offspring. He and the "second duchess" raised eight little Munger lords and ladies.

Unlike his Omaha partner, he led a big life, fishing in the rivers and wilds of various continents for trout, bonefish, and Atlantic salmon, holding court at the California Club, and dominating a party, especially after a glass of wine. Ira Marshall recalled a soirée in Bel-Air: Munger was talking his way through a rambling, sonorous monologue—something about a thousand-year orgasm—which Munger found quite funny, when the host asked Marshall, "Can you get Charlie to *shut up*? No one can say a word."

Otis Booth, a close friend, would awake in the middle of the night on a fishing trip and Munger would be sitting up poring over a book, likely quite arcane. On an expedition with Booth and Marshall to the Australian rain forest, all the while as their jeep went bounding through the jungle Munger was reading an obscure work of paleontology. Then, at night, Munger lectured the group from his reading, "telling us out of the clear blue sky how the dinosaurs evolved into birds," Marshall recalled.

People, including many of Buffett's friends, were intimidated by Munger's weighty discourses on black holes and Einstein, not to mention his contemptuous manner. Buffett's friend Roxanne Brandt once remarked that the only hospital she knew of in Los Angeles was Cedar

Sinai Medical Center. Munger shot back, "That's because you're Jewish."

Yet Munger was a formidable armchair psychologist and, in particular, a student of behavior. He saw the devil in such phenomena as the inability of people to change their minds, or what he termed "first-conclusion bias":

"This is why organizations solicit public pledges. Hell, it's the reason for the marriage ceremony."[17]

Buffett was deeply influenced by such precepts of Munger's. Yet it was Buffett, not Munger, who had the more natural touch when it came to applying them. Indeed, Buffett was a master at overcoming a person's "first-conclusion bias."

In the Wesco matter, after Munger had failed with Vincenti, Buffett began to court the one director with the power to abort the merger. Elizabeth Peters, a San Francisco heiress, was Wesco's largest shareholder.[18] Peters's parents had founded the savings and loan and taken it public in the late 1950s. Her brothers being unsuited to the task, it had been left to Peters, an English major, to learn the business and protect the family interest. She found, first, that she was good at it, and second, that Wesco provided an agreeable contrast to her other pursuits, which included tending to a Napa Valley vineyard that produced a fine cabernet and reading Chaucer.

By the early seventies, Wesco had gone a bit flat. Peters was anxious to give it a kick, but the other directors had little interest, financial or otherwise. When Santa Barbara made its offer, Peters knew that the terms were sorry, but she reckoned that a merger might stir the pot.

Buffett sent Donald Koeppel, Blue Chip's president, to talk to Peters, but she remained adamantly in support of the merger. A short time after Koeppel left, Buffett called. He pleasantly introduced himself, and suggested a tête-à-tête.

A couple of days later, Buffett and Peters sat down in a lounge at the San Francisco airport. Buffett told her that in his opinion, Wesco stock would in time be worth far more than what Santa Barbara was offering. This was the refrain that Peters had heard from Koeppel, but from Buffett it sounded more persuasive. For one thing, Buffett spoke to her as a fellow owner. His capital was on the line with hers.

When Peters insisted that *something* had to be done to reinvigorate Wesco, Buffett said he'd like to try it himself. He talked some about his relationship with other companies, which he described as being one of partnership. He talked some about himself. He was calmly reassuring, pushing the right buttons.

Peters felt that *she* wouldn't mind being this guy's partner, either. She liked Buffett—liked him a lot.[19] And he was a ray of hope.

Peters had just one question. "Mr. Buffett, if I buy you, what happens if you get hit by a truck at the intersection?" Who would save Wesco then?

Buffett replied that he had a partner whose ability he considered equal to his own. He had arranged for this fellow to be in charge of Berkshire, and of Buffett's family interests, in the event of a "truck," and he felt that either of them could be trusted with Wesco.[20]

When Buffett finished, Peters had made up her mind. The merger was dead.

Buffett and Munger now felt an obligation to her, and decided to raise their stake in Wesco. They could have bought stock on the cheap, as, ordinarily, when a merger blows apart the stock will tank. But to chisel investors who were bailing out because of the deal's failure—a failure for which Buffett and Munger were directly responsible—would seem less than classy. Therefore, they told their brokers to be liberal about the price.

Blue Chip bid for Wesco at 17—the price that had prevailed before the deal had fallen through. Though this was highly unusual, according to Munger, "We decided in some quixotic moment that it was the right way to behave."

Blue Chip raised its stake to 24.9 percent. Subsequently, Wesco's shares fell, along with the general market, and Blue Chip made several tender offers. By the middle of 1974, Blue Chip owned a majority of the stock (Peters continued as a big minority holder). There matters seemed to rest. But unbeknownst to Buffett and Munger, their trail had been picked up by the Securities and Exchange Commission.

The first hint of trouble came in the fall of 1974. It arose, in part, from Buffett and Munger's intricate, but still informal, partnership. Buffett and Munger, separately, owned stock in both Blue Chip and Diversified Retailing. However, Munger was not involved in Berkshire. Thus, when Buffett spent money from his Blue Chip pocket, it was collaborative; when he reached into Berkshire—his front pocket—he was on his own. The interlocking ownership made for a confusing, conflicted mess.[21]

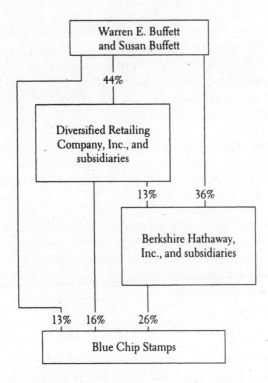

As a first step toward untangling these spaghetti strands, Buffett and Munger announced a plan to merge Diversified into Berkshire. But the SEC had questions. Lots of questions.

Munger, at first, presumed that the SEC was delaying them because Buffett and he were such "interesting" characters. He had a quaint image of a regulator scrutinizing Blue Chip as though it were an unusual bug that had crawled across its microscope. But as the months dragged on, Munger got testy. Writing to Charles Rickershauser, his and Buffett's lawyer at Munger's law firm, Munger had an aggrieved air, as though dealing with a plodding functionary at the bureau of motor vehicles:

I hope the foregoing will satisfy everyone at the SEC and that, if not, you can arrange that I receive the promptest possible response, preferably by direct telephone calls to me, so that we can clear up any problems and get our merger consummated.[22]

Alas, Munger had not read Kafka. Rickershauser sent a toned-down version of his letter to the SEC. In December, Munger got his prompt response—though not the one he expected. The SEC opened a formal investigation of the Prince of Omaha: *In the Matter of Blue Chip Stamps, Berkshire Hathaway Inc., Warren Buffet* [sic], *HO-784*. Buffett was now the target of a full-scale probe.

Blue Chip, Berkshire, Buffet [*sic*], singly or in concert with others . . . may have engaged in acts which may have, directly or indirectly oper-ated as a device, scheme, or artifice to defraud; or included an untrue statement of a material fact or omitted . . .[23]

The inquiry focused on whether Blue Chip had "manipulated" the price of Wesco's stock, a vague charge that can be difficult to resolve either way. Within the SEC's enforcement division, it was considered a big case, and it quickly broadened into a general investigation of ev-erything Buffett had touched.

Under subpoena, Buffett shipped three cartons of files to Washing-ton. His stock-transfer records, his letters to Blue Chip, his every memo to the textile mill and See's Candy and to Buffett's bankers—all of it was sucked into the SEC vacuum. In the opinion of Verne McKenzie, Berkshire's treasurer, "They had discovered a rich guy and decided he had to be a crook."

Buffett was concerned, but calm. He had the same unflappable pa-tience that he brought to investing, even when his reputation was on the line. Munger, in contrast, was nearly apopletic.

Roderick Hills, Munger's former law partner, was then serving as White House counsel. As the investigation gathered steam, word leaked out that Hills had been offered the job of SEC chairman. Rick-ershauser, Buffett's and Munger's lawyer, called Hills and pleaded with him to turn it down, arguing that if he took the job the SEC might feel compelled to bend over backward and judge them more harshly. "Is there anything there?" Hills asked, alluding to the investigation. Rickershauser said, "No, it's crap." Hills shrugged it off. Then Munger called a couple of times, berating Hills for supposedly abandoning Buffett in his hour of need. But Hills took the job.

Munger appeared at the SEC in March 1975, for two days of testimony. He grandly assured his interrogators, "If anything is wrong, Warren and I take full responsibility," as though that would put an end to it. He treated it as a test of character, frequently referring to the honor of various parties.

The young SEC lawyers, ignoring his tone, bored in on him. They intimated that Munger perhaps had conspired to sell short the stock of Wesco's suitor as a means of torpedoing the merger. Munger protested, "That is not our style of operation." He sounded shocked, like a confessor who has stumbled upon a policeman instead of a priest.

The SEC, in fact, suspected a plot. Specifically, had Blue Chip blown up the merger *in order* to take over Wesco for itself?

Q: For how long before February 26 had this approach [seeking control of Wesco] been under consideration by you and Mr. Buffett?

MUNGER: As I stated earlier, 98 percent of our attention was devoted to the task at hand. We are believers in Carlyle's Prescription, that the job a man is to do is the job at hand and not see what lies dimly in the distance.[24]

Undeterred by Carlyle, the SEC lawyers went to the heart. Why, that is, had Blue Chip paid more than necessary for Wesco?

Q: Why would you intentionally pay a higher price for something that you could get for less?

MUNGER: We wanted to look very fair and equitable to Lou Vincenti and Betty Peters.

Q: What about your shareholders? Didn't you want to be fair to them?

MUNGER: Well, we didn't feel our obligation to shareholders required us to do anything which isn't consistent with leaning over backwards to be fair. We have that Ben Franklin idea that—

if you will—the honest policy is the best policy. . . . You look puzzled.

Q: I am. It was my impression that businessmen always try to maximize profits for the corporation and shareholders that they serve.

MUNGER: Well, maybe we're trying to maximize profits over the long pull. If we hope to have a long and congenial working relationship with Louis Vincenti maybe it's just, in light of self-interest, to lean over backwards on deals where you might think he cared.[25]

This was similar to the theme that Buffett had struck with Betty Peters in San Francisco. A long-term investment was more than merely a bet on a stock; it was a form of partnership. A big shareholder—a partner—gave as well as got. To Buffett, the very word "partner" had a powerful implication, suggesting a raft of unspoken responsibilities and loyalties, such as he had felt toward the investors in Buffett Partnership.

The modern portfolio manager saw stocks in two dimensions; they flickered across the screen, and at the push of a button they disappeared. Buffett and Munger wanted a larger role. They often talked about how managing money was not enough. As Munger recalled, "I said to Warren, 'We don't want to be like Russell Sage, a shrewd, miserable accumulator.' We didn't want to be remembered by friends and family for nothing but pieces of paper."*

The SEC lawyers were incredulous. It looked to them as if Blue Chip had been propping up Wesco's stock—i.e., "manipulating" it—presumably to sell at a higher price. But as Blue Chip hadn't sold, the lawyers were mystified. Now, they tried with Buffett.

Q: From a business point of view, wouldn't it have been better to let the price go down and buy it at the cheaper price?

BUFFETT: On that single transaction it might, but I think if you look at the overall Blue Chip picture, having the people at Wesco

*Munger liquidated his partnership in 1976. His compound annual growth rate from 1962 to 1975 was 20 percent.

feeling that shareholders had been fairly treated . . . I think the general business reputation of Blue Chip would not have been as good.

Q: How about your responsibility to the shareholders of Blue Chip?

BUFFETT: I own a fair amount of stock. It has an impact on us. We're not spending other people's money entirely.

Q: You think it might have looked bad if right after the merger blew up, you went into the market and the price went down?

BUFFETT: I think someone might have been sore about it.

Q: I'm extremely puzzled by this rationale that somehow you thought the management of Wesco would be upset or sore at you. . . . I'm saying why should you care, why should Blue Chip care, why should the management of Wesco care?

BUFFETT: It's *important* how the Wesco management feels about us. You can say, well, we own the controlling interest so it doesn't make any difference. But it does make a difference. Lou Vincenti doesn't really need to work for us. He likes working with us. And I enjoy working with him, and it's a good relationship. If he felt that we were, you know, slobs or something, it just wouldn't work. It isn't based solely on the salary he's getting.[26]

It is implausible that a government agency would have badgered, say, J. P. Morgan, Sr., for paying too *much* attention to his reputation. "*Why should you care?*" To Morgan's contemporaries, the question would have been unthinkable. But so much of that era had been lost. Indeed, Buffett's dialogue with the SEC was suggestive of a colloquy across different centuries. The agency, and the buttoned-down lawyers whom it was accustomed to dealing with, defined corporate affairs as a series of transactions. Each action was discrete: today's partner could be tomorrow's adversary. Buffett preferred to think in terms of relationships, some of them lasting. He stubbornly stuck to his antique code like a rolltop desk for which he had a quaint fondness. Perversely, it was seen as grounds for suspicion.

The fact that Buffett had a doppelgänger merely heightened the SEC's suspicions. They had found the co-conspirator; now they merely needed the crime. Naturally, they looked for it in the mysterious-seeming alliance of Buffett and Munger.

Q: Who at Blue Chip makes the investment decisions?

MUNGER: It would usually be Mr. Buffett. He would ordinarily consult with me and get my approval before he went ahead.

Q: Now, after Mr. Buffett placed the order for the first purchase, did he tell you that he was going to keep purchasing the stock of Wesco Financial?

MUNGER: That type of thing is so natural to us that frequently we don't have to talk to one another or discuss what our future intentions are.

Q: Did you ask him?

MUNGER: I don't have to. I understand how his mind works.

Q: Would you consider yourself Mr. Buffett's—like—alter ego?[27]

The casual phrasing was disingenuous. The SEC had heard the term from Betty Peters. They tried it on Buffett, too.

Q: Did you consider him sort of like an alter ego to yourself?

BUFFETT: Well, it depends on what area you're talking about. We differ on some investments, you know. On most investment decisions, we tend to agree.

Q: From the time you became sort of *investing philosophers* in the same manner would you say you consulted with him on most of your investments?

BUFFETT: No, I wouldn't. . . . I would say there was a trend in that direction.

Q: Okay. So that you both discuss many investments, philosophies, what you're investing in.

BUFFETT: Sure.

Q: So you know basically what he is buying and selling most of the time [and] he knows what you are buying and selling?

BUFFETT: He knows what I got an *interest* in buying or selling. I know some of the things he has an interest in. In terms of keeping track of what he is actually doing at a given time, I have no idea.[28]

Buffett's tenor was unhurried. He returned to the SEC, informally and on several occasions, and seemed to go out of his way to *help* his interrogators. He patiently explained the Blue Chip jigsaw puzzle to Lawrence Seidman, an SEC attorney. When they took a break for lunch, Buffett told Seidman about his youth in Washington. Here and there, he sprinkled in a dose of the Buffett philosophy. Soon Seidman was caught in Buffett's gossamer web, just as Betty Peters had been. Seidman recalled:

> I sat around a table with him a number of times, charting it out. He'd say, "You're wrong here, this company doesn't own this," or, "That belongs over here." I spent a lot of time with him. I didn't view it as adversarial. He was a superb person to deal with—even though we were on the other side.

For the modern chief executive, the idea of wandering into the SEC unaccompanied by a lawyer and taking up one's case with a junior investigator—and, indeed, supplying him with information—would be so out of the question as to be ludicrous. Even if he had a mind to do so, the executive's lawyers would protest and doubtless restrain him. The modern spirit is a hesitant one. Spontaneity has given way to cautious legalisms, and the age of heroes has been superseded by a cult of specialization. We have no more giants; only obedient ants.

Buffett was at least a bit larger. He was a throwback to the age—long, long past—when people had been willing to act without their lawyers. He sensed that these modern auxiliaries—not only the lawyers, but also the government-relations people, consultants, and myriad other advisers—did not merely help, they also controlled. And that was anathema to him. Succeed or fail, Buffett would permit no one else to set the agenda for him.

The beauty of his sweet solo act was that it worked. People responded to his openness, in addition to his considerable personal charm, and they were disarmed by his lack of contentiousness. Buffett did not confront Seidman; he turned him into mush.

"Larry," Buffett said finally, "if you look at it your way, you're right, there is a technical violation. If you look at it our way, there isn't. But we weren't out to do anything wrong. Now how do we solve it?"

The case dragged on through 1975. The SEC went fishing in a new area: Source Capital—yet another Buffett-and-Munger-controlled pool of funds. By now, Buffett was "sick to death" over his sundry complications.[29] If the nightmare of being under the lamp ever ended, he told the SEC, he yearned to simplify his affairs:

> So hopefully we would have the same businesses we have now, but less complications. I really don't like these complications. It seemed fairly simple while we were doing it, but not simple now.[30]

In December, Rickershauser, Buffett's lawyer, pleaded for an end, arguing that Buffett had done nothing to deserve such scrutiny. He trumpeted Buffett's unblemished record of preparing his own tax returns over three decades as a sort of contemporary object lesson on a par with Lincoln's log cabin.

> He has paid federal income taxes continuously since his paper-route earnings required them at age 14, aggregating several millions of dollars over that 30-year period, and his total deficiency assessments have been less than $200.[31]

In 1976—two years after the inquiry had begun—the SEC settled. The terms amounted to a slap on the wrist. The SEC formally charged that Blue Chip had purchased Wesco not merely as an investment, as it had disclosed, but also for the purpose of defeating the merger (which was true). It also alleged that Blue Chip had artificially propped up Wesco's market price over a three-week period. Blue Chip agreed not to do it again, without admitting or denying guilt, a common clause in such settlements. It also forked over $115,000 to certain Wesco shareholders that the SEC construed had been hurt by Blue Chip's trades.

The SEC did not take action against Buffett. But a few weeks later, it

named him to a blue-ribbon panel to study corporate disclosure practices. Possibly the agency was offering absolution. To say the least, it
was unusual treatment for a guy it had spent the previous two years
investigating.

Buffett got rid of, or simplified, his "complications" with the zeal of
a reformed sinner. He sold Blue Chip's interest in Source Capital
(which had doubled). He quit his sideline as a money manager for
FMC. He consolidated Wesco within Blue Chip (he would have
bought all of Wesco, but stopped at 80 percent at the request of Betty
Peters). And, after a further two-year hiatus, he went ahead and merged
Diversified into Berkshire.

Happily for Buffett, the merger formalized his union with Munger.
In exchange for his Diversified stock, Munger got 2 percent of the stock
in Berkshire. Also, Buffett named his pal vice chairman. Munger remained in Los Angeles, pursuing largely separate interests, and he was
modest about his role in Berkshire. "By a significant margin most of
the ideas come from Warren," he said. Yet for someone as insular as
Buffett, having the counsel of the brilliant Munger, who observed the
battle at a distance, was vital.

The merger also gave Berkshire a majority stake in Blue Chip
Stamps. In effect, Buffett had just one "pocket" left—Berkshire Hathaway. He had no portfolio on the side: virtually no personal investments.[32] But Berkshire, which he had rescued from the dead end of
textiles, was itself "personal."

In his first decade, Buffett had engineered a rise in Berkshire's net
worth from roughly $20 a share to $95. He had transformed the company, now unrecognizable as its former self, by acquiring an insurance
unit, a bank, a stock portfolio, and majority stakes in Blue Chip, See's,
and Wesco.

Another chief executive might have renamed the company to reflect
the changes—maybe "BH Corp." or "Berkshire Enterprises." But Buffett was not a changeling. He liked the name, which evoked the company's origins. Though an unsentimental man, he asked Ken Chace to
dig up the old directors' notes from the archives in New Bedford and
ship them to Omaha. As Buffett explained to the SEC, Berkshire was
something he intended never to sell.

> I just like it. Berkshire is something that I would be in the rest of my life.
> It is public, but it is almost like the family business now.[33]

Not long-term, but *the rest of his life*. His career—in a sense, his life—was subsumed in that one company. Everything he did, each investment, would add a stroke to that never-to-be-finished canvas. And no one could seize the brush from him, as Buffett had seized it from Seabury Stanton. By the late seventies, Buffett owned 43 percent of the stock, and Susie owned another 3 percent. To gain control of Berkshire and of its Blue Chip subsidiary, Buffett had invested $15.4 million. That was the equivalent of $32.45 per share of Berkshire.[34] And that was all the capital that Buffett would put into it. Any further refinement of that canvas—any rise in Berkshire's valuation, and any increase in Buffett's personal fortune—would flow from that investment of $32.45 a share, and from what he could do with it.

Chapter 10

WASHINGTON
REDUX

When Warren Buffett parachuted into her company, Katharine Graham was midway through the signal transformation of her life. Her father had purchased the *Washington Post*, the fifth newspaper in a five-paper town, out of bankruptcy, in 1933. Kay assumed control in 1963 when her brilliant, but ultimately deranged, husband put a shotgun to his temple. As little as anyone could prepare for such a blow, Graham seemed, more than most, at the mercy of events. The daughter of Eugene Meyer, a financier-cum-statesman and head of the Federal Reserve Board, and a worldly but indifferent mother, Graham grew up with the peculiar loneliness of the rich. She was raised in a world of governesses and private schools, and was accustomed to receiving replies to her letters from her mother's personal secretary.[1] As a young woman, Graham worked as a reporter, but had no expectation that the family paper would be hers to run.[2] With marriage, she turned to raising a family.

When she was catapulted to authority, she was shy, self-conscious, and painfully self-abasing. Her male colleagues were condescending,[3] and Graham herself proclaimed in an interview that, given the way the world worked, "a man would be better in this job than a woman."[4] She expected to be only an interim caretaker.[5] In fact, responsibility proved a tonic. The *Post*, at the time, was an intelligent but parochial newspa-

per. Graham hired Benjamin Bradlee, the Washington bureau chief of
Newsweek, to run the paper, and Bradlee, with significant support from
Graham, propelled the *Post* to the front ranks of American journalism.
In 1971, when the Post Co. was in the midst of an initial public stock
offering, Graham overrode her wobbly-kneed advisers and published
the Pentagon Papers, the government's secret history of the Vietnam
War, despite threats of indictment from the Nixon administration.[6]
(The U.S. government had already won a restraining order halting
publication in the *New York Times*, which had broken the story.) Then
Graham backed the *Post*'s investigation of Watergate, despite a challenge, presumably Nixon-instigated, to the Post Co.'s television li-
censes in Florida. When John N. Mitchell, Nixon's Attorney General,
observed with regard to a pending story, "Katie Graham is gonna get
her tit caught in a big fat wringer if that's published,"[7] Graham knew
that she had arrived.

But the second act of her metamorphosis had barely begun. Despite
its clout in political circles, the Post Co. was unimpressive as a business. Its flagship newspaper dominated the Washington market, yet its
profit margin was an uninspiring 10 percent. A like condition prevailed
at its television stations.

In 1971, when the Post had gone public, Graham had begun to shift
her attention toward the bottom line. But she had left financial matters
to her board chairman and adviser, the lawyer Fritz Beebe. As Graham
put it, "I sort of thought figures were for men." Then, in the spring of
1973, Beebe died. Graham now became the first woman chairman of a
Fortune 500 company. She gamely declared to security analysts that
she hoped to win a figurative Pulitzer Prize in management.[8] But the
world of Wall Street terrified her. As it happened, this was precisely
when Buffett began to buy her stock.

Graham had met Buffett once, through Charlie Peters of the *Washington Monthly*. Still, she had no idea who Buffett was or what he was
up to. Within the Post Co., the alarm was general. Kay's son Donald,
then working his way up the ranks, feared that the company was being
pursued by some "super-right-wing type from Nebraska."[9] Kay herself was petrified. She made inquiries about Buffett with publisher
friends—"stalked him like a dog circling a snake," according to Bradlee. This was unnecessary, because the Post had two classes of stock.
Only the Class B stock, which had very limited voting rights, traded

publicly. Control of the company rested in the A shares, which were owned by the Graham family. But Kay was new to the game. Peter Derow, senior vice president at the Post's *Newsweek* division, kept telling her, "Don't worry about it. You've got the A shares." But Graham was scared stiff. She'd say, "What is he up to? Someone is making a run for us!"

Buffett suspected that as a 10 percent shareholder he might ruffle some feathers. He wrote her a letter—"Dear Mrs. Graham . . ."—in which he recalled his escapades as a *Post* paperboy and disclaimed any hostile intent.[10] She took this to a couple of streetwise friends, André Meyer of Lazard Frères and Robert Abboud, a Chicago banker. Each warned that Buffett's charm could be a ruse, and recommended that she not go near him.

If anything, Graham relied too heavily on advisers. But in this case, she went with her instincts. She wrote to Buffett, suggesting that they get together, and when Graham was visiting the *Los Angeles Times*, Buffett drove up from his home in Laguna Beach. They spent what Graham recalled as a perfectly pleasant hour together. Buffett, sensing that she was apprehensive, offered to stop accumulating stock.[11] Though still uncertain about her suitor, Graham invited him to see the paper when he was in the East.

Warren and Susie checked into Washington's Madison Hotel, a block from the *Post*, during a tense time. The pressmen were in a slow-down, and cops and union men were squaring off in the streets. Buffett managed to borrow a black tie and scooted his wife to dinner *chez* Graham, where he sat between Barbara Bush and Jane Muskie. Then he waited for Graham to make a move.

But none came. Finally, Tom Murphy, the Capital Cities chairman and Buffett's pal, had lunch with Graham and suggested that she ought to invite Buffett onto her board. When Graham visited Buffett at Laguna, he was still trying to please. He bought an umbrella and beach chair—which got a big rise out of Buffett's family, who had never seen him near the water. Graham inched closer. She said, "Someday, I'd like you to be on the board." Buffett said, "Well, what are you waiting for?" When Buffett drove her back to Los Angeles, she said, "If you want to tell me something, do so, but do it gently. If people bark at me, I'm apt to curl up." Buffett did not need to be told.

Buffett became a director in the fall of 1974. The other directors—a clubby bunch including Graham relatives, Post executives, and Kay's friends—were wary of him. Quoting Derow, the *Newsweek* executive:

> Warren was an outsider from Omaha. He ponies up 10 percent of the company. Our reaction was, "How come we never heard of him?" It was a little scary. He was the first guy at the table who had bought his own seat.

Buffett, of course, knew this. He would tell the executives why he liked the Post Co. as an investment and how, in a personal sense, the paper was a homecoming for him. Like the new guy in the club, all he talked about was how thrilled he was to be there.

He signed his proxy over to Don Graham (letting Kay's son and heir cast Berkshire's votes)—an unusual show of faith in management. He also declared in writing that he expected Berkshire to keep its Post stock "permanently"—another of those phrases that would have mystified the modern portfolio manager.[12] In every way, Buffett intimated, as he had with Betty Peters, that he considered himself not just an investor but a partner.

And Buffett began to come to Washington often. The night before directors' meetings he would put up at Graham's stately Georgetown home. Bradlee, not exactly a rube, said, "We were stage-struck. We didn't know anybody who had that kind of dough."

> He seemed to be in awe of us, glamorized by us. And we were awed by him. For years all he wore was a blue suede jacket. Everybody used to shit on it. I think he wore it for that reason. At board meetings editors would come by and chat about stories. He really got off on that. He loved being involved. He liked the informal relationship that Kay and I had. Once, we were playing tennis and I drove her back into a fence. Warren said, "I have to admire anyone who drives his boss into a fence." He had a marvelous, contagious enthusiasm.

Post executives were used to thinking of themselves as journalists—doing the Lord's work, so to speak. Buffett began to sprinkle them with droplets of finance. One time, he popped into Derow's office and asked about *Newsweek*. Buffett gradually got around to explaining what *he* saw in the *Newsweek* franchise—and used the analogy of a hamburger chain, to keep it simple.

"By the time I finished, I understood it better," Derow said. "He was like a laser beam. He got you to focus. But he didn't make you feel as if you were stupid."

In particular, Buffett became a personal tutor to Graham. When he came to Washington, he would bring a stack of annual reports and take her through them, line by line. One day, Buffett sent her the back cover of a Walt Disney report, depicting a child asleep in a stroller. Buffett's note: "This is you after the 20th annual report." Some of her colleagues thought that Buffett was manipulating her, but Graham thought he made sense. He didn't tell her what to do. He advised, he counseled. The secret to his seduction was his patience. It seemed to exert a magnetic pull on her. And the more she got to know him, the more she liked his ideas.

Before long, Buffett made a major suggestion—that the Post buy back a big portion of its own stock. Graham thought this was crazy. If a company returned its capital, how could it grow? Buffett's point was that overall growth didn't matter—merely growth per share. It was like shrinking the number of slices in a pizza. If the shares could be retired cheaply—and Post stock was still quite cheap—there would be more cheese on every slice. Buffett took her through the math, penciling it out in the book-lined study in Georgetown.

When Graham was sold on the idea, she talked it up to other executives at the Post. They noticed that her vocabulary was becoming spiced with financial lingo. She would quote Buffett openly and, in the view of some, ad nauseam. She had an irritating way of responding to a suggestion from the staff by saying, "That's interesting—let's ask Warren."

A year after Buffett joined the board, Graham, who was eager to reduce the chronic overstaffing in the *Post* pressroom and to recapture control of it from the militant pressmen's union, decided to take a strike at the newspaper.[13] Some of the pressmen trashed the plant, and the strike turned bitter. (An infamous placard declared of Kay's late husband: "Phil Shot the Wrong Graham.") The *Post* put out a paper with the help of scabs; however, the second-place *Washington Star* began to steal its advertisers.

Graham feared that the *Post* would win the strike and lose the war. "What I needed," she said, "was someone I could rely on totally." That would be Buffett. He promised that he would monitor the business and warn her if he thought the strike was permanently jeopardizing the *Post*'s franchise—which was the *raison d'être* for his investment. He never did. After four months, the union was crushed, and the *Post* resumed its lead.

Later, Time Inc., which purchased the failing *Star*, asked the *Post* to consider a joint operating agreement, which would reduce costs and have the civic virtue of keeping Washington a two-paper town.* Under the formula proposed by Time, each company would take a designated share of the papers' combined profits.

Buffett strongly argued against it. In his view, the *Post*, which had 66 percent of the circulation in Washington, was on the verge of seizing the market, and had no need to make nice with number two. Largely because of Buffett,[14] Graham made a much tougher counteroffer, which the *Star* rejected. Soon after, the *Star* went out of business— creating a windfall for the *Post*.

Graham estimated that she talked to Buffett "maybe every other day or so, several times a week."[15] When Graham had to give a speech, which she found frightening,[16] she would call Omaha, and Buffett would deliver a perfectly metered response, off-the-cuff. She actually taped their conversations.

> He speaks in finished paragraphs. I'd say, "What?—Could you say that again?" He can't do it. It comes so fast he can't retrace it. It takes your breath away.

Don Danly, Buffett's high school pinball chum, was visiting Buffett in Omaha once when Graham called. She was worried about what *USA Today* could do to the *Post*, and he was consoling her. To Danly's amazement, she kept him on the phone for half an hour.

After Buffett had been on the board awhile, he began to push her to be more self-reliant. One time, she asked him to come to Washington to negotiate a swap of the *Post*'s television station in Washington, plus some cash, for a station in Detroit.

"No," Buffett told her. "You do it."

"Okay, tell me how much to give them," Graham said.

---

*The Newspaper Preservation Act of 1970 permits competing papers to combine the business side of their operations while retaining separate editorial staffs—if it can be shown to the Department of Justice that one of the papers may otherwise go under.

"No—you figure it out. You can do it."

But Buffett's influence was felt in virtually every major decision. In particular, he restrained Graham from jumping into the red-hot (and expensive) bidding wars for media properties. Graham, as a relative newcomer, was daunted by such media high-fliers as Tom Murphy, chairman of the quickly growing Capital Cities, and by Times Mirror, which seemed to be buying everything in sight. And she was sorely tempted to follow suit.[17] Buffett kept reminding her that it was okay *not* to spend the money.

When Barry Bingham, Sr., the Kentucky publisher, offered to sell the *Louisville Courier-Journal* and *Times* to the Post if Graham would match a bid by Gannett, she naturally put in a call to Buffett. He observed that the price was *awfully* high, but was careful not to give explicit advice.[18] In a subtle sense, he was more effective that way. The schoolmaster had trusted her; now the earnest pupil did not want to disappoint. "You have to know how *eager* Kay was," Don Graham said of the *Courier-Journal*. But Kay let it pass.

Another time, David Strassler, the investor who had once tried to buy Dempster Mill from Buffett, was pitching a cable company to the Post. He had dinner with Buffett and Graham in New York, and was impressed at how easily they worked together. But Strassler sensed that his mission was doomed.

"Kay had the hots for cable," he recalled. "She was sophisticated. She was thinking in strategic terms. But I said to myself, 'He won't let her pay these kind of numbers.'"

It should not be surprising that Graham began to rely on Buffett as more than just a business adviser. As a rich widow, she was mistrustful of potential suitors and somewhat cloistered. Her brittleness kept people at arm's length, as did her stiff, Brahmin enunciation. Charlie Peters, of the *Washington Monthly*, said, "I think Kay desperately needed a friend." She found Buffett unthreatening, and the two became intimate. Graham invited Buffett to her farm in Virginia and to her home on Martha's Vineyard. Buffett countered with invitations to Laguna Beach, and Graham began to attend meetings of Buffett's Ben Graham investors group.

The two of them had a certain playfulness, arising in part from their unlike backgrounds and levels of refinement. When Buffett talked Graham into visiting Omaha, he knew that she hadn't the faintest idea of where it was, and decided to poke some fun at her. When they got on the plane he asked her to draw a map of the United States, and to mark the location of Omaha. The map was so awful that he grabbed for it, intending to stash it as a keepsake, but Graham nimbly tore it to shreds.

Another time, when they landed at La Guardia, Graham was in a hurry to make a telephone call and asked if he had a dime. Buffett fished a quarter out of his pocket. Not wanting to waste the fifteen cents, he started outside to change it, like any other multimillionaire from Nebraska. Graham hollered, "Warren, give me the quarter!"

In Washington, which Buffett usually visited without his wife, he squired Graham around town. "Kay widened his circle enormously," according to the writer Geoffrey Cowan. Another friend said that "the Washington Post really changed his life. It changed whom he was exposed to." Suddenly, Warren Buffett of Omaha was mixing with the likes of Henry Kissinger. Liz Smith, the gossip columnist, reported that Buffett was the rage since emerging as "a frequent guest and adviser to the powerful Katharine Graham."[19] Smith added: "Washington society is agog because Mr. B. drinks Pepsi-Cola with his meals, no matter how chic the gathering." Buffett did not like splashy affairs, but he liked meeting bigwigs in the controlled setting of Graham's home.[20]

At one VIP dinner, a birthday party for Graham, Malcolm Forbes, the publisher–cum–cultural connoisseur, brought a fancy wine that had been bottled the year she was born, and that he intimated had cost him plenty.[21] When the waiter got to Buffett, the Pepsi drinker stopped him. "No thanks," he said, putting a hand over his glass. "I'll take the cash."

Graham told her cook to make hamburgers when Buffett was in town, and stocked her Manhattan apartment with Buffett's favorites—greasy peanuts and strawberry ice cream. "When he arrived," she said with reflexive snobbery, "it was only cheeseburgers and fried—what do you call them?—french fries, all of it doused with salt." Succumbing to the urge to refine, she got to him to try haricots verts and spruced up his wardrobe.

Buffett, on the other hand, took Graham to such cultural monuments as the Hathaway textile mill in New Bedford. "He wanted me to see it," Graham noted. She considered him her "closest friend" and relied on him for personal as well as business advice. Buffett also became a sort of uncle to Graham's kids. He was in Washington at least once a month and kept a change of clothes in the Graham guest room. Even Buffett's children were unsure what to make of it.

During an interview, Graham referred without prompting to the persistent rumors of a liaison. "I was still young enough"—fifty-seven when Buffett joined the board—"that it raised eyebrows." Tom Murphy called on Buffett, too, she said defensively. "If I used him it was sort of frowned on."

Buffett had an unusual number of woman friends—*Fortune* writer Carol Loomis, Ruth Muchemore, Barbara Morrow. Morrow thought him a "feminist," in the sense of treating women as people. "There is a sensitivity toward women," she said. Buffett had an aspect of the now so unfashionable chivalry. He detested coarseness and off-color jokes, though he did go in for a tactful variety of bedroom humor.*

Susie was very relaxed about Warren's having women friends. When someone called her attention to all the time that Warren was spending in Washington, Susie replied—Susie could say such things without blushing—that she wasn't interested in the form of things, but in the purity of your heart. (When the Buffetts were in Washington, both of them stayed at Graham's.)

But, by the mid-seventies, the Buffetts' lives had become somewhat disjointed. Susie had done so much catering to Warren; now, she told a friend, she wanted to arrange her own calendar.[22] She was active in a campaign to save a local high school, which was losing students due to racial problems. She also began to travel a bit by herself. She certainly had no interest in Warren's work. Peter, who was the last child at home, noticed that the household was getting pretty *loose*. Dad was often in Washington; Mom often seemed to be out. Peter was fixing a lot of his own dinners.

Buffett sensed that his wife needed a *Washington Post* in *her* life. At one point, referring to their nearly grown kids, he said, "Susie, you're like somebody who has lost his job after twenty-three years. Now what are you going to do?"[23]

Susie's dream was to be a chanteuse. This was no surprise to the

---

*One time in California, the Buffetts and Roy and Martha Tolles were strolling past a tourist shop that had a help-wanted sign next to some rather skimpy bikinis in the window. Buffett deadpanned, "I wonder if they need a fitter."

family, given her habit of traipsing around in song while Warren was working. Now that she had some free time, she worked out tunes with a local band, the Bob Edson Trio, and performed at some private parties. The prospect of going public unnerved her, but Warren pushed her, telling her that if she chickened out she'd regret it later.[24] In 1975, with the help of a friend, Eunie Denenberg, Susie overcame her fright and appeared for a run at the Steam Shed, a nightclub on the outskirts of Omaha.

After that, she took her lounge act to the French Café, a restaurant in Omaha's artsy cobblestone market district. The café was owned by a pair of well-traveled Omahans, Michael Harrison, a dancer, and Anthony Abbott, and was something of a cultural outpost. Susie had once used the café to host a benefit for Planned Parenthood (Charlton Heston turned up and ate nothing but caviar at $175 a pound). Another time, she staged a benefit for African relief—dressed, like her guests, in a billowing gingham dress, a bandanna, and bare feet.[25] In Omaha, it was considered odd, to say the least, for a fortyish housewife to take to the stage. But the town had known Warren's wife to be a free spirit before such things were popular.

At the French Café, Susie performed in a darkened stone cellar, looking slinky and sexy and glittering in sequins. She was prettier than when she had gotten married—high cheekbones, a great bob of brown hair, and big searching eyes. Her speaking voice was a bit thin, but when she sang it had a throaty character. She did stylized jazz and popular tunes, such as the melancholy Stephen Sondheim number "Send in the Clowns." Her first run lasted six weeks. She drew good crowds, and the audiences were responsive. Kent Bellows, an Omaha artist, said, "Susie was a cabaret singer—all passion and nuance. I remember seeing Warren there one night. Seeing the expression on his face. He was digging it."

When Susie was onstage, Buffett would watch with a beatific expression, as if overcome by rapture. He told a friend, "When Susie sings, it is so beautiful I can't breathe."[26]

Buffett would make similar doe-eyed remarks about their offstage lives. He often commented that he had been unhappy until he had met Susie, or that he wouldn't have turned out well without her.[27] As a couple, they did not fit a normal pattern. Though their interests, and increasingly their schedules, were separate, Buffett remained extremely attached to her. Even now, she would nestle next to him and take his hand in public as though they were teenagers. Knowing that she was his muse, she seemed incapable of saying no to him.[28]

Buffett's companionship with Kay Graham contrasted markedly. She depended on *him*, owing to her lack of financial experience, and also to her insecurity. And Buffett was helpful to her, as he was, if on a lesser scale, with other colleagues. He was intent on making a profit in the Post Co., of course, but that hardly diminishes the fact that he was animated by Graham, and that he was personally quite generous with her.

Stan Lipsey, the publisher, observed Buffett and Graham together on a trip to Niagara Falls. "I don't know the answer," Lipsey said, "but I didn't get the vibes you get from people who are sleeping together. Kay is very powerful, and also very shy. Nine hundred and ninety-nine out of one thousand people would think twice about what they are saying to her. Warren didn't. And they became confidants."

It is doubtful that either "answer" would explain why Buffett thrived in the relationship. The annual reports that he brought her probably had more to do with it. Buffett delighted in playing the teacher, as he had in his letters to his partners, and Graham was a very intriguing, very receptive student. A Post director said, "It was kind of goofy. She would have these pre-meeting dinners. And we'd all leave. And Warren wouldn't go. I never saw anything sexual about it."

What executives did see was that the Buffett-Graham alliance had a far-reaching impact on the business, and ultimately on Buffett's investment. It was impossible to get Graham to open her checkbook, a fact that they blamed, quite rightly, on Buffett. Joel Chaseman, the head of broadcasting, had a chance to buy a television station in Orlando, before the city's full explosion as a mecca for tourists, for $120 million. "It was a hell of a buy," he noted. "You could already tell it would be a great market. But somewhere in the murk and mist of the upper levels of the corporation it got turned down."

Murk and mist? Graham had called Buffett, who said it was overpriced.[29]

The litany of such forgone chances drove Post executives to despair. Buffett was cool to cellular and to cable TV because they required a lot of capital.[30] (The reason he had invested in the Post was that its publishing and television properties—as distinct from, say, an airline—pro-

duced *free* cash flow. The profits were not sucked back into the business.) He was skeptical of start-ups and of new technology because they
were, well, *new*. They'd be like switching from hamburgers to foreign
foods.

If Buffett couldn't *see* a business, he wasn't comfortable with it. It
wasn't enough for him to get an expert's assurance on a new project,
which is what the typical executive relies on. If *he* didn't understand a
venture—he, *personally*—he felt that he'd be speculating. And Buffett
wouldn't do that.

Graham's dependence on Buffett caused the Post to miss some opportunities. Tom Murphy, the self-assured CEO of Cap Cities, also
conferred with Buffett, but adopted his suggestions selectively. But
Graham, who presided over a revolving door in the executive suite,
went to Buffett even on matters that were outside his expertise. And
Buffett's conservatism came to permeate the board.

Chaseman, who before joining the Post had launched the all-news
format at WINS radio in New York, proposed in the late seventies that
the Post start an all-news cable program. Ted Turner was developing
the same idea. At the Post it never got past the first board meeting. "I
don't think they were prepared to buy *anything*. It was the antithesis of
an entrepreneurial company," Chaseman said. He was so frustrated
that he tried to spin off the Post's broadcasting unit into a separate company. Mark Meagher, the Post's president, wrote a long letter when *he*
resigned, urging that the Post go private—since, as he saw it, there was
no point in such a stodgy company holding public capital. Richard
Simmons, who replaced Meagher, dryly remarked after yet another
proposal had been killed, "The sage of Omaha has spoken again."[31]

The funny thing was, the Post executives didn't really dispute Buffett's reasoning. Meagher, in a comment that is typical of the bunch,
says, "I didn't disagree. Prices *were* high." Also, on a personal level, the
executives found Buffett impossible to dislike. Simmons, like some of
the others, made a pilgrimage to Omaha, a trip that invariably included a steak dinner, a leisurely tour of Buffett's childhood haunts,
and an earful of his wisdom.

Buffett didn't say much during the Post's board meetings. But occasionally a comment would spark him. At one meeting, Jeffrey Epstein,
a young M.B.A. who was scouting for new fields of investment, gave an
overview of what consumers were spending in each part of the media

and entertainment industry. His figure for home entertainment was $5 billion.

Buffett's bushy eyebrows went up about three feet. "That $5 billion is a pretty interesting number," he noted. "That means if there are twenty million teenagers in the United States they are all spending $20 every month on video." That was how his mind worked: numbers, numbers. It was suddenly clear that Epstein's figure, if true, was unsustainable. Needless to say, the Post did not go into video.*

It is striking how little the Post did do during Buffett's tenure on the board. Over eleven years, it started and folded a sports magazine; it bought a newspaper in Washington state and sold one in Trenton; and it acquired small interests in cellular phones and other areas, some of which were subsequently sold. But 98 percent of the profits derived, as before, from the *Washington Post, Newsweek,* and four television stations.

Meanwhile, its revenue grew at a solid but unspectacular rate of 12 percent a year. The only dramatic change was in the level of profitability. In 1974, the company earned an operating profit of ten cents for each dollar of sales; in 1985, the figure was nineteen cents. Similarly, the return on equity doubled.

Of course, the *Post* would have won the newspaper war in Washington without Buffett. And he had little to do with the doubling of profit margins at its television stations.

His main contribution came after the profits had been earned. Buffett gave the Grahams a way of thinking about the business that was oriented to the shareholders, and at a time when media companies were devoted to acquiring empires. He insistently reminded them—as he had Ken Chace, so many years earlier, outside the textile mill—that size was not the goal; the return to shareholders was. Opportunities were missed, but he saved the Post from the business error that is truly a tragic error—throwing the profits from a good business into a bad one.

Instead, at Buffett's urging, the Post used its excess cash to retire 7.5 million of its own shares, or about 40 percent of the total. Net profits grew seven times over, but the earnings *per share*—the cheese on each slice—grew by a factor of ten.

---

*The figure was based on shipments to stores—which vastly overstated actual purchases. Within a year, Atari, the kingpin of video, was rocked by losses and the industry suffered a shakeout.

Of course, media companies in general were prospering in those years. But by the single yardstick that mattered to Buffett—translating the profits into rewards for the investors—the Post outclassed the field.

Consider that over those eleven years, 1974 to 1985, the Post earned an extraordinary average of twenty-three cents for each dollar of the shareholders' capital. Cap Cities and Times Mirror each earned a none too shabby, but inferior, nineteen cents.

The Post's stock rose at the astounding compound rate of 35 percent a year. With dividends, the total return was 37 percent a year. Cap Cities did a heroic 32 percent, and Times Mirror a still-impressive 24 percent. But the Post was better. And by the end of 1985, when Buffett would leave the board, Berkshire's $10 million investment would be worth $205 million.

Shortly after Buffett joined the Post's board, he began to renew his interest in another old corporate flame, also in Washington and also from his youth. GEICO had been a tiny company when Buffett, while at Columbia, had taken the train to Washington and knocked on its door. In the ensuing years, it grew dramatically. Lorimer Davidson, who had patiently taken Buffett's questions that long-past Saturday, rose to chief executive, and GEICO became one of the biggest auto insurers in the country.

However, by the early seventies, Davidson had retired and GEICO had new management, led by Ralph C. Peck. The climate had also changed; insurers were being battered by new no-fault laws and rising inflation. Peck, trying to grow his way out of such problems, relaxed the company's historic policy of accepting only the lowest-risk drivers—even while maintaining its generally low prices.[32] Inevitably, premium volume soared and the cash poured in.

For a while, all seemed rosy. Alas, GEICO's higher-risk drivers, not surprisingly, were filing more claims. Moreover, inflation was raising the cost of fixing the bodies and cars that GEICO was insuring.

To compound the problem, GEICO's management didn't adequately reserve for losses. For a critical fifteen months in 1974 and 1975, the company denied, belittled, or lied about the problem—both to Wall Street and to itself.[33] Lorimer Davidson, still on the board, bitterly complained as the company was wrecked. But even he did not suspect how bad it was.

We found out when the board retained an independent actuarial firm. We got the report the day before Christmas, 1975. It was some Christmas present. We had $50 million to make up—to our horror—and we didn't have the money.

Early in 1976, GEICO announced a staggering $126 million loss for the previous year. As recently as 1974, the stock had hit a high of 42. Now it was quoted at 4⅞.

Buffett had long since sold his small holding in GEICO, but he had harbored a secret desire to revisit the company in a big way, just as he had the *Washington Post*.[34] For someone so rational, Buffett was sentimental about his past (though not so misty-eyed as to invest in GEICO when the stock was dear). But now, GEICO was cheap. What's more, it was in deep trouble. And Ben Graham, who had been chairman of GEICO when Buffett had been at Columbia, still had his savings in it. Helping to salvage the company would be a sort of double fantasy: following in Graham's footsteps and rescuing his company.

Graham was then living quietly and modestly with his mistress, Malou, part of the year in La Jolla and part in Aix-en-Provence. At his eightieth-birthday party, when his family gathered in La Jolla, he movingly looked back on his life, without mentioning his career on Wall Street. He spoke of the pleasure he had gotten from beauty, literature, and art, and also from varied female companions, and recalled, as a boy, seeing Mark Twain in *his* later years, "resplendent in his white suit and curly white hair."[35] However, Graham had not lost interest in stocks. He had an account in La Jolla, and though he rarely traded, the father of security analysis would go to his broker's and sit unobtrusively at a corner desk, reading his beloved Standard & Poor's. A broker who visited Graham found a book of Greek on his desk and a Rodin sculpture in the living room.[36]

At about the time of GEICO's troubles, Graham asked Buffett to coauthor a revised edition of *The Intelligent Investor*. They corresponded, but Buffett found that he and his teacher had some basic disagreements. Buffett wanted a section on how to identify "great businesses" (such as See's Candy); Graham didn't think the average reader could do it. Also, Graham recommended a ceiling of 75 percent of one's assets in stocks; the gamer Buffett was willing to invest his whole kitty if prices were right.[37] Buffett felt so strongly that he gave up being Graham's coauthor and instead was simply acknowledged inside the book as a "collaborator."

Ironically, no stock was as suggestive of their philosophical rift as GEICO. Graham would have said that it lacked a margin for safety—which, given that the company was on the verge of failure, it certainly did. Buffett sensed an opportunity if the management could be righted, and he was following its drama closely.

In April 1976, when GEICO held its annual meeting, four hundred shareholders jammed into the Washington Statler Hilton, where they all but hooted the officers off the premises.[38] Within a month, Peck was booted out, and John J. Byrne, Jr., a forty-three-year-old veteran of Travelers, was tapped to succeed him. Byrne moved with exceptional force. In New Jersey, he visited James J. Sheeran, the state insurance commissioner, to demand a rate increase. When it was clear that Byrne was getting nowhere, he pulled a paper from his pocket, slammed it on Sheeran's desk, and said, "Here's your fucking license. We are no longer a citizen of the state of New Jersey." Then he summarily fired seven hundred employees and notified 300,000 policyholders in the state to find another insurer.

Nationwide, Byrne closed one hundred offices and cut the workforce nearly in half.[39] But it wasn't enough. The insurance superintendent in Washington, D.C., was threatening to shut him down unless GEICO could get other insurers to pick up a portion of its policies (providing what is known as reinsurance). Byrne appeared to have gotten their okay, but early in July, State Farm, the industry leader, backed out on him, as did Travelers.[40]

GEICO's fortunes were now at a low. Buffett was *acutely* interested in getting involved—though, as usual, he had someone else smooth his entree. Kay Graham, doing his bidding, called Byrne and said, "I have a houseguest I'd like you to meet." Byrne said some other time. Then Byrne got a call from Lorimer Davidson, GEICO's elder statesman, who asked if it was true that Byrne had snubbed Warren Buffett. Hearing that he had, Davidson snapped, "How can you be so dumb? Get your ass down there."

Byrne showed up at the Graham mansion in July, the night before a Post board meeting. GEICO's stock was at 2.* This once seemingly

---

*For comparison with current prices, as of 1994 GEICO had split five-for-one.

invincible company was on the brink of becoming the biggest failed insurer ever—in Buffett's words, "the Titanic of the insurance world."[41]

As Buffett led Byrne to the stately, high-ceilinged library, he had an eerie recollection of when he had banged on GEICO's door twenty-five years earlier and been led by a janitor to Lorimer Davidson. Though his circumstances were vastly changed, his modus operandi was not. Once more, he was eager to learn all he could about GEICO. As the ruddy-faced Byrne recalled, Buffett pumped him for hours.

> We talked to maybe 2:00, 3:00 A.M. He wanted to know the things I would do. What did I think of our ability to survive? I remember we talked late at night about families, other stuff. But mostly the conversation was GEICO. I'm sure I did 80 percent of the talking.

There was little Byrne could tell Buffett that he didn't already know. GEICO had the same low-cost method of operation (based on not having sales agents) that had always given it an edge. In rough terms, GEICO spent fifteen cents of each premium dollar on expenses, whereas other insurers spent an average of twenty-four cents.[42] This enabled GEICO to charge less, and thus be more selective about choosing customers. In recent years, of course, GEICO had abandoned this surefire formula. But its underlying cost advantage was intact. Buffett figured that if it survived the present crisis, its profitability would return.

Buffett's genius was to see this even when GEICO was in total chaos and on the verge of bankruptcy. Like American Express in the sixties, it was "a magnificent business going through a time of trouble."[43] And even in that troubled time, he could envision the storm's passing.

On this evening, Buffett wanted to take the measure of Byrne personally. And Byrne impressed him. He spoke like an owner as distinct from a manager or bureaucrat. He was decisive and energetic, as the crisis required. Perhaps he was too volatile to lead the troops in peace. But as a wartime general, Buffett thought him a brilliant choice.

> I didn't ask, "How long is it going to take, Jack?" In the end, you can't predict. [But] Jack clearly understood the dimensions of the problem.[44]

Somehow, Byrne would get it done. And if he did, the stock could prove to be a tremendous bargain—maybe even better than that.

Buffett got up a few hours after Byrne left and called Ronald Gutman, his broker at Goldman Sachs. He bought 500,000 shares at 2⅛ and left a standing order for shares "in the multimillions."[45] At the Post board meeting, a light-headed Buffett confessed, "I've just invested in something that might go under. I could lose the entire investment next week." But once he had started it was not in his nature to stop. Berkshire quickly invested more than $4 million in GEICO stock.

Byrne said later, "That night at Kay's was the turning point." But GEICO was far from out of the woods. It needed, first, to convince the regulators to give it time, and second, to persuade competitors to provide it with reinsurance and thus limit GEICO's exposure to losses.

Buffett took a piece of the reinsurance for Berkshire, and also paid a call on Maximilian Wallach, the D.C. insurance superintendent.[46] In essence, Buffett argued that if Berkshire thought enough of GEICO's future to stake a few million bucks on it, maybe Wallach shouldn't be so quick to close it down.

Byrne, meanwhile, got other insurers to agree to take the reinsurance—but only with a big "if." As part of the deal, GEICO had to raise new capital. Byrne went to eight firms on Wall Street and was bounced out of every one. In desperation, he turned to Salomon Brothers, a still-smallish trading firm.

John Gutfreund, Salomon's blunt-spoken second-in-command, had already rejected GEICO. However, a junior research analyst named Michael Frinquelli had invited Byrne to give a presentation to Salomon over lunch. Since Byrne was going to be in the building anyway, Gutfreund agreed to let him come by his office when he was done.

When Byrne sat down, Gutfreund removed his cigar and gave him a pouting sneer. "I don't know who'd ever buy that fucking reinsurance treaty you're trying to sell," Gutfreund said.

Byrne, answering in kind, replied, "You don't know any fucking thing you're talking about."[47]

Impressed with this display of virility, Gutfreund showed Byrne the door and told Frinquelli, the Salomon analyst, to research GEICO and write up a recommendation. Frinquelli concluded that GEICO could be saved, and *ought* to be saved. If restored to health, he said, it would be valuable to policyholders and profitable for investors. Gutfreund also was reassured by the news of Buffett's investment.[48]

In August, Gutfreund agreed to underwrite a $76 million offering of

GEICO preferred. This was a gutsy move. GEICO was thought to be
so risky that no other firm would join in a syndicate, as usually occurs,
meaning that if the offering failed, Salomon would be on the hook for
the entire $76 million.

When a lawyer on the deal pestered the bankers over some detail,
Gutfreund snapped, "What are *you* worried about? It's only your job.
It's our *money*."[49] In November, days before the offering, it appeared
that Salomon would take a major loss.[50]

Shortly before the underwriting, Buffett told Gutfreund that he'd be
willing to take the entire allotment—and named his price.[51] Byrne
wanted to sell it at $10.50 a share, but Gutfreund, knowing Buffett's
ceiling, insisted on $9.20. He wouldn't budge—not by a penny. Buffett
was his backup.

The offering turned out to be a hit. Buffett took 25 percent of it, giving Berkshire a total investment of $23 million. Thanks to a curious
Catch-22, the investment, once made, was no longer risky—because
the fact of the added capital took GEICO out of peril. In Byrne's view,
the hero of the rescue was Gutfreund, who had stepped up with capital
when no one else would.[52] Buffett also was impressed with him. Gutfreund evidently was his kind of investment banker.

Within six months, GEICO rose to 8⅛—a quadrupling. That was
only a faint indication of its potential. Over the next few years, Berkshire doubled its stake, making Buffett the controlling investor.
GEICO seemed to go through a Buffett mold—Buffett had that effect
on companies. GEICO, like the Washington Post, repurchased its own
shares; GEICO's boss, too, made a habit of calling on Buffett. It was
Buffett-ized. Byrne was an experienced pro, but his business relationship with Buffett was not so very different from Kay Graham's. Quoting
Byrne:

> I'd ask him all kinds of things. He showed me sensible ways to finance.
> He was generous with his time. But he never—*ever*—made suggestions.
> Warren figured out a long time ago that he could make a lot more
> money for Berkshire by being a benevolent shareholder. This guy made
> a lot of money by backing up the truck.

Once a year, Buffett would do a Q&A with GEICO's executives.
Onstage, he was a natural. He had the Casey Stengel technique of

avoiding overliteralness by treating questions as general prompts. He would segue into a little story, which usually had an investment moral, but which he told in an utterly simple style. He was informal, yet picked his words with exquisite precision. You couldn't not be drawn in.

Byrne swears that people at GEICO canceled vacations so as not to miss the show. One time, Buffett said an investor should approach the stock market as if he had a lifetime punch card. Every time he bought a stock he punched a hole. When the card had twenty holes he was done—no more investing for life. Obviously, the investor would filter out every idea but the best. Lou Simpson, who was managing GEICO's portfolio, said this parable had a profound impact on him.

Buffett, in fact, had this punch-for-life conviction in GEICO, and went out of his way to let Byrne know it, both privately and in Berkshire's published reports. In an era when managers were increasingly under the gun to raise their stock or face a takeover, Buffett wanted Byrne to manage for the long term, and emphasized that he *wouldn't* sell him out.

This was put to a test when a Fortune 500 company made a serious bid to acquire GEICO. Byrne called Buffett and asked what he thought. Buffett said, "It's up to you." Byrne said, "Oh, come *on*—you gotta give me more than that." Buffett said nothing, but agreed to accompany Byrne to a late-night bargaining session at the Waldorf-Astoria, in New York.

The suitor and his bankers naturally addressed themselves to Buffett, the controlling stockholder. Buffett said, "You're talking to the wrong guy. He [Byrne] is the one you have to convince." Byrne took Buffett aside and pleaded, "At least whisper a *price* in my ear." Buffett stayed mum.

"It was amazing," Byrne said. "We were talking a billion dollars or so. He left it in my hands."

Finally, Byrne named a price that was out of the buyer's range, and the talks ended. That was surely the outcome that Buffett, who figured that GEICO's best days were still ahead, had wanted. So why had he played around? "It's hard to know what's going on in Warren's mind," Byrne admitted.

No doubt, Buffett wanted Byrne to know that he trusted him. And he must have guessed that if he showed his faith, Byrne would not want to let him down. One could say that Buffett was lucky, except that he got lucky too often.

Reminiscing on the GEICO roller coaster, Walter Schloss, Buffett's buddy from Graham-Newman, said the entire saga "was pathetic in a way. Some people became millionaires, some didn't benefit at all, and others went broke."[53] Leo Goodwin, Jr., the son of GEICO's founder, bailed out at the low, a bankrupt. And Ben Graham kept his GEICO to the bottom. In September 1976, just before the bailout was completed, Graham died at his home in France. He was eighty-two.

After Graham's death, commentators often remarked on Buffett's departure from Graham's methodology. Quite obviously, Buffett evolved. He was influenced by Charlie Munger and by the writer-investor Philip Fisher, each of whom stressed good, well-managed companies as distinct from statistically cheap ones.[54] And he was influenced by his own experience.

Buffett analyzed companies more subjectively than Graham, and he found "intrinsic value" in companies, such as See's Candy, that Graham would not have touched. But these deviations tend to obscure a larger fidelity. The very idea that a stock had an "intrinsic" worth, independent of the tape, Buffett got from Ben Graham. Indeed, it is nearly impossible to imagine Buffett's quitting the partnership at the height of the Go-Go years, or jumping back in during the 1974 market depression, had he not read Graham's liberating parable of Mr. Market. Buffett's eulogy for Graham, written for the *Financial Analysts Journal*, stressed, precisely, the *endurance* of Graham's approach:

> In an area where much looks foolish within weeks or months after publication, Ben's principles have remained sound—their value often enhanced and better understood in the wake of financial storms that demolished flimsier intellectual structures.[55]

Some years later, Buffett admitted that the stocks he was buying were entirely different from those that Graham would buy. What he had retained from Graham was "the proper temperamental set"—that is, the principle of buying value, the conservatism embedded in Graham's margin of safety principle, and the attitude of detachment from the daily market gyrations.[56]

Buffett did not stop thinking of himself as one of Graham's followers, nor did he lose his personal feeling for the teacher who had treated him with an "open-ended, no-scores-kept generosity."[57] Much later, when Buffett was speaking to the author about Buffett's own career, he remarked with unmistakable affection: "The best thing I did was to choose the right heroes. It all comes from Graham." When the author mentioned that he had spoken to some of Graham's children, Buffett's voice suddenly broke. "I wish you could talk to Graham," he replied.

Chapter 11

PRESS LORD

A few days before Christmas, 1976, Buffett met with Kay Graham, her son Donald, and Mark Meagher, president of the Post newspaper division, in the *Newsweek* offices in New York. A party was going on at *Newsweek*. The Post directors retreated to a private room and ushered in a visitor—Vincent Manno, a newspaper broker.[1] Manno was hoping to interest the Post in making a bid for the *Buffalo Evening News*. Afternoon papers were a dying breed, but the *Evening News* had thrived, owing to its strong reputation and to Buffalo's demographics. In blue-collar Buffalo, people rose early and did not read a paper until after work.

The *Evening News* also had several negatives. It did not publish on Sundays—the day readers tended to linger over their paper and, increasingly, the day most sought after by advertisers. Buffalo, a rusting steel town, was itself considered a negative—too old and cold. Worst of all, the paper's employees were represented by a total of thirteen unions that had won increasingly good contracts; of 131 newspapers represented by the Newspaper Guild, employees at the *Evening News* had the seventh-highest pay.[2]

For all that, the *Evening News* was precisely the dominant, big-city paper of Buffett's dreams. It reached a higher percentage of local households than any other big-city daily in the country.[3] And Buffalo was a city where habits died hard. Most of its people were *from* Buffalo, and had grown up reading the *Evening News*. Despite its reputation as a dying city, Buffett knew that its stable population was a plus. What's more, he was hungry—not to advise a newspaper owner, but to be one. He wanted Graham to know in advance: if the Post didn't buy the *Buffalo Evening News*, then Warren Buffett might.[4]

Founded in 1880, the *Evening News*, which was establishment and Republican, had been run by the Butler family, which also owned a local television station and a fortune in American Airlines stock. In recent decades, the proprietor had been Kate Robinson Butler, a grande dame who traveled with her poodle in a Rolls-Royce. Butler had built a lavish printing plant, rimmed with distinctly nonnative tropical plants, and had gone to similar expense to avoid trouble with unions.[5] Employees who had once tied the papers by hand had continued at their posts after the work was automated. As papers came off the runway, the workers would pass their hands over the conveyors, as if offering a sacrament. They were known as "blessers."[6] But the family's stewardship had ended with Butler's death, in 1974. Now the paper was up for sale by her estate.

After the meeting at *Newsweek*, Graham concluded that the Post, having just crushed a strike, would be unwelcome in such a union town. The Tribune Co. of Chicago similarly decided not to bid.[7] Manno, the broker, cut the asking price from $40 million to $35 million. Shortly after, he got a call from Buffett.

"Do you work on Saturdays?" Buffett inquired.

Manno asked if it was important.

"I think you'll consider it important."[8]

Buffett and Munger arrived at Manno's home, in the quaint community of Weston, Connecticut, the first Saturday after New Year's Day, 1977. They had lunch at Manno's club, which was warmed by a blazing fire. When they got back to the house, Buffett cut to the chase. Bidding on behalf of Blue Chip Stamps,* he offered $30 million for the *Evening News*. Manno demurred. Buffett raised the bid to $32 million. Still no dice.

Buffett and Munger left the room. Their offer was extraordinarily

---

*At the time, Blue Chip had more free cash than Berkshire did. Blue Chip was already controlled by Berkshire, and it would soon become a majority-controlled subsidiary of it.

high, relative to the paper's meager profits. The *Evening News* had earned only $1.7 million, pretax, in 1976. But Buffett knew that it was capable of earning more. He knew that in city after city, strong papers had gotten stronger while weaker ones had floundered or failed. And the *Evening News* virtually owned the town. It had twice the daily circulation of its morning competitor, the *Buffalo Courier-Express*, and 75 percent more advertising revenue.[9]

When Buffett and Munger returned, a moment later, Munger scribbled out a formal offer of $32.5 million on a single sheet of yellow legal paper. That might do, Manno said.[10]

Directly, an omen arrived in the form of the worst snowstorm in Buffalo's history. When Buffett and Munger arrived to iron out a contract, the city was still digging out. Munger was uneasy—the *Evening News*, after all, was their biggest purchase by far. Touring the extravagant printing plant, Munger snapped, "Why does a newspaper need a *palace* to publish in?"[11] Buffett jokingly dubbed it Taj Mahal East. But the *Evening News* was a big step for him. It was not a stock-market investment but a business owned in entire. Buffett would not have Kay Graham to take the punches for him; he would be personally on the line.

Even before the sale closed, Buffett seemed to have a strategy in mind for the paper. When he introduced himself to Murray Light, the chain-smoking, Brooklyn-born managing editor, Buffett asked, "How do you feel about a Sunday paper?" Light said he had been urging the publisher to start one for years. Buffett hid his cards, but Light sensed that he agreed.

After the closing, Light threw a welcoming party for Buffett at his home. A gaggle of employees approached the new owner, standing in the backyard in the warm light of spring. Buffett remarked, "News happens twenty-four hours a day, seven days a week"—an unmistakable clue that he was thinking of expanding to Sundays.

Rumor had it that the *Evening News* had refrained from publishing on Sundays because of a tacit agreement between the Butlers and the Conners family—owners of the rival *Courier-Express*. The latter paper was older (the *Express* had once been owned by Mark Twain),[12] more liberal, and of marginal to no profitability. Its Sunday paper was its life-blood, as was evident from the two newspapers' respective circulations:[13]

EVENING NEWS	DAILY COURIER-EXPRESS	SUNDAY COURIER-EXPRESS
268,000	123,000	270,000

The advertising numbers told a similar tale. The *Evening News* out-sold the *Courier-Express* during the week by a four-to-one margin.[14] Only the latter's Sunday paper kept it in business.

Buffett and Munger thought this balance was unstable. Without a Sunday edition, they believed, the *Evening News* eventually would lose its dominant franchise and possibly, in time, go under. That summer, the nearby *Toronto Daily Star* announced that it would start a Sunday paper. As Buffett knew, in addition to the *Evening News*, only the *Cincinnati Post*, the *Cleveland Press*, and the *New York Post*—dinosaurs all—remained as big-city dailies without a Sunday edition.[15] Dashing off a note to Munger, he humorously warned that they should not be the last.

> Susie used to say, about my crew cut, that she didn't mind my being the next-to-the-last fellow in the country with a crew cut, but she had strong objections to my being the absolute last. I think our course of action in Buffalo should be obvious.[16]

Soon after, Buffett, who held the position of chairman at the *Evening News*, told Murray Light to design a Sunday paper—pronto. Light set up a special task force, and Buffett would drop in on them every month or so. Quoting Light:

> I'd see my colleagues reach into their jackets to pull out facts and figures which had been forwarded to Warren's office. When they faltered, Warren would interject and fill in the blanks. He knew more about the reports than the guys who had written them.

Buffett was on one of his highs, helping to design a newspaper, getting involved with ad rates, promotional schemes, pricing. He dashed off a note to a certain publisher friend: "Kay, I'm having so much fun with this it is sinful."[17]

However, people in Buffalo were afraid that the depressed local economy would not be able to support two papers in a head-on clash. As the November start-up neared, some stores, partly for civic reasons, made plans to advertise in both Sunday papers. Keith Alford, who ran a department store, said, "Nobody wanted to lose a paper—from an advertising standpoint or a news standpoint." According to Ray Hill, the Newspaper Guild representative and an *Evening News* columnist, "We knew the time had come—one or the other paper would be out of business."

The *Courier-Express* knew it too. Two weeks before the fateful Sunday, it launched a surprise attack, suing the *Evening News* for violating the Sherman Anti-Trust Act. Boldly, it demanded a preliminary injunction to handcuff the new Sunday edition before its scheduled November 13 debut.

The suit charged the *Evening News* with classic monopolist behavior. It alleged that Buffett was planning to use his strength during the week to subsidize a money-losing paper on Sunday—analogous to a chain store cutting prices in the one locale that is across the street from a mom-and-pop competitor.

> Mr. Buffett's Evening News [is] engaged in . . . a concerted effort to use its monopoly power to eliminate the Courier as a competitor in Buffalo.[18]

The evidence was said to include the *Evening News*'s plan to sell seven papers for the price of six during a five-week promotional period, and its intention to sell the Sunday paper for only thirty cents. The *Courier-Express*, like papers in Syracuse, Rochester, Albany, and Binghamton, charged fifty cents.

Buffett flatly disputed the charge. The *Evening News*, he asserted, fully intended to earn a profit on Sunday. He argued that a new edition would *promote* competition, not inhibit it, and made the obvious point that the *Evening News* had as much right to publish on Sunday as anyone, regardless of its effect.[19] Put differently, it was not Buffett's job to keep a competitor in business. But he had been badly caught off guard.

Transcripts of the legal papers were printed verbatim in the *Courier-Express*, which treated its lawsuit as the story of the century. Also, Frederick Furth, the *Courier-Express*'s flamboyant San Francisco litigator, aroused public opinion against the out-of-town Buffett, casting him as a carpetbagger out to wreck a local institution.

The law required the *Courier-Express* to show that its rival intended to destroy it. Certain business practices, such as pricing below cost, were considered unfair, and might weigh in the *Courier-Express*'s favor, but the line between merely competitive tactics and illegal ones was fuzzy. The key question was whether the *Evening News* had an *intent* to monopolize.

As Furth understood, the *Courier-Express* needed a villain in whom the evil intent could be personified. Warren Buffett—"Big Brother from Omaha," as Furth referred to him in court[20]—was his ace in the hole. The guts of his case were that Buffett was a numbers-crunching millionaire who had no concern for Buffalo, and who was intent on driving the *Courier-Express* out of business to enhance the value of Buffett's own paper.

Buffett answered in personal terms. As a prelude to appearing in court, he filed an affidavit citing his grandfather's and father's associations with newspapers, his background as a paperboy, the *Sun*'s Pulitzer:

> It is much more than just a business to me. I want to achieve business success in newspapers but will be unhappy unless it is accompanied by journalistic success.[21]

On November 4, 1977, as a hard rain came whipping in from Lake Erie, Buffett took the stand in the federal courthouse. The gallery was packed with *Courier-Express* employees and their family members, who saw the hearing as a last chance to keep their livelihoods, and saw Buffett as a viper. Furth hammered away at him. Buffett replied evenly, separating out the needles that were intended to bait him and responding with facts, facts, facts. He was like a human backboard; nothing riled him.

FURTH: Now, at the time that Blue Chip Stamp Company decided to acquire the *News*, you made an analysis, did you not, of the profit and loss of the *News*?

BUFFETT: I made a mental analysis of the position of the *Buffalo News*, its publishing strengths and weaknesses, its past history of earnings, its future potential, the price paid for newspapers, and other markets. There were a lot of variables that went into the calculation.

FURTH: Well, are you saying you didn't do a written analysis, you simply massaged the figures, as the current financial term, is that—

BUFFETT: That is your term. I don't think I massaged them at all. I tried to analyze the future potential of the *Buffalo Evening News*.

FURTH: You looked at the income for the previous year, didn't you?

BUFFETT: I looked at the income for the previous five years, the history of circulation, advertising, a number of factors.[22]

It was an odd sort of trial: the criminal was known—all that mattered was the motive. Furth's strategy was to destroy Buffett's stated rationale and supply his own. Thus: Buffett did not have an economic basis for buying the *Evening News*; he had not made much of an effort to learn about the paper—all he had cared about was getting his hands on it, so he could kill its competitor.

Buffett patiently countered that he had bought the *Evening News* on the basis of his own mental analysis of the facts and figures. The rationale was in his *head*. This played to Furth's strength.

FURTH: And you purchased the newspaper just on the information that [Manno] gave you, is that right?

BUFFETT: No, we purchased the newspaper based on some information he gave us, some information we dug up ourselves, and a general knowledge of the newspaper business.

FURTH: You did not come and inspect the plant, the facilities, the presses, talk to the people and do things like that?

BUFFETT: No, we did not.

FURTH: Now, sir, you had contemplated, had you not, even prior to the acquisition, coming out with the Sunday newspaper?

BUFFETT: I thought it was most unusual that a major metropolitan newspaper did not have a Sunday edition. I certainly intended to investigate the possibility.

FURTH: Did you have a study done?

BUFFETT: I don't have studies done, basically. I look into them myself.

FURTH: You just did it all yourself?

BUFFETT: Right. The circulation figures and the linage figures are available from trade publications.[23]

Perhaps it is necessary to add that the typical businessman does not spend $32.5 million without commissioning a study, often several of them. They provide him with a sense of security—the blessing of supposed experts—even if it is a false security. Ultimately, *someone* has to evaluate the facts. The someone ought to be the CEO, though it takes a rarely self-assured one to appear before a board without a prop. Buffett's instinct was to remove the layers between the decision and himself. Yet as one who dispensed with the normal props, he could be made to seem suspect.

FURTH: All right, sir, how many days did you spend here in Buffalo?

BUFFETT: Probably once a month on average.

FURTH: So you have been here maybe five, six times?

BUFFETT: Something like that.

FURTH: And you made your cost estimates based on the five days that you have been here since you acquired the paper?

BUFFETT: Not based on the five days. Based on regular financial statements I read, based on phone conversations I had, based on a knowledge of the newspaper business plus a knowledge of some of the aspects of the *Buffalo Evening News*'s operation.

FURTH: Plus your overall knowledge of newspapers, the *Washington Post*, the *Trenton Times*, and all of the other business that you, your father and grandfather have accumulated?

BUFFETT: My grandfather didn't have much to do with it.[24]

It occurred to Furth's associate, Daniel Mason, that Buffett was wholly unlike what he had expected. Nothing in his unassuming manner or rumpled suit gave him away—Mason would not in a million years have thought that the witness was rich.[25]

Buffett spoke informally, and also believably. He contended that people in Buffalo would benefit from having a second Sunday paper. When the judge, Charles L. Brieant, Jr., asked him to explain why he thought the *Evening News* would trail the *Courier-Express* on Sunday, Buffett reached for a couple of those earthy metaphors that he seemed to keep in his pocket.

BUFFETT: Well, you assume that the *Courier* has been publishing for many, many, many years, all alone in the market—that people's habit patterns are very strong. I shave my face on the same side every morning and put on the same shoe first and people are creatures of habit. And the product that they have been receiving every day for a great many years has an enormous advantage.[26]

That was how he spoke in private—say, to Kay Graham. Even on the stand, he talked about business schematically, in big, broad brushstrokes. However, it was not in Buffett's interest to look too clever. And by the time that Furth went for the knockout, it was obvious to everyone in the courtroom that Buffett knew more about the economics of the *Buffalo Evening News* than any other soul alive.

FURTH: Now, sir, did you consider whether or not your coming out with this newspaper, the Sunday newspaper, might put the *Courier-Express* out of business?

BUFFETT: No, sir.

FURTH: Never ever thought whether it would or not?

BUFFETT: I think the *Courier-Express* is going to be in business a long time.

FURTH: That was never discussed; right?

BUFFETT: No, sir.[27]

Now Furth had his hook in. Approaching the bench, he waved a copy of a recent *Wall Street Journal* article profiling Buffett. Furth read aloud a passage corroborating that, in a general sense, monopoly newspapers had been very much on Buffett's mind:

"Warren likens owning a monopoly or market-dominant newspaper to owning an unregulated toll bridge. You have relative freedom to increase rates when and as much as you want."[28]

The quote was from Sandy Gottesman, Buffett's friend at First Manhattan. Buffett tried to dance around it, but the toll-bridge metaphor was just too good. Everyone knew where it came from.

FURTH: Now, sir, did you ever tell him that owning a monopoly newspaper is like owning an unregulated toll bridge?

BUFFETT: I probably said that owning a monopoly, a small monopoly newspaper, specifically in a town like Fremont, Nebraska, [with] no television competition, is absolutely a great business. Whether it is like a toll bridge I don't remember, but it is a great business. It may be better than a toll bridge in Fremont.

JUDGE BRIEANT: What is significant about Fremont, Nebraska?

BUFFETT: Your honor, the newspaper in Fremont, Nebraska, exists in an advertising vacuum. You can't make a television buy in Fremont.

JUDGE BRIEANT: Do you own a newspaper in—

BUFFETT: No. I wish I did.

FURTH: What you are saying is that owning a monopoly or market-dominant paper in a small community is like owning an unregulated toll bridge; is that right?

BUFFETT: I won't quarrel with that characterization. It is a very, very good business.

FURTH: Because you can raise rates as much as you want, isn't that true?

BUFFETT: I wouldn't put it quite that strongly, but you have the power to raise rates.

FURTH: That is the kind of business you like to own; isn't that true?

BUFFETT: I don't own any, but I would like to own one.

FURTH: Now, sir, you have used that word, unregulated toll bridge, with others, haven't you? Isn't that *one of your phrases*?

BUFFETT: I have said in an inflationary world that a toll bridge would be a great thing to own if it was unregulated.

FURTH: Why?

BUFFETT: Because you have laid out the capital costs. You build the bridge in old dollars and you don't have to keep replacing it.

FURTH: And you used the term unregulated so that you can raise prices; is that right?

BUFFETT: That is true.

FURTH: And the toll bridge, you assumed, had the monopoly over the river; is that what you are saying?[29]

Though Furth couldn't have known it, Buffett had fancied toll-booths ever since, as a boy, he had gazed at the traffic cruising past his friend Bob Russell's house. And Blue Chip actually did own 24 percent of the stock of Detroit International Bridge Co., the owner of the Ambassador Bridge between Detroit and Windsor, across Lake Erie from Buffalo.[30] It was a *real* toll bridge—the only one owned by stockholders in the United States—and Buffett controlled a quarter of it. Furth had missed it. Still, he had drawn blood.

Blue Chip's lawyers thought Buffett had made an outstanding, and credible, witness. But had he been too credible? Had he revealed too much of his keenness for dominant businesses? The vivid toll-bridge metaphor hung over the court.

On November 9—four days before the inaugural Sunday—Judge Brieant ordered an injunction against the *Evening News*, pending a trial. Though technically he did not grant all of what the morning paper sought, his lengthy opinion—delivered with what seemed remarkable speed—was devastating.

Judge Brieant ruled that the *Courier-Express* would likely be able to prove at a trial that its rival was adopting unfair tactics, that it was doing so with the intent to monopolize, and that if not stopped the *Courier-Express* would fail:

> There are only two newspapers now. If the plan works as I find it is intended to work, there will be but one left.[31]

Buffett appears in the judge's rather awestruck opinion as an impressive but archetypal financier—supremely shrewd but darkly enhanced. Page for page, Buffett can barely take a breath without its reeking of motive. Judge Brieant, unaware that Buffett made a habit of buying businesses on the numbers, views even his failure to visit the newspaper plant or to talk to the employees as "evidence of specific intent to monopolize." Even the judge's subtitle, *Mr. Buffett Comes to Buffalo*, has a loaded ring. The judge elegantly acknowledges, "Intent exists only in the unfathomable human mind." But he has no problem discerning intent from Buffett's footprints:

> Mr. Buffett made no secret of his economic motivations and his acute awareness of the value which would be attached to ownership of the Evening News were it to become a monopoly. But for the awareness of this likelihood, it seems the acquisition of the Evening News for this price, all in cash, and in this manner, makes no economic sense.[32]

The injunction permitted the Sunday paper to go ahead, but severely restricted its ability to promote, market, and circulate the edition to readers and advertisers. While these half measures hurt, Judge Brieant's strongly worded opinion did the real damage, costing the *Evening News* dearly in public support, and at a crucial time. The verdict was splashed all over the *Courier-Express*, along with an approving photograph of the judge and a flurry of favorable stories and testimonials. The president of the local AFL-CIO Council, representing 122,000 Buffalonians, was quoted on the front page as saying: "Don't buy that Sunday newspaper." Just to make sure that no one forgot whom it was fighting, the *Courier-Express* slapped a new nameplate on the front page: "Buffalo Family Owned and Operated."

On the eve of the new edition, Buffett showed up at the *Evening News* for a bash in the newsroom, accompanied by a blue-jeaned

Susie. He pressed a button, and the presses rolled. But sales had been measurably slowed by the bad publicity. Readers and advertisers, fearing the loss of jobs if the *Courier-Express* went under, were rallying to the weaker paper. Most painfully, employees at the *Evening News* could not respond to the bad press, as they were legally enjoined from making defamatory remarks about the *Courier-Express*. By December 18—the fifth Sunday of publication—the *Evening News* had only 147 inches of ads, as compared to 579 for the *Courier-Express*, despite having 40 percent more news space.[33] In short, Buffett's newspaper had suffered a crushing setback. To put it in perspective, Berkshire Hathaway's share price, which had rebounded in 1977, was trading at 132 a share, so Buffett's net worth was in the neighborhood of $70 million. About a fifth of his personal fortune was sunk into the *Evening News*.

Both papers plunged into an all-out, old-fashioned newspaper war, which in Buffett's opinion only one of them was likely to survive.[34] The *Courier-Express*, sensing that the injunction had bought it time, modernized in a hurry. Typesetting was automated, equipment upgraded. Douglas Turner, the executive editor, said, "They gave me things I'd been asking for for years: split pages, outlook sections, bigger comics, a bigger magazine. I built up the payroll by 25 percent."

The news staffs combed the city like rival fifth columns. Robert McCarthy, a reporter for the *Evening News*, said, "You didn't dare show your face if the *Courier* beat you on a story. You stayed all night to beat them." One of the few things that Buffett could control was the size of the news hole, and he went at it full blast. "We made a point of having more news than the other paper," Buffett recalled. "If they had eight pages of sports, we were going to have more. All the traditional ratios—I told 'em to hell with it."[35]

In the newsroom, people had a sense that this owner would be different. As one veteran put it, "Warren seemed to take a real interest." He occasionally sent a note commending a story, and he showed up at a staff picnic wearing, of all things, a T-shirt. The reporters, a cynical bunch, loved his skepticism. Rather than pontificate on the redeeming value of capitalism, he tipped the paper to a story on a topic that concerned him much more—namely, how greedy and perhaps unethical he considered his fellow tycoons to be.

The story concerned a secret encampment in Santa Rosa, California, known as Bohemian Grove. Each summer, conservative business types such as Merv Griffin, Gerald Ford, and Ray Kroc flew out in corporate jets to meet in the redwoods and bewail the fate of Western civilization. According to Lee Coppola, the *Evening News*'s crack investigative reporter, "The angle Buffett wanted was to examine whether or not the businessmen were taking a tax deduction for the jets. It was during the gas crisis. He thought it was wrong." Coppola, who wrote a page-one blowout, turned down a job offer partly because of his high hopes for how the paper would be run under Buffett.

But in the financially crucial battle for Sunday supremacy, the paper continued to hurt. In 1978, the *Courier-Express* trounced the *Evening News* by 100,000 papers every Sunday. As Buffalo fell into a recession, the sight of laid-off factory workers enhanced people's fears that the *Courier-Express* would fold. "The community had bought their line," the editor Murray Light recalled. "I'd call Warren on Wednesday or Thursday to tell him how many ads we had for Sunday. And there were only a handful."

Buffett would frequently call Light—his eyes and ears in Buffalo—at Light's home, and pick his brain over how to jump-start the Sunday paper. An hour was a short conversation. "He had enormous interest in every facet of the Sunday product," Light said. Buffett came to town and met the big advertisers and retailers. He approved promotional series, contests—"We did everything," Buffett recalled.

We had these special circulation teams. All week they would tell me, "We got 828 starts this week, 750 starts this week." Then, on Friday night, I would get the draw for Sunday and we'd be down to 412 or something.[36]

Buffett's instinct in such a jam was to turn to a Man Friday, a Harry Bottle or a Ken Chace. The guy he wanted was in Omaha—Stan Lipsey, his buddy and the publisher of the Omaha *Sun*. Lipsey, though, had no desire to go to Buffalo.

"What about just going up there once a month doing whatever you think needs done?" Buffett asked.

Lipsey thought to himself, "What kind of a job description is that?"

Buffett, reading his mind, added, "The place will just *run* better if you're there."

Lipsey went to Buffalo. He spent a week there each month, in theory as an assistant to the publisher, who was a holdover from the previous owner.

But the *Evening News* remained badly hampered by the injunction. Judge Brieant required the paper to show a signed customer order authorizing each and every Sunday delivery. And every word that was uttered by an *Evening News* salesman, executive, or other employee was picked over by opposition lawyers in the hope of finding a violation of the court order. One time, the *Evening News* was found in contempt—a serious matter. Mason, a lawyer for the other side, said, "Things didn't go well for the *News*. We had the ability to police their activities. We had discovery, we had access to their records." Essentially, the paper was operating at the mercy of a federal judge.

In 1978, the *Evening News* lost $2.9 million pretax—easily Buffett's biggest hit. Lipsey, who would regularly phone him from Buffalo, was amazed at how upbeat Buffett remained. "He's put all his money in. He's got a Sunday section going to zip. He's got an antitrust action. He'd be encouraging. He'd say thanks for calling."

Munger was another story. After the contempt citation, Munger called Murray Light in a state of high agitation, with the supposedly big news that Buffett was planning to give a speech someplace. "Talk to Warren," Munger said excitedly. "You have more influence than I do. Get him to be more careful with some of the things he's saying." Munger lived in mortal fear of another toll-bridge comment. Buffett shrugged it off.

But Munger saw that the paper was no longer in control of its destiny. In Blue Chip's annual letter, he even allowed the possibility that the paper might not make it.

> Litigation is notoriously time-consuming, inefficient, costly and unpredictable. The ultimate security of the Buffalo Evening News remains in doubt, as it will for a very extended period.[37]

In April 1979, two years after Blue Chip's purchase, the U.S. Court of Appeals in New York reversed the injunction and the contempt citation and strongly rebuked Judge Brieant.

> Taking first the issue of intent, we find simply no evidence that Mr. Buffett acquired the News with the idea of putting the Courier out of busi-

ness as distinguished from providing vigorous competition, including the invasion of what had been the Courier's exclusive Sunday market. . . . All that the record supports is a finding that Mr. Buffett intended to do as well as he could with the News and was not lying awake thinking what the effect of its competition on the Courier would be. This is what the antitrust laws aim to promote, not to discourage.[38]

Legally, Buffett was vindicated. But in practical terms, the suit had served its purpose. Though the *Evening News* remained by far the dominant paper during the week, the *Courier-Express*'s lead on Sunday was holding fast at 100,000 papers. And two months after the appellate reversal, the morning paper was sold to the Minneapolis Star & Tribune Co., owned by the Cowles family of Minneapolis. Now the *Evening News* faced a protracted war against another, also deep-pocketed out-of-town owner. In 1979, the *Evening News* lost a whopping $4.6 million. For the first time, Buffett and Munger were losing serious money. Munger recalled, "I went through the calculations personally—I figured out exactly how much my share would cost me and exactly how much the Munger family could afford to lose."

In 1980, Lipsey moved to Buffalo full-time.* Buffett hadn't *asked* him to do it, but Lipsey knew that Buffett, in his none too casual way, wanted him there—badly. And Lipsey had gotten hooked on the battle with the *Courier-Express*.

When Lipsey took charge of the *Evening News*, the paper faced a new crisis with labor. Prior to Buffett's purchase, the paper's thirteen unions had played the company off against itself, resulting in what Munger termed a "leapfrogging of benefits."[39] Determined to break this pattern, Buffett and Munger sent a message, presumably intended for the unions, in the Blue Chip report that appeared early in 1980:

> If any extended strike shuts down the Buffalo Evening News, it will probably be forced to cease operations and liquidate.[40]

The teamsters decided to test them. Late in 1980, the delivery truck drivers demanded new manning requirements and pay for work even if not performed,[41] hot-button issues that were really about control. Buf-

---

*Buffett sold the *Sun*, the chain of Omaha weeklies of which Lipsey had been publisher. Subsequently, Buffett went on the board of his hometown daily, the *Omaha World-Herald*.

fett turned them down. At the eleventh hour, a Monday evening in December, Ray Hill, who represented the Newspaper Guild, the largest union at the paper, was called from a church meeting to come down to the paper and try to help avert a strike. Hill knew Buffett, and sensed that he wasn't bluffing. He advised the teamsters not to play poker with him. The teamsters' representative was Martin Brogan, a former bar bouncer and a ringleader in the only previous strike in the paper's history. Brogan figured that Buffett wouldn't risk a strike in the midst of the battle with the *Courier-Express*. Someone called a mediator, who showed up drunk. The talks lasted all night. Finally, the mediator turned to Hill and said, "Look, Ray, they want to strike." At 6:00 A.M. Tuesday, the teamsters walked.

The *Evening News* started to put out a paper, with the help of other unions, who crossed the picket line. Then the pickets sacked a delivery truck, and the pressmen stopped work and pulled the page plates.[42] The paper shut down, and subscription calls lit up the *Courier-Express*. The nightmare in Buffalo had hit bottom.

Buffett, according to a close confidant, was sweating. He knew that if the paper shut down for long, it would suffer a ruinous loss of market share.[43] He had to reopen it soon or never. On the other hand, if he gave in, twelve other unions would demand the same deal.

Early Tuesday, he announced that if the paper didn't publish he couldn't meet a payroll, and ordered the entire staff to leave. What's more, he said, if the drivers didn't return for the all-important Sunday edition, he would close the paper for good. Richard Feather, the *Evening News*'s chief bargainer, hung up the phone feeling certain that Buffett meant it.

Brogan, who was under pressure from the other unions, was sweating, too. Hill told him, "Marty, whatever you're fighting for, you're taking everyone over the side." Finally, Brogan blinked. The teamsters accepted a face-saving concession, and the *Evening News* was back on the streets by Thursday afternoon.

Hill said, "Warren, when this is over, I want our cooperation recognized."

"Ray, an empty sack doesn't stand very tall."

Hill took this to mean that if the paper recovered from the war with the *Courier-Express*, his members would be rewarded. But the balance of power had shifted in Buffett's favor. As Hill said, "Things are never the same after a strike."

Both papers were hurting badly from the recession, which had hit Buffalo hard. And the war of Sundays dragged on. The *Evening News* made some gains, but it did not close the gap. After five years, it trailed in circulation, 195,000 to 265,000.[44] And it continued to lose money, though at a diminished rate. Since Buffett had bought the paper, pretax losses had amounted to $12 million.[45] Early in 1982, Munger concluded that they had dug a hole from which they would never recover.

> We would now have about $70 million in value of other assets, earning over $10 million per year, in place of the Buffalo Evening News and its current red ink. No matter what happens in the future in Buffalo we are about 100% sure to have an economic place lower than we would have occupied if we had not made our purchase.[46]

In the next few months, Sunday circulation crept over 200,000, though it remained far below the *Courier-Express*. Meanwhile, Buffalo was rife with rumors that one or the other paper would fold. Buffett vehemently denied that he would even consider it.[47] But the city could not support two papers. The question, again, was who would blink first. And then, in September, the *Courier-Express* did; it folded.

The morning paper had been losing $3 million a year, twice as much as the *Evening News*. Otto Silha, chairman of the *Courier's* parent Minneapolis Star & Tribune Co., said the decisive factor was that its flagship Minneapolis paper also was doing badly. In contrast, he knew that Blue Chip could be sustained indefinitely by the increasingly lucrative See's Candy.

The day the *Courier-Express* died, the *Evening News* changed its name to the *Buffalo News* and started a morning edition. Within six months, Sunday circulation topped 360,000—far surpassing the peak Sunday readership of its rival. Ad rates, reflecting the surviving paper's higher readership—and its monopoly—surged. The paper became a gold mine, or perhaps even a toll bridge. It was soon clear that Munger had been wrong; the paper would be not merely profitable, but immensely so.

The *News* earned $19 million, pretax, in its first year without competition. (Those profits belonged to Berkshire Hathaway, which fully absorbed Blue Chip Stamps in a merger.) By the late eighties, the *News* would earn more than $40 million a year—more than Buffett had invested in Berkshire and Blue Chip combined. His ascent up the investment food chain had a certain inexorable momentum: stamps provided the cash for See's Candy; the profits from candy fueled the *Buffalo Evening News*, and the *News* could bankroll an even bigger prize still.

Buffett disabused the employees of any illusions over who would share in that prize. Soon after the *Courier*'s demise, Buffett attended a meeting for the newspaper's middle-level managers, in Buffalo's Statler Hotel. "What about profit-sharing for people in the newsroom?" Buffett was asked. On its face, this seemed reasonable. The newsroom had certainly done its bit.

Buffett replied coldly, "There is nothing anybody on the third floor [the newsroom] can do that affects profits." The staff was shocked, though Buffett was merely living up to his brutal-but-principled capitalist credo. The owners of the *Buffalo Evening News* had run very great risks. Employees had not come forward during the dark years to share in the losses. Nor, now, would they share in the gains.

Alvin Greene, a night editor who was present at the meeting, said, "I was just *stunned*. It sort of sent a message to everyone in the newsroom."

Employees got a catch-up raise, but not the home run they had hoped for. As Greene said, "The big disappointment was, we won the battle. We got one fairly good raise and then nothing [out of the ordinary]."

In the years after the *Courier-Express* folded, the pay scale at the *News* slipped to thirtieth among Guild papers nationwide—down from seventh when Buffett had bought the paper.[48] Still, Ray Hill, the Guild unit chairman, judged that Buffett had delivered on what he promised. Had the roles been reversed, Hill said, he would not have behaved much differently.

As the sole survivor in Buffalo, the *News* faced a problem that had been unthinkable during its war with the *Courier*. As Buffett noted in an annual letter to Berkshire, a monopoly newspaper has no *economic* incentive to maintain its quality.

Owners, naturally, would like to believe that their wonderful profitability is achieved only because they unfailingly turn out a wonderful product. That comfortable theory wilts before an uncomfortable fact. . . .
Good or bad [a dominant paper] will prosper.[49]

Buffett pledged to keep it a good paper anyway, and in a statistical
sense he kept his word. The *News* continued to publish the same number of news columns as advertising, giving it the highest news ratio of
any comparable daily in the country.[50]

Buffett also remained a close friend of Stan Lipsey's. But he went to
the newspaper less often, and reporters stopped hearing that he was
reading their stories. Gradually, the staff came to feel a certain disappointment. Buffett was a decent owner, probably no tighter than others. But the reporters had hoped that Buffett would be more—a larger
presence if not a more munificent one. And the wartime spirit of the
paper was lost.

Lee Coppola, the investigative sleuth who had been so motivated by
Buffett, left the paper, went into broadcasting, and eventually became
an assistant U.S. prosecutor in Buffalo. He continued to exchange an
occasional note with Buffett. His feelings—like those of others who had
invested Buffett with expectations not of Buffett's doing—were mixed.
"The dream that I had was not fulfilled," Coppola said. But, he added,
"To this day, I respect the man."

A decade after its war with the *Courier-Express*, the *News* reached
three-fourths of the households in Buffalo—the highest such ratio of
any metropolitan paper in the country.[51] But Buffalo was the poorer for
having one newspaper instead of two, and total newspaper readership
in the city was much less than when the *Courier-Express* had been
alive.[52]

Certainly, Buffett had every right, and also every reason, to start a
Sunday paper. And given what has occurred in other cities, there was
little chance that two papers could have survived even had Buffett
not come to town. In effect, he had merely given the Invisible Hand
a push. Still, a paper had been buried and jobs had been lost. And in
some remove of "the unfathomable human mind," Buffett must have
suspected, even in court, that it would turn out that way. Consider
his words to a colleague on the survival prospects of second newspapers:

In years past, hundreds of newspaper owners, putting up their own money, as well, I am sure, as most of the "experts", felt that large cities would sustain more than one healthy newspaper. It just wasn't so.[53]

Buffett wrote that in 1972, five years before the *Evening News* was even a glimmer in his eye. He had known, all along, that second papers were doomed. In Buffalo, he merely proved it.

On the shores of Lake Erie, memories of the war died hard. Long after the event, veterans of the *Courier-Express* were bitter about the paper's demise. Even their children harbored a resentment against Buffett's paper, but they subscribed to it seven days a week, just as did the children of the victors. As Daniel Mason, Furth's associate and later his partner, muttered, "At the end of the day, Buffett got his monopoly."

Chapter 12

PARTNERS, REDUX

As Buffett was jetting off to New York or Washington or Buffalo, he and his wife were leading increasingly separate lives. Susie was getting serious about her singing. Neil Sedaka heard her in Omaha and suggested that she turn professional, and Susie was game to do it.[1] Bill Ruane, Warren's investment manager friend, arranged for her to audition at Manhattan nightclubs, including Tramps and the Ballroom. The Buffetts' New York friends discovered that she could sing. According to Roxanne Brandt, who was also a singer, "If you had walked in off the street you wouldn't have said this was a rich guy's wife."

Invited back to New York for a return engagement, Susie began to talk about polishing her act and going on extended tour. She even signed up with William Morris, the talent agency.[2]

In the spring of 1977, as Buffett was purchasing the *Buffalo Evening News*, Susie was doing another stint at the French Café, in Omaha. On occasion, after the show, the staff would go to the Buffetts' for a nightcap. Warren would join them for a few minutes and then disappear to his study, leaving Susie to play hostess.[3] "I have a picture of Mom and the French Café people coming over," Peter said. "Dad was like the dad. He was upstairs reading. Mom and her friends were like the kids."

The Buffetts' schedules were so divergent that, when they celebrated their silver anniversary, in April 1977, Stan Lipsey had a cartoonist draw a wry card depicting the two of them whirling past each other on the top of a wedding cake.

While they had always had different interests, as the house emptied of children Susie was more aware of a sense of missing something. Kent Bellows, an artist friend who was hanging around the house, thought Warren and Susie had "a great marriage"; they were a case of opposites attracting. Yet so much of the time, Warren seemed to be in a shell—present physically, but not much more. He would be enveloped in a volume of Standard & Poor's or preoccupied with his thoughts.[4] In an emotive sense, he was, indeed, Susie's opposite. Susie said to Bellows, "All Warren needs to be happy is a book and a sixty-watt bulb."

Susie, of course, wanted more, much more. She was so giving, so wrapped up in emotional involvements. It was her nature to live for others, which she had done for Warren more than for anyone. Their daughter said, "Mom spent a lot of time supporting Dad so he could do his thing. Dad was so intent, so *focused*. He just did the same thing all the time." Peter, more pointedly, said, "Mom suffered for living for other people." Susie's time was late at night, when she would stay up alone, listening to music.[5]

In a rare public interview, when the *Omaha World-Herald* was writing up her stage career, Susie spoke appreciatively of Warren's support for her singing. Yet her description of him—the story was published two days shy of their twenty-fifth anniversary—was restrained. Recounting the story of their courtship, she noted that she had been "madly in love with somebody else," but had followed her father's advice and discovered that Buffett was "just an extraordinary person."[6] She said nothing about being mad for him. Nor did she mention that she still had wistful memories of her romance with Milton Brown, and that, a quarter century later, she still ruminated aloud, now and then, on what her life would have been like had she married Brown instead of Buffett. (Brown had become a successful food broker in Des Moines.)

By then, the Buffetts were alone. Their daughter was married and working for Century 21, in Irvine, California, near the state university where she had attended college. Howie, meanwhile, had dropped out of Augustana College, in Sioux Falls, South Dakota. He was launching his own business, Buffett Excavating, near Omaha, and had cashed in his Berkshire stock to purchase earthmoving equipment. Young Peter had enrolled at Stanford.

In September 1977, the elder Susie did a one-night performance at the Orpheum, an ornate former vaudeville house in Omaha that had been host in the 1930s to Al Jolson and Barbara Stanwyck. On this particular evening, facing a hometown crowd, Susie was at her slinky, sensuous torch-singer best. She cooed, "Let's feel like we're in love, okay?"[7]

A short time later, forty-five-year-old Susie walked out on her husband. That is, she moved out of the Buffetts' home on Farnam Street, left Omaha, and rented an apartment in San Francisco. She told her children (Howie was stunned, Peter almost expected it) that she was not "separating," legally or in other respects, from Warren. But day to day, she wanted to live on her own.

To Buffett, this was an immeasurable blow: stunning, devastating, irreparable. It undid the finely spun cocoon that had sheltered him from whatever was unpleasant, or distracting, and had given him the comfort to pursue his work. It emptied his home of gaiety and warmth, and of Susie's soul-penetrating closeness. There was no one who could remotely take her place. He told his older sister, "Susie was the sun and the rain in my garden for twenty-five years."

Left to himself, Buffett was mystified about why she had left and miserably lonely. He burst into tears on the telephone with her. Susie, soothingly, explained her move as an evolutionary adjustment—not a total break. They still could talk on the phone, travel together, even share regular vacations in New York and Laguna Beach. She talked and talked to him. They were still husband and wife, she assured him. But the gist of it was, "We both have needs."[8]

Warren's daughter came home to spend a couple of weeks with him. Young Susie had Warren's sunny, matter-of-fact temperament, and she adored her dad. Coincidentally, she was in the process of ending her own, short-lived marriage. She filled out his suddenly empty house and helped him through domestic issues such as eating something other than popcorn and having clean clothes. Buffett, who was nuts about "little Susie," expressed amazement that she could get the laundry done in a single afternoon. He didn't say much about Susie's mother. Young Susie recalled:

He has a hard time verbalizing feelings. I only remember him sitting in his chair and reading, talking about the laundry. At some point, I said, "Really nothing has changed. If you had a tape playing of Mother opening and closing the door and yelling, 'I'm home,' you'd think she was here."

Among the Buffetts' family and friends, who had tended to idealize the Buffett household, there was a sense of shock, and also sadness. But Warren and his wife were not, in the ordinary sense, broken. Though Susie was in California, they talked to each other virtually every day.[9] At Christmas, they reunited with their kids at the beach house in Laguna. In the spring, Warren and Susie took their usual two-week trip to New York.

Things got easier, his daughter said, as Buffett came to realize that his life was not so *very* different. Implicitly, it was the prospect of change that terrified him. He considered moving to Southern California, nearer to much of his family, but couldn't bring himself to do it, partly because it would mean working without his bland but faithful longtime secretary, Gladys Kaiser.[10] In a larger sense, he was loathe to change his routine, leave the familiar, or reinvent himself in any way.

Susie, on the other hand, was living in a modest, almost student-like apartment, outfitted with girlish accouterments such as a Mickey Mouse telephone. She had the exultant sense of freedom that comes with living alone, especially to someone who has had to delay it until middle age. There were aspects of Susie's personal life that she did not share with Warren, and that Warren preferred not to confront. People in the family knew, and understood that Susie, too, had needs. They formed a kind of protective conspiracy around him—the better for him to do his life's work—as, indeed, they always had. As Roberta, his younger sister, noted, "We are very protective to Warren. I don't know how it started, but it was that way even growing up."

Susie sheltered Warren more than anyone. She still cared for him, and in her own way, she was as good at weaving a web around people as her husband. Susie even suggested to several women in Omaha that they call Warren for a movie, or maybe fix him dinner.[11] One of those women was Astrid Menks, a blond, soft-spoken thirty-one-year-old waitress at the French Café. Astrid fixed Buffett a couple of homemade soups and began to look in on him. Susie gave them a push.[12]

If anyone in Omaha moved in different circles than Buffett did, it was Astrid Menks. She lived in a loft in the market district, an arty neighborhood perpetually in transition from head shops to cappuccino bars. Born in Latvia, she had come to Omaha as a girl. She had lost her mother when she was young, and her father, a waiter, had entrusted his children to an orphanage.[13] The most common description of Astrid was "survivor." Witty and street-smart, she was an habitué of antique stores and thrift shops and inevitably managed to look striking even in secondhand threads. She had a small frame and a sharply lined face that hinted at her origins. In the winter, she would pick her way through the mounds of snow and swirling Omaha winds, bundled up in an afghan and a fur coat and leading a reddish dog and looking like a character from *Doctor Zhivago*.[14]

Astrid seemed to know everyone in what passed for bohemian society in Omaha. Tom Rogers, a nephew of Buffett's who lived above the French Café, recalled, "When there was a blizzard and people were snowed in—Omahans are sort of spiritual about snow—Astrid would get together with the chef at V Mertz and organize a big dinner for everyone." She liked to make herself useful, but behind the scenes. When Susie sang at the French Café, Astrid had brought her tea between the sets. She had a cool attentiveness, and modesty was second nature to her.

Within a year of Susie's moving out of Buffett's home, Astrid moved into it. Warren's new arrangement baffled his son Howie. It baffled *everyone*. Kent Bellows, the artist, who knew Astrid as a thrift-shop fiend, was astonished that she had hooked up with the richest guy in town. Bellows very brassily asked her, "So what *is* this with you and Warren? Do you?"

There was talk that Buffett had hired her as a "cook," but in fact, they were a couple from the start.[15] Temperamentally, Astrid and Buffett suited each other. They had a kidding, easy way together. While Buffett was looking for bargain stocks, Astrid would stalk the junk stores, or scavenge the supermarkets looking for bargains on the millionaire's Pepsi-Cola. When Buffett was in his study, Astrid would be in the garden. She liked being at home, and she freed him from having to think about the practical details of living. If Peter came in on a late-night train, Astrid would meet him.

Perhaps because she had lived alone so much, Astrid had a way of catering to Buffett without seeming subservient or losing her grace. She stood up to him, but in a light, understated way. Of course, the trade-off was rather strange. Astrid had security and companionship. Buffett had a partner to come home to, or to share a steak with. Yet from the day she moved in, Astrid knew that Buffett did not envision remarrying, and that he was still attached to his wife. She made a home for him, yet she would see him off with neatly laundered shirts when he left town to be with Susie.[16]

At first, Astrid would leave Omaha rather than stay in the empty house.[17] After a while, she got comfortable with his comings and goings, and with people in Buffett's family. Remarkably, she also got to be chummy with Warren's wife. When Susie came to Omaha, she and Astrid did lunch, though Susie did not stay at Farnam Street. At an annual meeting of Berkshire Hathaway, the two women sat side by side, making small talk while their common friend presided onstage.

This mostly unlikely trio developed a rhythm. Astrid took care of Buffett day to day; Susie was with him if Buffett was accompanied outside of Omaha. In New York and California, Warren and Susie saw their usual friends. Also, at any formal occasion, such as the biannual meetings of Buffett's Ben Graham investors group, Buffett brought his wife.

To outward appearances, Warren and Susie's personal chemistry was unchanged. Joe Rosenfield, the Iowa retailer who often joined them in California, said they "acted like a regular married couple." The younger Susie said her parents' "basic relationship" was the same. Peter thought it "surreal"—the fact that they lived fifteen hundred miles apart seemed to have changed nothing.

Buffett even got a kidding tribute from Howard Newman (the son of Ben Graham's partner) for having two women. "Ben wanted to do that, but you pulled it off," Newman joshed. Yet Buffett was hardly the romantic Casanova that such a comment suggests. He alternated between his female leads in a methodical, compartmentalized fashion, almost as though it were scripted. In fact, Astrid and Susie were different people, not actresses and not really interchangeable. It was all very jarring to Buffett's friends, and though they became accustomed to his domestic triangle, they still found it inexplicable.

One wonders to what extent Buffett himself was willing to explore his marriage (Peter, for instance, questioned whether his mother had been talked into marrying his father from the start, a notion Buffett disputed), or whether he simply rearranged his supporting cast so as to best continue working. But however much it perplexed his friends, the fact is that Buffett found, or contrived, a solution that worked for *him*. Hanging on to Susie, even at a distance, gave him the continuity he had always craved, even as a boy when he had run back to Omaha. It spared him the trauma of divorce, or of a hateful search for new frontiers.

This deliberateness was characteristic of him. "I really like my life. I've *arranged* my life so that I can do what I want," he once observed to a reporter. Typically, he was not concerned with appearances, even now, when flouting the deepest of social conventions. He did not try to explain his *ballet à trois*; in his one published comment, he merely noted that it suited the three people directly involved: "If you knew everybody well, you'd understand it quite well."[18]

Buffett did make a point of telling friends that Astrid had Susie's blessing. Don Danly, Buffett's old pinball partner, visited him in Omaha after Astrid had moved in, and naturally wondered about her. Danly could hardly help but notice that she and Buffett went off at night. Buffett told him that the two women were friends. Danly said, "I think it was important to him. He was telling me he wasn't doing anything underhanded."

In Peter's view, Buffett's first years without Susie were a gray time. "For a while he was empty and sad," Peter said. An intimate woman friend thought Buffett "achingly lonely." But to her, the interesting thing was how he coped with it. No one outside a small circle had any glimpse of that grayness. According to his son, Buffett himself did not always see it. He focused on his work, and he "tap-danced" through his new, carefully plotted life as though he had "blinders."

In a previous crisis, when as a boy he had been marooned in Washington, Buffett had thrown himself into delivering newspapers. Though he was an owner of some of those papers now, not much else about his work had changed. He couldn't rise early enough, as though a bundle of papers still awaited him at the office. Nourished, now, by two supportive women, he would unfailingly answer the telephone with a verbal high-five, as if he had never known an unhappy moment. Joe Rosenfield, an old and dear friend, never saw Buffett despondent— not once. "He's so wrapped up in Berkshire," Rosenfield noted.

Far from slacking off amid his personal troubles, Buffett experienced
a creative resurgence. In the late seventies, and with his usual unpredictable timing, Buffett (on behalf of Berkshire) made a staccato burst
of investments. Energized, as always, by a depressed stock market, he
began to shovel the float from Berkshire's insurance company into
stocks, including Amerada Hess, American Broadcasting Cos., more
GEICO and then still more, General Foods, Knight-Ridder Newspapers, Media General, SAFECO, F. W. Woolworth, and then again still
more.

It was said that the rumor that Buffett was buying was enough to
boost a stock by 10 percent. General Foods "went winging up," according to the broker Art Rowsell. "Warren wouldn't acknowledge that he
was buying it. He kind of waited everybody out, and it came back
down, and he started buying it again. Charlie [Munger]—he was rant-
ing: 'The sonuvabitches are following us again.' "*

As Buffett was investing, he also began to write, occasionally for business magazines, but primarily in the Berkshire Hathaway annual reports. He had always had an urge to chronicle his progress, but his pen
had been strangely silent since the days of Buffett Partnership. Now,
increasingly, he used the letters to sketch lucid business primers that
ranged over investing, management, and finance.

There was no single beginning, though when Buffett later bound a
collection for reprint, he began with the 1977 letter, written early in
1978, which coincided with Susie's leaving home. This letter was a
primer of the most basic sort, and it is doubtful that too many people
read it. Buffett explained that he evaluated stocks exactly as he would
an entire business: he looked for companies he understood, run by
honest and competent managers, with favorable long-term prospects,
and available at a decent price. He made no attempt to anticipate the
short-term price action.

The inspiration for this missive—and for Buffett's buying spree—was
the strange world of Wall Street of the late 1970s. Stocks of the type that
Buffett described were there for the picking, yet once again, nobody
wanted them. By the summer of 1979, the Dow had crashed to the mid-
800s—remarkably, below its level of 1969. As in the mid-seventies, the
country was in a funk in matters economic, and the headlines spoke of

*Berkshire disclosed big investments at year-end.

despair. The dollar had been routed by the mark and the yen; there were fundamentalists in Iran, Reds in Nicaragua, a revivified OPEC, energy shortages at home, and a pervasive sense of the country in decline. Instead of the duplicitous Nixon as President, America now had the virtuous but sorely ineffective Jimmy Carter. His eye on the White House, George Bush expressed shock at the level of federal debt. He promised, if elected, to balance the budget in his first term.[19]

It comforted no one that Wall Street had survived a similar brush with Armageddon only five years before—or that the earlier slump had been followed by one of the greatest rallies ever. Financial cycles are apparent only in retrospect. As it unfolds, each swing of the market, cloaked in the vestments of the moment, appears unique. The peculiar curse of the late seventies was inflation, which hit an all-time high of 13 percent. On Wall Street, the prime rate was in double digits. In the hinterlands, there was a new species of snake-oil salesman—the doomsday profiteer. He peddled gold, diamonds, art, real estate, rare metals, freeze-dried foods, jojoba beans, and advice on surviving the next depression. His message was: "Get out of paper."

The poor soul who dared protest that stocks represented the country's earning power was greeted with a snicker. In a letter dated 1979, Buffett noted with astonishment that pension fund managers, "a group that logically should maintain the longest of investment perspectives," had put only 9 percent of their available funds into stocks that year—a record for cowardice.[20] He could hardly help but add, "We confess considerable optimism" regarding Berkshire's portfolio.[21]

Few disputed that stocks were cheap. But as in bear markets past, fund managers were waiting until the outlook was "clear." Manufacturers Hanover had 60 percent of its funds out of the market. Victor Melone, a senior investment officer, explained, "There are further questions to be answered."[22] Heinz H. Biel, vice president of Janney Montgomery Scott, joined the chorus:

Knowing that stocks are cheap does not impel one to go on a buying spree; the future is clouded by many ugly questions.[23]

The pinnacle of worry-wart prognostication was claimed by *Business Week*, which in August 1979 ran a celebrated cover: "The Death of Equities." It was a seminal piece—a carefully wrought obituary for the stock market. Henceforth, according to *Business Week*, people would invest in money markets, fast-food franchises, or rare stamps. Stocks, apparently, were history. That shares were cheap was a "disincentive"—proof that the market was not merely down but dead.

> For better or for worse, then, the U.S. economy probably has to regard the death of equities as a near-permanent condition—reversible some day, but not soon.[24]

Buffett could not have disagreed more. The same week, he penned an essay for *Forbes*, attacking the herd instincts of pension-fund managers and their age-old rationalization.

> The future is *never* clear; you pay a very high price in the stock market for a cheery consensus. Uncertainty actually is the friend of the buyer of long-term values.[25]

The *Forbes* essay reflected Buffett's reawakened urge to decipher business in print, and on a deeper level than he had in the sixties. He noted that pension-fund managers had flocked to corporate bonds, then paying 9½ percent. Their reasoning was simple: stocks had no coupons at all, and were considered more risky, especially in light of the market's recent performance.

To Buffett, there was less to this distinction than met the eye. In fact, stocks, then, were *less* risky, not more so. The origin of this singular insight was that Buffett looked beneath the *form* of a security to its economic substance. A stock, like a bond, was a claim on a corporate asset. A stock also bore a "coupon," at least implicitly—the underlying corporate earnings.

The companies in the Dow Jones Industrial Average, for instance, earned 13 percent on book value, a figure that for the group had held pretty constant. And those stocks were trading at less than book. When he shut his eyes, Buffett could see the stocks in the Dow as a "Dow Bond" with a "coupon" of 13 percent—clearly superior to the return on bonds. And for the patient investor, stock prices would eventually reflect the buried 13 percent.

Buffett's own stock had risen despite the bear market. Berkshire was now at $290 a share, giving Buffett a paper fortune of $140 million. But the curious fact was that Buffett, whose salary was only $50,000, couldn't *live* off his Berkshire. He refused to sell even a single share of his precious "canvas." Nor would he permit the company to pay a dividend. To bleed it of capital would have been sacrilege—shaving off a corner of his work-in-progress to pay the rent.

Feeling the pressure of having to support two households, he complained to Charles Heider, an Omaha broker, "Everything I got is tied up in Berkshire. I'd like a few nickels outside."

In the late seventies, he bought a few stocks for his own account. He was a bit more of a swinger with his personal money. For instance, in the case of Teledyne, Buffett invested in options—a strategy with a higher chance of either failing or making a killing.[26] According to one associate, he also bought copper futures—an outright speculation.

"It was almost frightening, how easy it was," a Berkshire employee said. "He analyzed what he was looking for. All of a sudden he had money." When a friend suggested that Buffett try his hand in real estate, Buffett grinned. "Why should I buy real estate when the stock market is so *easy*?"[27] According to the broker Art Rowsell, "Warren made $3 million like bingo."

Even with his now immense fortune, Buffett continued to live simply, at least in Omaha. He drove his own car, a Lincoln, to the modest suite at Kiewit Plaza, where he and a staff of five ran the corporate affairs of Berkshire. His principal diversions were bridge, reading business books, and watching sports and talk shows. When he and Astrid went out, it was usually to Gorats, an unprepossessing Omaha steakhouse, owned by a former grade-school classmate of Buffett's.

Increasingly, though, Buffett's world—his friends, his companies, his writing—extended beyond Omaha. His fortieth-birthday party had been on a golf course in Omaha; for his fiftieth, in the summer of 1980, Susie threw a black-tie bash at the Metropolitan Club in New York. Buffett got a giant bag of popcorn from Stan Lipsey and a succession of gags. Jerry Orans, his friend from Penn, was there, and Don Danly, from high school, Walter Schloss, aide-de-camp at Graham-Newman, Sandy Gottesman—he of the infamous toll-bridge quote—Kay Graham, Carol Loomis, and Marshall Weinberg. Buffett brought a copy of the balance sheet from Wilson Coin Op, his first business. Susie, the torch singer, sang an ode to her man. There were tributes from cronies, ending with a poignant toast from Munger.

Underneath the partygoers' merriment, there was probably no one

Howard Buffett and Leila Stahl
COURTESY UNIVERSITY OF NEBRASKA

The future capitalist with his sister Doris, probably 1931
COURTESY DORIS BUFFETT BRYANT

The Buffetts posed for a photographer in 1942, after Howard's upset election to Congress. Warren, then twelve, looked less than thrilled about his forced move to Washington. OMAHA WORLD-HERALD

Unshakably ethical, Congressman Howard Buffett refused to keep the salary increase that Congress awarded to itself. But Warren broke from his father's ultra–right wing politics.
COURTESY THE JOHN F. SAVAGE PHOTOGRAPHY COLLECTION, OWNED BY WESTERN HERITAGE MUSEUM, OMAHA

Roberta, Doris, and Warren in Washington. The house in the background is a neighbor's.
COURTESY DORIS BUFFETT BRYANT

"Likes math . . . a future stock broker."
WOODROW WILSON HIGH SCHOOL YEARBOOK, 1947

Though Buffett was a loner on campus, his witty friend Jerry Orans had him looking all very rah-rah for the cover of a campus magazine.
COURTESY THE UNIVERSITY OF
PENNSYLVANIA ARCHIVES

Ben Graham with his third wife, Estelle, in about 1950, the year
Buffett enrolled in Graham's investing class. Professor Graham
gave Buffett an A+; Estelle gave Buffett her money.
COURTESY MARJORIE GRAHAM JANIS

Charlie Munger, the
philosopher-king.
Buffett and his part-
ner thought so much
alike it was "spooky."
COURTESY CHARLIE MUNGER

Susie, sporting a Jacqueline Kennedy hairstyle, had strong objections to Warren's being "the absolute last" person in America with a crew cut. In 1962, they posed in the Buffetts' solarium at an anniversary party for Susie's parents. COURTESY TOM ROGERS

Seabury Stanton's heart was in tex-tiles. Buffett's wasn't.
COURTESY SPINNER PUBLICATIONS, INC.

The Berkshire Hathaway mill, distinguished by a clock tower, is nestled between three-story tenements in New Bedford's South End, a once-thriving commercial district. The water is to the right.
JOSEPH D. THOMAS

Buffett arriving at the New Bedford
airport for the fateful board meeting
at which he took control of Berkshire

The pigeons in Sevilla, Spain,
were drawn to Ben Graham no
less than his students back
home were. The picture was
taken in 1964.
COURTESY BENJAMIN GRAHAM, JR., M.D.,
AND JANET LOWE

Warren and Susie in Laguna, California, 1966

His ear to the phone, Buffett looked like nothing so much as an overeager chipmunk. By age thirty-five, he was worth $7 million.

One of the early "annual meetings." Buffett hosts a
dinner for some of his partners at his home on
Farnam Street, 1969.
COURTESY TOM ROGERS

The charter members of Buffett's
"Graham Group" were hoping to
get advice on the soaring stock
market of 1968, but when
Professor Graham showed up at
the Hotel Del Coronado, he gave
them a true-false test instead.
Left to right: Buffett, Roy Tolles,
Ben Graham, David "Sandy"
Gottesman, Tom Knapp, Charlie
Munger, Jack Alexander, Henry
Brandt, Walter Schloss, Marshall
Weinberg, Ed Anderson, a half-
obscured Buddy Fox, and Bill
Ruane. COURTESY JACK ALEXANDER

Ben Graham, father of security analysis, about 1970
COURTESY MARJORIE GRAHAM JANIS

The Buffetts strike a characteristic pose: Susie in Warren's lap. The picture was taken in the early 1970s.
COURTESY TOM ROGERS

Buffett in the mid-1970s with his two passions: Susie and a glass of Pepsi
COURTESY TOM ROGERS

Howie, Susie, and Peter with their folks, shortly after Buffett folded up the partnership. The coffee cup must have been a prop. COURTESY PETER BUFFETT

Onstage, the sequined Susie was *"all passion and nuance."*
OMAHA WORLD-HERALD

After Buffett invested $10 million in the Washington Post, *he charmed his way onto the board, befriended the company's number-shy chairwoman, Kay Graham, and took her to school. Buffett's investment in the company soared to more than $400 million.* COURTESY KAY GRAHAM

A dashing Buffett is feted at the Metropolitan Club in New York in 1980. By his fiftieth birthday, Buffett was worth close to $200 million.

COURTESY TOM ROGERS

"Commodore" Munger shows off a spotted grouper in Cape York, Australia. He earned the sobriquet in Minnesota, when he capsized a fishing boat with Buffett aboard, nearly drowning him.

IRA MARSHALL

Mrs. B, who quit Buffett's store in a rage and set up shop directly opposite, was the only business partner of Buffett's who ever ran out on him. She was ninety-five at the time. OMAHA WORLD-HERALD

Buffett was always smiling when he was with Tom Murphy—the CEO he admired most, and one who made more than $1 billion for him. They are shown at a Capital Cities/ABC retreat in Phoenix. Courtesy Capital Cities/ABC

Warren bought a farm for his son Howie and charged him a market rent.
Courtesy Howard Graham Buffett

As a youngster, Peter felt his investor-father was in his own solar system. Later, when Peter achieved success in music, he and Warren learned how to talk with each other.

COURTESY PETER BUFFETT

At American Express, the patrician Jimmy Robinson violated nearly every one of Buffett's rules. Buffett's friends were shocked when he invested with Robinson.

COURTESY JAMES D. ROBINSON III

*John Gutfreund, the "King"
of Wall Street* LARRY BARNS

*Buffett loads up on his favorite
cocktail at the Berkshire annual
meeting.* LaVERNE D. RAMSEY

in the great, wood-paneled room who did not feel that Buffett, in some way, was to leave a mark. With his scuffed shoes, grown-in but receding hair, and prominent beak, he looked more the professor than ever. Still slender, he had the unruly eyebrows of a thinker. Indeed, the revelers' affection was fused with an excitement, even a certain idolatry. Whosoever owned stock in Berkshire—now quoted at $375 a share—was getting *rich*.

The next year, Buffett had a dangerous close call. The wife of Rick Guerin, a money-manager chum of Buffett's and Charlie Munger's, died suddenly and tragically. Buffett, who was in Omaha, called Guerin at his home in California.

"I'm hurting," Guerin said.

"I know how you feel," Buffett replied. "I felt the same way when my father died, like someone beating me."

After a pause, he added, "Look, why don't you and your son get on an airplane and we'll meet up at Charlie's island. We'll just sit around for three or four days."[28]

Buffett and the others met at Munger's cabin, on a lake in Minnesota. Munger took them fishing in an outboard motorboat, and as he was maneuvering in reverse, water rushed in over the gunwale. Guerin warned him to slow down, whereupon the half-blind Munger obstinately turned up the throttle. In an instant, the boat was underwater—and Buffett was trapped beneath it. The athletic Guerin managed to pull him out from under. Though they all made light of it—Charlie's new sobriquet was "Commodore Munger"—Buffett was visibly shaken by his near-drowning.

Guerin, though, was deeply touched by Buffett's willingness to drop everything for him. "He has enormous compassion," Guerin said, "but people don't see that. To me it was just an amazing gift—the gift of time."

On Wall Street, Buffett's letters had begun to circulate beyond the clique of his Rick Guerin–like admirers. Bankers were photocopying the reports and passing them around chain-letter style. For the first time, Buffett had a bit of a *public* following. As he wryly observed, Berkshire had "one-share subscribers" who bought a single share just to get the report.

Munger said it was an accident that Buffett was running a public company—that he could have happily run a private portfolio from Omaha. But this does not take account of Buffett's entertainer's calling. In his letters, he found his stage. He would seize on an aspect of Berkshire—a wrinkle in its accounting, a problem in insurance—and veer off into a topical essay. In that respect, the letters were corporate oddities. One read the annual report of General Motors to learn about General Motors, not about the prejudices of any resident author-executive. The usual pose was Protestant and sober—what one would have expected from a Seabury Stanton. Buffett's were replete with sardonic observations on sex, greed, human fallibility—and himself. The syllabus was that of the Harvard Business School, but the spirit was *Poor Richard's Almanac*. And rather than explain business to just Kay Graham, he could do so for Wall Street, and for people across America.

Jack Byrne, who knew Buffett, had the sensation as he read the letters of the scales falling from his eyes. Richard Azar, a young entrepreneur from Trinidad who did not know him, experienced an epiphany: when he was nineteen, Azar wrote, "God sent a blessed gift to me that came in the form of a Berkshire Hathaway Annual Report."[29]

One explanation is that these tours through American capitalism and the exploits of Berkshire had no parallel. Tycoons there had been, and also men of letters, but here, in one package, was a J. P. Morgan writing with the irreverence of Will Rogers. Buffett leavened the essays with cracker-barrel witticisms and nimble quotations (belying the notion that he was some sort of hick) from cultural icons such as Pascal, Keynes, Mae West, and Yogi Berra. But these were mere truffles. What set the essays apart was his knack for unbuttoning a complex subject and clearly explaining it.

Through the early eighties one can discern three recurring themes. One was Buffett's dread fear of inflation, inherited from his father. He seemed to have taken to heart Lenin's dictum that the way to ruin capitalism was to ruin its money, and he doubted that politicians had the willpower to slow the printing press. Thus, Buffett saw inflation—as it turned out, erroneously—as a permanent affliction. "Like virginity, a stable price level seems capable of maintenance, but not of restoration."[30] Indeed, he feared that inflation might spell the demise of the long-term bond.[31] This proved to be dead wrong.

However, Buffett's insights enabled him (and more attentive readers) to minimize inflation's devastating consequences. His appreciation of its effect on the insurance business was especially dynamic. Inflation *was* destroying bond values, and the insurance industry had most of its capital in bonds—which previously had been the prudent course. What Buffett grasped was the vicious toll that the insurers' investments exacted on their main business. As bond losses mounted, Buffett saw that insurers would be unwilling to follow their usual course of selling assets to pay off claims, because any company that unloaded bonds would have to admit to a crushing loss of capital. Then again, he recognized, the money that insurers had invested in bonds was not theirs to keep.

> For the source of funds to purchase *and hold* those bonds is a pool of money derived from policyholders and claimants (with changing faces)—money which, in effect, is temporarily on deposit with the insurer.[32]

The alternative method of raising cash was for insurers to write more policies, which Buffett judged would cause the industry to write as much business as possible, driving premiums down to unprofitable levels and spurring huge losses in underwriting. All this unfolded as writ. Berkshire itself had minimal exposure to long-term bonds, the purchase of which, Buffett noted, was equivalent to "selling money" at a fixed price for thirty years. In an inflationary era, this was no less suicidal than agreeing to set a price on Hathaway yarn for the year 2010.

Alas, understanding inflation did not provide immunity to it. Buffett pointed out, with no little agony, that when he had taken over Berkshire the book value of one share could have bought one half-ounce of gold and that, after fifteen years in which he had managed to raise the book value from $19.46 a share to $335.85, it would still buy the same half-ounce.[33]

The best that he could do was to invest in companies that might resist inflation's ravages, such as General Foods and R. J. Reynolds Industries. Buffett figured that well-known consumer brands, such as Post cereals and Winston cigarettes, would be able to raise prices at a pace with inflation. He also bought hard-commodity stocks, such as Aluminum Co. of America, Cleveland-Cliffs Iron, Handy & Harman, and Kaiser Aluminum & Chemical. But as Buffett would remind his readers, neither Berkshire nor anyone had a "remedy" for the problem.

Inflation was a "gigantic corporate tapeworm" that "preemptively consumes its requisite daily diet of investment dollars regardless of the health of the host organism."[34]

On Wall Street, inflation had triggered a frantic hunt for corporate assets. Companies, like people, were desperate to convert money to anything other than cash, igniting the takeover mania of the early eighties. Venerable names, such as Del Monte, National Airlines, Seven-Up, Studebaker, and Tropicana, were being swallowed up at huge premiums. This spurred the multimillionaire Buffett to adopt the unlikely role of one of Wall Street's most scathing critics.

In his view, the vanity of corporate CEOs was leading to irrational deals. CEOs were, by natural Darwinian selection, excessively energetic sorts, seldom "deficient in animal spirits." They measured themselves by the *size* of their castle, rather than by Buffett's yardstick of profitability (which to him was the *only* rational goal). Instead of buying small pieces of companies on the cheap, as Buffett did, these CEOs preferred to take full bites at more than full prices. Not to worry, though—these CEOs, being by the same Darwinian process an egocentric bunch, believed that their talents would justify their paying such lofty prices:

> Many managements apparently were overexposed in impressionable childhood years to the story in which the imprisoned handsome prince is released from a toad's body by a kiss from a beautiful princess. Consequently, they are certain their managerial kiss will do wonders for the profitability of Company T(arget). . . . We've observed many kisses but very few miracles.[35]

Buffett wrote that for the 1981 report, when the merger wave was new. The next year, he could not resist a reprise. Many CEOs were paying for acquisitions by issuing shares. Buffett subjected this seemingly innocent technique to a rather savage dissection. In the first place, he observed, the acquiring CEOs weren't only buying, they were also *selling*. With the issuance of new shares, each ongoing stockholder wound up owning proportionately less of the company than before. The CEOs disguised this fact by using the language of a buyer: "Company A to Acquire Company B." However, "Clearer thinking about the matter would result if a more awkward but more accurate description were used: 'Part of A sold to acquire B.' . . ."[36]

Why was this disguise employed? Most stocks, including most acquirers' stocks, were cheap. In such a case, an acquiring CEO was shopping with unattractive currency, like an American in Paris when the dollar was undervalued. As he collected corporate trinkets he was parting with his own company on the cheap.

Buffett suggested that such managers and directors could "sharpen their thinking" by asking if they would be willing to sell *all* of their company on the same basis as they were selling part of it. And if not, why *were* they selling part of it?

> A cumulation of small managerial stupidities will produce a major stupidity—not a major triumph. (Las Vegas has been built upon the wealth transfers that occur when people engage in seemingly-small disadvantageous capital transactions.)[37]

What got under Buffett's skin was that CEOs were enlarging their personal empires at the expense of shareholders—the very group they were pledged to serve. Such managers "might better consider a career in government."[38]

Buffett likened corporate kingpins to bureaucrats precisely because he knew it would taunt them. In life, Buffett was friendly with many of those CEOs; he sat on their boards. In his letters, he was careful not to name them. Still, he divorced himself from his natural corporate allies. (On white-collar crime: "It has been far safer to steal large sums with a pen than small sums with a gun.")[39] There was a whiff about him of Dust Bowl progressivism, yet Buffett was anything but a Prairie socialist. Where the latter loathed businessmen as capitalists, Buffett arrived at his critique via the opposite route. He attacked CEOs for being wards of the corporate state—that is, for being *insufficiently* capitalist and self-reliant.

This suggests Buffett's most pervasive theme, which was the proper relationship between corporate managers and shareholders, i.e., between the stewards of capital and its owners. In his view, the mangers of other people's money bore a heavy burden, which he demonstrated in 1980, when a change in federal law forced Berkshire to divest the Rockford bank into a separate company. Buffett calculated that the bank was worth 4 percent of Berkshire; then he allowed each shareholder to choose between keeping his or her proportional stake in Berkshire and in the bank, or to take more of one and less of the other, depending on which slice (bank or Berkshire) a holder might prefer. The only one who did *not* get a choice was Buffett; he would take whatever shares were left. The principle was that he who cut the cake should be happy with the last slice.

In the same spirit, in 1981, Buffett introduced a novel corporate charity plan, conceived by Charlie Munger. For each of its one million shares, then trading at $470, Berkshire would contribute $2 to charities *of that shareholder's choice.* Someone who owned one hundred shares could designate the recipients for $200 in gifts, and so on. At other public companies, the choice of charities came from the CEO and the directors. (Only the money came from the stockholders.) Buffett saw this as sheer hypocrisy; not only did the CEO give away his stockholders' dough, he then got to play the big shot at his alma mater, etc. Thus, "Many corporate managers deplore governmental allocation of the taxpayer's dollar but embrace enthusiastically their own allocation of the shareholder's dollar."[40]

By such words and deeds, Buffett was shaping Berkshire into a very personal vehicle. In effect, he was re-creating it as a public form of the Buffett Partnership. Some of his two thousand or so shareholders were in fact his ex-partners, though most were not. But one purpose of his letters was to attract and knit together a shareholder group who would behave like his partners—in other words, who would stick with him.

The uniqueness of this approach is hard to overstate. At virtually every public company in America, high share turnover is not only the rule, it is devoutly encouraged by the executives. The typical CEO thinks of his investors as a faceless and changeable mass—to use Phil Fisher's analogy, like the diners in a highway road stop. At Berkshire, the turnover was extremely low, which—as was clear from Buffett's letters—was how he wanted his "café" to operate: "We much prefer owners who like our service and menu and who return year after year."[41]

Buffett scribbled his 7,500-word letters on a yellow legal pad, during family removes at Laguna Beach. He liked to imagine that his sister Roberta had been overseas for a year, and that he was writing to bring her up to date on the business.[42] The letters were edited by Carol Loomis, his friend at *Fortune,* but they were Buffett's creations and in fact sounded much as he did in conversation, full of homespun expressions and homilies.

The reports were printed on coarse matte paper and bore merely the company name and a vertical black stripe on the cover. Inside, there were no snapshots of chocolates at See's Candy, no photographs of Buffett and Munger with the pensive gaze that chief executives unfailingly employed for such occasions, no pyrotechnics with graphics—just a mass of type.

In part, Buffett was good at writing annual reports because he was good at reading them. Such reports typically are slick public relations documents, intended to put a gloss on management's performance and to attract new investors. Most contain only a perfunctory message from the CEO, and even that is typically ghostwritten. What Buffett missed in the hundreds that he read each year was a sense of the chief executive talking to him personally, and without the intrusion of professional hand-holders.

> Your Chairman has a firm belief that owners are entitled to hear directly from the CEO as to what is going on and how he evaluates the business, currently and prospectively. You would demand that in a private company; you should expect no less in a public company.[43]

He was most unhappy with CEOs who resorted to that old Buffett bugaboo, changing the yardstick. When results disappointed, they adopted "a more flexible measurement system": i.e., "shoot the arrow of business performance into a blank canvas and then carefully draw the bullseye around the implanted arrow."[44]

His primers on accounting in particular had a moral tone. Given that Wall Street cheers appearances, a CEO with the slightest Pavlovian impulse will be tempted to dress up his company before taking it out. The danger is that, having fooled the public, the CEO will do likewise unto himself.[45] Many run the business so as to maximize not the economic reality but the reported results. "In the long run," Buffett warned, "managements stressing accounting appearance over economic substance usually achieve little of either."[46]

What *should* a CEO say to the public? In theory, he ought to describe the business from the same perspective that its managers did. Just as Buffett expected Ken Chace to give him a candid account of the textile mill, Buffett owed a similar candor (though not the same level of detail) to his public investors.

Berkshire's reports, in fact, disclosed enough information for readers to evaluate the company on the least favorable of terms. As during the partnership, Buffett repeatedly assured investors that there was no chance of maintaining prior rates of success. He was still the dutiful parishioner; confession soothed him. If there was a flaw in the reports, it was that Buffett was occasionally cloying and autoreferential. There was a winking quality to some of his gags, as though he were looking over his own shoulder. Moreover, his confessions of error and tongue-in-cheek self-immolations had a falsely modest ring. His humility wasn't going to fool anyone—not with the stock in the stratosphere.

In 1982, that stock hit $750 a share. This gaudy number reflected the gain in Berkshire's stock portfolio, and that, in turn, was taking wing from developments in Washington. Paul Volcker, the Federal Reserve chairman, had been squeezing liquidity out of the system. The first effect was a recession, the second, an ebbing of inflation. By 1982, Volcker was sufficiently confident to loosen his grip on interest rates. The White House, meanwhile, was a picture of optimism. Ronald Reagan laughed off a would-be assassin and pushed through a tax cut.

For so long, Wall Street had known nothing but fear. Now, as if a cat-footed clerk in a basement of its stone fortresses had thrown a master switch, brokers and bankers arrived at their desks with confidence. In the summer of 1982, interest rates tumbled . . . and tumbled . . . and tumbled. Treasury bills, quoted at 13.32 percent in June, stood at 8.66 percent in August. Stock prices, at first, resisted this stimulus. In August, stocks fell for eight straight days. The Dow stood at 777—well below its level of *fifteen years* prior. The Dow finally broke its losing string on Friday the 13th, gaining 11 points. Optimism was muted. On Monday, the Dow eked out a few points more. Then, on Tuesday, at precisely 10:41 A.M., Henry Kaufman, the perpetually gloomy Salomon Brothers economist with the coveted crystal ball, did a volte-face. Kaufman—a.k.a. Dr. Doom—declared that, counter to his previous sooth-sayings, he now expected interest rates to continue falling. The news sparked a buyers' panic in stocks. The Dow rose 38.81 points—the biggest one-day rise in its history. The next day's *Wall Street Journal* presciently reported: "Some are saying this is the start of the 1980s boom."[47] The earth had moved.

By Labor Day, the market had risen 100 points more. By October, yet another 100. In 1983, economic growth resumed, and inflation retreated to a nostalgic 3 percent. The world discovered that it had not too little oil, but too much. The surge in bonds continued, driving long-term rates down to 11 percent, from 15 percent two years earlier. Meanwhile, the stock market experienced a phenomenon unseen since the sixties—a sustainable rally. New issues, out of favor since the Go-Go era, surged. Mutual-fund sales, yet another ghost from the Wall Street closet, revived. By May, the Dow was at 1,232, or 366 points higher than when *Business Week* had prematurely buried it. The magazine now proclaimed the *rebirth* of equities. As Buffett had predicted, those who had sat out the gloomy interval to wait for a "cheery consensus" had paid a dear price indeed. They had missed a 42 percent move. "The news that *Business Week* had rediscovered the stock market sent tremors of trepidation tripping through the Street," Alan Abelson of *Barron's* jested wickedly. "Panic set in, widows wept, orphans wailed and sell orders flooded the market with a mighty rush."[48]

Among the soaring stocks in Berkshire's portfolio, Washington Post, purchased at an average, split-adjusted price of 5¹⁵⁄₁₆, skyrocketed to 73; Affiliated, acquired at 5, when no one else would touch it, closed the year at 38. Interpublic, the ad agency, was up from 6⅜ to 52. GEICO, bought in its darkest hour, had multiplied ninefold. Time, purchased within the previous two years, had doubled; RJR was up 17 percent; General Foods, 40 percent. Here and there, Buffett did have losses. Berkshire dropped $3 million on Vornado, a discount retailer, and lost money on Sperry & Hutchinson, a green stamp purveyor, both purchased in the 1970s. And Buffett did not do well on some inflation-hedge metal stocks. But in sum, where Berkshire once had not had *any* portfolio, by the end of 1983 it had $1.3 billion worth of marketable stocks. And it had all been assembled from the tiny stream of cash that Buffett had diverted from textiles.

Berkshire's own stock was something to watch that year. It opened for trading at 775. By spring, it was 15 points shy of 1,000. On September 30, it was quoted at 1,245. This, as it happened, was 12 points higher than the Dow. When Buffett had taken it over, Berkshire had been quoted at 18; the Dow, at 931, had been fifty times higher. Now they were neck and neck. The Dow finished the year in game fashion, at 1,259, but by then, it was plainly visible in the rearview mirror. Berkshire had risen to $1,310 a share. Buffett suddenly was worth $620 million. According to *Forbes*, he was one of the richest Americans.

Shareholders pressed Buffett to split his stock. The rationale—and it is an article of faith at virtually every public company—is that a lower share price is more affordable and thus tends to enhance the public's interest in a stock. But in his 1983 letter, Buffett ruled out a split. Slicing the pie into more pieces would hardly increase its value. (Try it with a pizza.)

To be sure, a split would attract new investors and stimulate trading. It might even lift the price of Berkshire's stock, at least for a while. But this would merely *reapportion* one investor's share of the corporate wealth to another. If some traders exited at a higher price, others would pay more to buy in. But *as a group*, Berkshire's owners would not be any richer, because the value of what they owned, See's Candy, the *Buffalo News*, and all the rest, would not be affected. "These expensive activities may decide who eats the pie, but they don't enlarge it."⁴⁹ Indeed, in the aggregate, Berkshire's owners would be poorer by the sum of increased brokerage commissions. Brokers, themselves, praised high turnover in the guise of "liquidity." But, as Buffett derisively added, such trading merely helped the "croupier"; it inflicted a "tax" on the customer.

His attitude may seem extreme, but Buffett wanted no false notes that might conflict with his "ownership philosophy." Most CEOs do not have such a "philosophy," nor is it a matter to which they give much thought. But Buffett had thought about it quite a bit. He was consciously trying to assemble a tribe of like-minded shareholders, who would focus, as he did, on long-term value. If people bought for reasons that had nothing to do with value—such as a stock split—so, too, would they one day sell. As much as possible, Buffett wanted to dissuade such infidels from becoming his partners. This suggests the depth of Buffett's commitment to Berkshire; it was a "job" to him in the sense that England was a job to Churchill.

In the same annual letter of 1983, Buffett published a list of "principles," partly intended to attract and keep the investors he wanted. There was nothing outwardly exceptional in these rules; boiled down, they amounted to a pledge that he and Munger would be straight with their investors and prudent with their capital. The spirit that underlay them would have been familiar to Oliver Chace, Buffett's nineteenth-century corporate progenitor. But it was inconsistent with the spirit of Buffett's own, more restless age. His aim was to profit from the long-term growth of (hopefully) well-chosen businesses, but not from nimbly entering and exiting them, or from financial legerdemain, or from various forms of pie-splitting and (at foolish prices) pie-acquiring. In the sense of abhorring change for its own sake, it was profoundly conservative. Buffett confessed a reluctance to go into debt or to play investment musical chairs even at the *certainty* that his attitude would penalize Berkshire's return:

> Regardless of price, we have no interest at all in selling any good businesses that Berkshire owns, and are very reluctant to sell sub-par businesses as long as we expect them to generate at least some cash and as long as we feel good about their managers and labor relations. We hope not to repeat the capital-allocation mistakes that led us into such sub-par businesses. . . . Nevertheless, gin rummy managerial behavior (discard your least promising business at each turn) is not our style.[50]

In a calmer time, this would have been unremarkable. But the 1980s were no ordinary period in finance. America was home to the hostile takeover, the junk bond, the leveraged buyout. The archetypal business figure was no longer the rough-and-ready entrepreneur, the Oliver Chace, but the slicer and dicer on Wall Street. The mantra of this age was "liquidity"; not only corporate shares, but whole companies, too, were flipped like trading cards (indeed, flipped, and then dissected, and then reassembled and repartitioned). The ethos of the age was transience; credit was its catnip, instability its offspring. Supposing, for a moment, that Chace could have returned to his once-prudent world, one may imagine his horror. And yet, had he chanced to read some of his company's letters, might he not have felt, with astonishment anew, that it was not all lost?

Chapter 13

THE
CARPET
WOMAN

One question Buffett always asked himself in appraising a business is how comfortable he would feel having to compete against it, assuming that he had ample capital, personnel, experience in the same industry, and so forth.[1]

It was after such an appraisal that, in the summer of 1983, he strode into the Nebraska Furniture Mart, a sprawling store opposite Ross's Steak House. He made his way through the acres of convertible sofas and dining-room sets to the carpeting department, and there, amid the vast field of powder blues and placid beiges, he spied the store's owner, a woman all of four feet ten inches, and slightly stooped at that. But as measured by Buffett's yardstick, she might have been ten feet tall.

Rose Blumkin, known to Omaha as Mrs. B, was patrolling the store in her golf cart. She motored down the aisle, haranguing an employee and gesturing with her arms with the vigor of a woman half her eighty-nine years. Her cheeks were flushed, and her auburn hair, done up in a bouffant, showed gray only at the temples. Buffett reckoned that he would "rather wrestle grizzlies" than compete against Mrs. B, and that was why he had come.

Speaking deliberately, Buffett asked if she would like to sell the store to Berkshire Hathaway.

Mrs. B said, "Yes."

"How much?" Buffett asked.

"Sixty million," Mrs. B spat out.

They shook hands, and Buffett drew up a one-page agreement—Buffett's biggest acquisition by far. Mrs. B, who could not write in English and barely could read it, made a mark at the bottom. Merely a few days later, Buffett presented her with a check for 90 percent (the Blumkin family kept a minority share). She folded it without a glance and, by way of concluding matters, declared, "Mr. Buffett, we're going to put our competitors through a *meat grinder*."[2]

So well did Mrs. B incarnate Buffett's business ideal, she seemed to have sprung from the pages of his letters, as though he had invented her to illustrate the plain virtues that he most admired. Mrs. B had the toughness, determination, and common sense that Buffett had seen in his grocer grandfather, in the retailer Ben Rosner, and in other Buffett heroes. Her story was the familiar, and distinctly American, story to which Buffett thrilled. It was a Horatio Alger script, set to the score of *Fiddler on the Roof*, yet magnified almost beyond belief.

Rose Gorelick was born on the eve of Hanukkah, 1893, in a village near Minsk in czarist Russia.[3] She and seven brothers and sisters slept in one room, on straw. Her father was a rabbi, but his piety was wasted on Rose, who observed that his prayers did not provide the family with a mattress.[4] She would awake in the middle of the night to see her mother, who ran a grocery, slaving over an oven baking bread. Hating to see her mother work so hard, she helped her in the store from the age of six. Her other formative experience was of the Cossacks, who now and then would lay siege to the Jews in bloody pogroms.

The Gorelicks had no money for school (Rose never saw the inside of a classroom), but she learned to read and do figures at the home of a rich family. From her mother, she acquired a conviction that begging was ignoble. At thirteen, she talked her way into a job at a dry-goods store in Minsk. At sixteen, she was running the store, a slip of a girl supervising five men. She married Isadore Blumkin in 1914 and saw him off to America, intending to follow. But the war broke out before she could go. In the desperate winter of 1917, with Europe aflame and Russia tottering, she boarded the trans-Siberian railroad. At the Chinese frontier, a Russian guard stopped her. Mrs. B, who did not have a passport, told him she was buying leather for the army, and promised to bring him a bottle of vodka on her return. Then she crossed Manchuria to Japan and gained a berth on a peanut boat. Six weeks later she set foot in Seattle.

In 1919, she and her husband settled in Omaha. Though penniless, she sent for her parents and siblings, who moved in under the same roof. Isadore ran a pawnshop and secondhand-clothing store. To supplement this meager living, Mrs. B sold furniture out of her basement. She spoke not a word of English, but her kids, who picked it up at school, taught her.

In 1937, at the age of forty-four, she scratched together $500 and rented a storefront, on Farnam Street, one block east of the original Buffett grocery. Thinking big, she dubbed it Nebraska Furniture Mart. A photo from the time shows a determined face, the black hair drawn in a bun, the jaw set firmly. Her method was her motto: "Sell cheap and tell the truth."

Brand-name manufacturers considered that her ultralow prices were bad for business, and refused to supply her. But Mrs. B was an adroit bootlegger. She would hop a train to Chicago or Kansas City, where retailers such as Marshall Field would sell their excess merchandise to her at a little above their cost.[5] When she was out of stock, she dragged the furniture out of her home. One time, one of her grown daughters got a call from Mama. "Empty the baby's storage chest. I got a *customer*."[6]

When she applied for credit, the banks would refuse her with a snicker, out of which experience Mrs. B developed an enduring hatred of "big shots." What kept her going was her will. She worked seven days a week, fifty-two weeks a year, never a day off. In addition, she found that she had an affinity for her working- and middle-class customers, whom she referred to as "the vunderful American people." These loyal customers always came up with cash when Mrs. B had bills.

In 1949, Mohawk Carpet Mills hauled her into court, accusing her of violating fair-trade laws.[7] Mohawk, a manufacturer, set a minimum retail price on one of its carpets of $7.25 a yard. Mrs. B was charging only $4.95. "*So what's wrong with that?*" Case dismissed. The next day, the judge walked into Nebraska Furniture Mart and purchased $1,400 worth of carpet.

The next year, Mrs. B couldn't pay her suppliers. A friendly banker gave her a ninety-day $50,000 note. In a desperate bid to stay afloat, she rented a hall, unloaded $250,000 of furniture in three days, and vowed never to borrow again. And so, at age fifty-seven, Mrs. B was on her way.

She was merciless with her staff, including those in her family. "You worthless *golem*!" she would scream. "You dummy! You lazy!" What saved her from herself was her gentleman son, Louie. Louie was just as keen as his mother, but his manner was mild. When Mrs. B ripped into a salesman, Louie would buck him up. Mrs. B would fire the help; Louie would hire them back. "Mama was very tough," Louie noted. "I liked to smear on the honey." Isadore died, but Louie stayed in the store. Whatever Mrs. B said, he would answer with honey. "Mama, you know best."

Mrs. B's formula was irresistibly simple; she bought in volume, kept expenses bone-trim, and passed on the savings. Typically, she sold at 10 percent above her cost, but was known for making exceptions. When a young couple came in, misty-eyed at the prospect of their very own convertible, Mrs. B, who had memorized the wholesale price of every item, would slash her price on the spot. And that couple would come back.

The Mart became a rite of passage, the coda to weddings, births, promotions. Omahans who had furnished homes at Mrs. B's store would return when they moved, or when their kids moved. Advancing age didn't slow her in the least. When a tornado took her roof off, she kept selling. When a fire scorched the store, she handed out free televisions to the firemen.[8] Mrs. B never took a vacation. "I never lied," she said. "I never cheated. I never promised I couldn't do. That brought me luck."

Susan Buffett was friendly with the Blumkin family, and Warren heard from her of the wondrous store that was furnishing half of Omaha.[9] Buffett tried to buy it, early in his career, but Mrs. B dismissed his offer as "too cheap."[10]

But the rejection merely stiffened him. He kept a close eye on the store and observed that Mrs. B was running one competitor after another out of business. Driving around town with the writer Adam Smith, in the early seventies, Buffett pointed out the store and reeled off its operating statistics—the volume, floor space, turnover, and so on.

"Why don't you buy it?" Smith wondered.

"It's privately held."

"Oh."

"I might buy it anyway," Buffett added. "Someday."[11]

When the day arrived, Louie and his three sons were running the store. Mrs. B remained its chairman and full-time boss of the carpet department. Buffett, having heard that she was ready to sell, went to see Louie first—to sound him out on price and ensure that he understood Mrs. B's thickly accented English.[12]

Before the sale, Buffett looked at the Furniture Mart's tax returns, which showed that it was earning about $15 million a year pretax. He did none of the usual checking, such as asking for an audit or examining the inventory, receivables, or property titles. The average home buyer probably looks at more pieces of paper than Buffett did in spending $60 million. His approach seems strange in a modern context, but it was in accord with the notion of J. P. Morgan, Sr., that the principal judgments in business are those concerning character. In Buffett's terms, if he couldn't trust the Blumkins, why become their partner?

One was tempted to ask, as so often with Buffett, were things really so *simple*? The answer is that he had a genius for keeping them simple. In his 1982 letter, just before the deal with Mrs. B, he printed a "Want Ad" describing his criteria for acquisitions. He promised to respond to offers quickly—"customarily within five minutes." What Buffett was saying was that he wouldn't pursue a close call. A business had to grab him by the throat—and this the Blumkin business surely did.

The Mart was the biggest furniture store in the country, with $100 million in annual sales. In Omaha, it accounted for an astounding two-thirds of all furniture sales—a percentage that leading stores in other markets did not come close to matching.[13] Indeed, department store chains such as Dillard's ($4 billion in annual sales) refused to sell furniture in Omaha because Mrs. B was too tough a competitor.[14] As Buffett might say, she had a toll bridge to the living rooms of Omaha.

The Mart was so dominant that it ferried sofas out-of-state in unmarked trucks so as to avoid angering merchants in other cities. "If somebody else advertises Maytag washers she tears out their ad and puts it on *her* Maytag washer," Buffett marveled. "It is *hell* to compete with her."[15]

Don Danly, Buffett's pinball partner, was in Omaha the day of the purchase. After a ritual steak dinner, Buffett took Danly through the

Furniture Mart, recounting the saga of "the amazing Blumkins" in exquisite detail. Another visitor, Norman Lear, the Hollywood producer, said, "Warren's admiration for Mrs. B is like a child's. He talks about her the way a small boy would talk about his grandmother."

Since Buffett had no wish to run a store himself, or even to closely supervise one, he wanted managers who would "feel like I do," ready to tap-dance at the start of the workday.[16] Mrs. B was a sort of exaggerated version—almost a caricature—of that self-made, self-motivating ideal. Buffett, who had upped his own salary to $100,000 a year, paid $300,000 to Mrs. B.[17] He routinely referred to her as one of his "heroes."

He must have seen in her an unpolished—but in the essentials, quite faithful—rendering of himself. It was not just her obsessive habits (in her nineties, she continued to work every day of the year, ten to twelve hours a day), or her native suspicion of credit (the forty-three-acre store site was unmortgaged), or, as Buffett put it, that she "started with five hundred bucks and put everyone else out of business."[18] It was her utter singularity of purpose. When the *Omaha World-Herald* inquired as to her favorite movie, Mrs. B replied, "Too busy." Her favorite cocktail? "None. Drinkers go broke." Her hobby, then? Driving around and spying on competitors.[19]

A reporter who found Mrs. B at home noted that her living room looked like an extension of the showroom. The twin love seats, the reflecting glass coffee table, the assortment of crystal and brass figurines were arranged as they were in the store. Price tags dangled from the lampshades.[20] Mrs. B didn't spend much time there and never entertained. "I don't like rich society people," she noted. "Rich people are rude to you when you're poor; I don't forget that."

As an unlettered immigrant, she underscored all that Buffett had been writing about the folly of needless complexity. She knew nothing about B-school retailing concepts such as "elasticity," but she could tell Buffett her cash balance down to the penny.[21] Buffett told an audience at Columbia Business School that Mrs. B knew depreciation and accruals "better than anybody in this room," though she did not understand them in accounting terms. In his view, she had a native genius, which consisted of staying focused on the one area of her expertise.[22] This was very similar to how Buffett saw himself. (At Buffett's prompting, New York University granted Mrs. B an honorary doctorate of commercial science, an honor she shared with Fed chairman Paul Volcker and Citicorp CEO Walter Wriston.)

A visitor found her at work on a Sunday afternoon, attired in a sweater and blue pinstriped suit, with a carpet sample in her basket. She had a lively sense of humor and a poignant memory, and vividly described the day that she had seen two of the czar's daughters in Minsk, shortly before they were shot.

When she spied a young woman fingering a rug, she burrowed over to her like a motorized rat. An expression of alertness, bordering on suspicion, was etched onto her face.

"Thirty-nine dollars. It's a *beauty*."

"I have blues and pinks," the woman said uncertainly.

"It will go with *anything*."

Mrs. B motored toward the counter. A saleswoman was on the phone with a customer who hadn't paid for a carpet.

"Hang up," Mrs. B volunteered. "Let him go to hell. Got to be ashamed of himself."

The saleswoman was trying to work it out.

"Hang up! No sense talking to him."

The saleswoman was straining to hear the details—something about the wrong color.

"I make my life being honest. Say 'Goodbye' and *hang up*! The guy's going to get a cancer 'cause he's such a crook."

Aside from her prominent veins, she looked far less than her nine decades plus. She subsisted on a diet of fruits and vegetables, rose at 5:00 A.M., did not exercise, and, other than having had her knees replaced, was in perfect health. That was probably the trait Buffett admired most.

He couldn't bear the thought that ill health (or death) would force him to give up working, and often joked that he planned to rely on séances as a management tool. (Buffett invariably vented his most anxious feelings with humor.) For someone so conscious of his mortality, the sight of Mrs. B must have provided a sort of cover. Writing to his shareholders, Buffett openly made the link between Mrs. B's advancing age and his own:

It's clear to me that she's gathering speed and may well reach her full potential in another five or ten years. Therefore, I've persuaded the

Board to scrap our mandatory-retirement-at-100 policy. (And it's about time: With every passing year, this policy has seemed sillier to me.)[23]

Mrs. B's blemish was her disposition, which was increasingly brutal. She was badly at odds with two of her grandsons, who were the store's heir-apparent managers. One of them, Ronald Blumkin, was so fed up with his grandmother's scoldings that the two of them had stopped speaking. This fly in the Blumkin ointment was easy—perhaps too easy—for Buffett to ignore, because the Mart consistently earned a high return.

Buffett regarded the Blumkin clan so highly that Berkshire bought a *second* family business: the Omaha jewelry store Borsheim's. Borsheim's was truly a case of lightning striking twice. In 1948, the then tiny store had been purchased by Mrs. B's sister and brother-in-law, Rebecca and Louis Friedman, who had escaped Russia on a westward odyssey via Latvia. Borsheim's became the second-biggest-selling jewelry store (trailing only Tiffany's in New York) in the United States.[24] Like the Furniture Mart, it perfected the high-volume/low-price formula—which, once in place, tends to be self-perpetuating. Of course, the profits on diamonds were considerably higher than those on carpets.

From Buffett's vantage, the stores had similar strengths. Each enjoyed a protective "moat" that kept competitors at bay.[25] (Buffett's hatred of competition, evident in the Buffalo newspaper drama, was a mainstay in his career.) And nobody could take on the Furniture Mart without a very substantial investment and lengthy battle—which is the sort of chin-deep moat that dissuades would-be competitors from even trying.

Indeed, it gave Buffett a thrill just to stand by the counter at the Furniture Mart and watch it ring up a sale.[26] He made a ritual of taking out-of-town guests to Mrs. B's; he even provided buses for the annual meeting of Berkshire, so his shareholders could visit the store. In a spiritual sense, the Mart replaced the red-brick New Bedford textile mill as the company's flagship. In fact, Buffett made about as much money in fifteen months in furniture as he had in nineteen years in textiles.

The comparison is illustrative, because the Hathaway mill was everything the Mart was not. The mill was *indistinguishable* from its competitors; the end consumer didn't know it existed. As Buffett would bitterly joke, no one went into a men's store and asked for "a pinstriped suit with a Hathaway lining."[27]

Whereas the fast turnover at Mrs. B's resulted in precious little capital being tied down in inventory, the textile mill *consumed* capital. Every time one manufacturer upgraded its plant, Berkshire's mill and all the rest were forced to match it. Thus, no one would gain any advantage—any moat—but every manufacturer would have sunk in more capital.

Though Buffett knew better, he occasionally had been seduced into thinking that a little more capital could turn it around. In the mid-seventies, he even bought another textile plant, in Manchester, New Hampshire. On paper, the purchase was a steal. But it turned out to be a disaster. Retrospectively, Buffett realized that textiles were a trap:

> Viewed individually, each company's capital investment decision appeared cost-effective and rational; viewed collectively, the decisions neutralized each other and were irrational (just as happens when each person watching a parade decides he can see a little better if he stands on tiptoes).[28]

Shareholders increasingly questioned why he stayed in textiles. Buffett replied that the mills were big local employers, the unions had been cooperative, and he had hopes for modest profits. Also, he felt a loyalty to Ken Chace, who had run the operation from the start. As he reminded shareholders, it had been Chace's efforts in textiles that had provided the fuel for Berkshire's growth.[29] But in private, Buffett would occasionally warn Chace: "It looks like the mill is going to start using cash. I don't want that."

Chace continued to labor mightily—almost (not quite) as doggedly as Mrs. B. He switched product lines and fabrics. He upgraded machinery. He improved relations with union leaders (who knew that his boss in Omaha was a skinflint). But he couldn't outrun the competition, of which the supply seemed unending. Buffett drew from this a broad maxim: a good manager was unlikely to overcome a bad business.[30] This led to a truism about problem businesses in general: " 'turnarounds' seldom turn . . ."[31]

In 1980, Buffett halted production in Manchester and cut the number of looms in New Bedford by a third. Still, in 1981, textiles lost $2.7

million, rivaling some of the worst years of the Seabury Stanton era. Buffett told Chace, "If you can't cut the overhead I'm going to shut you down." But Chace—to Buffett's rueful surprise—pulled it off.

The purchase of the Furniture Mart, in 1983, put Buffett's mill mistakes in stark relief. He finally (though obliquely) admitted in public that his devotion to Ben Graham had caused him, for too long, to stick with brick-and-mortar assets such as textiles at the cost of overlooking Mrs. B–style franchises.

> My escape was long delayed, in part because most of what I had been taught by the same teacher had been (and continues to be) so extraordinarily valuable.[32]

But now, his thinking had "changed drastically." The next year, Chace retired. His replacement, Garry Morrison, an M.B.A. with a degree in textiles, argued for an infusion of fresh capital. Buffett refused. And without new money, the mill, clearly, would continue to bleed. In 1985, Buffett shut it down.

Its four hundred workers, mostly skilled, ethnic Portuguese, got a few months' notice and job retraining, though many, if not most, ended up in lower-paying work. They asked for severance above what the contract guaranteed and, as David Lima, secretary-treasurer of the New Bedford Textile Workers Union of America, recalled, got a month or so. "For guys who were losing their jobs, it wasn't worth a hill of beans," Lima said.

The union also asked to see Buffett personally. He coldly responded that he saw no reason to meet.[33] In Garry Morrison's view, "Warren wanted to be fair. He was fair, but not overly generous."

Buffett was sensitive to just such a characterization. In an epilogue to the affair, he noted that during the previous five years, 250 other mills had also closed.[34] During that time, Berkshire's mill had lost more than $5 million. Buffett fancied that by running the mill so long, he had found a "middle ground," less ruthless toward the workers' interests than (the original) Adam Smith but more so than Karl Marx—that is, willing to endure "subnormal profitability" but not "unending losses."

Of course, as between the two, Buffett had his "Marxist" tendencies rather well hidden. He was willing to *moderate* Adam Smith, and to sacrifice "a fraction of a point" on his rate of return—but not to abandon Smith. Indeed, the point of his essay was that to forsake Smith—to forsake capital—could be ruinous. The ill-disguised hero of Buffett's essay was himself, for having followed Smith and diversified out of textiles. Its devil was another yarn mill: Burlington Industries. Burlington, he noted, had not diversified; it had stuck to its knitting. During Buffett's bountiful score and one years at Berkshire, Burlington had reinvested $3 billion back into textiles. It was now the biggest U.S. textile company, but that was a dubious prize. For over those twenty-one years, Burlington's stock had pitifully crept from 60 to merely 68. Adjusted for inflation, its investors had lost two-thirds of their purchasing power. Marx might have approved, but Smith—and Buffett—did not.

> This devastating outcome for the shareholders indicates what can happen when much brain power and energy are applied to a faulty premise. The situation is suggestive of Samuel Johnson's horse. "A horse that can count to ten is a remarkable horse—not a remarkable mathematician."[35]

And a brilliantly run textile firm was not a brilliant business.

Ken Chace, in retirement on the Maine coast, judged that Buffett had run the plant ten years too long. He stressed that he treasured his experience with Buffett—"It's hard to describe how much I enjoyed working for him"—but was wistful for an expressiveness that Buffett had never shown. "One thing that's always bothered me," Chace admitted. "I never knew why he picked me. When I resigned, he said, 'I remember you were absolutely straight with me from the first day I walked through the plant.' That was all he ever said."

The mill's subsequent fate confirmed Chace's verdict that Buffett had been slow to close it. The equipment was auctioned to carrion hunters for the laughable sum of $163,122. Looms purchased in 1981 for $5,000 apiece were sold in 1985 as scrap for $26 each.[36] But Buffett insisted on keeping the real estate on Cove Street. The mill space was leased to tiny firms making silk screens, stage assemblies, data-processing forms—and others with no memory of the heyday of textiles. The old headquarters, where once Seabury Stanton had proudly reigned from the Ivory Tower, would serve as the office of BHR Inc.—Berkshire Hathaway Realty—its name a flickering reminder of the once-great mills that sit like rotting ships in the city's south end.

Chapter 14

THE
EIGHTIES

In 1984, Buffett dropped in on J. Richard Munro, the chief executive of Time Inc., at the company's stately headquarters in New York's Rockefeller Center. Berkshire owned 4 percent of Time, and Buffett and Munro often talked media together. Now, as both of them knew, Time was rumored to be a takeover target.

Buffett thought he could help the magazine giant keep its independence. "How would you like a white knight?" he asked. In the parlance of the eighties, Buffett was proposing a deal. In Munro's words:

> Warren would have been a major shareholder and agreed to never sell. He would have been our guy. We took it to our board, and they said, "Who is Warren Buffett?"

It was still possible for a company, especially an institution such as Time, to think of itself as immune. "That was before anything hit the fan, before we were lying awake nights," Munro noted. Later, Time would discover that it was anything but immune. Menaced by a hostile bid, it would merge with Warner Communications and, in the process, thoroughly wreck its balance sheet. Indeed, Time would be the most prominent example of the self-destructive tactics of the merger era. In hindsight, Munro said of Buffett's offer, "It's too bad we didn't do it."

As Munro—and so many others—would discover, dramatic changes were afoot. At First Boston, a sleepy firm where four people had worked on mergers and acquisitions a decade earlier, a staff of 110 were cranking out deals by the hour. And the pace was accelerating. In 1975, Wall Street had racked up $12 billion in deals; in 1984, $122 billion. Investment bankers, long seen as staid, suddenly were objects of envy and resentment. Young, rich, smugly powerful in red suspenders, they indulged in battlefield metaphors and terrified Main Street executives.

For a century, the Street had provided financing at the behest of corporate clients. Now the tables had turned. Wall Street's matchmakers were seizing the initiative; Main Street was merely fodder for their deals. Hostile raids were being backed by a novel form of finance, the junk bond, which had been pioneered by the renegade Drexel Burnham Lambert, and which investors were accepting as payment for whatever inflated sum the raiders offered. In this respect, the eighties bore a resemblance to previous speculative eras. Indeed, Fred Carr, the fallen archetype of the Go-Go market, had resurfaced as the head of First Executive, the most ardent promoter of Drexel's junk.

Of course, speculation was not new to Wall Street, nor was merger mania. But the architecture of Wall Street *had* changed. Fortune 500 companies were now, overwhelmingly, controlled by professional shareholders such as pension and mutual funds. And such investors uniformly took the high bid and ran. Once upon a time, at least at well-performing companies, the major shareholders' commitments to management had been a force inhibiting takeovers. By the mid-eighties, such commitments had the half-life of a cup of coffee. Andrew Sigler, the CEO of Champion International, complained that his stockholders changed so fast he didn't know who they were.[1]

Buffett's perspective had also changed. At one time, his view of the Street had been exclusively that of a shareholder. Now, in middle age, he also identified with CEOs—with the Dick Munros and Andy Siglers. He was suspicious of the raiders and of the havoc they caused in corporate boardrooms, and wary of stock prices inflated by takeover fever. Once again, he felt that Wall Street was going too far, as it had during the Go-Go era. But this time Buffett had no thought of quitting. In fact, he was hoping to do some very big deals.

Buffett's entry in the grand game can be dated—February 26, 1985. In Washington for a couple of days, Buffett got a call from Tom Murphy, his friend and the chairman of Capital Cities.

"Pal, you're not going to believe this," Murphy began. "I've just bought ABC. You've got to come and tell me how I'm going to pay for it."[2]

Thomas S. Murphy, like Buffett, was the son of a politician. His father was a Brooklyn judge and had exposed Tom to visitors such as Thomas Dewey and Al Smith. After a charmed youth—summers in the country, golf at the family club—Murphy went to the Harvard Business School. A classmate, James Burke (later chairman of Johnson & Johnson), thought Murphy was a natural for politics, too. Tall and balding, Murphy was almost irresistibly affable. He had an easy, unpretentious manner and addressed people as "pal." After a stint at Lever Brothers, he took an $18,000-a-year job with Hudson Valley Broadcasting, managing a bankrupt UHF station in Albany.

The humble Hudson Valley, which broadcast out of a home for retired nuns, managed to acquire another station and went public in 1957, at seventy-two cents a share. A few years later, Murphy moved to New York, settling into a cozy brownstone office, and tapped Daniel Burke (James's younger brother) as his second-in-command. They operated as a team, with Murphy focusing on strategy and deal-making and the harder-edged Burke on operational details. The company, now known as Capital Cities, gradually acquired an empire in broadcasting, cable, and publishing. Its style, though, was anything but imperial. Murphy and Burke delegated ample authority to their far-flung properties and ran a corporate office that was bone-trim. Cap Cities had no legal department and no public relations staff. Murphy was so frugal that he had once painted only the two sides of his Albany headquarters that faced the road—not the sides facing the Hudson River. His and Burke's blend of vision and cost-attentiveness produced consistently superior profits.

Buffett, who had met Murphy in the early seventies, knew that anyone who didn't waste paint on his headquarters was his sort of guy. He bought 3 percent of Cap Cities for Berkshire in 1977, but after a run-up in the stock he sold—a decision Buffett would later attribute to "temporary insanity." Meanwhile, Murphy and Burke began to check with Buffett before each big move. One time, when Walter Annenberg was mulling the sale of his publishing empire, which included such gems as *TV Guide* and the *Daily Racing Form*, Buffett said, "Murph, how about the two of our companies buying it on a fifty-fifty basis?"[3] They went to see Annenberg in Beverly Hills and offered $1 billion.

Annenberg turned them down, and Buffett and his "pal" went to a Swensen's—just a couple of regular guys with a billion bucks to burn—and drowned their sorrows over milk shakes. But Buffett's dream of becoming Murphy's partner didn't die. He often declared that the Murphy-Burke ensemble was the best in corporate America.

Buffett also had shown more than a passing interest in ABC. In the late sixties, ABC had agreed to be bought by International Telephone & Telegraph, but the Justice Department had blocked it. Buffett had been at the Pacific Stock Exchange when the deal had fallen through. He turned to Ed Anderson, Munger's associate, and said, "You know, Ed, ABC is totally in the hands of arbitrageurs. Anyone could get control. I sure wish I had the money." He bought a slice of ABC in 1979, and again in 1984. When Buffett took Murphy's call, Berkshire already owned about 2.5 percent of ABC's stock.

Murphy was equally keen on ABC, which had lucrative local stations and the prized jewel of a national network. Late in 1984, it became apparent that the Federal Communications Commission was going to raise the ceiling on television station ownership by a single company, making a merger possible. Soon after, Murphy dropped in on Leonard H. Goldenson, the seventy-nine-year-old architect and chief executive of ABC, at the ABC building in New York. "Leonard," he began, "I don't want you to throw me out of the thirty-ninth floor, but I have an idea."[4] Goldenson did not throw him out. ABC, he knew, was being stalked by raiders who, if successful, were likely to dismantle the company that had been his life's work. If he had to sell, better to someone like Murphy, who would keep the company intact.[5]

Two days later, Buffett met Murphy and Burke in New York.

Buffett began with a word of caution. "Think about how it will change your life," he warned. Murphy and Burke instantly understood. Cap Cities, which owned such properties as *Women's Wear Daily* and the *Kansas City Star*, was little known outside its industry, and Murphy and Burke led private lives. Now, Murphy, a devout Catholic who liked to stop at St. Patrick's Cathedral on his way to work, would be thrust in the company of network executives who rode to work in limousines.

Murphy was impressed that Buffett's first thought had been "the personal equation."[6] But Murphy wanted to go ahead.

Buffett had another concern, which neither Murphy nor Burke had anticipated. If Cap Cities bought ABC, then, by the perverse jungle code on Wall Street, Cap Cities would itself be in play.

"What do we do about that, pal?" Murphy asked.[7]

Buffett said, "You better have a nine-hundred-pound gorilla. Somebody who owns a significant amount of shares who will not sell *regardless of price*." Obviously, that somebody would have to be very rich, and totally loyal.

"How about you being the gorilla, pal?"

In a later account, Buffett said he had not, until that moment, envisioned a role for himself.[8] But what other gorilla could he have had in mind? Indeed, Burke's impression was that he had thought it all through. No sooner did Murphy pop the question than Buffett raised two obstacles to his going in.

Cap Cities owned a television station in Buffalo. If Berkshire became its "gorilla," then, because of FCC rules, either the station or the *Buffalo News* would have to go. Buffett said he couldn't sell the *News*. "I've got my life invested in that thing," he noted. Murphy agreed to sell the station.

The second issue was stickier. Again, under FCC rules, Buffett could not be on the boards of both the Washington Post and Cap Cities. He had strong feelings about the Post, and also about the Graham family. He wanted to mull it over.

They parted, and Buffett flew back to Omaha. Thinking it through, he decided that if he left the Post board but kept his stock, his relationship with the Post could continue.*

That night, he called Murphy. Having worked out the numbers in advance, Buffett immediately proposed that Berkshire buy three million shares of Cap Cities at $172.50 a share.[9] That was the current market price (up from the original seventy-two cents).† Murphy instantly agreed. Buffett now had a deal to buy 18 percent of Cap Cities for half a billion dollars—eight times as big as his most recent deal, with Mrs. B, and fifty times the size of his first big media investment, in the Washington Post. Cap Cities, in turn, would use Berkshire's infusion of equity to finance its planned purchase of ABC.

---

*Buffett's friend Bill Ruane took his Post board seat. The merger required Cap Cities to divest its cable systems; they were sold, at Buffett's prompting, to the Post.
†The prices do not reflect a ten-for-one split in 1994.

But the talks with ABC hit a snag. Bruce Wasserstein, cochief of mergers at First Boston, was representing the network. The plump, disheveled banker could be prone to goading clients into overpaying, but when working for a seller he was brilliant. Cap Cities' first offer was $110 a share, but under Wasserstein's prodding, Murphy, Burke, and Buffett grudgingly went to $118—twice as much as ABC's recent market price. Still, Wasserstein demanded more. On March 12, Murphy trudged over to the black Third Avenue skyscraper of Skadden Arps Slate Meagher & Flom to tell Joseph Flom, ABC's attorney, that Cap Cities was pulling out. But Flom wouldn't let Murphy leave. He insisted that the deal could be saved.[10]

That afternoon, both sides reconvened at Skadden. The group was an eighties set piece, starting with Flom, a pioneer in the tiny hostile raids of the 1950s. Now, no takeover was complete without him. His friend and perennial rival in the merger wars, defense specialist Martin Lipton, was working for Cap Cities. Wasserstein, the *ne plus ultra* of deal-makers, led a team of bankers for ABC. (Cap Cities, in accordance with Buffett's and Munger's prejudice, did not use an investment bank.) Filling out the powwow were principals from ABC and Cap Cities.

But the real talking was handled by two: Buffett and Wasserstein. Michael Mallardi, the chief financial officer of ABC, was struck by the contrast: the disarming, informal Midwesterner, and the bright, intense, Brooklyn-born banker—younger, but not at all intimidated. Wasserstein noticed that Buffett dispensed with the histrionics customary to negotiations and lightened things up with jokes. He enjoyed doing battle with him. But they were $100 million apart. Now the banker's tone got a little tense. He insisted that, in addition to cash, ABC's stockholders should get warrants to buy Cap Cities stock. In other words, Wasserstein wanted them to have the option of *keeping* a piece of the company they were selling. "Our view was, if Buffett was such a clever fellow—if he's buying why are we selling?" Wasserstein recalled. "We wanted a kicker."

Buffett was dead-set opposed. He gave a little speech, saying that he hated to issue stock, a practice that he had criticized in his annual reports and, indeed, that had been *verboten* at Berkshire. Then Wasserstein gave a speech, arguing that ABC's shareholders deserved a piece of the upside. Then he led the ABC group outside. The talks were at an impasse.

When the ABC team returned, Buffett blinked. "I know I'll regret doing this," he began—and declared that Wasserstein could have the warrants. The ABC people were stunned. Now each side had to figure out what the warrants were worth. Wasserstein's computer mavens began to crunch a series of numbers. Buffett, handling the calculations for Cap Cities, simply did them in his head.[11]

Buffett had saved an investment banking fee, but Wasserstein had gotten the better of him. Unlike Munger, who affected a vague lack of interest, Buffett may have wanted ABC—of which he would now be the biggest individual owner—a bit too much. As Buffett predicted, he *would* come to regret the warrants.*

Also, Buffett's price for Cap Cities—sixteen times earnings—was steep for a Graham disciple. As he admitted to *Business Week*, "Ben is not up there applauding me on this one."[12] Buffett was betting that Murphy and Burke would be able to trim the fat from ABC's stations and boost their profits. And in truth, Buffett was running out of opportunities. Stock prices were rising, and, as Berkshire grew, Buffett needed to make *big* investments; small ones had become irrelevant. Outside the oil patch, the $3.5 billion ABC deal was the biggest merger ever.

This record was not on the books for long. A raft of deals followed, many of them hostile. Investment banks, breaking a time-honored code, went after former clients. Corporate minnows gobbled up whales. Wall Street had become a war zone.

The raiders obtained a certain celebrity. They styled themselves as champions of the little guy, or, at least, the little shareholder. The week of Buffett's big deal, T. Boone Pickens appeared on the cover of *Time*, declaring himself an enemy of "entrenched" corporate executives.[13] A paper entrepreneur such as Pickens did not actually acquire, much less reform, any of his targets. He merely bought enough of their stock to drive them into the arms of other suitors—at an immense profit to himself.

But the tactics of target CEOs were no less self-serving. Many of them forked over greenmail, a bribe (paid from the pockets of their shareholders) to induce the raiders to go away and leave the CEOs their jobs. Even big companies, such as Walt Disney (greenmailed by

---

*The warrants enabled each holder of ten ABC shares to buy one share of Cap Cities at $250. Initially valued at $30, the warrants later soared to a peak price of $207.75.

Saul Steinberg), were cowed into paying up. Others, such as Phillips Petroleum, bedeviled by Carl Icahn, were so intent on making themselves unattractive to the bad guys that they went deeply into debt, wrecking their own balance sheets before the raiders could do it to them.

This strange game presented an opening for Buffett. He was hearing from quite a few CEOs that they were under siege.[14] It occurred to Buffett that Berkshire could make an attractive baby-sitter. It had a reputation as an unmeddlesome, and stable, owner. And, not needing financing, it could move fast. For a desperate CEO, selling to Buffett could be a third route between succumbing to a raider and resorting to self-immolation via greenmail. With this in mind, Buffett, in his letters, regularly touted Berkshire as a safe harbor: "For the right business—and the right people—we can provide a good home."

In the fall of 1985, Buffett got his chance. Scott & Fetzer was an obscure but not small Ohio-based conglomerate, with units ranging from *World Book Encyclopedia* to Kirby vacuum cleaners. Wall Street had ignored it until 1984, when Ralph Schey, the chairman, tried to buy it in a $50-a-share leveraged buyout. His offer was cheap (only $5 above the market price), and speculators, sensing that it would be topped, bid the stock to 53. Within a fortnight, a bid, at $60, did appear—from Ivan Boesky, the arbitrageur. Boesky, an obsessive and haughty trader, had become super-rich on the strength of his connections to Drexel. It was not yet known, of course, that Boesky was trading on illegal stock tips (for which he would go to prison), merely that he epitomized Wall Street's fast-money culture. Schey, a nuts-and-bolts type, was repelled at the thought of working for Boesky, and put off by Boesky's insistence that a deal include a $4 million "break-up fee" for Boesky.[15] Schey turned him down—but now he had a problem. Boesky, who owned 7 percent of the stock, would sell to the next bidder.

Schey cobbled together a new LBO, at $62, but the plan collapsed. What was worse, his wheeling and dealing had driven the stock into the hands of the "arbs," the short-term speculators (like Boesky) whose first, last, and *only* interest was to sell the company. Now Schey had to find a buyer before the arbs did. In the summer of 1985, Schey, to his horror, learned that Steven Rales, a thirty-four-year-old financier, and Mitchell, his twenty-nine-year-old brother, controlled 6 percent of the company. The Rales were emblematic of a new breed of postpubes-

cent raiders. With little equity (but plenty of debt), they had taken over
a chain of small companies, and now, convinced of the limitless power
of leverage, they were batting their eyes at the prospect of Scott Fetzer.
Ralph Schey, meet the 1980s.

Buffett had also coveted Scott Fetzer—and had also bought a chunk
of the stock. The company had a high cash return, and *World Book* was
the sort of publishing franchise that Buffett craved. (It didn't hurt that
he had read it as a boy.) And having followed Schey's travail in the
newspaper, Buffett sensed an opening. In October, he dispatched a
brief letter: "We own 250,000 shares. We have always liked your company. We don't do unfriendly deals. If you want to pursue a merger call
me."[16]

For Schey, this was manna from heaven. He agreed to meet Buffett
and Munger in Chicago, where they discussed a deal over dinner. The
next morning, October 23, Buffett made a cash offer of $60 a share.
Schey had two demands: no "material adverse changes clause" (a con-
tractual loophole that allows the faint-of-heart to back out at the altar)
and no "break-up fee." Normally, such demands would have been
relayed to the investment bankers, but Buffett didn't have an investment banker. He simply shrugged and suggested that Schey write up a
contract. A week later, for a total price of $315 million, Buffett had a
very rich new prize.

Buffett's cash came from yet another deal, also in October: Philip
Morris's shotgun (and unfriendly) takeover of General Foods. Berkshire, the food company's biggest holder, gleaned a $332 million profit.
"I'm not unhappy," Buffett chortled.[17] His stock hit a new high, $2,600
a share. That same month, Buffett made the *Forbes* list of billionaires,
trailing, among others, Sam Walton, Ross Perot, and Harry Helmsley.

Takeovers, obviously, had made Buffett a good deal richer. But despite
his handsome profits, he was atypical of the deal age. When compared
to Ronald O. Perelman, who epitomized the takeover artists, Buffett
was closer to its inverted image.

Both men were highly acquisitive and were shrewd judges of compa-
nies, and they shared more traits as investors than one might suppose.
Perelman eschewed high-tech and looked for strong cash flow. Like
Buffett, he took a long-term view and was, at heart, a financial person,

not a manager. He once told *Forbes* that he carefully read ten annual reports a week.[18]

On the other hand, the blustery Perelman did unfriendly deals; Buffett did not. Perelman was attracted to leverage; Buffett shunned it. Finally, Buffett participated in deals only as a shareholder in a public company, and his take was proportional to that of other shareholders. This was not true of the vast majority of deal-makers, who profited in ways (such as fees) that were available only to insiders.

Perelman, in particular, had frozen out shareholders of Technicolor and MacAndrews and Forbes—the two companies that made him rich—allegedly at grossly unfair prices, and was besieged by lawsuits following each. Buffett had agreed to testify as an expert witness against Perelman, on behalf of one claimant, his friend Bill Ruane, who had owned MacAndrews and Forbes stock. In the words of a lawyer involved in related litigation, Buffett was expected to say that Perelman "screwed the shareholders."[19] Perelman vigorously denied that he had done so. But the case was settled, averting what might have been an interesting face-off.[20]

Simultaneous to Buffett's takeover of Scott Fetzer, Perelman demonstrated the new rule of Wall Street—that once in play, a company, as an independent entity, was doomed. As Connie Bruck observed in *The Predators' Ball*, Perelman's assault on Revlon had elements of class war. Michel Bergerac, the cosmetic company's aristocratic chairman, regarded the cigar-puffing Perelman and his Drexel financiers as "pawnbrokers." He curtly waved them off, saying the company was not for sale. Perelman sneered back, depicting the lackluster Bergerac, who kept a butler and a suite in Paris (his "castle," Perelman called it), as an archetype of corporate waste. In a normal time, the raid would have been sheer fancy. Pantry Pride, Perelman's vehicle in the fight, had a net worth of only $145 million, while Revlon was worth over $1 billion. But Perelman, financed with junk bonds, prevailed. Revlon was his, and Bergerac was out of a job. He had been wrong in saying that Revlon was not for sale. *Everything* was for sale.

In November 1985, a week after Perelman claimed his prize (he decided, actually, to keep the butler and the castle),[21] Buffett appeared at a seminar on hostile takeovers at Columbia Law School. The panel and audience included CEOs, bankers, mergers and acquisitions lawyers—among them Marty Lipton, licking his wounds from his unsuccessful defense of Revlon—and a coterie of academics.[22] Takeovers were in their salad days. The Cap Cities/ABC deal was only eight months old—the merger had not even closed—and five larger deals had already surpassed it. The day before, Henry Kravis had stood before the Beatrice board and offered $6.2 billion to take the company private. A Beatrice director, sensing the inevitable, burst into tears in the boardroom.[23] Money was flying around the Street so fast (Revlon spawned $120 million in lawyers' and bankers' fees) it was a wonder that anyone had come uptown, much less to have dinner on an ivy-covered campus. But they wanted to see Buffett.

No doubt the audience was thinking of Revlon, but Buffett did not refer to it. Appearing without notes, he spoke, instead, about See's Candy, and about himself. He had been investing for more than forty years, since he had purchased three shares of Cities Service at age eleven. In that yellowed, far-off memory, he recalled, the stockholder's position "as unquestioned boss" had seemed very simple to him.

> I wanted to see that little piece of paper that said I was the owner of Cities Service Company, and I felt that the managers were there to do as I and a few other co-owners said. And I felt that if anybody wanted to buy that company, they should come to me.[24]

As an adult, he had felt the same way. If the manager at See's got an offer and didn't tell him about it, Buffett would have felt "a little put out." *Someone* had to make the decision on whether to sell—it had to be the shareholders. It was their capital. It could not be the CEOs—the Bergeracs of the world—any more than the guy behind the counter at See's.

Nor could he deny that shareholders were benefiting from takeovers. Buffett himself had reaped an immense profit in General Foods. What's more, he said, "because my mother isn't here tonight, I'll even confess to you that I have been an arbitrageur."* So he was profiting from deals in that respect, as well. And Buffett, in the past, had scorned "entrenched" CEOs in terms not dissimilar from the raiders'.

Yet now that the raiders were in the ascendant, he was deeply trou-

---

*Buffett limited arbitrage to companies that had agreed to merge. Classic "risk arbitrageurs," such as Boesky, speculated on rumored deals and helped to put targets in play.

bled. CEOs were now his peers—in many cases, his friends. At a visceral level, he was uneasy with the raiders' confrontational style. But his concerns went deeper.

> I had this idea that some sort of economic Darwinism would work and that if offers were made, it was the invisible hand working and that it would improve the breed of managers. And then over the years I've been troubled by two things I've observed—and I don't know exactly where this leads me—I'll just tell you what bothers me. The first thing is that over a good many [years] the very best-managed companies I know of have very frequently sold in the market at substantial discounts from what they were worth that day. . . .

Takeovers, in theory, were a curative, the system's method of pruning corporate deadwood. In the neat economic model, assets flowed to the highest bidder because, by definition, the high bidder was the one who could put them to best use.

But the stock market was not always neat. Shares of even very good companies, such as Cap Cities, occasionally could be had for a song. A raider could gobble them up—not because Murphy and Burke were managerial deadwood, but because their stocks were subject to the depressive fits of Mr. Market. Even Boone Pickens, in a too-candid moment, blamed the oil takeovers on the simple fact that it was cheaper to drill for oil "on the floor of the New York Stock Exchange" than in the ground.[25] One day it was oil; the next it was something else. To Buffett, it was not corporate Darwinism but corporate roulette. It could not be good for the Tom Murphys of the world to be replaced by asset shufflers.

His other troubling observation was that takeovers were distorting prices. Businessmen, like politicians and anyone else, spent other people's money more freely than their own. CEOs—quite a few confided in Buffett—purchased better aircraft on the company's tab, and they ate at better restaurants.

> And I also notice that when they eat companies, they behave a little differently with the shareholders' money than they would with their own.

A raider with access to somebody else's dough would pay a lot more than a company was worth. And Wall Street's soaring appetite for junk bonds was providing a vast supply of easy money. Junk bonds had become a kind of "phony currency" (phony because bond buyers were thoughtlessly, and naïvely, financing borrowers beyond their means). Whoever could borrow the most was winding up with the store. To Buffett, this was truly vexing. The trouble with debt was that it worked *too* well; people got hooked and carried it too far. And he allowed that the new borrowers would repeat this pattern. "I personally think, before it's all over, *junk bonds* will live up to their name."

For 1985, this was strong talk. Junk bonds were thriving, and defaults had been rare. Investors were or would soon be lining up for such sure-fire credits as Allied Stores, Continental Airlines, Macy, and Trump's Castle (and many more that later would file for bankruptcy).

Michael Bradley, a University of Michigan finance and law professor at the Columbia seminar, protested. "I am troubled by the use of the pejorative term *junk* to describe these high-yield securities." Bradley argued that the risks on such bonds were offset by their (high) interest rates, just as was true on a triple-A bond. There was no such thing as a *bad* bond.

In a theoretical sense, Buffett agreed. The previous year, Berkshire had made a lot of money buying the (then cheap) bonds of a highly troubled creditor, Washington Public Power Supply System. Bankrupt credits often were attractive on a price-to-value basis; Michael Milken, Drexel's junk-bond impresario, had gotten his start trading just such "fallen angels." Junk bonds of recent vintage had the crucial distinction of not having yet fallen: they were weak credits issued at par (full price), with a long way to fall and little upside.

Buffett, continuing in his "pejorative" vein, pointed out that the issuers of those junk bonds were raking in very fat fees, as were the deal promoters. To him, the takeover game resembled an addiction, and Wall Street was pushing junk-bond "needles" to keep the Street in a stupor. "It won't die out without a big bang," Buffett predicted. "There's too much money in it."

All this was very much on Buffett's mind in January 1986, just after the Cap Cities merger closed, when he made a surprise showing at the annual retreat for Cap Cities' managers in Phoenix. Noting that many big investors were reexamining their loyalties "every hour on the hour depending on the stock price," Buffett pledged that his investment in

Cap Cities would follow him to the grave—and, in fact, a bit beyond the grave.

> I get asked what happens if I get hit by a truck. I usually say I feel sorry for the truck. I have it arranged so that not a share of Berkshire Hathaway stock needs to be sold on my death and [so] the behavior will conform to the promises I have made.[26]

Buffett's "promises" were designed to thwart any possible designs of a Perelman, Pickens, or Kravis. He not only gave Murphy and Burke the proxy power over his Cap Cities stock, he also gave Cap Cities the legal authority over Berkshire's freedom to sell. Buffett wouldn't even be free to change his mind.

Buffett tried to rationalize this unusual setup on economic grounds. He made the point that Murphy would be able to focus on the business without worrying about a raid. But Buffett was personally, as well as professionally, motivated. Murphy, with whom Buffett spoke virtually every week, was a close friend. In this investment, the "personal equation" was just as important. Buffett remarked to an interviewer:

> I will be in Cap Cities as long as I live. It's like if you have a kid that has problems—it's not something we're going to sell in five years. We're partners in it.[27]

The deal did have problems, even before it closed. Television ad sales collapsed, and ABC went into free fall. The network finished third in the ratings, in both prime-time programming and news. Then it faced losses on baseball, football, the Winter Olympics, and two ill-conceived dramatic specials. And its costs were out of control.

A friend of Buffett's said, "I don't think Warren had any idea of the extravagance, of how poorly managed ABC was." Peter Buffett recalls his dad's reviewing expenses and flipping out over a $60,000 florist charge. Burke got a similar shock when he walked into the stylishly appointed ABC building before the closing: the walls had been stripped bare of their Jackson Pollock and Willem de Kooning paintings—which had been sold to pad the network's year-end results.[28]

In the first year after the sale, a projected network profit of $130 million melted into a $70 million loss. It would have been far worse had

Murphy and Burke not taken a scalpel to costs. On Murphy's first visit to Los Angeles, the entertainment division sent a white stretch limo for him. Thereafter, Murphy took cabs.[29] At the New York headquarters, the private dining room was closed. Months later, Murphy and Burke sold the whole building to a Japanese speculator (for a record $365 per square foot). They also laid off fifteen hundred employees.

Buffett lent an ear, but did not intrude. One time, he was in New York when ABC was renegotiating rights to *Monday Night Football.* Burke figured ABC would lose $40 million on it. But having already cut back on glamour events, including sports, he didn't want to lose the National Football League's showcase. "Warren stumbled in," Burke recalled, "and it was obvious he thought we should hold the line." Buffett didn't *say* much; he merely looked, in Burke's words, "like he smelled an odor." Only as they were waiting for the NFL to call back and finalize the deal did Buffett speak up. "Well," he said glumly, "maybe they'll lose our phone number." (They didn't. Losses on the contract were even worse than expected.)

Murphy and Burke were able to cut costs significantly. However, the entire media business was becoming more competitive, due to a plethora of new outlets in both television and print. The three major networks were gradually losing viewers to cable and home video. One time, as Buffett and Murphy were watching *Monday Night Football* on a large-screen TV, Buffett exclaimed, "Isn't that a great picture?" Murphy allowed, "I liked it better on an eight-inch black-and-white screen when there were only three networks."[30]

Buffett, needless to say, would have been happier with *one* network. But despite turning bearish on media ahead of the pack,[31] he made no attempt to get out. A couple of years after the merger, Walter Annenberg flew to Omaha to get Buffett's opinion on whether to sell his magazine empire to Rupert Murdoch. Buffett advised him that media, though still a good business, was weakening. Annenberg got out at the top, but Buffett made no attempt to lighten up on his own holdings.

In Burke's view, Buffett paid a price for it. Cap Cities' stock soared to 630—at which point, Burke maintained, Buffett had to know it was overpriced. "He could have sold," Burke said. Within a year, the stock had plunged to 360.

One of the best young money managers thought Buffett had sort of lost it. "Warren has had three careers," this investor-critic explained.

"In the old days, he was a scavenger. He looked for value. Then it got hard to find stuff and he became a franchise investor; he bought great businesses at reasonable prices. And then he said, 'I can no longer find good businesses at even acceptable prices, and I will take advantage of my size and teach the world a lesson about long-term investing.' We think he screwed up. It's stupid."

Buffett and Munger doubted that they could have done better trying to dance in and out.[32] For one thing, a buy-and-hold investor put off the tax man—over time, a very big saving.* For another, their long-term approach created opportunities: a Mrs. B or Ralph Schey was more inclined to sell to an owner such as Buffett. And, knowing that divorce was not an option, Buffett was a bit—quite a bit—more circumspect in choosing a partner. To the extent that he, or any investor, is not thinking about how and when he will get out, he will be more selective on the way in. As in a marriage, this is apt to lead to better results.

But the *reason* for Buffett's policy, "stupid" or not, was that selling left him hollow, whereas staying with "Murph" he found infinitely satisfying. As he expressed it to *Business Week*, selling a familiar stock was "like dumping your wife when she gets old."[33] This was a strong comment from a guy who, in fact, had refused to dump his wife after she had moved out on him. Buffett revisited this metaphor in one of his letters: here, selling a good stock was like marrying for money—a mistake in most cases, "insanity if one is already rich."[34]

Buy-and-hold did have a financial logic, but at Buffett's extreme it can only be seen, as he put it, as a "quirk" of character, appealing for "a mixture of personal and financial considerations."[35] He liked to *keep* things—stocks, "pals," anything that lent a sense of permanence. To turn around and sell because someone offered "2× or 3×" was "kind of crazy."[36] Any other investor, such as his young critic, would have deemed that Buffett was the crazy one. But Buffett had always craved, and had always felt enriched by, continuity: to work with the same people, to own the same stocks, to be in the same businesses. Hanging on was a metaphor for his life.

Buffett carried his avoidance of debt to a similar—highly personal—

---

*Buffett did sell stocks, of course, but usually after long holding periods. Berkshire's investments in three select stocks—Cap Cities, the Post, and GEICO—and its wholly owned businesses, such as See's Candy, were deemed by Buffett to be "permanent."

extreme. In 1986, Exxon, which enjoyed a triple-A credit rating, had four times as much equity as debt. Berkshire had *twenty-five* times, a ratio that would have put a Puritan to sleep.[37] But then, debt could lead to the supreme discontinuity, one perhaps more painful than "dumping your wife"—losing control of Berkshire. As Buffett explained in Phoenix, debt was the financial temptress, the fatal "weak link":

> It's a very sad thing. You can have somebody whose aggregate perform-ance is terrific, but if they have a weakness, maybe it's with alcohol, maybe it's susceptibility to taking a little easy money, it's the weak link that snaps you. And frequently, in the financial markets, the weak link is borrowed money.[38]

This prejudice for what was enduring, enlightened by a sense of his-tory, drove Buffett's critique of the LBO promoters. From the moment a deal was hatched, these escape artists had in mind an "exit strat-egy"—a "quaint term," he called it, for the deal-maker's eagerness to flip his creation to the first willing sucker (usually the public).[39] Since Buffett defined investing as an attempt to profit from the results of the enterprise, as distinct from the price action,[40] the LBO artists did not really qualify as "investors." They merely transferred assets from one pocket to the next. They did not "create" value, which Buffett defined as adding to the sum of socially useful or desirable products and ser-vices. Most often, their profits stemmed merely from the huge tax sav-ings that derived from converting equity to debt (interest payments being deductible).

Buffett disapproved, both because the raiders' bounty seemed un-deserved and because society was the poorer for the loss of tax dollars. Embedded in his critique was a strongly conservative bias that Mrs. B's sort of work was more useful to society than what went on at Merrill Lynch—that creating pies was more useful than slicing pies. The LBOs, he argued (at another Cap Cities retreat), did not "make the steaks taste better"; they didn't "make the clothes warmer or last lon-ger":

> Now when you read about Boone Pickens and Jimmy Goldsmith and the crew, they talk about creating value for shareholders. They aren't *creating* value—they are transferring it from society to shareholders. That may be a good or bad thing but it isn't creating value—it's not like

Henry Ford developing the car or Ray Kroc figuring out how to deliver hamburgers better than anyone else. . . . In the last few years . . . one [company] after another has been transformed by people who have understood this game. That means that every citizen owes a touch more of what is needed to pay for all the goods and services that the government provides.[41]

At Cap Cities/ABC, Buffett was trying to re-create a world where people would not be thinking about "exit strategies." Following the deal, ABC, once the rockiest of the networks, became the most stable one financially, and a consistently strong player in daytime soaps, evening news, and prime time. By contrast, CBS and NBC struggled with repeated management shake-ups and continuing doubts about the commitment of their respective owners, Larry Tisch and General Electric. In Burke's view, Buffett's investment provided a margin of comfort, without which "we would have felt differently," particularly during the industry's severe recession. The company would have been more leveraged and less able to maneuver. Possibly, it would have met a fate similar to Time's. In the event, Murphy and Burke continued to wring out superior profits, and Buffett's faith in them was vindicated by a spectacular rebound in Cap Cities' stock.

Chapter 15

PUBLIC
AND PRIVATE

By the time of the Cap Cities deal, Buffett had a following. There were fifty Buffett-made millionaires in Omaha and hundreds elsewhere around the United States.[1] When he showed up at Columbia Business School to speak on investing, two hundred fans were turned away. *Forbes* called him a "folk hero."[2] There was a dog in Kansas City named Warren and another in New York answering to "Buffy." William Oberndorf, a Stanford business student, saw Buffett once, turned down a job at McKinsey & Co., and made a watershed decision to enter investing. Christopher Stavrou, a money manager, christened his son Alexander Warren. Then there was Douglas Strang, an Omaha stockbroker who idolized Buffett but had never met him. When his wife, Marsha, went into labor, Douglas reached for a copy of *The Money Masters* and read aloud to her from the chapter about Buffett, as though his wisdom might explain the cosmic mysteries of their daughter's birth.[3]

By early 1986, Berkshire had broken $3,000 a share. In the twenty-one years that Buffett had been turning the veritable dross of a textile mill into gold, the stock had multiplied 167 times; meanwhile, the Dow had merely doubled. On Wall Street, Buffett was regarded with awe. When he told David Maxwell, chairman of Fanny Mae, that he had invested in his company, Maxwell felt an urge to rush to the window and shout, "Warren Buffett's buying our stock!" *Forbes* unashamedly asked, "He doesn't walk on water?"[4] Headline writers dubbed him a "Midas," a "wizard," the "sage of Omaha," and (the alliterative favorite) the "oracle of Omaha."

Perfect strangers besieged him with "deals." A Pakistani émigré pitched him a newsstand; a woman in Jackson, Mississippi, offered an antebellum mansion.[5] ("With my idea and your money, we'll do OK," Buffett quipped.)[6] Unnervingly, a man from Lincoln, Nebraska, requested a $100 million "loan" to buy a "ranch." When Buffett declined, the man showed up at Kiewit Plaza with a pistol-toting gunman. FBI agents, tipped off by the companion, arrested the man as Buffett sat calmly at his desk.[7]

Though in the public spotlight, Buffett was standing guard over a still uncommonly private life. So unlike the modern CEO, he did not block out his time in advance, preferring to keep it unencumbered. When Bill Graham (a son of Kay) asked when he might stop by, Buffett replied, "Come *any* time. I don't have a schedule." Richard Simmons, president of the Washington Post Co., was amazed by the quiet in Buffett's emerald-green inner sanctum, which was sparely outfitted with miniature sculptures of bulls and bears, an antique Edison stock ticker under a glass dome, a citation for the *Sun*'s Pulitzer, family pictures (and one of Ben Graham), and a plaid couch from which a cloud of dust issued at the merest pretext.[8] He did not have an electronic calculator, a stock terminal, or a computer. "I am a computer," he noted to an interviewer.[9] When Buffett was in his office, Simmons said, "Nothing seems to happen, except Bill Scott [Buffett's trader] pokes his head in to say, 'Ten million dollars at 125⅛; yes or no?' The phone doesn't ring much. Buffett has so much more *time* than the average CEO." His day was a veritable stream of unstructured hours and cherry colas. He would sit at the redwood horseshoe desk and read for hours, joined to the world by a telephone (which he answered himself) and three private lines: to Salomon Brothers, Smith Barney, and Goldman Sachs.[10]

No matter who told it, the story of first seeing Buffett had a ring of innocence reclaimed. Seth Klarman, a young investment manager, met the billionaire for breakfast at the Ritz-Carlton in Boston. Klarman found him "as advertised"—waiting by the maître d' stand, with no one fussing over him or aware of who he was. "He ate link sausage and eggs—the last person in America who ate sausage." Norman Lear, the Hollywood producer, saw the slightly pudgy billionaire at the Omaha airport, holding his car keys, and mistook him for a chauffeur—a plain-faced fellow in tortoiseshell glasses with thinning, unkempt hair. Only the untamable eyebrows suggested an independence of spirit.

The writer Adam Smith found "a certain nostalgia in this triumph of Middle America."[11] Buffett was a billionaire who drove his own car, did his own taxes, and still lived in a home he had bought in 1958 for $31,500. He seemed to answer to a deeply rooted, distinctly American mythology, in which decency and common sense triumphed over cosmopolitan guile, and in which an idealized past held firm against a rootless and too hurriedly changing present. It seemed fitting that Berkshire's shareholders included not only famous money managers such as Mario Gabelli but also Eppie Lederer, a.k.a. Ann Landers, the columnist from Sioux City, Iowa, who had met and befriended Buffett and who dispensed homespun advice to millions of ordinary Americans. Buffett was the advice columnist of Wall Street.

By the mid-eighties, Buffett was (paradoxically) becoming celebrated for his common touch. He was the subject of adoring profiles with such folksy titles as "Aw, Shucks, It's Warren Buffett" and "The Corn-fed Capitalist."[12] Such articles accented his self-deprecating wit and modest lifestyle. A newspaper profile written by a friend of Carol Loomis maintained, "Buffett does not relish the role of celebrity that has been thrust upon him."[13] But that was no longer true. When asked if his boss had changed, Verne McKenzie, who had been Berkshire's treasurer since the sixties, singled out Buffett's delight onstage. "I never would have predicted that he would have enjoyed the limelight and publicity," McKenzie said.

Actually, he always had—but before, his stage had not been as public. Buffett had always been a talker, an entertainer, a self-chronicler. He was a marvelous interview, relaxed, self-effacing, mocking himself as, say, a poor dresser. He was always telling vignettes from his career; he seemed to have a compulsion to tell and retell, to *mythologize* his past, whether with friends or giving a talk. He sugarcoated his past, just a bit, not seriously distorting it but occasionally embossing it around the edges, as if to *perfect* his past. Don Danly, Buffett's high school chum, remembered that he, Danly, had bought the first pinball machine on his own; as Buffett told the story later, they did it together.[14]

Bob Russell, from grade school, recalled their racing sheet, *Stable-Boy Selections*, as a one-time affair, etched in pencil. Buffett described it in more grand terms, as a "published" tip sheet.[15]

The thrust of Buffett's autobiographical shadings was less to exaggerate his success than to strip it, somewhat, of the element of ambition and calculation. For instance, Buffett cast his enrollment at Columbia in terms of his enchantment with Ben Graham—not as a cool decision to settle for second best after Harvard rejected him.[16] Similarly, he liked to recall that he had resigned from Graham-Newman and returned to Omaha with "no master plan,"[17] and had organized Buffett Partnership only at the behest of relatives. This gives too little credit to Buffett's own initiative; by the time the *Omaha World-Herald* reported that Buffett had returned from New York, the partnership had been up and running for three weeks.[18] Then, too, he liked to portray the idea of being Tom Murphy's "gorilla" as coming from Murphy, when Buffett's footprints were all over it.[19] He seemed to want to depict his success as partly the result of serendipity, rather than his intense, lifelong drive to get rich.

Actually, what friends liked about Buffett was his absolute *lack* of casualness—his never being halfhearted. Norman Lear said, "He simply delights in his life. There is not a false bone in his body." What gave rise to such impressions was Buffett's genuine, even juvenile, enthusiasm. He was informal but not "casual," unaffected but not in the least blasé.

Buffett tended to turn even ordinary pleasures into fetishes. A profile in *New York* magazine happened to note that he was "a chronic guzzler of Pepsi-Cola, preferably laced with cherry syrup."[20] Don Keough, Buffett's former neighbor in Omaha who had once refused to invest with the young Buffett, chanced to read the article—and was incensed. Keough by now was president of Coca-Cola Co. He wrote to Buffett, offering samples of the "nectar of the gods,"[21] and after further correspondence, Buffett agreed to sample the new "Cherry Coke," then in the testing phase. "He sort of became a Cherry Coke fiend," Keough said. Indeed, Buffett began to drink about five bottles of the stuff a day (Pepsi was gone; it vanished) and would scribble an occasional note to Keough exclaiming his rather boyish delight. He stocked the office with potato chips and what a visitor described as "thousands" of bottles of Cherry Coke.[22] When Keough ran into Buffett—at a 1986 White

House reception—he thought his old neighbor unchanged: "a person-able guy who loved life."

Buffett reached his psychic peak at the annual meetings of Berkshire Hathaway. In the early years in Omaha, only a handful of shareholders had attended these meetings, which had been held in the cafeteria of its National Indemnity subsidiary. As a trickle of holders began to come from out of town, Buffett switched the meetings to the basement of a hotel, the Red Lion. Then the trickle became a tide. In 1986, Buffett rented the mausoleum-shaped pink-marble Joslyn Art Museum. Share-holders, clutching copies of his reports, descended on Omaha like birds of spring—Buffett groupies, money men, Graham disciples, New York bankers, retirees now rich and young investors aspiring to be rich. They came in suits and shirtsleeves; they came from the East, the South, the West Coast. While most annual meetings attract virtually no one (for the reason that most are a waste of time), attendance at Berkshire's was 450. After the meeting, Buffett shooed them to the Fur-niture Mart, where Mrs. B unloaded a couple of oriental rugs for $10,000.[23]

The meeting itself was a sort of Bartles & Jaymes gathering. Tables were set up with coffee urns and tubs filled with cans of Cherry Coke, the company's "official drink." Ninety-five percent of the shareholders had been in the stock for at least five years[24]—a level of devotion unique on Wall Street—and most had the vast bulk of their savings in this one stock. The investors, then, were unusually beholden to it, and to its high priest. They were a sect, a cult of which Buffett was the object. They noted his every gesture and casually offered remark as though it were suitable for framing. They felt a vicarious brilliance, as if *they* de-served a bit of the credit—if not for being geniuses, then for having found one. The cult had its own dogma ("Graham-and-Dodd" invest-ing), and its members had the felt superiority of true believers.

There was James Lake, a metallurgical engineer from Tucson who had read Graham and Dodd, and Ronald Melton, who ran an insur-ance firm in Pocatello, Idaho, and Michael O'Brien, a photographer from Austin who had met Buffett on assignment, read his letters, and bought the stock. Then there was Thad McNulty, a Jacksonville money manager who so revered the man from Omaha that he brought his wife—to celebrate their wedding anniversary.

It was a faith healing, too, for Tim C. Medley, a Jackson, Mississippi, financial planner. His wife drawled in astonishment, "You're going to spend $1,000 to go all the way to Nebraska to hear a man *talk*?" Medley only owned one share. "Maybe I'm a little crazy about this," he admitted, "but if you practice a faith, you go to the church. Buffett energizes me."

Medley caught his first sight of Buffett in an archway of the Joslyn. Buffett was greeting investors in a blue blazer and gray slacks. His hair was tousled and his belt was worn thin from notch marks. He could have been a high school basketball coach: a "plain man" of whom Medley was in awe.

As Buffett and Munger went to the podium, the crowd settled into a reverential silence. A quart of Cherry Coke stood on the dais like a sacrament. Buffett raced through the formal business of the meeting and opened the floor to questions. He deadpanned that anyone who had to leave early should do so while Munger—not Buffett—was talking. Then the two of them embarked on a rambling, uncut version of the annual reports, taking questions on Berkshire and on business in general for hours.

Munger played the dour sidekick. He sprinkled his remarks with references to "the civilization," which he seemed to feel was in peril. He said at one meeting: "The intelligence in this room is remarkable." But he did not go in for the meetings' carnival aspect. Adulation struck him as unseemly.[25]

Buffett ate it up. He cracked joke after joke, and as he panned the crowd his eyebrows seem to waltz about his forehead. He loved seeing the same faces—people he had known for years, people he had made rich beyond all dreams, people such as the humble Doc Angle, who was now worth $15 million.[26] Buffett told a friend that he felt as if he were painting a vast, open picture that everyone he knew could admire.[27] This messianic attachment to Berkshire explains why he was unwilling to sell even a single share, and also, perhaps, why he turned the meetings into a ritual. He talked about inflation, Mrs. B, and management. He took questions on investing, Cap Cities, and Ben Graham. Now and then, he would respond with a story that was concise and to the point, yet so easy on the ear that one imagined the speaker to be sitting back in his rocker on a lazy summer's afternoon.

One time, when Buffett was speaking off-the-cuff to a group at Cap Cities, he was asked what techniques he recommended to managers.

He launched into a tale about a stranger in a small town. The fellow wanted to get acquainted with folks, so he went over to the village square and saw an old-timer with "kind of a mean-looking German shepherd." Buffett continued:

> He looked at the dog a little tentatively and he said, "Does your dog bite?" The old-timer said, "Nope." So the stranger reached down to pet him and the dog lunged at him and practically took off his arm, and the stranger as he was repairing his shredded coat turned to the old-timer and said, "I thought you said your dog doesn't bite." The guy says, "Ain't my dog."[28]

The moral for managers: It's important to ask the *right* question.

Buffett was forever dropping these little "pearls," even in small, private settings. One Saturday, Steven Gluckstern, a touted but reluctant prospect for Buffett's insurance company, flew in for an interview. It was a bitter-cold Omaha morning. Gluckstern, who had read Buffett's press notices, was nervous about what he would be like in person. Buffett greeted him in a flannel shirt and khaki pants, and immediately put him at ease. He didn't really *interview* him. He talked to him, in conceptual terms, about risk-taking. "Hey, Steve," he said, "you know, when you go into a poker game, you look around, there is always one patsy. If you look around and you can't tell who the patsy is, that's 'cause it's *you*."[29]

This was Buffett's way of warning him not to broker risks he didn't understand. Gluckstern felt his host was like the author of those annual letters—dropping one-liners which, in context, seemed highly meaningful. He accepted on the spot.

One thinks of the young Warren who had stood in the corner at fraternity parties, taking the other fellows' questions, or who had sat in the Brandts' Manhattan living room with cronies at his feet. "Jesus and the apostles," Roxanne Brandt had called them. Then he had been entirely private. Though now he was also a public person, he was surrounded by apostles still.

In Buffett's case, this usual distinction between private and public was blurred. His friends were also his apostles. They called on him regularly for advice and counsel. Stan Lipsey turned to Buffett for advice on how to disentangle himself from a girlfriend. Richard Rainwater, the Texas financier, went to him for periodic "reality checks." In 1986, Buffett urged Rainwater, then at a crossroads, to stay away from anything even remotely unseemly; a few extra dollars weren't worth it, he warned. Rainwater found it memorable when, a short while later, some of Wall Street's leading lights were dragged away in handcuffs. Jack Byrne spoke of Buffett as though he were some sort of national treasure. "Some people who know Warren don't share him," Byrne complained. "I deserve some credit for *sharing* him."

Every odd year, Buffett's inner circle—the so-called Graham group—convened at a resort. In the beginning, it had just been Buffett and a bunch of investment pals—very stag and very cheap. At the second meeting, in Palm Beach, Florida, a bellhop was so ticked off by one of their chintzy tips that he heaved it against a door.[30] Another time, the ultrarich Sandy Gottesman hooked up with the group at the airport, expecting to fly first-class. But no one else was; Gottesman stammered something about his secretary having made a mistake and switched to coach.[31]

More recently, the seminars had gotten tonier and less inbred. They met in places like Scottsdale, Arizona, Sun Valley, Idaho, and on board the *Queen Elizabeth 2*. Also, Buffett invited spouses and friends—such as Carol Loomis and Tom Murphy—who were not narrowly financial. One time, the group went rafting on the Colorado River, whereupon the patrician Key Graham was moved to remark, "I have never had my ass this wet in my life."[32]

Buffett considered these retreats with friends to be especially enjoyable times, and rather private ones. He was extremely fond of his friends, as they were of him. Yet the gatherings had a reverential aspect not wholly dissimilar from the annual meetings. These few dozen friends, though highly successful on their own, willingly regrouped under Buffett's mantle—almost in celebration of him. The guest list was Buffett's: only *he* decided who could come. One longtime member said, "There is a palpable desire of people to be seated at the same table with him. You get the feeling—will he sit at my table?" Peter Buffett, a young musician, sensed that his father's friends yearned to be in his company. Relaxing in his studio beneath a picture of John Lennon and Yoko Ono, Peter likened them to a group of talented but lesser musicians with his Beatles idol. Ed Anderson, a charter member, regarded Buffett as "a sort of miracle man." While Buffett's demeanor at these get-togethers was unassuming, there was a sense in which these private friends—some of them, at least—were a more familiar form of the "audience" that Buffett had with public shareholders.

Most of Buffett's older friends also were his shareholders. This set him at the curious remove of being responsible for many of his friends' and family members' wealth. They talked about Buffett, and about the stock, obsessively. Indeed, at every step of the way, they agonized over it. Marshall Weinberg, Buffett's stockbroker friend, urged a client to wait for a better price when Berkshire was at $77, and repeated this counsel at $105.[33] Henry Brandt, another longtime Buffett pal, was forever polling fellow disciples about the outlook for Berkshire. At $1,700, he panicked and sold his *wife's* stock.

Conceptually, selling was at odds with the reason for owning Berkshire—which was to let Buffett manage the money, rather than to make such calls oneself. But the stock's rise was so out of the realm of ordinary experience that people lost their nerve. Keith Wellin, the president of Reynolds Securities, had bought some Berkshire at $40, and a little more at $43. When it went to $50, he decided to wait for the price to fall. He waited . . . and waited. He finally bought some more at $3,000 a share.

Weinberg, a friend for decades, obsessively analyzed the possible financial consequences to himself of Buffett's dying. How much would the stock go down—$1,000 a share? $2,000? And Weinberg was hardly alone. It was as if Buffett's health were merely a financial concern. Witness the exchange at an annual meeting:

QUESTIONER: I'm thinking of making a purchase of Berkshire but I'm concerned about something happening to you, Mr. Buffett. I cannot afford an event risk.

BUFFETT: Neither can I.[34]

The blurring of Buffett's roles extended to his family. In writing his annual letters he envisioned that he was writing to Roberta, his adored younger sister. But when he was with Roberta, he kept her at a respectful distance. Roberta, who lived in California, was conscious of not wanting to intrude on her brother, and she took care to be succinct when she asked him a question.

She found his answers "wonderful," but she couldn't adopt "the usual format," as she would with "regular people." She was acutely aware of "interrupting," Roberta explained. "He wants to get back to what he's thinking about. It's like a cloud of concentration, a physical cloud, is surrounding him."

Buffett acknowledged that he had public and private personas—or, as he put it, that he was an introvert at home and an extrovert on the road.[35] This division was mirrored, in a rough sense, by his two female companions. Susie was Buffett's first lady in more public settings, such as the Graham group seminars, or the Berkshire annual meetings, or with their scores of friends in New York and California.

Susie herself was extremely outgoing. Though she had moved into a tonier apartment in San Francisco, she did not spend much time there. When one of her kids or a friend needed help, or if someone was sick or even dying, Susie would simply pick up and move in for weeks on end. When Bella Eisenberg, a friend in Omaha and an Auschwitz survivor, wanted to revisit the camp site, Susie thought nothing of hopping on a plane with her. She traveled widely, including (owing to her interest in population control) to such removes as India, Turkey, and Africa. As Susie said, she lived "in the sky."[36] She also looked after people in San Francisco, where she took an AIDS patient into her home. But the connective tissue in her later, nomadic life was not home or routine but being on loan to people who needed her—including her husband. "The mystery," one of Buffett's associates remarked, "is that he is still madly in love with her."

Astrid, his partner in Omaha, was quite private—as Buffett was when in Omaha. She spent her mornings at the local zoo, working on the plant life, and usually could be found there in jeans and a sweatshirt, digging in the dirt. She and Buffett didn't socialize much. When Buffett was at home, he hung out in his "pit," a small, private space off the living room, formerly the family sunroom, where he kept his papers and books and had a large TV. For meals—breakfast included—he often grabbed a ham sandwich or ate vanilla ice cream out of the container. Their quiet companionship suited Astrid, whose upbringing had been so unsettled. Once, at a holiday gathering, Warren's sister Doris bluntly asked Astrid how it was going. She blushed and said Warren was "the most wonderful man to live with."

Buffett's hunger for solitude, and its offshoot, simplicity, was palpable on the fourteenth floor of Kiewit Plaza—what he wryly termed the "world headquarters" of Berkshire Hathaway. Though it was now a Fortune 500 company, Buffett's corporate staff in the mid- to late eighties totaled merely eleven people: two secretaries, a receptionist, three accountants, the trader, a treasurer, an insurance manager, Gladys Kaiser (his longtime assistant), and the boss. Berkshire had no lawyers, no strategic planners, no public relations or personnel people—no support staff such as guards, drivers, messengers, or consultants. There were no rows of analysts tethered to cathode ray tubes—none of the sacred totems of the modern corporate village.

This spartan style was part of a deliberate effort to minimize what Buffett termed "institutional dynamics."[37] If he had hired a floor of traders, they would have found something to trade; lawyers, no doubt, would have found someone to sue.

> A compact organization lets all of us spend our time managing the business rather than managing each other.[38]

For a Wall Street investment banker, the trek to this citadel of capitalism was not easily forgotten. John Otto, a Bear Stearns man, got his first shock at the Red Lion. Otto had come with a client who was selling a company in the natural gas business. When he told the hotel doorman they were going to Berkshire Hathaway, the fellow gave him a blank stare. When they did manage to find Kiewit Plaza, Otto was surprised to see a "five-and-dime building" opposite a pizzeria. There was no sign, either outside or in the lobby, indicating that it was the domicile of Warren Buffett, Inc.

Buffett greeted his visitors in Kmart-style shoes. After a little small talk, he beckoned Otto's client to make his pitch. Now Buffett's features became totally concentrated. He pursed his lips and furrowed his brow, practically driving the thickets of his eyebrows into his spectacles. After listening for ninety minutes or so, Buffett began to ask some questions. The economics of natural gas are complicated; regulation is involved; there are legal issues, social issues. Otto had sent Buffett a package of information, and Buffett knew it cold. As the client divulged new material, he recalculated the economics on the run. Otto noticed that he had not brought notes with him; he had no minions running in and out to prop him up with data. *It was all solo.* After three or four hours, Buffett made an offer, subject to some fact-finding. Otto was stunned again—executives do not make offers on the basis of a single session. (Ultimately, the deal fell through.)

This ability of Buffett's to cut through the clutter suggests a certain genius. Buffett focused so exquisitely on his object, and his simplicity was a counterpart to that genius. He recognized that layers of added executives—though each might be bright, earnest, well-intentioned, etc.—would blur his focus. Much of the "work" they might "accomplish" would be unnecessary work. (A Buffett aphorism: "That which is not worth doing is not worth doing well.")[39] He did not like protracted decision-making or drawn-out and contentious bargaining. His negotiating style was to seek or propose offers on a take-it-or-leave-it basis. And once he made a decision he did not reverse it.

Buffett and Bill Scott alone handled the investing—a job that at other firms was divided among scores of traders and analysts. Scott was not even full-time; he left the office at three to practice in a polka band. In any case, Buffett did the research, and Buffett made the decisions, in sweet solitude (consulting by telephone, of course, with Munger). By contrast with this one-and-a-half-man band, the Harvard University endowment, which had roughly the same size portfolio, had a staff of more than one hundred.

Buffett's Kiewit coworkers were little more than a backdrop—unobtrusive, robotlike, and unerringly dependable. According to daughter Susie, "All of the people in that office are the same. They don't talk. They just do their work."

The most essential one to Buffett was Gladys Kaiser, his secretary and assistant. She kept intruders at bay and brushed off inquiries in a flat monotone.

The treasurer, Verne McKenzie, a native of Fremont, Nebraska, with a wispy frame and steely blue eyes, typified the staff's loyalty. McKenzie had never—not once since the 1960s—asked Buffett for a raise. "If I ever felt I wasn't making enough and he didn't agree, then I must have been wrong," McKenzie said dryly. (In the sixties and seventies, Buffett paid him skimpily. But by 1986, McKenzie was making $198,000.)

In all the time since the early seventies, when McKenzie had returned from New Bedford to Omaha, Buffett had never raised his voice in McKenzie's presence. Nor had he given McKenzie an inkling of his inner thoughts. "I wouldn't talk if I thought it would hurt him," McKenzie noted, "but Warren is such a private person I don't think it'd be possible."

There was no intellectual peer among this trusty crew—no one who might break Buffett's sweet seclusion. He was cheerful with the staff, but not talkative, as he was with his pals. Save for when he had a visitor, he lunched alone, often sending a secretary to McDonald's ("Quarter Pounder with cheese and french fries"). Buffett had talked to his sons about joining him, but he simply had no place for an understudy. Munger said it was lucky that the heads of Berkshire's operating units, such as See's Candy, did *not* work in the same office. Close up, comparing oneself to Buffett would be "hard on the human ego."⁴⁰ His intensity was better at a distance.

The one time that Buffett took an apprentice, he hired Daniel Grossman, a young tennis star who had grown up in Omaha and gotten an M.B.A. at Stanford. Grossman would not discuss the experience, but according to colleagues, he seemed to have been overwhelmed. Most likely, Buffett was a remote mentor. He seemed to converse only when he had a *purpose*. "The motor was always running," a lawyer in Omaha said of Buffett. "There had to be an analytical content."

What Buffett expected from the relationship with Grossman isn't clear. Peter said, "It was the first attempt at my dad's passing stuff to the next generation. It was just botched. He didn't know how to do it." Buffett did not assign projects to staffers or work with them. "If Dan was hoping to watch how he worked and to learn from it—that's not what happens there," Buffett's daughter noted. "You can't watch it. It's in his head." Most of what "happened there" was Buffett thinking and reading.* Grossman ultimately quit and became a successful investor in California.

In 1986, Buffett departed from form and bought a used Falcon aircraft. As corporate jets go, this one was modest (it cost $850,000), but it was

---

*Buffett's reading included first of all the *Wall Street Journal*, and then the *Omaha World-Herald*, the *New York Times*, *USA Today*, the London-based *Financial Times*, various magazines and industry journals, and massive quantities of financial statements.

the type of corporate frill that he had long criticized. He kiddingly disclosed its purchase in tiny letters in the annual report and damned it as "very expensive" and a "luxury."[41] However uncomfortable he was with the *idea* of the jet, he loved the jet itself. Nor was it really a departure, since it extended the isolation of Kiewit Plaza to the air. As Buffett explained to a pal, he had been traveling more, and other passengers had begun to recognize him. Often they had tried to feel him out on the market—an intrusion he abhorred.[42]

Buffett's eccentricities, though the stuff of a gifted investor, worked against him as a manager. He was better with abstractions than with operational detail, better with numbers than tangible problems, too jealous of his independence to be intimately involved with others on a daily basis.

And by 1986, he was managing a huge conglomerate—certainly a role he had never aspired to. Buffett tried to offset his managerial shortcomings by restricting his role at *World Book*, See's Candy, and such to a very few big decisions.[43]* He liked to say that one didn't need a big "circle of competence"—but it was important to know where the "perimeter" was.[44] And Buffett was unusually aware of his own limitations. As applied to managing, he picked the chorus line but didn't attempt to dance (no "advice" on carpets for Mrs. B). Where other managers often created problems by interfering, Buffett's native genius for simplicity averted them.

Buffett did not require his various unit managers to forecast their earnings. (Computer models of such things were deceptive: they lent the future an air of "false precision.")[45] He did not schedule meetings. (Chuck Huggins, the president of See's Candy, didn't set foot in Omaha for twenty years.) Nor did Buffett attempt to impose a Berkshire corporate "culture" from above. At Scott Fetzer, the Harvard-trained Ralph Schey used the full panoply of modern business tools: budgeting, planning, and so on. Mrs. B used . . . well, other methods. But Schey and the Blumkins appreciated Buffett for an identical reason—he allowed them to run their businesses nearly without strings.

> We have no one—family, recently recruited MBAs, etc.—to whom we have promised a chance to run businesses we have bought from owner-managers. And we won't have.[46]

---

*Two exceptions to his hands-off policy: Buffett often determined price increases for See's Candy and the *Buffalo News*.

In all this, Berkshire was a most odd conglomerate. In fact, it was odd as a modern *institution*. The modern era is one of specialization; it has, in fact, made a cult of specialization. This is why historians churn out dissertations on shoe sizes in Bonapartean France and why the average pro football team now has a larger staff than did President Coolidge. In the corporate suite, its manifestation is chronic overstaffing. The common thread is that historians, football coaches, and CEOs are equally fearful of shouldering, or even delegating responsibility for, big decisions.

Buffett's Berkshire bore more structural likeness to King Arthur's court. Power was concentrated at two levels—that of the operating chiefs, and that of Buffett himself. As CEO, Buffett hired (and, potentially, fired) the operating managers. He controlled their capital in-flow or out-flow. His third, unspoken job was motivating his managers— some of whom, such as Stan Lipsey, were his friends, but many of whom were not.

Ralph Schey knew Buffett only through work. He sent him a monthly financial report (which Buffett demanded from all his businesses, and which he virtually memorized). Occasionally, Schey wrote a narrative to give Buffett a hands-on feeling for the business. And once a month or so, they talked on the phone. But Schey had to initiate such calls. Buffett *never* called him. And Schey had a latitude that would have been unthinkable elsewhere.

When Schey proposed a plan to reorganize *World Book*'s sales managers, Buffett was skeptical but let him go ahead. The shake-up was disastrous to morale and spurred a 20 percent drop in sales.[47] "It never should have happened," Schey conceded. Still, Buffett didn't second-guess him.

The inspirational power in this approach is not to be taken lightly. Except on June 30 and December 31, when Schey was obliged to transfer his profits to Omaha, he felt as if the business were his. In a practical sense, he was free to run it for the long term, as a private owner would. Like Berkshire's other, low-salaried managers, he had a potentially lucrative incentive clause (the exceptions were Buffett and Munger, whose compensations were fixed at $100,000). But Schey was also motivated by Buffett personally. Like a kid on report-card day (Schey's own analogy), he hated to bring Buffett bad news.

"The personal responsibility he creates is unique," Schey explained. "We don't govern Scott Fetzer the way Berkshire governs us. We have forty people in *our* corporate office. We have budgets, we have annual plans, long-term plans. We make up rules. We don't have any of that with Berkshire."

If managers had a complaint with Buffett, it was that he was too remote. He never interceded, and when asked for advice, he was often elliptical. He would "drop a pearl," as one of them said—a verse from his Zen of capitalism intended to shed some light, as if his managers, too, were "apostles."

For some of the managers, pearls were not enough. When the head of Borsheim's, the jewelry store, died, he was succeeded by his greenish son-in-law, Donald Yale. Yale needed a bit of help. He found that Buffett was good with the numbers but was not willing, or not able, to walk him through the business. When Yale asked an operating question, Buffett would generalize or give a self-effacing dodge.[48]

As far as is known, Buffett had never fired a manager—rather remarkable, given the breadth of his career. He was clearly displeased with George Aderton, the president of a tiny Buffett holding, Citizen State Bank of Mount Morris, Illinois, in the 1970s. (Buffett wrote Aderton how "irritating" and "annoying" he found his allegedly inaccurate reports—for Buffett, strong words.)[49] But rather than get rid of Aderton, Buffett got rid of the bank.

A cautious approach to firings makes good business sense, particularly compared to the Steinbrenner fire-at-the-ready alternative. But Buffett's extreme fidelity suggests that, as with holding on to stocks, "personal" considerations were a factor. He was much better at motivating with a carrot than with a stick; while he disliked confrontation, he was a master flatterer. In a typically adroit paean, Buffett wrote:

> When I call off the names of our managers—the Blumkin, Friedman and Heldman families, Chuck Huggins, Stan Lipsey, and Ralph Schey—I feel the same glow that Miller Huggins must have experienced when he announced the lineup of his 1927 New York Yankees.[50]

While his individual businesses racked up exceptional returns on capital, they grew at only modest rates, for which Buffett deserves some blame. He was chary of reinvesting in them, possibly because of his failure in textiles. Thus, *World Book* was slow to put out an electronic edition, and Borsheim's ignored the opportunity to exploit its reputation by adding stores.

Buffett did not rule out expansion; he simply demanded that a Blumkin, a Lipsey, or a Schey convince him that said manager could do more by retaining a dollar of earnings than Buffett and Munger could do by investing it elsewhere. The manager who did not convince sent a dividend to Omaha. Buffett applied the same equation to himself at the corporate level. That is, if he and Munger could not find superior investments, it would be time for Berkshire to stop growing and to pay dividends to shareholders.

Chapter 16

CRASH

*I have never met a man
who could forecast the market.*

WARREN BUFFETT,
BERKSHIRE HATHAWAY ANNUAL MEETING, 1987

By the mid-1980s, Berkshire was being driven by the engine of insurance. Its group of property and casualty companies, which was headed by National Indemnity, and which had offices in Omaha, New York, and elsewhere, was providing vast sums of dollars for Buffett to reinvest. Those dollars, as he put it, were being traded for "promises"—cash today, as against indeterminate future claims. The calculations involved in such exchanges were second nature to him. Buffett thought of everything in terms of odds: horse races, plane crashes, even nuclear war. Once, at a meeting of the Graham group, with twenty-five of his confreres, he bet Carol Loomis that at least two people in the room would have the same birthday.[1] She was shocked when Buffett proved right. The simple (but surprising) explanation was that the mathematical odds of this occurring were 60 percent. Insurance, similarly, reduced all experience in life to mathematical probabilities. Buffett's buddy and fellow insurance executive Jack Byrne never forgot when Buffett met him at the University Club in Washington with three mysterious dice, each with an unusual assortment of dots. Buffett made a proposition: Byrne could pick whichever die he wanted and Buffett would take one of the two that remained. Buffett assured him that if they then rolled twenty times, Buffett would win. "I got out my H-P calculator," Byrne recalled. "I wasn't going to be shown up in my own business."

I added up the probabilities. I picked one and Warren takes one of the other two and wins fourteen times. Then he says, "You want to do it again—for lunch?" So this time, I pick the die that Warren won with. Now he wins sixteen times. So I go back to the H-P. He's sitting there with a shit-eating grin on his face.

For each die, one of the other two would always beat it. If you picked the right die and rolled enough times, you simply couldn't lose. That was insurance: if you figured out the odds of a hurricane, or a three-car fatal, and *priced your policies accordingly*, you were playing with loaded dice.

Buffett had always been more involved in insurance than in his other entities, and had always known that—unlike, say, candy—insurance had the potential to grow off the charts. But in no other business had growth been accompanied by so many setbacks. In the 1970s, Berkshire had been burned by auto insurance fraud in Florida and disastrous levels of workers' compensation claims in California. Its subsidiaries in Texas, Minnesota, and Iowa had been shut down altogether. And the growing tendency of juries to ladle out big awards had resulted in discomforting shocks. When Buffett met with his managers at National Indemnity, he would make a simple plea: "Tell me the *bad* news."[2] But despite their best efforts, his underwriters were repeatedly overly optimistic in estimating losses.[3]

In 1982—in effect, acknowledging his failure to manage the business—Buffett had asked Michael Goldberg, a thirty-six-year-old former McKinsey & Co. consultant who had been at Berkshire a couple of years, to run the insurance group. Goldberg was the exception to Buffett's far-flung managers; he worked in the adjacent office in Kiewit Plaza. If anyone was suited for this impersonal terrain, it was Goldberg. As Goldberg said, Buffett was looking for "people with no ego." Goldberg fit the bill.

A thin, intense New Yorker, Goldberg was physically evocative of Woody Allen. A colleague said it wouldn't have surprised him if Goldberg's IQ was 180. But, as a graduate of the elite Bronx High School of Science, he was used to being around smarter people still. From Buffett's angle, his virtue was that he was even more allergic to risk than Buffett. A worrywart who lived for his work, Goldberg drove a dilapidated Oldsmobile that was so banged up that a subordinate once tore his coat on the chrome.[4] At the time, Goldberg's bonus was $2 million.

He and his wife, who were childless, lived in a modest duplex not far from Buffett's home. However, he and Buffett rarely socialized.

Their relationship was strictly insurance. Buffett liked to kick around mathematical puzzles with Goldberg (always in Goldberg's office, so that Buffett was free to leave when he wanted). And Goldberg occasionally took policies to Buffett to get his okay. But Buffett made it clear that he didn't want to spend a lot of time answering questions.[5] What he did do was provide Goldberg's group with a strong sense of direction.

Berkshire's favored (but not exclusive) niche was "reinsurance." This in effect is a wholesale business. Instead of selling thousands of small policies to homeowners or drivers, the reinsurer sells a few very big policies to other insurance companies, thus assuming a portion of the risks that its customers have underwritten. It is typically a "long-tail" business, meaning that claims are slow to develop. Thus, a reinsurer can reinvest the "float" from premium payments over long periods, only at the end of which will its profit (or loss) be known. It is hardly surprising that many reinsurers err toward optimism. Buffett put it rather wittily:

> Initially, the morning mail brings lots of cash and few claims. This state of affairs can produce a blissful, almost euphoric, feeling akin to that experienced by an innocent upon receipt of his first credit card.[6]

The perennial problem is competition. As Buffett noted, all it took to increase the "supply" of insurance (unlike that of physical commodities) was the willingness of a provider to sign its name.[7] Therefore, when prices were high, new entrants rushed in. This led to frequent, cyclical bouts of price-cutting. The first half of the eighties was one such period, with woefully inadequate prices. Buffett's response to the slump, though, was unlike anyone else's.

As Buffett liked to relate the business to poker, it is illustrative to consider his response to an actual wagering proposition. Every other year, he got together with Tom Murphy, Charlie Munger, and some other pals for a golf and bridge weekend in Pebble Beach, California. The men did a lot of betting, and at one session, in the early eighties, Jack Byrne, the GEICO chairman, proposed a novel side bet. For a "premium" of $11, Byrne would agree to pay $10,000 to anyone who hit a hole-in-one over the weekend. Everyone reached for the cash—everyone, that is, except for Buffett, who coolly calculated that, given the odds, $11 was too high a premium. His pals could not believe that he—by then, almost a billionaire—would be so tight and began to razz him for it. Buffett, grinning, noted that he measured an $11 wager exactly as he would $11 million. He kept his wallet zipped.[8]

Now, cut to insurance. While other companies cut prices to hang on to market share, Buffett recognized this as betting against the odds. So he and Goldberg refused to play. From 1980 to 1984, they allowed their business to shrink from $185 million in premiums to $134 million. If the business was unprofitable, Buffett didn't want the business. Someday—he wrote this in 1982—losses would force providers to pull back, and prices would rise. In the meantime, he would wait.

It is natural to wonder why *every* insurer didn't adopt such an approach. Their shareholders, and their managements, had been schooled on the principle of "steady" growth. To turn down business would violate the culture. At Berkshire, insurance operatives responded to a very different imperative. (In insurance, Berkshire did have a "culture.") Constantine Iordanou, a division president in New York, said that when he wrote a policy, he was quite conscious that he was playing, as he put it, "with Warren's checkbook." This tended to inhibit Iordanou from betting against the odds.

In 1985, the insurance market did turn. The industry suffered severe losses and insolvencies, and many companies cut back the coverage they offered. The ability to provide insurance, in Buffett's phrase, is "an attitudinal concept, not a physical fact."[9] By 1985, both the "attitude" of insurers and their capital reserves were depressed, and prices soared.

Buffett now reaped a double payoff for his prior conservatism. Big commercial customers realized that a promise from a potentially insolvent provider is no promise at all. There was a flight to quality, and Berkshire, which had six times as much as capital as the average carrier, had the soundest balance sheet of any insurer in the country.[10] Thus, just as prices became attractive, Berkshire was very much in demand.

In mid-1985, Buffett took out a nervy advertisement inviting big commercial customers (who were hard pressed to find coverage) to submit policies for *any* type of risk with premiums of $1 million or more. There was a twist: respondents had to name their price. If Buffett (or Goldberg) deemed a proposal to be unreasonable, he would throw it out with the understanding that he would not grant a second chance. This poker ploy generated more than $100 million in premiums.

The strong-get-stronger scenario was even more pronounced in reinsurance. With their losses mounting, conventional insurers were scrambling for protective cover. But reinsurers, too, had been burned by losses. Few were able to answer the call, and fewer still were willing. Having lost money when prices were low, they were fearful of writing coverage at *any* price. Buffett likened them to Mark Twain's cat: "Having once sat on a hot stove, it never did so again—but it never again sat on a cold stove, either."[11]

Berkshire was now in a position to write *very big* policies, thanks to its capital and to Buffett's "attitude." He was perfectly willing to risk losing large amounts of money, even as much as $10 million on a single event such as a fire or earthquake, *as long as* the odds—the prices— were favorable. In the 1985 letter, one can hear him gloating: "Now the tables are turned: we have the underwriting capability whereas others do not."[12] In 1986, Berkshire's premiums soared to $1 billion, seven times the level of two years earlier.[13] This translated to $800 million of "float" (dollars available for reinvestment), and to more than $1 billion the following year.

By 1987, Berkshire was stuffed with cash. However, it was far from clear what Buffett would do with it. He would "rather buy a good stock than a good jet,"[14] he quipped, but he could not find one that was cheap enough. The bull market was in its heyday. In the spring, when Berkshire staged its annual meeting, the Dow was at an eye-opening 2,258 (and Berkshire at $3,450 a share). Buffett had quietly sold every stock in the portfolio save for the "permanent" three: Cap Cities, GEICO, and Washington Post. But he was stumped for a place to reinvest.

Buffett mistrusted forecasts—as he reminded shareholders, Ben Graham had been bearish when the Dow was at 400. But Buffett could not suppress his pessimism; in response to a question, he said he would not be surprised if the market—then at a precarious twenty times earnings—fell 50 percent. Share prices had lately been rising at a far, far faster clip than the 12 to 13 percent equity "coupon" that companies were actually earning. To Buffett, this suggested "a danger zone."

A shareholder with a long memory asked if the climate resembled that of 1969, when Buffett had folded Buffett Partnership. At that time,

Buffett recalled, "Opportunities were not available. I shoved the bottle away and returned the capital to my partners."[15] But now he could not cork the bottle; Berkshire's operating subsidiaries—insurance, Mrs. B, et al.—continued to feed him cash. Buffett needed a place to put it.

Throughout the spring and summer, the stock market rally continued. In July, the Dow hit 2,500; in August: 2,700. There were snickers from the bulls; those, such as Buffett, who were on the sidelines were missing the rally of the century. Shares of Berkshire touched a new high—$4,270 a share. It hardly mattered. As in 1969, Buffett was shoveling money into municipal bonds.[16] He had no decent alternative. Then he got a call from John Gutfreund, the chief of Salomon Brothers.

Since the bailout of GEICO a decade earlier, Gutfreund and Buffett had been in increasing touch.[17] Lonely at the top, Gutfreund often called Buffett for advice. Buffett, in turn, admired Gutfreund as a cut above the average investment banker. Though known for his scalding sarcasm, Gutfreund was conservative in his approach to business. He had refused to let Salomon underwrite junk bonds and had generally avoided hostile raids, despite the lucrative fees associated with each. Instead, the firm had concentrated on trading. To Charlie Munger, Gutfreund evoked all that was noble in Salomon's tribal culture, particularly its willingness to lay its capital on the line. He had a grandeur that the newer breed of executive lacked.

During the summer, Buffett had mentioned that he might be interested in buying stock if Salomon's shares got cheaper.[18] Though the stock had dropped by a third, it wasn't at Buffett's level yet. But the business was having trouble.

And Salomon's biggest shareholder, Minerals and Resources Corp., or Minorco, was making restive noises. Minorco, controlled by South Africa's Harry Oppenheimer, had retained Felix Rohatyn, the investment banker, who had let it be known that Minorco was anxious to sell. Though Minorco was sitting on 14 percent of his company, Gutfreund had let the matter drift—a fatal habit. Then, in mid-September, he learned that Rohatyn had found a potential buyer. Gutfreund was stunned to learn the buyer's identity: Ronald Perelman's Revlon.

Gutfreund had recently given in to his bankers and agreed to let Salomon enter the takeover business. How little he had suspected that *he* could be a target was evident from his breezy performance, earlier that year, in a roundtable on takeovers with Boone Pickens, merger lawyer Joe Flom, Drexel CEO Fred Joseph, prosecutor Rudolph Giuliani, raider Sir James Goldsmith, and Buffett.[19] The moderator, Lewis Kaden, had conjured up the image of "Harry," a typical, old-fashioned CEO, dedicated to building long-term values, who is suddenly threatened by a raider.

GUTFREUND: Let's not waste a lot of time on Harry.

MODERATOR: [*adopting the role of Harry*]: What do you mean? I invented this company in my backyard.

GUTFREUND: You did a wonderful job. You were great in your time. Sorry, that's life. The board will throw him out.

MODERATOR: Is that fair, to throw him out?

GUTFREUND: Fairness has nothing to do with it. There is no way you can turn the clock back. Now whether management is improved and does its own job or whether it's taken over by somebody else . . . Harry is gone.

Now, when Gutfreund looked in the mirror, "Harry" stared back.

Gutfreund agreed to meet Perelman, who assured him that his intentions were "friendly" and that he would want Gutfreund to stay. However, Perelman added that he would want two seats on the board and intimated that he might buy up to 25 percent of the stock. Gutfreund was cool.[20]

Gutfreund's supporting cast at Salomon was quick to note that Perelman was being represented by Bruce Wasserstein and feared that if Perelman won control, "Bruce" would soon be in charge.[21] Perelman scoffed at the idea that he would spend his own money to get Wasserstein a job. He maintained, in an interview, that his motive was misunderstood. However, he was vague about what his motive was, beyond a general appreciation for Salomon's business. In any case, Gutfreund didn't trust him, and neither did Salomon's brass.[22] "They viewed him as Attila the Hun," Rohatyn noted. Perelman was then in the midst of a second, very unfriendly raid on Gillette, from which he had already extracted greenmail.[23] Martin Leibowitz, Salomon's house mathematician, said, "People *couldn't* have worked for Perelman. It was not who we were."

Alas, it was late in the day for such high-mindedness. Minorco would sell to the first bidder that offered it a premium. Salomon could not itself afford to buy the block, and Perelman was ready to pay $38 a share (the market price was in the low 30s), or roughly $700 million. This was early in the week of Monday, September 21. Rohatyn figured that Salomon had until the weekend to find another investor. Gutfreund called Omaha.

Buffett arranged to meet Gutfreund and Gerald Rosenfeld, Salomon's chief financial officer, a night or two later in New York, at the office of lawyer Marty Lipton, Gutfreund's adviser. Buffett loped in *tout seul*, with a newspaper under his arm, in a white-and-blue seersucker, the lining of which was torn. Seeing his slouched frame, Rosenfeld drew a breath: *this* was Salomon's savior?[24]

Buffett and Gutfreund went off by themselves to feel each other out. After half an hour, Rosenfeld joined them, and Buffett began to ask him about Salomon's prospects, including where he thought the stock would be in five years. While they both agreed that the mid-60s was a likely number, Buffett thought Salomon too dicey for him to buy the common stock.[25] However, he was willing to invest in a "convertible preferred," as long as Berkshire could expect to make an after-tax annual profit of 15 percent. As they talked, it became clear that Buffett had the terms of such an issue in mind.

Convertibles are the half-breeds of Wall Street. They have attributes of a bond: a fixed coupon and security of principal. They also enable a holder to *convert* to common stock. They are aptly described as Treasury bills with a lottery ticket attached. The holder has a safe investment and a chance to make a killing—though not as big a profit as on ordinary common.

Buffett insisted that Berkshire get a 9 percent coupon and a pair of seats on Salomon's board—one for him, one for Munger. Salomon's senior managers had a heated discussion over the terms, which they thought far too sweet for Buffett. "The feeling was, it had a very small premium [the conversion price was $38] and a very high dividend. Warren had it both ways," William McIntosh, the head of Salomon's Chicago office, recalled. As a bonus, Berkshire's $63-million-a-year dividend (like all such payments received by corporations) would be mostly tax-exempt. On the other hand, Buffett's capital would enable Salomon to buy out Minorco at a premium—and rid it of the threat

from Perelman. In the minds of Salomon's executives, the choice between Perelman and Buffett was no choice at all.[26]

On Saturday evening, Gutfreund met Perelman again, for a drink at
the swank Hotel Plaza Athenée on the Upper East Side. This time Gutfreund declared, politely but bluntly, that Perelman would not be welcome as an investor.[27] Two days later, the offended Perelman indicated
that he would accept the same security as Buffett, and with less attractive terms—but threatened, if he was rejected, to buy a controlling
stake on the open market.[28] Once again, Gutfreund snubbed him.

Then Gutfreund told his directors that they could either approve the
Buffett deal, which would make Berkshire Salomon's biggest share-
holder, or find a new CEO.[29] Prophetically, Gutfreund argued that
Buffett would be a help to him in running the company. One director,
Maurice Greenberg, strenuously objected,[30] but the board went along.
The only rationale for this rather expensive deal was the uncertain
premise that somehow, down the road, Salomon would be better off
with Buffett in control than Perelman.

When the news broke, in late September, Wall Street was stunned.
The *Wall Street Journal* commented: "All the players seemed to fit—
except one."[31] Buffett was putting $700 million—his biggest bet ever—
into a firm of traders. His respect for Gutfreund figured heavily.
"Charlie and I like, admire and trust John,"[32] Buffett noted soon after.
Moreover, the form of the security seemed safe. Ace Greenberg, the
streetwise CEO of Bear Stearns, thought Buffett had made "a great
deal for the shareholders of Berkshire Hathaway." If Gutfreund had
given away the store, that was his problem.

Still, Buffett took some heat. *Forbes*'s Allan Sloan pointed out
that Buffett's financing had enabled Salomon to pay greenmail to
Minorco.[33] And Buffett's fans felt let down that Buffett had joined
forces with Wall Street. A year earlier, he had disdainfully written that
if a graduating M.B.A. had asked him how to get rich in a hurry, he
would have held his nose with one hand and pointed to Wall Street
with the other.[34] Now, even the stalwart Carol Loomis was moved to
write in *Fortune*:

> The most fascinating aspect of Buffett's Salomon investment is that it
> puts him in bed with Wall Streeters, whose general greed he has
> scorned in the past.[35]

It was soon apparent that Buffett had badly misjudged the business. As an important and well-treated customer of Salomon's, he had an overly rosy view of it. Two weeks after the deal, Salomon disclosed that it would lay off eight hundred employees and fold two departments, moves that would cost it $67 million. There was a sense that Gutfreund was not in control. And this was echoed by a sudden and general nervousness in stock and bond markets.

For five glorious years, the bull market had roared. Though interest rates had risen through most of 1987 (depressing intrinsic business values), the stock market had ignored them. By August, stock prices were at the historically unsustainable level of twenty-two times earnings.

As each lunatic has his vision, each bull market has its rationale. In 1987, it was that excess "liquidity" would hold prices up. This was a version of the greater-fool theory: the cash ("liquidity") of nameless others would save the day. Japanese stocks, then at sixty times earnings, were said to provide cover. No matter how absurd the prices at home, since Japanese stocks were *more* absurd, U.S. stocks were held to be safe. Of course, such rationales had not kept previous rallies from abrupt and unpleasant endings. But a bull market is a bit like falling in love. When you are in one, it has never happened to anyone before.

Binkley C. Shorts, a senior vice president of Wellington Management, was representative of the pack. Shorts had a Harvard M.B.A., three kids, and a finger on the pulse of Wall Street. He acknowledged that stocks were rich, but was strong of heart:

> Foreign money's attracted to our market because it's less expensive than their own. So maybe the market can go up regardless of fundamentals.[36]

No one disputed that prices were high, but the bull market had become an article of faith. *Business Week* suggested that "yesterday's yardsticks" were no longer apt.[37] Buffett felt that money managers were not using *any* yardstick. They had abandoned the effort to value stocks at all: "For them, stocks are merely tokens in a game, like the thimble and flatiron in Monopoly."[38]

With computerized trading, fund managers were now buying groups of stocks by the bucketful in market "baskets"—a few million GM, a couple of million AT&T, and a dab of Westinghouse, on rye, please. A parallel trend was the emergence of stock-index futures in the commodity pits in Chicago. These new futures contracts, which traded next to pork bellies and cattle, enabled speculators to bet on the direction of the entire stock market. To a Graham-and-Dodd investor, of course, a stock derived its value from the underlying, individual *business*. But the new breed of "investor," who was buying the market whole, did not even know which stocks he owned. Security analysis was irrelevant.

On Wall Street, if not in Omaha, "asset allocation" was the rage.[39] Instead of looking for individual issues, the portfolio manager first decided how much to invest in "stocks," treating them as a generic class. The total could be and was continually rejiggled, resulting in sudden wholesale shifts. As an offshoot, managers were letting computer models influence and even make their buy-sell decisions. Prophetically, *Institutional Investor* warned in September 1987 of the "false sense of security" from relying on technological masters.[40]

But few paid notice. "Portfolio insurance," a high-tech nostrum for fund managers, was said to be a fail-safe. Under this strategy, managers determined in advance to *automatically* sell increasing amounts of stock-index futures whenever markets fell. The theory was that futures could be sold more readily than stocks. By quickly selling futures, portfolio managers would hope to cut their losses before a drop became severe.

V. Kent Green, an investment adviser at First Bank System in Minneapolis, noted that when one wanted to sell, "some of your stock positions could be very illiquid"—meaning that no one would be around to buy them. But Green was sleeping soundly; if the need arose, he could get out by the side door, in Chicago. "Futures," he noted, "are about four times more liquid than stocks at the current time."[41]

What escaped Green's attention was that he did not need to sell futures "at the current time"; he would need to sell when markets tumbled—when, presumably, everyone else would be selling, too. When the hour came, according to a subsequent White House study, chaired by investment banker Nicholas F. Brady, some $60 billion to $90 billion of futures were poised on the same delicate trigger as Green's.[42]

In retrospect, what was memorable about October was not its suddenness, but the degree to which it had been advertised in advance. Cassandras abounded. Charles Allmon, a newsletter writer, had talked of "a huge debacle of the magnitude we saw in 1929."[43] The bears knew that prices were high; the bulls knew it, too. But everyone wanted the last drink. From January 1 to the August peak of 2,722.4, the Dow rose an astonishing 44 percent. The refrain was maddening. Byron R. Wien, investment strategist at Morgan Stanley and one of Wall Street's most-watched beacons, was ready to throw away the rule book. Even bad news, he suggested in August, might send stocks higher:

> . . . some profoundly mysterious forces have enabled the market to advance. . . . So perhaps the link between reality and stock prices isn't as tight as they taught us in business school.[44]

Alas, within a week or so, reality showed its face. There were hints of inflation, a naggingly stubborn trade deficit, and a worrying drop in the dollar. The Federal Reserve, hoping to stem inflation fears and to prop up the dollar, ushered in Labor Day by hiking the discount rate, the widely watched rate at which the Fed lends money to banks. Bond markets, taking their cue, went into a tumble. The stock market gave back 38 points in a day.

By early October, the yield on long-term bonds had risen to nearly 10 percent—up from only 7.4 percent as recently as March. On October 6, the Dow plunged 91.55 points, a one-day record. Markets had entered the vaporous territory in which events take on a life of their own and historical accidents may occur. In short, things were becoming serious.

On about October 12, Buffett cashed out the stock portfolio of at least one of Berkshire's profit-sharing plans. It cleaned the larder of stocks, save for his permanent three. According to a Buffett associate, "It was a clear edict: 'Sell everything.' "

Buffett was not making a forecast; he was merely obeying two cherished rules. Rule No. 1: "Never lose money." Rule No. 2: "Never forget Rule No. 1." Munger said, "Warren would never claim that he could call the market." But perhaps Buffett had been glancing a bit more anxiously at the newspaper clipping on his wall—the one from 1929. In the week following, interest rates climbed above 10 percent. Japanese shares continued to rise, but now no one on Wall Street cared about Japan. On Friday, October 16, the Dow plunged 108 points.

Washington was on edge. Whenever markets failed, bureaucrats could be counted on to look for a culprit outside their ken—speculators, the gnomes of Zurich, whomever. An official resentfully blamed the fall on "twenty-nine-year-old technicians."[45] The Treasury Secretary, more mindful of appearances, told a weekend television audience that he did not expect further tightening from the Fed. But it was too late.

On Monday, October 19, sell orders jammed the market. Eleven of the thirty stocks in the Dow average could not open during the first hour of trading.[46] In the interim, portfolio insurance sell programs had been triggered automatically. The futures market went into free fall, which, of course, touched off a sympathetic drop in stocks.[47] In the end, it did matter where the selling occurred. The door was too small to admit everyone through, and the vaunted portfolio insurance failed to save the day. By late afternoon, the panic had become a rout.

In Boston, people lined up outside Fidelity Investments to redeem shares. Newspapers spoke of "hysteria."[48] But the New York financial district was quieter than usual. People were indoors, tethered to electronic screens. Black Monday may have been the first postmodern historic event; it seemed not to have a tangible center. The Dow fell 508 points, or 22.6 percent.

Buffett's net worth dropped by $342 million. He must have been one of the few investment people in America who did not have a minute-by-minute account of the crash. At one point, Buffett went into Mike Goldberg's office and calmly told him where Berkshire was trading. Then he went back to his desk.

Two days later, Buffett's Graham group convened in Williamsburg, Virginia. The market was still turbulent, but the group was curiously detached. No one left the seminar room to check on prices or even spoke much of them. They toured a plantation under a resplendent fall sky, admiring the foliage. Wyndham Robertson, a university administrator and journalist in the group, asked Buffett what the crash had "meant." All he could say was "Maybe the market had gotten too high."

Compared with Black Thursday, the great collapse of 1929, Black Monday was oddly hollow. No depression or other economic tide followed in its wake. At first it was thought that the crash would prove a socioeconomic milestone. Columnists cheered the end of the casino era, and especially of the nouveau riche captains of investment banking. But after a brief pause, Wall Street rolled on. Indeed, in 1988, bankers would cut more deals than ever, and stocks would recoup most of their lost ground. The crash seemed to leave no footprint, save for the jagged slant on the screens of traders.

Its "meaning" was evident only on a small scale. A week before the fall, Berkshire had traded at $4,230 a share. On Friday the 16th, it closed at $3,890. In the madness of Monday, it fell to $3,170. Berkshire had been worth close to $5 billion, laboriously built up over twenty-two years. Nothing in the company had changed: Stan Lipsey sold the same number of papers in Buffalo; *World Book* was nestled, as ever, on pupils' shelves. Yet in the space of a week, 25 percent of the company's market value had been wiped out. A quarter of the fruits of a generation's work had vanished. Something was wrong.

Chapter 17

A BRIEF
INTRODUCTION
TO DARTS

Without due recognition of
crowd-thinking (which often seems
crowd-madness) our theories of
economics leave much to be desired.

BERNARD BARUCH

Ben Graham had likened the behavior of stocks to that of a kindly but fickle fellow named Mr. Market. Now manic, now depressive, Mr. Market's next quotation was anybody's guess. The trick for the investor was to ignore his unpredictable mood changes. But on October 19, 1987, investors had fallen dumbly under his spell, selling stocks—any stocks—tick for miserable tick.

This proved to Buffett what he had already known—that Graham had been abandoned. He had been shelved for academic "witch doctors" who peddled "arcane formulae" and "techniques shrouded in mystery." Though "Ben's allegory" was a fitting-as-ever prophylactic against the "super-contagious emotions that swirl about the market-place," scarcely a business school in the country used Graham's texts. Instead of price and value, Buffett lamented in a postmortem, "professionals and academicians talk of efficient markets, dynamic hedging and betas."[1]

The crash had exposed Wall Street along its intellectual seam, but the debate had been festering there for decades. Since the sixties, Graham-and-Dodd investors, led by Buffett, had been waging a war with modern financial theorists. Oddly, the most successful investor of the age, and perhaps ever, had come to be belittled and ignored by the foremost scholars in his field. The monks of finance had shunned him as a heretic, while in Buffett's eyes, these abbots and friars were engaged in an incestuous effort to prove, with ever greater elegance and seeming precision, that the earth, indeed, was truly flat.

The premise of Buffett's career was that stockpicking, though difficult and subjective, was susceptible to reasoned analysis. Occasionally, certain stocks sold for far less than they were "worth." An astute investor could profit by buying them.

In place of that rather modest maxim, scholars had substituted a seductively simple but unifying design, the Efficient Market Theory. In a nutshell, the theory said that at any moment, all the publicly available information about a company was reflected in the price of its stock. Whenever news about a stock became public, traders pounced, buying or selling until its price reached equilibrium. Underlying this truism was an assumption that the old price had been as "wise" as traders could make it. Therefore, the new price—and each succeeding new price—would be wise as well. The traders merely did the work of Adam Smith's Invisible Hand.

Since everything worth knowing about a company was already in the price, most security analysis was, to cite a popular text, "logically incomplete and valueless."[2] The future course of a stock would depend on new (as yet unknowable) information. A stock, then, was unpredictable; it followed a "random walk."

If markets were random, investing was a game of chance. Buffett, then, was a lucky investor but not a skillful one, just as the person who repeatedly got heads when flipping a coin was a lucky—not a skillful—flipper. This challenged nothing less than the validity of Buffett's career.

Buffett's record also posed a challenge, for it was the inconvenient fact that failed to follow the form. Buffett would taunt the scholars with the evidence of his career, and implicit in his taunts was a simple question: "If you're so smart, how come I'm so rich?"

Nonetheless, at business schools and economics departments, the Efficient Market Theory acquired the power of sacrament. Its truths were regarded as absolute, whereas competing doctrines were virtually banned. The theory also permeated Wall Street, as well as the investing culture as received in financial talk shows and advice columns. It is, indeed, the intellectual basis for the eggs-in-a-thousand-baskets approach of extreme "diversification," which is the prevailing bias of most investors today.

The theory fermented at various sites, but from similar yeasts, during the 1950s and 1960s. Among the pioneers was Paul A. Samuelson, the popular Massachusetts Institute of Technology economist and textbook writer. Samuelson was a Keynesian, but where the sardonic Lord Keynes viewed the stock exchange as a casino, Samuelson put faith in market prices. Around 1950, Samuelson subscribed to a tip sheet that charged $125 a year. He soon decided, logically enough, that if the tout service had really "known," it would have charged far more than $125 or kept its tips to itself.[3] This was a forerunner of the Efficient Market Theorist's joke in which two economists, walking across a campus, spot a $10 bill on the ground. As one bends to retrieve it, the other says, "Don't bother. If it were really worth $10, it wouldn't be there." Samuelson's landmark "Proof That Properly Anticipated Prices Fluctuate Randomly," published in 1965, adorned this notion in scholarly cloth. His intriguing gambit was that future events "cast their shadows before them"—that is, they are reflected in current prices.

> If one could be sure that a price will rise, it would have already risen. . . . You never get something for nothing.[4]

Two years later, Samuelson appeared before the Senate committee looking into mutual funds. As noted, funds of the Go-Go era were charging exorbitant fees, yet it was hard to see that their managers merited any fee at all. The typical fund did not even beat the market averages. As Samuelson explained it, "intelligent people" were "constantly shopping around for good value," buying bargain stocks and selling dear ones and, in the process, eliminating such opportunities even as they arose.[5] The funds' records were such that they could have done as well throwing darts. John Sparkman, the committee chairman, was stunned. Did Samuelson say *darts*?

MR. SAMUELSON: What my report says is that the median fund having access to this high-paid management has, in fact, done just as well and no better than twenty random stocks selected from the stock market.

THE CHAIRMAN: When you say twenty random stocks, are you referring to stocks that you just close your eyes and reach down and touch?

MR. SAMUELSON: Yes. Precisely.

THE CHAIRMAN: Or is some expert economist such as you picking them?

MR. SAMUELSON: No. Random. When I say "random," I want you to think of dice or think of random numbers or a dart.

The professor, however, did not *advocate* using darts to pick investments. For one thing, he knew, the Efficient Market Theory had some problems. Stock prices were far more volatile than the expected cash flows of the underlying companies, of which they were, in theory, a mirror. And Samuelson was corresponding with Conrad Taff, the Graham student and early Buffett devotee, who insisted that the theory was bunk. Buffett, who actually had a dartboard in his office for a while,[6] was beating the darts every year, Taff would tell him. Samuelson was intrigued, and gradually became a "Warren watcher,"[7] the first of many Efficient Market Theorists who puzzled over Buffett rather as an astronomer might wonder about a mysterious star.

But Samuelson did not change his mind. Part of the theory's allure was that it extended the classical economics of Adam Smith to financial markets. Investors such as Buffett thought of intrinsic value as an inherent quality; it lay "behind, or beneath, the prices observed in the marketplace."[8] The prices themselves were approximations. But to a classicist, the Invisible Hand was perpetually driving market prices and value together. In the extreme view, value only emerged—in a sense, only *existed*—at the point when buyer and seller agreed on a price. If IBM was trading at $120 a share, then IBM was "worth" $120; it could not be more or less. Of course, this implied that the buyer and seller were acting rationally.

Buffett's view, of companies and of human behavior, was more circumspect. In the first place, value was not so precise; another also rational investor might value IBM at $130. More to the point, investors were not always rational. At times, and especially under the influence of crowd psychology, investors might pay $160 for IBM—or agree to sell it for only $80.

The Efficient Market Theory had, in fact, begun as an attempt to debunk an aspect of the market's irrationality. From the time of Graham, Wall Street had peddled the work of so-called technical analysts.

By gazing into charts of *previous* prices, these would-be Merlins deigned to predict the future. Their lexicon was widely adopted; thus, commentators would speak of a stock's "testing a crucial barrier," which in fact was not a barrier but an inferred line on a chart. The Efficient Market Theorists exposed the chartists as frauds or, as the University of Chicago economist Eugene F. Fama put it, "astrologers."[9] The price "patterns" were patterns only in retrospect; no one could tell, looking at a chart, whether a stock that had fallen 10 percent would rebound or fall by 10 percent more. (For reasons known only to themselves, Merrill Lynch, Morgan Stanley, Salomon Brothers, and the rest continue to employ such soothsayers down to this day.)

But the theorists replaced the chartist voodoo with a voodoo of their own. They defused the idea that prices foretold the future, but ascribed to those same prices an unerring appraisal of the present. Prices, that is, were never wrong. They incorporated, with as much perfection as humans could manage, *all* there was to know of a company's long-term prospects. Studying those prospects was therefore pointless. Thus, the theorists' attack spread from the chartists to "fundamental analysts," such as Buffett, who combed through corporate reports looking for undervalued stocks. Quoting Fama:

> If the random walk theory is valid and if security exchanges are "efficient" markets, then stock prices at any point in time will represent good estimates of intrinsic or fundamental values. Thus, additional fundamental analysis is of value only when the analyst has new information . . . or has new insights concerning the effects of generally available information. . . .[10]

Taken at face, the qualifier offered a gaping loophole. Obviously, the analyst with neither new information nor new insights did not have an edge. But the rogue phrase "new information" was not to be taken at face. The implication was that investors with superior records must have had inside dope, or at least dope that was not widely known. Thus, the theory was intact: not even a perfect market could be expected to digest information before it was public. Indeed, the *Economist*, which reported each twist and turn of the theorists as received wisdom, asserted that stockpicking smarts were "either rare or nonexistent," although, the magazine sneered, "it helps to have the kind of inside smartness that Ivan Boesky had."[11] Samuelson was explicit:

> In the same way, experience has persuaded me that there are a few Warren Buffetts out there with high rent-earning ability because they are good at figuring out which fundamentals are fundamental and which new data are worth paying high costs to get. Such super-stars don't come cheap: by the time you spot them their fee has been bid sky high![12]

As Samuelson knew, Buffett did not charge a fee. In any event, Buffett got his "data" chiefly from annual reports, which were available to anyone. By ignoring this, Samuelson could attribute Buffett's success to information-gathering, and thus avoid the issue of whether Buffett might have a talent for *analyzing* the "data." It was as if he were merely a good librarian.

But Samuelson, a Nobel laureate in economics, knew he was more than that. At some point after his Senate testimony, Samuelson bought a big stake in Berkshire Hathaway,[13] a just-in-case hedging reminiscent of Voltaire's deathbed acceptance of the Church. Samuelson declined to comment, but he was hardly alone. Armen A. Alchian, a noted economist at the University of California at Los Angeles, also invested in Berkshire. Yet Alchian, in a letter to a fellow economist, maintained:

> I remain convinced that no investment funds, no matter for what kind of new activity or area, can claim demonstrable superior talent. Luck, Yes. But Superior Talent, No. . . . No, it's a world in which all reliably predictable events are priced right, with only surprise left. And surprise is "random" by definition.[14]

But Alchian devoted considerable energy to explaining Buffett's results. Ultimately, he decided that the secret lay in a wrinkle in Nebraska insurance law that, according to Alchian, permitted Nebraska insurers to take a greater role in monitoring their investments than out-of-state insurers.

> I attribute his success entirely to that fortunate, happenstance position, and not to any superior (relative to his competitors) skills.

It is difficult not to marvel at Alchian's leap of faith. Samuelson at least allowed that "Warren may be as near to a genius at investing as I have observed."[15] Yet that was also a sort of damnation. Genius was not method—and Samuelson disclaimed his method. "Warren gave a talk and said, 'Any fool could see that the *Washington Post* was under priced,' "Samuelson noted. "I'm not a fool. I don't find it credible." Why, then, had Buffett bought the *Post?* Samuelson replied, "That's the difference between genius and talent." As a genius—a sort of freak—Buffett could be dismissed. The Efficient Market Theory would still hold true for mortals. Thus, Stanford's William F. Sharpe wrote Buffett off as a "three-sigma event"—a statistical aberration so out of line as to require no further attention.

From the foundation of the Efficient Market Theory, scholars erected the elaborate construct of modern finance. Finance is the inverse of investing; it describes the capital-raising function from the corporate point of view. It is a useful discipline, but inexact. But now, like investing, finance was seen as a quantifiable social science, far more precise than the actual world it purported to explain. One theorist depicted a formula for a stock's return, R, with M standing for the market, a and b standing for constants that may vary from stock to stock, and u signifying a random error:[16]

$$R = a + bM + u$$

The economist hastened to add that this was only a model "in its simplest form." There was no shortage of models as impenetrable as the Dead Sea Scrolls or a verse from the Koran.

This "science" was grounded in the only evidence that scholars considered relevant: the data of (supposedly perfect) stock prices. It ignored all of the myriad and changing factors—such as a company's strategy, products, market strength, and management—that are central to valuing a business in the real world. Such variables are subjective and imprecise; but they are, of course, the stuff that investor-analysts such as Buffett reckon with every day.

One might have imagined that a few business schools might have turned to Buffett's reports, at least as a guide, in discussing such topics. But save for an occasional guest lecture, Buffett was a nonperson in academia. This hit him in a sensitive spot. While most investors are content to make the money, Buffett very much wanted recognition for being *right*. It was important to Buffett, ever the teacher, that Graham—and Buffett—be seen as a useful model. Quoting from a letter:

In my opinion, the continuous 63-year arbitrage experience of Graham-Newman Corp., Buffett Partnership, and Berkshire illustrates just how foolish EMT is. . . . the three organizations traded hundreds of different securities . . . we did not have to dig for obscure facts . . . we simply acted on highly-publicized events. . . .[17]

In what for Buffett must have been an excruciating defection, Graham himself, near the end of his life, voiced strong doubts about whether, given the growing abundance of stock research, security analysis would still pay off. Shortly before his death, in 1976, Graham told an interviewer:

I am no longer an advocate of elaborate techniques of security analysis in order to find superior value opportunities. This was a rewarding activity, say, 40 years ago, when our textbook "Graham & Dodd" was first published; but the situation has changed. . . .[18]

Since Graham had also attacked the "random walk," and specifically the notion of efficient prices, only six months before,[19] the best that one may surmise is that he continued to recognize inefficiency in a *theoretical* sense, but doubted that one could take advantage of it. Buffett never alluded to Graham's semi-apostasy, but then Buffett always idealized Graham, and Graham was always braver as a teacher than as an investor.

In contrast, neither Buffett nor the campus theologians entertained any ambiguity. As Buffett noted, economists treated the theory as "holy scripture."[20] Richard Brealey and Stewart Myers's *Principles of Corporate Finance*, the most widely used textbook of recent times, captured the unquestioning spirit. The authors spoke of the "discovery" of efficient markets as though the theory had been a natural element awaiting its Marie Curie. Their claim for it was remarkably sweeping:

In an efficient market you can trust prices. They impound all available information about the value of each security.[21]

One wonders how a flesh-and-blood trader would react to Brealey and Myers's idealized depiction of the stock market. Their traders were ever calm, their speculators ever dispassionate:

In an efficient market there are no financial illusions. Investors are unromantically concerned with the firm's cash flows and the portion of those cash flows to which they are entitled.[22]

Scholars did subject the theory to cross-examination, but in an entirely trivial sense. They studied various exceptions to the appearance of random pricing, but these exceptions—so-called anomalies—were formulaic in nature, such as a pattern of stocks showing gains in January, or on certain days of the week, or at smaller companies. The discovery of such a less-than-random pattern wide enough to leave the theory with a pinprick prompted cries of scholarly amazement and feverish demands for more such detailed, arcane studies. Yet in this vast epistemological literature there were no studies of the "anomaly" that might have left the theory with a mortal puncture—the consistently superior record of Buffett and of others such as Keynes, Graham, John Templeton, Mario Gabelli, John Neff, and Peter Lynch, to cite only the better-known names.

The records of such investors were ignored or wished away. Tony Thomson, an investment manager at Bankers Trust, airily dismissed Buffett as a "red herring." Buffett's record signified nothing; absent *seventy-five years* of quarterly data, Thomson argued, one couldn't "establish" whether he had done it with brains or luck. "Thus, the jury is out on Mr. Buffet [*sic*]."[23] Burton G. Malkiel, a Princeton economist, popularized this notion in his best-selling *A Random Walk down Wall Street*:

> But while I believe in the possibility of superior professional investment performance, I must emphasize that the evidence we have thus far does not support the view that such competence exists. . . .[24]

Malkiel saw no evidence of "competence" beyond that of coin-flippers able to disguise their luck as talent. "God Almighty," Malkiel proclaimed, "does not know the proper price-earnings multiple for a common stock."[25]

This fetching comment introduced a straw man. Graham-and-Dodders did not claim to know the *proper* price for a stock. Theirs was a rough science, at best. What they said was that *on occasion* a stock was so out of line that one could leap in without any claim to precision. Such instances might be rare. Graham-and-Dodd investors typically owned only a dozen or so stocks from among the thousands available. But those few could make one rich. Quoting Buffett:

Observing correctly that the market was *frequently* efficient, [EMT adherents] went on to conclude incorrectly that it was *always* efficient. The difference between these propositions is night and day.[26]

One striking contrast was in the rival camps' definition of "risk." Risk, to Buffett, was the risk of paying more than a business would prove to be worth. And the range of variables was nearly infinite. Was a company dependent on too few customers? Did the chairman drink? Since the sum (or even the number) of such risks could not be figured with precision, Buffett looked for companies—the very few companies—in which the risks seemed tolerable even allowing for error.

The theorists recognized no such nuances; risk, in their view, was measurable. Since stock prices were right, they simply assumed that the foreseeable risks in a business were incorporated in its price. Every change in outlook was immediately matched by a change in price. Therefore, the best proxy for the "riskiness" of an investment was the historical riskiness of its stock. Risk, then, equaled price volatility. It was defined in precise mathematical terms, as the degree to which a stock had bounced around, relative to each bounce of the market as a whole. As if to sanctify its algebraic properties, it was christened with a Greek letter, beta. A stock with a beta of 1.0 bounced around as much as the general market; one with a beta of 1.2 was quantifiably more volatile, and one with a beta of 1.5 more volatile still.

The theorists' logic now proceeded on a dizzying spiral. Investors did not like risk. Therefore, the investors who bought high-beta stocks, being ever-rational, must have done so because such stocks held the prospect of above-average returns—indeed, with returns that would exceed the norm *in precise arithmetic relation to their betas*. Conversely, investors in lower-beta stocks would "pay" for the past tranquillity of such issues by accepting lower returns. Indeed, since there could be no free lunch, the *only* way to consistently earn a higher profit was by accepting added "risk"—that is, higher betas.[27] Now the totemic nature of modern finance begins to emerge. The *only* factor necessary to calculate the expected relative return on a stock was its beta. Nothing about the fundamentals of a company mattered; the one number, beta, computed from past stock prices, was the only relevant issue. "What is your beta?" the scholars asked. It was like a mantra. And Wall Street analysts slavishly paid heed. Virtually every brokerage in the country required its analysts to assess their stocks in terms of "betas" and of "risk-adjusted"—meaning "beta-adjusted"—returns.

To Graham,[28] and to Buffett, this was a madness. That a stock bounced around did not make it risky to a long-term holder. In fact, beta turned "risk" on its head. Consider that when Buffett invested in the Washington Post, the market was valuing the Post at about $80 million. Had the stock fallen by half before his purchase, it would have been more volatile—and hence, to an Efficient Market Theorist, "riskier." Buffett tartly observed, "I have never been able to figure out why it's riskier to buy something at $40 million than at $80 million."[29]

Columbia Business School brought the two sides face to face in 1984, the fiftieth anniversary of Graham and Dodd's textbook. Buffett was asked to speak on behalf of Graham-and-Dodders, the University of Rochester's Michael C. Jensen for the theorists. A devout believer, Jensen had written in 1978:

> I believe there is no other proposition in economics which has more solid empirical evidence supporting it than the Efficient Market Hypothesis.[30]

Indeed, he had warned dissenters that the theory was "accepted as a fact of life, and a scholar who purports to model behavior in a manner which violates it faces a difficult task of justification."[31]

Since Jensen's encyclical, the theory, and particularly the concept of beta, had come under attack. Now, at Columbia, Uris Hall was stacked with Buffett's fellow investors. Surveying the crowd, Jensen adopted a gracious tone. He felt "like a turkey must feel at the beginning of a turkey hunt."

But the turkey was hard to pin down. First, Jensen made an absolutist claim: *no* profit could be systematically earned from analyzing public information. Then he gave some ground. Exceptions had popped up; he seemed to grant that a superior analyst might exist. Still, he ridiculed the profession in general. People consulted security analysts, like priests, owing to their "psychic demand for answers."

> When science responds by saying there is no known answer, or worse yet, there is no answer, people are not satisfied. . . . In such circumstances people are perfectly willing to make up answers, or even to pay others to make them up for them.[32]

Security analysts, then, were the spiritual descendants of "the medicine man, mystics, astrologers, gurus." As opposed to these pagan stockpickers, Jensen claimed for "science" the Efficient Market Theory. Noting that the "star pupils of Graham and Dodd" were in attendance, Jensen still claimed that it was hard to tell if "any" were really superior, due to the well-known "selection-bias problem."

> If I survey a field of untalented analysts all of whom are doing nothing but flipping coins, I expect to see some who have tossed two heads in a row and even some who have tossed ten heads in a row.

Buffett could not have asked for a better setup. The failure of most money managers to do better than coin-flippers had been invoked at every turn. But on reflection, there was less to this than met the eye. Since pros accounted for most of the trading, the *average* stockpicker could not do better than average. The meaningful question was, were there enough gaps in the market's efficiency so that some preidentifiable group could beat the market, and beat it consistently?

Borrowing from Jensen, Buffett envisioned a "national coin-flipping contest." Each day, everyone in the United States flipped a coin, with those who flipped tails continually dropping out. After twenty days, only 215 flippers would be left.

> Now this group will probably start getting a little puffed up about this, human nature being what it is. They may try to be modest, but at cocktail parties they will occasionally admit to attractive members of the opposite sex what their technique is, and what marvelous insights they bring to the field of flipping. . . . But then some business school professor will probably be rude enough to bring up the fact that if 225 million orangutans had engaged in a similar exercise, the results would be much the same. . . .[33]

But what if the surviving orangutans largely came from the "same zoo," located, conveniently, in Omaha? One would suspect that the zookeeper had something to do with it. Buffett's proposition was that a concentration of head-flippers *did* hail from one zoo—from the "intellectual village" of "Graham-and-Doddsville." Then he laid out the records of nine Graham-and-Dodd money managers—that is, all of those with whom Buffett had had a personal, and long, association. Their particular tastes varied from cigar butts (Walter Schloss) to franchise stocks (Bill Ruane). But each of the nine had beaten the market over an extended period. And each had been preidentified as a Graham-and-Dodder; that is, each had spent his career looking for discrepancies between market price and intrinsic value. None had paid attention to whether stocks did better on Monday or Thursday, or in January or August.

Buffett found it "extraordinary" that academics studied such things. They studied what was *measurable*, rather than what was meaningful. "As a friend [Charlie Munger] said, to a man with a hammer, everything looks like a nail."

Buffett seemed especially resentful about the theory's hold on his alma mater. He was willing to give a lecture at Columbia, and did so every year or two, but refused to donate money to it. John C. Burton, the business school dean, said, "He told me very frankly he didn't think education was enhanced by money and secondly that he didn't think business schools were teaching the things he wanted to support. He was very hostile to the idea of efficient market research."

Burton, who owned a few shares of Berkshire, thought Buffett's reason was genuine, but incredibly myopic. Buffett often cited his personal debt to Graham, yet when Burton pressed him to give something back—to endow, perchance, future Grahams and future Buffetts—the billionaire would turn him down.

Columbia's program was less one-sided than most. It hired Wall Street pros as part-time lecturers, some of whom used a Graham-and-Dodd approach. But the finance program was, as Buffett maintained, dominated by Efficient Market Theory. A stroll through the business section of the university bookstore suggested that a student could get an M.B.A. at Columbia without ever hearing the names Graham and Dodd, and without even a faint exposure to value investing. Eventually, Columbia established a Graham-and-Dodd chair, but oddly assigned it to Bruce Greenwald. Greenwald, an MIT-trained economist, had married into money, made a million or two in bond futures, lost a similar sum in oils, and quit at the insistence of his in-laws. "At investing I'm a complete idiot," he noted, rather affably, adding that it was speculating that turned him on. He invited Buffett to give a guest lecture but did not think him imitable. "I'm sympathetic to the Graham-and-Dodd point of view," Greenwald said, "but I'm not really a Graham-and-Dodder."[34]

On Wall Street, meanwhile, the theory made remarkable inroads. There was a trend toward making security analysis "precise." Brokerages emphasized groups of stocks, rather than selecting individual winners. In a remarkable comment, circa 1979, the chief strategist at Drexel Burnham said his aim was to make the analyst less like an independent entrepreneur who worked alone judging stocks.[35] Less, that is, like a Warren Buffett.

The introduction, in the 1980s, of stock-index futures marked the theory's coming-of-age. Academics had preached that investors could not pick stocks. Now they needn't try; they could heave a single dart at the entire market. Buffett urged Rep. John Dingell, chairman of the House Subcommittee on Oversight and Investigations, in 1982, not to permit such futures. "We do not need more people gambling in nonessential instruments identified with the stock market," Buffett wrote.[36] In a prophetic aside, he warned that futures could lead to speculative excesses and sour the public on stocks altogether.

It is easy to lose sight of the distinction between "futures" and stocks—after all, are they not both investments? This is arguable. Futures are zero-sum bets on the market direction. They do not raise capital for business, which is the essential purpose of the stock market. They do not represent a stake in a business—merely a stake in a wager.

In the eighties, money poured into futures as well as into "index funds" designed to mimic the market averages (by owning every stock or a reasonable proxy). Money managers were giving up investing for trading the market whole—thus abandoning the job assigned them by markets, which is to keep prices "right" by searching out bargains and winnowing out the overpriced. By 1986, well over $100 billion was managed "passively," meaning it was not managed at all. It was chained to the Ouija board of various market indices.

In the summer of 1986, there were, finally, cries that the trend had gone too far. The occasion was a then-shocking 62-point drop in the Dow. Perhaps too many people had been looking at Ouija boards? Burton Malkiel, writing in the *Wall Street Journal*, demurred. If markets were efficient, automaton investing was a cause for celebration.

: . . I am proud to have been at least partly responsible [for] a growing faith in the efficiency of stock markets and a trend toward passive portfolio management.[37]

Buffett countered in the *Washington Post*, arguing that new-age trading was fulfilling Keynes's dark prophecy of the market as a casino. Speculation had so overwhelmed markets that their proper, value-discovering role was being swamped by hyperactive trading. The new, esoteric instruments were not "investments"; they served no social agenda; they did the work not of the Invisible Hand but of "an invisible foot kicking society in the shins." Now Buffett trotted out a rather savage satire; he fantasized that a boat of twenty-five brokers were shipwrecked and forced to live out their days on an uninhabited island.

> Faced with developing an economy that would maximize their consumption and pleasure, would they, I wonder, assign 20 of their number to produce food, clothing, shelter, etc., while setting five to endlessly trading options on the future output of the 20?[38]

As a remedy for the "casino society," Buffett proposed what Jonathan Swift would have called "a modest tax": 100 percent of the profits on stocks and futures held for less than a year. This idea disappeared without a trace. But fears about hyperactive trading did not. In 1987, with markets restless, worries of a meltdown escalated. Malkiel, writing in the *New York Times*, again defended push-button trading as fostering "liquidity." Alluding to the market's jumpiness, he added, "but the market only seems more volatile because of a scale effect."[39] His timing was off; three weeks later, the market crashed. The Brady report on Black Monday uncovered a truism that Malkiel had missed: when everyone lined up on the same side of a trade, the liquidity provided by futures was an "illusion."[40]

Malkiel had praised professional investors for using futures to "shift and control risk and to respond to market movements." In Buffett's vision, true risk—the risk, say, that sales of carpets or of *World Book* would hit a slump—could not be "shifted." Such risk was inherent to owning Berkshire. Nor did market movements call for a "response." He blamed the crash on the very people Malkiel had praised:

> We have "professional" investors, those who manage many billions, to thank for most of this turmoil. Instead of focusing on what businesses will do in the years ahead, many prestigious money managers now focus on what they expect other money managers to do in the days ahead.[41]

The market survived the crash, but the theory was badly wounded. How could prices have been rational both before and after? No new information had surfaced to account for such a drop. There had been no sudden change in expected future profits. Indeed, for the people who sold stocks on October 19, corporate profits were not a remote consideration. According to Robert J. Shiller, a Yale economist who surveyed nearly one thousand investors soon after Black Monday, the only news that investors had been aware of that day was news of the crash itself. In place of the cold, "unromantic" investor of Brealey and Myers, Shiller's respondents reported sweaty palms, rapid pulse rates, and hypertension. On average, they had checked prices thirty-five times. The survey presented a microcosm of crowd psychology in action, with 40 percent of the institutional investors experiencing "a contagion of fear from other investors."[42]

In another blow, Eugene Fama demonstrated that the beta of a stock had *no* relation to its actual return.[43] Nobel prizes had been awarded for treatises on beta; now, it developed, beta was useless. But analysts and academics continued to use it. Definitions were rejiggled here and there, but the structure was left intact. Indeed, as the *Economist* reported, the theory itself lived on, despite the "awkward" facts.

As Charles Goodhart, of the London School of Economics, points out, no one has thought up a better theory. Instead, academics have tried to reinterpret the awkward evidence in less-threatening ways.[44]

The post-crash edition of Brealey and Myers was unreformed. It conceded, in a brief passage, that Black Monday posed some problems. But on the same page, the authors again advised, ". . . you can trust prices." But *which* prices—of the morning of October 19, or of six hours later? Never mind; the theory was "remarkably well-supported by the facts."[45]

In a broader sense, the theory retained its hold on the investing culture. Wall Street pros continued to flock to esoteric new instruments, and advisers continued to counsel extreme "diversification." Berkshire shareholders, in particular, were continually being advised that they should "diversify"—that is, should sell. J. P. Morgan was trustee for one woman who had virtually all of her money in Berkshire. As her portfolio soared into the millions, her man at Morgan repeatedly (but vainly) urged her to lighten up. It did not occur to him that one investment might be better than another. He affixed a note to her statement to cover himself: "Co-trustee/beneficiary *refuses* to sell Berkshire Hathaway. . . ."

In a narrow sense, the persistence of the theory was a boon to Buffett's career. Thousands of his potential competitors were taught that studying securities was a waste of time. "From a selfish point of view," Buffett wrote after the crash, "Grahamites should probably endow chairs to ensure the perpetual teaching of EMT."[46] But Buffett would have preferred that schools perpetuate the teaching of Buffett. In academia, he was still an "anomaly," a "red herring," a "three-sigma" irrelevancy. "No one," he wrote of the theory's proponents,

> has ever said he was wrong, no matter how many thousands of students he has sent forth misinstructed. EMT, moreover, continues to be an integral part of the investment curriculum at major business schools.[47]

And Buffett was not. But in the aftermath of Black Monday, Buffett was to give his most convincing lesson ever.

Chapter 18

SECRETS OF
THE TEMPLE

In the fall of 1988, Coca-Cola noticed that somebody was buying its stock. Roberto C. Goizueta, the chairman, and Donald Keough, the president, were more than mildly curious about who it was. The stock had fallen 25 percent from its pre-crash high, and the mysterious investor was gulping down shares by the caseload. When Keough saw that a broker in the Midwest was doing the buying, he suddenly thought of his former neighbor. "You know," he told Goizueta with a start, "it could be Warren Buffett." Goizueta urged Keough to call him.

"Well, Warren, what's going on?" Keough began. "You don't happen to be buying any shares of Coca-Cola?"

"It so happens that I am," Buffett replied.[1]

Buffett asked Keough to stay mum until he was required to disclose his stake. In the meantime, he continued to accumulate the stock. By the next spring, Berkshire had acquired $1.02 billion worth, or 7 percent of the Coca-Cola Co., at an average price of $10.96 a share. When the news broke, Buffett passed it off on his Cherry Coke dependency, quipping that the investment was "the ultimate case of putting your money where your mouth is."[2] Otherwise, he was delphic:

It's like when you marry a girl. Is it her eyes? Her personality? It's a whole bunch of things you can't separate.[3]

A Wall Street analyst termed it a "very expensive stock."[4] But in a mere three years, Buffett's stake in Coca-Cola would soar to an astounding $3.75 billion—roughly the value of *all* of Berkshire when it had begun investing in Coca-Cola.

What happened to Coca-Cola in those three years? Income per share rose 64 percent—a heady gain, but hardly enough to justify the near quadrupling of its stock. What did the trick, more nearly, was a sea change in Wall Street's perception of the business. It suddenly dawned on investors that as popular as Coke was, it had barely scratched the surface in the planet's most populous regions. The average American was guzzling 296 Cokes a year, compared to only thirty-nine drinks for the typical foreigner. And Coca-Cola was rushing to close the gap, aggressively expanding in markets such as Eastern Europe, France, China, and the entire Pacific Rim. It was already earning more in Japan than it was at home.[5] In places such as Indonesia, where the per capita intake was only four Cokes a year, the potential was vast. Keough crowed, "When I think of Indonesia—a country on the equator with 180 million people, a median age of eighteen, and a Moslem ban on alcohol—I feel I know what heaven looks like."[6] By 1991, judging from its stock, Wall Street did, too.

But what had inspired Buffett to become the biggest single owner of Coca-Cola just before its surge? What had inspired him to invest more—much, much more—in Coca-Cola than in any previous stock? Was it just a lucky dart? Or was it, as Buffett maintained, as close to a sure thing as he had ever seen?[7]

Many of his previous investments had hinged on specific events, or on values that could be tabulated from a balance sheet. The Washington Post had been selling for a mere fraction of its liquidation value, while GEICO, acquired for next to nothing, had been an absolute steal if one was convinced that the then troubled company would survive. Coca-Cola was different. Buffett couldn't derive its value from the balance sheet. He couldn't *compute* the value. But he could see it.

He was often asked, how did he determine the "value" of a stock? Conceptually, Buffett likened it to that of a bond. A bond's value was equal to the cash flow from future interest payments, discounted back to the present. A stock's value was figured the same way; it equaled the anticipated cash flow per share,* except that the investor had to fill in a crucial detail:

> If you buy a bond, you know exactly what's going to happen, assuming it's a good bond, a U.S. Government bond. If it says 9 percent, you know what the coupons are going to be for maybe thirty years. . . . Now, when you buy a business, you're buying something with coupons on it, too, except, the only problem is, they don't print in the amount. And it's my job to print in [to figure out] the amount on the coupon.9

With this notion of value in mind, Buffett tried to find stocks whose "value" was greater—significantly greater—than their price. Buffett's guides to finding such a stock could be summarized quickly:

- Pay no attention to macroeconomic trends or forecasts, or to people's predictions about the future course of stock prices. Focus on long-term business value—on the size of the coupons down the road.
- Stick to stocks within one's "circle of competence." For Buffett, that was often a company with a consumer franchise. But the general rule was true for all: if you didn't understand the business—be it a newspaper or a software firm—you couldn't value the stock.
- Look for managers who treated the shareholders' capital with ownerlike care and thoughtfulness.
- Study prospects—and their competitors—in great detail. Look at raw data, not analysts' summaries. Trust your own eyes, Buffett said. But one needn't value a business too precisely. A basketball coach doesn't check to see if a prospect is six foot one or six foot two; he looks for seven-footers.
- The vast majority of stocks would not be compelling either way—so ignore them. Merrill Lynch had an opinion on every stock; Buffett did not. But when an investor had conviction about a stock, he or she should also show courage—and buy a *ton* of it.

---

*Buffett defined cash flow as reported earnings plus depreciation, depletion, amortization, and certain other noncash charges, *less* the average annual capital expenditures required for a company to maintain its unit volume and competitive position.8

Buffett did that. After the Cap Cities deal, in 1985, he sat for three long years without buying a single common stock.* And then, when Coca-Cola fell to attractive levels, he staked a fourth or so of Berkshire's market value on that one stock.

The question was: why then? Coca-Cola's stock, after all, had been cheaper years before, and the global reach of its drink was hardly new. Robert Winship Woodruff, the Georgia tycoon who became Coca-Cola's president in 1923, had been determined to make Coke available everywhere on earth. In 1928, it was bottled in China. During World War II, the company persuaded the U.S. government to ferry fifty-nine bottling plants overseas, theoretically to boost troop morale and not incidentally to spread the soda.[10] In 1949, nine Buddhist priests presided over the opening of a plant in Bangkok. Such was Coke's universality that in 1956, an enterprising Coke publicist set forth to find an innocent to whom he could introduce the drink. He trekked 150 miles into the Peruvian back country, encountered an Indian woman in the jungle, and, through an interpreter, explained his mission. The woman reached into a sack and pulled out a bottle of Coke.[11]

Buffett was exposed to this wondrous beverage in about 1935. "Of a certainty," he wrote to shareholders,

> it was in 1936 that I started buying Cokes at the rate of six for 25¢ from Buffett & Son, the family grocery store, to sell around the neighborhood for 5¢ each. In this excursion into high-margin retailing, I duly observed the extraordinary consumer attractiveness and commercial possibilities of the product. I continued to note these qualities for the next 52 years as Coke blanketed the world. During this period, however, I carefully avoided buying even a single share, instead allocating major portions of my net worth to street railway companies, windmill manufacturers, anthracite producers, textile businesses . . . and the like.[12]

Coca-Cola was the sort of "simple" business—one with pricing power and a protective "moat"—that Buffett came to crave, particularly in the 1970s, as his taste began to shift from "anthracite" to franchise companies such as See's. Coca-Cola's main business was not selling Coke; it was providing concentrate and syrup to bottlers and soda fountains. Such a business (unlike bottling) required little capital. What's

---

*Does not include arbitrage or undisclosed small purchases.

more, its name recognition was unique, especially overseas, where Coke outsold Pepsi four-to-one.[13] In Buffett's terms, the brand name was a sort of a universal toll bridge.

However, by the seventies, though the drink had blanketed the world, the company was adrift. Sales overseas had been left to the individual bottlers, not all of whom were up to the job. Also, certain cultural proclivities slowed Coke's acceptance (in France, opponents of Americanization made common cause with vineyards).[14] Even worse, J. Paul Austin, the chief executive, did not know what to do with Coca-Cola's surplus cash. By mid-decade, that was a $300 million problem. Austin, a handsome, red-haired Olympic rower from Harvard, by then secretly ailing from Alzheimer's and Parkinson's,[15] invested in a string of un-cola diversifications: water purification, wine, shrimp farming, plastics, whey-based nutritional drinks, and fruits and vegetables. Buffett thought such moves were squandering precious capital.[16] And, indeed, the average annual return on Coca-Cola's stock during the seventies was a miserable 1 percent.

Goizueta, a Cuban-born chemical engineer, took over in 1981 and made Keough, a broad-smiling salesman, his number two. Goizueta's first instinct was to continue diversifying.[17] In 1982, Coca-Cola branched into movies by acquiring Columbia Pictures, a sideshow that Buffett disliked.[18] Its annual report for that year devoted six pages to its film studio (including a full-page photo of a sunburned Dustin Hoffman) and wine business and only three pages to overseas cola sales.

The company also was rolling out diet Coke, which proved to be a winner. Goizueta soon began to shift his focus to the burgeoning battle for the U.S. cola market.[19] He was so caught up in fighting Pepsi-Cola that in 1985 Coca-Cola ditched the syrup formula that had served it for a century and unveiled "New Coke." This stupendous error paid an unexpected dividend. The old drink was, truly, brought back by popular demand.

Buffett switched his drink from Pepsi to Cherry Coke at about the same time. The stream of cherry-flavored fizz seems to have had a catalytic effect, and he began to look at Coca-Cola's stock with increasing interest.[20] The New Coke fiasco merely made the company more compelling to him. As Buffett explained it, Coca-Cola *knew* that Americans had preferred the sweeter New Coke, but when people were told about the switch, they wanted their old Coke back. The drink had "something other than just the taste—the accumulated memory of all those ballgames and good experiences as children which Coke was a part of."[21] As Buffett dug into his research, he read everything on Coca-Cola he could find. One paragraph in a *Fortune* story caught his eye:

> Several times every year a weighty and serious investor looks long and with profound respect at Coca-Cola's record, but comes regretfully to the conclusion that he is looking too late.[22]

This had been published way back in 1938 (when the stock, adjusted for later splits, cost forty-six cents a share). Even then, Coke had been seen as "a sublimated essence" of all that America stood for;[23] even then, the sound of a nickel dropping down the slot, followed by "a whir and a clunk" and an ice-cold bottle sliding out the chute, had been something to behold. And it had been known, even in 1938, that the potential thirst of people overseas was far from quenched. That was the thing that got to Buffett.

By the mid-eighties, he saw that the light had finally dawned on Coca-Cola's management. Goizueta was divesting the company's un-cola side ventures. And the Yale-educated sugar baron's son, who had begun his career at a bottling plant in Havana, was paying more attention to marketing Coke overseas.

A case in point was the Philippines, where the San Miguel brewery, which bottled Coke as well as beer, had neglected soft drinks and allowed Pepsi to take the lead in colas. The home office invested $13 million to become a partner in its bottler, and Coca-Cola soon won back two-thirds of the market.[24]

Spurred by success in the Philippines, Coca-Cola moved to strengthen bottling operations in Brazil, Egypt, Taiwan, China, Indonesia, Belgium, Holland, and Britain. In France, where the per capita was a dismal thirty-one drinks a year, Coca-Cola began a lengthy fight to sack its bottler. Also, the company became more attentive to margins. In Mexico, a big market with subpar profits, prices were hiked and earnings soared. The change in focus was hardly a secret—in fact, it screamed out from the pages of Coca-Cola's annual reports. The cover of the 1986 report depicted three Coke cans perched on top of the world. Inside, the company hungrily eyed its future:

The potential appears limitless, and the Coca-Cola system is aggressively implementing . . . soft drink availability, affordability and acceptability around the world.

The numbers in those reports showed that Coca-Cola's strategy was reaping a substantial payoff. From 1984 to 1987—that is, *before* Buffett invested—the total of gallons sold overseas rose 34 percent.[25] Profit margins on each gallon rose, too, from 22 percent to 27 percent, thus providing a double dip. In all, foreign profits surged from $607 million to $1.11 billion.

The larger picture was of a company redirected. Whereas in 1984 Coca-Cola had earned just a shade more than half (52 percent) of its profits overseas, by 1987 a full three-fourths of its income was international. And the untapped potential remained vast. In the fast-growing Pacific Rim, people still drank fewer than twenty-five Cokes a year; in Africa, even fewer. Even in Europe and Latin America, where Coke had been served for decades, the per capitas were less than one hundred.[26] Moreover, the profits per drink in those populous and far from sated areas were much, much higher than at home. To Buffett, it amounted to a convincing case that the "coupons" on Coca-Cola would be rising for a very long time. "What I then perceived," Buffett wrote after his investment but before the stock had really taken off,

was both clear and fascinating . . . What was already the world's most ubiquitous product [had] gained new momentum, with sales overseas virtually exploding.[27]

In addition, Goizueta was using the company's excess cash to buy back stock—the same approach that Buffett had urged on Katharine Graham at the Post. He was also grading his managers according to their return on capital. Sounding remarkably like Buffett, Goizueta, who had no training in finance, would later remark, "I learned that when you start charging people for their capital, all sorts of [good] things happen."[28] Buffett recognized a kindred spirit.[29]

By the latter part of 1988, Coca-Cola was trading at thirteen times expected 1989 earnings, or about 15 percent above the average stock. That was more than a Ben Graham would have paid. But given its earning power, Buffett thought he was getting a Mercedes for the price of a Chevrolet. In his own mind, he was not abandoning Graham—far from it.

> I felt as sure of the margin of safety with Coke as when I bought Union Street Railway at 40 percent of net cash. In both cases you're getting more than you're paying for. It's just that one was easier to spot.[30]

In fact, every analyst on Wall Street had spotted it. What Buffett knew about Coca-Cola was disclosed in detail in company reports and was understood, intuitively, by the average fourth-grader. Coke, simply, was *the* best-known brand in the world. But with a couple of exceptions (First Boston's Martin Romm called Coca-Cola a "strong buy"), the analysts dithered. It wasn't their research that failed them, it was nerve. Dean Witter's Lawrence Adelman observed, "Coca-Cola has the potential to expand profits at a rate *significantly* higher than the S&P 500 over the next five years."[31] But Adelman couldn't pull the trigger; he sent his clients a waffling "buy/hold" opinion on the stock. Roy Burry, Kidder Peabody's man on the beat, also expected strong profit growth, but Burry was dissuaded from recommending the stock by "*uncertainty about the near-term movement of the dollar.*"[32]

A more interesting case was PaineWebber's Emanuel Goldman, who liked Coca-Cola but preferred the more diversified PepsiCo.[33] Goldman showed the Wall Street disease of paying too close attention to the trees. Pepsi, he noted, could expect a boost from higher Frito Lay prices, better results with Mountain Dew, home delivery of Pizza Hut, a forty-nine-cent meal at Taco Bell, and healthier fare at Kentucky Fried Chicken. Buffett also looked at Pepsi (which would also turn out well).[34] But he did not have the same degree of *certainty* about pizza, chicken, and tacos. He could reduce Coke's virtues to a sentence:

> If you gave me $100 billion and said take away the soft drink leadership of Coca-Cola in the world, I'd give it back to you and say it can't be done.[35]

After Buffett invested in Coca-Cola he became one of its directors, but his role on the board was passive.[36] In short, anyone could have bought the stock when he did and gotten the same result. Yet Wall

Streeters were dubious that much could be learned from Buffett. They maintained that he got his ideas from a network of tipsters that they, of course, could not hope to crack. As an Omaha broker said, with a knowing air, "Warren had the best *network.*" This fulfilled the hoariest of Wall Street clichés: that the little guy was no match for the savvy pro.

A few of Buffett's negotiated deals, such as Salomon, did arise from personal connections, and Buffett's circle of such contacts was extensive. But most of his investments were market-traded stocks. And, in fact, he instructed his brokers not to distract him with their hot ideas.[37] According to Munger, he used his contacts to investigate prospects after he had a lead.

Given Buffett's usual holding period, tips would have been of dubious value—it is hard to conceive of a "tip" that would be relevant five years later. However, the "tips" rationalization absolved others who had not thought of the same ideas, and who resented Buffett's success. Once, when an investor put in an order for yet more Berkshire, his Manhattan broker snapped, "*Warren* makes mistakes, too." It is hardly a surprise that Buffett was resented, since he made a point of mocking the complex "tools" on which other money managers relied. And some of these others, being less than anxious to slog through annual reports, were reluctant to believe that Buffett found his stocks the way he *said* he did. One financial editor inquired about Buffett's "secret"—a black box, perhaps, hidden in the bowels of Kiewit Plaza?

Buffett kept insisting that he had no mysterious shortcut, no crystal ball. Once, a broker who was buying a house asked for his outlook on interest rates. Buffett jokingly replied, "Only two people understand that. Both of them live in Switzerland. However, they're diametrically opposed to each other."[38]

Most of what Buffett did, such as reading reports and trade journals, the small investor could also do. He felt very deeply that the common wisdom was dead wrong; the little guy *could* invest in the market, so long as he stuck to his Graham-and-Dodd knitting.[39] But people, he found, either took to this approach immediately or they never did. Many had a "perverse" need to make it complicated.[40] This truism extended to Buffett's family.

His elder sister Doris once tried to juice up her income by selling "naked options"—precisely the sort of market roulette that Buffett had scorned. Come Black Monday, Doris, who rather liked living on the edge, found herself $1.4 million in debt.[41] Warren agreed to reorganize a family trust that he administered for Doris, so that she would now get a monthly stipend from it. But he flatly refused to pay off the debt—leaving Doris no choice but to default. She was badly hurt by Warren's refusal, and he was hurt by her subsequent spell of coolness. But bailing out a speculator went against his grain—and Warren would not break his rules, not even for his sister.

Of course, following Graham and Dodd would not make Doris—or most anyone else—as gifted as Buffett. At the mere mention of a stock—any stock—he could spit back a fact-filled summary of it, just as the young Warren had once recited from memory the populations of cities. Similarly, his ability for figures left his colleagues stunned.[42] (Buffett explained his penchant for mental math by saying that if he didn't understand a figure *in his head*, he didn't "understand" it; thus, no computer.)[43]

People habitually referred to his mental processes in mechanical terms. Doris, herself, reflexively remarked how quickly information appeared on Warren's "screen"; Mike Goldberg spoke of his "iterating" insurance policies through his memory. This agile sifting of mental index cards enabled him to recognize past patterns and, through untold repetitions, develop an investing instinct. Alas, the average investor is not endowed with a mental calculator or an on-line encyclopedia.

This does *not* imply that Buffett could not be a useful model. (A clinic with Ted Williams should make one a better hitter, even if not a .400 hitter.) Anyone is free to adopt the approach of evaluating a stock as a share of a business, rather than a blip on a screen, just as anyone is free to trade options. Munger said the Buffett style was "perfectly learnable."

> Don't misunderstand. I do not think that tens of thousands of people can perform as well. But hundreds of thousands can perform quite well—materially better—than they otherwise might. There is a duality there.

Part of the "duality" was that people confused "simplicity" with "ease." Buffett's methodology was straightforward, and in that sense "simple." It was not simple in the sense of being easy to execute. Valuing companies such as Coca-Cola took a wisdom forged by years of experience; even then, there was a highly subjective element. A Berkshire stockholder once complained that there were no more franchises like Coca-Cola left. Munger tartly rebuked him. "Why should it be easy to do something that, if done well two or three times, will make your family rich for life?"[44]

Buffett said it did not require a formal education, nor even a high IQ.[45] What mattered was temperament. He would illustrate this with a little game at business schools. Suppose, he would tell a class, each student could be guaranteed 10 percent of one of their classmates' future earnings. Whom would they choose? The students would start to scrutinize one another intently. They weren't looking for the smartest, necessarily, Buffett would observe, but for someone with the intangibles: energy, discipline, integrity, instinct.

What mattered most was confidence in one's own judgment, from which would flow the Kiplingesque cool to keep one's head "when all about you are losing theirs." In market terms, if you *knew* what a stock was worth—what a *business* was worth—then a falling quote was no cause for alarm. Indeed, before he invested in a stock, Buffett wanted to feel sufficiently comfortable so that if the market were to close for a period of years and leave him with *no* quoted price at all, he would still be happy owning it.[46] This sounds extraordinary, but one's house is not quoted day-by-day, and most people do not lose sleep over its value. That is how Buffett looked at Coca-Cola.

The disclosure of his investment, in March 1989, seemed to inject the stock of Berkshire Hathaway with an unusually bubbly carbon dioxide. Berkshire, at the time, was trading at $4,800 a share. In a mere six months, it rose 66 percent, to $8,000.

Buffett, now worth $3.8 billion, seemed born to his new investment. He quickly became a fount of Coca-Colaisms. He would recite to any who would listen Coke's "per capitas" in countries around the globe, or dissect a can of Coke according to its financial ingredients. He knew the sales, the growth rates. He got a rush from gazing at the red-and-white cases stacked up in a supermarket, and he took comfort, he explained to a visitor, in knowing that people were drinking the product at that very moment, as they were sitting there in Buffett's office.[47] He knew the figures by rote: a penny of profit on each eight-ounce serving, 700 million servings a day, 250 billion a year.

Chapter 19

HOWIE BUFFETT'S CORN

In 1980, Buffett had written a scathing article in the *Omaha World-Herald* blasting the self-indulgence of the superrich. To Buffett, a vast pool of wealth, such as his own, represented a pile of "claim checks," which ultimately should benefit society. He zeroed in on Hearst, who had squandered his claim checks on the grandiose San Simeon, thus diverting "massive amounts of labor and material away from other societal purposes."

Buffett was just as critical of the superrich for leaving fortunes to their heirs. The latter-day Du Ponts, for example, had "contributed very little, if anything, to society while claiming a great many times their pro rata share of its output." With a typically egalitarian flair, Buffett noted that the Du Ponts "might believe themselves perceptive in observing the debilitating effects of food stamps for the poor" but were themselves living off a "boundless" supply of "privately funded food stamps."[1]

The Du Ponts would not have recognized the Buffett clan. Warren had a cousin who drove a cab, a nephew who played in a jazz band, and so on. Some of them owned stock in Berkshire, but Buffett went out of his way to avoid giving favors or tips. His familial relationships, he felt, would be "cleaner" without the distorting element of financial dependency.

Most of all, he wanted his grown children to lead normal, independent lives. This forced him, at least as he saw matters, virtually to cut them off from financial support. He was so wary of spoiling his likable kids with "food stamps" that he refused them even the dollop of financial help that children of moderately wealthy parents receive as a matter of course.

His attitude baffled his millionaire friends (save for Munger, who came close to agreeing with him). When the Graham group debated what was the "right amount" to leave to one's children, Buffett said a few hundred thousand ought to do it.[2] Larry Tisch protested, "Warren, that's *wrong*. If they aren't spoiled by age twelve, they won't be spoiled." As Kay Graham, who was grooming her son to take over the Post, recalled, "That was the one thing we [Buffett and she] argued about."

Buffett did care very deeply about his kids. Moreover, he was a tolerant, in some respects an enlightened, father. He encouraged his kids to follow their stars, and he was patient when one of them suffered a disappointment—in a career, for instance, or in a marriage. But where money was involved he was impersonal and at arm's length, as though his kids were merely junior financial partners. There was a good deal of sanity in his approach—a billionaire *should* set limits—but Buffett, as in his professional life, was blind to any middle ground. When Susie needed $20 to park at the airport, she had to write her father a check. When Buffett gave his kids a loan, they had to sign a loan agreement, so that it would be plain, in black and white, that they were legally on the hook to him.[3]

Many Berkshire holders gave substantial gifts of stock to their kids—but not Buffett. He simply gave $10,000—the tax-deductible limit—to each child and to any of their spouses at Christmas.

Such restraint sent them a message, just as giving them millions would have. When the kids were toddlers, Buffett had written to Jerry Orans that he wanted to defer any largesse at least until he could see "what the tree has produced." In young adulthood, Susie, Howie, and Peter must have grasped that their father still viewed his saplings as unfinished. Philosophically, they defended his approach, and with considerable pride. But they also wondered, as Howie put it, why he couldn't "lighten up," and at times seemed to resent his unsubtle efforts to motivate them.

The Buffett kids had open, direct manners that put one in mind of their father (none drank anything stronger than Coke). They also had his eagerness, but were slow bloomers. Each dropped out of college, and each entered into an early, ill-fated marriage. Financially, they had inherited a grubstake from Warren's father, which Warren had invested for them in Berkshire. Thus they could have been millionaires without working a day.

Susie, alas, sold some stock (when it was under $1,000 a share) to buy a Porsche. After her marriage dissolved, she moved to Washington. There she made contact with Kay Graham, who took it upon herself to help her get an administrative job at *The New Republic*.[4] In 1983, Susie remarried, to Allen Greenberg, a public-interest lawyer and future congressional aide. Warren and his wife were ecstatic about Greenberg, a wry, mild-mannered sort, whom they referred to as "Allen-the-perfect-son-in-law."[5]

By the time the Greenbergs moved into a townhouse near Dupont Circle, Susie had used up her Berkshire. The young couple rented out part of their home and had just a tiny kitchen—*very* tiny. When Susie became pregnant, she wanted a larger kitchen for when the baby came—something she could fit a table into, with a door to the backyard. She had plans drawn up and got an estimate of $30,000. Knowing that her father wouldn't spring for it, she asked him for a *loan*, at prevailing interest rates.

Warren turned her down.

"Why not go to the bank and take a loan out like everyone else?" he suggested.

They had a long discussion, in which Warren explained that if he were the quarterback of the Nebraska football team it wouldn't be fair of him to pass down the job to a son or daughter, and that he felt the same about his money. This was a "rational" response with his daughter's "best interests" in mind. That was the rub; it was too rational, as if Susie had been just anyone. His daughter was troubled by it.[6]

When Susie was expecting her second child, she spent much of the time bedridden. "Mrs. Graham"—an ally—would come to dinner with her cook in tow, ferrying glazed monkfish and poached peaches up the steps to Susie's bedroom. Noticing that Susie had only a small black-and-white television in the room, Graham suggested that she get a bigger, color set—and was horrified to learn that Buffett's daughter couldn't afford one. Warren, after all, had a large-screen TV in *his* house. Graham promptly called Warren, and this time he relented and bought Susie a proper TV.7 Still, Graham had had to shame him into it.

Perhaps because money was the pivotal motivator in *his* life, Buffett acted as though money were a similarly pervasive and overriding focal point for others. He seemed to think that Susie would see a new television in terms of dollar signs (as he would), or that such a gift could somehow mar his daughter's open and unspoiled character. To her, it was just a TV.

But Susie deeply admired her father and probably had the easiest time accepting him. Dark-haired and vibrant, she recounted the saga of her kitchen as consistent with everything she knew of him. "He has a flat-out thing," she said, as if to explain him. "He just doesn't give us money."

For Howie, living up to his father was more of a struggle. He had an open-collared, sneakered informality that recalled his dad, but there was a flaw in the likeness, in that Howie was a good deal heavier. Having sold *his* Berkshire to finance his earthmoving venture—Buffett Excavating, which proved to be short-lived—as well as a house, Howie had gone to work for See's Candy in Los Angeles. In the early eighties, he had returned to Omaha, remarried and started a family, and gotten a job in real estate. As an aside, he rented some land and planted crops.

As Warren knew, what Howie really wanted was a farm. After "torturing" himself, as a friend put it, Warren made what for him was a truly generous proposal. He offered to buy a farm and rent it to Howie on standard commercial terms (Howie would have to fork over a percentage of his farm income and pay the taxes).

Howie asked his mother why Warren was getting involved.

"Don't ask," Susie advised. "Just get the farm."

But that was not so easy. Warren announced a ceiling to what he would pay for a farm, depending on its potential income. Howie went to farm after farm, making bids "of insulting proportion." When he'd seen about one hundred of them, he began to despair of getting one, but Warren refused to bend on the price. Finally, in 1985, they bought a farm for about $300,000 in Tekamah, Nebraska, forty-five minutes north of Omaha.

"It was a typical Warren Buffett purchase," Howie observed. "We bought it at the absolute bottom of the market. I think part of his motivation was to teach me a little about negotiation."

Howie didn't even have a telephone at the farm, but it was a joyful refuge for him. He would go out in the spring and fall, often taking his family, working columns of corn and soybeans with a John Deere tractor. But he couldn't get Warren to share the experience with him. "I can't get him to come out and see how the crops are going," Howie said plaintively.

Warren went only twice in six years. He would laugh off Howie's invitations, saying, "Send me a rent check, and make sure it's big enough." Though he had been thoughtful enough to *buy* the farm, he couldn't give Howie the fatherly recognition that he craved in other than financial terms. He could look at Howie's books, but not at his crops—which is what Howie cared about. To Warren, it was just a business. Inasmuch as corn and soybeans are commodities, Warren was blunt about the farm's being not a very good business at that, sardonically observing, "No one goes to the supermarket to buy Howie Buffett's corn."[8]

Warren did use the farm to "teach" Howie something; he agreed to lower his rent for any year in which Howie got his weight below a specified ceiling. (Warren was obsessed with staying slim, which he associated with longevity. He made similar "weight deals" for money with his wife and daughter.) In most years, this blatant attempt to manipulate Howie's weight with financial plums failed.[9]

Warren was more helpful when Howie turned to him for guidance, as he often did. After he got the farm, Howie decided to run for election as a county commissioner (as a Republican, like Warren's father). Howie was worried that Warren would be seen either as trying to buy the election or—what would be worse—as not supporting him at all. Warren defused this concern by declaring that he would simply contribute 10 percent of whatever Howie raised elsewhere—and Howie won.

Their relationship improved as Howie had kids of his own and, particularly, as Howie's career began to blossom.[10] After his election, Howie was appointed to a state board in charge of promoting ethanol. Ethanol politics put him in touch with Dwayne Andreas, the politically connected chairman of Archer Daniels Midland. Eventually, Andreas hired him, and Howie became a jet-setting executive. Warren bragged to a friend that Howie was "making more" than Warren was, which was his way of showing pride in Howie.[11] Seeing his kids succeed on their own "was a real issue with him," Howie observed—just as getting approval from Warren was a real issue for Howie.

Warren's younger son acknowledged this openly. Peter had quit Stanford to start a sound studio and, ignoring his father's sage advice, had sold *his* Berkshire to buy a $30,000 twenty-four-track tape recorder. He soon realized that he did not have the income to justify it, but he and his wife slowly built a music-production company, Independent Sound, in San Francisco. Later, they moved to Milwaukee. Though mostly a jingle producer, Peter scored the fire-dance scene for the movie *Dances with Wolves* and recorded several well-received albums of New Age music.

On a wintry Milwaukee morning, Peter ducked out of a soundproof glass studio, where two musicians were cutting a commercial, and began to talk about his father. He recounted one rather clumsy attempt by Warren to influence him. Warren had invited Peter to the Alfalfa Club, a very exclusive annual dinner in Washington, but stipulated that Peter cut his ponytail. Peter said no thanks. "He likes to have strings attached," Peter observed.

In recent years, Warren had started giving his $10,000 Christmas gifts to his kids in various stocks, which Peter felt carried a "message." "Again—there was a string on it. He was saying this isn't just money to spend. If you invest it, it will grow to be more. To test our patience.

"I sold most of my [Berkshire] stock. I'm glad I did," Peter added, the ponytail neatly tucked in a rubber band. "It's so nice to say I've gotten to this point without it." But a moment later, he said he regretted that his father had not told him—or perhaps that he had not heard his father say—that he could have simply borrowed against his Berkshire and held on to it.

Peter had an unassuming, even inquisitive, manner—as if he, too, were curious about Warren's character. He was extremely proud of his father's accomplishments and moral standards. He recalled that Warren had once told him, "Someday you're going to have to tell your dad to go to hell." Establishing himself in a new city and selling his Berkshire were part of that, he said. Had Warren ever told *his* father to go to hell? Peter acknowledged that he didn't know.

Peter got to know his father better as he had success as a musician.

When he played the piano with a fifteen-piece band, before an audience of seven hundred, in Milwaukee, Warren attended and praised him profusely. At one point, he told his son, "We do the same thing"— to Peter, an overwhelming tribute.

By the late eighties or so, Peter, who as a boy had purchased *The Father's Handbook* for his remote-seeming dad, felt that Warren and he had finally learned how to talk to each other. When Peter's marriage broke up, Warren counseled him, and with more empathy than he had shown in the past. One night, they were shooting the breeze at Farnam Street. Around midnight, Peter broached the subject of Peter's mother, in intimate terms. Warren talked about how he hoped that Susie would spend more time with the Buffett Foundation—more time in *his* world. "We talked about how Mom had this great opportunity to do what she wants," Peter said. Warren suddenly grew silent—for him, a sign of emotion. "We talked until 2:00 A.M.," Peter recalled. "When it was over I remember thinking, 'Wow, Dad was emotional.' You could see it in his expression, his lack of words. It blew me away."

Warren's renewal with his family may have stemmed in part from a gradual healing with his wife. He had heard more, from Susie directly, about her reasons for leaving him. They had an understanding and a greater openness. As Tom Rogers, a close nephew, put it, the Buffetts didn't have to "try anything in their relationship. They are each other's alter ego. Aunt Susie is as much able to cut emotion out of a decision as he is."[12]

Warren was in constant contact with his wife. He saw her often, and with as much affection as ever. After an evening at Tom Murphy's home in Westchester County, when the Buffetts shared a limousine with Stan Lipsey back to Manhattan, the two sat quietly in the back, holding hands the entire way. Susie told a mutual friend it had "worked out great," meaning that Warren had gotten what he wanted—to stay married to Susie.[13] Even now, years after Susie had moved out, she was the one—the only—person in the world he fully trusted.

In 1987, Warren took a big step toward the family by offering Allen Greenberg, his son-in-law, the job of managing the Buffett Foundation. As usual, the carrot had a string—Susie and Allen would have to move to Omaha.[14] This they did, buying a home a few blocks from Warren. Susie was soon bound up in Warren's supportive web. When he wanted a car, Susie went to the dealer and picked it out. At annual-meeting time, Susie helped to organize his social schedule. She was there for him.

As Warren was paying his son-in-law only $49,846 a year, young Susie's life was no different from those of other Omaha mothers juggling young children and civic involvements. The author happened to visit on a day when her son had chicken pox. Susie was bathing him; she had no nurse or nanny. Ironically, Susie was always fending off fund-raisers who were under the mistaken notion that she had the keys to the fortune.

One time, when Warren was escorting the billionaire wunderkind of Microsoft, William Gates, through the Borsheim's jewelry store, they noticed a box in the corner labeled "Buffett Lay-Away." When Warren asked what it was, an employee sheepishly confessed that Susie had asked them to save a string of pearls, which she was buying on installment. As a birthday gift, Buffett paid off the balance. It began to dawn on him that spending money—particularly at Borsheim's—could be fun. Another time, he remarked, as if discovering the wheel, "Gee, Suz, women really *like* jewelry."

With Susie around, Warren had a greater sense of extended family. Susie often dropped her kids off at Warren's for Astrid to look after, which tended to knit Astrid into the Buffett family. In fact, Susie even urged Astrid to redo Warren's house, which still had the sunshiny (but now faded) look given it by Susie's mom. Astrid and the younger Susie redecorated together, giving it a more subdued style, with Astrid's signature collection of antique toasters lining the kitchen. (Warren's wife and at-home girlfriend were closer than ever. This unlikely duo would send presents to Buffett relatives accompanied by a card signed by "Warren, Susie and Astrid.")[15]

The younger Susie, and her kids, were around Warren a lot. They seemed to humanize him. He would come to the Greenbergs in a worn jogging suit, get down on the floor, and play with the grandkids. At dinner, he would listen to the family chatter with a distracted look, pursing his lips, bobbing his chin, occasionally inserting a wisecrack, and salting (and resalting, after every bite) his hamburger. He told Kay Graham that Susie's return to Omaha had changed his life.[16] He even gave her a ruby bracelet—for Warren, hardly a casual gesture.

In a sign that he was becoming comfortable with "what the tree produced," he made his daughter a director of the Buffett Foundation and modestly relaxed his inheritance policy. The kids would get *something*—maybe three million or so apiece.[17] (He didn't tell the children how much.)

Whatever the figure, it would not allow Susie, Howie, and Peter to lead the despised life of the "superrich."[18] Wholly apart from its effect on his kids' lives, he simply didn't think they were *entitled* to vast amounts of money. It would confer too much power, which in his view belonged to the public. "The idea that you get a lifetime supply of food stamps based on coming out of the right womb strikes at my idea of fairness," he said.[19] Ultimately, the claim checks should go to society.

But philanthropy posed as large a dilemma to Buffett as giving money to his kids. The idea of bestowing a handout—even to charities—made him edgy. James Burke, a friend who had left Johnson & Johnson to run Partnership for a Drug-Free America, said Buffett had a "block." If he gave the money away, he was "giving away the chips he could use to make money."

The Buffett Foundation was for many years rather a joke. In 1979, when Buffett had a net worth of $150 million, the foundation's total endowment was merely $725,000. Its gifts that year were a trifling $38,453.[20] But after Buffett began the Berkshire charitable program, in 1981, Susie and he used it to fund the foundation. And Buffett steadily raised the corporate gift, though it did not rise as quickly as Berkshire's share price. By 1990, each stockholder could allocate $6 a share from the Berkshire treasury to a favored charity, meaning that Warren and Susie were indirectly giving away $3 million.

As exemplary as this corporate program truly was, it didn't require Buffett to take out his wallet. Of his private, non-Berkshire money, of which he had many tens and perhaps hundreds of millions,[21] Buffett did not give his foundation so much as a penny. And even his indirect gift, via the Berkshire program, was inconsequential compared to his $4 *billion* fortune.

Buffett's tightness was a sore spot with his friends. They knew that he was socially conscious. They knew he didn't spend it on himself. And on a personal level, they thought of him as "generous"—a word they often used. In an exceptional case, Buffett made small but anonymous Christmas payments (discovered via a bank error) to the mother of his boyhood chum Bob Russell. More typically, he showed a generosity of spirit in nonfinancial gestures, such as writing thoughtful, handwritten notes to people, or acting as their sounding board. But when even close friends asked for *money*, and for worthy causes, Buffett sent them packing. The writer Geoffrey Cowan called Buffett when he learned that *Weekend Edition*, the lively National Public Radio news show, was facing a funding crisis. Without a fast $50,000, *Weekend Edition* might go off the air. Most people would have given something, if only because of social pressure, but Buffett, in his sweet independence, was perfectly comfortable saying no. He didn't give the news show a dime.[22] Another friend, Ann Landers, frequently urged Buffett to loosen up. She tried her "darnedest," she said, to get him more interested "in what he could do for the world."

> What he does is piling and heaping and heaping and piling. So what is this all about? He did buy a plane, and he *loves* it. So I try to use the plane as an example. I say: "Look how much fun you're having with the plane. Maybe if you gave some of it away you'd have fun with that."

But Buffett would shake her off with a chuckle.

Buffett's skepticism of philanthropy was shaped in part by an experience in the 1970s with Grinnell College. His friend Joe Rosenfield had persuaded him to join the board, and Buffett turned this small Iowa liberal arts college into a financial powerhouse. Under Buffett's direction, the Grinnell endowment bought a television station in Dayton for $13.6 million and sold it four years later for $48 million. But Buffett was horrified that Grinnell actually *spent* some of this windfall—far too much, to his liking. As he saw it, the money was being spent in ways that did not enhance the students' educations, and the professors had it rather easy.[23]

This soured him on higher education. He did give scholarships to numerous individual students. But, as Greenberg said, "Warren would rather choke to death than write a check to a university." When a fundraiser from his own University of Nebraska stopped by the office, Buffett—despite being a diehard Nebraska football fan—wouldn't even open the door for him.[24]

In fact, Buffett approached philanthropy more or less as he did investing. He refused to "diversify," preferring that his foundation give to a few "high-leverage" causes that he hoped would reap the biggest social bang for the buck. Sensibly, he wanted to focus his giving, and he recognized that in the case of many charities, too much may be spent on administrator lunches and so forth. Once, hosting a crowd of friends at Laguna Beach, Buffett asked in none too casual a way: "If you had to give money to one charity to do the most good, which would it be?"[25]

He seemed to be searching for the Coca-Cola of charities—a home run that would take society's investment off the charts. This worked for him in stocks, but was less suited to philanthropy. Many of the types of projects that seek funding—in medical research, for example—are apt to make gains in fits and starts. A benefactor must be willing to take some losses. In other areas, such as the fine arts, doing "the most good," as Buffett put it, may not even be a meaningful concept. (But doing "some good" is meaningful. Society would certainly be the poorer if no one endowed museums.) Put differently, social progress cannot be measured as easily as the profits of Coca-Cola. But Buffett wanted to see "concrete results."[26]

Given these constraints, he found it hard to find suitable charities.[27] The Buffett Foundation, which was managed by Greenberg but jointly steered by Warren and his wife,[28] salted away much of its revenue for *future* giving. In 1990, the foundation's receipts from Berkshire and from income on its portfolio totaled $3.8 million. But it donated just $2.3 million to charities. Meanwhile, its assets were ballooning to $18 million. It resembled nothing so much as a miniature Berkshire—its outlays kept to a carefully chosen few while its assets were "piling and heaping."

Buffett had two pet causes. The danger of nuclear war had bothered him since Hiroshima, but disarmament did not seem a goal that private citizens could further in any substantial way. Buffett briefly underwrote the research of George F. Kennan, the famed ambassador to the Soviet Union who, while at Princeton, was an advocate of drastic nuclear arms reductions. Then, in 1984, Buffett learned that William Ury, an expert on negotiation at Harvard Law School, was working on ways to prevent accidental war. Buffett invited Ury to meet him for breakfast at the Boston Ritz-Carlton and described to him, in very human terms, his fear of Armageddon. Peering over the china, Buffett asked Ury to envision that thousands of white marbles were lying on the table, with one black marble lying among them. Suppose, he added, somebody picked up a marble every day. Sooner or later—maybe a century later—they would reach for the black one. That would be nuclear war.

Ury had proposed setting up "risk reduction centers" in Moscow and Washington. These would be equipped with faxes and phones and would be able to provide a communications channel during a crisis. However, Ury noted that the United States, in those early Reagan years, was hostile to working with the Soviets.

Buffett said, "Look, these are human beings on the other side, and we've set up these systems which could set the world aflame." Almost instantly, he added, "I'm going to fund you. I'm going to give you a hundred grand." (The foundation ultimately gave $200,000.) Risk reduction centers were approved about a year later, at the Reagan-Gorbachev summit in Geneva, and are still in place.[29] But with the end of the Cold War, there was less that Buffett could do about disarmament.

The mother of all Buffett causes was population control. In 1990, for example, about $1.7 million, or 75 percent of that year's gifts, was devoted to family planning, sex education, birth control, abortion rights, and so on. Susie and Warren were both firm believers, but their emphases differed. While Susie was largely inspired by the poor living conditions of people, and particularly women, that she had seen in the Third World,[30] Warren conceptualized in macroeconomic terms. He had a Malthusian dread that overpopulation would aggravate problems in all other areas—such as food, housing, even human survival.[31]

As pragmatic as this view was, it is striking that both of Buffett's "causes" were aimed at alleviating or preventing *future* sources of grief, such as a future war or a future oversupply of people. Virtually none of his immense resources went to help people who were already born—people who were here and now poor, sick, living in urban blight, illiterate; or people raising money for here-and-now concert halls, museums, universities, and hospitals (save for endowments of abortion or family planning programs).* Buffett's almost exclusive focus on such macroeconomic, futuristic issues gave his philanthropy a detached—almost a dehumanized—quality.

Traditional charities would have "spent" his money. On the other

---

*An exception: in 1982, Buffett gave $100,000 to a library in West Point, Nebraska, named for his maternal grandfather. More typical was a $400,000 gift in 1993 to the Columbia University School of Public Health, which was earmarked for a family planning clinic.

hand, giving to population control could be construed as "investing"—sort of a global share buyback—because it would reduce the number of future divisors clamoring for the social pie. Charlie Munger, who was equally Malthusian, articulated this mind-set at a party for Keith Russell, a doctor who had been a Munger-Buffett ally in the *Belous* abortion rights case in California. After some of Russell's patients presented a toast to the many babies he had delivered, Munger rose, glass held high, and solemnly declared, "I want to toast Dr. Russell for the thousands of babies he *didn't* deliver."[32]

The strangest aspect of Buffett's focusing on population control was that he did not get the pleasure of seeing his money help people. He often *asked* people if they had any good ideas for philanthropy—as if the world had a shortage of such—but it didn't lead anywhere. He was hung up on the notion that the recipients might be unworthy—that charity was a "food stamp" that would likely corrupt both donor and donee. Interestingly, Buffett was equally uneasy receiving a handout. He once ordered a chocolate malt at the Goodrich Dairy in Omaha and discovered—too late—that he had nothing smaller than $100 bills, which the Goodrich couldn't change. An older woman who knew Buffett happened to be at the dairy, and she graciously paid for his malt, which cost all of $1.50. Buffett *insisted* that he would reimburse her for the malt. But, to Buffett's supreme agony, he couldn't remember the woman's name. It must have weighed on his conscience, because he eventually found out and did repay her.[33]

The one philanthropic stroke that seemed to give Buffett real pleasure was an annual $10,000 award to each of fifteen Omaha public school teachers. The award was named for Buffett's Aunt Alice, the teacher who had cared for him when he lived with his grandfather, and the winners were chosen on the basis of merit, which appealed to him. Buffett liked to point out that rich people threw money at their colleges in return for getting their names on buildings, but did nothing for their elementary schools, which were trusted with more formative years. He thought of the award as a thank-you to Omaha.

However, his nonparticipation in the standard Omaha charity drives was a sore spot among the city fathers. Robert Daugherty, a local manufacturer, said, "Warren is *renowned* for not giving money away." Omaha had no tangible evidence that it was home to one of the country's richest men. There was no Buffett wing in the Joslyn museum, nor was there a Buffett park in Omaha, nor a Buffett chair at the local college.

In 1990, after years of seeming indifference, Buffett did endow a second trust, the Sherwood Foundation, solely for charities in Omaha. It was much smaller than the Buffett Foundation, but it suggested that Buffett—now sixty—was becoming aware that for all that Omaha had done to shape him, he had given virtually nothing back.

What confounded the pillars of Omaha was that in spite of Buffett's parsimony, he obviously had a strong sense of community. Politically, his disdain for handouts did not result in the expected conservatism, but in a strong belief that government should work on behalf of society as a whole, rather than hand out goodies to its individual members. In 1977, long before it was common to attack "special interests," Buffett pointedly criticized the "propensity of major groups in our society to utilize their electoral muscle to shift, rather than solve, economic problems."[34]

Thereafter, he wrote occasional quite creative proposals for dealing with economic issues, which were published in the *Washington Post*. The general theme was to promote "pie enlarging," rather than "pie rearranging" (just as he was scornful of "pie-rearranging" takeovers on Wall Street). One of his ideas would have wiped out the trade deficit in a single stroke, without resorting to quotas, tariffs, or red tape. Under this elegant scheme, the free market would have sorted out how many Nissan trucks to import and how many Adidas running shoes, but all within a framework that (with one, simple governmental edict) would have limited the total of such imports to the total of exports.[35] Buffett's premise was that society had a stake in an *overall* trade balance, but not in playing referee between various industries—a job that it does rather poorly.

Though he did not oppose actual "food stamps," he was generally skeptical of government transfers. One of his most piercing essays was an allegorical warning set in "Static Island"—a fictional society with a static population in which the members grew ample amounts of rice and wine for all. Since it was "an island with a heart," the workers guaranteed fixed rations for their nonworking elders. Alas, as the number of retirees grew, Buffett showed, by simple math, that the workers would have to toil backbreaking hours and give up wine for themselves to meet the generous quotas legislated by their forebears.[36]

Most of his proposals followed the neoconservative tactic of trying to harness people's selfishness, rather than relying on their "goodness." Unlike his wife, Warren was wary of do-gooders. In the seventies, Susie had befriended Larry King, an Omahan who ran a credit union with the ostensible aim of providing credit to blacks. King, who drove a white Mercedes, threw lavish parties, and swaddled himself in gold watches, zebra skins, and a leopard muumuu (all on a $16,200 salary), managed to con half of Omaha, including Susie.[37] But he did not fool Warren, who immodestly remarked, "I knew that King was a phony and I think that he knew I knew. I'm probably the only person in Omaha he never asked for money."[38] By then, King was in prison for looting millions.

Another time, Susie asked Warren to help Charles Washington, an Omaha civil rights activist. Warren was dubious but lent him $24,900. Washington defaulted in six months. Warren felt so bad about being suckered out of this trifling sum that he took Washington to court—the only time he had ever sued anyone.

On a national level, Buffett was friendly with quite a few politicians, such as Daniel Patrick Moynihan, Bill Bradley, and Bob Kerrey. But, like few other executives, Buffett did not try to curry favor with them.[39] The textile trade group repeatedly asked Buffett to help it lobby for import protection, but Buffett never did, even though his mill could have used the help.[40]

In a more dramatic case, Berkshire's savings and loan was a member of the United States League of Savings Institutions. The league, like all such groups, viewed its mission as grabbing for its members the biggest possible share of the government pie. It even had the effrontery to lobby against requirements for stronger levels of capital just as the S&L scandal was coming to light—that is, just as its members were running up a $100 billion bill to the taxpayers.

Buffett and Munger, having the quaint view that even lobbyists should have social consciences, quit the league in protest. Munger, who had been warning of danger signs on the S&L front for years,*

---

*In a remarkably prescient forecast, six years before the scandal broke, Munger observed in the Wesco letter for 1983 that "an agency of the U.S. government (F.S.L.I.C.) continues to insure savings accounts in the savings and loan industry, just as it did before. The result may well be bolder and bolder conduct by many savings and loan associations. A sort of Gresham's law ('bad loan practice drives out good') may take effect for fully competitive but deposit-insured institu-

released to the press an acid letter accusing the league of "furnish[ing] self-serving nonsense."

> Because the League has clearly misled its government for a long time, to the taxpayers' great detriment, a public apology is in order, not redoubled efforts to mislead further.[41]

Though skeptical of government bailouts, Buffett definitely did not share the neoconservative faith that marketplace judgments were inherently correct. He did *not* subscribe to the now fashionable view of the free market as the ultimate arbiter of individual worth. People who did not have powerful jobs, women in particular, noticed that Buffett treated them without any hubris or air of self-importance. Once, likening himself to his secretary, Buffett allowed that she

> raises children just as well and contributes just as much to her community. Her talents—and they are many—in a market society just are not bid up in the same way. Take me and stick me in Afghanistan or someplace and we'll find out how talented I am.[42]

For a billionaire, he was quite radical. His politician friends were Democrats, of course, but some of his ideas were far, far to the left of theirs. Once, at a Q&A at Cap Cities, Buffett was asked how he would rewrite the tax code. "If I really could do it, it would shock you," he said. He'd tax the hell out of personal consumption—at progressively higher rates—and impose an "enormous" inheritance tax.

> If I want to run around in a jet, which I do, fine, I have the claim checks to pay for it, but that should be taxed *heavily*, because I am withdrawing people, fuel and so on—resources—from society.[43]

Given such a liberal outlook, people could not understand why Buffett didn't *do* more. Munger, who shared his skepticism of philanthropies, was a generous giver and got heavily involved in his hospital as well as in a private school. But Buffett refused to be *enlisted*. Norman Lear once asked Buffett to make a brief introduction at an award cere-

---

tions. If . . . 'bold conduct drives out conservative conduct,' there eventually could be widespread insolvencies caused by bold credit extensions come to grief."

mony for a group called Business Enterprise Trust. Buffett contributed to the group, which honors socially responsible businesspeople, and he was planning to be there in any case. But he flatly refused to make a presentation, saying he got fifty such requests a month. Lear was dismayed. He added, disbelievingly, "It's twelve steps to the podium for a thirty-second introduction."

From Buffett's viewpoint, everybody wanted a piece of him, like camera-toting tourists pursuing a colorful native. His defense, as Kay Graham recognized, was to set his *own* agenda, in philanthrophy as in so much else. Holding on to his money was a way of keeping control. Even as a boy, when he hadn't owned a part of Kay Graham's newspaper but had merely delivered it, he wouldn't let his mother touch the money.

The adult Buffett felt the same way about his 474,998 shares of Berkshire.[44] Bill Gates occasionally sold some of his Microsoft stock, Lee Iacocca some Chrysler, and so on. But Buffett would not parcel off even a sliver of his brilliant canvas. Over a quarter century, he had not sold a single share. The ironic result is that Berkshire's extraordinary growth did not put so much as a dime in Buffett's pocket.

From society's point of view, he argued that it was a good thing. The dimes that he could give now were not merely dimes—to Buffett, they represented the quarters and the half-dollars that a dime could become down the road. "When I am dead," he observed, "I assume there'll still be serious problems of a social nature as there are now."[45] He planned to leave his stock to Susie; whichever one died last would bequeath it to the foundation. Society would get a greater benefit from his money then, after he was done heaping and piling. This was irrefutably logical, but obsessive. By the late eighties and early nineties, Buffett could have been peeling off tens of millions for society's "serious problems" every year and still would not have diminished his pile of chips by even 1 percent.

One wonders if his desire to control those chips related, at least in part, to his desire to control not only his life, but also his death. It is only human to hope, and perhaps to believe, that one will not die in the midst of a great journey. In Buffett's "unfathomable human mind," his command of Berkshire may have provided a sense of protection from that lifelong fear. Perhaps, like Lincoln, he would not be called while the battle was still joined. And as long as he continued to heap and pile the job would not be done.

Chapter 20

RHINOPHOBIA

As the memory of Black Monday faded, Wall Street basked in an Indian summer. Stocks surged to new highs and deal-makers hatched a fresh wave of LBOs, compared to which the earlier waves had been no more than innocent ripples. The math of the late 1980s was simple. Any company that exchanged its equity for debt was immediately worth more, courtesy of the U.S. tax code. And *every* company was thought to be ripe for such a maneuver.

In a sure sign that greed had overtaken fear, investment banks had plunged into "merchant banking," not only brokering LBOs but buying companies themselves, with their own capital at risk. In another sign, John Gutfreund, the traditionalist at Salomon Brothers, had jumped into the game. This gave Buffett and Munger a window seat on the later stages of the deal era.

The two played the good-cop/bad-cop bit to perfection. When a deal was proposed, Buffett, the "good" director, would diplomatically question Salomon's bankers. Munger would try to rip the deal to shreds. Of one proposal to buy a chain of gasoline stations, which never made it past the board, a senior executive said Buffett and Munger "tore the presentation apart."

Michael Zimmerman, the head of merchant banking at Salomon, said, "Warren's attitude was, if it didn't make sense to do a deal with equity it didn't make sense to do it with debt." Buffett's point was that the bankers should focus on finding good businesses, rather than on balance sheet reengineering. But by no means did he oppose every deal.

In October 1988, on a Sunday evening, Buffett, who was at home in Omaha, got a call from Gutfreund. The latter was at his Fifth Avenue apartment with a group of Salomon bankers. The previous Wednesday, F. Ross Johnson, the swashbuckling boss of RJR Nabisco, the maker of Winston and Salem cigarettes, Ritz crackers, and Oreo cookies, had proposed to take his company private. Johnson's banker was Shearson Lehman Hutton, a subsidiary of American Express. No sooner had this giant LBO been hatched than every other house on Wall Street started scheming for a piece of the action. Now, Salomon Brothers was mulling a competitive bid. The group at Gutfreund's wanted to know: would Buffett, as a Salomon director and big shareholder, give his blessing? And secondly, would Berkshire put up $100 million of its own and join the deal as a general partner?[1]

Unbeknownst to the bankers, Buffett had placed an order for RJR Nabisco shares in the past few days, on the heels of Ross Johnson's announcement.[2] And, of course, Buffett had owned the stock in the early eighties. When Jay Higgins, Salomon's top investment banker, started to explain the company's merits, Buffett's Midwestern twang crackled over the speakerphone.

"Don't tell me about the economics—I know they're great. You make a product for a penny, you sell it for a dollar, and you sell it to addicts. And it has tremendous brand loyalty."[3]

Buffett and Munger had once come close to buying Conwood Co., a Memphis-based chewing-tobacco maker. But they didn't want to be principals in tobacco, they had decided. Such thoughts were on Buffett's mind as he talked to the bankers.

"The product—it's got some problems," he continued wryly. "I don't think I'd want it on my tombstone that I was a partner in it." But Salomon could go ahead without Buffett.

The next day, Kohlberg Kravis Roberts launched a bid of its own. Then Salomon joined forces with the Shearson–Ross Johnson team, and a bidding war the likes of which Wall Street had never seen burst into the open. The mother of deals was at hand, and the merger fever, which had been so long in building, rose to a climax. Now that the fever was at its apogee, no price was too much to pay for an Oreo.

At the eleventh hour, KKR sweetened its bid by promising that sometime after the deal had closed, it would "reset" the interest rate on the junk bonds it sold to finance the LBO. The *worse* that RJR Nabisco fared, the *higher* the rate that it would pay. (Imagine buying a house with a "reset" mortgage: lose your job and the interest rate doubles.) It is hardly a secret why KKR agreed to such a deal. Regardless of how its investors fared, KKR would immediately pocket $75 million in fees.[4]

Gutfreund had a chance to match the KKR "reset," but to his credit he refused. It cost his side the deal.[5]

Once KKR had it locked up, Buffett bought more RJR Nabisco—a short-term arbitrage (a bet that the deal would fly). Berkshire would make a fast $64 million on it.[6] Given Buffett's well-known criticisms, it seemed, to some, hypocritical of him. It did not seem that way to Buffett. Once a deal was on the table, he analyzed the risks and rewards with his usual indifference to anything but profit and loss. He also made arbitrage profits on Beatrice, Federated Department Stores, Kraft, Interco, Southland, and other deal stocks.[7]

But Buffett, who had learned arbitrage from Ben Graham, deviated from Wall Street's arbitrageurs in one Graham-like respect. As the action got hotter, Buffett was less eager to go along. Years earlier, at the Columbia seminar on takeovers, he had warned that bankers using phony currency would one day push the bidding to unsound levels. After the $25 billion RJR Nabisco deal, he judged that this was a prophecy no more.

Deal-makers were financing LBOs with "zero-coupon bonds," a type of funny money that enabled buyers to borrow huge sums and defer their interest payments (and reality) for years. Given the ease with which such scrip was printed—and the willingness of investors to suspend disbelief—it is hardly surprising that deal prices had made for the stratosphere. Quoting Buffett:

> Some extraordinary excesses have developed in the takeover field. As Dorothy says: "Toto, I have a feeling we're not in Kansas any more."[8]

Buffett wrote that in February 1989, just as the RJR Nabisco deal was closing. He had made his profit; now he wanted nothing more of arbitrage. The deals were too unsafe.

> Considering Berkshire's good results in 1988, you might expect us to pile into arbitrage during 1989. Instead, we expect to be on the sidelines.[9]

With the stock market soaring, Buffett (who was just buying his last Coca-Cola shares) was on the sidelines there, too. But he needed someplace to put his cash. And this had become a much tougher problem with Berkshire's greater size. Ever since the early years of the Buffett Partnership, Buffett had been prophesying the day when the law of averages would finally catch him—prophesying it, yet somehow putting it off. But as he warned his stockholders, "A high growth rate eventually forges its own anchor."[10] To have any chance of continuing his gravity-defying act he had to put his money to work.

Such a compulsion to invest can be dangerous. It has been wittily defined as *rhinophobia*, an investors' disease meaning "the dread of ever having any cash."* Buffett admitted to such feelings; having cash around was "an enormous temptation."

> There is an itch that comes about, and I get it, I confess. There is an itch
> to do things, particularly when you haven't done anything in a while.[12]

In the second half of 1989, Buffett did something. In a sudden spurt, he fashioned three big deals—with Gillette, USAir, and Champion International—totaling $1.3 billion. As a group, they were below his par. While Gillette, the world's dominant razor blade seller, was a typical Buffett investment, USAir and paper producer Champion were capital-intensive cash absorbers and not at all the stuff of his past success. (Champion had something in common with his failures, though. Buffett thought it might be an inflation hedge.)[13]

In each case, Berkshire bought a new convertible preferred stock, just as it had with Salomon Brothers. Save for Gillette, a consumer-brand company in the mold of Coca-Cola, Buffett did not have a strong opinion on the companies' prospects.[14] That is why he structured them as convertibles (with fixed dividends). Indeed, he admitted, rather gloomily, "If I had four more Coca-Colas to buy, I wouldn't be buying these."[15]

The threat of takeovers, once again, was behind these deals. Gillette

---

*The term is from Fred Schwed, Jr.'s quaint classic *Where Are the Customers' Yachts?* Schwed seemed to have known a Buffett or two in his day. He observed that rhinophobia is apt to strike "economical souls who do not believe in frittering away their money on food and drink and momentary pleasure. If they play bridge of an evening for a quarter of a cent and lose $17, they are liable to go home in a pretty depressed state of mind."[11]

had been stalked by Ronald Perelman; USAir had been put in play by Michael Steinhardt, a New York money manager; and Champion was thought to be a target. "When you've got an able management," Buffett told the *Washington Post*, "they should have time to play out their hand."[16] Now each of those companies would have Buffett as its protective "gorilla." In return, Berkshire would get a fixed coupon, on average 9 percent, and an option to convert to common stock (a "lottery ticket") if the shares should rise.

But Buffett's latest moves were unpopular. At Cap Cities, Buffett had bought the common stock, as anyone could, but in the new deals, he had negotiated a special security, available only to him. Linda Sandler, writing in the *Wall Street Journal*, charged that Buffett was pocketing rich coupons for Berkshire in return for safekeeping the other CEOs' jobs:

> Many Wall Street investors say Mr. Buffett's special deals amount to a kind of gentlemanly protection game. In the old days, these investors say, corporate raiders such as Saul Steinberg got paid "greenmail" to go away. But Mr. Buffett is getting "whitemail" to stick around and hold management's hand.[17]

Such sweetheart deals with the CEOs, so the argument ran, were depriving the stockholders of the freedom to sell out in takeovers. According to *Forbes*,

> Buffett gets a special deal, but so does management. . . . Put differently, how much does Warren Buffett charge for takeover protection?[18]

Buffett, of course, was not *responsible* to the shareholders of Gillette, USAir, and Champion. He was supposed to make good deals for Berkshire. But moralists get judged by tougher standards, and Buffett, suddenly on the defensive, seemed anxious to defend the high ground. In a letter to his holders after the "whitemail" deals, he argued:

> . . . the other shareholders of each investee will profit over the years ahead from our preferred-stock purchase. The help will come from the fact that each company now has a major, stable, and interested shareholder. . . .[19]

The trouble with this argument is that it assumes that every CEO—or every CEO that Buffett likes—will be deserving of protection, and will deal fairly with the inherent conflict of interest. But not every CEO is a Tom Murphy. Buffett himself, at the Columbia seminar, had argued that as imperfect as the takeover process may be, ultimately, the decision had to be up to the folks who owned the "little piece[s] of paper"—the stockholders.

Champion was a particularly dubious case. Andrew Sigler, its CEO, was a vocal critic of takeovers and an active member of Business Roundtable, a lobbying group for big business. At Champion, he had poured money into the company's mills but failed to deliver for his shareholders. Over the previous decade, a great one for stocks in general, Champion's had risen by an abysmal 3 percent a year. Even among other paper companies, its return ranked as one of the poorest.[20]

The only person with much to show for Sigler's poor record was Andrew Sigler. In 1989, a lackluster year, Sigler paid himself an $800,000 salary, plus "incentive compensation" of $425,000. *In addition,* he took advantage of Champion's depressed stock price to award himself options on 31,000 shares. The next year, Champion's earnings fell by half. Sigler upped his take to $1.2 million, plus $28,000 so he wouldn't have to pay for his personal tax adviser, plus options on 47,000 more shares.

Buffett, of course, had been a fierce critic of options,[21] particularly when doled out to poorly performing CEOs. If anyone had been desirous of taking over Champion, it's hard to see why Buffett would have wanted to stop them.

The managements of Gillette and USAir were a different story. USAir was building a national system with hubs in middle-market cities, but had yet to consolidate. It seemed to have the sort of strategy that warrants time and a little "protection." Gillette, quite simply, was minting money.

Although Buffett's terms *were* richer than what an ordinary Joe could have gotten on open-market issues,[22] the deals were not as sweet as his critics claimed. Berkshire was locked into each security for a decade, which on Wall Street is an eternity and then some. Indeed, most money managers would have rejected Buffett's "sweetheart" arrangements.

Nonetheless, the deals had an unwholesome aspect. They had an odor of insidership—of Buffett's standing too close to his pals in corporate boardrooms. It may be no coincidence that he bought a swankier corporate jet that year, for $6.7 million. In his annual letter, Buffett went to lengths to poke fun at himself for this singular perk (without alluding to his exceptionally modest $100,000-a-year salary). He noted that if the cost of replacing his plane continued to rise "at the now-established rate of 100% compounded annually, it will not be long before Berkshire's entire net worth is consumed by its jet."[23] But the jet, which he wittily dubbed the *Indefensible*, underscored the fact that he was spending more time out of town and in very elite company.

By the late eighties, down-home Warren Buffett seemed to know everyone. He would jet out of town to a board meeting, or the Super Bowl, or a party where he might run into Paul Newman or Senator Edward Kennedy.[24] He played bridge with the Corporate America team, a celebrity CEO group, including a match against members of Parliament at Old Battersea, the splendid seventeenth-century London home of Malcolm Forbes. When Buffett was asked, during a talk, what financial advice he might give to the President, he could respond that, as a matter of a fact, he had been to a dinner with President Bush the previous Saturday.[25]

Warren's wife insisted that it was time for him to get some "decent clothes," as she told their daughter. When the elder Susie was in Omaha, the two women dragged Warren to a store and fitted him into a $1,500 Zegna suit. The Italian-made Zegnas became his uniform—a fetish like his Cherry Cokes and his jet. (But he refused a salesman's entreaty to order them custom-made, preferring to drop into Zegna's New York branch sans appointment and buy a bunch at a time off the rack.)[26]

His new circle was astonishingly wide. In Boston, he would hobnob with the likes of John Kenneth Galbraith and *Globe* editor Thomas Winship. Winship said, "Warren's a great *collector* of friends"—an interesting comment about a guy who collected and hung on to stocks. Buffett had a gang in Washington, and another in California. Susie and he would visit the Big Apple with a sort of "program," as one friend put it, to squeeze everybody in. "They are not like other people," she noted.

Buffett's inner circle—a group that included Graham, Loomis, Murphy, Munger, and Ruane—was as before. But his friends in Omaha, such as Dick Holland, noticed that he wasn't around as much. Verne McKenzie estimated that his boss was out of town one or two days a week.

So uncontemporary in other respects, Buffett jetted from coast to coast like one of the glitterati. He dined at the Oscars with Dolly Parton.[27] He flew into Martha's Vineyard for a gathering at Kay Graham's with the likes of Nancy Reagan and *60 Minutes* correspondent Mike Wallace.[28] Another time, he picked up his wife and swooped into Walter Annenberg's Palm Springs, California, estate, abloom in the desert with silver-leafed tamarisk trees and sculpted shrubs. Sam Walton came, too.

Buffett was popular in this crowd because he seemed to be unaffected by his money. He still spoke in homey expressions that vaguely recalled the 1930s ("I'm on the wire" instead of "I'm on the phone"). At the 1988 Winter Olympics in Calgary—where he was a guest of Murphy and of ABC—Buffett ducked an invitation for lunch by the pristine Lake Louise to hole up in town and work. At the Olympics, Agnes Nixon, a soap opera creator for ABC, met Buffett and decided he was "the reincarnation of Will Rogers." She invited him to New York to do a cameo on *Loving*, a daytime soap opera. After the taping, Buffett, Nixon, and others from ABC went out to dinner at Bravo Gianni, an East Side northern Italian restaurant. As they were leaving, Nixon noticed that John Kluge, another billionaire, was exiting, too. Kluge ducked into a waiting limousine while Buffett stepped off the sidewalk and hailed a cab.[29]

Buffett liked to portray himself as a sort of provisional traveler in high society. He was full of stories that accented his supposed innocence, such as one regarding a dinner party at which he found himself seated next to Carolyne Roehm, the socialite designer, then married to Henry Kravis. Roehm said, "Can you cut my meat for me?" Buffett didn't know if this was a new form of upper-class affectation or—worse—a come-on. He ignored her the entire evening—until, to his horror, as her barely nibbled roast was carried away, he saw that she had a cast on her wrist.[30]

He liked his homespun image and seemed uncomfortable with the reality that he now was something of a celebrity. After Buffett appeared in an episode of television's *Lifestyles of the Rich and Famous*, he was so embarrassed that he told people that the producers had spliced it together without his having known about it. But that was untrue. In fact, Buffett had donned a microphone and been formally interviewed.[31]

In 1989, Buffett also was in the news in Omaha. Mrs. B—the carpet woman—was stripped of her authority in carpets by her grandsons Ronald and Irvin, who by now were running the Furniture Mart. She quit the store in a rage, denounced Buffett for selling her out, and publicly called her grandsons "Hitlers."[32]

In Omaha, the spat got the sort of attention elsewhere reserved for Charles and Princess Di. Mrs. B accused her grandsons of being spoiled ingrates who wasted their time in "meetings" and lived like "millionaires." Besides, she added poignantly, "It hurts when you're a nobody."[33]

The ninety-five-year-old dynamo spent a few months at home. Then she opened a new store, "Mrs. B's Warehouse," adjacent to the Furniture Mart—now her blood rival.

"It breaks my heart," Mrs. B remarked one Sunday, motoring past a sea of carpets in her new store. She added that she now was working "for spite."

Buffett felt terrible about it. He took two dozen pink roses to Mrs. B on her birthday to try to patch it up. But as a business matter, he backed his management. Reporting on the unhappy affair to shareholders, he praised Louie, Mrs. B's son, as well as Ron and Irv, as "outstanding merchants."

> Mrs. B probably has made more smart business decisions than any living American, but in this particular case I believe the other members of the family were entirely correct: Over the past three years, while the store's other departments increased sales by 24%, carpet sales declined. . . .[34]

Nonetheless, one has the sense that if Buffett had been in Mrs. B's shoes, he would have wanted to go out the same way, kicking and screaming—and that at some level he admired her for it. Shortly after her break, he spoke about her with considerable empathy:

> She hasn't lost her marbles in any way, shape or form. She happens to be—improperly, in my view—very negative on a couple of the grandchil-

dren that work in the store. Every now and then they want to take a day off with their families. Believe me, they are marvelous guys, but they can't work as hard as Mrs. B did. . . . It's a human tragedy in the sense that she couldn't have a better family than she had. But they had it easier than she did—nothing you can do about it.[35]

Mrs. B's departure did not hurt Berkshire, which hit an all-time high in September 1989 of $8,750 a share. But it is a strange truism of Buffett's career that he felt most apprehensive during bull markets. He was gloomy about the lack of opportunities, and gloomy even about Berkshire.

His response was nothing short of brilliant. In a mirror image of his deals with Gillette, USAir, et al., Buffett raised $400 million by selling bonds that were convertible into shares of Berkshire. The people who bought this paper got a fixed return and a "lottery ticket" on Berkshire's stock.

This time, Buffett's terms were sweeter than sugar. His interest rate was only 5.5 percent. The low rate was a measure of the investors' faith that Berkshire's share price would continue rising. (They were betting on the lottery ticket.)

What's more, since these were "zero-coupon" bonds, Berkshire would owe interest, but not actually pay it, until the bonds matured, fifteen years later. But owing to a quirk in the tax laws, Berkshire could deduct the interest all along, as though it *were* paying.

And there was more. Berkshire could redeem the "zeros" in three years. Thus, the investors were betting not just that Berkshire's stock would rise, but that it would do so *in a hurry*. Lost in the shuffle was the fact that Buffett was making exactly the opposite bet.

Two weeks later, in October, a proposed LBO of United Airlines collapsed. Arbitrageurs—Buffett had quit the game months before—suffered huge losses. The stock market plunged 191 points in a day. The junk-bond market crashed; the takeover game stopped in its tracks. Within months, Drexel Burnham was dead. Wall Street's long love affair with debt was over. By early 1990, the Street was in the tank, and Berkshire was under $8,000.

In his annual letter, Buffett confirmed his gloominess, predicting that Berkshire's net worth was "almost certain" to drop (for the first time in his tenure) in one of the next three years. He tied together

Berkshire's recent history and Wall Street's current crisis with a seemingly innocent thread: many of the now-toppling LBOs, such as Federated, the corporate parent of Bloomingdale's, had also been financed with zeros. Of course, Buffett had a larger theme in mind. On Wall Street, it was often the good ideas that got you into trouble, for what the wise did in the beginning, "fools do in the end."[36] Thus it was with LBOs and zero-coupon bonds.

As was his style in such essays, Buffett started small and in the distant past. He invited readers to "travel back to Eden, to a time when the apple had not yet been bitten."[37]

> If you're my age you bought your first zero-coupon bonds during World War II, by purchasing the famous Series E U. S. Savings Bond, the most widely sold bond issue in history.

Nobody called it a zero-coupon, but that's what the Series E was. The interest was paid in a lump sum, when the bond matured. The ordinary Americans who bought the Series E were no fools. Since the Treasury was the surest possible credit, they slept soundly, knowing that their money was safely compounding at 2.9 percent per annum.*

In the 1980s, investment banks invented a zero-coupon for large lenders. These—like Berkshire's—were rated Triple-A. Then the bankers discovered that zeros and the equivalent pay-in-kind (PIK) bonds could be used to finance LBOs. The appeal was obvious: since no cash payments were required for years, bidders could be induced to borrow any sum at all. Buffett's description rendered this shell game suddenly self-evident:

> To these issuers, zero (or PIK) bonds offer one overwhelming advantage: It is impossible to default on a promise to pay nothing. Indeed, if LDC governments [Mexico, Brazil, etc.] had issued no debt in the 1970's other than long-term zero-coupon obligations, they would now have a spotless record as debtors.

Buffett suggested that investors offer the bankers a taste of their own medicine, a signature Buffett stroke that made it intuitively clear, even

---

*One skeptic was Rep. Howard Buffett, who in 1951 proposed a bill to protect holders of the Series E bonds against inflation.

to a person on Main Street, that Wall Street was dealing in extremely funny money.

> Our advice . . . zip up your wallet. Turn the tables by suggesting that the promoter and his high-priced entourage accept zero-coupon fees, deferring their take until the zero-coupon bonds have been paid in full. See then how much enthusiasm for the deal endures.

Such essays, though, were guides to the broad strokes; of his strategy they revealed nothing. Indeed, Buffett was a master dissimulator.

At the very moment that his junk-bond critique was rolling off the press, Buffett was scooping up one of the largest bundles of junk bonds ever—$440 million of RJR Nabisco paper. RJR Nabisco's bonds had collapsed with the general market, but in Buffett's view, the market had overreacted. (After all, RJR Nabisco was still selling a high-margin product to "addicts.") His purchase of junk bonds might seem hypocritical, but it was not. Buffett saw a moral hazard in *selling* a junk bond that would likely never be repaid. Buying a bond was different. To the investor, no financial instrument was "evil per se";[38] it was a question of price.

After the purchase was disclosed, Dr. Benjamin Graham, the son of Buffett's mentor and a Berkshire stockholder, wrote to protest Berkshire's investment in tobacco. Buffett replied that while he wouldn't manufacture cigarettes, he had no problem with owning traded tobacco securities—or, for that matter, a newspaper that advertised the product. "I'm not sure that this is strictly logical," he admitted, but in a complex world, he deemed it a practical way to draw the line.[39]

With Iraq's seizure of Kuwait, in August 1990, the "credit crunch" snowballed into a full-blown recession. New decades do not necessarily portend new eras, but this one did. In the eighties, spirits had run high. Buffett, conversely, had hewed to caution. In the nineties, Wall Street rediscovered fear. People who had lent money wanted it back; companies that once could have borrowed millions found the window slammed shut.

Corporate bankruptcies and junk-bond defaults (the "big bang" that Buffett had predicted at Columbia in 1985) lit up the map. Fred Carr's insurance company—stuffed with junk bonds—became the biggest insurance failure in history. Banks, just reborn from the foreign-debt crisis, found they were up to their ears in homegrown deadbeats, such as LBOs and commercial real estate. A contagion of bank failures moved like a storm front from Texas to Colorado, New England, and the mid-Atlantic states. Serious people gathered at investment seminars and discussed whether Citicorp or Chase Manhattan would fail.

From Buffett's point of view—Buffett and Fred Carr were always out of synch—it was an ideal time to take a little risk. Berkshire's stock, it was true, had collapsed with the rest (its low for the year was $5,500, down almost 40 percent from its peak). But it was at such times that Buffett was at his best. Rhinophobia might get hold of him when prices were high. But when the world turned gloomy, his instinct was deadly.

During 1990—the worst year for banking since the Great Depression—Buffett bought 10 percent of the stock of Wells Fargo, the San Francisco banking giant. California real estate was just beginning to turn down; the misery of its banks was expected to be deep and long-lived. And Wells Fargo had lent more money to California real estate than any bank in the country.

Buffett, of course, knew that. Generally, Buffett did not like banks. An outsider had no way of gauging the soundness of their loans until it was too late. But he had been pining for *this* bank for years.[40] Wells Fargo had a strong franchise in California and one of the highest profit margins of any big bank in the country. Its chairman, Carl Reichardt, was a cost-cutter in the Tom Murphy mold. During an earlier rough period, Reichardt had sold the company jet—a sacrifice Buffett could appreciate—and frozen the salaries of the top brass. And Reichardt had largely avoided the periodic fads, such as lending to Latin America, that had undone other banks. As Buffett knew, Reichardt and Paul Hazen, the bank's number two, had cut their teeth on property loans in the 1970s and had escaped the real estate debacle of that decade with barely a scratch.

None of this meant that the outlook for Wells Fargo over the next year or so was rosy. But Buffett was thinking about a much longer period than the next year or so. The bank was well capitalized; it ought to survive the current trauma. Indeed, Buffett reported, a bad year "would not distress us."[41]

And because other people *were* distressed, Buffett was able to pick up $290 million worth of stock at the fire-sale average price of $58 a share, or five times earnings. That was down from a recent high of $84.

After Buffett invested, Wells Fargo's portfolio began to take in water. Wall Street wrote it off; Barton Biggs, the chief strategist at Morgan Stanley, said he had no idea if Wells Fargo would survive and Warren Buffett didn't either.[42] In the spring quarter of 1991, Wells Fargo took a massive reserve against the possibility that loans would not be repaid. Earnings plunged to twenty-one cents a share, compared with $4.40 in the corresponding quarter a year earlier. Buffett responded with aplomb; in fact, he asked for regulatory approval to *double* his investment.

Wells Fargo, by then, was the darling of short-sellers. It had almost $15 billion in commercial real estate loans—two and a half times as much, per dollar of equity, as its neighbor Bank of America. Half of Wells Fargo's real estate loans were in the terra infirma of Southern California, the new fault line of American credit. In Los Angeles, where the boom economy had turned to bust, developers were quixotically racing to complete new skyscrapers that they now had no hope of renting. In Orange County, 22 percent of the office space was vacant. A bear on Wells Fargo, writing in *Barron's*, sardonically observed that the "Sage of Omaha, Warren Buffett" would be stuck with all that.[43]

Even many within Buffett's crowd saw the bet on Wells Fargo as a breaking of the faith. Scott Black, a Graham-and-Dodd-style money manager, said, "It upset me. Warren made a *mistake*," as though the heavens should have forbidden it. People who had been appalled by the excessive leverage of the eighties had an emotional stake in seeing the guilty get their just deserts—and real estate lenders were "guilty."

Buffett also disapproved of excessive leverage, but he stripped the emotion out of his calculations. At a certain price, he was happy to buy a bank, or even a junk bond. During the height of the gloom, a Manhattan friend called to "warn" him that the smart money was saying that Wells could go under. Buffett said calmly, "We'll see who's right."

Unhappily for Buffett, the gloomy times were over all too soon. When the United States opened fire on Iraq, early in 1991, the stock market rallied. The fighting ended in six weeks, but the rally did not. By July, the Dow had broken 3,000. The combination of more cash at Buffett's disposal and fewer places to put it could be counted on to induce a new spell of rhinophobia. When Buffett got a call from James D. Robinson III, chairman of American Express, he was all ears.

Robinson, the courtly son of an Atlanta banking family, was a fellow Coca-Cola director and a social chum of Buffett's. An habitué of boardrooms who held thirteen directorships, Robinson projected a refined, statesmanlike air. His dark-wood, river-view office seemed to whisper "old money." Personally, Buffett was fond of Robinson. What he thought of him as a CEO of American Express was not so clear.

The company's charge cards and traveler's checks had remained a very good business. During the most recent decade, their profits had galloped ahead at an 18-percent-a-year clip. But Robinson's shareholders had never seen that 18 percent.

Robinson had frittered away the profits of this very good business on a series of bad ones—in insurance, banking, brokerage, even an art gallery specializing in nineteenth-century American paintings. Eager to follow the 1980s fad for "financial supermarkets," Robinson had pumped a staggering $4 billion into Shearson. But supervision was lax (Shearson "invested" $26 million in a "conference center" at a Colorado ski resort), and the investment bank had repeatedly needed bailing out. To make matters worse, American Express had a habit of not coming clean with the bad news until after the fact.[44]

Robinson had managed to elude the blame for such miscues, partly thanks to his busy public relations department and partly because he had stacked the board with captive directors. One such captive, Henry Kissinger, pocketed $350,000 a year in consulting fees from the management he was supposedly overseeing.

Despite Robinson's good press, Buffett was hardly unaware of his record. In 1985, Buffett had attended an American Express board meeting, when the company was considering selling its Fireman's Fund insurance unit to a group that included Buffett. Buffett gave the board some advice: it should sell Fireman's to *somebody* and focus on American Express's one truly splendid business.[45] A bit later, when insurer GEICO bought a chunk of American Express's stock, Buffett had called GEICO to express his concern. Though Buffett didn't put it in such terms, Robinson's record was a compendium of the managerial sins that Buffett had bewailed in his letters.

But when Robinson called, all this was forgotten. Buffett hopped on the *Indefensible* for New York—seized, apparently, by one thought: the memory of his investment in American Express a quarter century earlier, which had been the first big gusher in his career. Now, as before, the company was in trouble. Just weeks earlier, its credit had been downgraded. When Robinson asked for a $300 million investment, Buffett quickly agreed.

As Buffett noted at the time, with the market at a high, he was finding few things he liked, and he *did* like American Express's basic business. Still, it is hard to account for his saying "We're buying to be in with Jim [Robinson]."[46] Buffett's friends were stunned. He had even agreed—reluctantly, but nonetheless—to a term that capped Berkshire's potential upside. Jack Byrne, who was an American Express director, told *Business Week* he would have thought that Buffett's "genes" would have forbidden such an agreement.[47]

When they spoke privately, Byrne realized that Buffett regarded his earlier American Express investment as a milestone in his career and was eager to play a part in restoring the company. Buffett told him, "This is coming home again." Of course, he had also come home to GEICO and to the *Washington Post*. He liked these old shoes, just as he liked investing in the soft drink that he had delivered as a boy. Replaying these ventures transported him to a comforting time, when he had been young, and had had the likely prospect of many more years ahead. It had also occurred to Munger that his partner's career was full of "odd coincidences." "Warren likes his past," Munger admitted.

By August 1991, many of the recent additions to Buffett's portfolio were troubled. Wells Fargo was on the verge of a disastrous quarter. There was major trouble brewing at American Express, which was facing a revolt by restaurants, a decline in the number of card holders, and slumping profits.

Among the much-criticized "whitemail" deals, Gillette had soared, enabling Berkshire to convert to common stock. Other Gillette holders were also better off, since the stock was twice as high as what Perelman had offered for it. Peter Lynch, the mutual-fund manager and a Gillette shareholder, said, "The deal with Buffett helped everyone."

Few would have said the same of Buffett's deal with Champion. Earnings had plunged by 85 percent, though Berkshire wasn't suffering, since its dividend was fixed. Meanwhile, Sigler, the CEO, had awarded himself options on 250,000 *more* shares at a price well below the company's book value.

USAir was doing worst of all. Almost on the day that Buffett had invested, a fare war had broken out. Then, in the wake of the Persian Gulf War, air travel had collapsed. USAir found itself with high employee costs at a time of intense cost pressure. It lost a staggering $454 million in the year after Buffett's investment, and its bleeding was far from over.

At one point, Seth Schofield, the chief executive, called Buffett to apologize for the way his investment was turning out.

"Seth, I want you to remember one thing," Buffett shot back. "I called you, you didn't call me. So I have no one to blame but myself if it doesn't work out, and let's let it go at that."

Buffett blamed himself in a deeper sense, too. He had understood the dynamics of airlines—lots of competition, high fixed costs—but invested anyway. In public, he was up-front about this mistake. With a touch of Will Rogers, he wrote to his shareholders, "No one pushed me; in tennis parlance, I committed an 'unforced error.' "[48] It was easily his worst investment, and violated Buffett's own guidelines. Ironically, the investment was probably a good thing for other USAir holders, as it injected the deeply troubled airline with much-needed capital.

These blemishes in Buffett's portfolio were easily outweighed by the likes of Coca-Cola, Gillette, and the RJR Nabisco junk bonds—on which he turned a fast profit of roughly $200 million.[49] Berkshire's net worth continued to rise, in defiance of Buffett's prophecy. And the stock rebounded smartly; by August, it was at $8,800. What's more, the problems at his companies did not require Buffett to get personally involved. He liked to say that he had "arranged" his life so that he needn't do anything he didn't like. In the summer of 1991, this was true. He said his biggest worry was Nebraska's upcoming game with Colorado.[50]

Buffett's broad defense of the whitemail deals—that the companies would benefit from having "a major, stable, and interested shareholder"—had yet to be tested. Perhaps it never would be. But the controversy had faded. Even the first one, often-troubled Salomon Brothers, was enjoying a record year.

Chapter 21

THE KING

*John Gutfreund runs an
extremely good operation
at Salomon.*

WARREN BUFFETT,
BERKSHIRE HATHAWAY ANNUAL MEETING, 1991

Appropriately enough, the origins of Salomon Brothers lay in a family quarrel. Ferdinand Salomon was born in Alsace-Lorraine, where the Salomons were money brokers. He emigrated to New York in the late nineteenth century and carried on the family trade, arranging short-term loans for securities firms. At the dawn of the new century, three of his four sons joined him. In those days, Wall Street was open for half a day on Saturdays. Ferdinand, who was orthodox, observed the Jewish sabbath; the sons insisted on working. In time, their rift became irreconcilable, and in 1910, the sons raised $5,000 and struck out on their own.[1]

Setting up shop at 80 Broadway, the brothers went from bank to bank each morning, inquiring as to who had surplus funds and placing these funds with brokers. Gradually, they moved into corporate bond trading. Though its pedigree relegated it to a backwater, Salomon Brothers soon discovered a client that did not discriminate—the U.S. government. In 1917, Salomon became a registered dealer in Treasury securities. Later, it would be said that being a partner in Salomon was "the closest thing to being a partner in the U.S. Treasury."[2] But the firm remained small for many years. Two pivotal decisions would trigger its growth—and ultimately, would bring Warren Buffett to its door.

From its inception, Salomon was scrappy and sharp-witted. Despite its humble origins, Arthur Salomon, one of the brothers, was one of the few people on Wall Street with whom J. P. Morgan, Jr., consulted. Once, while getting a shave, Salomon learned that Morgan needed to see him. With his whiskers yet untrimmed, he wiped the soap from his face and dashed to Morgan's office. In return for such obeisance, the House of Morgan occasionally tossed a bone—such as a minuscule piece of a corporate bond underwriting—Salomon's way.

But Salomon was not content playing second fiddle. During the Depression, when the Morgans of Wall Street went on a "capital strike" to protest against the newly created SEC, Salomon stepped into the breach and got a toehold in underwriting.[3] By such acts of brashness, coupled with its partners' willingness to risk their capital, the firm prospered.

Such was its growing strength that by the postwar era, a "marketable" bond was said to be one on which Salomon would bid.[4] But it was still a niche player. Though feared as a bond trader, it remained an outcast in the snootier lines of underwriting and investment banking.

In 1958, William Salomon revolutionized the firm in a single, brilliant stroke. A second-generation partner, Salomon decreed that each partner would have to leave his capital in the firm, save for a 5 percent annual draw. Younger partners, often eager to buy a home, would beg for an exception. The poised, dark-haired Billy Salomon would turn them down.[5] The partners' fates were thus intertwined, and a clannish spirit emerged. Moreover, the firm's capital, then $7.5 million, began to grow.

Salomon used its burgeoning capital to substitute for the corporate relationships that it had never had. It muscled its way into equities and investment banking, alongside the blue-blood Morgans and Kidder Peabodys. As recalled by Bruce Hackett, who was hired in 1968 as one of Salomon's first stock salesmen:

> We were the last major house to get into research, the last to establish an investment bank. It wasn't based on being close to customers. It was based on being close to markets. We were a pricing machine.

In 1979, IBM asked Morgan Stanley to relinquish its traditional role as a sole manager of underwritings and comanage a $1 billion debt offering with Salomon. When Morgan refused, IBM stunned the old guard by choosing Salomon to lead the underwriting.[6] There was no more dashing from barber stools to take calls from Morgan; Salomon had arrived. Its capital, by then, had soared to $200 million.

By this time, Wall Street's private firms had sensed the need for capital and had begun to sell shares to the public. Billy Salomon, who thought the discipline of the partnership was essential, was vehemently opposed to selling out. His protégé John Gutfreund agreed. Overhearing the partners discussing such a move one day, Gutfreund brusquely cut in, "If you fellows are thinking of doing anything like that I quit right now."[7]

Gutfreund had grown up in the tony suburb of Scarsdale, the son of a wealthy meat-truck-company owner who occasionally golfed with Billy Salomon. Intellectual and withdrawn, Gutfreund majored in English at Oberlin and considered a career in teaching. When he returned from service in Korea, Billy Salomon invited him downtown. Charmed by the energy of the trading floor, the stocky young man took a job as an apprentice.

Working his way up through municipal bonds and syndicates, Gutfreund became a partner at thirty-four. He guided Salomon through a meteoric rise in underwriting, but was never quite one of the boys on Wall Street. During the Vietnam War, a bearded Gutfreund led a peace march through the financial district.[8]

As if to compensate for being out of step, he developed a gruff, even a crude, exterior. Once, at a black-tie reception, he was introduced to Roland Machold, who ran New Jersey's state pension fund. Dissatisfied with the amount of business he was getting from Trenton, Gutfreund blurted out, "Well, it ain't worth fucking around with the state of New Jersey."[9]

Colleagues thought his rough language had a forced ring, as though, armadillo-like, it was covering up a shyness. Gedale Horowitz, a good friend at the firm, said, "John's problem was he didn't want people to know he was compassionate. He couldn't get rid of the shell."

Billy Salomon, who thought Gutfreund would outgrow his bluster, tapped him to run the firm in 1978. Nothing could have prepared Salomon for the day in 1981 when Gutfreund, Henry Kaufman, and a third partner flew out to Salomon's beachfront home in Southampton, New York. Salomon greeted them in casual slacks. His visitors were in pinstripes. They brought bitter tidings: they were selling the partnership to

Phibro Corp., a publicly owned commodities trading firm. (Gutfreund had been reluctant to sell, but had bowed to his colleagues.)[10] Salomon's seventy partners reaped an average of $7 million apiece.

Though Gutfreund could not have imagined it, the road from Southampton led inexorably to Omaha. Following the sale, Salomon had access to capital in the public markets, and the firm grew as never before. But the firm's culture changed in ways that could not be undone. The executives continued to call each other "partners," but that was a fiction. Now they had no money in the firm—no stake in it. "All of a sudden," Billy Salomon recounted, "you had guys with five, six, ten million dollars. They were watching their money as much as the business."

Gutfreund assumed a dual chairmanship with David Tendler, the chief executive of Phibro. But Salomon hit its stride just as Tendler's side of the business collapsed. Gutfreund promptly ousted him. By the mid-eighties, not only was Salomon's traditional bond business soaring, but it was throwing its weight around in equities. It led the pack in underwritings and was enthroned by *Business Week* as "King of Wall Street." Prophetically, the magazine added, "if for some reason the company stumbles and profits dwindle, Salomon is the kind of place where the long knives could come out in a hurry."[11]

Stumbling was the last thing on anybody's mind. These were the years when Gutfreund ran the company from a desk in the fabled gym-sized trading room overlooking the Statue of Liberty. Short and thick-lipped, he would stroll past rows of traders, trailed by a vaporous cloud of cigar smoke. With his plum-sized jowls, he would lacerate underlings in full view of their peers. "He'd take someone to task," a partner recalled. "He could turn you into a pile of shit on the floor."

Gutfreund was said to have dared his star bond trader, John Meriwether, to bet $1 million on a single round of liar's poker, a game that traders played during lulls in the bond market. The incident, described in *Liar's Poker*, a best-selling insider's account of the firm, was probably invented, but it enshrined Gutfreund's image as a trader's trader.*

---

*Eric Rosenfeld, one of Meriwether's traders, says he witnessed the incident, and that it involved Meriwether and John O'Grady, a veteran salesman, since deceased. After O'Grady repeatedly challenged Meriwether to play him during a busy day of trading, Meriwether dared him to one round for $1 million, "no tears." Meriwether beat him, in front of a group of spectators. According

When not playing poker, Meriwether's bond wizards, some of whom held Ph.D.s, made million-dollar bets on changes in interest rates using complex trading formulas. Gutfreund encouraged them to take risks and was manly about the inevitable loss. He inspired not only fear, but also intense loyalty.

"It was striking how John dominated," said Martin Leibowitz, the house mathematician. "He would walk the aisles. The electricity followed his path."

Gutfreund's towering pride suffused the firm. His traders believed that a single moral lapse would be their last, and, indeed, Salomon went unscathed by the insider-trading scandals that sullied Drexel, Kidder, and Morgan Stanley. Imbued of old-school ethics, Gutfreund turned away clients that he deemed unsavory and rejected deals that he thought unsound.[12]

And yet, eventually, he caved in, just as he had on selling the partnership. Giving way to his bankers, he let Salomon sponsor LBOs of Revco and Southland and authorized a junk-bond loan to TVX Broadcast. His vacillating—so at odds with his gruff facade—resulted in a trio of humiliating failures.

Underneath, Gutfreund did not really have control. Departments were virtually unbudgeted. Salomon did not even have a chief financial officer until 1987. When the bond market collapsed that year, Gutfreund discovered—too late—that he had built a bloated staff. Since going public, the firm had tripled to 6,800 people. Gutfreund had poured capital into equities and investment banking but had yet to earn a decent return on them. In an eerie foreshadowing, he told the *New York Times*, "My problem is that I am too deliberate on people issues."[13]

His partners saw a pained quality to him, as in the doomed figures in the histories he devoured. Surrounded by antic traders, he strutted about the office like a stuffed bird. At a partners' retreat on Cape Cod, Leibowitz espied him alone, brooding over a drink. When he asked what the matter was, Gutfreund said, "I can see my job will require me to hurt people I don't want to hurt."

---

to Rosenfeld, the bet was clearly in fun. Gutfreund, he says, was not present. However, Gutfreund frequently did play liar's poker with other traders, though for less impressive stakes. "He never played during the middle of the day," Rosenfeld said. Michael Lewis, the author of *Liar's Poker*, later attributed his account to Meriwether, "among others." Meriwether and Gutfreund both denied Lewis's version.

Struggling to get a grip, Gutfreund shook up the management time and again. Lewis Ranieri, a close colleague, had been running the mortgage department with virtual autonomy, as suggested by his traders' habit of winging slices of tomato across the trading room. Gutfreund brutally fired him. But Salomon boiled over with rivalries between the lordly bond traders and the lesser-ranking bankers and salesmen. Well-known stars, such as deal-maker Ira Harris and bond-market guru Henry Kaufman, walked out. The long knives came after Gutfreund, too. There was a plot to unseat him, though it fizzled.

At the heart of this Machiavellian infighting was the annual divvying up of bonuses. Gutfreund tried to hold them down, but he was continually bullied by Salomon's princes, archdukes, vassals, and assorted subchieftains into raising the kitty.

His troubles were inflamed by a seeming parallel between his business and private lives. Coincident with selling the partnership, Gutfreund had remarried, to a onetime Pan Am flight attendant and determined socialite. Previously retiring, Gutfreund became a Gatsby, and he and his wife spent an estimated $20 million on a Fifth Avenue duplex, which became the scene of fabulously lavish soirées. To top it off, Susan Gutfreund, blond and sixteen years her husband's junior, bought a pied-à-terre in an eighteenth-century mansion on Rue de Grenelle, so that the Gutfreunds would have a place to repose in Paris.[14]

The oft-repeated slap that she diverted him from Salomon was undeserved, but she aggravated a strain between Gutfreund and his partners, who felt they had to compete for the boss's ear. Susan even overhauled their cherished executive meeting room, ditching their easy, bulky sofas for fluffy couches and antique ashtrays without so much as a word. "It looked a like a French bordello," one partner groused. "I was walking around with a cigar in my mouth and I didn't know where to put the ashes."

Increasingly, Gutfreund sought his counsel outside the firm. By the late eighties, he was dialing Omaha a couple of times a week. Buffett, his biggest shareholder, was inevitably supportive, and as Gutfreund confessed to *Institutional Investor*, he trusted Buffett more than he did his partners.

I view Warren as a resource. I go to him if I've got something that I can't ask anybody inside the firm about and get a reliable answer. Or, more than that, if I don't trust the answer that I can get in the firm to be truly objective. Warren is a terrific call.[15]

Buffett had been a fan of Gutfreund's since the latter's role in rescuing GEICO, in the mid-1970s. He had repeatedly cited Gutfreund's "integrity."[16] But he and Munger were aghast at the chaos within the firm. They and the other directors did not even get an up-to-date balance sheet.[17]

In 1990, Salomon Brothers' profits plunged by $118 million. When Gutfreund then *raised* the total bonus pool by $120 million, Buffett was appalled. Salomon Brothers was earning 10 percent on equity pretax, far below the average of American industry. Its stock was mired in the low 20s—unchanged from eight years earlier (over which time the Dow had nearly tripled). Not a nickel of value had been built for stockholders, yet bonuses had risen in every year. As Buffett might have put it, the investment bankers were getting lavish "food stamps" at the expense of the stockholders. This violated everything Buffett believed in, and he was extremely unhappy about it.

Late in the year, Buffett met with the executive committee—for him, a rare intervention in management—and told them to cut back. "I don't care how you pay it—you can pay it all to one person," said Buffett, who was one of three directors on the compensation committee. "But the overall number is wrong."

Gutfreund, who for once did not have Buffett in his hip pocket, ordered his managers to submit lower numbers. But by the time his underlords were through with him, Gutfreund had approved a revised bonus plan that was $7 million *higher*.[18]*

Buffett voted against the bonus plan—a singular instance of his voting against one of his managers. The other committee members voted in favor, averting a showdown. But the news that Buffett had voted against Gutfreund rocketed through Salomon like a thunderbolt. As Buffett explained later, he feared that an irrational pay scale was not a containable problem; such lopsided rewards would tend to produce "irrationalities" throughout the firm.[19] And Salomon's was very irrational; despite its poor results, no fewer than 106 executives had made at least $1 million.

One trader in Meriwether's elite bond arbitrage group had taken

---

*Gutfreund also instituted a useful reform, according to which a significant portion of bonuses would be paid in stock.

home $23 million! Though the group, and the trader, had earned immense profits for Salomon, news of his bonus raised an egalitarian uprising among other young traders, who were getting by on merely seven figures. In particular, Paul Mozer, the head of Salomon's government bond desk, went "ape-shit."[20]

Mozer, given his thirty-four years, was in a position of considerable trust. An intense man with narrow-set eyes and wire-rim glasses, Mozer had grown up on Long Island and gotten an M.B.A. at Northwestern University. He joined Salomon as a bond salesman in 1979.

In 1988, after a two-year stint in Meriwether's group, Mozer was persuaded by Gutfreund to take over the government desk, a job he said was "second best."[21] Nonetheless, he worked constantly. He and his wife, who also worked on Wall Street, took an apartment in Battery Park City, within walking distance of Salomon. He installed a trading screen in his bedroom and customarily rose at six to take a call from London. Mozer made $4 million in 1989 and $4.75 million in 1990.[22]

Even for a trader, Mozer was uncommonly edgy. When John McDonough, Salomon's auditor, informed him that the government desk was due for an audit, Mozer exploded.

"Look, my business runs fine."

"Paul, you don't have authority to say you don't want to be audited," McDonough pointed out.

"Every fucking time we try to do something intelligent we get beaten back," Mozer stormed.

When Meriwether, who was Mozer's superior, was told about the incident, he chuckled, "You have to take Mozer with a grain of salt."[23] But no one questioned Mozer's dedication.

Mozer's job was bidding for bonds at U.S. Treasury auctions and trading the bonds after they were issued. Treasury securities are the world's biggest market, with some $100 billion in daily trading, compared to $8 billion or so on the New York Stock Exchange. The market was dominated by the "primary dealers," a group of firms chosen by the Federal Reserve Bank of New York with which the bank did its trading. Though anyone could bid at a Treasury auction, only the primary dealers could also submit bids on behalf of clients. Thus they tended to know a great deal in advance about the tone of the market. And of the thirty-nine primary dealers, Salomon, the most venerable, took by far the biggest share of bonds.

In return for its valuable imprimatur, Salomon, like the other dealers, was expected to help the government float its debt smoothly and to keep officials abreast of the bond market. Its traders chatted with their peers at the Federal Reserve virtually every day.

The relationship was informal, and something of a throwback to a clubby, less regulated era of gentlemanly trust. Every quarter, a group of dealers and investors, including Salomon, were invited to the Treasury, where they were informed of the government's funding needs and asked for advice on how to proceed. (The dealers were on their honor not to call their offices or trade on the news.) Then traders and bureaucrats would retire to the Madison Hotel for dinner, customarily of lamb chops.[24]

Only at auctions were they on opposite sides, the dealers aiming for the lowest winning bid, the Treasury seeking the maximum price. Before each auction, traders such as Mozer frantically canvassed customers to size up demand. Meanwhile, Salomon and the other dealers stationed "runners" by a bank of phones in the Italian Renaissance Fed building. Seconds before the one o'clock deadline, the runners got their orders and wrote them out by hand. They dropped the bids into a wooden box. As the clock struck one, a Fed clerk put his hand over the slot.

This baroque system had successfully financed the U.S. government debt since World War I. In 1990, the Treasury auctioned $1.5 trillion of bills, notes, and bonds. The single hitch had occurred in 1962, when a Morgan banker bid for half of an auction of T-bills. The Treasury Secretary feared an attempt by Morgan to corner the market; for obvious reasons, the Treasury did not want to become dependent on only a few dealers.[25] After that, it imposed a 35 percent limit on awards to each account.

Usually, winners did not get that much, since awards were prorated. But the canny Mozer found a loophole. Recognizing that *awards* were limited to 35 percent but *bids* were not, he submitted a bid in June 1990 for double the total of notes on auction. Even after prorating, Mozer got the lion's share.

Michael Basham, the white-shirted mandarin who was in charge of the Treasury auctions, immediately called Mozer and told him not to do it again.[26] Not surprisingly, he assumed that was the end of it.

But two weeks later, at a $5 billion bond auction, Mozer submitted a bid for $10 billion. Basham was stunned; he could not believe that a dealer would openly defy the U.S. Treasury, much less the dealer that had been partaking of its lamb chops for three-quarters of a century. Rejecting Mozer's bid, Basham proclaimed that bids, too, would be limited to 35 percent.

Mozer, as Charlie Munger would say, now began to exhibit delusional behavior. He threatened to go above Basham to the Treasury Secretary. Then he squawked to the press—a breach of the gentlemanly code that infuriated the Treasury. Now alarmed, Salomon higher-ups arranged a breakfast with Robert Glauber, the Treasury undersecretary for finance, intending for Mozer to apologize. But Mozer couldn't pull it off; he affected an aggrieved air.[27] Salomon was so concerned that it ordered him to ring back and say he was sorry. Then Mozer was shipped to London for a brief cooling off.

But Mozer was in deeper than Salomon knew. At an auction in July and again in August, Mozer had inflated his awards by bidding on behalf of customers who had not, in fact, authorized him to do so.[28]

Then, in December 1990, at an auction of four-year notes, Mozer submitted a phony $1 billion bid on behalf of a customer, Mercury Asset Management. A clerk was told, either by Mozer or by a Mozer deputy, to "sell" the bonds from the unwitting Mercury's account to Salomon, as though Mercury had really bid for the bonds and later sold them. To cover Mozer's tracks, the clerk wrote "No Confirm" on the trade ticket, so that Mercury would not be advised of the trade.

Continuing in this pattern, in February 1991 Mozer submitted 35 percent bids for two customers—Quantum Fund and Mercury—again without authorization, as well as a genuine bid for Salomon. Salomon and its "customers" were awarded 57 percent of the auction.

The Treasury, of course, had no idea that all of the bonds were going to one party—in explicit violation of its rule. But in April, a Treasury official reviewing the auction sent a routine housekeeping letter to Charles Jackson, a Mercury executive. A copy was sent to Mozer. One may imagine his alarm. The letter referred to Salomon's bid in February "on behalf of Mercury Asset Management." Mercury knew of no such bid.

Desperate to cover himself, Mozer called Jackson, coyly telling him that the bid was the result of an error by a clerk, which Salomon was correcting. He asked Jackson not to embarrass him by responding to the Treasury. Jackson let it pass.

To play it safe, Mozer told Meriwether that he had submitted a single false bid, and described his effort to hush it up. Meriwether, who was stunned, said it could end Mozer's career.

"Is there anything else?" he inquired.

Mozer lied. He said it was the only time, and begged for another chance.

A few days later, on April 29, Meriwether huddled with Gutfreund, Salomon president Thomas Strauss, and general counsel Donald Feuerstein in Salomon's new headquarters, a massive pink-granite-and-glass spire in the shadow of the World Trade Center.[29] Gutfreund was shocked by what he heard.

"How could you misuse a customer's name?" he wondered.[30]

Meriwether defended Mozer as a hardworking manager who had goofed. Yet they knew that Mozer's behavior was not completely isolated. There had been his perverse battle with Basham, which the group discussed, and his outburst at the company auditor.

Feuerstein said the false bid probably was criminal. Though not required to do so, Salomon should report it, he thought. But Gutfreund hesitated. He belabored the issue of whether to report to the Treasury—an unpalatable option, in light of the Mozer-Basham spat—or to the Fed. A phone call right then to Gerald Corrigan, president of the New York Fed, would have ended the matter. But perhaps they could break the news more gently in a personal visit. The group agreed that Mozer's misstep *should* be disclosed, but didn't decide who would do it or when. Remarkably, Mozer was left in charge of the government desk.

Anyone else in Mozer's shoes would have operated discreetly, at least for a while. But discretion was not a part of Mozer's playbook. In May, at an auction of two-year notes, Mozer bid an unexpectedly high price and was awarded an astonishing $10.6 billion worth, or 87 percent, to be split among Salomon and two Salomon customers. This was clever, but too clever.

Many other dealers who had commitments to deliver the notes could not get hold of them. They were "squeezed." This set off a scramble for the "May two-years," and the price soared. Mozer made about $18 million on the squeeze (in addition to $4 million or so from his earlier, phony bids).

But traders complained—loudly and, in some cases, directly to

Washington—that Salomon had cornered the market. Squeezes are not illegal unless a trader conspires to manipulate prices. Nor are they uncommon. But the squeeze in May triggered widespread losses and put a few traders out of business.[31]

The Treasury still knew nothing of Mozer's false bids, but Basham and his colleagues had been watching Mozer. Now, to Basham's amazement, he saw what looked to him like a brazen attempt to manipulate the market by the Treasury's supposed partner.[32] Just before Memorial Day, he tipped off the SEC.

As Washington busied itself with cherry blossoms, its investigative machinery quietly began to churn. The SEC and the Justice Department secretly began a probe of Salomon's role in the squeeze.[33] Subpoenas went out to Salomon's clients.

Meanwhile, the Treasury was getting heat from Rep. Edward J. Markey, a subcommittee chairman who had heard griping from traders. The Massachusetts Democrat was preparing a bill to tighten supervision of the Treasury market.

Stephen Bell, Salomon's profane but effective Beltway lobbyist, was worried about the legislation. When Bell saw press reports of a squeeze, he knew it was trouble.

Dialing Salomon's government desk, Bell, a New Mexican given to cowboy boots, hollered into the phone, "What the fuck is this?"[34] Mozer said Salomon had done nothing wrong. For nothing, Bell thought, Washington was pretty upset.

Early in June, at Bell's urging, Gutfreund paid a courtesy call on Glauber, the Treasury undersecretary. Despite repeated reminders from Salomon's lawyer,[35] Gutfreund still had not disclosed the phony bid. But to do so now, when the Treasury was concerned with the squeeze, would have been . . . well, awkward. Sitting stiffly, under the gaze of Glauber's dark oil portraits, Gutfreund defended Salomon's behavior and offered to be helpful. He did not mention that the head of his government desk had lied to the Treasury. Glauber wondered why he had come.[36]

Gutfreund may have hated to blow the whistle when Salomon, finally, was enjoying a revival. And he now had the matter of explaining his own delay. Like a witness who is too long silent, he began to act as though he himself were guilty. He still intended to disclose the bid, he confided to Strauss, but he contended that it was a "minor" matter.[37]

Incredibly, it did not occur to him that the U.S. Treasury, Salomon's oldest and most valued partner, might see matters differently.

Then, late in June, Gutfreund learned that Salomon was the target of a civil—and a criminal—probe. He promptly hired the law firm Wachtell Lipton Rosen & Katz to investigate Salomon's behavior in the squeeze. Yet he didn't tell Wachtell Lipton about Mozer's false bid. Gutfreund was still tiptoeing, even with his lawyer. Only on July 12, when a Wachtell Lipton attorney found evidence of false reporting, did Salomon come clean.[38]

During the next month, Wachtell Lipton uncovered six bidding violations. Marty Lipton, the firm's senior partner and a Gutfreund confidant, also advised Gutfreund that he had no obligation but should make disclosure anyway. Gutfreund agreed. In his own mind, he was doing—and had done—the right thing. He expected, if not congratulations, at least a muffled approval.[39]

On Thursday, August 8, Salomon gave its directors the news. They got hold of Buffett at an outdoor pay phone, next to a restaurant in Lake Tahoe.[40] What little Buffett heard didn't overly concern him. Munger, who was dining at his cabin in Minnesota, pushed harder for an explanation.[41]

The same night, Gutfreund and Strauss made the long-delayed call to Corrigan at the New York Fed, giving him a sketch of Wachtell Lipton's findings and mentioning that they had known of one false bid for a while. Corrigan was cool. Gutfreund made similar calls to SEC chairman Richard Breeden and to Glauber.[42]

On Friday, Salomon went public with a press release. But the Wachtell Lipton attorneys, who wrote the release, had picked up the habit of tiptoeing. They failed to mention that Gutfreund and Strauss had known of an illegality for months. What the release did say it said confusingly and incompletely. Nor did Gutfreund say more to the staff. Salesmen and traders left for weekend homes with the reassuring thought that the matter was contained to Mozer and his deputy, who had kept his knowledge of a false bid quiet. Both had been suspended.

On Monday, August 12, the tone changed. The *Wall Street Journal* focused on the purported roles of Gutfreund and Strauss:

> Said one person familiar with the firm: "It's hard for me to believe—it's inconceivable—that [Salomon's management] wouldn't know how much was bid for."[43]

The implication that Gutfreund had been in on the bidding was incorrect. But reading those words, Gutfreund rightly sensed that the spotlight would shift from Mozer to himself.

Immediately, he summoned Deryck Maughan, who chaired a Monday meeting of Salomon's investment bankers, and William McIntosh, who ran the weekly sales meeting. Gutfreund told the two to reassure the troops that the problem was "contained." Maughan and McIntosh did as told. But it was not contained. Salomon's stock opened lower. Worse, traders began to back away from its commercial paper, the short-term IOUs that Salomon depended on to fund its operations.[44]

By the end of the day, markets were awash in rumors. McIntosh confronted Gutfreund and Strauss again; now they admitted that there were more violations—and that they had known of one since April. McIntosh, a balding veteran of thirty years, boldly suggested that Gutfreund resign.[45] Gutfreund refused, but allowed that if McIntosh thought he could write a better, second press release, to give it a try.

On Tuesday, McIntosh called Maughan. "Deryck, I found something out and I'm terribly uncomfortable," McIntosh began. "You're the one person I can trust."[46]

Maughan, a Britisher, had built Salomon's Tokyo office into a major profit center. He had recently been called back to New York to revive the corporate finance department. A coal miner's son, educated at the London School of Economics, the forty-three-year-old Maughan was already thought to be Gutfreund's likely heir.

The day before, Maughan had vouchsafed for Gutfreund's integrity. Now both he and McIntosh felt they had been sandbagged. His cheeks reddening, Maughan called Zachary Snow, a Salomon attorney who worked for Feuerstein.

"Zack, I need to talk to you. I need facts. If you don't come, that's a message."

Meanwhile, a letter from the Fed was being hand-delivered to Gutfreund. Corrigan also needed facts—and hinted that Salomon's primary dealership was in jeopardy. Alarmed, Gutfreund and Strauss called Corrigan, and found him in an unfriendly state. The beefy central banker was furious that a scandal had broken on his watch. Even during that call, Corrigan felt that he was getting the facts "in dribs and drabs."[47] He is said to have huffed at Strauss, "How could you do this to me?"

Salomon's brass regrouped Tuesday night at Wachtell Lipton. Amid some heated arguing over Gutfreund's culpability, the executives drafted a second press release. This one weakly admitted that "senior management" had had prior knowledge. Then Munger came on the line and said, "Let's not just say 'senior management.' Let's say who!"[48] That settled it.

A week before, Gutfreund had been Wall Street's most feared executive. By Wednesday, his career hung by a thread. The disclosure that he had known of a violation in April—and had left Mozer in place for further mischief—set off a chain reaction. In the minds of regulators, lawyers, reporters, and Salomon's own employees, the firm began to resemble the still-fresh corpse of Drexel Burnham, which had collapsed after a lengthy battle with the government the previous year.

On Thursday, customers began to desert. The Wisconsin investment board cut Salomon off. Moody's announced a possible downgrade. Corporate clients told Salomon not to bother calling until they saw a change at the top. Gutfreund, who was cloistered with loyalists on the forty-third floor, had become a leper.

Thirteen floors below, the closely cropped Maughan was issuing makeshift orders like a platoon sergeant cut off from his command. But Maughan could not calm markets. Salomon's stock had dropped from 37 to under 27 in a fortnight. The bond market, too, had turned on its former king. Salomon's medium-term paper had plunged from 60 points off the Treasury curve to 300 points off.[49] Its credit was unraveling. People were telling Maughan that he had to call Buffett—whom he had never met.

On Thursday night, Corrigan and Gutfreund spoke again. This time, Corrigan made it clear that he was preparing to yank Salomon's status as a primary dealer.[50]

People in high places, especially those with pieds-à-terre in Paris, may find it hard to fathom that the bell can toll for them. Certainly, Gutfreund had never imagined that *he* could be jeopardized by Mozer's petty machinations. But without Corrigan, he doubted that he could go on.

On Friday, Gutfreund awoke to see his picture atop the *New York Times*. It occurred to him that he was looking at his obituary. At six-thirty, he phoned Corrigan, who did not discourage him from quitting. Then he called Lipton, who was shaving. Lipton, always eager to help his friend—though Salomon, not Gutfreund, was his client—pleaded with him to reconsider.

The once and sometime king sped to his office. Shortly before seven, Omaha time, he called Buffett at his home, waking him. Gutfreund said he had decided to quit—it was his decision alone—and wanted Buffett to step in.

Buffett hesitated. He had always been careful to avoid such entanglements. In Omaha, he had his life neatly arranged. Once, when Tom Murphy was on the verge of acquiring ABC, Buffett had cautioned, "Think about how it will change your life." Undoubtedly, he now had the same thought about himself.

"You got to come to New York," Gutfreund insisted. "I just read my obituary. Look at the paper."

"Well, let me think about it."[51]

Buffett showered, dressed, and cruised the familiar route to Kiewit Plaza. In his mind, he ran through Salomon's balance sheet. He knew that it had $150 billion or so of assets, only $4 billion of which was equity. Salomon had more liabilities than any company in the United States save Citicorp. Then Buffett began to think about Salomon's intangibles. The business was making money—as a business, it wasn't going broke. *The crisis was that top management was being eliminated overnight, in a business where confidence is enormously important.*[52] The directors would be meeting Sunday to accept Gutfreund's and Strauss's resignations. They would need someone to take the reins.

Buffett's confidants were skeptical as to whether he should do it. Ron Olson, his lawyer at Munger, Tolles & Olson, warned that it was "a very high-risk proposition," and that Buffett's reputation would be forever damaged if it turned out badly.[53] Howie prophetically told his father, "Everybody who ever wanted to take a shot at you is going to do it now."

The safe course would be to give Salomon a quiet burial. True, Buffett had a $700 million investment in Salomon preferred. But the preferred stock was far safer than the common; neither Munger nor Buffett thought they would lose much money in a liquidation.[54]

But Buffett stood to lose something nonetheless. His entire career, he had argued for a sort of compact between shareholders and corporations. Gutfreund had failed the trust, through weakness and hesitation. But the compact worked both ways. As Salomon's biggest owner, Buffett also had responsibilities. He had a *duty*, which at the extreme resembles fate.

By midday, Buffett was aloft in the *Indefensible*, racing toward New York.

For most of that Friday, trading in Salomon's stock was halted. Its ordinary business stopped. The top executives huddled in the board-room. Gutfreund came in at noon and said, "Warren is the CEO." The others hung around, waiting. According to Maughan:

> The whole firm had put down their phones. They knew there was a meeting of the office of the chairman going on. We had this curious suspended animation while we were waiting for the CEO to get here on his plane.

The executives knew they were days, perhaps a week, from seeing the firm go down the tubes. They were beady-eyed and stale from too many meetings. Donald Howard, the chief financial officer, said, "We were in a state of shock."

Late in the afternoon, Buffett poked his head into the boardroom and gave a hearty "Hi there." He managed a joke about "the little prob-lem we have," as though the firm had lost a valued attendant in the mailroom. Thinking aloud, he added, "I'm really sorry about John and Tommy. Is there any way we can save JM [Meriwether]?"[55]

Buffett knew none of the details of the scandal, for which he would now be responsible. But he made no attempt to grill anyone. Glancing about the boardroom, he said it was obvious that people were tired and should get some rest. His relaxed manner had a calming effect. For the first time in a week, the executives felt their spirits lift.[56]

"This is only a temporary setback."

He said it as if he knew.

Then Buffett went to the auditorium for an assembly of Salomon's managers. Gutfreund spoke first. He said the firm was fortunate to have Buffett stepping in, and that Gutfreund would be rooting for them. He did not show sentiment—only a hint of the old defiance. He had com-mitted no crime; now he was gone. Leibowitz thought his dour fare-well was "horribly sad." Richard Barrett, an investment banker, said it was "pure John—making a bad moment worse." Nobody forgot Gut-freund's final words. "Apologies," he said, "don't mean shit."

After a pause, Buffett faced the troops for the first time. They had seen their firm brought to its knees. They were desperate for leadership, but unsure of where they wanted to be led. Now, Buffett told them, Salomon Brothers would have to do more than obey the rules. His standard would be far stricter.

"Anything not only on the line, but near the line, will be called out."[57]

It was a warning but also a challenge, evoking a muffled memory of the firm's long-lost pride. According to witnesses cited in the next day's *Times*, it was what they wanted to hear:

> After Mr. Buffett's discussion, in which he told the managing directors that the firm would have to follow the laws closely, the firm's executives burst into applause for the man who would soon be their chairman.[58]

Chapter 22

SALOMON'S
COURT

I—Crisis

Friday evening, Buffett leaves Salomon with Gutfreund and Strauss. Their limousine snakes through the financial district, pushing against the six-o'clock tide of homeward-bound commuters. At the Federal Reserve, Corrigan greets them austerely. Stressing that Salomon's dealership is at risk, he makes clear he wants not just the phony bids cleared up but a *broad* reform. He has had it with Salomon's swagger. Buffett pleads for time. Otherwise, he is contrite as a fallen samurai.[1]

In the morning, Buffett reconvenes with a dozen of Salomon's brass at the midtown office of Wachtell Lipton. Eyeing the group—some of whom he has never met—he coolly announces that he intends to pick one of them to manage the company.

"I'm going to meet with you one at a time," Buffett declares. "I'll ask you all the same question: 'Who should run this firm?' Come in any order you like." Then he walks into an adjoining room and shuts the door.[2]

All but two of the executives nominate the same man. Maughan says, "I'm afraid it may have to be me."

When Buffett reappears, Lawrence Pedowitz, a Wachtell Lipton partner, gives a briefing on the Mozer case. Buffett asks about Meriwether. The general view is that Salomon's top producer has done nothing wrong but that, given the cry for a clean break, he may have to go. Later, Buffett sees Meriwether in private. "JM"—the first incidental casualty—resigns.

Now, Saturday night, the scene shifts to Christ Cella, a bustling steakhouse on Manhattan's East Side. Buffett, Munger, and Gutfreund are dining. The latter offers his consulting services, gratis. Buffett graciously responds that he will need all the help he can get. The King of Wall Street lifts his glass and toasts to the new regime.[3]

Cut to ten o'clock Sunday morning, outside 7 World Trade Center. The directors push through a phalanx of photographers and head for the boardroom on the forty-fifth floor. But events are moving ahead of them. As they gather around the burled-walnut table, the directors learn that the Treasury has just banned Salomon from its auctions.

The board meeting is disjointed. One director is participating via a speakerphone at a lodge at Mount McKinley. Another is on the phone from Maine. Buffett repeatedly darts out to take calls from government officials, including Nicholas Brady, Secretary of the Treasury, Jerome Powell, the assistant secretary, and Corrigan, who are also in conference with one another and with Fed chairman Alan Greenspan.[4] Buffett pleads with the regulators for a show of grace, and he reminds them that Salomon's king-sized $150 billion balance sheet is almost entirely financed with short-term money. It rolls over an astounding $50 billion every day, of which $1 billion is secured only by Salomon's name—a rapidly depleting asset.[5] If it cannot refinance, it will have to liquidate. At this very moment, Wachtell Lipton is preparing bankruptcy papers.[6] Although it is morning in New York, the opening of markets in Tokyo is only hours away. Buffett is afraid that the Treasury's banishment of Salomon will trigger a funding crisis in Japan and, ultimately, the firm's collapse.[7] He needs *some* evidence that Salomon—or Buffett— has the government's faith.

Meanwhile, as news of Salomon's expulsion flashes over the wires, employees drift onto the trading floor, like family members awaiting the last rites of a relative. Eric Rosenfeld, a bond trader, Lawrence Hilibrand, the $23 million arb, and McIntosh are going over options for emergency funding. Maughan is talking to Japan. John Macfarlane, the thirty-seven-year-old treasurer, having just finished a triathlon, has raced to the office. He is trying to figure out how much cash Salomon will need in the coming days. Above the vast trading room, a trio of electronic clocks tick off the seconds in New York, London, and Tokyo. "Your life," Macfarlane says, "flashes in front of you."

In the boardroom, Gutfreund has resigned, and Buffett has taken control. His sense of humor has left him, but he is running the meeting with his customary calmness and sense of purpose. Dwayne Andreas, a director, takes heart from the fact that Buffett has so much of his own money invested in Salomon. Another board member is cheered by the thought that Buffett, at least, knows the government officials personally. For varying reasons, each of the directors is convinced that Buffett is the one person who has the combination of reputation, financial clout, experience, and inner strength to save the firm.[8] All of his prior career—particularly, his habit of making lonely decisions—now seems but a preparation for this moment.

But Buffett is not certain that he wants the job. If Salomon remains on the Treasury's blacklist, Buffett will be little more than Salomon's undertaker. Munger is vehement that Buffett should refuse such an assignment.

Around midday, Secretary Brady calls. As Buffett ducks out of the boardroom, Munger snarls, "You'd be crazy to take it!"

Brady is at a summer home in Saratoga, where he has been trying to assess the damage to markets if the biggest firm on Wall Street fails. Buffett takes the call in a side room with antique pottery and lavender walls. He ticks off the changes at Salomon: Mozer fired; Gutfreund and Strauss resigned; specific new procedures to prevent a recurrence. In addition, Buffett delivers a *personal* promise to clean house thoroughly:

> I told him there were going to be controls that he could hold me responsible for in the future. . . . Similarly, that we were planning a future that would be considerably different than our past.[9]

But if the Treasury cuts Salomon off, Buffett adds, it may not make any sense for him to become its chairman.[10]

Brady understands that Buffett has issued a threat, but his instincts tell him that Buffett is not a quitter. "He has never walked away from any investment before," Brady tells himself.[11]

Brady is relatively unperturbed by the prospect of Salomon's demise.

The system has survived Black Monday, the collapse of Drexel, and similar traumas. "No one is bigger than the U.S. government," Brady thinks.[12]

But Brady, of course, knows Buffett. He is the same Nick Brady who, as a Harvard M.B.A. student, wrote a thesis on his family firm, Berkshire Fine Spinning. Though he sold his stock before Buffett's arrival, he is all too aware of what Buffett has done with it since. In recent years, Brady has rubbed shoulders with Buffett at Katharine Graham's dinner parties and, like Graham herself, has occasionally called Buffett for a "reality check." Though shrugging off what he regards as Buffett's bluff, he puts immense stock in his promise to clean up Salomon Brothers. The call breaks off without resolution.

The board meeting lurches on until midafternoon, when Buffett is due in the auditorium for a press conference. As he exits the boardroom he collars Deryck Maughan. "You're the guy," he says with a nod. Salomon, the colossus of Wall Street traders, is now in the hands of a Midwesterner who once proposed a 100 percent tax on short-term trading and a onetime British civil servant and career administrator.

Introducing himself and Maughan to the press, Buffett explains that he will be an interim, unsalaried chairman, for as long—but only as long—as it takes to get Salomon out of trouble. Then he delivers a bit of good news: Brady has just reversed himself and announced that Salomon may bid at Treasury auctions for its own account, though still not for customers. This is a limited but hugely important reprieve.

Softening up his inquisitors, Buffett says he is ready to take the reporters' questions and will "attempt to do it in the manner of a fellow that has never met a lawyer."[13] Buffett still has only a sketchy outline of the scandal. But fielding questions, he is in his element, fluid and witty as at his annual meetings. Now contrite, now gently remonstrative, Buffett already has a strategy. He wants to apologize for the past, but also to disassociate it from the future.

REPORTER: I am curious if you have read *Liar's Poker*?

BUFFETT: Yes, a long time ago.

REPORTER: Any book review?

BUFFETT: No. I want to make sure there is not a second edition.

The pressing question is whether Salomon's culture is to blame—whether Mozer is merely a symptom. Buffett defends Salomon as generally honorable. It was not "pouring out criminal acts in any way, shape or form." Still, he recognizes that the question of motivation is inherently obscure, and that the culture may have played a part. "I don't think the same thing would have happened in a monastery," he admits.

The most delicate interchange concerns Gutfreund. Buffett declares that his silence regarding Mozer was "inexplicable and inexcusable." But otherwise, he does not back down from his previous, admiring characterization of his friend.

REPORTER: Do you think you misjudged Mr. John Gutfreund, and do
             you regret having invested in Salomon Brothers?

BUFFETT: The answer to both of those is "No."

Buffett's three-hour performance goes over well. The press conference over, he pops into a room with the senior executives and delivers an unmistakable message. "Deryck's running this firm, so don't call me. He decides who gets promoted and who gets fired. That's all—see ya."[14]

Then he departs for the nearby Marriott Hotel. In one day, Buffett has had a taste of regulators, the press, the executives, and the staff. Saving Salomon will require that he satisfy each of these constituencies—and the company's customers and creditors, too. In the recent past, no investment bank that has wrestled with such a crisis has managed to survive.

II—Wartime

"For Salomon, the tough times are only beginning,"[15] Monday's *Wall Street Journal* intoned. One might have asked why they were beginning. The crime had been foiled; the perpetrator was gone. Yet the *Journal* proved sage. In Washington, regulators pledged a full-scale probe. Salomon's debt was downgraded. The firm remained frozen out of commercial-paper markets. And more customers—Connecticut, Massachusetts, the California Public Employees Retirement System, and the World Bank—cut Salomon off. Individually, these blows were glancing, hardly worthy of advancing a plot. Yet stitched together they wove a familiar thread. To wit, a "scandal" was in progress, and it had transformed Gutfreund's bond house into a pariah.

Buffett struck back on several fronts.

Early Monday, he distributed his home telephone number to Salomon's top managers, with a letter instructing them to call him at any sign of further misconduct. Though largely symbolic, this was a characteristically simple and powerful stroke. Most CEOs do not like to be called at their homes.

The same day, he and Munger went to see Richard Breeden, chairman of the SEC, the lead agency investigating Salomon. Breeden, a regulatory hawk, was trying to expand the SEC's jurisdiction into the Treasury market. In keeping with his macho reputation, he warned his visitors that he was prepared "to dig up an entire beach looking for a grain of sand."

"Call us anytime someone doesn't give you what you want," Buffett replied evenly. "You'll have a new person to deal with in twenty minutes."

Breeden was impressed.[16]

Returning to New York, Buffett took steps to generate cash. Salomon hiked the interest rate that it charged its traders, inducing them to sell securities. By the end of the first week, a company-wide liquefaction of assets was in progress.[17]

Then Buffett demanded that Feuerstein, the general counsel under Gutfreund, resign. Buffett implored Robert Denham, a partner at Munger Tolles in Los Angeles, to drop his practice and replace him. The squeaky-clean Denham had been Buffett's lawyer on Berkshire matters for fifteen years. "Bob, I really need you," Buffett said. Denham felt he couldn't refuse.

The biggest worry was the threat of prosecution by the Justice Department. Buffett knew that Salomon wouldn't be able to run its business while fighting an indictment, and he figured that the firm would be nearly as devastated were it to plead guilty to one.[18] (Many fiduciaries are forbidden from doing business with felons, and few would choose to do so.) That left one hope: play ball with the government so fully that Justice might grant a reprieve. Wachtell Lipton deduced that this was "a real long shot."[19] The government rarely passed up a chance to prosecute a high-visibility case.

But the strategy was the only one Buffett could have followed. Instinctively, he shrank from confronting his adversaries, but he was superb at winning them over without a fight. He did not so much convince; he disarmed, he co-opted. Though fearful of hostility, he knew what many are slow to learn—that a sustained demonstration of good faith is apt to be returned in kind, *if it is not undermined by any conflicting behavior*. That is how he had induced Kay Graham to trust him, and Stan Lipsey to go to Buffalo and save his newspaper, and the SEC to drop its investigation of Blue Chip. Now he had to cooperate with Salomon's investigators, bow down before its accusers, actually help Justice prove its case. He had to assume, very publicly, as only Buffett could, a personal responsibility for the scandal—to show that the stain was not only purged but deeply and sincerely regretted.

There was a political element to the case, and the political climate was overtly hostile. The public had been predisposed—by previous scandals, and by *Liar's Poker*—to believe that all of Salomon was rotten. Also, regulators and many in Congress, who were embarrassed at having slept through the S&L fiasco, viewed the Salomon case as an opportunity to demonstrate their "toughness." Their outrage seemed to run ahead of the revelations. Rep. J. J. Pickle, a Texas Democrat investigating Salomon, actually issued a statement declaring, "My fear is that this isn't the only runaway train on the tracks, and that the real wreck [at Salomon] is yet to come."[20] At the SEC, Breeden was treating the Salomon affair as a replay of Drexel, and had dashed off 135 subpoenas and requests for information.[21]

Compared with Boesky or Milken, Mozer, of course, was very small beer. But his blunt defiance of the Treasury was the picture of Wall Street arrogance—and arrogance, more than any specific crime, is what turned the public's stomach. In one respect, Salomon was the most arrogant of all. "We screwed around with securities of the U.S. government," noted Gedale Horowitz, a longtime Salomon executive. "Not even Milken did that."

As summer wound down, Washington was abuzz over "the Salomon scandal" as only Washington can be. Rep. Markey, having booked a hearing for two days after Labor Day, had bagged Buffett as the star witness. The Senate had scheduled a hearing for a week later.

Bell, Salomon's capital lobbyist, shrewdly took Buffett to see some of his interrogators in advance. A few had tough questions about the Salomon board's lack of oversight. Buffett said, you know, he wished he had paid more attention to it at the time. He was humble, sort of hat-in-hand, laying on that killing kindness. He reminded them that he was a congressman's son, and poked fun at the fact that he had gotten himself in a stew.[22]

He freely admitted that Salomon had been in the wrong, and persuaded the legislators that he was on their side. After meeting with Buffett, Senator Jake Garn turned to an aide and said, "You know, we shouldn't go flying off the handle."

It hardly hurt that Buffett was friendly with some of the key players, such as chairman Markey. Nor did it hurt that, unlike many businessmen, he had never lectured Congress on the evils of regulation—Buffett believed in government, and had long said so.

The usual tactic at a congressional hearing is to lob grenades at the witness. But the congressmen were wary of slinging mud at Buffett. Despite his $700 million investment in Salomon, they saw him as a figure from without Wall Street—from the Plains. "Half the people think Omaha's a farm town," Bell noted.

Bell, who spent a lot of time with Buffett in preparation, was astounded by his inside knowledge of Washington. He thought him far more complicated than his Rousseauian image:

> He's genial. He's not outwardly crusty. But I had the impression that Buffett was an old New England Yankee—the eighteenth-century ethic that success in business was a sign of God's grace. There was no equivocation in morals. No room for sentimentality. He does what he wants, very logical. He has no problem with the word "no." There is not a lot of pretense in the SOB. There are contradictions, but those are different. He's all of a piece—but it's a very complex piece.

A hearing, like a trial, has a carnival spontaneity. Whatever happens, there is no second chance. Even before the doors opened on the sweltering afternoon of September 4, a crowd had formed in the hallway of the Rayburn House Office Building. Then reporters, lobbyists, onlookers burst into Room 2123. They filled the seats and stood in the aisles—the same hearing room where a glowering Michael Milken had pleaded the Fifth. The front was filled with the technical paraphernalia of journalism—television cameras with their blinding spotlights, tape recorders, photographic equipment. The audience picked out Buffett, in a dark suit, seated at the witness table, and Katharine Graham, sitting in front. Now, in their preambles, the congressmen ascended to spasms of telegenic outrage. *An arrogant disdain . . . the American people . . . ripped off by a few aggressive traders . . . Ivan Boesky . . . Michael Milken . . . our financial culture . . . these disgraceful episodes . . .*[23]

Rep. Jim Slattery addressed the witness. *Mr. Buffett, you have an opportunity to provide a great service for the taxpayers of this country. . . . And I am pleased that you have moved quickly to fire [sic] the upper managers that appear to be responsible. . . . And I only hope that we won't learn in the future about any sweetheart deals with these managers that are being fired now. . . . And as far as I am concerned, those responsible deserve absolutely nothing from Salomon Brothers, not a dime in severance pay, not a dime in remuneration of any kind, and not a dime to pay for their defense, either . . . nothing but a swift kick in the butt out of Salomon Brothers and onto the street. . . .*

Having hanged the old regime, they rushed to praise the new. *Mr. Buffett, I want to congratulate you. . . . Mr. Buffett, you are a man of unquestioned integrity. . . . Mr. Buffett . . . who has followed the path of the straight and true. . . .*

Rep. Peter Hoagland, of Omaha, rose to introduce his neighbor. *A man who is typical of the people we grow and nurture in the Midwest. . . . He continues to live in a quiet, tree-lined street in Omaha. . . . He files his own tax returns. . . .*

Buffett loped his way to the dais, trailed by a score of photographers and cameramen. He shook hands with chairman Markey, and there was a click-click-clicking like a swarm of summer cicadas. His profile was filled out now, slightly paunchy. His eyebrows danced above his eyeglass frames, and his hair was a mop of pepper and salt. He spoke in a tremulous voice, shadowed by a nervous laugh.

Norma Jean Thurston (a.k.a. "Peroxide"), seeing Buffett, on camera, for the first time since high school, instantly recognized his mannerisms and wit. Harry Beja, his friend at Wharton, saw the testimony live, in Mexico, where Beja had become a successful businessman. Beja recognized Buffett's "brightness of spirit," but thinking of his friend's shyness, Beja winced.

Buffett sat in the witness chair, facing the members. As he began to speak, his left arm swung in a decisive arc:

I would like to start by apologizing for the acts that have brought us here. The Nation has a right to expect its rules and laws will be obeyed. At Salomon, certain of these were broken.

The baldness of his apology would outlive all that followed. Captains of Wall Street had been appearing in Congress since J. P. Morgan, Sr.'s, defiant performance in the Pujo hearings of 1912. Until now, none had ever said he was sorry.

A dozen shutters click-click-clicked. Buffett made a pitch for Salomon's eight thousand employees, most of whom were "hardworking, able, and honest." He promised new measures to ensure compliance with the law. But in the end, he recognized, "the spirit of compliance is as important, or more so, as the words." Speaking of his vision for the new Salomon, Buffett reached for one of those vivid images that seemed to spring from the lectern into America's living rooms:

I want employees to ask themselves whether they are willing to have any contemplated act appear on the front page of their local paper the next day, to be read by their spouses, children and friends. . . . If they follow this test, they need not fear my other message to them: Lose money for the firm and I will be understanding; lose a shred of reputation for the firm, and I will be ruthless.

Buffett's emphasis on reputation was oddly reminiscent of Morgan's testimony that character—not money—was the basis of credit. There the similarity ended. Morgan, whatever else, epitomized Wall Street. Buffett, who had made a fortune in the stock market, was hailed as a Main Street antidote to Wall Street's excesses. It is doubtful that Salomon could have found another living American who represented both these extremes.

The hearing, and also the follow-up in the Senate, was remarkably gentle. The subcommittees saved their powder for the regulators. *So the Fed knew all along what was going on? Is that correct, Mr. Corrigan?* . . . As Buffett left the House committee room he was pursued by a mob of reporters. But he ducked into a limousine, bound for the *Washington Post*.[24]

Salomon's "fired managers" had not been kicked onto the street. Gutfreund and Strauss had been fixed up with an office and a secretary on an otherwise empty floor of Salomon's former headquarters. The company had been paying their legal bills.

Buffett had called Gutfreund a few times since taking over. An associate of Gutfreund's said, "I think he was being kind—telling John he didn't consider him to be scum." But the day before the House hearing, Gutfreund, in the interest of propriety, suggested that the two stop speaking.

The day after the hearing, Salomon's directors met in New York. Buffett raised the topic of benefits for Gutfreund and the other former managers. With Rep. Slattery's bombast ringing in their ears, the board cut off severances, bonuses, legal fees, office space, secretaries, and health benefits—the works. Gutfreund stoically told friends that he understood that Buffett was trying to save the firm. When a colleague called to see how he was doing, Gutfreund said, "You have to distance yourself from me—you and the firm."[25]

Buffett, meanwhile, was working in Gutfreund's office and being waited on by his former secretary. He had his friend's olive-wood Italian desk and his sweeping view of the Hudson and East rivers. But he found it all unfamiliar and stressful.[26]

On Friday afternoons he could barely wait to board the *Indefensible*, knowing that when he landed in Omaha, Astrid and his family would be waiting for him at Gorats.[27] Then, in the comfort of his steakhouse, where the organist had been playing forever and where the people knew nothing of finance, he would unwind by telling stories of his week on Wall Street.

The most nerve-racking aspect of Salomon was that Buffett had to contend with so many outside forces. He had to reassure bankers, credit agencies, investors, the press. He could not *control* events at Salomon, as he did at Berkshire. "It's like waiting for the other shoe to drop—on a centipede," he quipped to a friend.[28] For one of the few times, Buffett was having trouble sleeping.[29]

His intimates worried about him, knowing that he had always been so careful to stick to his knitting and avoid the unfamiliar. Save for the time when Buffett's wife had undergone surgery, Munger had never seen him so distressed. Rick Guerin, who had saved Buffett's life during the boating mishap, said, "People don't understand the enormity of his gift to Salomon Brothers." Another chum, less charitably, said, "Warren is great at peace. We'll see if he's good in wartime."

Buffett was a reluctant warrior, but he had certain qualities of gener-alship, such as confidence, perspective, an unsurpassed ability to focus on his object, and a gift for communicating all this to the troops. Now he needed these qualities in spades.

The SEC wanted Salomon to turn over Wachtell Lipton's report, the most damning evidence in the case. Like any attorney-client com-munication, the report was immune from subpoena power.

Salomon's outside lawyers urged Buffett to refuse. That is what any lawyer in America would advise. According to Bell, the lawyers said, "We're going to have liability. We can't admit to this. It'll be a night-mare."

"I don't want to hear that stuff," Buffett retorted. He didn't care about the civil liability—the money could be earned back. In his mind, the legalistic details were far less important than that he uphold his promise to the Feds.

"This is our position," Buffett went on. "We did wrong. We're going to *show* how we did wrong. We've signed the charge sheet."

Then he turned to Bell. He wanted him to fire Salomon's paid polit-ical consultants.

"Can we talk about that?"

"Yeah, sure."

Bell explained that the consultants were Beltway insiders with a keen grasp of politics. Salomon could use their expertise.

"You have a point," Buffett said. "But this is what we're going to do."

The consultants were gone. Buffett hated these professional hand-holders. They would obscure the grand message which, like a lone horseman, he was intent on delivering *personally*.

This, and, indeed, Buffett's every move was aimed at winning for-bearance. He ordered Salomon to stop trading with Marc Rich, the fugitive oil trader. He ended political gift-giving, to avoid the appear-ance that Salomon was buying favors. He sacked Wachtell Lipton, which was linked to Gutfreund.

He repeatedly warned Salomon's traders that they had to operate "way, way away from the line"—another of Buffett's simple but potent images. Within weeks, a half-dozen of Salomon's traders had gone to Buffett to see if a planned stratagem met his definition of "the center of the court."[50]

Eric Rosenfeld, the bespectacled trader and former Harvard professor who had replaced Mozer, proposed a trading strategy to profit from discrepancies in tax laws. Rosenfeld had been working on the idea for months, had gotten it blessed by lawyers, and felt it would be highly lucrative.

Buffett said, "Eric, I'm not comfortable with it." He said it was probably legal but *"too close to the line."*[31]

By repeating such moralistic exhortations, Buffett was subtly trying to lift the employees' self-image. Thomas Hanley, the firm's banking analyst, had never seen Salomon pull so much in unison. He felt that Buffett was "brilliant."[32]

But Buffett couldn't get the story off the front page. Salomon kept disclosing new details of Mozer's wrongdoing, and the government kept announcing new, or expanded, investigations (five federal agencies and various states got into the act). The press kept speculating that other, unrelated sins at Salomon were soon to be exposed; Salomon was hit by dozens of civil suits; its bank lines were cut. The basic story didn't change, but the surface impression was of an ever-widening scandal.

Alarmingly, fear was spreading among Salomon's customers, who were loath to give business to a firm that might be indicted on the morrow. British Telecommunications sacked it from a major underwriting. Bond-trading customers defected.[33] Trying to reassure the CEO of a big corporate customer, Buffett had to literally put his hand across his heart and swear, "There are no more bombshells coming."[34]

After five weeks, when the crisis seemed to be stabilizing, Robert E. Allen, chairman of American Telephone & Telegraph, one of America's most respected CEOs, landed a blow from left field, publicly denouncing Salomon's moral laxity as "unforgivable."[35] Salomon was like the proverbial dog with a can tied to its tail: it raised a ruckus wherever it ran. The next day, September 24, the stock hit a low, 20¾.

Two days later, Buffett took off to meet with the Graham group, which had mushroomed to fifty-odd of his friends and spouses, including the young Bill Gates, in Victoria, British Columbia. The others were surprised that Buffett took the time, but for him the trip was a tonic. He stayed at the inn while they toured Victoria's lush, beautiful gardens—but Buffett would have skipped the gardens anyway. He did attend the seminar. The topic, assigned just before the scandal broke, was "The Dumbest Thing I Have Done in Investments or Business."

In New York, the scandal was taking a toll on morale. A manager complained, "It's tough to come in in the morning and open the paper. You just wonder when it is going to stop."[36] Rosenfeld, the able new chief of the government desk, went to a restaurant frequented by young professionals on the Upper East Side. He overheard people talking about Salomon—"Isn't it disgusting?" one said knowingly—as if the firm were shot through with crooks.

Early in October, Buffett held a pep talk with the staff. He asserted *unequivocally* that he was feeling good about their prospects. The employees, most of them, were living through a crisis for the first time. Buffett had been there before.

I have seen a couple of companies taken into the emergency ward. . . . American Express in 1963 and GEICO in 1976. . . . At GEICO a few people made mistakes. It went from being an organization with enormous pride to an organization that was in doubt. Policyholders were leaving by the tens of thousands. I have to tell you that the period did last for some time. Jack Byrne had to wrestle with one alligator after another.[37]

GEICO's stock, he noted dryly, had risen since then from 2 to about 194. As in buying a stock in a falling market, he told the employees, they had to look beyond the passions of the moment to a future for Salomon that he insisted would be bright.

On Wall Street, the betting now was that Salomon would survive, but as a shrunken firm—as *Business Week* put it, "smaller, less profitable, less powerful."[38] It was feared that Buffett, while cleansing Salomon, had emasculated it. He had overseen a sell-off of $50 billion in assets, easing its credit worries, but reducing its ability to make the big, blustery bets that had been its trademark. Larry Tisch pointedly asked Buffett, "Who's going to be the risk-taker in the Gutfreund sense of the word?" Buffett did not have an answer.[39]

Buffett was not a *physical* presence at Salomon. He occasionally wolfed down a ham sandwich in the executive dining room, where the others dined on veal paillard, but there was none of Gutfreund's stalking the aisles. And, as the case dragged on, Buffett spent more of his time in Omaha.

He had close contact with only a handful of employees: Rosenfeld, the whiz-kid trader, who was surprised by Buffett's detailed knowledge of arbitrage, and the treasurer, the chief financial officer, general counsel Denham, and Maughan, who relied on Buffett as a corporate encyclopedia.

The executives initially mistook Buffett's gracious exterior for softness. But they discovered that Buffett was tougher than his image (a reversal of their experience with Gutfreund). "It's a perfect contrast with John," said William Jennings, a senior vice president. "Warren is not easy to convince. John had trouble saying no."

But Buffett refused to *manage* Salomon. He admonished Maughan, "I don't want to disappoint you, but I didn't grow up wanting to run an investment bank."[40] In effect, Buffett re-created the same role for himself—a concerned but distant overseer—that he played at See's Candy.

Unlike most CEOs, he did not identify with the other executives. He was less a manager than an investor with a ringside seat. And as an investor he was profoundly unhappy. In October, Buffett told Maughan, "You may be a wonderful company, but you're a lousy stock." That was a tipoff. Over the previous five years, the return on Salomon's shares had ranked a miserable 445th among the S&P 500. But now, Buffett's focus was slowly shifting—from the scandal to the stock.

III—Agony

Viewing Salomon as a long-term owner, Buffett saw a picture that was anything but pretty. Its assets had ballooned, yet its return on capital had vastly diminished. It had consistently profitable areas, such as the Tokyo branch, arbitrage and bond trading, and underwriting. But its well-paid investment bankers had been losing money for years. In equities, it was a profit one year, a loss the next.[41] On balance, a huge engine had been assembled, capital employed, labor expended, all for an enterprise that yielded a pittance.

Buffett was convinced that the problem was rooted in Salomon's extravagant bonuses. Gutfreund had let the executives take home nearly three-quarters of the firm's profits—as if he had never sold the business and the executives had still been partners in it.[42] The real partners—the shareholders—had been left out. This failure to hold managers accountable had sent a distorted signal, just as Buffett had once feared that too much allowance would distort the message to his kids. With their bonuses rising, managers had allowed entire divisions to run with "inadequate or nonexistent returns."[43]

To break this pattern, Buffett decided to act boldly. On October 29 he took out a remarkable two-page ad in the *New York Times*, the *Wall Street Journal*, the *Washington Post*, and the *Financial Times*, reproducing Salomon's third-quarter report. The heart of it was a letter from Buffett denouncing the company's pay scale. He emphasized that he had no problem with extraordinary pay for extraordinary performance. But Salomon's "share-the-wealth" system was subsidizing all—even the mediocre—at the shareholders' expense.

Having said this, Buffett dropped a bomb. He was lopping off $110 million from the pool set aside for bonuses for 1991. As a result, although profits that year (earned before the scandal) were double those of 1990, bonuses would be slightly *less* than in 1990. Those who didn't like it could walk.

> Our pay-for-performance philosophy will undoubtedly cause some managers to leave. . . . In the end we must have people to match our principles, not the reverse.[44]

A quarter century earlier, standing in the shadows of the Hathaway mill, Buffett had told Ken Chace that he wanted employees who thought like owners. Now, in the glass-and-steel splendor of Wall Street, he told Maughan that he was quite prepared to lose large numbers of staff. Maughan wondered how many. Buffett said, "Deryck, we can't buy loyalty."[45]

Buffett's manifesto generated a groundswell of support from people outside Salomon, many of whom hoped that it might—finally—bring some reasonableness to Wall Street's pay scales. Inside Salomon it was a different story. The employees felt they were being made to take the fall for Mozer, and they deeply resented Buffett's going public. The day the ad ran, Gary Goldstein, a headhunter, got a torrent of calls from Salomon executives who were, indeed, quite willing to have their loyalty priced.

What's more, the size of the cuts—amid a record year on Wall Street—stunned them. Maughan slashed bonuses for 70 percent of Salomon's managers.[46] Investment bankers were shaved by an average of 25 percent, with some taking *cuts* of as much as $500,000. In addition, Buffett and Maughan laid off eighty professionals and two hundred support staff.[47]

Quite quickly, sentiment toward Buffett soured. People were grateful to him for saving Salomon. Now they'd had enough of him. They thought he was pandering to the regulators and blamed him for putting Gutfreund out in the cold. A veteran analyst said, "Some of us who have been here a long time felt a certain affection—a strong one—for John Gutfreund. Warren was a savior. You know how you feel about saviors. You love 'em but you also resent them."

Of Gutfreund's barons, none had been more protected than Stanley Shopkorn, Salomon's head stock trader. Gutfreund used to smoke cigars in Shopkorn's office while the heavyset, bejeweled horse player traded stocks. On Wall Street, Shopkorn's reputation for trading big positions and playing his hunches had given him a certain aura.

However, the equities department, which he ran, was a poor performer. Buffett, totally unmoved by Shopkorn's Runyonesque charm, ordered him to sell a couple of losing stocks and to quit his speculations. Shopkorn resigned.

His departure triggered a wave of defections in equities. After the group's paltry bonuses were announced, Bruce Hackett, Shopkorn's replacement, got on the squawk box and hollered to his troops, "I'm mad as hell. I leave it to you to figure out why." Buffett's rush to remake the firm seemed to have opened a trapdoor in Salomon's attic, through which all of the demons accumulated over the past decade were suddenly tumbling forth.

The fourth quarter of 1991 was a disaster. Salomon's share of stock underwritings collapsed from 8 percent before the scandal to 2 percent. The timing was awful. Wall Street was doing a record business in underwritings and bonuses were up all over the Street. But at Salomon, the salesmen and analysts had nothing to pitch, and the bankers had no deals. So they left.

"Warren doesn't realize how easy it is for people to leave—he thought he was so goddam smart," a departing banker fumed, reclining in the leather-backed chair of a men's club. "He's running it like a stock. He doesn't care about the people."

Warming to his subject, the banker continued, "Do you think *his* entire record could go on the front page? He'd have to be almost inhuman. A saint or something."

In January 1992, Buffett faced a crisis. Tom Hanley, the banking analyst previously enthralled by Buffett's team spirit, threatened to defect to First Boston unless his pay was doubled to $2 million. Hanley had used similar ploys to extract raises in the past (including a 40 percent hike in 1991). Though a prima donna, Hanley was a valued analyst, and influential in winning business from banks. Buffett let him go.

Four other analysts left the same week. It touched off a panic. The cream was gone; now rivals were threatening to pick the department clean. At Maughan's urging, Buffett backpedaled a bit and guaranteed bonuses for six younger analysts. It was the first time he had blinked.

Meanwhile, Buffett and Maughan were trying to design a system that would link bonuses in each group to the group's return on capital. This was not so easy. Salomon had never bothered to calculate how much capital each of its various units was using. To Buffett, it was a fatal oversight.

Rather strange, frankly, to me, to think of having a business that employs close to $4 billion of equity capital and not knowing exactly who is using what.[48]

In the midst of the battle over bonuses, Jack Byrne's son Patrick, a doctoral student in economics and philosophy at Stanford, stopped off to see Buffett, and the two had a long chat about motivation. Buffett encouraged young Byrne to question the dogma of his textbooks. People—at least some people—he maintained, were not the purely economic creatures depicted by economists. They could also be motivated by loyalty.

To put it mildly, this was less than obvious on Wall Street. People became investment bankers to make money. If you didn't pay them they would leave. Nick Brady, himself a former investment banker, thought Buffett was out of his element: "It's like running an opera. You're dealing with people with big egos, with prima donnas. I don't think he understood the business completely."[49]

Many shared this view, some adding the twist that Buffett was putting on his Midwestern morals for public relations purposes. Yet their criticism betrayed a level of discomfort that Wall Street had always felt with Buffett. Rub the critics deeply enough and they, too, were uneasy about their profession's pay and overall behavior. The CEO of a major, nonpublic Wall Street competitor sarcastically remarked that Buffett "came in as Mr. Clean, the open-eyed boy from Omaha."

> The guy was anything but. He's a canny, shrewd operator. But his attempt to rationalize pay was naïve. [Then a nervous giggle.] Some—a lot of it made sense. I agree, the compensation isn't rational. I'd hate for my pay to be on a public proxy. [Another giggle.] He was quite right— you've got to run it like a business.

As Howie had predicted, people who had been waiting for the chance to take a shot at his father came out of the woodwork. *Business Week*, citing "lemons" such as Wells Fargo and Salomon (and omitting Coca-Cola), asserted early in 1992 that Buffett had lost his touch as an investor.[50] Three weeks later, *Business Week* decided that Buffett had also blown the job at Salomon. While acknowledging that he had, in fact, saved it, the magazine slammed him for "a series of mistakes." He had embittered employees, backtracked on pay, killed the firm's taste for risk, and, interestingly, was lacking in "leadership and trust."[51]

Some of the criticism was intensely personal. A *Wall Street Journal* profile played up Buffett's mistress and implied that his folksy image was something of a fraud.[52] In this revisionist view, Buffett crafted his annual letters so as to deflect "tough questions"; he levitated his stock by manipulating his image; he owed his success to his nonpareil circle of contacts. The *Journal*, quoting Michael Price, a competing money manager, saw Buffett as "one of the biggest invisible market operators going, big arbitrages and all, getting better market information than anybody—and all people see is this homespun, down-to-earth guy."

Buffett, who had been used to the press fawning over him, "was really upset" by the article, according to Peter, who added, "I was with him. He was obsessed with it." Buffett wrote a letter to the *Journal* contesting numerous points in the article, but he was typically unwilling to show his hurt publicly and insisted that the letter not be published.

Next, Michael Lewis, the author of *Liar's Poker*, smeared Buffett in *The New Republic*.[53] In "Saint Warren: Wall Street's Fallen Angel," Lewis charged Buffett with a series of investing and ethical flaws so all-encompassing that an unknowing subscriber might have supposed that he was reading of one of the century's great swindlers—and one of its great failures, to boot. Lewis took the Efficient Market Theory as gospel and dismissed Buffett's career as a run of lucky coin flips. That aside, "Fallen Angel" was rife with actual errors.*

Buffett was livid over the Lewis piece. Morey Bernstein, the author of *The Search for Bridey Murphy* and a Ben Graham devotee who had known Buffett casually, wrote Buffett a sympathetic note, damning Lewis's article, apparently in profane terms. Buffett—ever careful with words—responded: "Morey—Thanks for the empathy re the Michael Lewis piece. He is everything you say he is."[54]

The interesting question is, what was Lewis's gripe with Buffett? There is a clue in *Liar's Poker*, and it reflects on Wall Street's discomfort with Buffett as well. In the book, Lewis, describing his life as a young bond salesman, seems to celebrate his unloading of $86 million of unwanted Olympia & York bonds on a gullible client. Yet he admits to a hint of embarrassment over it. He has stuck his "best customer," and one who trusted him, with bonds that Lewis "probably wouldn't touch with a barge pole"—save for the "glory" that will redound to him at Salomon.

> I knew it was awful. But I feel much worse about it now than I did at the time.[55]

Now, the conclusion of his essay on Buffett:

> You can frighten people into behaving themselves for a while. But in the long run he's wrong. . . . Thus we arrive at what might be called Buffett's Dilemma: the choice between doing good and making money.

In fact, it was Lewis who had made that choice. Buffett, under extremely trying circumstances, was attempting to do both. Buffett's repeated exhortation—"Good profits simply are not inconsistent with

---

*Lewis said, "In the middle of 1988 [Buffett] broke with his strict rule of long-term investing and became an arbitrageur. . . ." In fact, Buffett had done arbitrage since 1954 and had often written of it. Lewis said Buffett had offered to finance the RJR Nabisco deal; in fact, he had refused to back it. Lewis, making light of Buffett's disclaimer, said: "He even once suggested, in 1985, that his bogey was merely to outstrip the average returns of corporate America." Buffett did not "suggest it once," he had explicitly stated it in each annual report for years. Lewis said Buffett invested in bonds of RJR, "nearly . . . the largest bankruptcy in history." That was true—but Buffett had invested *after* the bonds had fallen, and had made a killing on them.

good behavior"[56]—was a challenge to Lewis's (and other cynics') rationalizations.

By the time of Lewis's piece, mid-February 1992, Salomon was in limbo. The stock had recovered to 30. Customers such as the World Bank and state pension funds had returned. The management had been overhauled, and Buffett was spending most of his time in Omaha.

But Salomon's corporate business continued to bleed. Morale was suffering from speculation that Salomon was losing its core viability, and by rumors that Buffett was planning to return the firm to its bond-trader "roots" and close up everything else, such as its investment bank. One hundred employees defected in February alone. Of those who had been on the payroll in August, a third of the people in equities and a fourth of the bankers were gone.[57] Even Denis Bovin, who had been Buffett's banker in his first dealing with Salomon, in the early seventies, and who had been a fan of Buffett's personally, jumped to Bear Stearns.

As painful as such betrayals were, Buffett relentlessly insisted that Salomon was on track. When the dust settled, he maintained, Salomon would be stronger, in *all* areas, than ever. No one on the staff saw him waver, even in the slightest. This was Buffett's essential virtue—the courage to stick to his course. Don Howard, the chief financial officer, said, "He conveyed to me that every problem was surmountable."

Inwardly, it was killing him. Perhaps the most stressful aspect was that Buffett was not used to working with people who were not personally loyal to him. "It's agony," Munger said that spring. "It's just bloody murder. Salomon is losing key employees even as we speak." For as long as the Treasury case remained open, there was scant hope of stemming the tide.

IV—First Love

It had dawned on Buffett that the government was punishing Salomon by making it wait. He pleaded with the Treasury to bring the case to a head, though he was careful as always not to pressure anyone. "Take your shots," he would say. "We just don't want to bleed to death while you're making up your mind."[58]

The Justice Department and the SEC were demanding that Salomon plead to a felony and pay $400 million in fines. Gary Naftalis,

Salomon's criminal lawyer, considered that to be shockingly stiff. Kidder Peabody, which Naftalis had defended in the 1980s, had paid only $25 million, and had not been charged with a crime, after Martin Siegel, its star deal-maker, had confessed to pervasive insider trading. All the government had on Salomon was phony bidding. (The more serious charge of manipulating the market in the squeeze had been dropped for lack of evidence.)

The boyish-looking Naftalis even kidded government lawyers about the case's seeming smallness, remarking, "What baby died over this?"

An assistant U.S. attorney replied, "You lied to the government. That's worse than insider trading."

The decision was up to Otto G. Obermaier, the U.S. attorney in Manhattan. Unlike his predecessor, Rudolph Giuliani, who had handcuffed investment bankers in daylight, Obermaier was a legal scholar and thought to be dovish. But prosecutors live in a world of deterrents. Obermaier wanted a guilty plea.

As Naftalis and the U.S. attorney's office began to negotiate, Naftalis realized that Buffett had presented him with a subtle weapon. In August, Buffett had promised to cooperate. In the government's view, he had kept his word. If Obermaier were to prosecute Salomon now, Naftalis argued, Buffett's openness would be seen as naïve. In effect, the prosecution would then deter not future crimes but future cooperation. Buffett had made his own behavior—not Mozer's or Gutfreund's—the issue in the case.

In April, as the case was nearing a climax, Naftalis played his ace. He, Denham, and attorney Ron Olson brought Buffett to the U.S. attorney's office, a squat, brownish building by the federal courthouse, for a meeting with Obermaier. As this was to be Buffett's show, the lawyers held their tongues.

Buffett began unassumingly, giving Obermaier a sense of his career.[59] He didn't argue the case, and yet, like a country lawyer who may defend a man accused of murder by pointing out the upstanding nature of his client's family, he was arguing it all the same. He sketched in the milestones in his relationship with Salomon—how it had once raised money for Berkshire, how it had continued to be his broker ever since, how Gutfreund had bailed out GEICO. In Buffett's experience, Salomon was a proud firm, of which his own twenty-year tie to it was emblematic. Though not belittling the moral and financial depths to which Salomon had fallen at the hour of Gutfreund's desperate call to him, Buffett argued that, in both senses, the firm had recovered. "The firm is totally different than it was in August," Buffett insisted.

Obermaier asked just one question: how long would Buffett be around?

Now, Buffett talked about his philosophy of investing for the long term—of treating his companies like partners—as he had done in his early years and right through the rip-roaring eighties. He hadn't just sucked the blood out; he had stuck with them. And now and in the future he would be on Salomon's board, invested in the company and watching over it. As on the Sunday when he had pleaded with Brady— as in the entire Salomon episode—Buffett presented the case in personal terms.

Obermaier would insist that the facts were sufficient to indict.[60] Nonetheless, in May he announced that he would not bring charges. Concurrently, the various federal agencies announced a civil settlement with Salomon. To a man, the top officials had been personally won over. Powell, the assistant Treasury secretary, said, "I think every Salomon shareholder should have a little picture of Warren Buffett by their night table."[61]

The settlement cost Salomon $290 million (including $100 million set aside for private suits)—then the second-largest penalty ever levied against a U.S. securities firm.

The final SEC complaint detailed ten "extremely serious" bidding violations. Breeden gravely noted that he had issued four hundred subpoenas and taken thirty thousand pages of testimony to ferret them out. Yet the SEC had done more to prove Salomon's integrity than its guilt. Its exhaustive probe had turned up no evidence of affirmative wrongdoing other than that by Mozer—the full extent of which Salomon had uncovered and disclosed itself.

In June, Buffett stepped down from the chairman's post he had held for nine months. The stock was at $33⅝—25 percent higher than in August 1991. Buffett stunned the Street by picking Bob Denham, his tight-lipped lawyer, to succeed him.

The bland, soft-spoken Texan was a Wall Street outsider whose loyalty was to Buffett, and whose mission would be to preserve Buffett's reforms. Deryck Maughan would continue to run the business, but the power behind the throne was unchanged; it would be Buffett himself.

Having ridden into Salomon with fanfare, Buffett slipped away with none. Merely a note, scribbled by Bill McIntosh:

"I'm with Salomon" has always been said with pride, and thanks to you it will be for many years to come.

Buffett bought more stock in Salomon, raising Berkshire's stake in it to 20 percent. After rising to 50, the stock fell sharply after Buffett's purchase, but it remained above its high for the period that he had been chairman.

The Treasury market underwent modest reform. The Fed retained Salomon as one of its primary dealers, but post-scandal changes diluted the club's importance. The wooden box at the Fed went the way of the horse and buggy.

Paul Mozer admitted that he had lied to the Treasury. He served four months in a low-security jail, paid $1.1 million in various fines, and was permanently banned from the securities business.

The SEC brought an action against Gutfreund for failing to supervise Mozer. He settled for a $100,000 fine and a stipulation that he would not run another securities firm. In exile, he grew bitter at what he considered his unjust railroading and at the loss of his social standing. His friendship with Buffett dissolved. In an ugly aftermath, Gutfreund brought a claim against Salomon for money and stock he said he was owed in severance, options, and bonuses—an amount that swelled with Salomon's rising share price to $55 million. In an effort to hash it out, Gutfreund met Buffett and Munger, in California, and lost his temper with them.[62] An arbitration panel ruled against Gutfreund—leaving him with zero.

Gutfreund was commonly depicted as a managerial giant with an ethical flaw. Ironically, that was doubly off the mark. He was an upright but weak manager who built little of enduring value for stockholders. His procrastination over Mozer was simply one more management failure.

Salomon recouped some, though not all, of its market share in underwritings and rebuilt its staff. Though the swagger was gone, it made gains in investment banking and reestablished itself as a player in worldwide markets.

In the two years following the scandal, Salomon had record profits.

Then, during the tumultuous bond market of 1994, it suffered wrenching losses. It was increasingly apparent that some of the damage from the scandal had lingered. The best of Meriwether's former traders, including the talented Eric Rosenfeld, defected to join Meriwether in a new arbitrage venture. Salomon's own arbitrage group was decimated. And, after a couple of years of sanity in the payroll, bonuses again exploded out of control, forcing Buffett to eat humble pie and again overhaul the compensation system—triggering a new round of defections. Salomon eventually returned to profitability, but as an investment for Buffett it was distinctly mediocre. In sum, the jury remained out on Buffett's decision to rebuild the entire firm and to entrust it to a colorless administrator such as Maughan, rather than return Salomon to its bond trader "roots," which had always been its strength. Moreover, Buffett had yet to answer Tisch's question: who, if anyone, could replace Gutfreund as Salomon's "risk-taker"?

When he stepped down, though proud of having rescued the firm, Buffett was rather eager to have the burden lifted. Peter spoke to him after the settlement and thought he sounded like a different person. Soon after, Warren and his wife flew into Buffalo for a *Buffalo News* picnic, where Warren stood for a pie-throwing contest. Then Stan Lipsey, the publisher, led Warren and Susie on a tour. It had just rained, and Lipsey turned to make sure that his guests were dodging the puddles and saw them walking arm in arm. They went through an old graveyard, where Warren gazed at the headstones, and to the foot of the Albright-Knox Art Gallery, where a jazz band was playing. After a while, Lipsey and Susie went to see the art, and a relaxed Warren stood on the steps, listening to the jazz. Then they met Lipsey's girlfriend and the editor Murray Light and his wife for steaks—which Lipsey had ordered from Omaha.

Buffett was thrilled to get his life back. The Salomon escapade, he wrote, was "interesting and worthwhile," but "far from fun."[63] Now the sanctuary of Kiewit Plaza beckoned. To his shareholders, Buffett left no doubt: "Berkshire is my first love and one that will never fade."[64]

Chapter 23

BUFFETT'S
TROLLEY

*Forecasts may tell you a great deal
about the forecaster; they tell you
nothing about the future.*

WARREN BUFFETT,
BERKSHIRE HATHAWAY INC.,
1980 ANNUAL REPORT

Buffett's moves of the early nineties may be quickly sketched. After the Soviet Union collapsed, there was talk of a peace without end, and defense stocks were cheap. Buffett scooped up 14 percent of General Dynamics at 11 a share.[1] Rather soon, a civil war raged in the former Yugoslavia, utopia was put on hold, and General Dynamics went to 59⅛.*

Buffett raised his stake in Wells Fargo. When the recession in real estate ended, the bank recovered. Its earnings soared, and Buffett's much-maligned investment, acquired at an average of 62 a share, took wing to 216.

Buffett also bought big stakes in two familiar-type companies—Guinness, the distiller of Johnnie Walker and other consumer brands; and, most recently, newspaper empire Gannett.

Finally, Buffett bought three New England shoe manufacturers for about $600 million—a little-known but huge addition to Berkshire's portfolio. H. H. Brown and Dexter Shoe, the two bigger companies, had resisted the onslaught of imports by adhering to Rose Blumkin work habits and by developing specific product niches, such as work shoes and outdoor shoes. Both were well-managed, family-style companies up Buffett's alley.

*Share prices in this chapter are as of December 31, 1995.

Mrs. B herself made a détente with her grandsons and admitted publicly that she had made a mistake. Remarkably, she sold her new store to Berkshire for $5 million and returned to the fold.[2] At ninety-nine, she continued to work at the new locale, in charge of her own carpet business, seven days a week. "I am delighted that Mrs. B has again linked up with us," Buffett reported happily. "Her business story has no parallel."[3]

Among Buffett's other holdings, Gillette soared to 52⅛ and Coca-Cola climbed to 74¼, a quadrupling and near-septupling, each in six years' time.* Gannett quickly surged 25 percent and Buffett cashed out Champion at a profit.

American Express fired Jimmy Robinson. True to form, Buffett ploughed another billion dollars into this old favorite. By the end of 1995, his investment was up 47 percent.

USAir's total losses following Buffett's investment mounted to $3 billion. In 1994, it suspended its preferred dividend to Berkshire. After an upturn the following year, Buffett decided to cut his losses and bail out.

None of these stocks moved as dramatically as Berkshire itself. In June 1992, when Buffett stepped down from Salomon, Berkshire was at $9,100. In November, it broke $10,000. Late in the year, Buffett redeemed Berkshire's zero-coupon bonds—a signal that he thought the stock was cheap. During 1993, it was as if traded by the gods. By Valentine's Day, Berkshire had risen to $12,400. It soared, like a messenger to Olympus, through spring and summer, whence it reached a peak of $17,800. Then it gave some ground and closed at $16,325.

The young man who had once put pinball machines in barber-shops was proclaimed by *Forbes* to be the richest fellow in the land.[4] In 1994, Buffett relinquished the crown to the young Bill Gates. However, he did not exactly lose ground. Berkshire rose 25 percent (in a year in which the Standard & Poor's 500 inched up 1 percent.) Then, during the euphoric bull market of 1995, Berkshire rose a phenomenal 57 percent. The stock, which Buffett had begun buying at precisely $7.60 a share, finished at the astonishing figure of $32,100. At that price, Buffett was worth $15.2 billion, surpassing Gates.

*In 1996, Coca-Cola's stock split two-for-one.

Over thirty-one years, his stock has appreciated at a rate of 27.68 percent a year, compounded. Over the same span, the Dow Jones Industrial Average, including dividends, has a growth rate of 10.31 percent a year, and the Standard & Poor's 500 of 10.7 percent.[5] Put differently, if in 1965 one had put $10,000 into Berkshire and like amounts into the S&P 500 and crude oil, the Berkshire at year-end 1995 would have been worth $17.8 million, the S&P portfolio $224,000, and the crude oil $72,000.

If one tacks on the record of Buffett Partnership, Buffett has been doing it for four decades, without much leverage, without speculating or taking undue risks, and without suffering a single down year.[6] Although nay-sayers continue to greet his each new investment with a chorus that "this time" Buffett has finally blown it, no one else has a record over a similar span that compares. Arguably, no one is close.

Among history's great capitalists, Buffett stands out for his sheer skill at evaluating businesses. What John D. Rockefeller, the oil cartelist, Andrew Carnegie, the philanthropic steel baron, Sam Walton, the humble retailer, and Bill Gates, the software nerd, have in common is that each owes his fortune to a single product or innovation. Buffett made his money as a pure investor: picking diverse businesses and stocks.

When he took over Berkshire, in 1965, the once-great yarn mill was fading. He redeployed its capital into insurance, candy, department stores (a mistake), banking, and media. These were followed by tobacco, soft drinks, razor blades, airlines (another mistake), and various whole businesses from encyclopedias to shoes. In sum, he built an industrial empire now worth $38 billion entirely from what miserable trickle of cash he could wrest from a dying textile mill, before that mill was sold for scrap. Though still run by a corporate staff of twelve, Berkshire, ranked by market value, is now the nineteenth-largest company in the United States, worth more than household names such as American Express, Citicorp, Dow Chemical, Eastman Kodak, General Mills, Sears Roebuck, Texaco, and Xerox.[7]

Investors counting on Buffett to stay in orbit should keep in mind his perennial complaint about the burden of size. So far, it has not affected him. Over the last decade, Berkshire's rate of appreciation has been a whisker better than Buffett's overall rate of 29.2 percent.

But the depressing truth is that allocating capital will get tougher as Buffett's assets grow.

Also, the themes that have provided his biggest winners—consumer franchises and newspapers and television—could be getting long in the tooth. The societal trend toward discount, private-label shopping poses a real challenge to brand names. In 1994, Buffett discovered that Guinness's well-known drinks were not so impervious to competition as he had figured—and he abruptly sold the stock, taking an estimated 15 to 20 percent loss. In the not-too-distant future, it is not unthinkable that Coca-Cola and Gillette, in which Buffett has much bigger investments, will face serious threats to their profit margins.

Similarly, if the futurologists are even partly right, newspapers and networks will have to contend with a proliferation of new outlets, and even with new forms, of news and entertainment. Though it is far too early to single out winners and losers, it is a good bet that once-safe media companies will find their "toll bridges" under attack.

Perhaps that helped to explain Buffett's quick response to Michael Eisner, chairman of Walt Disney, in summer 1995. Buffett and Eisner were guests at investment banker Herb Allen's annual retreat for entertainment moguls and family members in Sun Valley, Idaho. Eisner was packed and ready to leave the pristine resort, but on his way to the parking lot he bumped into Buffett and blurted out, "What do you think about selling ABC for cash?"

Buffett had sworn never to abandon Tom Murphy, his friend and the Cap Cities/ABC chairman. But Buffett's instincts told him that Murphy, who had resisted such overtures in the past, might be ready, particularly if Eisner could be persuaded to pay in stock. And Buffett himself thought the company was ripe. Though still Cap Cities' biggest shareholder, he had recently sold some of his stock at $63 a share.* By the time he saw Eisner in Sun Valley, the stock, benefiting from a cyclical upturn in advertising, had vaulted to $102.

"Sounds good to me," Buffett shot back. "Why don't we talk to Murph?" Coincidentally, Buffett was on his way to play golf with Murphy and also with Bill Gates, and suggested that Eisner come along.

*Prices of Cap Cities/ABC shares are adjusted for a ten-for-one split in 1994.

Murphy seemed unsure. But at the right price, the prospect of combining ABC's network with Disney's famous brand name and product line was irresistible. After the retreat, Eisner and Murphy, counseled as usual by Buffett, began to negotiate in earnest. Murphy's main concern was that his own shareholders get a chance to participate going forward—what he called a "ticket on the horse race."

Incredibly, they cut a deal in only two weeks. Disney would acquire Cap Cities/ABC for $19.5 billion—the second biggest deal in history, trailing only RJR Nabisco. Cap Cities shareholders—Berkshire included, of course—got $127 a share, seven times Buffett's going-in price of 17¼. (As Murphy and Eisner had compromised and made it a part-stock, part-cash acquisition, Berkshire became a big investor in Disney, one of the best of Buffett's early stocks in the 1960s.) Buffett's total profit from investing with Murphy, long his favorite CEO, was just over $2.5 billion.

And Buffett had a big idea for what to do with his profit—to finally close the loop with GEICO, the investment that had bewitched him literally from the start of his career, in Ben Graham's investment class. As a salesman starting out in his father's brokerage, he had bought the stock for himself and touted it to customers. In 1951, the *Commercial and Financial Chronicle* had published Buffett's write-up of GEICO next to a mug shot of the buttoned-down, cherubic twenty-one-year-old under the apt title "The Security I Like Best."[8] By the 1980s, Berkshire owned half of GEICO.

Buffett had occasionally given thought to buying the rest, which traded publicly. But in the 1990s, GEICO had been a disappointment. Its success had been based on direct marketing to low-risk automobile drivers, but it had stumbled by going into new areas such as finance, home insurance, and aviation insurance. And William Snyder, the CEO who succeeded Jack Byrne, had bought a couple of insurance companies that weren't direct marketers. Its profit slumped, due partly to Hurricane Andrew; worse, GEICO seemed to have lost its focus.

Buffett, plainly unhappy, aired his concern with two influential GEICO directors, Samuel Butler and Lou Simpson.[9] Buffett even said he was thinking of selling his stock—a comment certain to alarm them. Butler and Simpson, who had been worried about

GEICO even before, now decided that Snyder should be eased out as CEO a year ahead of his planned retirement. Buffett backed them and Snyder did step aside. Buffett's silent coup complete, GEICO began to reform itself to Buffett's liking. It quickly moved to dump its unsuccessful and distracting sidelines and to put more capital into its core auto lines.

By 1994, Buffett was sufficiently pleased that he opened merger talks with Butler and Simpson. A year later—just after the Disney deal—Buffett struck again, agreeing that Berkshire would acquire the rest of GEICO for $2.3 billion. Superficially, it was a rich price, but given Buffett's time horizon and GEICO's renewed growth prospects, it was not so rich as it seemed. And Buffett now owned all of the security he had "liked best" for forty-four years. Jack Byrne said it was "predestined."

Even before the GEICO deal, Buffett had been sending signals of his renewed enthusiasm for insurance—the game of odds that so suits him. In particular, Berkshire's in-house insurance operation, which will be increasingly important to Berkshire's future, has for some time been writing special reinsurance policies, known as "super-cats," which is Buffett-speak for super-catastrophics.

Insurance companies buy super-cats for protection against a mega-disaster that would require them to pay claims on a great number of policies. Berkshire got into the business in 1989, after the twin calamities of Hurricane Hugo and the World Series–shattering earthquake in San Francisco. With insurers devastated and premiums soaring, Buffett sensed the sort of bad news–cum–opportunity that has always aroused his interest.

Since then, Berkshire's super-cat business has grown to be enormous. In most years, it is extremely profitable. But in an unusually bad year, one with a series of big disasters or a single blow such as a Hurricane Andrew, Berkshire could be stuck with *gigantic* losses, possibly as much as $600 million.[10] (Few insurers write super-cats, because the stakes are so big.)

Buffett and Ajit Jain, the Indian-born, Harvard-educated star of Berkshire's super-cat business, who works in Connecticut, frequently chat about the odds of a major earthquake in New Zealand, a flood in the Midwest, or a radical change in long-term climatic patterns.[11] But super-cats occur too infrequently for the odds to be figured with precision, so Buffett and Jain must rely on judgment and on an informed reading of history.

Who would have guessed, Buffett recently wrote, that the United States' most serious quake would occur in New Madrid, Missouri? It did, in 1812—an estimated 8.7 on the Richter scale. "Now you know why I suffer eyestrain: from watching The Weather Channel."[12]

Thanks largely to super-cats, Berkshire's insurance float has multiplied tenfold over a decade. In 1995, the float was $3.6 billion, a figure which will nearly double with the addition of GEICO. This money may be thought of as a low-interest loan, which is Buffett's to play with until claims are made. In recent years, Buffett has had the use of this immense sum at an effective cost that is lower than the rate on long-term government bonds. This gives Buffett a huge advantage.

Though normally reluctant to talk up the future, Buffett has been predicting a rosy one for his insurance operation. He has said that he and Munger expect it to be their "main source of earnings for decades to come," and has hinted that he thinks its value is enormous.[13] But as Buffett freely admits, it will be hard to evaluate his bet on super-cats until decades of loss experience can be toted up.

Given this embarrassment of riches—from Disney to GEICO to super-cats—it is small surprise that the public's expectations for Berkshire were becoming inflated. By early 1996, its share price was swelling toward $40,000. Buffett was worried that the shares were becoming bait for speculators, and he was highly agitated by the plans of a couple of promoters to take advantage of Berkshire's unusual share price by peddling low-priced "clones." (The promoters intended to create investment trusts that would purchase shares of Berkshire and then sell low-priced units to the public.) Obsessed, as usual, with controlling every aspect of Berkshire, Buffett decided to beat these promoters to the punch with a baby Berkshire of his own.

In a sort of do-it-yourself stock split, Buffett devised a new issue of Berkshire—Class B common stock—worth $1/30$ of the old shares and expected to trade at $1/30$ the price. Shareholders could hang on to the ordinary common, now known as Class A, or (at any time) convert—one A share for thirty B shares. (Buffett would keep the high-priced variety.) Of course, in value terms they were identical: the same pizza cut in thirty slices.

But given that small investors attracted to his celebrity might be especially tempted to hop aboard the "cheaper" B stock, Buffett did what virtually no chief executive has ever done—he warned that the price of his stock (then $36,000) was more than he would pay for it. Berkshire's intrinsic value had continued to grow at an impressive rate, but its stock, in recent years, had overperformed it, Buffett warned in his latest annual report. *"Inevitably, there will be periods of underperformance as well."* In short, investors who pay too much for Berkshire—or any stock—implicitly are betting on its high performance to continue, perhaps for many years into the future.

Discussion of such an extended time period makes Buffett's shareholders uncomfortable. It reminds them of the one "super-cat" they fear the most. As one shareholder and longtime friend admitted bluntly, "All of us have a vested interest in Warren's good health."[14]

Among the stockholders, the size of the "Buffett premium"—that is, the amount above fair value that Buffett's presence adds to the stock—is a subject of endless debate. It is feared that his death could be followed by panic selling, though, as Buffett would be quick to point out, his death would not affect the value of Berkshire's Coca-Cola stock or of any of its other assets. Save for rare occasions, such as his recent annual letter, Buffett does not comment on what *he* thinks Berkshire is worth. His policy is to disclose what he will about the company and let trading follow its course.

But the obsession with Buffett's longevity is one that Buffett, though for different reasons, feels more keenly than anyone. He repeats at every turn the quip that he plans to run Berkshire for at least a few years after his death, via séances. (No saying goodbye to Berkshire, even then.)

When Doris, his elder sister, researched the Buffett family tree, Warren said the only thing *he* wanted to know about his ancestors was how long they had lived.[15] Another time, he remarked to a friend that although scientists had not found a correlation between age and wealth, he didn't think they had ever studied age and *super*wealth.[16] Still again, when a shareholder asked what his goal was, now that he had become the richest man in the country, Buffett spit out, "To become the oldest one."[17] Even in his private life, he married a woman with a singular interest in helping people cope with death.

It is scarcely implausible that Buffett's fear of death has contributed to his drive to accumulate. Agnostic and hyperrational, he has few other opiates. His one passion has been to collect—not money, precisely, but tangible evidence of himself. He clings to his friends, his house, his old foods and stock lines, and his stocks themselves. Notably, he says he does not enjoy running businesses; he enjoys *owning* them.[18] In the view of his friend Barbara Morrow, the formative trauma of his life was when he was yanked out of Omaha to go to school in Washington—a forced separation. He has been accumulating assets, but hardly ever selling or disengaging from them, ever since. As he commented in a recent letter, "We like to buy. Selling, however, is a different story."[19] In a sense, his whole career has been an act of holding on—of refusing to say goodbye.

One sees him in Omaha, on a spring Sunday morning, the day before Berkshire's annual meeting. An ersatz trolley car, not too different from the one Buffett rode as a boy, is making the rounds of Omaha's hotels, picking up his guests. Buffett is at the front of the trolley. He heartily greets his visitors—the widow of a longtime friend from Wharton, a fellow student of Ben Graham's, the CEO of a company Buffett owns—who step from various stages of his life as from the pages in an album. Buffett, who is dressed casually and is in a jovial mood, guides the trolley to his country club, where he is throwing a brunch for more than one hundred of his closest disciple-friend-admirers.

In the afternoon, the festivities, now open to all shareholders, continue at Borsheim's. Tables of caviar, raspberry-and-kiwi tarts, cheesecake, and horseradished roast beef are set beside the jewelry and fine china. A string quartet entertains, and tuxedo-clad porters ease among the crowd ferrying velvet-cased diamonds and trays of champagne.

Buffett has been in a back room, playing bridge with some pals. As the party picks up steam, he quietly saunters in and stakes out a position against a rack of diamond earrings. Shareholders screw up their courage and wander over in groups of twos and threes. Buffett gets a charge out of it, not from the aspect of spectacle, exactly, but from the feeling that all of these people are *included* in his personal show.

Most of the faces at Borsheim's are familiar to Buffett. He mentions that he knows a relative of 90 percent of Berkshire's 7,500 shareholders on sight. He greets James Earl, a balding astronomy professor, and proudly recalls that Earl's parents invested with Buffett in the partnership back in 1957. Indeed, Buffett tracks the destiny of every one of Berkshire's million-plus shares—a level of familiarity that no other public CEO would dream of or, for that matter, even remotely desire. But Buffett knows them all. Each time a share of Berkshire trades, Buffett makes a mental note of it, as though someone were getting on and off his trolley.

This helps to explain Buffett's hold on his admirers. As uncanny as his success has been, his sense of fidelity is even rarer. His faithfulness to old friends and old habits illuminates his entire career. Consider, for a moment, the advice of John Train in his best-selling *The Money Masters:*

> Everything has its season, which does not last forever. The world changes its spots, and the investor must change his.[20]

Few people on Wall Street would disagree, or even give it a second thought. The former disciples of debt, the Kravises and the Perelmans and the rest, have already lost their taste for leverage and in the nineties are selling equity.

Yet Buffett has spent a lifetime wearing essentially the same spots. He has never opted for investment fashions, be it the Go-Go stocks of the sixties, the high leverage of the eighties, or the derivatives of the nineties. He has continued to hunt for the irreducible kernel that his teacher labeled "intrinsic value."

Much has been made of Buffett's metamorphosis away from Ben Graham, from "value" stocks to "growth" companies. The Street is fond of such pigeonholes, just as the critic of art is quick to recognize a Blue Period or a cubist phase. But such boundaries are irrelevant to the artist. To Buffett, the growth/value distinction has always been illusory. He sees the growth potential of a business as a *component* of its value, just as its assets are a component.[21] At a price, Coca-Cola's potential represents good value; at some higher price, it does not.

The point is that Buffett views *all* investing, and all that he has ever attempted, as "value investing." Anything else, he wrote a year after the Salomon episode, is unworthy of the name:

What is "investing" if it is not the act of seeking value at least sufficient to justify the amount paid? Consciously paying more for a stock
than its calculated value—in the hope that it can soon be sold for a
still-higher price—should be labeled speculation. . . .[22]

The world has largely lost sight of that distinction. The treasurer
of Orange County, California, thought nothing of borrowing heavily
and then speculating with the funds for public schools, roads, and
waterworks on esoteric interest-rate derivatives, as a consequence of
which the county recently went into bankruptcy. Indeed, the notion
of *intrinsic* value is itself something of a lost ideal. In a world of
shifting benchmarks and changing "spots," value is not intrinsic but
ephemeral; the painting cannot be appreciated until the critic weighs
in, and beauty is truly up to the beholder. In Orange County, beauty
was whatever the treasurer or Merrill Lynch, his broker, said it was.
Neither really knew, and therefore both were willing to speculate. At
the other end of the spectrum, this lack of conviction results more
commonly in cowardice and mediocrity.

If we have lost the people with Emersonian inner conviction, it is
because we have lost the fixed stars that formerly guided them. The
modern relativism has reduced us all to being timid specialists, peep-
ing out from cubbyholes marked "growth" and "derivative." For similar reasons—the lack of intrinsic value systems—educators waffle
and juries seem unable to convict. They retreat, as it were, into ambiguity, complexity, and cacophony. Where one conviction is lacking,
a thousand opinions will do—indeed, they become a necessary re-
course. Our captains seem the smaller for it, not only on Wall Street
but in industry, education, government, and public life in general.

Buffett, in contrast, seems the larger for his rare independence. As
he expressed it, "I don't have to work with people I don't like."[23]
There are few people, CEOs and statesmen included, who would say
the same.

We see him in his inner sanctum, without advisers or lackeys, opposite the framed and fading newspapers and the looming picture of
his father, who counseled him toward just such sweet Emersonian
solitude. Hours pass without interruption; the telephone scarcely
rings. He is looking not for patterns on a screen but for the fundamental values, the time-honored merchants, the shoe companies,

the Horatio Alger–Rose Blumkins, the Ben Rosner retailers, the *World Books*, the salt–of–New Bedford Ken Chaces, the scrupulous Tom Murphys, the universal Coca-Colas. He judges them not according to the "season," but by the sound principles and aphorisms that his father or grandfather or Ben Graham might have recognized. Buffett has not always lived up to his heroes. He is only human, and he certainly has strayed. But he has at least been able to evoke their memory.

When Buffett is called to *his* reward, it is likely that his bequest will dwarf the legacies of Carnegie, Ford, Rockefeller, and all that have gone before him.[24] The Buffett Foundation will probably find itself with the largest endowment in the country (the Ford Foundation, the biggest, has assets of $7 billion). But the legacy that preoccupies Buffett is not what will happen to his money, but what will happen to Berkshire itself. He harbors a ghoulish fantasy that once he is in the grave, Berkshire will continue to operate as in the past. Indeed, he has taken pains to assure investors that whether he or his wife dies first, "in neither case will taxes and bequests require the sale of consequential amounts of stock."[25]

If Buffett and Munger are leveled by the same truck, or if Buffett does not get around to grooming a successor, the company, at least temporarily, will be run by a "third man," chosen by Buffett. The identity of this Harry Lime has long been secret, even to Buffett's children.* But after the GEICO deal, Buffett revealed that GEICO's Lou Simpson would be called on to pinch hit for Berkshire "if something were to happen to Charlie and me."[26]

Beyond that, Berkshire will be in the hands of its board, which Buffett has handpicked. He has recently appointed his wife and son Howie as directors, steps that he hopes will perpetuate the company's sense of mission. (The other directors are Buffett; Malcolm G. Chace III, the son of the former chairman; Munger; and Omaha businessman Walter Scott, Jr.) His family members will represent the controlling owner, presumably the foundation. "All in all," Buffett wrote recently, "we're prepared for 'the truck.' "[27]

At sixty-five, Buffett is in excellent health, though he seems to have slept through the dietary revolution of the professional classes.

---

*Harry Lime was the mystery figure played by Orson Welles in the 1949 film classic *The Third Man*.

It is not uncommon for him to greet the morning with a bowl of peanuts and a Cherry Coke. During a Super Bowl weekend organized by Tom Murphy, Buffett ordered vanilla ice cream and chocolate sauce for breakfast. When his friends started kidding him about his health, he responded stagily: "What I want people to say when they pass my casket is—'*Boy*, was he old!' "[28]

Though still absorbed in his work, Buffett has become a tad less intense with his success. His sons say he is more relaxed than in years back; Peter is no longer aware of the clock ticking in his father's head.

Some of this may be attributable to Astrid, with whom Buffett has grown highly comfortable. Buffett thinks that he has helped her self-esteem,[29] and no doubt draws pleasure from a sense of reciprocity. When Buffett and Astrid go out, say, to Gorats, Buffet looks like any Omaha gentleman and his wife, sometimes draping an affectionate arm around her.[30] Astrid has a sense of humor about her role and has told one of Buffett's relatives that living with Warren is "the best job" she has had. Joe Rosenfield, Buffett's octogenarian friend, says, "Astrid is what he needs now. He can go off and leave her and she doesn't mind. She's a free spirit—a girl of quality."

For all that, Warren is deeply attached to Susie, with whom he reunites in one corner or another (such as in Paris for a board meeting of Coca-Cola) every month or so. Warren also has a sense of humor about the arrangement; he told a friend that he couldn't divorce Susie because she is too rich.[31]

Recently, Buffett has somewhat loosened his purse strings. He spent $1.25 million of his own money for a 25 percent interest in Omaha's minor league baseball team—effectively an act of charity to keep the team in town.[32] In 1993, on the occasion of Mrs. B's hundredth birthday, Buffett eschewed his usual gift of flowers and See's candy and presented a check for $1 million to the Rose Blumkin Performing Arts Center, an abandoned vaudeville house Mrs. B was converting into a children's theater. He also spends a bit more personally, such as on his travel and on his pricey suits, though the latter seem to develop rumples even in his closet. But in relative terms, his spending (as well as his philanthropy) remains a flyspeck.*

---

*In 1994, Buffett's two foundations gave away just a shade more than the $7 million they received from the Berkshire gift program and from interest and dividend income combined. In 1995, Buffett raised Berkshire's per-share gift from $11 to $12.

His life is his work; food and shelter are minor matters. Buffett still drives his own car, a blue Lincoln Town Car. He has no fancy automobiles or homes, and he would not be interested in them if he had. On a recent two-week stay at his ocean-view home in Laguna Beach, he went out of the house but three times—twice to a movie and once to have lunch (his daughter counted). He still plays bridge, but usually via a computer (which he refuses to use for work) many miles away from his partners.[33]

In Omaha, Buffett has become a curiosity. People drive by Farnam Street very slowly, sometimes slowing to a stop, gaping with wonderment at the incongruously modest house by the blinking light. Buffett can see them from his kitchen, where he might be scooping out some ice cream, or grabbing a Cherry Coke to take to his "pit," to settle in with papers and annual reports. He and Astrid are alone in the house. Buffett has no flunkies or hangers-on, and the two of them have no butlers or household staff—only a maid who comes every other week.[34] Astrid still prowls the stores for bargains, and loads up her station wagon with Cherry Coke when she finds it on sale.

Buffett does enjoy being a billionaire, but in offbeat ways. As he put it, though money cannot change your health or how many people love you, it lets you be in "more interesting environments."[35] Buffett mixes with a rarified crowd of CEOs, politicians, and others. Gary Kasparov, the world chess champion, who has an interest in developing capitalism in Russia, has called on Buffett in Omaha. The end of summer 1994 found Buffett on Martha's Vineyard, golfing with Bill Clinton, after which he and the President had a quiet dinner at Kay Graham's. Most notably, Buffett has developed an intriguing friendship with Bill Gates, his junior by twenty-six years and his financial rival. Though Gates is a technology freak and Buffett is anything but, they plainly have fun together. Both are fiercely competitive, genuinely curious, unusually boyish as CEOs go, and insanely rich. Having broken the ice at a Nebraska football game, in 1995 the two traveled together, and with their wives, to China.

And Buffett finds a receptive audience when he wants to distill the Zen of Warren Buffett. He goes around quite often now, at college campuses, at his companies, even in smaller, informal groups, launching into his liturgy, retelling his stories, serenading as many onto his trolley as he can.

Much about this life is strange, and much about Buffett remains obscure. Perhaps, as a judge in Buffalo once remarked of his purported monopolist aims, the private man may be secreted "in the unfathomable human mind."

But the public legacy is secure. Buffett's uncommon urge to chronicle made him a unique character in American life, not only a great capitalist but the Great Explainer of American capitalism. He taught a generation how to think about business, and he showed that securities were not just tokens like the Monopoly flatiron, and that investing need not be a game of chance. It was also a logical, commonsensical enterprise, like the tangible businesses beneath. He stripped Wall Street of its mystery and rejoined it to Main Street—a mythical or disappearing place, perhaps, but one that is comprehensible to the ordinary American.

As opposed to the dark side of Wall Street, to which the public was so accustomed, Buffett's was a face not often seen. He was one of the few capitalists who got fabulously rich without leaving a trail of those he had victimized. (His adversaries in Buffalo were a singular exception). In Munger's phrase, he strove to be more than a "miserable accumulator," in particular by treating investors and investees as partners, with no fingers crossed and no "exit strategies."

And it is here that Buffett begins to transcend finance and to claim a space on a broader canvas. His comment that his favorite holding period was "forever" was a stunning breach of the usual horizon both on Wall Street and off it. "Forever" has an embarrassing ring to postmodern ears; the word seems to belong to dime novels and fairy tales.

Buffett made that pledge to his candy business, his newspaper, to Tom Murphy and Kay Graham and many more. In an age of fraying loyalties, he turned investments into relationships, almost into a form of social contract. As he wrote to his partners in 1969, with regard to Berkshire Hathaway:

> I certainly have no desire to sell a good controlled business run by people I like and admire, merely to obtain a fancy price.[36]

Such a sentiment was unheard-of on Wall Street and blasphemous in academia, but rare on Main Street as well.

It is more stunning today because it is more rare; it deviates not only from the fickleness of mutual funds, but from all in society that is transient. Today, the frenetic trading at Wall and Broad may be seen as a metaphor for the rapidity with which once-firm social connections, to job, neighborhood, family, civic affiliation, and the past itself, become unglued. And unglued each day all the faster. When Andy Warhol predicted fifteen minutes of fame for each of us, he did not get the half of it. In these restless times, it is not only our fame that disappears in a quarter of an hour, but, seemingly, every relationship that once was enduring or valued for its ongoing character. Professional partnerships splinter apart, athletic heroes desert their teams, employers overhire and then overfire, and even our universities, the supposed repositories of our past, race to reinvent the canons that had served for a near-millennium. In our daily walks of life, the faces on the trolley change overnight. Investors seek their exit strategies, but they are hardly alone. Viewed in this light, Wall Street's mania for shuffling paper is only the most blatant sign of the general rush to put a price on once-lasting commitments. This is why Buffett filled a hollow. More than most, he reclaimed the rewards that spring not from trading commitments one for the next, but from preserving them.

AFTERWORD

January 2008

Some months after *Buffett* was published, in the spring of 1996, I made the pilgrimage to Omaha for the Berkshire Hathaway, Inc., annual meeting. Before the formalities got under way, Buffett was seated at a small table greeting shareholders, many of whom bore books, annual reports, and memorabilia for him to sign. Having spent three-plus years writing his biography, without as yet having gotten any feedback, I thought the moment had arrived. I fetched one of my own copies of *Buffett* and joined the queue. As I did so, I remembered what Buffett had told me years before when I was doing my research—that he would not attempt to block me, but neither would he give me any help. And so as I handed him the book, as well as a ballpoint, I said emphatically, "Now I *will* ask for something." He grimaced as if he were cornered. Then he flung the book open to the title page, etched the words "Warren Buffett" in his trademark scrawl, and shut the volume tight, as though sealing it against any protest I might utter, any plea for an intimacy or for a response that might, at the very least, reveal something of his reaction.

When readers ask if there is anything I would change about the portrait of Buffett in this book, I often think of that bare-bones autograph. Bill Ruane, his since-departed friend, remarked around that time, "I'm not sure if you captured just how *tough* Warren is." Perhaps Bill was right. Buffett did not build a company worth $220 billion (sixth largest in the United States) by being an easy mark; in particular, he did not dodge every investment land mine of the past half century without possessing a hard outer shell—a unique ability to say no to all manner of investment promoters, bubble profiteers, and well-meaning but deluded brokers. And even to inquiring biographers. He answered to no one but himself.

The other question that arises, with increasing frequency, is "Will there be a sequel?" That one is easier. Very little in the portrait, and nothing in the investment profile, has changed. That may sound strange, given the relentless expansion of Berkshire's assets, not to mention the astounding continued rise in its stock. At year-end 1994, Berkshire Hathaway was trading at $20,400 a share; thirteen years later, the stock has hit the eye-popping figure of $141,600. (To update the set of figures in the introduction, an original partnership investor who had given $10,000 to Buffett in 1956, which in the dollars of that day would have paid the salary of a baseball star such as Ted Williams for two weeks, today would be worth $550 million, or enough to sign an Alex Rodriguez for twenty seasons.)

As lofty as it is, the current share price is actually evidence of a marked deceleration. In the first three decades after Buffett dislodged Seabury Stanton and began to transform Berkshire from a sleepy New England textile manufacturer into a media, insurance, and industrial conglomerate, the stock rose at a rate of 27 percent a year (which means that it doubled every third year). Alas, since the initial publication of *Buffett*, the stock has advanced at merely 16 percent per annum. The "slowdown" is not news; it is exactly what Buffett predicted. The laws of mathematics assured that as Berkshire grew larger, each new investment would have a smaller impact on the whole. The growth rate would *have* to diminish. What *is* news, or at least cannot fail to impress, is the extent to which, even at the slower gait of his septuagenarian years, Buffett has left the market in the dust. Which is to say, post 1994 the broad market average is up two times, Berkshire *six* times.

The more recent performance is a testimony to Buffett's consistency, which may be his least appreciated trait. His first rule ("Never lose money") was expressed so glibly that it may have been taken for a lighthearted quip; with the perspective of more time, it emerges as one of the keys to his success. The last dozen years, in particular, have seen more than their share of investment folly. We need only recall the ill-fated rush to lend to the teetering, newly capitalist Russia of the 1990s, or the collapse of the meteoric hedge fund Long-Term Capital Management (LTCM), or the madness of the dot-com bubble. During the last of those episodes, shares of companies with no prospect of realizing earnings soared while Berkshire's stock, confounding all logic and despite steadily rising earnings, was cut in half. The public became obsessed with twenty-something website promoters, and it was commonly said that Buffett was outmoded, an old-economy relic, and so forth. To Buffett, it was a replay of the Go-Go era of the 1960s; the speculative mania, rather than tempting him into taking more risk, redoubled his innate sense of caution. Seeing the apparent profits of their neighbors, investors who knew better jumped into the game, but not Buffett. "Never lose money" is an unyielding standard; it forecloses the option of taking *any* speculative risks. This is why Buffett has so outdistanced investors who earn impressive returns in many years but who, on occasion, succumb to speculation and suffer punishing losses. The effect of even an occasional severe loss on cumulative returns is devastating.

In 2007, Berkshire stock vaulted 29 percent (making Buffett once again the U.S.'s and now, most likely, the world's richest man). The outsize gain seemed a belated recognition of Buffett's prudent approach. As investors panicked and fled to safety, T-bills fetched a premium and so—almost as if it were a branch of the Treasury Department—did Berkshire Hathaway. The context is worth revisiting, if only because the script is so familiar. America was in the throes of yet another financial crisis, this one triggered by waves of mortgage defaults and foreclosures, which themselves were the fruit of a sharp escalation in housing prices that had given rise to unsound lending practices. Even financial institutions not generally associated with mortgage lending were deeply implicated, because they had invested in mortgage-backed securities.

When the real estate market finally cooled, the losses were horrendous. Virtually every major financial institution—from Citigroup to Merrill Lynch to Bear Stearns to General Electric—was burned. Berkshire had owned a big piece of Freddie Mac, the mortgage giant, but Buffett had sold it years before, out of concern that it was trying to grow too fast. In the debacle of 2007, Berkshire was not only unscathed, it emerged with $45 billion in liquid assets, as well as an unblemished, triple-A credit rating. Devastated bond insurers reached out to Buffett for relief, and there were frequent rumors that Berkshire would come to the rescue of this or that beleaguered lender. Buffett, of course, had recapitalized Salomon Brothers when it was on the skids, and in 1998 he came very close to inking a deal to rescue (on advantageous terms) the hedge fund LTCM. By the time of the mortgage crisis, he, or his company, had become a unique American institution—akin to that of J. P. Morgan, Sr., a century earlier. It was, or was uniquely capable of being, a lifeboat to Wall Street's fallen, the firm whose credit was invariably soundest when the system was under its greatest stress. As if to seal this legacy, at year-end '07 Berkshire made a $4.5 billion acquisition of diversified assets—its biggest outside of the insurance industry ever. At the age of seventy-seven, Buffett was reaping the benefits of the watchword of his distant forebear Zebulon: "Save your credit, for that is better than money."

His corporate empire (which begins, as always, with insurance, and includes dozens of businesses ranging from private aviation to carpeting to water treatment products to household paints) is larger today and more diverse than a decade ago. Berkshire also has invested overseas, in countries as disparate as Israel and China. And the relative concentration of industries has shifted—away from the newspapers he loved as a boy and other media assets, which have been hit hard by the Internet. In recent years, with his usual astute sense of timing, Buffett has acquired huge interests in energy. But Buffett has always followed opportunity, and as he still adheres to the price and value discipline that he learned at Ben Graham's knee, nothing about his approach has changed.

Buffett is also more celebrated today as a public figure. In the early 1990s, people often asked me to repeat the name of my subject, as though trying to commit a strange new word to memory. No such obscurity shrouds Buffett today. His avuncular face—more rounded with age—stares out from magazine covers and television specials; his comments are headlined on CNBC; he is friendly with baseball stars (indeed, with A-Rod) and with Democratic politicians from Hillary Clinton to Barack Obama. But the change has been evolutionary, not sudden, and the urge to command a public audience was always there, even in his twenties, when his friends would gather at his feet and listen to his financial sermons in awestruck silence.

Buffett has made one truly significant change — a reworking of his estate. Ironically, though this is a personal matter, it is likely to influence his public legacy more than any investment he has made. Half a century ago, as a Pepsi-Cola-imbibing young man, Buffett agonized (as he admitted to Jerry Orans) over what to do with his fortune — a fortune he had not yet obtained but that he was sure would one day be his. The problem nagged at him for fifty years, looming larger as his assets grew. Always he had the cushion of believing that his wife, Susie, would outlive him, and that if need be she would dispose of their assets. However, in 2004 Susie died of a stroke. Buffett married his longtime companion, Astrid Menks, but the inheritance issue could no longer be postponed. In 2006, Buffett stunningly reversed his intention to hang on to his assets until death — and announced a plan to slowly give away (with annual bequests) 85 percent of his Berkshire stock. Five-sixths of the money will go to the Bill and Melinda Gates Foundation, which is primarily dedicated to fighting disease in the developing world. The rest will go to four family foundations (one that was his and Susie's and three others, each of which is run by one of the Buffett children).

The plan to transfer stock to Gates was a lightning bolt that only Buffett could have conceived of. Combining his money with that of his close friend — in recent years the only American richer than he — will create by far the world's largest foundation. The size of Buffett's annual gifts will depend, of course, on the future level of Berkshire stock, but at current prices, Buffett has a fortune of $64 billion — probably the greatest on earth. And yet, what is truly notable about the plan is its modesty. It is not just that the bulk of Buffett's money will be administered by someone else, and that no hospitals will bear the Buffett name, nor will researchers, scientists, and doctors around the globe associate their funding with the Oracle of Omaha. It is his trademark insistence on staying within his "circle of competence" — on doing only what *he* is good at. By temperament, he was a poor philanthropist. He was too fearful of not getting good value to feel easy about writing checks (or perhaps, to use a Buffettism, he was simply too cheap). In any case, his refusal to give, or to give in proportion to his means, has long been a sore spot to his friends. And so, turning his logical mind to his own estate, he coolly decided to give his money to someone better equipped to dispense of it than he — a trusted friend who in all likelihood should have decades remaining to oversee the bequests and who, most important, has conceived of a purpose worthy of Buffett's billions: ridding the poorest regions of the globe of disease. As a portfolio manager, Buffett has always tried to concentrate on a few stocks — a *very* few — that he both understood and felt comfortable with. With his estate, similarly, it is as though Buffett sees in the Gates couple, Melinda as well as Bill, a superstock of philanthropy — a nondiversified vehicle through which his assets will, conceivably, do more to improve human health, and perhaps even human living standards, than anyone's money ever. The man who taught America how to invest is writing a new chapter on giving it away.

NOTES

In the notes that follow, names appearing without reference to any published works, public gatherings, or archival materials indicate an interview with the author.

"SEC File No. HO-784, *Blue Chip Stamps, et al.*" refers to a 1974–76 Securities and Exchange Commission investigation of Blue Chip, Berkshire Hathaway, and Buffett. Notes beginning with "SEC File No. HO-784" followed by a slash "/" indicate materials which, while unrelated to the case, were collected by the SEC and released to the author under the Freedom of Information Act.

INTRODUCTION

1. Figures are based on total returns, 1957–1995. The "major" averages are the Standard & Poor's 500 and the Dow Jones Industrial Average, as calculated by S & P and Lipper Analytical Securities. Buffett Partnership had a compound annual gain of 29.5 percent for 1957–69 inclusive, before fees to Buffett. From 1970 through 1995, shares of Berkshire Hathaway advanced at a compound rate of 29.2 percent.

2. The calculation assumes that one invested $10,000 in Buffett Partnership prior to 1957, Buffett's first full year, and that when the partnership disbanded, at the end of 1969, one used the investment (then worth $160,270) to buy 3,909 shares of Berkshire Hathaway, then priced at $41 a share, and held to December 31, 1995.

3. Berkshire Hathaway Inc., 1989 *Annual Report*, 21.

4. Peter Derow.

5. Berkshire Hathaway Inc., 1982 *Annual Report*, 11.

6. Jack Newfield, *Robert Kennedy: A Memoir* (New York: Dutton, 1969), 19.

7. Wyndham Robertson.

8. Peter Lynch.

Chapter 1. OMAHA

1. Doris Buffett Bryant researched the family lineage.

2. Lincoln initially designated the neighboring city of Council Bluffs, Iowa, as the terminus. However, the site was changed to Omaha. George R. Leighton, "Omaha, Nebraska: The Glory is Departed," *Harper's Monthly*, July and August, 1938; Lawrence H. Larsen and Barbara J. Cottrell, *The Gate City: A History of Omaha* (Boulder, Colo.: Pruett, 1982).

3. Leighton, "Omaha, Nebraska."

4. John Taylor, "Grocery Will Close After 100 Years," *Omaha World-Herald*, October 29, 1969 [italics added].

5. Robert McMorris, "Leila Buffett Basks in Value of Son's Life, Not Fortune," *Omaha World-Herald*, May 16, 1987.

6. Leila Buffett's memoirs.

7. Ernest Buffett, letter to Clarence Buffett, March 28, 1930.

8. Leila Buffett's memoirs.

9. L. J. Davis, "Buffett Takes Stock," *New York Times*, April 1, 1990.

10. Leila Buffett's memoirs.

11. Ibid.

12. Robert Falk.

13. "The Money Men: How Omaha Beats Wall Street," *Forbes*, November 1, 1969; Davis, "Buffett Takes Stock."

14. Bob Russell.

15. Warren's sisters attested to his fear.

16. Carol J. Loomis, "The Inside Story of Warren Buffett," *Fortune*, April 11, 1988.

17. Warren's sisters declined to discuss their mother's "moods" in detail, but confirmed that Leila had such outbreaks and provided background.

18. Peter Buffett.

19. Stuart Erickson.

20. Arthur W. Baum, "Omaha," *Saturday Evening Post*, September 10, 1949.

21. "Omaha: A Guide to the City and Environs" (unpublished, part of the American Guide Series, Federal Writers' Project, Works Progress Administration, 1930s). For descriptions of Depression Omaha, see also A *Comprehensive Program for Historic Preservation in Omaha* (Omaha: Landmarks Heritage Preservation Commission, 1980); Baum, "Omaha"; Larsen and Cottrell, *The Gate City*; and Leighton, "Omaha, Nebraska."

22. "Buffett Files for Congress, Fights 'Political Servitude,'" *Omaha World-Herald*, June 29, 1942.

23. Davis, "Buffett Takes Stock."

24. Ibid.

25. Doris Buffett Bryant.

26. Berkshire Hathaway Inc., *1985 Annual Report*, 10.

27. Ernest Buffett, letter to Clarence Buffett, March 28, 1930.

28. Gladys Mary Falk.

29. Charles Munger.

Chapter 2. RUNAWAY

1. Leila Buffett's memoirs.
2. For an account of Warren's time in Washington, see "The Corn-fed Capitalist," *Regardie's*, February 1986.
3. Doris Buffett Bryant.
4. Roger Bell; Doris Buffett Bryant; Roberta Buffett Bialek.
5. "Corn-fed Capitalist."
6. Warren Buffett, speech to newspaper circulation managers, June 11, 1985.
7. Ibid.
8. Adam Smith, *Supermoney* (New York: Random House, 1972), 180.
9. Robert Dwyer.
10. "Corn-fed Capitalist."
11. John Train, *The Money Masters* (New York: Harper & Row, 1980), 4.
12. "Corn-fed Capitalist."
13. Sam Fordyce.
14. Patricia E. Bauer, "The Convictions of a Long Distance Investor," *Channels*, November 1986.
15. "Buffett Asks U.S. Policy," *Omaha World-Herald*, March 26, 1944.
16. On aid to Britain, *Journal of the House of Representatives*, 79th Congress, 1st Session (Washington: U.S. Government Printing Office, 1946), 197–98; on school lunches, *Journal of the House*, 79th Congress, 2nd Session, 101–3; on grain exports, *Omaha World-Herald*, September 11, 1947; and on Bretton Woods, *Omaha World-Herald*, March 10, 1945.
17. Leila Buffett's memoirs.
18. "Buffett Lashes Marshall Plan," *Omaha World-Herald*, January 28, 1948. See also "Buffett Sees Stalin Trick," *Omaha World-Herald*, March 18, 1947.
19. Don Danly.
20. Warren Buffett, letter to Jerry Orans, August 4, 1950.
21. Martin Wiegand.
22. Davis, "Buffett Takes Stock."
23. Buffett, speech to circulation managers, 1985.
24. Anthony Vecchione.
25. Harry Beja.
26. Richard Kendall; Robert Martin; Anthony Vecchione.
27. Anthony Vecchione.
28. Robert Martin and Laurence Maxwell had the same recollection.
29. Davis, "Buffett Takes Stock."
30. Warren Buffett, letter to Jerry Orans, August 31, 1949.
31. Buffett, speech to circulation managers, 1985.
32. Warren Buffett, letter to Jerry Orans, January 30, 1950.
33. Warren Buffett, letter to Jerry Orans, April 29, 1950.
34. Warren Buffett, letter to Jerry Orans, July 19, 1950.
35. Buffett, speech to circulation managers, 1985.
36. Smith, *Supermoney*, 180.
37. Warren Buffett, letter to Jerry Orans, May 1, 1950.
38. Loomis, "Inside Story."
39. Warren Buffett, letter to Jerry Orans, August 4, 1950.
40. Wood was unsure of when the conversations took place. Loomis ("Inside

Story") said Buffett read *The Intelligent Investor* early in 1950, or when Buffett and Wood were living in Lincoln.

Chapter 3. GRAHAM

1. Elaine Sofer Hunt [Benjamin Graham's daughter].

2. Barbara Dodd Anderson.

3. The Germanic-sounding surname was changed during World War I.

4. This account draws on Irving Kahn and Robert D. Milne, *Benjamin Graham: The Father of Financial Analysis*, Occasional Paper Number 5, Financial Analysts Research Foundation.

5. Douglas W. Cray, "Benjamin Graham, Securities Expert," *New York Times*, September 23, 1976.

6. Kahn and Milne, *Benjamin Graham*, 12–16.

7. John Kenneth Galbraith, *The Great Crash* (1st ed. 1954; Boston: Houghton Mifflin, 1988), 70.

8. Ibid., 108–9.

9. Howard Newman.

10. Kahn and Milne, *Benjamin Graham*, 22.

11. Benjamin Graham and David L. Dodd, *Security Analysis* (New York: McGraw-Hill, 1934), 5.

12. Benjamin Graham, "Should Rich but Losing Corporations Be Liquidated?" *Forbes*, July 1, 1932.

13. Lawrence Chamberlain and William W. Hay, *Investment and Speculation*, as cited in Graham and Dodd, *Security Analysis*, 8.

14. Gerald M. Loeb, *The Battle for Investment Survival* (1st ed. 1935; New York: Hurry House, 1955), 22, 73, 65, 23.

15. Ibid., 57; see also 64–67.

16. Ibid., 33, 61–63, 68, 75.

17. Graham and Dodd, *Security Analysis*, 341.

18. Ibid., 22–23.

19. Benjamin Graham, "Are Corporations Milking Their Own Stockholders?" *Forbes*, June 1, 1932.

20. Graham and Dodd, *Security Analysis*, 3.

21. Ibid., 493 [italics added].

22. Ibid., 19; see also 14, 18.

23. Ibid., 22.

24. Graham, *The Intelligent Investor* (1st ed. 1949; 4th rev. ed., New York: Harper & Row, 1973), 277.

25. Ibid., 107.

26. Ibid., 108.

27. "How Omaha Beats Wall Street"; Robert Dorr, "Investor Warren Buffett Views Making Money as 'Big Game,'" *Omaha World-Herald*, March 24, 1985; Smith, *Supermoney*, 181.

28. Janet Lowe, *Benjamin Graham on Value Investing: Lessons from the Dean of Wall Street* (Chicago: Dearborn Financial Publishing, 1994), 158.

29. Jack Alexander; Loomis, "Inside Story."

30. Roger Murray.

31. Jack Alexander.

32. Kathryn M. Welling, "The Right Stuff: Why Walter Schloss Is Such a Great Investor," *Barron's*, February 25, 1985.

33. Walter Schloss; Loomis, "Inside Story."

34. Warren Buffett, talk at Columbia Business School, October 27, 1993.

35. Ibid.

36. Warren E. Buffett, "The Security I Like Best," *Commercial and Financial Chronicle*, December 6, 1951.

37. Buffett, talk at Columbia, 1993.

38. Graham, *Intelligent Investor*, 287.

39. "Corn-fed Capitalist."

40. Elaine Sofer Hunt.

41. Marjorie Graham Janis; Elaine Sofer Hunt; Benjamin Graham, Jr.

42. Warren Buffett, speech to Graham and Dodd commemorative seminar, Columbia Business School, May 17, 1984.

43. Warren Buffett, 1989 Capital Cities/ABC management conference.

44. Warren Buffett, 1992 annual meeting of Berkshire Hathaway.

45. "Columbia Business School, 1986" (annual report), 21.

46. Wayne Eves; Walter Schloss; Lowe, *Benjamin Graham*, 160.

47. Ron Chernow, *House of Morgan* (1st Touchstone ed. 1991; New York: Simon & Schuster, 1990), 581.

48. Barbara Morrow.

49. Robert Berkshire.

50. Al Pagel, "Susie Sings for More Than Her Supper," *Omaha World-Herald*, April 17, 1977.

51. Ibid.

52. Ibid.

53. Milton Brown; Dorothy Thompson Rogers.

54. Faith Stewart-Gordon.

55. Barbara Morrow.

56. Barbara Morrow; Marshall Weinberg.

57. Susan and Warren Buffett, eulogy for Daniel Cowin, 1992.

58. Lorimer Davidson; John J. Byrne, *Government Employees Insurance Company: The First Forty Years* (New York: Newcomen Society, 1981), 14 [account of Newcomen Society dinner, Washington, D.C., 1980]; Berkshire Hathaway Inc., 1995 *Annual Report*, 9.

59. Buffett, talk at Columbia, 1993.

60. Don Danly; Wayne Eves; Dan Monen.

61. Real estate: "2 Omaha Firms File Incorporation Papers," *Omaha World-Herald*, July 30, 1952. Texaco: Warren Buffett, 1992 annual meeting of Berkshire Hathaway.

62. "Columbia Business School, 1986," 21.

63. Robert Dorr, "Investor at 11, Warren Buffett Controls $45 Million Fund at 35," *Omaha World-Herald*, May 29, 1966.

64. Dan Monen; Leland Olson.

65. Leila Buffett's memoirs.

66. Doris Buffett Bryant.

67. Wayne Eves.

68. Lowe, *Benjamin-Graham*, 163.

69. Martin Mayer, *Wall Street: Men and Money* (1st ed. 1955; New York: Harper & Brothers, 1959), 118.

70. Tom Knapp. Graham articulated his fear in "The New Speculation in Common Stocks," *Analysts Journal*, June 1958.

71. Buffett, talk at Columbia, 1993; Tom Knapp.

72. Buffett, talk at Columbia, 1993.

73. Walter Schloss. Buffett referred to a personal holding in Union Street Railway in an August 1957 letter to Jerry Orans.

74. Berkshire Hathaway Inc., *1988 Annual Report*, 15.

75. Howard Newman.

76. Irving Kahn; Walter Schloss.

77. Lowe, *Benjamin Graham*, 169.

78. Ibid., 167.

79. Ibid.

80. Lorimer Davidson.

81. Lowe, *Benjamin Graham*, 162.

82. Walter Schloss.

83. Lowe, *Benjamin Graham*, 166.

84. Walter Schloss; "Walter & Edwin Schloss Associates, LP's," *Outstanding Investor Digest*, March 6, 1989.

85. U.S. Senate, Committee on Banking and Currency, 84th Congress, 1st Session, "Factors Affecting the Buying and Selling of Equity Securities," Statement of Benjamin Graham, March 11, 1955.

86. Tom Knapp.

87. Graham-Newman letter to stockholders, February 28, 1946; Walter Schloss; Kahn and Milne, *Benjamin Graham*, 43, 46. Figures for Graham-Newman are net returns to stockholders. Note that as G-N generally did not allow reinvestment of dividends, the figures for G-N and the S & P are average returns, not compound returns.

88. Davis, "Buffett Takes Stock."

89. Linda Grant, "The $4-Billion Regular Guy," *Los Angeles Times*, April 7, 1991.

90. Norton Dodge; Train, *Money Masters*, 10.

91. Ed Anderson.

Chapter 4. Beginnings

1. Warren Buffett, letter to Jerry Orans, June 19, 1957.

2. Warren Buffett, letter to Jerry Orans, May 26, 1957.

3. Wiesenberger was the principal of Wiesenberger & Co., a well-known firm that evaluated mutual funds.

4. Lee Seemann [Edwin Davis's son-in-law].

5. Deficiencies were carried forward; thus, if the partnership earned zero in one year, it would have to make 8 percent in the next before Buffett could draw a share. Buffett's other partnerships were structured similarly, though the precise formulas varied. After 1962, when the partnerships merged, all investors got the first 6 percent of the profits and shared any remaining profits with Buffett on a 75–25 basis.

6. Warren Buffett, letter to Jerry Orans, March 12, 1958.

7. "Sam Reynolds Home Sold to Warren Buffetts," *Omaha World-Herald*, February 9, 1958.

8. Doris Buffett Bryant.

9. Jack D. Ringwalt, *Tales of National Indemnity Company and Its Founder* (Omaha: National Indemnity Co., 1990), 6–7.

10. William Angle.

11. Dan Monen.

12. Warren Buffett, letter to partners, January 30, 1961.

13. Ibid.

14. Train, *Money Masters*, 10.

15. Donald Keough.

16. Dan Monen.

17. Warren Buffett, letter to partners, January 18, 1963.

18. David Strassler.

19. Warren Buffett, letter to partners, January 24, 1962.

20. In his letter to partners of January 24, 1962, Buffett wrote: "You will not be right simply because a large number of people momentarily agree with you." Compare this to Graham's comment on disagreeing with the crowd on page 44.

21. Warren Buffett, letter to partners, January 24, 1962.

22. Ibid.

23. Hugh S. Hord.

24. Keith McCormick.

25. James Koley; Gordon Ryan.

26. Peter Buffett; Tom Rogers; Thama Friedman.

27. Doris Buffett Bryant.

28. Ibid.

29. Peter Buffett.

30. Eunice Denenberg.

31. Yale Trustin.

32. Eunice Denenberg.

33. Warren Buffett, letter to partners, January 24, 1962.

34. Roy Tolles.

35. Lee Seemann.

36. Richard Holland.

37. Robert Dorr, "Ex-Omahan Traded Law for Board Room," *Omaha World-Herald*, August 31, 1977.

38. Warren Buffett, letter to partners, January 18, 1963.

39. Ibid.

40. Dorr, "Investor at 11."

41. Bob Billig; Ed Anderson.

42. Warren Buffett, appendix to letter to partners, 1964.

43. Warren Buffett, letter to partners, January 18, 1963.

Chapter 5. PARTNERS

1. Warren Buffett, letter to partners, January 20, 1966.

2. Frederic Sondern, Jr., "Checks That Never Bounce," *Reader's Digest*, August 1963.

3. "Credit: Toward a Cashless Society," *Time*, November 5, 1965.

4. American Express Co., *1963 Annual Report*, 22.

5. Howard Clark.

6. See the Pulitzer-prize-winning account of Norman C. Miller in the *Wall Street Journal*, "How Phantom Salad Oil Was Used to Engineer $100 Million Swindle," December 2, 1963; Murray Kempton, "The Salad Oil Mystery," *New Republic*, July 24, 1965.

7. Josephine Lorella [owner of Ross's].

8. "How Omaha Beats Wall Street."

9. Graham, *Intelligent Investor*, 283.

10. Smith, *Supermoney*, 193.

11. Howard Clark.

12. Davis, "Buffett Takes Stock."

13. Warren Buffett, letter to partners, January 20, 1966.

14. Warren Buffett, letter to partners, January 18, 1965.

15. Warren Buffett, letter to partners, January 18, 1963.

16. Warren Buffett, letter to partners, January 18, 1965.

17. Warren Buffett, letter to partners, January 18, 1963.

18. Ibid.; Warren Buffett, letters to partners, January 18, 1965.

19. William Brown.

20. Warren Buffett, letter to partners, January 24, 1962.

21. Warren Buffett, letters to partners, January 18, 1964, and January 18, 1965.

22. Warren Buffett, letter to partners, January 18, 1965.

23. Ibid.

24. Warren Buffett, letter to partners, January 20, 1966.

25. Ibid.

26. Ibid.

27. Graham, *Intelligent Investor*, 282.

28. Warren Buffett, letter to partners, January 18, 1965.

29. Richard Holland.

30. Marshall Weinberg.

31. Martha Tolles.

32. Smith, *Supermoney*, 182; Richard Holland.

33. "Buffett Enthusiastic Birch Member," *Omaha World-Herald*, April 1, 1961.

34. Keith McCormick.

35. Elizabeth Flynn, "Panel Cracks Wall of Prejudice with Humor, Common Sense," *Omaha World-Herald*, March 30, 1962. Similar groups had been organized in Kansas City and Des Moines.

36. U.S. Senator Bob Kerrey [D-Neb.].

37. Dan Monen.

38. Howard Graham Buffett.

39. The phrase is from Peter Buffett.

40. Marshall Weinberg.

41. Ibid.

42. Barbara Morrow.

43. Tom Rogers. The younger Susie recalled that when the Buffetts went to Disneyland, Warren would sit on a bench and read and join the family at lunchtime.

44. "How Omaha Beats Wall Street"; Barbara Morrow.

45. "How Omaha Beats Wall Street."

46. Smith, *Supermoney*, 193.

47. Warren Buffett, talk at Kenan-Flagler Business School, University of North Carolina, October 20, 1994.

48. Warren Buffett, letter to partners, January 20, 1966.
49. Warren Buffett, letter to partners, January 25, 1967.
50. Warren Buffett, letter to partners, January 20, 1966.
51. Dorr, "Investor at 11."
52. Jack Hyde, "Buffett Means Business," *Daily News Record*, May 20, 1965.
53. Ann Seemann Drickey.

Chapter 6. Go-Go

1. Warren Buffett, letter to partners, January 20, 1966.
2. Warren Buffett, letter to partners, July 12, 1966.
3. Ibid.
4. Warren Buffett, letter to partners, January 25, 1967.
5. Ibid.
6. John Brooks, *The Go-Go Years* (New York: Weybright & Talley, 1973), 210.
7. "The Ghost of Fred Carr," *Business Week*, August 25, 1973.
8. "A Fund Wizard Builds an Empire," *Business Week*, May 3, 1969.
9. Warren Buffett, letter to partners, January 25, 1967.
10. Ibid.
11. Benjamin Rosner.
12. Warren Buffett, letter to partners, July 12, 1967.
13. U.S. Senate, Committee on Banking and Currency, "Mutual Fund Legislation of 1967," August 2, 1967.
14. John M. Keynes, *The General Theory of Employment, Interest and Money* (1st ed. 1936; New York: Cambridge Univ. Press, 1973), 154–55.
15. *The Collected Writings of John Maynard Keynes*, vol. 12, ed. Donald Moggridge (New York: Macmillan, 1983). See ch. 1, "Keynes as an Investor."
16. Keynes, *General Theory*, 156.
17. All discussions of crowd psychology—including this one—are indebted to Gustave Le Bon's small-shelf classic *The Crowd: A Study of the Popular Mind* (1st trans. 1896; London: Ernest Benn, 1938).
18. This version of the tale, which Buffett knew in the sixties, is from Berkshire Hathaway Inc., 1985 *Annual Report*, p. 5.
19. Galbraith, *The Great Crash*, 47.
20. Brooks, *Go-Go Years*, 280–85.
21. Ford Foundation, 1966 *Annual Report*, vii.
22. I. Ross, "McGeorge Bundy and the New Foundation Style," *Fortune*, April 1968.
23. Warren Buffett, letter to partners, October 9, 1967.
24. Warren Buffett, letter to partners, January 24, 1968.
25. Loomis, "Inside Story"; Davis, "Buffett Takes Stock."
26. Buffett, talk at UNC, 1994; Berkshire Hathaway Inc., 1995 *Annual Report*, 16.
27. Warren Buffett, letter to partners, January 24, 1968.
28. Warren Buffett, letter to Graham group, January 16, 1968.
29. Warren Buffett, letter to Graham group, January 2, 1968.
30. Charlie Munger; Davis, "Buffett Takes Stock."
31. Warren Buffett, letter to partners, October 9, 1967.
32. Buffett discussed his continuing fidelity to Graham's ideas in the Berkshire Hathaway 1983 *Annual Report*, p. 4.
33. Lowe, *Benjamin Graham*, 3.

34. Jack Alexander.

35. Warren Buffett, talk at Columbia, 1993.

36. Warren Buffett, letter to partners, January 24, 1968.

37. Brooks, *Go-Go Years*, 183–84.

38. Warren Buffett, letter to partners, July 11, 1968.

39. Brooks, *Go-Go Years*, 267–68.

40. Warren Buffett, letter to partners, January 24, 1968.

41. Warren Buffett, letter to partners, January 22, 1969.

42. "Expert on Investing Plans to Slow Down," *Omaha World-Herald*, February 25, 1968.

43. Ed Anderson.

44. Robin Wood.

45. *Wall Street Transcript*, January 1969; Burton G. Malkiel, *A Random Walk down Wall Street* (1st ed. 1973; New York: Norton, 1991), 173; Brooks, Go-Go Years, 267–70.

46. *Wall Street Transcript*, January 1969.

47. Warren Buffett, letter to partners, January 22, 1969.

48. *Wall Street Transcript*, multiple issues.

49. *Wall Street Transcript*, interview with William R. Berkley, December 8, 1969.

50. Warren Buffett, letter to partners, January 22, 1969.

51. "Fund Wizard Builds an Empire."

52. Warren Buffett, letter to partners, May 29, 1969.

53. Dan Monen; Charlie Munger.

54. Warren Buffett, letter to partners, May 29, 1969.

55. Estimated from a partnership filing of January 1, 1969.

56. Warren Buffett, letter to partners, May 29, 1969.

57. Robert Dorr, "Buffett Plans to Shut Down Finance Firm," *Omaha World-Herald*, June 2, 1969.

58. C. J. Loomis, "Hard Times Come to the Hedge Funds," *Fortune*, January 1970.

59. Smith, *Supermoney*, 198–99.

60. Fran Burton. Burton's father supported Buffett's entry.

61. Jonathan R. Laing, "The Collector: Investor Who Piled Up $100 Million in the '60s Piles Up Firms Today," *Wall Street Journal*, March 31, 1977.

62. The reference to *Belous* is from Supreme Court of the U.S., No. 70-18, 1971 Term, *Roe v. Wade*, Brief for Appellants, 108–9.

63. Evelyn Simpson, "Looking Back: Swivel Neck Needed for Focus Change Today," *Omaha World-Herald*, October 5, 1969.

64. Brooks, *Go-Go Years*, 261.

65. Lipper Analytical Services; "Ghost of Fred Carr."

66. Brooks, *Go-Go Years*, 4.

67. Warren Buffett, letter to partners, February 18, 1970.

68. Leland Olson.

69. Warren Buffett, letter to partners, February 25, 1970.

70. Warren Buffett, letter to partners, December 5, 1969.

71. Ibid.

Chapter 7. BERKSHIRE HATHAWAY

1. Herman Melville, *Moby-Dick* (1st ed. 1851; New York: Bantam, 1986), 40.

2. *Spinner: People and Culture in Southeastern Massachusetts*, vol. 4 (New Bedford: Spinner Publications, 1988), 185.

3. Bess Zarafonitis, "When Cloth Mills Made City's Gold," *New Bedford Standard-Times*, August 18, 1985.

4. Horatio Hathaway, *A New Bedford Merchant* (New Bedford: private printing, 1930), 3–10; Zarafonitis, "When Mills Made Gold"; "The New Mill of the Hathaway Manufacturing Company," *New Bedford Evening Standard*, December 24, 1888.

5. *People and Culture*, 185; Zarafonitis, "When Mills Made Gold."

6. *People and Culture*, 185.

7. Ibid., 186.

8. Seabury Stanton, *Berkshire Hathaway Inc: A Saga of Courage* (New York: Newcomen Society, 1962), 15–16 [account of Newcomen Society dinner, Boston, 1961].

9. Stanton, *Saga of Courage*, 17–18; *People and Culture*, 186.

10. Malcolm Chace; "The Chace Tradition," *Warp and Filling* [Berkshire Hathaway magazine], Autumn 1965.

11. Stanton, *Saga of Courage*, 10.

12. Ibid., 11.

13. Kenneth V. Chace.

14. Ibid.

15. Jack Stanton.

16. Ralph Rigby.

17. Stanton, *Saga of Courage*, 20; Ken Chace.

18. Value Line, reports of Richard N. Tillison, March 18, 1963, June 17, 1963, and September 13, 1963.

19. "The New Team at Berkshire Hathaway," *Warp and Filling*, Autumn 1965.

20. Susan and Warren Buffett, eulogy for Daniel Cowin.

21. "New Berkshire Interests Plan No Policy Shift," *New Bedford Standard-Times*, May 11, 1965.

22. Ken Chace; Jack Stanton. *Warp and Filling*, published by Berkshire, reported in the Autumn 1965 edition that Buffett had been "suddenly revealed" as the controlling shareholder.

23. Malcolm Chace.

24. "New Berkshire Interests Plan No Policy Shift."

25. Ibid.; Joseph L. Goodrich, "K. V. Chace Heads Berkshire Hathaway," *Providence Journal*, May 11, 1965.

26. "Seabury Stanton Resigns at Berkshire," *New Bedford Standard-Times*, May 10, 1965.

27. Berkshire Hathaway, *Letters to Shareholders, 1977–1984*, 1.

28. Berkshire Hathaway Inc., *1985 Annual Report*, 8.

29. Berkshire Hathaway Inc., *1966 Annual Report*, 3.

30. Ringwalt, *Tales of National Indemnity*, 3.

31. Ibid., 46.

32. Robert Dorr, " 'Unusual Risk' Ringwalt Specialty," *Omaha World-Herald*, March 12, 1967.

33. Ringwalt, *Tales of National Indemnity*, 62–63.
34. Berkshire Hathaway Inc., 1969 *Annual Report*, 2.
35. Ralph Rigby.
36. SEC File No. HO-784, in the matter of *Blue Chip Stamps, et al.*
37. Ibid. [italics added].
38. Berkshire Hathaway Inc., 1970 *Annual Report*, 1.
39. Warren Buffett, letter to partners, December 5, 1969.
40. Ken Chace.
41. See, for instance, Buffett's letter to partners of January 20, 1966: "Berkshire is a delight to own."

Chapter 8. RETURN OF THE NATIVE

1. Train, *Money Masters*, 9.
2. Warren Buffett, letter to John Spears, July 6, 1971.
3. Loomis, "Hard Times."
4. Doris Buffett Bryant.
5. Jack Z. Smith, "Warren Buffett: Corn-fed Capitalist," *Fort Worth Star-Telegram*, June 7, 1987.
6. Caroline Mayer.
7. Layne Yahnke.
8. SEC File No. HO-784, *Blue Chip Stamps, et al.*/Charles E. Rickershauser, Jr., letter to Stanley Sporkin, December 1, 1975.
9. SEC File No. HO-784, *Blue Chip Stamps, et al.*/Warren Buffett, letter to Lawrence Seidman, March 4, 1975.
10. SEC File No. HO-784, *Blue Chip Stamps, et al.*/Warren Buffett, letter to Ambrose Jackson, April 2, 1973.
11. George Rushing. As a minority-owned venture, the bank failed. It was ultimately sold to Norwest Corp., at a 90 percent loss to the original stockholders.
12. Charles Heider; Sam Thorson, "Warren Buffet [sic], Omahan in Search of Social Challenges," *Lincoln Journal & Star*, March 18, 1973.
13. Thorson, "Omahan in Search."
14. Charlie Peters. One of the editors was Taylor Branch, later the biographer of Martin Luther King, Jr.
15. Stan Lipsey.
16. Previously, Boys Town's report was combined with that of the Archdiocese of Omaha.
17. SEC File No. HO-784, *Blue Chip Stamps, et al.*/Warren Buffett, letter to Martin J. Burke, October 27, 1972.
18. Laing, "The Collector."
19. Stan Lipsey.
20. There is a record of Berkshire's stock purchases in SEC File No. HO-784, *Blue Chip Stamps, et al.*
21. Peter Buffett.
22. Barbara Morrow.
23. Peter Buffett; Tom Rogers [the Buffetts' nephew].
24. Buffett, 1984 Graham and Dodd seminar.
25. Norman Williamson.

26. William H. Schumann III, Executive Director, Corporate Development, letter to author, September 21, 1992. Buffett's compound average gain was 8.6 percent. The year-by-year record: 1973, −14.2 percent; 1974, −12.6 percent; 1975, +33 percent; 1976, +45.4 percent; 1977, +4.1 percent. FMC also hired several other value managers at Buffett's suggestion.

27. SEC File No. HO-784, *Blue Chip Stamps, et al.*/Donald Mutschler, letter to Warren Buffett, August 29, 1973.

28. Buffett, 1984 Graham and Dodd seminar.

29. *Wall Street Transcript*, May 7, 1973.

30. SEC File No. HO-784, *Blue Chip Stamps, et al.*/Warren Buffett, letter to William Taylor, October 1, 1973.

31. 1986 Capital Cities/ABC management conference.

32. "Pension Fund and Money Managers," *Wall Street Transcript*, December 23, 1974.

33. Carl Spielvogel.

34. Verne McKenzie; Conrad Taff.

35. Ed Anderson; Walter Schloss.

36. SEC File No. HO-784, *Blue Chip Stamps, et al.*/Warren Buffett, letter to Eugene Abegg, January 23, 1974.

37. Berkshire Hathaway Inc., *1974 Annual Report*, 4.

38. *Wall Street Transcript*, April 23, 1973.

39. William G. Shepherd, "The Size of the Bear," *Business Week*, August 3, 1974; William Gordon, "Poppa Bear Market," *Barron's*, August 26, 1974.

40. *Wall Street Transcript*, January 1974.

41. Howard Stein, "Some Thoughts for Financial Analysts," reprinted in *Wall Street Transcript*, June 17, 1974 [italics added].

42. Benjamin Graham, "Renaissance of Value," as reprinted in *Barron's*, September 23, 1974.

43. Reprinted in *Wall Street Transcript*, September 1, 1974.

44. "Look at All Those Beautiful, Scantily Clad Girls out There!" *Forbes*, November 1, 1974. *Forbes* prudishly substituted "harem" for "whorehouse."

Chapter 9. Alter Ego

1. Charlie Munger.

2. James Gipson.

3. George Michaelis witnessed the interchange.

4. Berkshire Hathaway Inc., *1991 Annual Report*, 9–10; Robert Flaherty; SEC File No. HO-784, *Blue Chip Stamps, et al.*, testimony of Warren Buffett, March 21, 1975, p. 22.

5. SEC File No. HO-784, *Blue Chip Stamps, et al.*/Warren Buffett, letter to Charles N. Huggins, November 29, 1974.

6. SEC File No. HO-784, *Blue Chip Stamps, et al.*/Warren Buffett, letter to Charles N. Huggins, December 13, 1972.

7. SEC File No. HO-784, *Blue Chip Stamps, et al.*/Warren Buffett, letter to Donald Koeppel [president, Blue Chip], May 8, 1972.

8. SEC File No. HO-784, *Blue Chip Stamps, et al.*/Warren Buffett, letter to Donald B. Koeppel, April 6, 1972.

9. SEC File No. HO-784, *Blue Chip Stamps, et al.*, testimony of Buffett, p. 26.

10. Ibid., 24–26.

11. Ibid., 42–43.

12. SEC File No. HO-784, *Blue Chip Stamps, et al.*, testimony of Buffett, pp. 63–64; testimony of Charlie Munger, March 19–20, 1975, p. 53.

13. SEC File No. HO-784, *Blue Chip Stamps, et al.*, notes of Louis R. Vincenti, February 7, 1973.

14. Ira Marshall.

15. *California v. Belous*, Amici Curiae in Support of Appellant. Joan Babbott; Mary Ripley; Ruth Roemer; Dr. Keith Russell.

16. Joan Babbott.

17. Charles Munger, "Bad Judgments, Common Causes," talk at California Institute of Technology, February 17, 1992.

18. SEC File No. HO-784, *Blue Chip Stamps, et al.*, testimony of Elizabeth Peters, March 20, 1975, pp. 19, 32–40.

19. Elizabeth Peters.

20. Ibid.; SEC File No. HO-784, *Blue Chip Stamps, et al.*, testimony of Peters, pp. 38–39.

21. Berkshire Hathaway and Blue Chip Stamps, 1975 proxy statements; Berkshire *Prospectus*, November 27, 1978.

22. SEC File No. HO-784, *Blue Chip Stamps, et al.*, Charles Munger, letter to Charles E. Rickershauser, Jr., October 22, 1974.

23. SEC File No. HO-784, *Blue Chip Stamps, et al.*, Order directing private investigation, December 10, 1974.

24. SEC File No. HO-784, *Blue Chip Stamps, et al.*, testimony of Munger, pp. 51–52, 73, 87–88.

25. Ibid., 111–14.

26. SEC File No. HO-784, *Blue Chip Stamps, et al.*, testimony of Buffett, pp. 98–102.

27. SEC File No. HO-784, *Blue Chip Stamps, et al.*, testimony of Munger, pp. 17, 30–31, 36–37, 193.

28. SEC File No. HO-784, *Blue Chip Stamps, et al.*, testimony of Buffett, pp. 70–71, 133–34.

29. SEC File No. HO-784, *Blue Chip Stamps, et al.*, testimony of Munger, p. 195.

30. SEC File No. HO-784, *Blue Chip Stamps, et al.*, testimony of Buffett, p. 157.

31. SEC File No. HO-784, *Blue Chip Stamps, et al.*, Charles Rickershauser, letter to Stanley Sporkin, December 1, 1975.

32. SEC File No. HO-784, *Blue Chip Stamps, et al.*, testimony of Buffett, p. 161.

33. Ibid.

34. SEC, *Schedule 13D*, Berkshire Hathaway Inc., July 28, 1983. The $32.45 is based on Buffett's interest in Berkshire following the 1983 conversion of Blue Chip shares into Berkshire.

Chapter 10. WASHINGTON REDUX

1. Lynn Rosellini, "The Katharine Graham Story," *Washington Star*, November 13 and 14, 1978 [first two of five-part series].

2. Robert G. Kaiser, "The Strike at The Washington Post," *Washington Post*, Feb-

ruary 29, 1976; Pat Munroe and Caryl Rivers, "Kay Graham Talks About Her Job at the Helm of Washington Post," *Editor & Publisher*, May 2, 1964.

3. Kaiser, "Strike"; Carol Felsenthal, *Power, Privilege, and the Post* (New York: Putnam, 1993), 228–31.

4. Richard Cohen, "A Woman of Influence," *Women's Wear Daily*, March 27, 1969.

5. Katharine Graham, "Learning by Doing," *Bulletin of the American Academy of Arts and Sciences*, May 1989; Jane Howard, "Katharine Graham: The Power That Didn't Corrupt," *Ms.*, October 1974; Felsenthal, *Power, Privilege, and the Post*, 226–28.

6. Graham, "Learning by Doing."

7. Carl Bernstein and Bob Woodward, *All the President's Men* (New York: Simon & Schuster, 1974), 105.

8. "Remarks of Katharine Graham," *Wall Street Transcript*, April 1, 1974.

9. Geoffrey Cowan.

10. Katharine Graham; Larry Israel.

11. "Corn-fed Capitalist." Berkshire's stake would rise to 15 percent as the Post reduced the number of its outstanding shares.

12. Berkshire Hathaway Inc., 1975 *Annual Report*, 4.

13. Kaiser, "Strike."

14. Lloyd Cutler [then outside counsel for the Post].

15. *Buffalo Courier-Express, Inc., v. Buffalo Evening News, Inc.*, Civil Action No. 77-582, U.S. District Court, Western District of New York, Deposition of Katharine Graham, p. 34.

16. Rosellini, "Katharine Graham Story," November 16, 1978.

17. William Graham.

18. Donald Graham.

19. "Columnist Discovers Buffett," *Omaha World-Herald*, March 11, 1977.

20. Katharine Graham.

21. Ron Olson. See also "Corn-fed Capitalist."

22. Thama Friedman.

23. Pagel, "Susie Sings."

24. Ibid.

25. Michael Harrison.

26. Barbara Morrow.

27. Barbara Morrow; Roxanne Brandt.

28. Peter Buffett.

29. Kay Graham.

30. Alan Spoon.

31. Joel Chaseman.

32. Lorimer Davidson; Jack Byrne; Michael Frinquelli; Robert Sobel, *Salomon Brothers: 1910–1985* (New York: Salomon Brothers [corporate history], 1986), 149.

33. According to an SEC finding, GEICO "failed in material respects to disclose its deteriorating financial condition." Among other things, it failed to report a change in the formulas for calculating loss reserves which, over the second and third quarters of 1975, reduced reported reserves by $25 million. SEC file, *In the matter of GEICO, et al.*, p. 11, October 27, 1976.

34. Lawrence Seidman; John Steggles.

35. Remarks of Benjamin Graham, La Jolla, April 11, 1974.

36. Charles Brandes.

37. Ed Anderson; Walter Schloss; James Fogarty, "Buffett Questioned in IBM Suit," *Omaha World-Herald*, January 24, 1980.

38. William H. Jones, "Stockholders Questioning Often Angry," *Washington Post*, April 1, 1976.

39. Sobel, *Salomon Brothers*, 150.

40. If GEICO had failed, other insurers would have been forced to meet its liabilities by making contributions to state guarantee funds. Byrne thought GEICO was so feared that State Farm preferred to pay for its burial rather than to bring it back to health.

41. Byrne, *GEICO*, 14–15.

42. GEICO; A.M. Best Co.

43. Warren Buffett, 1987 Capital Cities/ABC management conference.

44. Ibid.

45. Ronald Gutman; Warren Buffett, 1987 Capital Cities/ABC management conference.

46. Jack Byrne.

47. Ibid.

48. Michael Frinquelli.

49. Ibid.

50. Sobel, *Salomon Brothers*, 151.

51. Jack Byrne.

52. Byrne, *GEICO*, 21.

53. "Walter & Edwin Schloss Associates, LP's."

54. Philip A. Fisher, *Common Stocks and Uncommon Profits* (New York: Harper & Row, 1960).

55. Warren Buffett, "Benjamin Graham: 1894–1976," *Financial Analysts Journal*, November–December 1976.

56. "Warren Buffett: Reluctant Billionaire," WNET/Thirteen, Adam Smith's *Money World*, broadcast June 20, 1988.

57. Buffett, "Benjamin Graham."

Chapter 11. PRESS LORD

1. *Courier-Express v. Evening News*, Civil Action No. 77-582, U.S. District Court, Western District of New York, Deposition of Graham, pp. 54–57; Deposition of Vincent Manno, pp. 161–63.

2. Guild collective bargaining manual, February 1, 1977.

3. *Courier-Express v. Evening News*, Affidavit of Richard C. Lyons, Jr., pp. 4–5.

4. Deposition of Graham, p. 61.

5. Deposition of Manno, pp. 98, 235.

6. Albert Mugel.

7. Deposition of Graham, pp. 64–73.

8. Deposition of Manno, p. 165.

9. 601 *Federal Reporter*, 2d series, p. 50, *Courier-Express v. Evening News*, appellate decision, April 16, 1979.

10. Deposition of Manno, pp. 61, 115–16, 165–80.

11. Murray Light.

12. Justin Kaplan, *Mr. Clemens and Mark Twain* (New York: Simon & Schuster, 1966), 99.

13. Audit Bureau of Circulation figures for 1976.

14. 601 F.2d 48 (1979) [appellate decision], p. 50. The *Evening News* published a weekend edition on Saturdays that attracted a large circulation but not a lot of ads.

15. Blue Chip Stamps, 1977 *Annual Report*, 3.

16. *Courier-Express v. Evening News*, Affidavit of Warren Buffett, Exhibit A, letter of Buffett to Charles Munger, July 26, 1977.

17. Deposition of Graham, p. 83.

18. *Courier-Express v. Evening News*, Plaintiff's memorandum in support of preliminary injunction, pp. 2–3.

19. Affidavit of Buffett, pp. 8, 18.

20. "5 Testify in Lawsuit by Courier," *Buffalo Courier-Express*, November 6, 1977.

21. Affidavit of Buffett, p. 3.

22. *Courier-Express v. Evening News*, testimony of Warren Buffett, pp. 12–13, 22.

23. Ibid., 22–23, 26, 28–29.

24. Ibid., 30–31.

25. Daniel Mason.

26. *Courier-Express v. Evening News*, testimony of Buffett, pp. 44–45.

27. Ibid., 46–47.

28. Ibid., 48. Furth was citing Laing, "The Collector."

29. Ibid., 50–52.

30. Blue Chip and/or Berkshire had owned stock in the bridge since the early seventies. After a failed attempt at buying the entire company, Blue Chip sold its interest in 1979.

31. 441 *Federal Supplement* 1977, p. 644, *Courier-Express v. Evening News*, November 9, 1977.

32. Ibid., 633, 634, 639, 641–42.

33. Dick Hirsch, "Read All About it," *Bflo.*, Winter 1978.

34. Berkshire Hathaway Inc., June 30, 1983 *Prospectus*, 48.

35. Warren Buffett, 1987 Capital Cities/ABC management conference.

36. Ibid.

37. Blue Chip Stamps, 1978 *Annual Report*, 2.

38. 601 F.2d 48 (1979), pp. 54–55, *Courier-Express v. Evening News*, U.S. Court of Appeals, second circuit, April 16, 1979.

39. Blue Chip Stamps, 1980 *Annual Report* (as reprinted in Berkshire Hathaway Inc., 1980 *Annual Report*, 45–46).

40. Blue Chip Stamps, 1979 *Annual Report* (as reprinted in Berkshire Hathaway Inc., 1979 *Annual Report*, 40).

41. Blue Chip Stamps, 1980 *Annual Report* (as reprinted in Berkshire Hathaway Inc., 1980 *Annual Report*, 46).

42. Richard Feather [labor negotiator for the *Evening News*].

43. Charlie Munger.

44. Audit Bureau of Circulation figures as of March 1982.

45. As of year-end 1982. Blue Chip Stamps 1982 *Annual Report* (as reprinted in Berkshire Hathaway Inc., 1982 *Annual Report*, 53).

46. Blue Chip Stamps, *1981 Annual Report* (as reprinted in Berkshire Hathaway Inc., *1981 Annual Report*, 46).

47. Stan Lipsey.

48. Guild collective bargaining manual, April 1, 1991.

49. Berkshire Hathaway Inc., *1984 Annual Report*, 8.

50. Ibid., 7.

51. Audit Bureau of Circulation.

52. In 1981, the *Courier-Express*'s last full year, the combined weekday circulation of the two papers was 396,000. A decade later, in 1991, weekday circulation at the *News* alone was 306,000, a decline of 23 percent. Similarly, combined Sunday circulation was 449,000 in 1981, compared to 383,000 for the *News* in 1991.

53. SEC File No. HO-784, *Blue Chip Stamps, et al.*/Warren Buffett, letter to Martin J. Burke, October 27, 1972.

Chapter 12. PARTNERS, REDUX

1. Michael Harrison; "Buffett Serious," *Omaha World-Herald*, September 14, 1976.

2. "Buffett Serious"; Peter Buffett.

3. Michael Harrison.

4. Sidney Wood.

5. Pagel, "Susie Sings."

6. Ibid.

7. Steve Millburg, "Williams Songs Outshine Voice," *Omaha World-Herald*, September 5, 1977; Michael Harrison.

8. Peter Buffett; Tom Rogers.

9. Roberta Buffett Bialek.

10. Susan Buffett Greenberg; Charlie Munger; Art Rowsell.

11. Susan Buffett Greenberg.

12. Peter Buffett; Joe Rosenfield.

13. Peter Buffett; Susan Buffett Greenberg; Roberta Buffett Bialek; Anthony Abbott.

14. Anthony Abbott.

15. Peter Buffett.

16. Ron Suskind, "Legend Revisited: Warren Buffett's Aura as Folksy Sage Masks Tough, Polished Man," *Wall Street Journal*, November 8, 1991.

17. Peter Buffett.

18. "Corn-fed Capitalist."

19. George Bush, speech to Hartford Society of Financial Analysts, October 5, 1979, as reprinted in *Wall Street Transcript*.

20. Berkshire Hathaway Inc., *1978 Annual Report*, 5.

21. Ibid., 4.

22. Laurie Meisler, "The Coming Rush into Equities," *Institutional Investor*, September 1979.

23. Heinz H. Biel, "What Alternative?" *Forbes*, June 25, 1979.

24. "The Death of Equities," *Business Week*, August 13, 1979.

25. Warren Buffett, "You Pay a Very High Price in the Stock Market for a Cheery Consensus," *Forbes*, August 6, 1979.

26. Art Rowsell.

27. Clifford Hayes; Art Rowsell.

28. Rick Guerin.

29. Richard Azar, letter to Louis Lowenstein, June 24, 1992.

30. Berkshire Hathaway Inc., *1981 Annual Report*, 6. On inflation, see also Berkshire reports for 1979 and 1980, and Warren Buffett, "How Inflation Swindles the Equity Investor," *Fortune*, May 1977.

31. Berkshire Hathaway Inc., *1979 Annual Report*, 9.

32. Berkshire Hathaway Inc., *1980 Annual Report*, 8–9.

33. Berkshire Hathaway Inc., *1979 Annual Report*, 3.

34. Berkshire Hathaway Inc., *1981 Annual Report*, 8.

35. Ibid., 4.

36. Berkshire Hathaway Inc., *1982 Annual Report*, 13.

37. Ibid., 13.

38. Ibid., 12.

39. Berkshire Hathaway Inc., *1988 Annual Report*, 5.

40. Warren Buffett, letter to shareholders, October 14, 1981.

41. Berkshire Hathaway Inc., *1979 Annual Report*, 11.

42. Robert K. Otterbourg, "Banishing Boredom," *Public Relations Journal*, July 1990.

43. Berkshire Hathaway Inc., *1979 Annual Report*, 10.

44. Berkshire Hathaway Inc., *1982 Annual Report*, 3.

45. Berkshire Hathaway Inc., *1983 Annual Report*, 2.

46. Berkshire Hathaway Inc., *1981 Annual Report*, 4.

47. Gary Putka, "In Binge of Optimism, Stock Market Surges by Record 38.81 Points," *Wall Street Journal*, August 18, 1982.

48. Alan Abelson, "Up & Down Wall Street," *Barron's*, May 9, 1983.

49. Berkshire Hathaway Inc., *1983 Annual Report*, 12–13.

50. Ibid., 2.

Chapter 13. The Carpet Woman

1. Berkshire Hathaway Inc., *1983 Annual Report*, 3.

2. Rose Blumkin; Louis Blumkin; Warren Buffett, talk at Columbia, 1993; Buffett, 1986 Capital Cities/ABC management conference.

3. Michael Kelly, "Mrs. B Cruises into Year 100," *Omaha World-Herald*, December 17, 1992.

4. Rose Blumkin.

5. Rose Blumkin; Joyce Wadler, "Furnishing a Life," *Washington Post*, May 24, 1984; Robert Dorr, "Break with Furniture Mart Begins to Heal," *Omaha World-Herald*, February 2, 1992.

6. Frank E. James, "Mrs. Blumkin's Secret: Sell Cheap, No Cheating," *Wall Street Journal*, May 27, 1984.

7. "Price Cutting Basis of Suit" and "Manufacturer Loses in Fair-Trade Suit," *Omaha World-Herald*, July 9, 1949, and June 4, 1951; James, "Mrs. Blumkin's Secret"; Wadler, "Furnishing a Life"; Berkshire Hathaway Inc., *1983 Annual Report*, 3.

8. Wadler, "Furnishing a Life."

9. Louie Blumkin.

10. Robert Dorr, "Furniture Mart Handshake Deal," *Omaha World-Herald*, September 15, 1983; Rose Blumkin; Don Danly.

11. Smith, *Supermoney*, 192.

12. Buffett, talk at Columbia, 1993.

13. Dorr, "Furniture Mart Handshake Deal."

14. Berkshire Hathaway Inc., *1988 Annual Report*, 8.

15. Warren Buffett, 1986 Capital Cities/ABC management conference.

16. Smith, "Reluctant Billionaire."

17. Rose Blumkin.

18. Warren Buffett, 1990 Capital Cities/ABC management conference.

19. "Getting Personal," *Omaha World-Herald*, June 12, 1977.

20. Chris Olson, "Mrs. B. Uses Home to Eat and Sleep," *Omaha World-Herald*, October 28, 1984.

21. Warren Buffett, 1986 Capital Cities/ABC management conference.

22. Donald Yale.

23. Berkshire Hathaway Inc., *1987 Annual Report*, 8.

24. Berkshire Hathaway Inc., *1990 Annual Report*, 8.

25. Buffett, talk at Columbia, 1993.

26. Donald Keough.

27. Tim Medley, "The Pilgrimage to Omaha," *Mississippi Business Journal*, June 10, 1991.

28. Berkshire Hathaway Inc., *1985 Annual Report*, 9.

29. Berkshire Hathaway Inc., *1977 Annual Report*, 2–3.

30. Berkshire Hathaway Inc., *1980 Annual Report*, 7.

31. Berkshire Hathaway Inc., *1979 Annual Report*, 5.

32. Berkshire Hathaway Inc., *1983 Annual Report*, 4.

33. Edward Clark [Amalgamated Clothing and Textile Workers Union].

34. Berkshire Hathaway Inc., *1985 Annual Report*, 7–10.

35. Ibid.

36. Ibid.

Chapter 14. THE EIGHTIES

1. Allan Sloan, "Why Is No One Safe? (From Hostile Corporate Takeovers)," *Forbes*, March 11, 1985.

2. Leonard H. Goldenson with Marvin J. Wolf, *Beating the Odds* (New York: Scribner's, 1991), 464. Goldenson's memoir includes recollections by Buffett, Murphy, and others.

3. Tom Murphy.

4. Tom Murphy, 1988 Capital Cities/ABC management conference.

5. Ken Auletta, *Three Blind Mice: How the TV Networks Lost Their Way* (New York: Random House, 1991), 26; Goldenson, *Beating the Odds*, 461–62.

6. Tom Murphy [interview and 1988 management conference].

7. Dan Burke; Tom Murphy. Dialogue is largely from Buffett, in Goldenson, *Beating the Odds*, 464–65, supplemented by Auletta, *Three Blind Mice*, 41–42.

8. Goldenson, *Beating the Odds*, 465.

9. Ibid.

10. Dan Burke; Tom Murphy.

11. Reconstruction from Dan Burke, Jeffrey Epstein, Ev Erlick, Michael Mallardi, Tom Murphy, Frederick Pierce, and Bruce Wasserstein.

12. Anthony Bianco, "Why Warren Buffett Is Breaking His Own Rules," *Business Week*, April 15, 1985.

13. John Greenwald, "High Times for T. Boone Pickens," *Time*, March 14, 1985.

14. John C. Coffee, Jr., Louis Lowenstein, and Susan Rose-Ackerman, eds., *Knights, Raiders, and Targets: The Impact of the Hostile Takeover* (New York: Oxford University Press, 1988), 22–23.

15. Ralph Schey.

16. Schey was paraphrasing the letter from memory.

17. Robert Dorr, "General Foods Proves Rewarding," *Omaha World-Herald*, October 3, 1985.

18. Robert McGough, "The Joys of Being an Insider," *Forbes*, December 31, 1984.

19. Gary Greenberg.

20. Fraud litigation brought by Cinerama, a former Technicolor holder, in 1983 was dismissed in 1995. Cinerama's appraisal claim against Perelman-owned MacAndrews and Forbes was still pending. See Connie Bruck, *The Predators' Ball: The Junk Bond Raiders and the Man Who Staked Them* (New York: American Lawyer/Simon & Schuster, 1988), 199–201; Ralph King, Jr., "Ron Perelman's $640 Million Unsure Thing," *Forbes*, October 30, 1984; and McGough, "The Joys of Being an Insider."

21. Bruck, *The Predators' Ball*, 237.

22. Louis Lowenstein, the author's father, was the moderator.

23. George Anders, *Merchants of Debt* (New York: Basic Books, 1992), 113.

24. Transcript of seminar; *Knights, Raiders, and Targets*, 11–27.

25. Greenwald, "High Times for T. Boone."

26. Warren Buffett, 1986 Capital Cities/ABC management conference.

27. Bauer, "Convictions." See also Berkshire Hathaway Inc., *1985 Annual Report*, 20.

28. Dennis Kneale, "Duo at Capital Cities Scores a Hit, but Can Network Be Part of It?" *Wall Street Journal*, February 2, 1990.

29. Ibid.

30. Medley, "Pilgrimage."

31. Bauer, "Convictions."

32. Charlie Munger.

33. Bianco, "Why Buffett Is Breaking His Rules."

34. Berkshire Hathaway Inc., *1989 Annual Report*, 7.

35. Bianco, "Why Buffett Is Breaking His Rules"; Berkshire Hathaway Inc., *1987 Annual Report*, 15.

36. Buffett, talk at Columbia, 1993.

37. Debt is defined as term debt plus short-term borrowings, exclusive of other liabilities. Berkshire's insurance unit makes a precise comparison somewhat fudgy, but the basic point holds.

38. Warren Buffett, 1986 Capital Cities/ABC management conference.

39. Warren Buffett, 1988 Capital Cities/ABC management conference.

40. *Knights, Raiders, and Targets*, 26.

41. Warren Buffett, 1988 Capital Cities/ABC management conference.

Chapter 15. PUBLIC AND PRIVATE

1. Robert Dorr, "Early Faith Made Many 'Buffett Millionaires,'" *Omaha World-Herald*, May 4, 1986.

2. William Baldwin and Jean A. Briggs, "We Love You, Ben Graham, but It's Time to Take a Vacation," *Forbes*, June 3, 1985.

3. Marsha Strang.

4. Jason Zweig, "Faces Behind the Figures," *Forbes*, September 4, 1989.

5. Robert Dorr, "Buffett Hears from Large, Small in His Search for New Businesses," *Omaha World-Herald*, December 3, 1986.

6. Robert Dorr, "Investor Warren Buffett Views Making Money as 'Big Game,'" *Omaha World-Herald*, March 24, 1985.

7. Terry Hyland, "Lincolnite Cohen Ordered to Trial in Extortion Case," *Omaha World-Herald*, February 18, 1987.

8. Robert Spass.

9. Davis, "Buffett Takes Stock."

10. Ronald Gutman.

11. Smith, *Supermoney*, 179.

12. Bernice Kanner, "Aw, Shucks, It's Warren Buffett," *New York*, April 22, 1985; "Corn-fed Capitalist" (*Regardie's*); and Smith, "Warren Buffett: Corn-fed Capitalist" (*Fort Worth Star-Telegram*).

13. Grant, "$4-Billion Regular Guy."

14. "Corn-fed Capitalist."

15. Davis, "Buffett Takes Stock"; Bauer, "Convictions"; Grant, "$4-Billion Regular Guy."

16. Kanner, "Aw, Shucks"; Laing, "The Collector"; "Corn-fed Capitalist." Harvard was often omitted from the story until Carol Loomis's probing interview in 1988 ("Inside Story").

17. Davis, "Buffett Takes Stock"; Dorr, "Buffett Plans to Shut Down Finance Firm."

18. "Buffetts in New Home," *Omaha World-Herald*, May 23, 1956.

19. Goldenson, *Beating the Odds*, 465.

20. Kanner, "Aw, Shucks."

21. Donald Keough.

22. Robert Spass [Salomon Brothers banker].

23. Berkshire Hathaway, *1986 Annual Report*, 21.

24. Warren Buffett, 1986 Capital Cities/ABC management conference.

25. Stan Lipsey; Charles Munger.

26. William Angle. The figure includes his wife's stock.

27. Richard Rainwater.

28. Warren Buffett, 1990 Capital Cities/ABC management conference.

29. Steven Gluckstern.

30. Walter Schloss.

31. Roxanne Brandt.

32. Tom Knapp.

33. Louis Lowenstein.

34. Tim Medley, "Medley on Money," *Mississippi Business Journal*, July 1989.

35. Doris Buffett Bryant.

36. Robert Dorr, "Buffetts Fund Efforts for Population Control," *Omaha World-Herald*, January 10, 1988.
37. Berkshire Hathaway Inc., *1989 Annual Report*, 22.
38. Berkshire Hathaway Inc., *1982 Annual Report*, 14.
39. William Snyder.
40. Charlie Munger; Loomis, "Inside Story."
41. Berkshire Hathaway Inc., *1986 Annual Report*, 21.
42. Thomas Winship.
43. Warren Buffett, talk at Columbia, 1993.
44. Warren Buffett, 1993 annual meeting of Berkshire Hathaway.
45. Warren Buffett, 1987 annual meeting of Berkshire Hathaway.
46. Berkshire Hathaway Inc., *1990 Annual Report*, 27.
47. Ralph Schey.
48. Donald Yale.
49. SEC File No. HO-784, *Blue Chip Stamps, et al.*/Warren Buffett, letter to George Aderton, January 14, 1975.
50. Berkshire Hathaway Inc., *1989 Annual Report*, 8.

Chapter 16. CRASH

1. Tom Knapp.
2. Quentin Breunig.
3. Berkshire Hathaway Inc., *1984 Annual Report*, 10–12.
4. Steven Atkins.
5. Michael Goldberg.
6. Berkshire Hathaway Inc., *1980 Annual Report*, 10.
7. Berkshire Hathaway Inc., *1982 Annual Report*, 9.
8. Jack Byrne.
9. Berkshire Hathaway Inc., *1985 Annual Report*, 15.
10. A.M. Best Co.
11. Berkshire Hathaway Inc., *1985 Annual Report*, 16.
12. Ibid., 16.
13. The 1986 total includes $233 million from a new contract under which Berkshire took 7 percent of the business written by Fireman's Fund. Excluding Fireman's, premiums were up sixfold.
14. "What Buffett Isn't Buying Now," *Fortune*, April 27, 1987.
15. John Constable, annual meeting notes.
16. Tim Medley, summer 1987 newsletter to clients.
17. Michael Zimmerman.
18. Laurie P. Cohen and Steve Swartz, "Salomon Buys Holder's Stake for $809 Million," *Wall Street Journal*, September 28, 1987; James Sterngold, "Too Far, Too Fast, Salomon Brothers' John Gutfreund," *New York Times Magazine*, January 10, 1988.
19. Coproduction of Channel 13 in New York and the Columbia University Seminar on Media and Society. The program was taped early in 1987 and aired on Channel 13, October 31, 1987.
20. Ronald Perelman; Felix Rohatyn; Sterngold, "Too Far, Too Fast"; Anthony

Bianco, "Salomon and Revlon: What Really Happened—How Perelman Drove Gutfreund into Buffett's Arms," *Business Week*, October 12, 1987.

21. Gedale Horowitz; Gerald Rosenfeld.

22. Jay Higgins; Gedale Horowitz; Martin Leibowtiz; William McIntosh; Gerald Rosenfeld.

23. Lisa Belkin, "Gillette Deal Ends Revlon Bid," *New York Times*, November 25, 1986.

24. Gerald Rosenfeld.

25. Berkshire Hathaway Inc., *1987 Annual Report*, 19.

26. William McIntosh.

27. Ronald Perelman; Sterngold, "Too Far, Too Fast."

28. Ronald Perelman; Felix Rohatyn; Laurie P. Cohen, "Revlon Offers to Buy Interest in Salomon Inc.," *Wall Street Journal*, September 29, 1987.

29. Gedale Horowitz; Sterngold, "Too Far, Too Fast."

30. Huey Lowenstein [no relation to author]; Jay Higgins.

31. Steve Swartz, "Home to Roost: Raid on Salomon Inc. Has Turned the Tables on Wall Street Firms," *Wall Street Journal*, October 2, 1987.

32. Berkshire Hathaway Inc., *1987 Annual Report*, 19.

33. Allan Sloan, "What Color Is Your Mail?" *Forbes*, October 19, 1987.

34. Warren Buffett, "How to Tame the Casino Society," *Washington Post*, December 4, 1986.

35. Carol J. Loomis, "The Wisdom of Salomon?" *Fortune*, April 11, 1988 (sidebar to Loomis, "Inside Story").

36. "The Money Manager," *Wall Street Transcript*, June 29, 1987.

37. Jeffrey M. Laderman, "Why the Bull Is Such a Long-Distance Runner," *Business Week*, August 24, 1987.

38. Berkshire Hathaway Inc., *1987 Annual Report*, 17.

39. Julie Rohrer, "Timing from the Top," *Institutional Investor*, February 1987.

40. Henny Sender, "Turmoil in the Trading Room," *Institutional Investor*, September 1987.

41. "The Money Manager," *Wall Street Transcript*, February 23, 1987.

42. Report of the Presidential Task Force on Market Mechanisms, January 1988, p. 29 [the "Brady report"].

43. "The Money Manager," *Wall Street Transcript*, April 13, 1987.

44. Byron R. Wien, "Investment Strategy," Morgan Stanley research report, August 11, 1987.

45. Peter T. Kilborn, "U.S. Aides Calm, but Worried," *New York Times*, October 17, 1987.

46. Tim Metz, Alan Murray, Thomas E. Ricks, and Beatrice E. Garcia, "Stocks Plunge 508 Amid Panicky Selling," *Wall Street Journal*, October 20, 1987.

47. Brady report; Scott McMurray and Robert L. Rose, "Chicago's 'Shadow Markets' Led Free Fall in a Plunge That Began Right at Opening," *Wall Street Journal*, October 20, 1987.

48. Alison Leigh Cowan, "Day to Remember in Financial District," *New York Times*, October 20, 1987.

Chapter 17. A BRIEF INTRODUCTION TO DARTS

1. Berkshire Hathaway Inc., *1987 Annual Report*, 14.

2. James H. Lorie and Mary T. Hamilton, *The Stock Market: Theories and Evidence* (Homewood, Ill.: Richard D. Irwin, 1973), 100.

3. Peter L. Bernstein, *Capital Ideas: The Improbable Origins of Modern Wall Street* (New York: Free Press, 1992), 115, 118–19.

4. Paul A. Samuelson, "Proof That Properly Anticipated Prices Fluctuate Randomly," MIT *Industrial Management Review*, Spring 1965, pp. 782–85.

5. Paul A. Samuelson, memorandum with testimony on mutual funds, U.S. Senate, Committee on Banking and Currency, August 2, 1967.

6. Thorson, "Omahan in Search."

7. Paul A. Samuelson.

8. Bernstein, *Capital Ideas*, 117.

9. Eugene F. Fama, "Random Walks in Stock Market Prices," *Financial Analysts Journal*, September–October 1965.

10. Ibid.

11. "The Stock-picking Fallacy," *Economist*, August 8, 1992.

12. Paul A. Samuelson, foreword to Marshall E. Blume and Jeremy J. Siegel, "The Theory of Security Pricing and Market Structure," *Journal of Financial Markets, Institutions and Instruments*, Vol. 1, No. 3, 1992, pp. 1–2.

13. Warren Buffett, private correspondence.

14. Armen A. Alchian, letter to Tibor Fabian, June 29, 1992.

15. Paul A. Samuelson.

16. Michael C. Jensen, "Random Walks: Reality or Myth—Comment," *Financial Analysts Journal*, November–December 1967, p. 7.

17. Berkshire Hathaway Inc., *1988 Annual Report*, 18.

18. "A Conversation with Benjamin Graham," *Financial Analysts Journal*, September–October 1976.

19. Kahn and Milne, *Benjamin Graham*, 38.

20. Berkshire Hathaway Inc., *1988 Annual Report*, 18.

21. Richard A. Brealey and Stewart C. Myers, *Principles of Corporate Finance*, 2nd ed. (New York: McGraw-Hill, 1984), 266, 272.

22. Ibid., 273.

23. Tony Thomson, letter to Louis Lowenstein, March 3, 1993.

24. Malkiel, *Random Walk*, 185.

25. Ibid., 98, 175.

26. Berkshire Hathaway Inc., *1988 Annual Report*, 18.

27. E.g., see Malkiel, *Random Walk*, 231–41.

28. Graham, *Intelligent Investor*, 60.

29. Recording of 1984 Graham and Dodd seminar; and Warren Buffett, "The Superinvestors of Graham-and-Doddsville," *Hermes* [Columbia Business School], Fall 1984.

30. Michael C. Jensen, "Some Anomalous Evidence Regarding Market Efficiency," *Journal of Financial Economics* 6 (1978), p. 95.

31. Ibid., 96.

32. 1984 Graham and Dodd seminar.

33. 1984 Graham and Dodd seminar; Buffett, "Superinvestors."

34. Bruce Greenwald.

35. Laurie Meisler, "Can Analysts Learn to Love MPT?" *Institutional Investor*, February 1979.

36. Reprinted in *Fortune*, December 7, 1987.

37. Burton G. Malkiel, "Why Markets Are Working Better," *Wall Street Journal*, August 22, 1986.

38. Buffett, "How to Tame the Casino Society."

39. Burton G. Malkiel, "But Markets Only Seem More Volatile," *New York Times*, September 27, 1987.

40. Brady report, vi.

41. Berkshire Hathaway Inc., *1987 Annual Report*, 17.

42. Robert J. Shiller, "Investor Behavior in the October 1987 Stock Market Crash: Survey Evidence," Working Paper 2446 (New Haven: Cowles Foundation, November 1987), pp. 11–12.

43. Eric N. Berg, "A Study Shakes Confidence in the Volatile-Stock Theory," *New York Times*, February 18, 1992.

44. "Beating the Market: Yes It Can Be Done," *Economist*, December 5, 1992.

45. Richard A. Brealey and Stewart C. Myers, *Principles of Corporate Finance*, 4th ed. (New York: McGraw-Hill, 1991), 297–300, 310.

46. Berkshire Hathaway Inc., *1988 Annual Report*, 18.

47. Ibid.

Chapter 18. SECRETS OF THE TEMPLE

1. Donald Keough.

2. Michael J. McCarthy, "Coke Stake of 6.3%, 2nd Biggest Held in Soft-Drink Giant, Bought by Buffett," *Wall Street Journal*, March 16, 1989.

3. Michael J. McCarthy, "Heard on the Street: Buffett's Thirst for Coke Splits Analysts' Ranks," *Wall Street Journal*, March 3, 1989.

4. Ibid.

5. Eben Shapiro, "Coke vs. Pepsi as an Investment," *New York Times*, October 23, 1991.

6. Roger Cohen, "For Coke, World Is Its Oyster," *New York Times*, November 21, 1991.

7. Warren Buffett, talk at Columbia, 1993.

8. Berkshire Hathaway Inc., *1986 Annual Report*, 24

9. Smith, "Reluctant Billionaire."

10. E.J. Kahn, Jr., "The Universal Drink," *New Yorker*, February 14, 1959, pp. 47, 66.

11. Ibid, 37, 38, 50, 52.

12. Berkshire Hathaway Inc., *1989 Annual Report*, 15.

13. Cohen, "For Coke, World Is Its Oyster."

14. Mark Pendergrast, *For God, Country and Coca-Cola: The Unauthorized History of the Great American Soft Drink and the Company That Makes It* (New York: Scribner's, 1993), 241–44.

15. John Huey, "The World's Best Brand," *Fortune*, May 31, 1993.

16. Buffett, talk at Columbia, 1993.

17. Coca-Cola Co., *1982 Annual Report*, 2.

18. Buffett, talk at Columbia, 1993.
19. Pendergrast, *For God, Country and Coca-Cola*, 343.
20. Donald Keough.
21. Buffett, talk at Columbia, 1993.
22. "The Coca-Cola Industry," *Fortune*, December 1938. Buffett quoted the *Fortune* piece in the Berkshire Hathaway Inc. 1993 *Annual Report*, p. 14.
23. Ibid. *Fortune* was quoting William Allen White.
24. Huey, "World's Best Brand."
25. Emanuel Goldman, "The Coca-Cola Company," PaineWebber research report, January 16, 1989.
26. Pendergrast, *For God, Country and Coca-Cola*, 375.
27. Berkshire Hathaway Inc., *1989 Annual Report*, 15.
28. Huey, "World's Best Brand."
29. Buffett, talk at Columbia, 1993.
30. Ibid.
31. Lawrence Adelman, "Coca-Cola," Dean Witter research report, February 6, 1989 [italics added].
32. Roy D. Burry, "The Coca-Cola Company," Kidder Peabody research report, July 25, 1988 [italics added].
33. Beverage Roundtable, *Wall Street Transcript*, December 26, 1988.
34. Ron Gutman.
35. Huey, "World's Best Brand."
36. Donald Keough.
37. Ron Gutman.
38. Art Rowsell.
39. Berkshire Hathaway Inc., *1987 Annual Report*, 18.
40. Buffett, "Superinvestors."
41. Caroline E. Mayer, "Doris Buffett Said to Invest at Failed Firm," *Washington Post*, October 28, 1987.
42. Denis Bovin; Ken Chace; Mike Goldberg; Ron Gutman; Art Rowsell; Alan Spoon; Marshall Weinberg.
43. "Corn-fed Capitalist."
44. 1992 annual meeting of Berkshire Hathaway.
45. *Lifestyles of the Rich and Famous* [television program], October 25, 1992; Buffett, talk at Columbia, 1993.
46. Berkshire Hathaway Inc., *1987 Annual Report*, 14; Buffett, talk at Columbia, 1993.
47. Edith Kenner; John Otto.

Chapter 19. HOWIE BUFFETT'S CORN

1. Warren Buffett, "Kiewit Legacy As Unusual as His Life," *Omaha World-Herald*, January 20, 1980.
2. Richard I. Kirkland, Jr., "Should You Leave It All to the Children?" *Fortune*, September 29, 1986.
3. Susan Buffett Greenberg.
4. Susan Buffett Greenberg; Kay Graham.
5. Ann Landers.

6. Susan Buffett Greenberg.

7. Ibid.

8. Peter Buffett.

9. Howard Buffett.

10. Ibid.

11. Joe Rosenfield.

12. Tom Rogers.

13. Joe Rosenfield.

14. Susan Buffett Greenberg.

15. Robin Wood.

16. Kay Graham.

17. Larry Tisch. In 1988, Buffett told Adam Smith ("Reluctant Billionaire") that "99 percent plus" of his money eventually would go to society. In 1991, by which time Buffett's fortune was considerably larger, he told Linda Grant ("$4-Billion Regular Guy") that his kids would get "substantially less" than half of 1 percent of his estate.

18. Robert Lenzner, "Warren Buffett's Idea of Heaven: 'I Don't Have to Work with People I Don't Like,'" *Forbes*, October 18, 1993.

19. Bauer, "Convictions."

20. Internal Revenue Service; Buffett Foundation report for year ending June 1980. Net worth calculated as of December 31, 1979.

21. His private wealth was, indeed, private, but the visible tip of the iceberg was sizable. Buffett netted $16 million in cash and stock from the sale of the Rockford Bank in 1985. In 1987, he disclosed a 5.1 percent stake in ServiceMaster Limited Partnership, worth about $40 million. Also at about that time, he told a friend that he had $50 million in liquid securities.

22. Geoffrey Cowan.

23. Richard Holland; Joe Rosenfield.

24. William Wenke. In 1989, Buffett did give Nebraska $10,000.

25. Geoffrey Cowan.

26. Dorr, "Buffetts Fund Population Control." The quote is from the elder Susan Buffett, who was speaking about Warren.

27. Warren Buffett, 1993 annual meeting of Berkshire Hathaway.

28. Allen Greenberg. Aside from Warren and Susie, the foundation board included Carol Loomis, Tom Murphy, and the Buffetts' daughter. Their son Peter was added to the board in 1994.

29. William Ury.

30. Allen Greenberg; Jeannie Rosoff [Alan Guttmacher Institute].

31. Susan Buffett Greenberg.

32. Keith Russell.

33. Eunice Denenberg.

34. Buffett, "How Inflation Swindles the Equity Investor."

35. Warren E. Buffett, "How to Solve Our Trade Mess Without Ruining Our Economy," *Washington Post*, May 3, 1987. Other *Post* op-eds include "The Age-Old Lesson of Static Island," September 28, 1982; "How to Tame the Casino Society," December 4, 1986; "Depositors' Insurance: A Little Help for the Feds," September 25, 1990; and "The 3 Percent Solution," September 14, 1993.

36. Buffett, "Static Island."

37. Kathleen Rutledge, "Franklin More Than Financial Story," *Lincoln Journal-Star*, March 19, 1989; Howard Buffett; Tom Rogers.

38. James Traub, "Other People's Money," *GQ*, December 1991.

39. Bill Bradley; Bob Kerrey.

40. Buffett, "How to Solve Our Trade Mess."

41. Charles T. Munger, letter to United States League of Savings Institutions, May 30, 1989.

42. Warren Buffett, 1989 Capital Cities/ABC management conference.

43. Ibid.

44. Lenzner, "Buffett's Idea of Heaven."

45. Ibid.

Chapter 20. RHINOPHOBIA

1. Jay Higgins; Michael Zimmerman.

2. Berkshire Hathaway Inc., 1988 *Annual Report*, 17.

3. Michael Zimmerman; Jay Higgins. See also the Bryan Burrough and John Helyar page-turner *Barbarians at the Gate: The Fall of RJR Nabisco* (New York: Harper & Row, 1990), 218.

4. Anders, *Merchants of Debt*, 216.

5. Michael Zimmerman; Burrough and Helyar, *Barbarians*, 493–99.

6. Buffett, as an insider, was prevented from buying stock while Salomon was bidding. As Buffett disclosed (1988 *Annual Report*, 17), his board seat "cost Berkshire significant money."

7. Tatiana Pouschine and Carolyn Torcellini, "Will the Real Warren Buffett Please Stand Up?" *Forbes*, March 19, 1990.

8. Berkshire Hathaway Inc., 1988 *Annual Report*, 17.

9. Ibid.

10. Berkshire Hathaway Inc., 1989 *Annual Report*, 5.

11. Fred Schwed, Jr., *Where Are the Customers' Yachts? or A Good Hard Look at Wall Street*, (1st ed. 1940; Burlington, Vt.: Fraser, 1985), 81.

12. 1990 Capital Cities/ABC management conference. See also Buffett's talks at Harvard (1991) and Columbia (1993).

13. Larry Tisch.

14. Berkshire Hathaway Inc., 1989 *Annual Report*, 17.

15. Davis, "Buffett Takes Stock."

16. Martha M. Hamilton, "Billionaire Buffett Puts $358 Million into USAir; Preferred Stock Can Become 12% Stake," *Washington Post*, August 8, 1989.

17. Linda Sandler, "Heard on the Street: Buffett's Savior Role Lands Him Deals Other Holders Can't Get," *Wall Street Journal*, August 14, 1989.

18. Pouschine and Torcellini, "Will Buffett Stand Up?"

19. Berkshire Hathaway Inc., 1989 *Annual Report*, 17.

20. Linda Sandler, "Heard on the Street: Knightly Warren Buffett Trips Up 'Rescued' Champion Shareholders," *Wall Street Journal*, December 15, 1989.

21. Berkshire Hathaway Inc., 1985 *Annual Report*, 12.

22. Richard Nelson, a convertible specialist at Lehman Brothers, examined the deals for the author. Nelson said Berkshire's dividends were a point or two higher than those on market-priced issues. Also, its conversion premiums were a tad

lower (and thus more attractive) than the usual 20 to 24 percent. Premiums on Buffett's deals were as follows: Salomon, 19 percent; Gillette, 20 percent; USAir, 15 percent; Champion, 20 percent.

23. Berkshire Hathaway Inc., 1989 Annual Report, 24.

24. Lee Seemann.

25. 1990 Capital Cities/ABC management conference.

26. Edward Devera [Zegna salesman, New York].

27. Ron Gutman.

28. Felsenthal, Power, Privilege, and the Post, 412–13.

29. Agnes Nixon.

30. Robin Wood.

31. Howard Buffett understood from talking to his father that Warren hadn't done a formal interview. Also, Liz Smith reported in Newsday ("Mr. Buffett Does TV," November 4, 1992) that Buffett was telling friends, "I don't give interviews, but they made it look as if I did." Leellen Childers, the show's producer, said that, in fact, Buffett had donned a microphone and been interviewed at Borsheim's jewelry store "in a room with lights and cameras." Donald Yale, CEO of Borsheim's, confirmed that.

32. Rogers Worthington, "Granny, 95, Takes On Grandsons; Buffett Neutral," Chicago Tribune, October 24, 1989; Robert Dorr, "Mrs. B: 'I Got Mad and Quit,' " Omaha World-Herald, May 12, 1989.

33. Dorr, "Mrs. B: 'I Got Mad and Quit.' "

34. Berkshire Hathaway Inc., 1989 Annual Report, 10.

35. 1990 Capital Cities/ABC management conference.

36. Berkshire Hathaway Inc., 1989 Annual Report, 19.

37. Berkshire Hathaway Inc., 1989 Annual Report, 18–21.

38. Ibid.

39. Warren Buffett, letter to Benjamin Graham, M.D., April 8, 1991.

40. Robert Wilmers.

41. Berkshire Hathaway Inc., 1990 Annual Report, 16.

42. Fred R. Bleakley, "Paper Losses: Some Savvy Investors Bought Bank Stocks, Now Look Less Savvy," Wall Street Journal, December 5, 1990.

43. Charles Biderman, "California's Real Estate Woes Pose Risk to Wells Fargo," Barron's, June 10, 1991.

44. Journalists have since made a subspecialty of cataloguing Robinson's failures, e.g., Linda Sandler, "Heard on the Street: American Express Dismantles Its Eighties Superstore," Wall Street Journal, January 9, 1990; Robert Teitelman, "Image vs. reality at American Express," Institutional Investor, February 1992; Brett D. Fromson, "American Express: Anatomy of a Coup," Washington Post, February 11, 1993.

45. Louis Lowenstein, Sense and Nonsense in Corporate Finance (Reading, Mass.: Addison-Wesley, 1991), 164; Jack Byrne.

46. David Greising, "For Buffett, Amex Is a Great Place to Stash Cash," Business Week, August 19, 1991.

47. Ibid.

48. Berkshire Hathaway Inc., 1990 Annual Report, 18.

49. An estimate. In March 1991 (*1990 Annual Report*, p. 17) the market value of Berkshire Hathaway's investment in RJR Nabisco was up by more than $150 million.

50. Donald Graham.

Chapter 21. THE KING

1. Sobel, *Salomon Brothers*, 1–17.
2. Ibid., 169.
3. Ibid., 21, 36–37, 46–50.
4. Brooks, *Go-Go Years*, 264.
5. William Salomon.
6. Chernow, *House of Morgan*, 626.
7. William Salomon.
8. Stephen Bell.
9. Roland Machold.
10. David Tendler.
11. Anthony Bianco, "The King of Wall Street," *Business Week*, December 9, 1985.
12. Michael Frinquelli; William Jennings.
13. Sterngold, "Too Far, Too Fast."
14. John Taylor, "Hard to Be Rich," *New York*, January 11, 1988.
15. Gilbert Kaplan, "True Confessions," *Institutional Investor*, February 1991.
16. Grant, "$4-Billion Regular Guy."
17. Donald Howard.
18. Jay Higgins; Warren Buffett, testimony, September 11, 1991, in "The Activities of Salomon Brothers, Inc., in Treasury Bond Auctions," Subcommittee on Securities of the Committee on Banking, Housing, and Urban Affairs, U.S. Senate, p. 68.
19. Warren Buffett, talk at Harvard, 1991.
20. Eric Rosenfeld.
21. Daniel Hertzberg and Laurie P. Cohen, "Scandal Is Fading Away for Salomon, but Not for Trader Paul Mozer," *Wall Street Journal*, August 7, 1992.
22. U.S. House of Representatives, Subcommittee on Telecommunications and Finance of the Committee on Energy and Commerce, "Salomon Brothers and Government Securities," Hearing, September 4, 1991, p. 70.
23. John McDonough.
24. David Wessel, "Treasury and the Fed Have Long Caved In to 'Primary Dealers,' " *Wall Street Journal*, September 25, 1991.
25. Chernow, *House of Morgan*, 540.
26. Michael Basham.
27. Robert Glauber.
28. The public record is extensive. See *SEC v. Salomon Inc. and Salomon Brothers Inc.*, 92 Civ. No. 3691, Complaint for permanent injunction and other relief, May 20, 1992. For a summary of the SEC's allegations against Mozer, see *SEC v. Paul W. Mozer and Thomas F. Murphy*, 92 Civ. No. 8694, December 2, 1992.
29. For a complete account of the meeting, see SEC File No. 3-7930, *In the Mat-*

ter of John H. Gutfreund, Thomas W. Strauss, and John W. Meriwether, Release No. 34-31554, December 3, 1992.

30. Peter Grant and Marcia Parker, "Hurtling Toward Scandal," *Crain's New York Business,* June 1, 1992.

31. Constance Mitchell, "Precise Roles of Salomon, Others in May Sale Probed," *Wall Street Journal,* August 19, 1991.

32. Michael Basham.

33. "Salomon Brothers," House Subcommittee, especially pp. 131–35 and 166–74. See also Michael Siconolfi and Laurie P. Cohen, "Sullied Solly: How Salomon's Hubris and a U.S. Trap Led to Leaders' Downfall," *Wall Street Journal,* August 19, 1991.

34. Stephen Bell.

35. SEC File No. 3-7930, *Gutfreund, Strauss, and Meriwether.*

36. Robert Glauber.

37. SEC File No. 3-7930, *Gutfreund, Strauss, and Meriwether.*

38. Ibid.

39. Laurie P. Cohen, "Benched and Blue: Gone from Salomon 16 Months, Gutfreund Finds Life Frustrating," *Wall Street Journal,* December 4, 1992.

40. Laurie P. Cohen, "Buffett Shows Tough Side to Salomon—and Gutfreund," *Wall Street Journal,* November 8, 1991.

41. Buffett in "Activities of Salomon," Senate Subcommittee, p. 64.

42. Events of August 8–18 were recounted by participants, supplemented by "Salomon Brothers," House Subcommittee; and "Activities of Salomon," Senate Subcommittee.

43. Michael Siconolfi, Constance Mitchell, Tom Herman, Michael R. Sesit, and David Wessel, "The Big Squeeze: Salomon's Admission of T-Note Infractions Gives Market a Jolt," *Wall Street Journal,* August 12, 1991.

44. John Macfarlane.

45. William McIntosh.

46. Deryck Maughan.

47. Gerald Corrigan.

48. William McIntosh.

49. Ibid.

50. Gerald Corrigan.

51. At a press conference two days later, Buffett said he "volunteered" for the job, a version he would repeat to associates. Gutfreund insisted that he asked Buffett. See, for example, his letter to the *New York Times,* June 8, 1992.

52. Buffett recounted the morning in talks at Harvard (1991) and Columbia (1993) and also in a family chat shortly afterward.

53. Ron Olson.

54. Charlie Munger.

55. Jay Higgins.

56. Leo Higdon; Deryck Maughan; William McIntosh.

57. Siconolfi and Cohen, "Sullied Solly."

58. Kurt Eichenwald, "Salomon's 2 Top Officers to Resign Amid Scandal," *New York Times,* August 17, 1991.

Chapter 22. SALOMON'S COURT

1. Gerald Corrigan.
2. Jay Higgins; Deryck Maughan; William McIntosh.
3. Cohen, "Buffett Shows Tough Side."
4. "Salomon Brothers," House Subcommittee, p. 174; Salomon directors; Gerald Corrigan; Jerome Powell.
5. John Macfarlane.
6. Wachtell Lipton attorney.
7. James Massey [Salomon executive and director].
8. Dwayne Andreas; James Massey; William May; Robert Zeller.
9. Salomon transcript of August 18, 1991, press conference.
10. Stephen Bell; Nicholas Brady; Charlie Munger; Jerome Powell; Salomon attorneys.
11. Nicholas Brady.
12. Ibid.
13. Transcript of August 18 press conference.
14. Jay Higgins; Deryck Maughan.
15. Siconolfi and Cohen, "Sullied Solly."
16. Richard Breeden.
17. John Macfarlane.
18. Deryck Maughan.
19. Told to Gary Naftalis by a Wachtell Lipton attorney.
20. Kurt Eichenwald, "Salomon Expects to Continue Finding Bidding Violations," New York Times, September 21, 1991.
21. "Salomon Brothers," House Subcommittee, p. 131. Breeden told the author that he considered the Drexel and Salomon cases to be "quite comparable."
22. Interviews with congressional staff; Stephen Bell.
23. 'Salomon Brothers," House Subcommittee, pp. 2, 3, 5–6, 9, 11–13, 67–68, 98–99, 164.
24. David C. Beeder, "Buffett Treated Like a Hero," Omaha World-Herald, September 5, 1991.
25. James Massey.
26. Robert Denham; Charlie Munger.
27. Susan Buffett Greenberg.
28. Faith Stewart-Gordon.
29. Jim Burke; Charlie Munger; Tom Murphy.
30. "Activities of Salomon," Senate Subcommittee, p. 73.
31. Eric Rosenfeld.
32. Thomas Hanley.
33. Eric Rosenfeld.
34. Warren Buffett, talk to Salomon employees, October 2, 1991.
35. Randall Smith and Michael Siconolfi, "Salomon Is Scolded by AT&T Chairman, Who Calls Bid Scandal 'Unforgivable,'" Wall Street Journal, September 24, 1991.
36. Floyd Norris, "Forcing Salomon into Buffett's Conservative Mold," New York Times, September 29, 1991.
37. Buffett, talk to Salomon employees, October 2, 1991.

38. Leah Nathans Spiro, "How Bad Will It Get?" *Business Week*, October 7, 1991.
39. Larry Tisch.
40. Deryck Maughan.
41. Donald Howard.
42. From 1987 to 1990, the average of compensation divided by compensation plus pretax income was 72.5 percent.
43. Salomon Inc., 1991 third-quarter report to shareholders.
44. Ibid.
45. Deryck Maughan.
46. Ibid.
47. Salomon Inc.
48. Warren Buffett, meeting with analysts, February 14, 1992.
49. Nicholas Brady.
50. Gary Weiss and David Greising, "Poof! Wall Street's Sorcerers Lose Their Magic," *Business Week*, January 27, 1992.
51. Leah Nathans Spiro and Richard A. Melcher, "Rescuing Salomon Was One Thing, but Running It . . ." *Business Week*, February 17, 1992.
52. Suskind, "Legend Revisited."
53. Michael Lewis, "The Temptation of St. Warren," *New Republic*, February 17, 1992.
54. Bernstein described the Lewis article as "a piece of s———" in a November 20, 1992, letter to Richard Lowenstein, the author's uncle, and copied to the author. He added that he also wrote to Buffett about the Lewis piece, and attached Buffett's response.
55. Michael Lewis, *Liar's Poker: Rising Through the Wreckage on Wall Street* (1st ed. 1989; New York: Penguin, 1990), 180–84.
56. Salomon Inc., 1991 third-quarter report to shareholders.
57. The figures refer to professionals in the United States and Europe.
58. Jerome Powell.
59. Gary Naftalis.
60. Stephen Labaton, "Salomon to Pay Phony-Bid Fine of $290 Million," *New York Times*, May 21, 1992.
61. Jerome Powell.
62. Charlie Munger.
63. Berkshire Hathaway Inc., 1992 *Annual Report*, 6.
64. Berkshire Hathaway Inc., 1991 *Annual Report*, 6.

Chapter 23. Buffett's Trolley

1. Buffett paid $36 a share, but $25 was returned in special distributions in a partial liquidation.
2. Robert Dorr, "Mrs. B Gets $4.9 Million for Building," *Omaha World-Herald*, January 22, 1993.
3. Berkshire Hathaway Inc., 1992 *Annual Report*, 19.
4. Lenzner, "Buffett's Idea of Heaven."
5. Lipper Analytical Securities; Salomon Brothers. Figures are calculated from May 10, 1965 (Buffett's first day at Berkshire), through December 31, 1995.

6. There have been years in which Berkshire's share price has fallen. But its book value, which Buffett has consistently used as a proxy for intrinsic value, has risen every year.

7. "Fortune 500," *Fortune*, April 18, 1994.

8. Buffett, "The Security I Like Best," *Commercial and Financial Chronicle*, December 6, 1951.

9. This account is from the GEICO proxy, December 20, 1995, and various interviews. See also Roger Lowenstein, "To Read Buffett, Examine What He Bought," *Wall Street Journal*, January 18, 1996.

10. Berkshire Hathaway Inc., *1993 Annual Report*, 13.

11. Buffett, talk at Columbia, 1993.

12. Berkshire Hathaway Inc., *1992 Annual Report*, 11.

13. Berkshire Hathaway Inc., *1992 Annual Report*, 12; see also *1993 Annual Report*, 12–13.

14. Ira Marshall.

15. Doris Buffett Bryant.

16. Barbara Morrow.

17. 1994 annual meeting of Berkshire Hathaway.

18. Louis Lowenstein.

19. Berkshire Hathaway Inc., *1992 Annual Report*, 13.

20. Train, *Money Masters*, 176.

21. Berkshire Hathaway Inc., *1992 Annual Report*, 14.

22. Ibid.

23. Lenzner, "Buffett's Idea of Heaven."

24. Ibid.

25. Berkshire Hathaway Inc., *1993 Annual Report*, 18.

26. Warren Buffett, 1989 annual meeting of Berkshire Hathaway; Alan Gersten, "Berkshire Chief Leads Annual Meeting: 1,000 Come to Hear Buffett," *Omaha World-Herald*, April 25, 1989. Berkshire Hathaway Inc., *1995 Annual Report*, 10.

27. Berkshire Hathaway Inc., *1993 Annual Report*, 18.

28. Tom Murphy.

29. Barbara Morrow.

30. Peter Buffett.

31. *Thomas Winship*.

32. Jim Rasmussen, "Buffett to Tap 'Personal Funds' for Royals Deal," *Omaha World-Herald*, July 16, 1991.

33. David C. Churbuck, "Games Grown-ups Play," *Forbes*, December 19, 1994.

34. Susan Buffett Greenberg.

35. Bauer, "Convictions."

36. Warren Buffett, letter to partners, May 29, 1969.

Index

About the Author

ROGER LOWENSTEIN is the author of three bestselling books and the forthcoming *While America Aged: How Pension Debts Ruined General Motors, Stopped the NYC Subways, Bankrupted San Diego, and Loom as the Next Financial Crisis.* He reported for the *Wall Street Journal* for more than a decade and wrote the *Journal*'s stock market column "Heard on the Street" from 1989 to 1991 and the "Intrinsic Value" column from 1995 to 1997. He is now a columnist for *SmartMoney Magazine* and writes for the *New York Times Magazine* and the *Wall Street Journal*, among other publications. He has three children and lives in Westfield, New Jersey.